Illumination of the Hidden Meaning

Maṇḍala, Mantra, and the Cult of the Yoginīs

Chapters 1–24

By Tsong Khapa Losang Drakpa

The American Institute of Buddhist Studies (AIBS), in affiliation with the Columbia University Center for Buddhist Studies and Tibet House US, has established the Treasury of the Buddhist Sciences series to provide authoritative English translations, studies, and editions of the texts of the Tibetan Tengyur (*bstan 'gyur*) and its associated literature. The Tibetan Tengyur is a vast collection of over 3,600 classical Indian Buddhist scientific treatises (*śāstra*) written in Sanskrit by over 700 authors from the first millennium CE, now preserved mainly in systematic 7th–12th century Tibetan translation. Its topics span all of India's "outer" arts and sciences, including linguistics, medicine, astronomy, socio-political theory, ethics, art, and so on, as well as all of her "inner" arts and sciences such as philosophy, psychology ("mind science"), meditation, and yoga.

The present work is contained in a related series comprising the Collected Works of Tsong Khapa Losang Drak pa (bLo bZang Grags pa, 1357–1419) and His Spiritual Sons, Gyaltsap (rGyal Tshab) Darma Rinchen (1364–1432) and Khedrup Gelek Pelsang (mKhas Grub dGelegs dPal bZang, 1385–1438), a collection known in Tibetan as rJey Yab Sras gSung 'Bum. This collection also could be described as a voluminous set of independent treatises and supercommentaries, all based on the thousands of works contained in the Kangyur and Tengyur collections.

THE DALAI LAMA

Letter of Support

The foremost scholars of the holy land of India were based for many centuries at Nālandā Monastic University. Their deep and vast study and practice explored the creative potential of the human mind with the aim of eliminating suffering and making life truly joyful and worthwhile. They composed numerous excellent and meaningful texts. I regularly recollect the kindness of these immaculate scholars and aspire to follow them with unflinching faith. At the present time, when there is great emphasis on scientific and technological progress, it is extremely important that those of us who follow the Buddha should rely on a sound understanding of his teaching, for which the great works of the renowned Nālandā scholars provide an indispensable basis.

In their outward conduct the great scholars of Nālandā observed ethical discipline that followed the Pāli tradition, in their internal practice they emphasized the awakening mind of *bodhichitta*, enlightened altruism, and in secret they practised Tantra. The Buddhist culture that flourished in Tibet can rightly be seen to derive from the pure tradition of Nālandā, which comprises the most complete presentation of the Buddhist teachings. As for me personally, I consider myself a practitioner of the Nālandā tradition of wisdom. Masters of Nālandā such as Nāgārjuna, Āryadeva, Āryāsaṅga, Dharmakīrti, Candrakīrti, and Śāntideva wrote the scriptures that we Tibetan Buddhists study and practice. They are all my Gurus. When I read their books and reflect upon their names, I feel a connection with them.

The works of these Nālandā masters are presently preserved in the collection of their writings that in Tibetan translation we call the Tengyur (*bstan 'gyur*). It took teams of Indian masters and great Tibetan translators over four centuries to accomplish the historic task of translating them into Tibetan. Most of these books were later lost in their Sanskrit originals, and relatively few were translated into Chinese. Therefore, the Tengyur is truly one of Tibet's most precious treasures, a mine of understanding that we have preserved in Tibet for the benefit of the whole world.

Keeping all this in mind I am very happy to encourage a long-term project of the American Institute of Buddhist Studies, originally established by the late Venerable Mongolian Geshe Wangyal and now at the Columbia University Center for Buddhist Studies, and Tibet House US, to translate the Tengyur into English and other modern languages, and to publish the many works in a collection called *The Treasury of the Buddhist Sciences*. When I recently visited Columbia University, I joked that it would take those currently working at the Institute at least three "reincarnations" to complete the task; it surely will require the intelligent and creative efforts of generations of translators from every tradition of Tibetan Buddhism, in the spirit of the scholars of Nālandā, although we may hope that using computers may help complete the work more quickly. As it grows, the *Treasury* series will serve as an invaluable reference library of the Buddhist Sciences and Arts. This collection of literature has been of immeasurable benefit to us Tibetans over the centuries, so we are very happy to share it with all the people of the world. As someone who has been personally inspired by the works it contains, I firmly believe that the methods for cultivating wisdom and compassion originally developed in India and described in these books preserved in Tibetan translation will be of great benefit to many scholars, philosophers, and scientists, as well as ordinary people.

I wish the American Institute of Buddhist Studies at the Columbia Center for Buddhist Studies and Tibet House US every success and pray that this ambitious and far-reaching project to create *The Treasury of the Buddhist Sciences* will be accomplished according to plan. I also request others, who may be interested, to extend whatever assistance they can, financial or otherwise, to help ensure the success of this historic project.

May 15, 2007

Illumination of the Hidden Meaning

Maṇḍala, Mantra, and the Cult of the Yoginīs

Chapters 1–24

By Tsong Khapa Losang Drakpa

INTRODUCTION AND TRANSLATION
by
David B. Gray

Treasury of the Buddhist Sciences series
Tengyur Translation Initiative
Complete Works of Jey Tsong Khapa and Sons collection

Published by
The American Institute of Buddhist Studies
Columbia University Center for Buddhist Studies
Tibet House US

New York
2017

Treasury of the Buddhist Sciences series
Tengyur Translation Initiative
Complete Works of Jey Tsong Khapa and Sons collection
A refereed series published by:

American Institute of Buddhist Studies
Columbia University
80 Claremont Avenue, Room 303
New York, NY 10027

http://www.aibs.columbia.edu

Co-published with Columbia University's Center for Buddhist Studies and Tibet House US

Distributed by Columbia University Press

Printed in the United States of America on acid-free paper.

27 26 25 24 23 22 21 20 19 18 17 1 2 3 4 5

ISBN 978-1-935011-09-5 (cloth)

Library of Congress Control Number: 2017939986

A complete cataloging record for this work may be found online by searching for the above Library of Congress Control Number (LCCN) at the Library of Congress Online Catalog (https://catalog.loc.gov), or directly via the permalink for this record: https://lccn.loc.gov/2017939986.

This work is gratefully dedicated to
all yoginīs everywhere, and especially to Diana, Karuna, and Clara

Contents

Appendixes

Glossaries

Selected Bibliographies

Indexes

Publisher's/Series Editor's Preface

This *Treasury* series is dedicated to making available in English and other languages the entire Tengyur (*bstan 'gyur*), the collection of Sanskrit works preserved in Tibetan translations, and the originally Tibetan learned commentaries and treatises based upon them.

We are very delighted to publish here the long-awaited first volume of Jey Tsong Khapa's master commentary on the *Cakrasaṁvara Tantra*, the *spas don kun gsal*, well translated by David Gray, who previously translated the abridged Tantra itself (Gray 2007). Building on the work of his eminent predecessors in India and Tibet, Tsong Khapa's *Illumination of the Hidden Meaning* (the first half of which is introduced and translated herein) clarifies the esoteric, often enigmatic contents of the abridged root Tantra, widely considered the most important of the "Mother Tantra" category of Unexcelled Yoga Tantras.

This work is famous among Tibetan Tantric scholar-practitioners, since it opens the door to the supreme of the "Mother" category of Unexcelled Yoga Tantras, the *Śhrī Cakrasaṁvara*. It is very explicit in its commentary on the sexuality-transforming yogas of the creation and perfection stages, even though Tsong Khapa was a Buddhist mendicant (monk) who pointedly declined to resign his robes once confident in enlightenment in 1398.

During the time he was writing this commentary, it is said that a "woman in red" would appear suddenly at night high in the mountain near Tsong Khapa's retreat house at the newly founded Ganden monastery. This is thought to explain his detailed description of female anatomy and his straightforward description of the specific type of sexual union employed by advanced Unexcelled Tantra yogis and yoginīs. Some have even thought that he took this "red lady" as a consort at this time, and subsequently only pretended still to be a monk.

Indeed, it is maintained by the Indian Buddhist Tantric tradition as explicated by his own scholarship that for a male yogi it is almost impossible to attain the highest—third, fourth, and fifth—stages of the perfection stage without the skilled partnership of a female yoginī of the equal level of realization. However, not only is it very unlikely that someone of Tsong Khapa's demonstrated character would have practiced such hypocrisy, but also his attainment on those levels was vividly demonstrated only at the moment of his death, when he was observed by his main disciples going through the male-female union processes needed for Vajradhara-hood in a glowing subtle body formage. As for the procedure for a monk who reaches that point to postpone taking the next step on the third perfection stage until the between (*bar do*) state after death, in order to keep his monk's vow until his death, it is matter-of-factly mentioned as a common option at the time by the Indian adept scholar Buddhaśhrī-jñānapada in his *Revelation of Mañjuśhrī*.

Dr. Gray's translation of the *Illumination* follows on his ground-breaking translation of the *Cakrasaṁvara Tantra* itself, and indeed much of it was completed during the process of that previous translation. We are very much relieved that now the first volume has finally come out, with the second volume also very close to completion. Only now have we succeeded in properly following H. H. the Dalai Lama's advice to us, that root Tantras of the Unexcelled Yoga category should not be published without being accompanied by extensive commentaries. This is because the root Tantras tend to have shocking statements about what are considered transgressive thoughts and acts, which can give rise to serious misunderstandings (indeed have often done so). On the other hand, with the commentaries from the scholar-practitioners of the tradition, we can see how the "thunderbolt words" (*vajrapada*) were interpreted in India and Tibet, and can thus begin to gain a clearer sense of the extraordinary world of the Buddhist Tantras; how they aim to fulfill, and do not depart from, the Mahāyāna bodhisattva drive to transform the world for the betterment of all sentient beings.

I must express my unstinting admiration for Dr. Gray's breadth of scholarship in accomplishing these landmark works. He is one of the single handful of contemporary scholars who have read very widely and carefully in the Indian and Tibetan Tantric scientific treatises. These still survive in a few cases in Sanskrit, but most of them must be studied in the Tibetan Tengyur, where the important works from the libraries of the great Indian Buddhist monastic universities have been preserved in translation. Therefore, Dr. Gray and his colleagues have accomplished a monumental effort in providing primary source evidence on which religious studies scholars interested in Tantra can base their interpretations.

This first volume of the *Illumination* is accompanied by a short translation of a summary commentary written by the 11th century Kashmiri scholar-practitioner Sumatikīrti, which Tsong Khapa himself quotes in his detailed commentary. This inclusion is a good omen, perhaps resonating with the general belief in Tibet that Sumatikīrti was a previous life of Tsong Khapa's continuum, which shows the Tibetan persistence in insisting that a human being can complete her or his work from one life in the others that follow!

Once again, I congratulate Dr. Gray for his great scholarly achievement, philological, historical, and philosophical, in producing this book, maintaining his focus through many years of strenuous labor and unrelenting critical insight. I also add my sincere thanks to the international group of fine scholars he remembers and thanks for their skilled assistance, and a special acknowledgment of the labor of love and skill given by Thomas Yarnall, our designer, scholarly colleague, and executive editor.

Robert A.F. Thurman (Ari Genyen Tenzin Choetrak)
Jey Tsong Khapa Professor of Indo-Tibetan Buddhist Studies, Columbia University
Director, Columbia Center for Buddhist Studies
President, American Institute of Buddhist Studies
President, Tibet House US

Ganden Dechen Ling
Woodstock, New York
February 27, 2017 CE
Tibetan Royal Year 2144, Year of the Fire Bird

Author's Preface and Acknowledgements

This book is the first volume of a two-volume translation of Jey Tsong Khapa's *Illumination of the Hidden Meaning, A Detailed Exegesis of the Concise Saṁvara Tantra called "The Cakrasaṁvara."* As the title indicates, it is his extensive commentary on the *Cakrasaṁvara Tantra*. This volume contains a translation of Tsong Khapa's magisterial introduction to the text, as well as his commentary on the Root Tantra's first twenty-four chapters. My translation of the remaining twenty-eight chapters will be contained in the companion volume that will follow this volume in the near future.

This volume is subtitled *Maṇḍala, Mantra, and the Cult of the Yoginīs* due to the content of the chapters translated within it. They cover the construction of the mandala and the performance of consecration ceremonies therein (chs. 2–3); the esoteric coding of various mantras (chs. 5–9); ritual actions employing these mantras (chs. 9, 12–13); the enumeration of the mandala's yoginīs (ch. 4); and the elucidation of the identifying characteristics of the various clans of yoginīs, as well as the secret verbal and physical signs employed for communication when they are successfully identified (chs. 15–24).

In composing his commentary Tsong Khapa employed all of the resources available to him. These included the various translations of the Root Tantra, the translations of the Indic commentaries, as well as the works of prior Tibetan scholars. Most of these sources are still available today, but several appear to be lost. This work is a monumental achievement of Tibetan scholarship, which set a standard which was and still is difficult to surpass.

* * *

This study could not have been written without the assistance that has been provided by many individuals and institutions. My work on the *Illumination of the Hidden Meaning* began in July 1995, when I was a young graduate student at Columbia University at the formative stage of my study of the Vajrayāna traditions of India, Nepal, and Tibet. At this time, I had developed a preliminary interest in the *Sarvatathāgatatattva-saṃgraha Sūtra*, an influential eighth century Indian work that later was identified as a Yogatantra. One weekend I journeyed to Prof. Robert Thurman's summer residence in Woodstock, NY, to begin reading this text with him. That weekend Bob was also hosting Lelung Rinpoche, then a young Geluk monk, who had a strong past-life connection to the Cakrasaṁvara tradition. This inspired Bob to suggest that we read Tsong Khapa's commentary on this work. I reluctantly agreed, but soon was entranced. The three of us read the first five folia of the text that weekend, and by the end of the weekend I had changed my mind, deciding instead to focus on the *Illumination of the Hidden Meaning* for my dissertation research.

I conducted this research on the *Cakrasaṁvara Tantra* at Columbia University, studying under Robert Thurman, who was my primary advisor, and also with Ryuichi Abé, Gary Tubb, and Matthew Kapstein. I had the good fortune of being able to spend a year studying in India and Nepal with the financial and logistical support of Columbia University and the American Institute of Indian Studies. While there, I received the hospitality of the Central Institute of Higher Tibetan Studies in Sarnath, the Office of H.H. The Dalai Lama Tenzin Gyatso, and the Library of Tibetan Works and Archives in Dharamsala. In Sarnath I read portions of this work with Geshe Yeshe Thapkay, and in Dharamsala I continued my studies under the guidance of Geshe Yama Tseden and Geshe Tenzin Dargyay at Namgyal Monastery. I am also indebted to the Central Institute of Higher Tibetan Studies, the Library of Tibetan Works and Archives, the Oriental Institute in Vadodara, the Kesar Library in Kathmandu, and the Institute for Advanced Studies of World Religions in Carmel, NY, for so graciously allowing me to study manuscripts and blockprints in their collections, and for providing me with microfilm and microfiche copies, as well as photocopies, of those that were essential for my work. I am particularly grateful to E. Gene Smith and the Tibetan Buddhist Resource Center for making available to me a number of scans of Tibetan texts that were essential for the completion of the this work.

My dissertation featured an edition and translation of the first four chapters of the Root Tantra as well as the introduction and first four chapters of the *Illumination of the Hidden Meaning*. Following my graduation from Columbia University, I received a Woodrow Wilson post-doctoral fellowship at Rice University. This fellowship enabled me to make great progress on both my translation and my edition of the Root Tantra. I completed both of these works shortly after joining the faculty of the Department of Religious Studies at Santa Clara University. Over the past twelve years I slowly completed my translation of the *Illumination of the Hidden Meaning,* finally completing this work in early 2017, almost twenty-two years after I initially undertook it. I am thus indebted as well for support provided to me by the Woodrow Wilson Foundation, Rice University, and Santa Clara University.

I would like to acknowledge the detailed, tremendous support provided by my mentor, Robert Thurman, who initially inspired me to undertake this work, continued to support me throughout, and encouraged me to complete it. This would never have been possible without his assistance. The editor of this volume, Thomas Yarnall, likewise has provided indispensable and meticulous editorial support and critical advice. This volume would not have been possible without their assistance. Any and all faults, however, are solely my own responsibility.

I would particularly like to thank my wife, Diana Iong, who encouraged me to begin work on this project when I was initially unsure about it, and who has ever since provided me with countless instances of support and assistance of the past two decades.

David B. Gray
Associate Professor of Religious Studies
Santa Clara University

March 3, 2017 CE

Abbreviations and Sigla

Note: Here I am listing the two-letter abbreviations and one-letter sigla that I use throughout this text. The names I provide here are the shorthand names that I use when referring to them, not necessarily their full titles. They are also listed alphabetically under these shorthand titles in the bibliography (p. 422 ff.), where complete bibliographic details are provided.

AC	Kāṇha, *Ālicatuṣṭaya*
AM	Abhayākaragupta, *Āmnāyamañjarī*
AU	*Abhidhānottara Tantra*
AV	Atiśa Dīpaṅkaraśrījñāna, *Abhisamayavibhaṅga*
B	TBRC scan of the *bla brang bkra shis 'khyil* print of the KS
BC	Bhavyakīrti, *Śrīcakrasaṁvarapañjikā Śūramanojñā-nāma*
CP	Jayabhadra, *Cakrasaṁvarapañjikā*
CT	*Cakrasaṁvara Tantra*
CV	Bhavabhaṭṭa, *Cakrasaṁvaravivṛtti*
D	TBRC scan of the *de dge dgon chen* print of the KS
DA	*Ḍākārṇava Tantra*
DV	*Ḍākinīvajrapañjara*
H	*Abhidhānottara Tantra*. IASWR microfiche no. MBB-I-100
HT	*Hevajra Tantra*
I	*Abhidhānottara Tantra*. IASWR microfiche no. MBB-I-26
IC	Indrabhūti, *Śrīcakrasaṁvaratantrarāja-saṁvara-samuccaya-nāma-vṛtti*
J	*Abhidhānottara Tantra*. Lokesh Chandra 1981 reproduction
JS	*Sarvabuddhasamāyoga-ḍākinījālasamvara-nāma-uttaratantra*
K	Kambala, *Sādhananidhi-śrīcakrasaṁvara-nāma-pañjikā* (Sanskrit)
KS	Tsong Khapa, *sbas don kun gsal*
KV	*Khyāvajravārāhī-abhidhāna-tantrottara-vārāhī-abhibodhiya*
L	*Saṁputa Tantra* (IASWR Microfiche edition)

LA Sumatikīrti, *Laghusaṁvaratantrapaṭalābhisandhi* (*Intended Import of the Laghu[saṁvara] Tantra*)

LT Vajrapāṇi, *Laghutantraṭīkā* (*Commentary Praising Saṁvara*)

MT *Mahāmudrātilaka Tantra*

MV Śūraṅgavajra, *Mūlatantrahṛdaya-saṁgrahābhidhānottaratantra-mūlamūlavṛtti*

NS Büton, *bde mchog rtsa rgyud kyi rnam bshad gsang ba'i de kho na nyid gsal bar byed pa* (*Illumination of the Hidden Reality*)

PG Sachen Kunga Nyingpo, *dpal 'khor lo bde mchog gi rtsa ba'i rgyud kyi ṭī ka mu tig phreng ba*. This photographic reproduction of the Tibetan text includes four folio sides per page. Citations to this text refer to the page number followed by the folio side number.

PD Vīravajra, *Padārthaprakāśikā-nāma-śrīsaṁvaramūlatantraṭīkā*

PK Vajraghaṇṭa, *Śrīcakrasaṁvarapañcakrama*

PM Prajñākīrti-Mardo revised translation of the CT (edited in Gray 2012)

PTT. Refers to the numbers assigned in the *Tibetan Tripitaka: The Peking Edition* (Suzuki 1955–1961)

Q The Otani reprint of the KS in the Tibetan Tripitaka, Beijing edition

RG Durjayacandra, *Ratnagaṇa-nāma-pañjikā*

RP Büton, *rgyud sde spyi'i rnam par gzhag pa rgyud sde rin po che'i mdzes rgyan zhes bya ba*

SG Vīravajra, *Samantaguṇaśālina-nāma-ṭīkā*

SL Sumatikīrti-Malgyo revised translation of the CT (edited in Gray 2012)

SM Sumatikīrti-Mardo revised translation of the CT (edited in Gray 2012)

SN Kambala, *Sādhananidhi-śrīcakrasaṁvara-nāma-pañjikā* (Tibetan)

SS Devagupta's *Śrīcakrasaṁvara-sarvaśādhana-sanna-nāma-ṭīkā*

ST *Saṁpuṭa Tantra*

SU *Saṁvarodaya Tantra*

T *bkra shis lhun po par rnying* edition of the KS

To. Refers to the numbers assigned in the Tōhoku Catalogue of the Derge Canon (Ui 1934)

TP Kāṇha, *Guhyatattvaprakāśa*

TV *Śāśvatavajra (rtag-pa'i rdo-rje), *Śrītattvaviśada-nāma-śrīsaṁvara-vṛtti*

UN Tathāgatarakṣita, *Ubhayanibandha*

VD *Vajraḍāka Tantra*

VP Puṇḍarīka, *Vimalaprabhā-nāma-mūlatantrānusāriṇī-dvādaśa-sāhasrikā-laghukālacakra-tantrarāja-ṭīkā*

VV Bhavabhaṭṭa, *Śrīvajradāki-nāma-mahātantrarājasya vivṛtti*

YS *Yoginīsaṁcāra Tantra*

Typographical Conventions

We have strived generally to present Tibetan and Sanskrit names and terms in a phonetic form to facilitate pronunciation. For Tibetan names, a complete list of phonetic-transliterated (Wylie) equivalents may be found in Appendix III.

For most Sanskrit terms—while we generally have kept conventional diacritics—we often have added an *h* to convey certain sounds (so *ś*, *ṣ*, and *c* are often rendered as *śh*, *ṣh*, and *ch* respectively). For Sanskrit terms that have entered the English lexicon (such as "nirvana" or "mandala"), we use no diacritical marks. In more technical contexts (notes, bibliography, and so on) we use full standard diacritical conventions for Sanskrit, and Wylie transliterations for Tibetan.

Throughout the translation, text in square brackets has been added by the translator for clarity. Words in bold represent text quoted from a root text (generally the CST, unless otherwise noted or evident from context). Light gray numbered outline entries have been inserted throughout from Tsong Khapa's general outline (*sa bcad*), the entirety of which may be found in Appendix I.

PART ONE

INTRODUCTION

Introduction

The Context of This Work

The Detailed Exegesis of the Concise Saṁvara Tantra, Called "The Illumination of the Hidden Meaning," is a general commentary or detailed exegesis of the *Cakrasaṁvara Tantra*, an important Indian Buddhist scripture of the Yoginītantra class also known as the *Laghusaṁvara* and *Śriherukābhidhāna*. It was composed by Tsong Khapa (1357–1419 CE), the great scholar-practitioner who founded the Geluk (*dge lugs*) order of Tibetan Buddhism. As such, it is an important work of Tibetan Buddhist scholarship, composed during the early fifteenth century, right at a turning point of Tibetan Buddhist history, as the second and final "latter transmission" (*phyi dar*) of Buddhism to Tibet was waning, and the Tibetan transformation of Buddhism was well under way. This process, as Ronald Davidson has argued, was "neo-conservative," thinly veiling genuinely Tibetan religious innovations with claims of authentic Indian origination.[1] Tsong Khapa's position at this point in Tibetan religious history is exemplified by this work, which attempts to maintain fidelity to the Indian commentarial traditions while advancing his own uniquely Tibetan commentarial agenda.

At some point during his sixty-third year, when he was at the peak of his teaching career as well as the end of his life, Tsong Khapa taught his lecture series that would be recorded as his *Complete Illumination of the Hidden Meaning* (*sbas don kun gsal*) commentary on the *Cakrasaṁvara Tantra*.[2] It should be noted that this work was not "written" by him, but orally composed and recited, and recorded by his "secretary" (*yi ge pa*) Kashipa Rinchen Pel.[3] It is thus a work that originated as an oral composition, and as such it differs considerably from written works of scholarship, such as those that Western academics in the twenty-first century are wont to compose. To say this is by no means to belittle Tsong

---

[1] Davidson makes this claim in his (2005) book.

[2] See Kaschewsky 1967, 329. Since Tsong Khapa lived for sixty-two years (1357–1419 CE), this event took place during the last year of his life, in 1418 or 1419 CE.

[3] This information is recorded in the text's colophon, which is translated at the end of volume 2 of this work.

Khapa's achievement. The work is highly erudite, and displays a deep familiarity with the root text itself, as well as a mastery of the large numbers of Indian and Tibetan commentaries that were available to him. Indeed, it is the work of a master scholar produced at the peak of his career.

I have often wondered what this teaching might have been like. The text's colophon reports that the teaching occurred at Ganden monastery, the institution founded by Tsong Khapa in 1409, where he spent much of the last decade of his life. Tsong Khapa's memory was likely prodigious, as was (and still is) often the case with scholars trained in the traditional Buddhist educational systems, which focus on mnemonic exercises.[4] Nonetheless, I suspect that he had several texts in front of him as he lectured on this topic. He probably had several translations of the root text to which he refers. While he clearly favors the Sumatikīrti-Mardo (SM) revised translation, this is perhaps the text that he is most likely to have memorized, and thus is the least likely to have been sitting before him. He refers frequently to the three revised translations of the root text, any or all of which may have been present before him. But the text that he is almost certain to have had was Büton's masterful and massive commentary on the root text, his *Illumination of the Hidden Reality* commentary on the *Saṁvara Mūlatantra* (NS). Tsong Khapa heavily relied upon this massive and masterful commentary on the root Tantra. Throughout his work, he often directly quotes and paraphrases it, and periodically takes issue with it. It is a major work to which Tsong Khapa responded in his lectures, and Tsong Khapa's work thus cannot be fully and properly understood without taking it into consideration.

Tsong Khapa's work is thus a synthetic one. He relied and drew upon the massive edifice of Indian scholarship on the *Cakrasaṁvara Tantra*, and he also seriously engaged with the smaller body of Tibetan works on the subject. It is a truly Tibetan work, as Tsong Khapa's sources were exclusively Tibetan—Tibetan translations and indigenous Tibetan works. It also makes a small but noticeable shift toward a distinctly Tibetan commentarial agenda, while maintaining the "neo-conservative" stance of total fidelity to the Indian tradition, as I will suggest below.

---

[4] For a discussion of the significance of memory and oral transmission in the traditional Tibetan monastic education system, see Dreyfus 2003.

Tsong Khapa's Sources

Tsong Khapa relied on a wide range of sources in the composition of his commentary. Regarding these, it seems almost certain that Tsong Khapa, unlike Büton, did not actually consult Sanskrit manuscripts of the root text or their commentaries.[5] Even if Tsong Khapa had access to such manuscripts, it is likely that he would not have sought them. Christian Wedemeyer has argued, on the basis of Tsong Khapa's commentary on the *Guhyasamāja Tantra*, that Tsong Khapa had little or no understanding of Sanskrit.[6] There are several instances in this commentary as well where Tsong Khapa makes mistakes with respect to Sanskrit equivalents of Tibetan words, betraying this lacuna in his education.

Tsong Khapa makes up for this by relying on all of the available Tibetan translations. First, he had access to, and frequently refers to, the original, unrevised translation made in the late tenth century by Lochen Rinchen Zangpo (958–1055 CE) and his Kashmiri collaborator, Padmākaravarman. This work, unfortunately, appears to be lost, surviving only in part via the numerous quotations made by commentators such as Tsong Khapa and Büton.

This translation was revised three times, and Tsong Khapa makes use of all three revised translations. Two of these revisions were made during the eleventh century, within a century of the Lochen's original translation. One is the revision preserved in all of the editions of the Tibetan Kangyur, (PM) revised translation undertaken by the Tibetan scholars Dro Lotsawa Sherab Drak, also known as Prajñākīrti, and Marpa Chökyi Wangchuk, who was also known as Marpa Dopa or Mardo (c. 1043–1138 CE). As I discussed in more depth in my edition of the Sanskrit and Tibetan texts, this is a generally good translation, although it is significantly different from the extant Sanskrit, apparently due to extensive interpolations from explanatory Tantras such as the *Abhidhānottara*.[7] Tsong Khapa was aware of these problems, and defends this

---

[5] These certainly did exist in Tibet; a manuscript of the CT was apparently preserved in the Potala palace, and is reportedly now in a highly restricted archival collection in Beijing. Such manuscripts were quite rare in Tibet, even in Tsong Khapa's time, and he likely did not have easy access to them.

[6] See Wedemeyer 2006.

[7] See Gray 2012, 28–34.

revised translation against accusations that it contains spurious interpolations. It is not, however, the translation that he preferred.[8]

Another revised translation was undertaken around the same time, circa the late eleventh century. This is the (SL) revision undertaken by the Tibetan translator Malgyo Lotsawa Lodrö Drakpa, who was active during the eleventh century, and the Kashmiri scholar Sumatikīrti, who was a disciple of Nāropā (956–1041 CE). Malgyo traveled to Nepal during the late eleventh century and studied with some of the disciples of Nāropā who were living there, including Sumatikīrti (Roerich 1976, 382). After returning to Tibet, he served as a teacher to Khön Könchok Gyalpo (1034–1102 CE), the founder of the Sakya school, as well as his successor, Sachen Kunga Nyingpo (1092–1158 CE), who wrote the important *Pearl Garland* commentary on *Cakrasaṁvara Tantra* (Davidson 2005, 293–315). This translation was not preserved in the standard Kangyur canonical collections. However, it was included in the Phugbrag manuscript Kangyur.[9] This is the translation preferred by the Sakya tradition, and it is the basis of Sachen's commentary. Tsong Khapa refers to it frequently, but does not privilege it.

Tsong Khapa's preferred translation is the (SM) "dual" revised translation undertaken by two members of the above translation teams, namely Sumatikīrti and Mardo. It is a text that was actually revised twice, according to its colophon. It was revised first in the eleventh century by the Indian scholar Sūryagupta and the Tibetan translator Gö Hlaytsay. Gö Hlaytsay, also known as Gö Kugpa Hlaytsay, lived during the eleventh century and was a student of Atiśa, and one of the teachers of Khön Könchok Gyalpo. This duo translated Kambala's *Sādhananidhi* commentary into Tibetan, and also revised Lochen's original translation of the *Cakrasaṁvara Tantra* on the basis of this work, which contains abundant quotations from the root text. It was further revised by Sumatikīrti and Mardo, most likely during the late eleventh or early twelfth century.[10]

It is clearly the last of the revised translations, as it draws upon both the SL and PM translations. Generally speaking, it tends to follow the PM text most closely, but it frequently assumes the SL reading,

---

[8] For an edition of this translation see Gray 2012.

[9] For a diplomatic edition of this text see Gray 2012.

[10] For an edition of this translation see Gray 2012.

especially when the latter accords most closely with the surviving Sanskrit text. It also avoids some of the excesses of the PM translation, such as the "spurious interpolations." It is overall, in my judgment, the best translation that maintains the closest fidelity to the Sanskrit. Tsong Khapa shared this preference, but due to what is likely an accident of history it is not the version that was selected for inclusion in the Kangyur editions. Evidently, careful comparison with the Sanskrit originals was not required for admission to the Kangyur. Fortunately, this text was preserved extra-canonically by the Geluk order, undoubtedly due to Tsong Khapa's preference for it. It was sometimes printed together with Tsong Khapa's commentary.

Tsong Khapa relies extensively on the Tibetan translations of the "explanatory Tantras" (*vyākhyātantra*) associated with the *Cakrasaṁvara Tantra* preserved from the Kangyur, as well as the numerous commentaries and ritual texts preserved in the Tengyur. Tsong Khapa had clearly read extensively in the literature associated with this tradition, and he abundantly quotes passages that support his arguments as he discusses various aspects of the text and its associated practice traditions. He largely, but not exclusively, focuses on the Cakrasaṁvara literature. He also quotes the closely related *Hevajra Tantra* and several of its commentaries, and ranges even further, quoting at times Mahāyāna śāstras such as Nāgārjuna's *Vaidalyaprakaraṇa* and Asaṅga's *Bodhisattvabhūmi* and *Abhisamayālaṁkāra*.

In his lengthy introduction, Tsong Khapa quotes repeatedly from the explanatory Tantras. He also quotes in its entirety a short précis of the root Tantra by his namesake, Sumatikīrti.[11] This text, the *Laghusaṁvaratantrapaṭalābhisandhi*, provides a short summary of the root Tantra. Since Tsong Khapa quotes almost the entire text, I have included as an appendix to this volume an annotated translation of it.

In the introduction he also summarizes the creation and perfection stage practice traditions associated with the *Cakrasaṁvara Tantra*, with focus on the meditative traditions attributed to the three mahāsiddhas who are believed to have founded Cakrasaṁvara practice traditions, namely Kāṇha or Kṛṣṇācārya, Lūipa, and Ghaṇṭapā or Vajraghaṇṭa. He

---

[11] Tsong Khapa's ordination name was *blo bzang grags pa*, which is a Tibetan equivalent to the Indian name Sumatikīrti.

quotes from the works attributed to these authors. Among these, he quotes most abundantly from Kāṇha's works, no doubt due to the fact that he was the most prolific author among the three. His summary is general, and he does not go into the details of the specific practice traditions, as he had lectured on these topics separately.

In his actual commentary on the text, Tsong Khapa primarily quotes from the four Tibetan translations as well as the ten Indian commentaries that comment on the entire root Tantra.[12] He also relies extensively on Tibetan commentaries, although he does not openly acknowledge this fact. Tsong Khapa mentions only three Tibetan works by name. These include a commentary composed by the translator Mardo, Sachen's *Pearl Garland* (PG) commentary, and Büton's (NS) commentary.

Mardo's commentary is almost certainly the earliest Tibetan commentary on the root text. Unfortunately, it appears to be lost, although a copy of the text was preserved, until recently, at Labrang monastery in China.[13] Tsong Khapa quotes it by name, and I suspect that it is the source for several of the quotations that I have not been able to identify. Tsong Khapa also mentions, and clearly consulted, Sachen's *Pearl Garland* commentary. While he does not quote it extensively, he does so periodically, and also at times takes issue with Sachen's interpretations.

The third Tibetan work that Tsong Khapa mentions, Büton's NS commentary, is the work upon which Tsong Khapa most relied. While he mentions the text by name at the beginning of the commentary, he does not cite it at the many instances in which he directly quotes or para-

---

[12] These are the commentaries composed by Bhavabhaṭṭa, Bhavyakīrti, Devagupta, Durjayacandra, Jayabhadra, Kambala, *Śāśvatavajra (rtag-pa'i rdo-rje), Tathāgatarakṣita, as well as the two commentaries by Vīravajra. Tsong Khapa also quotes from Vajrapāṇi's "bodhisattva commentary," but in the introduction rather than in the body of the text, since this work comments only on the first ten and a half verses.

[13] The nineteenth-century author Akuching Sherab Gyatso (1803–1875) prepared a catalogue of rare works preserved at Labrang monastery in his *dpe rgyun dkon pa 'ga' zhig gi tho yig don gnyer yid kyi kuṇḍa bzhad pa'i zla 'od 'bum gyi snye ma*, which was reproduced by Lokesh Chandra. Entry number 12165 in this catalogue is the following: *mar do lo tsā ba chos ki dbang phyug gi bde mchog rtsa rgyud kyi bsdus don dang ṭikka rgyas pa* (Chandra 1963, vol. 3 p. 552). This is almost certainly the *mar do'i 'grel pa* to which Tsong Khapa refers. Hopefully this work has survived the tumult of the twentieth century, and will come to light in the near future. I am indebted to Gene Smith for bringing this work to my attention.

phrases it. While this would constitute plagiarism in our current academic milieu, it did not in his. To a significant extent, Tsong Khapa's work is derivative, as he often simply repeats Büton's commentary when he agrees with it. He does not always agree with it, however; Büton is most often the "someone" (*kha cig*) with whom he disagrees. This is understandable if one takes into account the intellectual climate in which Tsong Khapa lived and worked. Büton (1290–1364 CE) was one of the brightest intellectual lights in fourteenth century Tibet.[14] Not only was he one of Tsong Khapa's "grand gurus," but Tsong Khapa was linked to him via numerous lineage transmissions, as he studied with a number of Büton's disciples.[15] Given this context, he could hardly have embarked on this teaching without seriously taking into consideration Büton's work. This consideration seems to have involved a selective summation of Büton's commentary; Tsong Khapa follows it closely at times, and at other times departs from it, or directly criticizes the work while maintaining the polite Tibetan convention of not directly naming the object of his critique.

Tsong Khapa's Commentarial Agenda

Despite Tsong Khapa's extensive reliance on Büton's work, his commentary is far from being entirely derivative. Not only does Tsong Khapa often disagree with Büton, but he also advances a distinctive exegetical approach. This approach is somewhat subtle, for the work, on the whole, functions as a *padārtha* commentary, explaining the meaning of the text of the root Tantra, typically via paraphrasis, and via detailed explanations when necessary. Here I will not waste the reader's time with a summary of the topics covered by this long and complex work, given the fact that this information can be obtained via an examination either of the "General Outline of the Text" (in Appendix I below) or the index. I would rather let Tsong Khapa's work speak for itself. Readers interested in specific topics can, naturally, consult the index or Tsong Khapa's

---

[14] Regarding the life of Büton, see Ruegg 1966.

[15] These include Chökyi Pelwa (1316–1397 CE), Chö Pelzangpo, Cholay Namgyal (1306–1386 CE), Shönu Sönam, Rinchen Namgyal (1318–1388 CE), and Sönam Gyaltsen (1312–1375 CE).

work. Here I would rather briefly discuss some interesting but not obvious features.

First, Tsong Khapa spent some effort establishing an authoritative basis for this work. Although Tsong Khapa undoubtedly enjoyed considerable prestige by his sixty-second year, it seems that he still needed to establish his authority to comment on the Yoginītantras. It was widely believed that texts such as the *Cakrasaṁvara Tantra* were not human creations, but rather the authentic speech of the buddhas that is periodically revealed in the world by mahāsiddhas such as Lūipa and Saraha, as Tsong Khapa discusses in section 3.3.3.1 of his text below. Moreover, for practitioners of these traditions, authority derives via lineage connections to the Indian mahāsiddhas. Tsong Khapa, like many other contemporary Tibetan practitioners, was the recipient of numerous transmissions of lineages deriving from the mahāsiddhas. Tsong Khapa, like most Tibetans Buddhists, saw India as the locus of spiritual authority, and like Tibetans of previous generations, he sought to travel to India to personally approach this source. However, Tsong Khapa was living in what was then still a new era in the history of Buddhism, in which pilgrimage to India was no longer safe or worthwhile for Buddhists, due to the destruction of the major centers of Buddhist learning there.[16]

His biographies relate that, during his thirty-ninth year, Tsong Khapa had been staying at Hlodrak Drawo monastery at the invitation of the Nyingma Lama Hlodrak Namka Gyaltsen, where he was receiving teachings from this lama. While there, he gave rise to a strong desire to travel to India to meet with the mahāsiddhas Nāgabodhi and Maitrīpa. The Nyingma Khenchen had the ability to communicate with the bodhisattva Vajrapāṇi, and consulted him on this issue. Vajrapāṇi wisely dissuaded Tsong Khapa from making this trip, which, by the late fourteenth century, would have been extremely dangerous, given the fact that by this time all of the major Buddhist sites in North India had been destroyed. Instead, Tsong Khapa and his entourage went on pilgrimage to Tsari Mountain, a sacred site in southeastern Tibet identified with the South Asian pilgrimage site of Cāritra, associated with the Yoginītantras such

---

[16] For a harrowing first person account of a Tibetan Buddhist pilgrim who witnessed the destruction wrought in North India by the Turks during the mid-thirteenth century, see Roerich 1959.

as the *Hevajra* and *Cakrasaṁvara Tantras*. While on pilgrimage at Tsari Mountain, Tsong Khapa refrained from drinking consecrated beer, apparently out of concern that this would be a violation of his monastic vows. As a result, the ḍākinīs who dwell there afflicted him with sharp pains in his feet, which were not relieved until he propitiated them.

This story was very well known; it is related in Tsong Khapa's biography,[17] and is retold by later scholars such as the Drukpa Kagyu master Padma Karpo (1527–1592 CE).[18] And as Toni Huber has brought to our attention, the story is retold by the contemporary Drukpa Kagyu yogīs who practice advanced Tantric meditative practices in the vicinity of Tsari Mountain, in order to illustrate the power of the site and the devotional attitude needed to safely approach it.[19]

I bring up this story not to disparage Tsong Khapa or cast doubt on his qualifications for composing a commentary on the *Cakrasaṁvara Tantra*. Such a judgment is not mine to make, nor is it one that I personally hold. But I bring it up due to a caricature of Tsong Khapa that seems to have originated in Tibet, reinforced by the telling and retelling of this story, which portrays him as a somewhat stodgy and spiritually uninspired scholar, who is more concerned with ethical conundrums (should a monk consume an alcoholic sacrament?) than the conduct appropriate to the consecrated environment of the ḍākinīs. In other words, he is portrayed as learned but not realized. This portrayal has been carried over into the West, where it is held by some scholars and practitioners of Tibetan Buddhism.

I begin with this story because it calls to mind an important distinction made in Tibetan religious discourse between the scholar (*mkhas pa*) and the practitioner (*grub pa*). Here, Tsong Khapa fills the role of the scholar, whose persistent adherence to discursive thought patterns lands him in trouble when he enters the world of advanced Tantric practice, where discursive thought is problematic and must ultimately be abandoned. This is an important distinction, which also calls to mind more general distinctions, such as between practice and knowledge. This latter

---

[17] See Kaschewsky 1974, 130–131, and Thurman 1982, 18–20.

[18] For a translation of Padma Karpo's account see Huber 1999, 62–63.

[19] See Huber 1999, 61.

category is highlighted in the Tibetan tradition in a fashion that is particularly meaningful here, via the distinction between the ordinary knowledge of a scholar, *shes pa*, and the gnosis that ideally results from practice, *ye shes*.

But while Tsong Khapa's achievements as a scholar were tremendous, he cannot simply be pigeonholed as a scholar. This is in fact a mischaracterization, as it fails to take into account his rich visionary life,[20] as well as his four-year and one-year retreats at Ölka Chölung (*'ol kha chos lung*).[21] And while the distinction between visionary practice and scholastic knowledge is a meaningful one in Tibetan culture, it tends to collapse as we explore the lives of Tantric practitioners, including those of both Tsong Khapa and his Kagyu critics. In fact, I will argue that Tibetan Buddhism, as it is practiced in both the early-modern and modern periods, tends to exemplify as its ideal not the "scholar" or the "practitioner," but rather the *mkhas-grub*, the "scholar-practitioner," who is widely learned as well as deeply realized. The great figures of Tibetan Buddhism, including both Tsong Khapa and his critics such as Padma Karpo, tend to manifest both of these ideals to varying but not insignificant degrees.

The integration of theory and practice is in fact a characteristic of Tantric Buddhism. The Tantric forms of Buddhism are fundamentally concerned with practice. The Tantras themselves are typically concerned with methodology, techniques of meditation and ritual. One of the early names for the Tantric movement in India was the *mantra-naya*, "the method of the mantras." This was not conceived to be an independent vehicle, but rather, a set of tools in the Mahāyāna repertoire, which augments, but does not replace, general Mahāyāna belief and practice.

Despite the general Tantric focus on practice, the Tantric traditions also require considerable scholarship. While it is not the case that every practitioner must master scholarship, those who do not invariably rely

---

[20] A short perusal of Tsong Khapa's biographies indicates that he did have a number of significant visions of spiritual entities such as bodhisattvas and siddhas brought on by his intensive practice. See Kaschewsky 1974, 107–117, 130. See as well Thurman 1982, 16–22, for descriptions of his visions of various buddhas, bodhisattvas such as Maitreya, Mañjuśrī, and Vajrapāṇi, and the mahāsiddhas Nāropā and Tilopa.

[21] See Thurman 1982, 17, 21–22.

upon the scholarship of their guru or the lineage tradition in which they are embedded. This is because the Tantras themselves are extremely cryptic documents that attempt to conceal, rather than reveal, the requisite details that any practitioner needs to know. Deriving order from the disorder of the Tantras takes a considerable amount of scholarship. As a result, while every Tantric tradition traces its origin to a siddha or realized practitioner, we almost always find scholars on these lists as well, often in one and the same person. Hence were find important figures in lineage lists, such as Atiśa and Nāropā, who were renowned for their mastery of Tantra from both perspectives. Not only did they transmit major practice lineages, but they also composed texts that aided those who would take up these practices. I would go farther than this and argue that the individuals who have made the greatest impact in Tibetan religious history have typically been among the most learned.[22]

Partly on account of this, the act of scholarship in the Tibetan context inevitably has political implications. Hence, I contend that we can shed light on Tibetan religious history by exploring commentarial literature, a genre of Buddhist literature that, in the Tantric context at least, has been largely neglected by Western Buddhologists. This neglect may be due to the impression that commentaries are tedious, an impression that, while subjective, is also misleading, as it assumes that commentaries are intellectual dead ends, cul-de-sacs in which long-dead scholars debated irrelevant issues. This neglect may also be due to the fact that a significant number of Western scholars of Buddhism are Buddhist, often of the sort who paradoxically idealize the practice that they are typically unable to engage in, due to pressures of the academic life.

Here it might be worthwhile to take note of the work of J.Z. Smith, who has challenged a fundamental assumption underlying the practice versus scholarship dichotomy, namely the belief that religions originate in some sort of primal experience that is concretized and routinized by subsequent religious historical development. As Smith argued:

---

22 There are, of course, many exceptions to this generalization. Notable exceptions include figures such as Milarepa, whose great fame was not due to his scholarship. Milarepa's guru and grand guru, Marpa "the translator" and Nāropā, were both scholar-practitioners, as was Milarepa's disciple Gampopa. He was thus embedded in a tradition that produced notable works of scholarship.

> I would propose an enterprise that would insist on the value of the prosaic, the expository, the articulate. It is to explore the creativity of…"exegetical ingenuity," as a basic constituent of human culture. It is to gain an appreciation of the complex dynamics of tradition and its necessary dialectics of self-limitation and freedom. To do these things…is to give expression to what I believe is the central contribution that religious studies might make,…the realization that in culture, there is no text, it is all commentary; that there is no primordium, it is all history; that all is application. The realization that, regardless of whether we are dealing with "texts" from literate or non-literate cultures, we are dealing with historical processes of reinterpretation, with tradition. That, for a given group at a given time to choose this or that way of interpreting their tradition is to opt for a particular way of relating themselves to their historical past and their social present.[23]

In other words, the study of commentary is not an irrelevant pursuit, but aids us in our attempts to understand religion in its socio-historical contexts. I contend that the study of commentaries such as Tsong Khapa's influential commentary on the *Cakrasaṁvara Tantra*, his *Illumination of the Hidden Meaning*, could also shed light on the religious world of early fifteenth-century Tibet.

This is an excellent example for making the case for the socio-historical relevance of commentarial literature. By the early fifteenth century, when Tsong Khapa wrote this text, the *Cakrasaṁvara Tantra* was one of the most popular Tibetan Buddhist practice traditions. Politically speaking, the situation in Tibet was exceptionally fluid. With the collapse of Mongol hegemony in Central and East Asia in the late fourteenth century, there was a rapid decline in the power of the Sakya school, which administered Tibet under the Mongols. By the early fifteenth century, when Tsong Khapa was active, there were numerous schools of Buddhism vying for influence. For this reason alone, a com-

---

[23] Smith 1987, 196.

mentary upon one of the most popular Tantras by a lama of rising influence was invariably seen as political, as an attempt to forge a distinct position on which to base the authority of one's tradition. This, in fact, is exactly what Tsong Khapa accomplished.

In order to do this, Tsong Khapa had to establish his own authority as a suitable exegete for the tradition. Tsong Khapa was, perhaps, open to criticism precisely because he was, like his grand guru Büton, an extremely ambitious generalist, rather than a specialist in the Cakrasaṁvara tradition.[24] Like Büton, Tsong Khapa was an intellectual synthesist. Indeed, this seems to be a characteristic feature of many of the Tibetan intellectuals of this period, who were faced with the challenge of making sense of the vast transmissions of Indian Buddhist texts and practices that preceding generations of scholars had accomplished.

As a result, Tsong Khapa discusses the issue of qualifications at several points in his commentary. One point he makes firmly is that one need not be an accomplished siddha to be qualified to comment on the Tantras. He wrote:

> Furthermore, it is the case that before developing an exegetical system on the intention of a Tantra, one first distinguishes the practice systems of that particular Tantra. However, it is not taught that it is necessary to obtain the supramundane cognitions in order to elucidate the meaning of the Tantra, provided that one has followed a tradition created by former [masters]. Some people say that to just comment on a Tantra one must have attained the supramundane cognitions, and that if one writes without them, one will go to hell. However, if one engages in Tantric commentary without even having attained a trace of supramundane cognition, one is just making a fool of oneself.[25]

Tsong Khapa here challenges the claim, apparently made by some of his contemporaries or predecessors, that one need be not only a practitioner

[24] Tsong Khapa's numerous and often lengthy retreats were necessitated by his ambitious attempt to master all four classes of Tantra.

[25] See section 3.1 of Tsong Khapa's text below.

of a Tantra but also a master of these practices in order to comment upon it. This is a very high bar to scholarship on the Tantras, to which he rightly objects. He also sensibly challenges the scare tactics employed by advocates of these positions. His view is that following a lineage tradition is sufficient qualification. He undoubtedly felt that intensive practice in a tradition was an essential requisite for commenting on that tradition. While he does not state this here, he himself set a practical example of a scholar-practitioner.[26] Tsong Khapa carefully outlines for the reader his qualifications with respect to lineage transmission, and shows how he himself is the beneficiary of lineage transmissions descending from the mahāsiddha Nāropā.[27]

Tsong Khapa was careful to present his position in the lineage, but this does not mean that he was a staunch traditionalist. Taking such a stance was in fact an essential political move within the unsteady and shifting political ground of early fifteenth-century Tibet. The *Cakrasaṁvara Tantra* was one of the most popular Tibetan Buddhist practice traditions. For this reason alone, a commentary upon it by a lama of rising influence would have been seen as political, as an attempt to forge a distinct position on which to base the authority of one's tradition. This, in fact, is exactly what Tsong Khapa accomplished in his commentary.

He achieved this by taking several radical stances in his interpretation of the scripture. The term "radical" is not often applied to Tsong Khapa, given his portrayal as a conservative reformer who sought to re-establish monastic discipline. The latter part of this portrayal is true; that is, he clearly was concerned with creating a firm institutional basis for the practice of monastic discipline, continuing the work begun by the great Indian saint Atiśa, who traveled to Tibet during the eleventh century for precisely this purpose. For Tsong Khapa, it was only from this firm foundation that both Buddhist scholarship and Buddhist practice could flourish.

However, he did not achieve this goal via conservative or traditionalist means only. In the case of his commentary on the *Cakrasaṁvara Tantra*, he took a quite radical approach, one that in several important

---

[26] A quick examination of Tsong Khapa's biography shows that he repeatedly went on practice retreats throughout his life. See Thurman 1982 for many examples.

[27] See section 3.2.3.3 of Tsong Khapa's text below.

instances broke from the venerable Indo-Tibetan commentarial tradition on this text. In the cases where he made these breaks, it was precisely because the classical approaches to understanding the text did not support his agenda.

If one reads through all of the Indian commentaries on this text, one will find, not surprisingly, that it is the presence of violent and erotic elements that aroused the greatest commentarial activity. Regarding the former, it appears to have been the general product of the cultural world of early medieval India that was increasingly characterized, as Ronald Davidson has argued, by the "idealization of warfare and the apotheosis of kingship."[28] The *Cakrasaṁvara Tantra* tended to provoke violent discourse directed at Hindus, largely because the text, at its inception, seems to have been heavily influenced by Śaivism. However, these issues were not of particular concern to Tsong Khapa, no doubt because he was operating in a largely Buddhist cultural world in which Hinduism presented no threat.

Sex, however, was an issue that maintained its controversial impact as the text and tradition was transmitted from the Indian to Tibetan cultural worlds. The *Cakrasaṁvara Tantra* contains numerous erotic passages that suggest that practices involving sexuality are essential for the achievement of both the worldly miraculous powers, *laukikasiddhi*, and the supreme achievement, *lokottarasiddhi*, of awakening. The Indian commentators generally confirm this, interpreting these passages in reference to perfection stage yogic practices conducted in sexual union with a consort. However, they are typically extremely secretive about the details of the practices. We can find an excellent example of this attitude in the earliest surviving commentary by Jayabhadra, the third abbot of the Vikramaśīla monastery active during the ninth century. Jayabhadra stated his position as follows:

> The "secret" (*rahasyam*) is that which should be hidden, i.e., so that there is no disclosure to all of the disciples, and so forth. Now, that which is achieved through the union of the wisdom and art is the secret. Moreover, the vajra, lotus, and awakening spirit are the three secrets.

[28] Davidson 2002, 68.

> *Ra* is said to mean "vajra," and the syllable *ha*, "lotus." *Syam* designates the seed of those two. This is because the syllable *ra* is shaped like the tip of the vajra, the syllable *ha* has the shape of a bird's beak, and the combination of the two syllables *sa* and *ya* has the form of the seed of the two.[29]

Jayabhadra unambiguously identifies the "secret" with sexual practices. He also scrupulously follows his own injunction, and refrains from providing any detailed descriptions of the secret practices to which he refers here. Such commentary has the cumulative effect of creating the impression that the great secret of the Tantra concerns sexual practices.[30]

This led to considerable controversy in both India and Tibet. Some scholars, most notably Atiśa, were concerned that the literal interpretation of the Tantras and the concomitant practice of sexual yogas inevitably led to cenobitic fornication. This sort of transgression was a great concern to the king of Western Tibet, Hla Lama Yeshe Ö, which led him to invite Atiśa to Tibet in the early eleventh century for the expressed purpose of reforming monastic discipline. Atiśa's efforts led to the development of the Kadampa school, a tradition that was noted for its efforts to restrict the study of the Tantras to those qualified on the basis of their dedication to moral and intellectual cultivation.[31]

It should probably be of no surprise that Tsong Khapa, who inherited the mantle of the Kadampa tradition and saw himself as a continuer of Atiśa's work, took a new approach to the interpretation of this scripture. What is surprising is the tack that he took, an approach that challenges the impression some have of him as a puritanical reformer. At issue here is the "secret" of the Tantra, the secret that the text promises to reveal in its very first line. For Tsong Khapa, like his Indian and Tibetan

---

[29] My translation from the following text in Jayabhadra's *Cakrasaṁvarapañjikā*: *āha rahasyaṁ gopanīyaṁ sarvaśrāvakādibhyo 'prakāśyatvāt /athāva prajñopāyor ekīkaraṇena yar sādhyaṁ tad rahasyam / athāva vajraṁ padmaṁ bodhicittaṁ ca etat trayaṁ rahasyam // repho vajram iti prokto hakāraḥ padmam ucyate / ubhayos tayor bījaṁ syam ity abhidhīyate // rephasya vajrasūcyākāratvāt / hakārasya khagamukhākāratvāt / sakārayakārayoḥ saṁyogasyobhayabījarūpatvāt* / (Sugiki 2001, 106).

[30] I argue this at length in my (2005b) article.

[31] See Gray 2007, 123–129.

predecessors, this secret concerns the realization of bliss. This is probably an inescapable conclusion; bliss is frequently mentioned in the Tantra.

For Tsong Khapa, the "bliss" to which this text refers is no mere sexual bliss. While the text makes use of sexual imagery and metaphor, for him, the bliss that it describes is far more profound. By this I do not mean that Tsong Khapa was a prude, and denied the existence of the sexual arts that the text seems to describe. Quite the contrary, Tsong Khapa describes these practices in a very matter-of-fact manner, often far more clearly than the Indian sources on which he relied. In other words, he did not seek to deny that these practices existed, or even to veil them under a mantle of esotericism. An example of this is his extensive commentary on the following line in chapter 26, which deals with the proper conduct that the male adept should exhibit with the "messenger" (*dūtī*) or consort:

> My messengers are omnipresent, always bestowing power above and below. These messengers bestow all powers, always looking, touching, kissing, and embracing. Especially at the seats of yoga, as long as there are bands of yoginīs, then there are those who produce all powers, it is said.[32]

Tsong Khapa comments on this as follows:

> In practicing the supreme, with whom does one practice? It is my messenger. She goes to all places through the mode of bestowing kisses and embraces, etc., to all for the purpose of achieving the aims of fortunate beings. If that messenger who is like this bestows all powers even by looking with the eye, touching with the body, or hearing, what need is there to mention her bestowing power through being propitiated continually and correctly? This is the explanation of the three scholars.[33]
>
> Regarding the messenger's system of bestowing power through looking, and so forth, it is through a process of giving rise to great bliss. The *Vajrapañjara* states:

[32] My translation of *Cakrasaṁvara Tantra* 26.2c–4b; cf. Gray 2007, 265–266.

[33] Tsong Khapa here expands upon Büton's commentary at NS 157a.

> There is bliss from the sight of the supreme woman, and true bliss even from hearing her song. The bliss from smelling her delicious scent is greater, and even greater is the bliss from touching her vulva. No one is able to turn away from the bliss of union, the draught of the supreme savor. (VP 57b)

> Thus, the blazing of great bliss from the sight, and so forth, of the supreme messenger is the "melting bliss" (*zhu bde*). One must melt the body's awakening spirit in order to give rise to that bliss, and for that [to happen] it is essential that the fury fire blaze. Since the fire is kindled through the force of the accumulated winds, if one is blessed by the supreme messenger, just as soon as she is seen one will generate great bliss continually and without reversal, even if there are contradictory conditions, through the force of the accumulated powers of wind that draw forth great bliss. Thus one will very quickly [progress on] the path of the messenger.

> One should always, i.e., continually, kiss and embrace the messenger. Furthermore, [one should] especially [kiss and embrace] the seat, i.e., distinctive place, in which occurs the yoga of the nondual union of bliss and emptiness, that is, the supreme lotus. It is there that the kissing should be done, meaning that one rubs it by moving about the tip of one's tongue. Having delighted one's mind with beer drinking, one should engage in love play, uniting the vajra and lotus. One engages in love play so long as one knows the yoga spoken by Vajrasattva, which is the host of sexual positions (*karaṇa*) explained in the treatises on love (*kāmaśāstra*). It is said that [doing this] causes the production of all powers.[34]

This commentary, far more detailed than any written in India, has the seemingly paradoxical effect of demystifying these practices. He

[34] My translation of the text in KS ch. 26, section 3.3.3.2.2.2.4.2.2. This will be presented in vol. 2 of my KS translation.

neither highlights nor attempts to hide them, raising them to the status of the "secret of secrets." Tsong Khapa here may have been acting strategically, for had he taken the latter approach, this very well may have undermined his efforts to reform monastic discipline.

For Tsong Khapa, the sexual arts are not the true secret, but rather a relatively mundane art. Here, and also at several other points in his commentary, he directs readers who wish learn more to turn to the *kāmaśāstras*, the secular literature on sexual love. What, then, is the "secret"? For Tsong Khapa, the true secret, the hidden meaning of the Tantra, is something that he refers to as the "union of emptiness and bliss." By this he means that the realization of the great bliss on which the text is so focused depends upon prior realization of emptiness. Tsong Khapa's addition of emptiness into the equation was radical. For one thing, the term is not mentioned once in the Tantra. Tsong Khapa ingeniously accounts for this as follows:

> Here the Yoginī Tantras teach primarily the inseparability of bliss and emptiness from the perspective of wisdom. The view of the reality of emptiness is taught in brief in the Tantras, since the Lord Nāgārjuna intended that there would be nothing left to explain aside from what he established extensively.[35]

In other words, since Nāgārjuna already stated everything that can be profitably said about emptiness, there is no need for the Tantras to say more on this subject. Instead, they focus on bliss as the "exoteric" topic to be stated. Emptiness thus remains the hidden, esoteric import of the text. This interpretation is almost certainly the product of Tsong Khapa's larger intellectual project, the proper interpretation of Madhyamaka philosophy, which was a major concern of many Tibetans at this time.[36]

While emptiness, arguably, may be the ultimate import of the Tantras, the realization of which is the *buddhajñāna*, or gnosis of a buddha, it is clearly not their overt focus. Instead, they focus on blissful union, *saṁvara*, as a useful if not necessary art, since its perfection results in the

[35] See KS ch. 24, section 3.3.3.2.2.2.3.5.4 below.

[36] For a fascinating study of the Tibetan discovery of Candrakīrti and the Tibetan creation of the Prāsaṅgika school of Madhyamaka philosophy, see Vose 2009.

rapid achievement of the *rūpakāya*, or buddha's physical form, that is a necessary adjunct to the achievement of the *dharmakāya*, a buddha's gnosis, which is a total realization of emptiness.

The concept of blissful union pervades the scripture, and is evoked by its title. The term *saṁvara*, literally meaning "binding," and, by extension, "union," is frequently translated in Tibetan as *bde mchog*, "Supreme Bliss," and in Tibet the text was most frequently referred to by its alias *Laghusaṁvara*, "Supreme Bliss Light," *bde mchog nyung ngu* or just *bde mchog*. Tsong Khapa comments on it as follows:

> "Union" (*saṁvara*, *sdom pa*) means "supreme assembly." Those that are to be united are the physical, verbal, and mental actions of all buddhas. They are the wheels of body, speech, and mind. Regarding the manner in which they are united, all of the things to be united are united as one, inseparably. It is the union of bliss and emptiness as one, and the union of body, speech, and mind into the single reality of the natural (*sahaja*) Heruka. The *Saṁvarodaya* states that:
>
>> Physical, verbal, and mental action is the ultimate union of all forms (*sarvākāraikasaṁvaraṁ*, *rnam pa thams cad gcig sdom pa*). Union (*saṁvaraṁ*, *sdom pa*) is supreme bliss, the awakening that cannot be spoken or shown. It is the secret of all buddhas, the assembly that is the supreme union (*saṁvaraṁ varaṁ*, *bde ba'i mchog*).[37]

For Tsong Khapa, the ultimate referent of the imagery of "union" is not necessarily physical union, but rather the abstract union of emptiness and bliss. In this he was supported with the later Indian tradition, which tended toward the interpretation of the "secret" of the text as an abstract realization of ultimate reality, rather than an actual embodied practice.[38]

Although Tsong Khapa had no textual basis for this interpretation in this Tantra, fortunately for him there are other Tantras that do support

---

[37] See KS introductory section 3.3.1.2 below.

[38] See Gray 2005b for a discussion of this trend.

his interpretation. It is here that Tsong Khapa's synthetic approach to the study of Tantras bore fruit. However, elucidating the "secret" of one Tantra with reference to another is a controversial exegetical approach. Tsong Khapa defended this strategy with a citation from Vajrapāṇi's commentary on the *Cakrasaṁvara Tantra*:

> In the *Commentary Praising Saṁvara*, [Vajrapāṇi] stated that [the abridged Tantra's import] should be realized, for the sake of those who have not had the good fortune of hearing the very extensive root Tantra, through reliance upon other Tantras that collect the profound vajra words of the Tantras, whose teachings have been collected from the extensive Tantra, or the commentaries of bodhisattvas, or the instructions of the guru.[39]

Tsong Khapa here refers to the following comments provided by Vajrapāṇi in his *Laghutantraṭīkā*: "Furthermore, due to its abundance of adamantine expressions,[40] learned ones desiring liberation should know it by means of the instruction of the holy guru, what is said in other Tantras, and the commentaries written by the bodhisattvas."[41] Elsewhere in the same work, Vajrapāṇi justifies commenting on one Tantra via another as follows: "[This] is the determination of the Tathāgata [stated] in other Tantras. One should understand [this] Tantra by means of other Tantras, since the Tathāgata stated them."[42] This seems like an eminently reasonable claim; if one accepts the Tantras as authentic speech of the buddhas, there is no reason why one could not comment upon one while taking account of what is stated in others. But this was definitely a political claim, particularly if we recall that the authors of the "bodhisattva commentaries" were advocates of the Kālacakra tradition, and, in commenting on

---

[39] See KS introductory section 3.1 below.

[40] "Adamantine expressions" (*vajrapada*) are the instances of symbolic speech found in the Tantras, which require detailed explanation.

[41] My translation of the following text: *sā ca vajrapadabahulatvāt sadgurūpadeśena tantratantrāntaroktena bodhisattvakṛtaṭīkaya jñātavyā vidvadbhir mokṣārthibhir iti* / (Cicuzza 2001, 52).

[42] My translation of the following text: *...iti tantrāntareṣu tathāgataniyamaḥ / tantraṁ tantrāntareṇa boddhavyaṁ iti tathāgatavacanāt* / (Cicuzza 2001, 124).

two of the most popular Tantras in early eleventh-century North India in light of the Kālacakra, they were arguably attempting to bolster the status of this new scripture by treating it not only as authentic, but as the ultimate teaching, the hermeneutical lens through which all other teachings could, and should, be interpreted.[43]

Tsong Khapa, however, was far less audacious than Vajrapāṇi, and while he does refer to other Tantras in his commentary on the *Cakrasaṁvara Tantra*, he does so in a very restrained fashion, largely restricting himself to the closely related *Hevajra Tantra*. It is in his general works, such as his masterful *Great Stages of Mantra* (*sngags rim chen mo*), that he allows himself the freedom to range throughout the canon to support his arguments.

Given Tsong Khapa's great prestige and influence, his interpretive stance did have political ramifications. Particularly, I believe that his insistence that the cultivation of bliss must be rooted in a realization of emptiness was linked to his institutional project. Tsong Khapa and his disciples were quite successful in creating a network of monastic institutions that emphasized a hierarchical approach to the study of Buddhism, one that is loosely based on the triple vow (*trisaṁvara*) system of Buddhist practice.[44] For Tsong Khapa, the practice of Buddhism rested on a foundation of moral discipline, a foundation that depended upon the cornerstone of the monastic order. This, in turn, supported the edifice of the Mahāyāna tradition that centered on the correct understanding of emptiness, which in turn was the basis for the development of great compassion. This, moreover, supported the pavilion of Tantric practice. For Tsong Khapa and the Geluk tradition in general, Tantric practice was best undertaken by well-prepared and well-educated monks, and, occasionally, by nuns as well.[45] This preparation would be both moral, by virtue of their mastery of monastic discipline, and intellectual and emotional, by virtue of realizing emptiness and cultivating compassion.

---

[43] For more on Vajrapāṇi and his *Laghutantraṭīkā* see Cicuzza 2001, 23–26. See also Gray 2009.

[44] Regarding this, see Sobisch 2002.

[45] Regarding the status of nuns in a contemporary Geluk community and the challenges they face in receiving advanced Tantric training see Gutschow 2004.

In other words, Tsong Khapa's "radical" reinterpretation of the *Cakrasaṁvara Tantra* was political, in that it served as a justification for the process of institution building in which he was engaged. We should note, too, that this institution building was directed toward the production of Buddhist masters who would exemplify the ideal of *mkhas-grub*, "scholar-practitioners." While only a small minority of Geluk practitioners would ever achieve this goal, this ideal was not limited to the Geluk tradition, but appears throughout the various traditions of Tibetan Buddhism. Great Drukpa Kagyu scholars such as Padma Karpo would also exemplify this, as would the eighteenth-century Nyingma master Jigmay Lingpa (1729–1798 CE), whom Geoffrey Samuel upheld as a paradigm of the "visionary-shamanic" perspective.[46] Jigmay Lingpa's beautiful writings, while inspired by his spiritual practice, clearly are also the product of his profound scholarship. Although there are many differences among these figures, they share a common link insofar as all three excelled in both scholarship and spiritual practice.

I would like to conclude by noting that this commentary is a work produced by one of Tibet's best-known and most productive scholars, at the peak of his teaching career. It definitely deserves serious study, by both scholars interested in the history of Tibetan Buddhism and practitioners interested in his views on one of the key Yoginī Tantras. I hope that readers of both types, scholars and practitioners, will find something of value in this work.

---

[46] See Samuel 1993, 546–551.

PART TWO

TRANSLATION

The Detailed Exegesis of the Concise Saṁvara Tantra, called *The Illumination of the Hidden Meaning*

[Outline of Tsong Khapa's Preface and Introduction]

Preface
Introduction
1. The general arrangement of all the teachings
2. The particular arrangement of the great bliss Tantras
2.1. Identifying the root Tantra, explanatory Tantras, and intertextual Tantras
2.1.1. Identifying the noncontroversial Tantras
2.1.2. Discussing the controversial explanatory Tantras
2.2. Showing the time and place of the original proclamation of the *Cakrasaṁvara Tantra*
2.3. The way in which the explanatory Tantras explain the root Tantra
2.3.1. Identifying the main points by which the explanatory Tantras explain the root Tantra
2.3.2. How the uncommon explanatory Tantras explain
2.3.2. 1. How the *Abhidhānottara* and *Vajraḍāka* explain
2.3.2. 1.1. How the *Abhidhānottara* explains
2.3.2. 1.1.1. How the creation stage is explained
2.3.2. 1.1.1. 1. How the creation stage is not clear in the root Tantra
2.3.2. 1.1.1. 2. How this explanatory Tantra explains clearly
2.3.2. 1.1.2. How the perfection stage is explained [in the *Abhidhānottara*]
2.3.2. 1.2. How the *Vajraḍāka* explains
2.3.2. 2. How the *Saṁvarodaya* and the *[Yoginī]saṁcāra* explain
2.3.2. 2.1. How the *Saṁvarodaya* explains
2.3.2. 2.2. How the *[Yoginī]saṁcāra* explains
2.3.3. How the common explanatory Tantras explain
3. Introduction to the way in which the concise root Tantra is explained
3.1. The explanation based on the instructions of the mahāsiddhas
3.2. Showing the method of explanation based upon them [the instructions of the mahāsiddhas]
3.2.1. Significance of the count of fifty-one chapters
3.2.2. Applying the threefold explanation to the fifty-one chapters
3.2.3. Showing the relevance of the summary of each chapter
3.2.3. 1. Showing the summary of each [chapter]
3.2.3. 1.1. The summary of bestowing consecration and showing reality therein
3.2.3. 1.2. The summary of the selection of mantras and achieving the powers
3.2.3. 1.3. The summary of attaining both powers through the kindness of the messengers
3.2.3. 1.4. The summary of impact-heightening conduct and the vow as a friend on the path
3.2.3. 1.5. The summary of the four mudrās such as mahāmudrā
3.2.3. 1.6. The summary on understanding the signs of the rapid attainment of the powers
3.2.3. 2. The arrangement in one of the stages of the path
3.2.3. 3. The method of the lineage from Nāropā

[Tsong Khapa's Preface]

[This is] a detailed exegesis of the concise *Saṁvara Tantra*, namely the *Cakrasaṁvara*, which is called the *Illumination of the Hidden Meaning*. I bow down with reverence and take refuge at the lotus feet of His Holiness Guru Mañjughoṣa. I bow down with reverence at the lotus feet of Her Holiness [Vajravārāhī] and great glorious Heruka who are like a rose dawn cloud embracing a great sapphire mountain. I bow down to the essence yoginīs, who, moved by love, always befriend the practitioner of this path, visiting him wherever he abides, by means of the force of their magic powers. Bless me, heroes and yoginīs, who always bless the practitioner, never withdrawing the appearance of your emanation bodies from the twenty-four supreme places such as Pullīramalaya. I respectfully bow to the gate and quarter goddesses,[47] who, with their inconceivably great power, defeat the demons that harass practitioners. May they enable me to accomplish my desired aims.

May I be blessed by guru Mañjughoṣa, who refreshes beings with his wondrous deeds, whose mind plays in the delight and bliss in administering the kingdom of the Dharma that is to be found within the teachings of the Buddha, and who, out of great compassion, pierces the heart with a flicker of his glance, breaking the tight bonds of the net of confusion in which we have been embroiled since beginningless time. I bow to the learned mentors of India and Tibet, such as Nārotapa, who upheld properly the system of the great saints who have touched [their heads] to the feet of the glorious Heruka.

The treasure of all the jeweled successes is arrayed as a series of waves of the many personal instructions in the ocean of the hidden currents of supreme bliss. How could one such as I ever cross it? However, I found a little bit of intellectual brilliance concerning how to connect the Root and explanatory Tantras, through the excellent explanation that descended to me through the lineage from the wise, so I feel some enthusiasm about this. For those who have ambition for investigating this method, I will expand upon it, as it is an elixir for the eyes, a sweet

---

[47] They are Kākāsyā, Ulūkāsyā, Śvānāsyā, Śūkarāsyā, Yamadāḍhī, Yamadūtī, Yamadaṁṣṭrī, and Yamamathanī.

message for the ears, and a miraculous delight for the mind, a mirror for viewing the meaning of the hidden Tantra.

Since the emanation of the mandala, which manifests the heroes and heroine Īśvarīs, still abides here in the twenty-four places of this very land of Jambudvīpa, one might rapidly attain their powers and virtues, for they still arise without any obstruction and without any decline in power, even up to the end of time.

The concise *Saṁvara Tantra*, called the *Śrī Cakrasaṁvara*, is famous as having blessings. In order to come to determination concerning this Tantra, there are three things: (1) the general arrangement of all scriptures, (2) the arrangement of the great bliss Tantras in particular, and finally, (3) the explanation of how one precisely engages in the explanation of the abbreviated root Tantra.

[Tsong Khapa's Introduction]

1. The general arrangement of all the teachings

First, (1) as for demonstrating that the teaching of the Victor is the sole entrance for those who desire liberation, and also, as for the teachings on the various ways of entering that, I have extensively explained this in the *Stages of the Path of Vajradhara*.[48] I have already taught extensively the arrangement of Father and Mother Tantras in books such as *The General Introduction to the Detailed Analysis of Guhyasamāja*[49] and so forth, so I will not bother with them here.

2. The particular arrangement of the great bliss Tantras

The second part has three sections: (1) identifying the root Tantra, explanatory Tantras, and intertextual Tantras; (2) showing the time and place of the original proclamation of the *Cakrasaṁvara Tantra*; and (3) the way in which the explanatory Tantras explains the root Tantra.

---

48 That is, his well-known *sngags rim chen mo*.

49 That is, his *mtha' dpyod*, or *rgyud kyi rgyal po dpal gsang ba 'dus pa'i rgya cher bshad pa sgron ma gsal ba'i dka' ba'i gnas kyi mtha' dpyod rin po che'i myu gu*.

2.1. Identifying the root Tantra, explanatory Tantras, and intertextual Tantras

The first part has two sections: (1) identifying the noncontroversial Tantras, and (2) discussing the controversial explanatory Tantras.

2.1.1. Identifying the noncontroversial Tantras

If we speak roughly about the arrangement of the noncontroversial Tantras of the literature of the *Śrī Cakrasaṁvara Tantra*, master [Vīra-]vajra explained that "there is a one hundred thousand-chapter root Tantra, a hundred-thousand-stanza *Khasama Appendix*, and the appendix of the appendix is the fifty-one–chaptered, seven-hundred-stanza version."[50] Some of the Tibetan lamas accepted that. However, there does not seem to be any proof based on an authoritative source.

Now, the *Ḍākārṇava* states that "in the *Laghusaṁvara*, which is derived from the three-hundred-thousand-stanza *Abhidhāna*, the chapters are linked to reality in accordance with the letters, from *a* until the letter *kṣ*."[51] This indicates that the *Laghusaṁvara Tantra* is derived from the three-hundred-thousand-stanza *Abhidhāna*.

The *Saṁcāra* states: "the *Saṁvara* that is abridged from the one-hundred-thousand[-stanza] *Abhidhāna Tantra* is said to be from within the *Khasama Tantra* of one hundred thousand [stanzas]."[52] This explana-

---

[50] This is in reference to Vīravajra's (PD) commentary on CT 1.2a, *uttarādapi cottaraṁ*. Now, *uttara* implies distance in time or space, in the former case implying something that came afterward or later, or, in the latter case, something that goes higher or beyond, connoting sublimity. This line is usually interpreted in the latter sense, and thus could be translated as "more lofty than the lofty." Vīravajra, however, takes it in the former sense as referring to an *uttaratantra*, an appendix, as follows: "Why is it 'later than the late'? There is the hundred-thousand-chaptered root Tantra, and subsequent to it is the hundred-thousand-stanza *Khasama*, and the fifty-one-chaptered [text] is the subsequent appendix" (PD 355b). He makes this point in several other places in this commentary, such as in his commentary upon the first word of the root Tantra, *atha*, which follows: "Since the fifty-one-chaptered [text] was taught after the hundred-thousand-chapter root Tantra and the hundred-thousand-stanza appendix were completed, 'and then,' etc., was stated" (PD 354b). He also makes the same argument on fol. 355a in commenting upon the line *samāsān na tu vistarāt* (CT 1.1b).

[51] See DA 242b–243a.

[52] This quote corresponds to the following passage in the *Yoginīsaṁcāra*: *lakṣābhidhānatantrasya uddhṛtaṁ tena saṁvaram / khasamatantraikalakṣasya tattvaṁ madhye tu*

(cont'd)

tion that the *Khasama Tantra* is a one hundred thousand [stanza Tantra] is in accordance with the former [statement by Vīravajra]. And it is explained that the *Laghusaṁvara Tantra* was abridged from the *Abhidhāna* of one hundred thousand stanzas. The one-hundred-thousand-stanza *Abhidhāna* from which the *Laghusaṁvara* was abridged and the *Khasama Tantra* are stated as being two distinct Tantras.[53]

A comment on these two from the *Herukābhyudaya* is, "The essence of the Tantra was taught abridged from a hundred and three hundred thousand [stanza texts]."[54] Since a commentary on this says that there was a three hundred thousand [stanza] extensive *Abhidhāna*, and an abridged one of one hundred thousand [stanzas], so therefore there is no contradiction.[55] Such being the case, there are two different extensive root Tantras.

The root Tantra states, "The hero stated it concisely as it is in the *Ocean of Spells*."[56] As for the *Ocean of Spells* mentioned here, Jayabhadra and Vīravajra explain that it refers to the Mahātantra.[57] Some

---

khyāpitam // (Pandey 1998, 123); */ ming gi rgyud ni 'bum sde las / / snying po bsdus par gyur pa yin / / nam mkha' dang ni mnyam pa'i rgyud / / 'bum gcig nang nas de bzhin bshad /* (YS 41a).

53 None of the six editions that I have consulted corroborate Tsuda's quotation (1974, 32) of Tsong Khapa's concluding phrase here as *rgyud gnyis so snor gsungs so*, the syntax of which seems unusual. The editions consulted here all read *rgyud gnyis so sor gsungs so*. If the latter is correct, Tsong Khapa is asserting that the 100,000-stanza *Abhidhāna* and the 100,000-stanza *Khasama* are distinct texts.

54 This is a quote from the ninth chapter of the *Śrīherukābhyudaya*. The text here as quoted by Tsong Khapa is ambiguous, but the version in Kangyur translation is somewhat clearer, as follows: */'bum dang 'bum phrag gsum du gsung / / rgyud kyi snying po mtha dag bsdus /* (HA 7a).

55 Tsong Khapa here paraphrases *Candrakumara's (zla-ba gzhon-nu's) *Śrīherukābhyudaya-mahāyoginītantrarāja-katipayākṣarapañjikā* at D fol. 105a.

56 Tsong Khapa here quotes the SM translation of CT 34.8ab. This text differs considerably from the extant Sanskrit as well as the other Tibetan translations.

57 The Tibetan translation of Jayabhadra's commentary identifies the *vidyārṇava* as a Mahātantra (CP 63b: *rgyud chen po*), although the Sanskrit identifies it simply as a Tantra. His commentary reads as follows: "As for the Tantra called the ***Ocean of Spells***, [the things] **taught** in it **succinctly in the manner of the hero** are clarified here. Moreover, **taught in the *Ocean of Spells*** means that the rites [taught] concisely here are [taught] extensively there" (Sugiki 2001, 134: *vidyārṇavaṁ nāma tantra tatra he vīra yathā samāsāt paribhāṣitaṁ tad atra vispaṣṭīkṛtam ity arthaḥ / athavā vidyārṇave paribhāṣitam atra saṁkṣepato vidhis tatra tu vistara ity abhiprāyaḥ //*). See also SG 195b.

Tibetans say that it refers to the one hundred-thousand-stanza Tantra.[58] From among those, however, now in this area we only have this one abridged root Tantra in fifty-one [chapters].

Many explanatory Tantras as well are abridged Tantras derived from their own extensive Tantras, though they are not root Tantras that are abridged Tantras, root Tantras such as [this] fifty-one [chaptered text]. As for the explanatory Tantras, Durjayacandra says, "the four, the *Ḍāka* (*mkha' 'gro*), the *Udaya* (*'byung ba*), the *Saṁcāra*, and the *Abhidhānottara Tantra*,[59] along with the *Saṁpuṭa Tantra*, should be understood to be explanatory Tantras."[60] The *Ḍāka* refers to the *Vajraḍāka* (VD),[61] and the *Uttara* (*bla ma*) is the *Abhidhānottara*. The [title] *kha sbyor* refers to the *Saṁpuṭa* (ST). In regard to the *Udaya* literature, in general there are the three, the *Herukābhyudaya* (HA), the [*Origin of*] *Vārāhī*, and the *Saṁvarodaya* (SU). I will explain which of the *Udaya* can be said to be explanatory Tantras.

Since taken in that way there are five explanatory Tantras, [the word] "along with" (*dang*) of "along with [the *Saṁpuṭa*] Tantra" should be interpreted as the [conjunction] *dang* that separates [items in a list]. Of the four explanatory Tantras mentioned in Atiśa's commentary [the *Abhisamayavibhaṅga*], three of them are the *Udaya*, the *Abhidhāna*, and the *Vajraḍāka*. As for the fourth one, he thought it should be taken as the *Saṁcāra* (YS).[62]

---

58 Sachen identifies it with the three-hundred-thousand-stanza *Khasama Tantra* (PG 92.1). I have not found any Tibetan sources identifying it with a one-hundred-thousand-stanza root text.

59 The title given here, *mtshan mchog bla ma'i rgyud*, appears to be an unconventional translation of the title *Abhidhānottaratantra* (AU).

60 See RG fol. 246b.

61 This is a plausible identification, but note that it could also be a reference to the *Ḍākārṇava* (DA).

62 Tsong Khapa here refers to a passage in Atiśa's *Abhisamayavibhaṅga*, a commentary on Lūipa's *Śrībhagavad-abhisamaya sādhana*, as follows: "I will explain gathering together the essential points from the *Abhidhāna[-uttara]* (*nges brjod*), the [*Heruka-*] *Abhyudaya* (*mngon 'byung*), and the *Ḍāka* (*mkha' 'gro*). Here the object of explanation is the stages of the path of definitive meaning, which is the topic of the Yoginī Tantras, including the *Khasama Mahātantra* and the four explanatory Tantras that elucidate it" (AV fol. 186a). Again, it is not clear if by *mkha' 'gro* he is referring to the *Vajraḍāka* or

(cont'd)

The disciple of Nāropā in India whose name was Dārika, and who was the guru of the Paṇḍita Thang-chuba, says that if both the *Caturyoginī Saṁpuṭa* and the *Ḍākārṇava* are added to the five, this makes seven explanatory Tantras. Some of the expert Tibetans claimed that the *Saṁvarodaya* commentary is a concise Tantra, an appendix (*uttaratantra*) , or even an explanatory Tantra, and that the *Saṁvarodaya* and the *Origin of Vārāhī*[63] are explanatory Tantras to the Tantra itself. Therefore those added to the former seven makes nine explanatory Tantras.[64]

In that regard, in the *Saṁvara Tantra*, the Root and explanatory Tantras are not determined to be two. Alaṁkakalaśa said that the explanatory and auxiliary Tantras are separate.[65] Buddhaguhya also takes explanatory Tantras and intertextual Tantras as separate.[66] Here these [comments] are not contradictory so we should take them as such. If we

---

the *Ḍākārṇava*. Atiśa makes no mention of the *Yoginīsaṁcāra*, but it may be implied and included within his "four explanatory Tantras," given the fact that Lūipa's *Śrībhagavadabhisamaya* is based on this Tantra.

63 Normally I give the Sanskrit equivalents to Tsong Khapa's shorthand names for Indian Tantras, but this is not possible in this case. Tsong Khapa does not use the shorthand name "Origin of Vārāhī" (*phag mo mngon 'byung*) to refer to the *Ḍākinīsarvacittādvayācintyajñāna-vajravārāhyabhibhava-tantrarāja* (To. 378), as one might expect. Rather, he uses it in reference to the *Khyāvajravārāhī-abhidhānatantrottara-vārāhyabhibodhi* (To. 377), which would be better abbreviated as *phag mo mngon byang*. Tsong Khapa here may be relying on an older translation of this text.

64 Tsong Khapa here seems to be referring to Büton's analysis in his RP commentary. In this work he lists and describes nine noncontroversial explanatory Tantras (of both the special and common types). See RP 396–429.

65 Alaṁkakalaśa mentions three categories of Tantras at the opening of his *Vajramālā* commentary (2b–3a), namely "root Tantras," "explanatory Tantras," and "auxiliary Tantras" (*yan lag gi rgyud*). He does not define the latter category, but I presume that it consists of Tantras that are deemed to be related to a given root Tantra, but not closely enough to be deemed an "explanatory Tantra."

66 Explanatory Tantras are Tantras that are thought to explain or expand upon the root Tantra, while "intertextual Tantras" (*cha mthun gyi rgyud*), literally "tantras with corresponding portions," are Tantras that contain parallel passages. These are not necessarily separate categories, for many of the explanatory Tantras contain parallel passages with their root texts. Apparently, the presence of parallel passages does not in itself make one Tantra an explanatory Tantra to the other. Unfortunately, I have not been able to find a discussion of this issue in Buddhaguhya's works.

do this, the three, the *Vajraḍāka*, the *Saṁpuṭa*, and the *Saṁcāra* are as we explained. As for the *Abhidhānottara*, in some commentaries it is an explanatory Tantra, and in other commentaries it is taken as a root Tantra. However, it should be taken as an explanatory Tantra.

As for the *Origin of Vārāhī*, it refers to itself as "the Origin of Vārāhī from the explanatory appendix."[67] The "explanatory appendix" is the *Abhidhānottara*. And there are a few places where they draw upon each other, such as in the case of the twelfth chapter of the *Abhidhāna* and the third chapter of the *Origin of Vārāhī*, meaning that [the latter] is derived from the *Abhidhānottara*. Therefore, it is not an explanatory Tantra separate from the *Abhidhānottara*.[68]

As for *Saṁvarodaya*, it is explained that the *Sahaja Kalpa* was taught from the three hundred thousand [stanza] extensive Tantra,[69] and as this is very important, it seems that it is taken as an explanatory Tantra in [these] commentaries. Durjayacandra and Atiśa, stating only "Udaya," are unclear. Several previous Tibetan lamas thought they referred to the

---

[67] Tsong Khapa cites the title given at the end of the KV as follows: *bshad pa'i rgyud phyi ma las phag mo mngon par 'byung ba zhes bya ba*. The following title is given at the end of the KV: *bshad pa'i rgyud phyi ma las phag mo mngon par byang chub pa zhes bya ba* (KV 60a). Tsong Khapa's version of the title, *mngon par 'byung ba*, versus the *mngon par byang chub pa* preserved in the Kangyur text, suggests that he either relied upon an alternate translation or incorrectly recalled the title of the text.

[68] With regard to Tsong Khapa's claim that the KV derives from the AU, in part upon the basis of the title preserved at the end of the KV, it is important to note that the KV begins with an expanded version of this title, as follows: "The *Vārāhī-abhibodhiya*, from the *Vārāhī-abhidhāna* Explanatory Appendix" (KV 52b: *phag mo mngon par brjod pa bshad pa'i rgyud phyi ma las/ phag mo mngon par byang chub pa zhes bya ba*). This suggests that the text is *not* claiming the AU as its source, but rather a mythical *Vārāhī-abhidhāna*, undoubtedly echoing the origin story of CT. While AU ch. 12 deals with yoginīs, his claim that the KV is derived from the AU seems unlikely.

[69] Tsong Khapa is here referring to a passage that occurs in the colophon of the SU. It does not refer to itself as the *Sahaja Kalpa*, but rather identifies this as the name of the massive text from which it derives. The SU text reads as follows: "This completes the Great King of Tantras, the *Śrī Saṁvarodaya*, which achieves through recitation the secret of all yoginīs, and which was selected from the *Sahaja Kalpa*, which is in the three-hundred-thousand[-stanza] *Śrī Herukābhidhāna mahātantra*" (SU 311a: *//dpal he ru ka mngon par brjod pa'i rgyud chen po 'bum phrag gsum pa las lhan cig skyes pa 'byung ba'i rtog pa las* [reading *yas* as *las*] *btus pa/ rnal 'byor ma thams cad kyi gsang ba bklags pas 'grub pa/ dpal sdom pa 'byung ba'i rgyud kyi rgyal po chen po rdzogs so/*).

Herukābhyudaya, which, although it is said to be an explanatory Tantra on [the subject of] bestowing consecrations, does not have any presentation of the consecrations that does not arise from the root Tantra, and moreover there do not appear to be any clear reasons it should be taken as an explanatory Tantra, so it is better to think of it as a Parallel Tantra.[70] As for the *Ḍākārṇava* and the *Caturyoginī Saṁpuṭa*, taking them as Parallel Tantras would, I think, be better.

Atiśa talks about four explanatory Tantras, thinking of the explanatory Tantras as the doors of *Cakrasaṁvara*. The followers of Malgyo uphold five explanatory Tantras following Pamting-pa and Durjayacandra, from [the latter's] quote "*Ḍāka*, *Udaya*, *Saṁcāra*," etc.[71] Guru Pamting-pa[72] held that there are five explanatory Tantras, which is good; this is the system of not counting the *Origin of Vārāhī* as separate from the *Abhidhānottara*.

2.1.2. Discussing the controversial explanatory Tantras

There are the twenty-four *Rali* explanatory Tantras of the body, speech, and mind wheels of *Saṁvara*, which together with the eight auxiliary Tantras constitute thirty-two.[73] In regard to these eight auxiliary

---

70 The *phyogs mthun rgyud* are Tantras that are parallel in the sense that they contain similar material to that contained in the root Tantra, but do not serve to further "explain" or elaborate on this material or provide new information, which is the primary purpose of an explanatory Tantra. These categories of Tantras are explained at considerable length by Büton in his RP commentary.

71 Malgyo Lotsawa Lodrö Drakpa was a Tibetan translator who studied the CT with Pamting-pa in Nepal, and produced a Tibetan translation of the Tantra. Upon his return to Tibet he was one of the teachers of Sachen Kunga Nyingpo. Tsong Khapa is clearly referring here to Sachen and his Sakya successors.

72 The *bla ma pham-thing-pa*, i.e., the "guru from Pharping," also known as Vāgīśvarakīrti, was a disciple of Nāropā and renowned eleventh-century Newari teacher of many prominent Tibetan translators, including Malgyo, Marpa, and Mardo. Regarding him and his prominent brothers, see Lo Bue 1997.

73 Büton lists and briefly describes all thirty-two of the *Rali Tantras* at RP 429–36. They are divided into four groups of eight: body, speech, mind, and auxiliary. The body Tantras are: *Śrī Guhyavajra-tantrarāja* (To. 383, PTT. 28), *Śrī Guhyasarvacchinda* (To. 384, PTT. 29), *Śrī Cakrasaṁvaraguhyācintya-tantrarāja* (To. 385, PTT. 30), *Śrī Khasama-tantrarāja* (To. 386, PTT. 31), *Śrī Mahākhā-tantrarāja* (To. 387, PTT. 32), *Śrī Kāyavākcitta-tantrarāja* (To. 388, PTT. 33), *Śrī Ratnamālā-tantrarāja* (To. 389, PTT.

(cont'd)

Tantras of the Tibetan scholars, someone adds a category of "nonturbid Tantras" and claims that there are eight of these. This person, not counting the *Mahābalajñāna Tantrarāja*, adds the two *Rigi-arali* to the "nonturbid" ones, making eight. As for *Rigi-arali*, there is no reason for it to be a Saṁvara explanatory Tantra. We should abandon mixing these as complements of those [actual explanatory Tantras].[74] The [other] "nonturbid" ones seem to be real [explanatory] Tantras. These were previously infamous as controversial Tantras, and some of them certainly seem to be untrue Tantras. Since there seems to be a ground of doubt regarding the others, they should be investigated.

The *Khasama Tantra*[75] is also doubtful, as are ten chapters in the *Ḍākinīsarvacittādvayācintyajñānavajravārāhyabhibhava-tantrarāja*,[76] as well as two chapters in the appendix [of that], as is the *Vārāhyabhibodhi*

---

34), *Śrī Mahāsamaya-tantrarāja* (To. 390, PTT. 35). The speech Tantras are: *Śrī Mahābala-tantrarāja* (To. 391, PTT. 36), *Śrī Jñānaguhya-tantrarāja* (To. 392, PTT. 37), *Śrī Jñānamālā-tantrarāja* (To. 393, PTT. 38), *Śrī Jñānajvala-tantrarāja* (To. 394, PTT. 39), *Śrī Candramālā-tantrarāja* (To. 395, PTT. 40), *Ratnajvala-tantrarāja* (To. 396, PTT. 41), *Śrī Suryacakra-tantrarāja* (To. 397, PTT. 42), *Śrī Jñānarāja-tantrarāja* (To. 398, PTT. 43). The mind Tantras are: *Śrī Vajraḍākaguhya-tantrarāja* (To. 399, PTT. 44), *Śrī Jvalāgniguhya-tantrarāja* (To. 400, PTT. 45), *Śrī Amṛtaguhya-tantrarāja* (To. 401, PTT. 46), *Śrī Śmaśānālaṁkāra-tantrarāja* (To. 402, PTT. 47), *Śrī Vajrarāja-mahātantra* (To. 403, PTT. 48), *Śrī Jñānāśaya-tantrarāja* (To. 404, PTT. 49), *Śrī Rājarāja-tantrarāja* (To. 405, PTT. 50), *Śrī Ḍākinīsaṁvara-tantrarāja* (To. 406, PTT. 51). The eight auxiliary Tantras are: *Śrī Ḍākinīguhyajvala-tantrarāja* (To. 408, PTT. 52), *Śrī Vajrabhairavavidāraṇa-tantrarāja* (To. 409, PTT. 53), *Śrī Agnimālā-tantrarāja* (To. 407, PTT. 54), *Śrī Vajrasiddhajālasaṁvara-tantrarāja* (To. 411, PTT. 55), *Śrī Mahābalajñānarāja-tantrarāja* (To. 410, PTT. 56), *Śrī Cakrasaṁvara-tantrarāja-adbhuta-śmaśānālaṁkāra-nāma* (To. 413, PTT. 57), *Anāvila-tantrarāja* (To. 414, PTT. 58), *Sarvatathāgatacittagarbhārtha-tantra* (To. 412). This list also occurs at Tsuda 1974, 41, with the exception of the last Tantra, which Tsuda did not identify, evidently because he only consulted the Otani reprint of the Beijing (Q) edition of the Kangyur, which does not contain that text.

[74] Tsong Khapa here gives a slightly abbreviated version of Büton's criticism, which occurs at RP 436, as follows: *ri gi a ra li ni rgyud sde gzhan yin gyi bde mchog gi bshad rgyud yin rgyu'ang med la / 'di rnams kyi zla la bsre ru'ang phangs so /.*

[75] Tsong Khapa evidently refers to the *Śrīkhasama-tantrarāja* (To. 386, PTT. 31), one of the *rali* Tantras previously mentioned.

[76] That is, To. 378.

of twenty-two chapters.[77] And it is said that there are two translations of Yeshe Zangpo that seem to be false Tantras. It is also said that the *Tied-up Topknot Tantra*,[78] which is a Mahāmāyājālā Tantra, and which was drawn from the three-hundred-thousand-stanza [text], called the *Mahāmāyā*, seems to be set aside as the *Laghutantra* of the *Maitrī Khecara*.[79] These matters should be investigated well, with subtle intelligence, caution, and manifold understanding.

2.2. Showing the time and place of the original proclamation of the *Cakrasaṁvara Tantra*

The commentary on the *Abhidhānottara* states that the *Saṁvara Tantra* was taught on the peak of Mt. Sumeru, and that the place for training disciples was Jambudvīpa.[80] According to the root Tantra commentary attributed to Indrabhūti, first it was stated on the peak of Mt. Sumeru, and later it was stated at Dhānyakaṭaka.[81] As for the time of the occasion, master [Vīra]vajra, in his commentary, asserted that it was taught in the Dvāparayuga at the time of the disciplining of Īśvara.[82] Yet

---

[77] Tsong Khapa mistakenly uses the abbreviated name *phag mo mngon 'byung*, instead of *phag mo mngon byang*, for the *Khyāvajravārāhī-abhidhāna-tantrottara-vārāhy-abhibodhi*. The nickname used by Tsong Khapa would render the Sanskrit *Vārāhy abhibhava*, which would more correctly refer to the *Ḍākinīsarva-cittādvayācintya-jñānavajravārāhy-abhibhava-tantrarāja*, a text Tsong Khapa already mentioned using its full name. That Tsong Khapa's abbreviation *phag mo mngon 'byung* refers to the former text is proven by an instance in which he uses the term to identify a quote that is in fact from that text. This could also have been a scribal or printing error.

[78] Perhaps the *ral pa gyen brjes kyi rtog pa chen po*, To. 724.

[79] Tsong Khapa here refers to the *Vidyādharīvajrayoginīsadhāna* (To. 380), and in fact directly quotes the first identifying line of that text, which occurs as follows: *'bum phrag gsum pa las 'byung ba'i sgyu 'phrul dra ba chen mo ral pa gyen du brdzes pa'i rgyud las sgyu ma chen mo zhes bya ba ste* / (D 72b). Evidently this text was considered a "root text" of the Maitrī Khecarī tradition, one of three *Khecarī/mkha' spyod* traditions attributed to Nāropā, Indrabhūti, and Maitrīpa. Presumably for this reason, it was included in the Kangyur rather than the Tengyur.

[80] Tsong Khapa is presumably referring to Śūraṅgavajra's (MV) commentary, but I have not been able to locate the passage in which he identifies the place of the Tantra's exposition.

[81] See IC 4a.

[82] See PD 356a. Note that Vīravajra identified it as the "time of disciplining of Rudra-Bhairava" (*drag po 'jigs byed btul ba'i tshe'o*), not Īśvara.

the Tibetan lamas claim that it was taught during the Kaliyuga.[83] In the *Ḍākārṇava* it says, "This Tantra that was propagated by the Lion of the Śākyas was taught by infinite buddhas within the world of the Kaliyuga."[84] Its commentary also explains that the Lion of the Śākyas taught the extensive Tantra of the *Ḍākārṇava* during the Kaliyuga,[85] further illustrating [this point].

While a commentary on the root Tantra states that it was not taught again,[86] the former [explanation, that it was taught again after its initial revelation,] is correct. It should be understood as is explained in the *Vajrapañjara Tantra*, which says that he taught it abbreviating from the expanded root Tantra in the time of the Kaliyuga, for the sake of those with short lives and intense addictions.[87] As for the teacher, it is Heruka, as is stated in the *Commentary Praising Saṁvara*.[88] The root Tantra also says, "The hero stated it concisely."[89] And that same text says that the interlocutor was Vārāhī.[90] But master Kambala held that Vajrapāṇi made

---

83 Tsong Khapa here repeats Büton's comments on the subject. Büton does not identify these Tibetan lamas. See RP 376.

84 See DA 264a.

85 Padmavajra, in his *Śrīḍākārṇavamahāyoginī-tantrarāja-vāhikaṭīkā*, commented that "The Lion of the Śākyas taught the 3,600,000 [stanza] *Abhidhāna Mahātantra* during the Kaliyuga." / *slar yang rtsod pa'i dus su rgyud chen po mngon par brjod pa 'bum phrag sum cu rtsa drug pa shākya seng ges gsungs so* / (D fol. 317a).

86 Tsong Khapa here is probably referring here to Bhavyakīrti's comments at BC 2b–3a.

87 This is not a direct quote, and I was unable to find an identical passage in the VP. For a passage that approximates this discussion see VP 43a.

88 The *Commentary Praising Saṁvara*, *bde mchog stod 'grel*, is Tsong Khapa's shorthand name for the *Laghutantraṭīkā* (LT), a commentary on the first chapter of the CT attributed to Vajrapāṇi. This highly influential work, though structurally limited to the first chapter, covers a wide range of important topics and interprets the Tantra from the perspective of the Kālacakra literature. It is one of the three so-called "bodhisattva commentaries," the other two being the *Vimalaprabhā* (To. 845), a Kālacakra commentary attributed to Puṇḍarīka, and the *Hevajrapiṇḍārthaṭīkā* (To. 1180), attributed to Vajragarbha. With respect to Tsong Khapa's point here, see LT 82a, Cicuzza 2001, 51.

89 Tsong Khapa here quotes a portion of CT 34.8.

90 See LT 82a, Cicuzza 2001, 51.

the request.[91] The root Tantra says, "Listen truly, hero, to the secret of form and action,"[92] in agreement with that. As for the compiler, the *Ḍākārṇava* states:

> Those who compile, and so on, achieve that which comes from me. Those that were collected by all of the mothers (*mātṛkā*, *ma mo*) were collected in the adamantine seats (*vajrapīṭha*, *rdo rje'i gnas*). They teach it from one to another, praying again and again. They delight in these words spoken by the Blessed Lord.[93]

It is said that Oḍḍiyāna was the adamantine seat in which it was collected by the yoginīs.

2.3. The way in which the explanatory Tantras explain the root Tantra

The third part has three sections: (1) identifying the main points by which the explanatory Tantras explain the root Tantra, (2) how the uncommon explanatory Tantras explain, and (3) how the common explanatory Tantras explain.

2.3.1. Identifying the main points by which the explanatory Tantras explain the root Tantra

Although there are many topics in the root Tantra explained by the explanatory Tantras, the main one is the perfection stage. In regard to the perfection stage, in the literature of the *Cakrasaṁvara*, there are the systems of the six branches of yoga and the five stages of the *Guhyasamāja*. The *Ḍākārṇava* states: "Withdrawal (*pratyāhāra*), meditation (*dhyāna*), breath control (*prāṇāyāma*), concentration (*dhāraṇā*), recollecttion (*anusmṛti*), and *samādhi* are the six types of yoga." It also says in that Tantra that:

---

[91] Kambala states that the Blessed Lord taught it to the 'Lord of Secrets' (*guhyapati*, *gsang ba'i bdag po*), which is clearly a name for Vajrapāṇi (SL 4b).

[92] Tsong Khapa here quotes CT 42.4cd. Regarding the interpretation of this passage, see Gray 2007, p. 340, n. 15.

[93] See DA 264a.

> Withdrawal is Kākāsyā (Crow Face), meditation is Ulūkāsyā (Owl Face), breath control is Śvānāsyā (Dog Face), and concentration is Śūkarāsyā (Pig Face). Recollection is Yamadūtī, and *samādhi* is Yamadāḍhī. Yamadaṇṣṭrī attains the expansive teaching. Yamamathanī creates the lord of all fruits. [By means of all of these] one is liberated from samsara.[94]

With the exception of Śūkarāsyā, the three gatekeepers together with Vārāhī make four. Together with the two quarter guardians, Yamadūtī and Yamadādhī, there are six, which are said to be in accordance with the six branches of yoga. Although this is easily understood from the commentaries, it is said that they should be understood from the guru's oral instructions.

In the commentary [by Tathāgatavajra] on Lūipa's [*Cakrasaṁvarābhisamaya*], known as the *Distinctively Illuminating*,[95] there is a presentation of the six branches of yoga in regard to the two stages stated in Lūipa's *sadhāna*. The *Ḍākārṇava* also says, "One's own body is like a magical illusion; this self-consecration is subtle. Vajra repetition has its own intrinsic nature, the treasury of the spirit of perfect enlightenment. Other than those the rest is integration (*yuganaddha*)."[96]

One's own body is like a magical illusion, and since this self-consecration is extremely difficult to understand, it is said to be subtle. The stage of self-consecration is the third stage, the magic body. The intrinsic nature of the vajra repetition is the stage of the vajra repetition, which is the first stage. The stage of manifest awakening (*abhisambodhi*)

---

[94] See DA 159a for both of the passages quoted here.

[95] Lūipa's *Cakrasaṁvarābhisamaya* (or *Śrībhagavad-abhisamaya*, To. 1427) is perhaps the most influential *sādhana* text in the Cakrasaṁvara corpus. A great many commentaries have been written on it, including two by Atiśa Dīpaṁkaraśrījñāna (To. 1490, 1492). Tsong Khapa himself wrote a commentary on the text, entitled *bcom ldan 'das dpal 'khor lo bde mchog gi mngon par rtogs pa'i rgya cher bshad pa 'dod pa 'jo ba zhes bya ba bzhugs so* (bkra shis lhun po par rnying ed. vol. ta). The text to which he is refering here is Tathāgatavajra's *Lūhipāda-abhisamaya-vṛtti-ṭīkā-viśeṣadyota* (To. 1510, PTT. 2225). Along with Atiśa's *Abhisamayavibhaṅga*, it is the commentary on Lūipa's *Abhisamaya* to which Tsong Khapa most often refers.

[96] See DA 159a.

is the fourth stage, another name of which is the clear light stage. As for "the treasury of the spirit," it is the mind isolation or mind objectification stage, which is the second stage. Beyond the previously explained four, the remaining one is the stage of integration, making five stages.[97]

Furthermore, there are the perfection stage Mahāyoga that occurs in Lūipa's treatise, the *Five Stages* written by Ghaṇṭapā, and the *Four Stages* written by Kāṇhapā.[98] The *Abhidhānottara* commentary states:

> In this Tantra the perfection stage is meditation on channels, winds, and drops, meditation on heat, and meditation on the spirit of enlightenment; these are the five conceptual meditations (*mtshan bcas sgom pa*). There are three more, which are the meditation on the ultimate truth store of wisdom that is like a magical illusion, clear light emptiness meditation, and integration meditation. The [former] five are *dhyāna* meditations that are the arts of pushing the life force into the central channel. The [latter] three are meditations on the ultimate truth store of wisdom.[99]

There are many explanations in which the terminology of *Guhyasamāja* perfection stages is applied to the *Saṁvara* perfection stages. Here [the text] differentiates between two occasions in the perfection stage, these being the art of inserting the life force into the central channel, and the meditation that depends upon it being thus inserted. One must understand that these two [occasions] are relevant not only in the *Saṁvara* [system] but also in the meditations of other Unexcelled [Yogatantra] perfection stage [systems].

---

[97] Tsong Khapa here goes through the list of the five stages of the perfection stage, *pañcakrama*, the *locus classicus* of which is Nāgārjuna's *Pañcakrama*. For a summary of these stages see Cozort 1986.

[98] The *Five Stages* (*rim pa lnga pa*) is Ghaṇṭapā's *Śrīcakrasaṁvara Pañcakrama* (PK), while the *Four Stages* (*rim pa bzhi pa*) is Kāṇhapā's *Ālicatuṣṭaya* (AC). These texts make different but equally influential attempts to schematize the stages of meditation of the Cakrasaṁvara tradition.

[99] This is from Śūraṅgavajra's commentary; see MV 145b–146a.

2.3.2. How the uncommon explanatory Tantras explain

The second part has two sections: (1) how the *Abhidhānottara* and *Vajraḍāka* explain, and (2) how the *Saṁvarodaya* and the *Yoginīsaṁcāra* explain.

2.3.2. 1. How the *Abhidhānottara* and *Vajraḍāka* explain

The first part has two sections: (1) how the *Abhidhānottara* explains, and (2) how the *Vajraḍāka* explains.

2.3.2. 1.1. How the *Abhidhānottara* Explains

The first part has two sections: (1) how the creation stage is explained, and (2) how the perfection stage is explained.

2.3.2. 1.1.1. How the creation stage is explained

The first part has two sections: (1) how the creation stage is not clear in the root Tantra, and (2) how this explanatory Tantra explains it clearly.

2.3.2. 1.1.1. 1. How the creation stage is not clear in the root Tantra

As [Ghaṇṭapā] says in the *Saṁvara Pañcakrama*, "I will explain the consecration process that is hidden in the *Cakrasaṁvara*."[100] This refers not only to the hiding of the perfection stages in the fifty-first chapter of the root Tantra but also to the hiding of the creation stage, as Kṛṣṇācārya says in his *sādhana*: "I am going to explain the *sādhana* here that is hidden by means of barbaric language, which collects all the secret mantras and practices, the secret import of the *Cakrasaṁvara*."[101]

---

[100] See PK 224b.

[101] This quote is from a text called the *Śrī Cakrasaṁvara-sādhana-nāma*, To. 1445, fol. 272b. Note that Tsong Khapa's version reads "barbaric language" (*kla klo'i skad*), while the text preserved in the Kangyur reads "symbolic language"(*brda yi skad*). Note as well that there was some confusion concerning the attribution of authorship to this text. The Tōhoku editors did not list an attribution for this text, while the editors of the Beijing Photographic edition attributed it to a "*Vratācārya." What the colophon actually says is *slob dpon chen po brtul zhugs kyi spyod pa'i zhal snga nas mdzad pa rdzogs so*, "written in the presence of the great master *brtul zhugs kyi spyod pa*." *brtul zhugs kyi spyod pa* almost certainly translates *caryāvratī*, a title of Kāṇha.

The *Saṁcāra* also states that many things on the topic of the creation stage are hidden.[102]

In this way, the second chapter of the root Tantra refers to the placement of the four-faced Heruka and Vārāhī couple in the navel of a lotus in the center of the mandala palace,[103] the placement of the twenty-four heroines in the directions and quarters, and likewise the placement of the heroes and the placement of the Mothers in the quarters and directions. This is the sixty-two-deity mandala.

As for the body colors of the principal couple, in the context of the performance [section] of the twenty-seventh chapter, "Always naked at night, one should ever be black and red."[104] The gurus claim that this shows that the Heruka's color is blue-black, and Vārāhī's color is red. Kambala's commentary also explains thus.[105]

The thirty-fourth chapter tells of the four essence yoginīs surrounding the four-faced lord of heroes, and the fifty-first chapter teaches the meditation on the Heruka with twelve arms, together with a host of heroes and heroines. These Herukas are taken to be the resultant Heruka. In the thirty-second chapter, there is a white, four-faced Heruka with four to one hundred thousand arms. There is a divine consort (*yum*), Vārāhī, who has the same color. Kāṇhapā says that this is a causal Heruka, though there are other ways of explaining as well.

Furthermore, in the fourth chapter, the names of the twenty-four heroines are stated, but while the heroes names aren't stated until the forty-eighth chapter, the hand implements and number of hands and faces of sixty deities [of the retinue] are not clear anywhere, nor are their colors clear. Likewise, there is no clarity about the consecration of the aggregates, elements, and media, the merit accumulated in the assembly

---

[102] The *Yoginīsaṁcāra* deals largely with the topics of the creation stage, particularly the topic of the body mandala and its relation to the macrocosmic mandala. There is a general statement regarding secrecy at YS 1.2. See Pandey 1998, 6, and YS 34a.

[103] Here I translate nonliterally the term *gzhal yas khang*, literally "immeasurable house," as "mandala palace," as it is the term for the palace at the center of the mandala that is the home of the mandala's deities.

[104] Tsong Khapa here quotes CT 27.14cd.

[105] See SN 44a.

field,[106] the meditation of the two protection wheels,[107] the stacking up of the levels of elements, and the creation of Mt. Sumeru and the mandala palace. With the exception of statements such as "in regard to the inhabitant mandala, in which the deities are created, you create Heruka upon Sumeru, in the navel of a variegated lotus, from the vowels and consonants," the way of creating the rest of the visualizations, such as the entry of the gnosis hero into the commitment hero, as well as the conferral of initiation, the sealing, the creation of the sacrificial cakes, are all unclear, and are not explained in a well-arranged manner.

2.3.2. 1.1.1. 2. How this explanatory Tantra explains clearly

With respect to the creation stage, the realization (*abhisamaya*), which is unclear in the root Tantra, is clearly explained in a well-arranged manner in the fourth chapter of the *Abhidhānottara*. That chapter comments on the place were one meditates on the creation stage, and, in order to meditate there, the invitation of the assembly field and the accumulation of merit. It also explains the blessing by the seventeen deities of the aggregates, elements, and media, both the common and uncommon protection wheels, the meditation on emptiness, the stacking up of the elements, the method of creating Mt. Sumeru, and the creation of the mandala palace from Vairocana atop Sumeru. After that, [portions of the creation stage] from collecting the stores up to the method of creating the mandala palace are not explained. I think that these explanations in the fourth chapter are common to all of those [creation stages].

As for the way of explaining the inhabitant mandala, once arrangement of some sort of mandala has been taught, it becomes important to understand the commentarial method of the creation stage. If we explain that a little bit, there is a mandala of thirty deities, [namely] the Body Saṁvara divine couple who are the principal deities, the four essence yoginīs, the sixteen body-mandala heroes and heroines, and the eight gate and quarter goddesses. Likewise, there is also a thirty-deity mandala consisting of the speech Saṁvara couple with the speech-mandala heroes

---

[106] The "assembly field," *tshogs zhing*, is the visualized host of the major figures of one's practice lineage and deities.

[107] These are the common and uncommon protection wheels.

and heroines, and so on, as above. The Mind Saṁvara divine couple, the sixteen mind-mandala heroes and heroines, and so on, also yields a thirty-deity mandala. The commitment (*samaya*) Saṁvara divine couple, the four essence yoginīs, and the eight gate and quarter goddesses yield a fourteen-deity mandala. Then there is the five- or six-deity mandala with the Saṁvara couple surrounded by the four essence yoginīs, [in which] the Saṁvara of gnosis or great bliss is taken as the principal deity. In these five mandalas, there are two kinds of Vajradharas, causal and resultant, and there is the entry of the gnosis hero, consecration bestowal, repetition of each [deities' mantra], the creation of both armors at the time of [the deities'] manifestation, and so on, all of which are explained.

Then there is explained a body mandala created from the Saṁvara manifest awakening [process],[108] mainly called "the mandala of the solitary hero" in the center of the mandala palace. There are no other deities other than a divine couple in the mandala palace, but since those two are on one seat, they are called the "solitary hero." One [normally] does not visualize the three defense perimeters in a body mandala, [but as] there is the meditation on the creation of the mandala palace with Mt. Sumeru and the stacked-up elements, and the creation of the fundamental Heruka from the manifest awakening [process], if some people think this is contradictory, that is due to their failure to understand well the explanatory Tantras.

Now, as for the sixty-two-deity mandala, there are many different kinds, and also many Saṁvara mandalas explained. As for the way of creating these mandalas, the habitat is the previously created mandala palace. The method of creating the inhabitant deities is then explained. All of the statements about these many mandalas of the Saṁvara creation stage in this explanatory Tantra are explanations of the creation stage itself that is stated in the root Tantra. Therefore, applying all of the occurrences of the creation stage in the root Tantra to the creation stage

---

108 That is, it is created via the *samvara-abhisaṁbodhi* (*bde mchog mngon byang*), the process of visualizing the creation mandala from the bottom up, starting with the elemental disks.

of either Lūipa [only] or Kāṇha [only], is to have the fault of being very narrow.[109]

2.3.2. 1.1.2. How the perfection stage is explained [in the *Abhidhānottara*]

The perfection stages of this Tantra are extremely unclear, even more so than the hidden things of the creation stage. Since coming to know how the explanatory Tantra shows the perfection stage in such and such an occasion in the root Tantra—that is, understanding its method for stating hidden things—is very difficult, I will explain this. Regarding the way the perfection stage is made clear in this explanatory Tantra, Ghaṇṭapā explains that the lines "always abiding in the heart," etc.,[110] teach the self-consecration stage. The fourteenth chapter indicates the perfection stage of the fury fire meditation, which is explained in the *Ālicatuṣṭaya*.[111] In the twenty-fifth and fifty-sixth chapters, there is an explanation of the Mahāyoga that is the perfection stage of Lūipa.

Furthermore, by the mode of being slightly unclear, there are many [places] where the perfection stage is only touched upon. Among those, it is necessary to know the method of inserting the life force into the central channel, and the great bliss developed thereby. There are many ways in which it recommends the view of emptiness, and the gnosis of the indivisibility of bliss and emptiness.

2.3.2. 1.2. How the *Vajraḍāka* Explains

In portions of the first and second chapter of the *Vajraḍāka*, and from the twelfth and fourteenth, various creation stages are repeatedly stated. In the eleventh chapter there is a brief statement about the yoga of fury fire. In the fifteenth is an extensive explanation by the mode of depending on the four chakras. Here again, one should understand the

---

[109] Tsong Khapa here is arguing that the numerous cryptic references to creation stage practice in the root Tantra do not refer only to the two mandalas most commonly employed in the Tibetan traditions, those of Lūipa and Kāṇha. He feels that the numerous types of mandalas described in the AU are intended by the root Tantra itself.

[110] Ghaṇṭapā quotes a passage from AU ch. 4, beginning with this line, which occurs at AU fol. 256a, J 26.1–2. See PK 225a.

[111] That is, Kāṇha's *Ālicatuṣṭaya* (AC).

method of inserting the life force into the central channel, and it having been inserted, the procedures of the perfection stage that are developed thereby. Furthermore, in the first chapter, there is much reference to the art and wisdom of bliss and emptiness. In the second chapter there is an extensive explanation of the definitive meaning of the root mantra of the father deity. In the forty-ninth chapter there are many statements [on topics] such as the differentiation between the four types of seals (*phyag rgya ma bzhi*), the way of binding the awakening spirit by the power of the different characteristics of their secret places, the way of holding the awakening spirit for a long time relying upon the fluid,[112] and performance of the sexual positions (*karaṇa*) explained in the sexological treatises (*kāmaśāstra, 'dod pa'i bstan bcos*). In the forty-second chapter there is a detailed explanation of most of the text of the first chapter [of the root Tantra]. The forty-sixth chapter expounds the many rites that are unclear in the second chapter of the root Tantra, as well as the many types of ritual actions from most of the other chapters [of the root text].

2.3.2. 2. How the *Saṁvarodaya* and the *[Yoginī]saṁcāra* explain

This first part has two sections: (1) how the *Saṁvarodaya* explains, and (2) how the *[Yoginī]saṁcāra* explains.

2.3.2. 2.1. How the *Saṁvarodaya* explains

The answer to the request for the creation stage in the first chapter of the *Saṁvarodaya* is stated in the second chapter. It states [the following topics]: in general, the four modes of birth; the realm of enjoyment of three [of the four] human continents; Jambudvīpa, which is the land of deeds, and Madhyadeśa, which is its principal land; and the four methods that enlighten though the method of detachment, which is dependent upon human life in Jambudvīpa. [It also states] that birth and death are

---

[112] This translates *rdzas la brten nas*, Normally the term *rdzas/dravya* is translated as "substance," but in the context of the sexual yogas it is better translated as "fluid," as it refers to the mixed sexual fluids that are to be absorbed and held by the yogī. In the context of the VD this is clearly the case. The passage Tsong Khapa is referring to reads as follows: "One should take up one measure (*srang*) of the fluid [consisting of] semen (*so ma*), uterine blood (*ra dza*) and turmeric all mixed together, and cook it in the manner of pure, clarified butter in accordance with the procedure previously stated" (VD 118b).

produced by the previous deeds of those who do not understand the illusionlike concentration, and that after death there is the between state, the method of womb birth from the union of the parents, and the method of birth from the womb into the outer world.[113]

The creation stage is not shown here, but the correspondences that are meditated upon in accordance with birth, death, and the between states in the creation stage are shown. Furthermore, this is the significance of the stages of the arrangement that explains quoting from this Tantra. The creation stage meditation that accords with the three [states of] birth, death, and the between state is clarified by this [text] from among the Saṁvara Tantras. Therefore, one needs to carry [this] into all of the creation stage visualizations of the wheels of the Saṁvara mandala. Due to this, at the occasion of the Saṁvara perfection stage, it is necessary to understand the meditation on clear light in conformity with the dying process, as well as the meditation on the magic body in conformity with the between state, and so forth.[114]

The creation stage that is meditated upon in conformity with these three correspondences is shown in the thirteenth chapter. It teaches the creation of the levels of the elements together with Mt. Sumeru, and on top of Mt. Sumeru, the universal vajra. On top of that is a lotus, in which, from the vowels and consonants, is Heruka with three faces and six arms. Together with his divine consort (*yum*), he is surrounded by the four yoginīs and eight gate and quarter goddesses. [This is taught] along with ancillary [matters]. It is the method of creating simultaneously the habitat and inhabitants, in the manner of Lūipa. Furthermore, the literature regarding the consecration rituals is taught in the seventeenth and eighteenth chapters.

As for the perfection stage, in the third chapter there is the method of instantaneously visualizing the deity of the perfection stage. [First,] "[Selflessness, as suchness,] is universal. Its art is powered by compas-

---

[113] See the edition and translation of this chapter in Tsuda 1974.

[114] Tsong Khapa here argues that the connection made by the *Saṁvarodaya* between creation and perfection stage practices and the life cycle of birth, death, and the between states should be applied to all systems of meditation associated with the Cakrasaṁvara.

sion. Their integration is spontaneous, the supreme essence mandala."[115] This verse [describes] the stage of integration. [Then,] "Conventionally arising, it is not nonexistent, since it is ceaseless; all innate things are self-arisen, innate joy in nature, and self-consecrated."[116] [This verse describes that,] since the production of the conventional magic body emerges from clear light, the self-consecration avoids the extreme of nonexistence and cessation. And "Great bliss is manifest awakening, and likewise [leads to] the supreme great seal (*mahāmudrā*)."[117] [This verse] describes the stage of clear light [or] manifest awakening.

In the fifth and sixth chapters, vajra repetition is taught, through mention of both the reality of mantra (*mantratattva*) and the reality of wind, together with the winds of the five lords such as the Padmanātha, and so on, in accordance with the stages of vajra repetition of the *Pañcakrama*. This is the definitive meaning of the mantra repeated in the root Tantra. The fifth chapter shows the perfection stage of visualizing the mantric drops in the heart, and the heart center vase-breathing. The thirty-first chapter teaches the great essential points of the fury fire [practice] based upon the four wheels. It mentions the method of injecting the life force into the central channel by these, following the vajra repetition. Relying on that method, the union of bliss and emptiness is extensively explained in the twenty-ninth and thirty-third chapters. Also taught in the thirty-first chapter are the characteristics of each of the four [types of] seal consorts (*phyag rgya ma*) and the different methods of playing with each of these four. The twenty-first chapter extensively states the method of doing practices after having attained heat.[118]

---

115 Tsong Khapa quotes SU 3.8c–9b. Tsuda's edition of this text reads as follows: */sna tshogs de bzhin nyid bdag med/ /thabs ni snying rje'i stobs yin te/ /zung 'jug pa rnam rtog bral/ /dkyil 'khor snying po mchogs yin no/* (1974, 171); *nairātmyā tathatā viśvam upāyaḥ karuṇābalaḥ // yuganaddham anābhogaṁ mandalaṁ sāram uttamam/* (1974, 78). Tsong Khapa's quote differs from the text preserved in the Kangyur; my translation follows the Kangyur reading and the Sanskrit. Note as well that commentators on this passage read *nairātmyā* as the goddess so named, and read *upāyaḥ karuṇābalaḥ* as a reference to Heruka. See Tsuda 1974, 244 n. 3.

116 Tsong Khapa quotes SU 3.13a–14a. See Tsuda 1974, 78 and 171.

117 Tsong Khapa quotes SU 3.16ab. See Tsuda 1974, 78 and 171.

118 By "heat," *drod*, Tsong Khapa is referring to the first of the four aids to penetration, which is heat, on the path of application. The path of application is generally correlated to

(cont'd)

2.3.2. 2.2. How the *[Yoginī]saṁcāra* explains

From the first to the tenth chapters of the *Saṁcāra*, the creation stage together with the branches are presented. Furthermore, it states in its fifth chapter [the following]:

> The best outer mandala should likewise be known internally. The [mandala that is] the collection of all essences should be applied in accordance with the laying down [of the mantric syllables].[119]

Accordingly, it teaches [the creation stage] in terms of the arrangement in both the outer and body mandalas. It teaches that one should arrange in the outer mandala the complete sixty-two deities, and the deities in the body mandala, not including the twelve mothers (*ma mo*) and the principal couple. Regarding not arranging the fourteen deities in the body mandala, since it is taught in *Saṁpuṭa*, and so forth, that one should arrange even these [deities], the body mandala also is complete with the deities.

It was intended [by Mahāvajradhara Buddha] that there be no instruction on the number of faces and body color of Heruka present in the root Tantra. It is said that each of the sixty deities after Vārāhī has one face and two arms. In the context of the twenty-four heroes, Mardo's translation has "embraced by his own sign," which is unclear. The translations of Lochen and Prajñākīrti have "embraces with vajra [and] bell," which is good, and it occurs likewise in the commentaries.[120] And

---

the four lower stages of the perfection stage, namely, physical, verbal, and mental isolation, and the impure magic body. Regarding this see Cozort 1986, 62.

[119] Tsong Khapa quotes YS 5.2. See YS fol. 36a, as well as the Sanskrit edited in Pandey 1998, 42.

[120] Tsong Khapa cites alternate translations for CT 51.15b. He attributes the following text to "Mardo's translation": *rang gi mtshan mas legs 'khyud cing*; to Lochen's and Prajñākīrti's translations he attributes the following: *rdo rje dril bus legs 'khyud cing*. However, all three extant translations read: *rdo rje dril bus sku la 'khyud* (PM, SL, SM). Note as well that this line is not describing the twenty-four heroes, as Tsong Khapa claims, but rather the central deity Heruka.

their implements are similar to Ghaṇṭapā's.[121] The body color of the divine mother is said to be red.

The statement that "the four yoginīs have various colors"[122] is not in reference to the body coloration of each one of them, but in terms of all four.[123] One should set aside the four quarter guardians from within the [group of] the eight gate and quarter goddesses. Since one is speaking in terms of the color of half of the group], one is able to understand that the four gatekeepers are blue in color, and so forth. If one understands it in this way, one is able to conclude that the four yoginīs are similar in color to the four gatekeepers by the virtue of the statement that the four gatekeepers are like the four yoginīs.

As for the color of the deities of the three wheels [of the mandala], the sixth [chapter says], "Thus, they all abide in the wheels. Their colors are differentiated in accordance with the ritual procedure."[124] This means that the body colors of all those who abide in the three wheels are differentiated in accordance with the ritual procedure, that is, with the clans.

It also means, as explained in the *Abhidhānottara*, "or rather make the colors as desired, with the distinctions of body, speech, and mind."[125] This means that one should make the colors however one desires by distinguishing body, speech, and mind. One should make the deities of the body wheel white, the deities of the speech wheel red, and the deities of the mind wheel blue. The sixty-two deities of these [wheels] are just like the deities of Ghaṇṭapā's body mandala.

---

[121] Tsong Khapa is likely referring here to Ghaṇṭapā's description of the central deities in his *Śrīcakrasaṁvara-sādhana*, which echoes this line as follows: *rdo rje dril bus yang dag 'khyud* (fol. 223a).

[122] Tsong Khapa's quote here reads *rnal 'byor ma bzhi la sna tshogs gzugs can*. It seems that he is referring to YS 11.1d. This line reads "has various colors, like jewels" (*viśvarūpo maṇir yathā*; *sna tshogs gzugs can nor bu 'dra*; see Pandey 1998, 101, 285; cf. YS D 39a). Note that the text quoted here is declined in the masculine singular case, and thus does not unambiguously refer to the four yoginīs as Tsong Khapa claims.

[123] In other words, it is not the case that each has variegated coloration. Tsong Khapa interprets "various colors" as referring to the four different colors of the four goddesses.

[124] Tsong Khapa quotes YS 6.15cd. See Pandey 1998, 67, 254; cf. YS 37b.

[125] This passage occurs in AU ch. 14. See Kalff 1979, 318, and AU 287b.

The method of creation is explained in Tathāgatarakṣita's commentary,[126] in accordance with creation from the five manifest awakenings in the system of Lūipa, the system of creating at one time the habitat and inhabitants. Therefore, it is good to do the method of creation from the manifest awakenings in the manner of Lūipa in the context of Ghaṇṭapā's body mandala as well.

The twelfth chapter glorifies natural gnosis and explains perfection stage Mahāyoga. Here it is necessary to understand the two perfection stages: the perfection stage of injecting the life force into the central channel, and the perfection stage created in reliance upon that injection. This I have extensively explained elsewhere. The fourteenth chapter shows the practice to be done having developed ability. Furthermore, it explains many things that are unclear in the root Tantra.

2.3.3. How the common explanatory Tantras explain[127]

"Genuine Union," "Kiss," and "Kiss Drop" are synonyms of the name of the *Saṁpuṭa Tantra*. There are eleven sections (*kalpa*) in it together with its appendix. A certain Tibetan lama asserted that it is an explanatory Tantra of the thirty-six hundred thousand Tantras by King Indrabhūti. It is said that it is an explanatory Tantra of sixteen Tantras that identifiably exist now.

As for the first assertion, the *Saṁpuṭa* commentary attributed to Indrabhūti states the following: "To begin with, it said that the '*Saṁpuṭa-tilaka*' is a short Tantra with eleven sections, extracted from the thirty-six hundred thousand extensive Tantras of the yogīs and yoginīs."[128] The meaning of [the statement that] the *Saṁpuṭa* is "extracted from the thirty-six hundred thousand Tantras" is uncertain. It appears to mean that it was abridged from thirty-six hundred thousand Tantras, but it is not established as an explanatory Tantra of those merely by that [assertion]. For

---

[126] This refers to Tathāgatarakṣita's *Yoginīsaṁcāranibandha*. See especially his commentary on the first ten chapters, edited in Pandey 1998.

[127] The expression "common explanatory Tantra" (*thun mong ba'i bshad rgyud*) refers to explanatory Tantras such as the *Saṁpuṭa* that are shared by two or more different Tantras.

[128] This quote is from the beginning of Indrabhūti's massive *Śrīsaṁpuṭatilaka-nāma-yoginī-tantrarājā-ṭīkā-saṁdarśanāloka-nāma*. See D 94b.

example, it could be like the abridgement of the short root Tantra from the one hundred thousand [stanza] *Abhidhāna*.

In regard to the second assertion, it does not seem to have an authentic basis. Another Tibetan lama said, "This Tantra is, in general, an explanatory Tantra of all Tantras, and, in particular, of forty Tantras." However, this does not appear to be in any way verifiable. Particularly, in regard to the explanations of the imports of other Tantras in the *Saṁpuṭa*, i.e., its serving as an explanatory Tantra for those various Tantras, the reasoning [for this] seems entirely uncertain. But fearing prolixity, I will not write further.

A commentary of this Tantra composed by Vīravajra states, "As this is an explanatory Tantra, it is an explanatory Tantra of nine Tantras, and furthermore it is an ordinary Tantra."[129] Regarding the nine Tantras, there seems to be a series of nine if one takes as threefold [the following three]: the narrative preface (*nidāna*), secret, and *Saṁpuṭa*, [which are mentioned in the text as] "the narrative preface of all Tantras, the secret, ...the *Saṁpuṭa*."[130] However, [this interpretation] does not seem to be reliable.[131] Thus, it is the explanatory Tantra that is common to the *Hevajra* and *Saṁvara* [*Tantra*s], as was explained by the previous lamas of Tibet.

As for the Saṁvara creation stage, the fourth chapter of the third section explains the creation of Saṁvara Vajrasattva with three faces and six arms from the five manifest awakenings, and [states] that he is surrounded by twenty-eight retinue deities. In regard to the eight goddesses such as Hāsavatī, [Abhayākara] stated in the *Āmnāyamañjarī* that "[it is

---

[129] Tsong Khapa here seems to be paraphrasing a passage from the introduction to Vīravajra's *Sarvatantranidānamahāguhyaśrīsaṁpuṭa-nāma-tantrarāja-ṭīkā-ratnamālā-nāma*. The passage that corresponds to Tsong Khapa's abridged paraphrase can be found at D 5b.

[130] Tsong Khapa quotes a fragment from the opening passage of the ST, which occurs as follows in full: "I would like to listen, oh Lord of Gnosis, to the narrative context of all Tantras, the secret, which is the defining characteristic stated in the *Saṁpuṭa*" (Skoruspski 1996, 216: *śrotum icchāmi jñānendra sarvatantranidhānam rahasyaṁ saṁpuṭodbhavalakṣaṇam*; *ye shes kyi dbang po rgyud thams cad kyi gleng gzhi'i gsang ba yang dag par sbyor ba las byung ba'i mtshan nyid nyan par 'tshal lo*).

[131] Tsong Khapa is here referring to Vīravajra's threefold interpretation of each of these three terms. See his *Sarvatantranidānamahāguhyaśrīsaṁpuṭa-nāma-tantrarājaṭīkā-ratnamālā-nāma*, D 5a.

said that] 'one should be aware of what is said in other Tantras.' Those who know much advise this."[132] Thus, the mandala of the thirty-seven deities together with the branches is stated [in this Tantra].

The fourth chapter of the sixth section states many things such as an explanation of sixteen syllables, *ra-ha-sya* and so forth,[133] as well as the application of the twenty-four lands to the inner body, the "spring drop" (*vāsantatilaka*), the principal syllables of the four cakras, the channels and elements of the body, and the inner applications of the stacked-up elements, the fire sacrifices, and so forth. It mainly deals with the fury fire [practice] that relies on the four wheels, and thus it reveals the generation of the four joys, and so forth. In regard to this one should know the two perfection stages, i.e., the method of inserting the life force into the central channel, and the generation [of the fury fire and four joys] that is dependent upon that insertion. In the final sections it also says much concerning consecration. In the previous chapter as well it also discusses the method of bestowing the higher consecrations.

Thus, since the numerous explanatory Tantras of the very unclear root Tantra are autocommentaries of the root Tantra,[134] it is extremely important to well unite the Root and explanatory Tantras.

3. Introduction to the way in which the concise root Tantra is explained

This third part has three sections: (1) the explanation based upon the instructions of the mahāsiddhas, (2) showing the method of explanation based upon them, and (3) the actual method of explaining the root Tantra.

---

[132] Tsong Khapa here directly quotes the *Āmnāyamañjarī* at AM 120b. Abhayākara, in turn, appears to be quoting Vajrapāṇi's comments on the necessity of relying on other Tantras in order to ascertain the meaning of any given Tantra. See Cicuzza 2001, 52, and LT 83a.

[133] Tsong Khapa is referring here to the sixteen-syllable esoteric narrative context of the CT, which is the text of CT 1.2cd: *rahasye parame ramye sarvātmani sadā sthitaḥ*.

[134] The claim that the explanatory Tantras are autocommentaries on the root Tantra is based upon the presupposition that all of these texts were composed by the Buddha Vajradhara.

3.1. The explanation based on the instructions of the mahāsiddhas

In general, in explaining root Tantras that are abridged from extensive Tantras, on what should one rely? It is said that there are three methods [for doing this]. In the *Commentary Praising Saṁvara*, [Vajrapāṇi] stated that [the abridged Tantra's import] should be realized, for the sake of those who have not had the good fortune of hearing the very extensive root Tantra, through reliance upon other Tantras that collect the profound vajra words of the Tantras, whose teachings have been collected from the extensive Tantra, or the commentaries of bodhisattvas, or the instructions of the guru.[135] The first type includes explanations that rely on other explanatory Tantras that were abridged from the extensive original Tantra (*āditantra*). The second type includes explanations that rely on the commentaries of bodhisattvas, like the *Commentary Praising Saṁvara*. The third type includes explanations depending on the personal instructions of those like Lūipa, Kāṇhapā, and Ghaṇṭapā, who are like the noble master and his students. Therefore, it is not the intention of the bodhisattvas that you should rely only on their commentaries. This literature does imply that commentary [on the Tantras] should only be done by those who have attained the supramundane cognitions. While this is not a statement concerning the many other ways of attaining such powers, there is the attainment of the five supramundane cognitions that are realized by the power of manifesting the meaning of reality by means of great bliss. This is in accordance with the explanations of Ghaṇṭapā and Ḍombiheruka.

Furthermore, it is the case that before developing an exegetical system on the intention of a Tantra, one first distinguishes the practice systems of that particular Tantra. However, it is not taught that it is necessary to obtain the supramundane cognitions in order to elucidate the meaning of the Tantra, provided that one has followed a tradition created by former [masters]. Some people say that to just comment on a Tantra one must have attained the supramundane cognitions, and that if one

---

[135] Tsong Khapa here paraphrases the following passage in Vajrapāṇi's LT commentary: "Furthermore, due to its abundance of adamantine expressions, learned ones desiring liberation should know it by means of the instruction of the holy guru, what is said in other Tantras, and the commentaries written by the bodhisattvas." My translation from the Sanskrit in Cicuzza 2001, 52, and the Tibetan at LT 82b–83a.

writes without them, one will go to hell. However, if one engages in Tantric commentary without even having attained a trace of supramundane cognition, one is just making a fool of oneself.

In that way, from among the three [approaches] here, I will explain based on two of them, the first and the third. I will conjoin the root [text] and its explanations relying upon the expositions of the creation and perfection [stages] of Lūipa, Kāṇha, and Ghaṇṭapā. Since I will explain relying on the personal instructions of Śrī Nārotapa, this explanation is distinctively excellent. Although the two stages are not shown clearly with respect to the text of the root Tantra in the expositions of Lūipa and Ghaṇṭapā, if you know well the instructions of these two, you will be able to understand, by relying on the instructions that join the root [text] and its explanations. I will explain this in the context of [my presentation of] the meaning of the text.

The *Vasantatilakā*, a text of Kāṇha, [states,] "Now I will explain, by means of both the outer and inner forms, the performance of the procedures of mandala, fire sacrifice, sacrificial offerings, repetition, meditation, and so forth, of the body of a Tathāgata."[136] In regard to this, "the body of a Tathāgata" is the body of any adept, and the mandala of his or her body is a body mandala. In that way, in regard to those listed from the mandala up until meditation, there are the two stages of outer creation stage and inner perfection stage. [The expression] "and so forth" includes selecting mantras, in regard to which there are two topics, the basis of selecting mantras and the repetition of the selected mantras.

Furthermore, from the *Vajraḍāka*, "In order to realize the authentic union, one should practice the contrived meditations and the contrived [mantra] repetitions."[137] In this way, [practices such as] meditation,

---

[136] Tsong Khapa here quotes VT 8.1 as follows: */de nas de bzhin gshegs pa gang yang rung ba'i sku'i dkyil 'khor dang / sbyin sreg dang mchod sbyin dang bzlas pa dang / bsgom pa la sogs pa'i cho ga'i bya ba phyi rol dang mthun par / nang gi ngo bos yang dag par rab tu bshad par bya'o/*. This is identical to the text as it occurs in Q at p. 222.5; the D print (fol. 303a) and Samdhong and Dwivedi's edition (1990, 106) read *gnod sbyin* instead of *mchod sbyin*, which does not make sense. The Sanskrit doesn't help here as it reads *yoga*, which does not correspond to either Tibetan variant. The Sanskrit occurs as follows in Samdhong and Dwivedi's edition: *athānyatam asya tathāgatakāyasya maṇḍalahomayogajapabhāvanādividhikriyāṁ sabāhyādhyātmarūpeṇa saṁpravakṣyāmi* // (1990:60).

[137] See VD 124b.

repetition, and so forth should be taken in terms of both authentic (*rnal ma*) and contrived (*bcos ma*) [varieties]. This has the same meaning as the previous [statement]. Here the pairs of outer and inner, contrived and uncontrived (*bcos ma bcos*), and interpretable and definitive are taken as synonymous. Even though in the text of the root Tantra there is no statement that reveals this inner, uncontrived perfection stage by means such as these, one should understand that it is necessary to take the root Tantra's references to the mandala, and so forth, in terms of both stages.

3.2. Showing the method of explanation based upon them [the instructions of the mahāsiddhas]

This second part has three sections: (1) significance of the count of fifty-one chapters, (2) applying the threefold explanation to the fifty-one chapters, and (3) showing the relevance of the summary of each chapter.

3.2.1. Significance of the count of fifty-one chapters

In this Tantra there are fifty-one [chapters]. The *Ḍākārṇava* [states,] "The *Laghusaṁvara*, extracted from the three hundred thousand–stanza *Abhidhāna*, is joined to reality by the sequence of chapters, from *a* up to *kṣ*."[138] This says that the exact process of the occurrence of the chapters in the root Tantra is connected to the letters from *a* up until *kṣ*, and it is also connected with reality. However, if you think that there is a contradiction since there are [only] fifty vowels and consonants, and [yet] there are fifty-one chapters, there is no fault, because the fifty apply to the reality of each of them, and the fifty-first is connected with the reality [of them all] in general.

In regard to the method by which they are joined with the reality of the vowels and consonants, the vowels are the side of art, and the consonants are the side of wisdom. Since these two are indivisible, all of the chapters of the Tantra are shown to have the nonduality of art and wisdom as their topic, and thus connect to the vowels and consonants.

Furthermore, the meaning of the vowels and consonants is relevant to the entire Tantra, from beginning to end, provided that they are understood in terms of the natural great bliss that is generated in dependence

---

[138] See DA 242b–243a.

upon the encounter of the red and white elements. This is in the oral transmission that should be realized. Having reflected on that, it says in the *Saṁcāra* that "If one desires this teaching without understanding the vowels and consonants, one's labor is useless, and one will not attain fruition."[139] As for the number of stanzas, it says in the *Commentary Praising Saṁvara* that there are seven hundred.[140]

3.2.2. Applying the threefold explanation to the fifty-one chapters

If, in this method of interpreting the concise meaning in each chapter set forth in the system of Nāropā, you take the testimony of the *Intended Import of the Laghu[saṁvara] Tantra* of the scholar Sumatikīrti, then you will reach the very pure commentarial style of Nāropā.[141] Moreover, *Intended Import of the Laghu[saṁvara]* states:

> First, all of the concise meanings with respect to the creation and perfection stages are summarized by the first chapter, stated in detail by the chapters from the second up to the fiftieth, and are brought together by the last chapter. The Blessed Lord said this. This explanation, which is applied threefold to the *Laghu[saṁvara] Tantra*, is the intention of Nāropā.[142]

The expression "applied threefold" is the explanation that connects the first chapter's summarization, the extensive explanation of [the chapters] from the second up to the fiftieth, and the fifty-first's unification of those chapter's meanings, brief and extensive.

---

[139] Tsong Khapa here quotes YS 16.5. See Pandey 1998, 142, and YS 42b.

[140] See LT 79a.

[141] Sumatikīrti's *Laghusaṁvaratantrapaṭalābhisandhi* (LA), referred to by Tsong Khapa as the *Intended Import* or *Intended Import of the Concise*, is a quite short text, amounting to only one and a half folios in its Tibetan translation. Despite its brevity it is an important and influential work, composed by the Kashmiri scholar who assisted in the translation of a number of Saṁvara texts, and who prepared a revision of the root Tantra itself. Tsong Khapa relied upon it so much that he directly quotes the entire text in this and the following few chapters. It is translated in Appendix II below.

[142] This quote is the first part of Sumatikīrti's LA, following the translator's salutation, and a brief one-line statement of the author's intent. Note that I follow Tsong Khapa's reading here. See Appendix II for my translation of the Tengyur version of the text.

Some Tibetans say that this "applied threefold" refers to Nāropā's system for explaining in terms of the three *Saṁpuṭa*s; this is an explanation that employs the terminology meaninglessly without ascertaining the *Intended Import*'s meaning. Also, some Tibetans seem to say that "applied threefold," that is, to the summary, explanation, and conclusion, occurs elsewhere. They seem to explain that in the first [chapter] there are summaries of what follows starting from the second, and that [the chapters] in their own context give an extensive explanation of that, and in the end the meanings are unified. Since the conclusion unifies the stages of the path that are the import of the fifty chapters, it clarifies what was previously extensively explained. But that is not Nāropā's way of explaining it.

3.2.3. Showing the relevance of the summary of each chapter

This third part has three sections: (1) showing the summary of each [chapter], (2) applying the threefold explanation to the fifty-one chapters, and (3) showing the relevance of the summary of each chapter.

3.2.3. 1. Showing the summary of each [chapter]

This first section has six subsections: (1) the summary of bestowing consecration and showing reality therein, (2) the summary of the selection of mantras and achieving the powers, (3) the summary of attaining both powers through the kindness of the messengers, (4) the summary of impact-heightening conduct and the vow as a friend on the path, (5) the summary of the four mudrās such as mahāmudrā, and (6) the summary on understanding the signs of the rapid attainment of the achievements.

3.2.3. 1.1. The summary of bestowing consecration and showing reality therein

The *Intended Import of the Laghu[saṁvara]* states that:

> "Having conferred consecration, show reality to him." This means that in the Mantrayāna, first there is consecration bestowal. The mandala is the preliminary stage

> for this, thus the second chapter shows the mandala,
> while the third shows consecration bestowal.[143]

The statement in the first chapter, **in the primordially established charnel ground, there one should draw the mandala (1.16cd)**, is explained by the second and third chapters.

If you show the reality of the two stages to one who has not been previously consecrated, this delays the powers. Therefore, the statement "having conferred consecration, show reality" indicates that there must first be a conferral of consecration with respect to the mantra. Just as Ghaṇṭapā stated that "Vajradhara said that bestowing consecration is preceded by the mandala,"[144] the need of the mandala beforehand is shown by the second chapter. This not only shows the habitat mandala, but also establishes the inhabitant mandala, and offerings made to it. Thus it states the characteristics and necessity of the vases.[145]

The third chapter shows the entry into the mandala, the casting of the flower, and the bestowal of the name, etc., consecrations, the secret consecration, and the third consecration.

Both the adherents of Mal and the explanation of Mardo claim that the fourth chapter, by teaching the four realities, explains the conferral of the fourth initiation.[146] In the *Intended Import of the Laghu[saṁvara]* it says, "the fourth [chapter shows] the reality that is the aim of consecration conferral."[147] This means that the explanation of the four realities by

---

143 See my LA translation in Appendix II below.

144 See Ghaṇṭapā's *Śrīcakrasaṁvaraṣekaprakriya-upadeśa*, D fol. 216b.

145 The vases, described at the end of CT ch. 2, contain offerings offered to the mandala's inhabitants.

146 Sachen discusses this at the beginning of his commentary on the fourth chapter, as follows: "The fourth chapter also shows the secret of the path, the substance, and the fourth initiation in order to pursue the relevance of the statement 'one shows the reality' connected with that for those thus engaged who have undergone consecration. This is due to statements such as 'And having conferred consecration, show reality' etc." */de ltar lam gyi gsang ba la 'jug pa dbang bskur ba sngon du song ba la/ de dang 'brel ba'i de kho na nyid bstan par bya'o zhes 'brel pa bsnyegs pa'i don du le'u bzhi pas lam gyi gsang ba dngos dang yang dbang bzhi pa yang ston te/ de yang dbang bskur nas ni de nyid bstan/ zhes pa la sogs pa gsungs pas so/* (PG 308.1).

147 See my LA translation in Appendix II below.

the fourth chapter is the reality of the meaning of that which is to be explained in the initiation conferral. Therefore, since they are in agreement, this [explanation] seems to be acceptable.

It also says in the *Intended Import*, "Thus the three chapters explain [the meaning summarized by the lines in chapter one] from **And now... the secret (1.1a)** up until **Listen (1.5d)**."[148] Some editions of this [text] say "the third chapter."[149] This refers to the third chapter of the extensive explanatory Tantra.[150] That chapter explains the meaning of the two stages that are taught by [expressions] such as **And now...the secret**. In an expansion on [the term] "explain," [Sumatikīrti states that]:

> This [indicates] the detailed exegesis of the mandala that is visualized by means of the preliminary [visualizations] such as **the dried** [dung] **in a cattle pen (32.10cd)** and so forth, which are thus stated [in the root text]. Since [this topic] is completed with this, it is not stated elsewhere than this [text].[151]

The creation of the stacked-up elements is indicated by [the expression] **cattle pen**, etc., which is stated in the thirty-second chapter. The mandala visualization that this precedes is explained in the second chapter. And while the explanation of the stacked-up elements visualization occurs afterwards, here he means that one should not say that it is a mandala visualization separate from that in the second [chapter].

3.2.3. 1.2. The summary of the selection of mantras and achieving the powers

According to the meaning of the summary from **And now...the secret** up to **Listen...**, the person who has thus properly attained

---

[148] See my LA translation in Appendix II below.

[149] That is, *le'u gsum pas* rather than *le'u gsum pos*.

[150] This statement is almost certainly a reference to the *Saṁpuṭa Tantra*, the third chapter of which is on the topic of the "secret"; it states and explains the root Tantra's *nidāna*.

[151] See my LA translation in Appendix II below. Note that my translation "Since [this topic] is completed with this" follows the Tengyur reading *'di nyid kyis zin pas*, rather than Tsong Khapa's reading *'di nyid yin pas*.

consecration does [mantra] repetitions and contemplations of meditation on the two stages, and is said to achieve the powers, as explained by the fourth chapter. [To achieve this one] needs mantras, and thus needs to select the [appropriate] mantra. As for the method of doing this, [the following] is stated in the *Intended Import*:

> Then, when commenting upon [the text] **successful with mantra repetition and meditative states (1.10.ab)**, one must show the selection of the mantras that are to be repeated, which are set forth in a scrambled order in the four chapters from the fifth through the eighth and from the twenty-fifth to the thirtieth [chapters]. You should understand that this is for the sake of preventing the repetition of the mantra [by someone who] lacks a master in the lineage.[152]

However, the [text] "*from* the twenty-fifth [*to* the thirtieth chapters]" is not correct, because it discusses elsewhere the topics shown by the four chapters from the twenty-sixth to the twenty-ninth. Therefore, it should be read as "*in* the twenty-fifth *and* [the thirtieth chapter]."[153]

Regarding that, the consonants of the root mantra of the father deity are selected in the fifth chapter, and the root mantra's vowels are selected in the seventh. And the twenty-fifth states the root mantra itself, joined with the initial [syllable] *oṁ* and the final [syllables] *hūṁ hūṁ phaṭ*. The sixth chapter simply enumerates the letters of the essence and quintessence mantras of the Father deity, and the selection of the Father's armor mantras. The eighth chapter gives the selection of the Father's essence mantra and the Mother's armor mantras. The thirtieth chapter shows both the selection of the mantra of the four-faced [Trailokya-vijaya] and the selected mantra.[154] The expression "scrambled order" (*go rim 'chol ba*) has to do with things such as showing the essence mantra in reverse order, and so forth.

---

[152] See my LA translation in Appendix II below.

[153] Tsong Khapa here corrects the reading *nyi shu rtsa lnga pa nas* to *nyi shu rtsa lnga pa dang*. Note, however, that the text preserved in the Tengyur has the latter, correct reading.

[154] That is, it gives the coding for the mantra, and then states the mantra itself at the end of the chapter.

In regard to the chapter that shows the time of achieving the fruit that "will be achieved," the *Intended Import* states [the following]:

> In this way, one should understand that the mundane powers are shown in the characteristics of the supreme and ordinary powers of repetition [that are described] from the ninth chapter until the end of the fourteenth, and from the forty-first until the fiftieth. By applying the three bodies to the above [descriptions], the supreme, supramundane success is revealed.[155]

"Powers of repetition" is an example; success is achieved from both [mantra] repetition and meditative states. In regard to that, chapter nine shows the attainment of mundane powers by means of the Father's root mantra, while [the latter section of] chapter ten shows the achievement of ritual actions with the Father's essence mantra. In chapter eleven there is an investigation of the one born seven times. And having taken the concretion (*rocanā*) from his heart, it shows the achievement of ritual actions with the essence mantra of the Father. Chapter twelve teaches the achievement of ritual actions by means of the Father's quintessence. Chapter thirteen shows the achievement of ritual actions by means of the armor mantras. Chapter fourteen shows the achievement of ritual actions of the one born seven times by means of the donkey-faced Heruka.

The [text] "from the forty-first" is clearly erroneous, because [the topics covered] in the four chapters from the thirty-ninth up until the forty-second are explained separately. Therefore, it should be read as "from the forty-third."[156]

Chapter forty-three teaches the achievement of ritual actions by means of the Father's quintessence, and chapter forty-four by means of the Mother's armor mantras and the Father's quintessence. Chapter forty-five shows how to achieve ritual actions by means of the heroines' armor mantras, and chapter forty-six does so relying on the five *ha* [mantra]. Chapter forty-seven teaches the achievement of ritual actions by means

---

155 See my LA translation in Appendix II below. Tsong Khapa's text reads "from the forty-first until the fiftieth"; this is incorrect, but he corrects it in his comments below.

156 As before, the text in the Tengyur preserves the correct reading.

of the *sarvabuddhaḍākinī*[157] mantra. Chapter forty-eight shows the actual *[sarva]buddhaḍākinī* mantra,[158] and teaches continual meditation on the four [essence] yoginīs and the twenty-four heroes. Chapter forty-nine extensively details the one born seven times, and chapter fifty teaches the achievements of ritual actions by the Vajravairocanī mantra.[159]

The supreme success is taught by a section of chapter ten, which demonstrates the attainment of the three bodies. This is summarized by [a statement] in the first chapter, **success is always attained (1.13b)**. And if we explain in more detail the three bodies of the path of the perfection stage, you will be able to understand that they will be attained by a process of step-by-step ascension.

In regard to the teaching of the two powers, it was said that "having developed enthusiasm for the common powers, when you attain them, it is for the sake of entry into the supreme." However, the principal disciples of Unexcelled [Yogatantra], having reached the end of the creation stage, do not seek mundane powers, [but seek instead] entry into the perfection stage; this is explained in many treatises. Therefore, [the above statement] is not correct. The attainment of mundane powers at the end of the creation stage is the method of Unexcelled [Yogatantra] disciples who have inferior faculties.

3.2.3. 1.3. The summary of attaining both powers through the kindness of the messengers

The *Intended Import* also explains that:

> In that way, the [chapters] from the fifteenth to the twenty-fourth explain **the messengers are natural and accomplished (1.7a)**, etc., in order to show here that the mundane and supramundane successes are based on the kindness of the yoginīs. So that one might understand

157 Here I read *sarva buddha ḍā ki ni* as *sarvabuddhaḍākinī*.

158 This mantra, which is only mentioned by name in ch. 47, is given in reverse order at the beginning of ch. 48.

159 Here I read *vajra bai ro tsa na'i* as *vajravairocanī*, which refers to Vajravārāhī's quintessence mantra. Note that there is no mention of this mantra in the text of ch. 50.

> the differentiation of the three [types of] yoginīs,[160] one should know the syllabic signs, the differentiation of the six classes, the enumeration of names, the characteristics of the ḍākinī clans, the lāma clan characteristics, the hand signs, the gazes, the body gestures, the signs and insignia, and the verbal signs. These ten particularities show the characteristics of the messengers in the ten chapters, respectively.[161]

This means that the ten chapters from the fifteenth to the twenty-fourth were stated in order to extensively explain the summary that one achieves success in dependence upon the worship of the clanswoman, i.e., [the verse] in chapter one from **the messengers are natural and accomplished (1.7a)** to **give rise to the achievement of pleasure (1.7d)**. [This is done] in order to show that both powers are achieved through the kindness of the yoginī.

Regarding [Sumatikīrti's claim that this is done] "so that one might understand the differentiation of the three [types of] yoginīs," although these chapters do not state the means for distinguishing each of these three individually, such as the mantra-born, etc., since one depends upon meeting with these ḍākinīs, one must know things such as "she is this one of the three yoginīs" and "this is that kind of place." One must recognize those things that are explained a bit by each of the ten chapters, which were shown very concisely, such as the signs, and so forth, in order to worship the ḍākinī clanswoman. And one will need to investigate them in order to recognize them. And when one has investigated them, one will come to understand the hero and the sister, via an investigation of chapters fifteen, twenty, twenty-two, and twenty-four, which are the means of knowing them. The signs of each syllable are shown by chapter fifteen, and the verbal signs that are aggregates of many syllables are shown by chapter twenty-four. Thus they are recognized by relying on speech.

---

160 The three types of yoginīs, explained by Tsong Khapa below, are the *kṣetraja*, "womb-born," the *mantraja,* "mantra-born," and the *sahaja,* "natural." See section 3.3.3.2.1.1.3.1.2 in chapter one.

161 See my LA translation in Appendix II below.

In order that they are recognized by means of physical signs, chapter twenty shows the physical signs, of which [those made with] the hands are principal, and chapter twenty-one relates the physical signs that are visual gestures. Chapter twenty-two shows the physical signs that are gestures distinctive to the hands. Thus these five chapters show how to understand the ḍākinīs' gestures.

Since understanding the yoginīs in general is not sufficient, it is necessary to investigate their particular clans. [This is addressed] in four chapters. Chapter sixteen teaches the characteristics of the six clans, so that one might worship them with the understanding of the clan harmonious with one's own affinity. Chapter seventeen shows via the enumeration of names the two sets of seven ḍākinīs, which constitute the ḍākinīs, and chapter eighteen shows the distinctions of the characteristics of the ḍākinī clan. Chapter nineteen shows the five differences that characterize lāmā clans. Although you might recognize the ḍākinīs through analysis, it is not suitable to perform reality worship[162] if they are not fond of you. Therefore chapter twenty-three shows the signs that they are devoted to you, as well as the symbolic insignia distinctive to the ḍākinīs.

In general, if messengers endowed with all of the characteristics assist all practitioners of unexcelled secret mantra, then the path is swift. And if those practitioners well understand the path of *Cakrasaṁvara* in particular, they are blessed by the ḍākinīs' distinguished messengers; assisted by them, the path is much swifter. And even though one might not now reach this practice directly, in another life there will arise the outstanding auspicious circumstance in which one will be able to directly employ the signs and their responses. Therefore, one should become skilled in these methods, and one should become thoroughly accustomed to them.

3.2.3. 1.4. The summary of impact-heightening conduct and the vow as a friend on the path

It also says in the *Intended Import* that:

---

[162] "Reality worship," *de kho na nyid kyi mchod pa*, *tattvapūjā*, is a topic briefly addressed in CT ch. 36, which is understood by the commentators to refer to sexual yogic practices.

> After that, in order to fulfill the meaning of [statements] such as **...should always protect the commitments (1.10c)**, chapter twenty-six shows the commitments that are guarded so as to please the messenger whom one has recognized. Chapter twenty-seven shows the conduct (*spyod pa*, *caryā*) performed at the command of the pleased seal that one has achieved. [It also demonstrates] the contrived conduct that fulfills the import of characteristic [statements] such as **the state of being a yogī (1.9c)**. Chapter twenty-eight and twenty-nine show the performance of the contrived conduct.[163]

As for the meaning of that, in order to extensively explain the meaning of the summary in the first chapter, [that one] **should always protect the commitments**, chapter twenty-six shows the eight commitments that are preserved so as to please the messengers, who are recognized in reliance upon the signs. That is just an example, as one must also preserve the pledges that protect against the root downfalls, etc. If you please the distinctive messenger, the contrived performance that is commanded by her is shown by chapters twenty-seven, twenty-eight, and twenty-nine.

It also says in the *Intended Import* that "Then the thirty-eighth extensively illustrates the uncontrived and extremely uncontrived conduct in order to fulfill the import of [statements] such as **the state of being a yogī**, etc."[164] The summary of [the topic of] "conduct" is provided in the first chapter by the statement that **the state of being a yogī is the supreme purifying merit that destroys sin (1.9cd)**. Furthermore, it says in the *Intended Import* that:

> Then, as an explanation of [the text] **there are honey and vermilion,...with camphor (1.11c)**, etc., the three chapters from the thirty-first show the commitments of eating necessary for all [modes of] conduct. Furthermore, one should also know hand worship, the names of the

---

[163] See my LA translation in Appendix II below.

[164] See my LA translation in Appendix II below.

> distinctive substances, and the differentiation of the three types of food procedures.[165]

Chapter thirty-one shows the hand offerings, chapter thirty-two the names of the distinctive substances, and chapter thirty-three the types of food procedures. These protect the commitments of eating. These two commitments illustrate as well the types of commitments on which one relies.

3.2.3. 1.5. The summary of the four mudrās such as mahāmudrā

It also says in the *Intended Import* that:

> After that, the four chapters from the thirty-fourth onward are commentaries on **the four [types of] worship; thus the great hero (1.14ab)**,[166] etc. One should investigate them in the order of the great seal (*mahāmudrā*), the reality seal (*dharmamudrā*),[167] and the subjugation of the actual seal (*karmamudrā*). The symbolic seal (*samaya-mudrā*)[168] is shown in accordance with the characteristics of visualizing the wheel of the mandala. Therefore, here it is not very extensively discussed separately from them.[169]

165 See my LA translation in Appendix II below.

166 Here I have translated the line from the first chapter's fourteenth verse as it occurs in the LA, Tsong Khapa's text, and the Kangyur, namely, *mchod bzhi dpa' bo chen po ni*. Elsewhere, however, I have translated it as "there are the four [types of] worship; thus the yoginīs and heroes," following the Sanskrit (*catuḥpūjā tathā yoginyo vīrāḥ*) as well as Kambala's commentary (SN 6a). The latter actually makes more sense in this context, as it makes more clear the connection between the four offerings and the four *mudrā*s.

167 In this tradition, the term *dharmamudrā* appears to refer to sonic or visual manifestations of the deity, in the form of mantras or images.

168 I translate *samayamudrā* here as "symbolic seal" because the term in this context appears to mean an internally visualized replacement of the actual seal [consort]. I thus interpret *samaya* here in its sense of "sign, hint, indication" (Monier-Williams 2002, 1164 col. 1), which is the sense that is also implied by the term *samayamaṇḍala*, the mandala paintings in which the deities are represented by their symbolic implements.

169 See my LA translation in Appendix II below.

The meaning of this is that the four chapters from the thirty-fourth up to the thirty-seventh extensively explain the summaries of the four seals (*mudrās*) such as the four offerings and the great hero. Furthermore, chapter thirty-four teaches about the great seal, and chapter thirty-five, the reality seal.[170] Chapter thirty-six shows the method of relying on the actual seal, and chapter thirty-seven the art of bringing the actual seal under one's control.

It is said that the symbolic seal (*samayamudrā*) is not shown separately from that [shown in the] setting forth of the Heruka deity couple in the center of the mandala that was previously explained. The symbolic seal is what is called the gnostic seal (*jñānamudrā*) in other texts; it is the goddess who is mentally visualized, such as Vajravārāhī. This does not contradict the claim by those who follow the systems of both Lama Mardo and Mal that chapter thirty-six shows both the symbolic and the actual seals.[171] This is because, as it is said, "while it is not that it does not show the symbolic seal in general, it does not do so in detail."[172] This means that it is not clearly shown separately from the actual seal.

3.2.3. 1.6. The summary on understanding the signs of the rapid attainment of the powers

It also says in the *Intended Import*, "Next, the signs of the powers common to the three yogas are taught from chapter thirty-nine to chapter forty-two."[173] The signs or indications of the rapid attainment of the supreme accomplishment common to the three yogas, i.e., conducts, are shown by the four chapters from the thirty-ninth to the forty-second.

---

170 Chapter thirty-five deals with ritual actions involving visualizations of the mantra, so it would appear that here *dharmamudrā* refers to sonic or mantric representations of the deities.

171 This claim is made at the opening of Sachen's PG ch. 36 commentary, as follows: "Chapter thirty-six shows, at the same time, both the meditation relying upon an actual seal for persons of inferior faculties, and [the meditation] relying on the symbolic seal, the [visualized] luminous spell [consort] (*'od kyi rig ma*), for those of middling faculties" (PG 357.4).

172 This quote does not occur in Sachen's commentary; Tsong Khapa may be referring to Mardo's commentary here.

173 See my LA translation in Appendix II below.

How is it that the meanings of the summary and the meaning of the fifty-first chapter are made to accord? It also says in the *Intended Import* that "The characteristics of the meanings that were shown thus both in summary and in detail are brought together by the fifty-first chapter, and were taught by the Blessed Lord. [This] is the guru's oral instruction."[174] The method whereby chapter fifty-one condenses into one the process of realization will be explained on the occasion of [commenting on] that [chapter] itself. Doing this in accordance with the concise meaning is indicated in the personal instructions of the very reverend Nārotapa.

3.2.3. 2. The arrangement in one of the stages of the path

Knowing to take as a path the meanings of the root Tantra from beginning to end with regard to the stages of practice is the supreme essence of the many explanations. Therefore, if we arrange them all as one and explain them, then [for example] one could well attain the initiation, the topics of which occur in the second and third chapters, and are filled out by the two explanatory Tantras. For this is the excellent method for becoming a suitable vessel, which is one who listens, contemplates, and meditates upon the two stages of the path along with their components.

When you have become such a suitable vessel, having brought together well the Root and Explanatory [Tantras], [connecting] the meaning of **And now I will explain the secret (1.1a)** and the meaning of the fourth chapter and the chapters on the four seals, then one should meditate on the two stages. That is sticking to the center of the path. You should also have a guide on this path who adheres to the commitments.

When one develops one's capability by meditating on that and adhering [to the commitments], one will come to meet with a distinctive messenger. At that time one should rely on her and practice according to her command—this is the excellent method of heightening impact on the path. When you take advantage of that impact by practicing in the contexts of each of the two stages, then you will rapidly attain both the ordinary and supreme powers. Since the oral instructions of the saints (*siddha*, *grub thob*) explain the thoroughly mixed-up and unclear root

[174] Note that Tsong Khapa's text here varies considerably from the text preserved in the Tengyur. See my LA translation in Appendix II below.

Tantra, they seem to fascinate the scholars, since they give unexcelled certainty on the path. Later scholars who rely on Nāropā's commentarial tradition should explain in accordance with that only.

3.2.3. 3. The method of the lineage from Nāropā

The superiority of this commentarial tradition is due to Śrī Nāropā. Although he had many students, he had four principal disciples of *Cakrasaṁvara*, who were named Mānakaśrījñāna,[175] Prajñārakṣita,[176] Pitong Hamdu, and Pamting-pa.[177] Regarding the first of them, Mardo says that he was known as the northern door guardian [of Nālandā], having become the door guardian after Nāropā. The third, [Pitong Hamdu], was the elder brother of Pamting-pa, and was called Dharmamati.[178] Having remained for twelve years in the presence of Nāropā, he evidently went to Wu-tai-shan in China. The fourth is the Newar Pamting-pa. In the Kathmandu valley[179] he was known as Aday Chenpo. He was also known as Abhayakīrti Bhikṣu.[180] He remained in the presence of Nāropā for nine years. Through *Cakrasaṁvara* he obtained inferior and middling powers. His younger brother, Kālacakrapa, served Nāropā for five years. His younger brother, Thang Chupa,[181] studied *Cakrasaṁvara* with Nāropā.

---

[175] His name occurs in the *Blue Annals* in the list of masters in the *Cakrasaṁvara* lineage received by Mardo. The *Blue Annals* cites his name as Manakaśrījñāna (Roerich 1976, 385).

[176] He was one of Nāropā's disciples. See Roerich 1976, 384.

[177] The label Pamting-pa (*pham-thing-pa*) is not a proper name, but a title meaning "the one from Pharphing," an important Buddhist pilgrimage site at the south edge of the Kathmandu valley. It is sometimes used as a name for one of the brothers, and sometimes used to refer to the brothers in general. Regarding this see Lo Bue 1997, 643–652.

[178] According to the *Blue Annals*, Dharmamati was the eldest of the Pamting-pa brothers. He studied under Nāropā for twelve years, and then went on pilgrimage to Wu-tai-shan in China. His remains are reported to be enshrined near mChod-rten-dkar-po on the Sino-Tibetan border. See Roerich 1976, 381.

[179] The Tibetan word *bal yul* traditionally referred to the Newar kingdom(s) in the Kathmandu valley, not to the modern state of Nepal.

[180] Some sources link the name Abhayakīrti with the older brother, a.k.a. Dharmamati, and connect the younger "Pamting-pa" with the name Vāgīśvarakīrti. See Lo Bue 1997, 644.

[181] His name is usually given as Tang Chungpa. See Lo Bue 1997, 644, and Roerich 1976, 381.

The Kashmiri Bodhibhadra, having served Nāropā, studied *Cakrasaṁvara*.[182] Kanakaśrī studied with Pamting-pa and the first two of the previous four.[183] He was also called the Newar Bhadanta.[184] Sumatikīrti of lesser omniscience[185] also studied with him, and also with Mānakaśrī and Pamting-pa. The Newar Mahākaruṇa studied with Kanakaśrī.

Although there are many ways in which lineages in Tibet derive from them, there were two [people] who most benefited Tibet. They were the Malgyo translator Lodrö Drakpa, and the translator known as Marpa Dopa, whose real name was Marpa Chökyi Wangchuk and whose secret name was Mañjuśrīvajra. Of them, Malgyo studied with the three Pamting-pa brothers, the Kashmiri Bodhibhadra, Sumatikīrti, and the Newar Mahākaruṇaka. Mardo listened to both Pamting-pa and Sumatikīrti. The Venerable Sakya Chenpo,[186] who studied *Cakrasaṁvara* with the translator Mal, the Translator of rMa, and the Lesser Translator of Pu-rangs, considered Mal's system to be authoritative. Mal and Sachen did not write about the root Tantra, but Sachen's explanations in conference with Mal were accurately edited by a certain disciple of theirs called Puṇyavajra in an extensive commentary on the root Tantra called the

---

[182] He was a fellow disciple studying with Pamting-pa under Nāropā. Roerich erred in identifying him as Pamting-pa's brother. See Lo Bue's (1997, 644) critique of Roerich's translation (1976:382). He was most likely the Kashmiri Paṇḍita Śrī Bhadra who is said to be a disciple of Nāropā in gTsang-smyon Heruka's biography of Marpa Hlodrakpa (Trungpa 1982:58).

[183] Regarding Kanakaśrī see Lo Bue 1997, 652–653.

[184] The Newar Bhadanta (misspelled in Tsong Khapa's text as *ba-dan-ta*) was, according to Shönu Pel, a servant to Pamting-pa's younger brother Tang Chungpa, who was instructed by Pamting-pa to meditate on Vāgiśvara. He did this and afterwards threw a flower into a stream as a test of his attainment. He did so thrice, and all three times it flowed upstream. He only noticed this, however, on the last throw, and hence attained only middling success. His servant, however, drank of the water downstream, and hence gained the success that his master failed to acquire (Roerich 1976:381). Tsong Khapa's identification of the Newar Bhadanta with Kanakaśrī appears to be incorrect. He evidently was an Indian from Magadha who studied at Vikramaśīla, and was a student of Nāropā. See Lo Bue 1997, 652.

[185] It seems that there was a Newar Buddhist figure of this name. There was also a well-known Kashmiri of this name who assisted with the translation of texts in the *Cakrasaṁvara* tradition, but he studied with Nāropā himself. See Lo Bue 1997, 649.

[186] That is, the great Sakya master Kunga Nyingpo (1092–1158).

Pearl Garland (*muktāvali*, *mu tig 'phreng ba*). Mardo wrote a commentary on the root Tantra.[187] His disciples Zewa, Demchok Dorje,[188] Namka Wangchuk of India, and Chogro Chökyi Gyaltsen[189] greatly propagated the *Cakrasaṁvara* [tradition].

Lama Phakpa Ö[190] gave the consecrations, instructions, and explanations of the system of Sakya, Lochung,[191] Sachen, as well as the system of Atiśa to the omniscient Büton. Since he also received the exegetical transmission of Mardo's system, he mastered Nāropā's explanatory style through the lineage of both the translators and the scholars. I myself heard the exegetical transmission (*bshad lung*) of the *Great Commentary on the Root Tantra* (*rtsa-gyud kyi rnam-bshad chen-mo*) from his disciple, the great lama Dechenpa.[192]

---

187 This would be the *Mar do lo tsa ba chos kyi dbang phyug gi bde mchog rtsa rgyud kyi bsdus don dang tikka rgyas pa*. This is text #12165 in Akuching Sherab Gyatso's *tho yig*, a catalogue of texts available at Labrang monastery during the early twentieth century, published in Chandra 1963. Unfortunately, this text does not seem to have come to light yet. Many thanks to Gene Smith for bringing this text to my attention.

188 Tsong Khapa here reads *gze ba bde mchog rdo rje*, which I read as a reference to two people, namely Mardo's disciple Zewa Loden, who is usually known as Zewa. Zewa's son, to whom he transmitted the Cakrasaṁvara teachings, was Demchok Dorje. See Roerich 1976, 384–285.

189 Regarding Chogro Chökyi Gyaltsen (1108–1176), see Roerich 1976, 386–387.

190 That is, his teacher Yönten Gyatso, also known as Kunkyen Phakpa Ö.

191 I presume that Tsong Khapa uses the title *lo-chung* in reference to Mardo rather than to Ngok Lochung Legpay Sherab, one of Rinchen Zangpo's disciples. He uses it in this way, quoting Sachen, in the context of chapter five, section 3.3.3.2.2.2.2.1.1.1.2.1.2 below.

192 This refers to Chö Pelzangpo, also know as Gongsum Dechenpa. He was a disciple of Büton who in turn taught Tsong Khapa.

CHAPTER 1

Chapter 1 Outline

3.3. The actual method of explaining the root Tantra
3.3.1. The meaning of the name
3.3.1. 1. The translation of the name
3.3.1. 2. The explanation of the name
3.3.2. The salutation of the translators
3.3.3. The meaning of the text
3.3.3. 1. The reason "Thus have I heard" is not stated in the beginning
3.3.3. 2. The actual explanation of the text's meaning
3.3.3. 2.1. The first chapter's introduction to the significance of the entire Tantra
3.3.3. 2.1.1. The actual text
3.3.3. 2.1.1. 1. The promise to explain the secret
3.3.3. 2.1.1. 2. The exhortation to listen to the secret
3.3.3. 2.1.1. 2.1. The secret that should be heard
3.3.3. 2.1.1. 2.1.1. Showing in brief the presentation of the secret
3.3.3. 2.1.1. 2.1.1. 1. Explaining the interpretable meaning
3.3.3. 2.1.1. 2.1.1. 2. Explaining the definitive meaning
3.3.3. 2.1.1. 2.1.2. Explaining the presentation [of the secret] somewhat more extensively
3.3.3. 2.1.1. 2.1.2. 1. The actual meaning
3.3.3. 2.1.1. 2.1.2. 1.1. Explaining the two lines [that begin with] "The secret...supreme" [1.2cd]
3.3.3. 2.1.1. 2.1.2. 1.1.1. Explaining in terms of the interpretable meaning
3.3.3. 2.1.1. 2.1.2. 1.1.1. 1. Explaining as applicable to the narrative preface "Thus have I heard..."
3.3.3. 2.1.1. 2.1.2. 1.1.1. 1.1. Stating the exact words of the narrative preface
3.3.3. 2.1.1. 2.1.2. 1.1.1. 1.2. Explaining their meaning
3.3.3. 2.1.1. 2.1.2. 1.1.1. 2. The explanation applicable to the creation stage
3.3.3. 2.1.1. 2.1.2. 1.1.2. Explaining in terms of the definitive meaning
3.3.3. 2.1.1. 2.1.2. 1.1.2. 1. The definitive meaning as applied to the narrative preface
3.3.3. 2.1.1. 2.1.2. 1.1.2. 2. The definitive meaning as applied to the creation stage
3.3.3. 2.1.1. 2.1.2. 1.1.2. 3. Explaining the sixteen syllables in reference to alchemy
3.3.3. 2.1.1. 2.1.2. 1.2. Explaining the four lines [that begin with] "made of all ḍākinīs" [1.3]
3.3.3. 2.1.1. 2.1.2. 1.2.1. The explanation applied to the goal
3.3.3. 2.1.1. 2.1.2. 1.2.2. The explanation applied to the perfection stage of the path
3.3.3. 2.1.1. 2.1.2. 1.3. Explaining the two lines that begin with "arising" [1.4a–b]
3.3.3. 2.1.1. 2.1.2. 1.3.1. Explaining the interpretable meaning
3.3.3. 2.1.1. 2.1.2. 1.3.2. Explaining the definitive meaning
3.3.3. 2.1.1. 2.1.2. 2. The difficult to obtain
3.3.3. 2.1.1. 2.1.2. 3. Showing an example of the union of bliss and emptiness
3.3.3. 2.1.1. 2.2. The actual exhortation to listen
3.3.3. 2.1.1. 3. The method for making progress in the secret of the path
3.3.3. 2.1.1. 3.1. Worship of the clanswoman

3.3. The actual method of explaining the root Tantra

This third part has four sections: (1) the meaning of the name, (2) the salutation of the translators, (3) the meaning of the text, and (4) the meaning of the conclusion.

3.3.1. The meaning of the name

This first part has two sections: the translation of the name and the explanation of the name.

3.3.1. 1. The translation of the name

This Tantra's name, from *śrī* to *nāma*, is in the Sanskrit language, one of the four language classes of India.[193] When this is translated into Tibetan,[194] *śrī* is *dpal*, "glory." *Heruka* means "blood drinker." Some take the *ru* [in *heruka*] as *rudhira*, which means "blood."[195] As [this interpretation] relies on the mere portion of a word, some people say it is not good to translate it as "blood drinker." The adherents of the system of Mardo make an etymological explanation wherein they add syllables to each of the three syllables [of *heruka*], by which they arrive at "blood

[193] The *skad rigs bzhi* are Sanskrit, Pāli, Prākṛt, and Apabhraṁśa.

[194] Tsong Khapa here follows the Sanskrit title as given in the SM revised translation. It reads as follows: *śrī he ru ka rā dza tsa kra saṁ ba ra bhi dha na yo gi ni rud ta ra sarva tantrod ta ra saṁ ba ra saṁ gra ha nā ma* (SM 1b). It differs considerably from that given in the PM and SL versions, as well as the surviving Sanskrit texts. See Gray 2012 for a comparison of these texts.

[195] Tsong Khapa repeatedly writes **rutira* for *rudhira*.

drinker," which is good. For example, ***helā*** means "dalliance,"[196] ***rudhira*** "blood," and ***kapāla*** "skull bowl." In brief, because he dallies in skull-bowl blood, [*heruka*] is translated as "blood drinker."[197]

Rāja means "king," and *cakra*, "wheel." *Saṁvara* means "binding," and *abhidhāna*, "text."[198] *Yoginī* is "yogini";[199] *uttara*, "highest";[200] *sarvatantra*, "all Tantras." The *o* vowel of the *trot* [of *tantrottara*] is formed from the conjunction [*sandhi*] of *-tra* with *ut-*.[201] *Uttara* means "highest." *Saṁvara* means "supreme bliss," *saṁgraha* means "compilation," and *nāma* means "called." Although there are many different [translations of the text's] name, this is similar to [the name in] Mardo's solo translation.[202]

3.3.1. 2. The explanation of the name

In the *Saṁcāra* it says that "*śrī* means 'nondual gnosis.' "[203] As nondual gnosis is to be desired and relied upon, it is glorious. I have already explained *heruka*, but I'll give some other explanations. The

[196] Tsong Khapa writes *he la*, no doubt referring to the Sanskrit term *helā*, which can mean "wanton sport, frivolity, amorous dalliance" (Monier-Williams 2002, 1305 col. 2).

[197] This alliterative etymology accounts for the common translation of *heruka* as "blood drinker" (*khrag 'thung*, 食血). This etymology clearly derives from India, as it occurs not only in Tibetan sources but also in Chinese sources, such as the Śubhakarasiṁha 726 CE translation of the *Subāhuparipṛcchā Tantra* (T.895.18.720a10). However, most commentators on the CT quote the famous alliterative etymology contained in the *Hevajra Tantra*, namely: "**śrī** is the nondual gnosis; **he** is the emptiness of cause, and so forth, **ru** is devoid of discrimination, and **ka** is nonlocality" (HT 1.7.27: *śrīkāram advayaṁ jñānaṁ hekāraṁ hetvādiśūnyatā / rukārāpagatavyūhaṁ kakāraṁ na kvacit sthitaṁ //*; ed. in Snellgove 1959, 2.24.25; see also YS 9.7–8, ed. in Pandey 1998, 87–88). See, for example, Büton at NS 150. Bhavabhaṭṭa quotes a variant of this text at Pandey 2002, 5.

[198] Here I read *bhi dha na* as *abhidhāna*.

[199] Here I read *yo gi ni* as *yoginī*.

[200] Here I read *rud ti ra* as *uttara*.

[201] Here I read *trod* as *trot* and *ud* as *ut*.

[202] Tsong Khapa uses the expression *mar do rkyang pa'i 'gyur* to refer to the SM translation, which alone preserves this unusual title for this text.

[203] YS ch. 9.7c: *śrīkāram advayaṁ jñānaṁ* (Pandey 1998, 87); *śrī ni gnyis med ye shes te /* (D fol. 38b).

"king" is the lord of all those who dally in skull bowl blood. "Union" (*saṁvara*, *sdom pa*) means "supreme assembly." Those that are to be united are the physical, verbal, and mental actions of all buddhas. They are the wheels of body, speech, and mind. Regarding the manner in which they are united, all of the things to be united are united as one, inseparably. It is the union of bliss and emptiness as one, and the union of body, speech, and mind into the single reality of the natural (*sahaja*) heruka. The *Saṁvarodaya* states that:

> Physical, verbal, and mental action is the ultimate union of all forms (*sarvākāraikasaṁvaraṁ*, *rnam pa thams cad gcig sdom pa*). Union (*saṁvaraṁ*, *sdom pa*) is supreme bliss, the awakening that cannot be spoken or shown. It is the secret of all buddhas, the assembly that is the supreme union (*saṁvaraṁ varaṁ*, *bde ba'i mchog*).[204]

The text is known as the *Cakrasaṁvara*. "Unexcelled yoginī" shows that it is a Mother Tantra, and that it is the highest of all Tantras, lofty and supreme. As for "Tantra," the *Samājottara* states that "*tantra* is known as a 'continuum,' and it has the three aspects of basis, nature, and nondeprivation. Its nature aspect is the cause, and nondeprivation is the fruit, and the base is the means. These three comprise the meanings of the [term] *tantra*."[205]

The definition of *tantra* is "continuity." In regard to that, "nature," refers to the "causal [aspect of] Tantra" (*rgyu rgyud*), which is the nature of the adept who is a jewel-like person. "Base" refers to the "tantra [as] art" (*thabs rgyud*), namely the four branches of service and practice of the two stages. Nāropā explained the "fruition [aspect of] Tantra" (*'bras*

---

204 SU 3.18a–19b: *kāyavākcetasāṁ karma sarvākāraikasaṁvaram / saṁvaraṁ sukhavaraṁ bodhir avācyam anidarśanam // // rahasyaṁ sarvabuddhānāṁ milanaṁ saṁvaraṁ varam /* (Tsuda 1974, 79); Tsong Khapa's quotation differs slightly from the text of the SU preserved in the Kangyur. Cf. Tsuda 1974, 171–172.

205 This quote is from the eighteenth chapter of the *Guhyasamāja Tantra*, which is also known as the *Uttaratantra*, *rgyud phyi ma*. The Sanskrit occurs as follows in Matsunaga's (1978) edition: *prabandhaṁ tantram ākhyātaṁ tat prabandhaṁ tridhā bhavet / ādhāraḥ prakṛtiś caiva asaṁhāryaprabhedataḥ // prakṛtiś cākṛter hetur asaṁhāryaphalaṁ tathā / ādhāras tad upāyaś ca tribhis tantrārthasaṁgrahaḥ //* (vs. 34–35, p. 115); see also D fol. 150a.

bu'i rgyud) as the body of integration, namely nonabiding nirvāṇa or Vajradhara, which cannot be taken away by any other [being]. Tantra, with respect to the aim [of awakening] (*don gyi rgyud*), thus has three divisions. Śāntipa and Abhayākara[206] say that the causal [aspect of] Tantra is the nature of the mind. "Tantra" is the word that expresses those three [meanings]. Here the latter [sense, in terms of fruition, is relevant].

Finally, the translation of *saṁvara* as "supreme bliss" would mean taking *saṁ* as *sukha*, "bliss," and *vara* as "supreme." Just as it says in the *Saṁpuṭa-uttaratantra*, "Regarding the meaning of the word *saṁvara*, *saṁ* is 'bliss,' and *vara* means 'particularly noble,' "[207] it is necessary that one knows both this and the former meaning of *Saṁvara*. "Abbreviated" means that it was stated by collecting words from the extensive root Tantra.

3.3.2. The salutation of the translators

Blessed Lord (*bcom ldan 'das*) and **glorious** (*dpal*) are easily understood. It says in the *Samāyoga* that "*vajra* is said to mean emptiness, and *sattva* is simply gnosis. The achievement of the nature of these is called Vajrasattva."[208] Accordingly, the salutation of the translator can be read as "Homage to the achievement of the entrance into the experiential unity of the two, the *vajra* that is ultimate emptiness, and the *sattva* which is gnosis."

3.3.3. The meaning of the text

This third part has two sections: the reason "Thus have I heard" is not stated in the beginning, and the actual explanation of the text's meaning.

---

206 Here I read *abhayākara* for *a bhyā ka ra*.

207 See the *Mahātantrarāja-śrīsaṁpuṭatilaka*, D fol. 163a and Q p. 283.3–4.

208 Tsong Khapa attributes this quote to the JS. Although this text focuses on Vajrasattva, I did not find an equivalent passage to Tsong Khapa's quote in the text preserved in the Tengyur. However, a passage very close to this occurs in Advayavajra's *Pañcatathāgata-mudrāvivaraṇa*, as follows: *vajreṇa śūnyatā proktā sattvena jñānamātratā / tād ātmya-manayoḥ siddhiṁ vajrasattvasvabhāvataḥ* / (Shastri 1927, 24, lines 5–6). This is likely a standard definition, present in a number of different works.

3.3.3. 1. The reason "Thus have I heard" is not stated in the beginning

Why is "Thus have I heard" not stated at the beginning of this Tantra? Bhavyakīrti provides [the following assertions]: (1) "that this Tantra was extracted from a one-hundred-thousand-verse extensive Tantra, and since *evaṁ*, etc., is stated in that text, it is not stated in the [text that is] an appendix (*uttaratantra*) of that. Others assert (2) that it is not mentioned in order to show that the Buddha is in the nonabiding nirvāṇa. Another says (3) it is not said in order to show that the teacher and that which is taught are one in regard to the unteachable reality, or that it was done [this way] (4) to teach the Mahāyāna in the manner of the *Mañjuśrīnāmasaṁgīti*, which lacks 'Thus have I heard.' Thus I set up the four systems asserted by others." In [Bhavyakīrti's] own system, it is [not stated] because the primal buddhas know no cessation, and this Dharma formulation has a beginningless continuum, existing before Śākyamuṇi; the ten million buddhas and ten million heroes stated this well. That's how it's said.

This means that the *Prajñāpāramitā* and such teachings disappear by the power of time and by the burning eon, and so forth, and Śākyamuṇi again states them. *Saṁvara* is not like that, since it is practiced without interruption in the inexpressible buddhalands, so it is said.[209] In regard to the first claim, it is refuted by a certain Tibetan, [who said]:

> Just as it says *evaṁ*, etc., in the *Dvikalpa*, which was taught separately, having been extracted from an extensive five-hundred-thousand-verse *Hevajra Tantra*, if it also says it in this Tantra taught separately, having been extracted from the hundred-thousand-verse version, then what is the contradiction?[210]

In regard to this, if you take its mere abbreviation from an extensive Tantra to be the reason, and you assert that 'thus,' etc., is not taught

[209] Tsong Khapa here closely paraphrases a long passage from Bhavyakīrti's commentary (BC 2b–3a). For a full translation of this passage, see Gray 2007, 30.

[210] While Tsong Khapa was closely following here Büton's discussion of this issue, and while Büton does refute this claim, he does not make this argument. Perhaps Tsong Khapa is quoting Mardo's commentary here.

separately from the extensive [version], although [you acknowledge] the fault there, that [reason] alone is not sufficient.

What, then [is the reason]? The Tantra begins with [the assertion]: **And now I will explain the secret**. The occurrence of the term "and now" (*atha*, *de nas*) at the beginning of an abbreviated Tantra like this [shows that it is] a continuation of the previous Tantra. While this means that it does not [explicitly] show "Thus," etc., if it is indeed a Tantra selected from an extensive one, I will not accept that "there is no mention of 'Thus,'" etc.

It also says in Kambala's commentary that the expression **and now** indicates that it was taught subsequently to the previous Tantra.[211] Therefore, if you refute as above in this system, then you do so without understanding the opponent's position. Someone said that, according to Kambala, "Thus have I heard" is stated in the three-hundred-thousand-verse *Cakrasaṁvara* root Tantra, and since this is an appendix extracted from that, it does not state it. This is unacceptable, for the *Vimalaprabhā* states that the extensive root Tantra lacks "Thus have I heard."[212] As for the argument that here "Thus have I heard" is not stated because this is an appendix that is condensed from an extensive Tantra that has "Thus have I heard," this position is completely devoid of understanding of the opponent's position. This is because *Vimalaprabhā* explains that there is no "Thus have I heard," etc., in the one-hundred-thousand-verse *Abhidhāna*, while there is in the three-hundred-thousand-verse *Abhidhāna*, and there is no contradiction in those two statements.[213] We have already

---

[211] Tsong Khapa here paraphrases the following passage from Kambala's commentary: "**And now**, etc., [shows] that this Tantra concludes another Tantra. The word **and now** refers to the previous Tantra" (SN D 1a). Sachen quotes both this quotation from Kambala and the one discussed in the following note, without attribution (PG 293.3–4).

[212] See VP 132b–134a. Tsong Khapa here refers to a passage written by Büton (NS 147). Büton refers to the following passage in Kambala's commentary: "Since the [tantra of] three hundred thousand stanzas states 'Thus have I heard,' the narrative context verse is not employed at the beginning of this [text], since it was used previously" (SN 1a). In his comments that follow, Tsong Khapa criticizes Büton for confusing the one hundred and three-hundred-thousand-verse versions of the *Abhidhāna*, i.e., root Tantra, the existence of which Tsong Khapa already argued for in the beginning of his introduction, section 2.1.1.

[213] The *Vimalaprabhā* discusses the extraction of an abbreviated Tantra from the "great 100,000 [-stanza] *Abhidhāna*" at VP 134a, but it makes no mention there of a 300,000-stanza version.

explained the sources that [claim that] there are two different extensive Tantras. Thus, it is totally unadvisable to seek for errors in the great saints of India, such as Kambala the "Blanketed." While there is also no clear expression of "Thus have I heard" in this concise Tantra, I will explain that it exists spoken by the Blessed Lord himself in an indirect way.

The second assertion is also not viable. Although according to the position of the philosophical *sūtra*s "Thus have I heard" indicates that it was compiled by a compiler after the Teacher's *parinirvāṇa*, here I will follow what is said in texts such as the *Vajramālā* explanatory Tantra and the *Sandhivyākaraṇa*, etc.[214] [They claim that] "Thus have I heard," etc., was spoken by the Teacher himself. Thus [the use of the expression] is not necessarily limited to [the instances of] gathering the texts after the *parinirvāṇa*. And as the Teacher in traditions such as the Guhyasamāja and so forth indeed is the Teacher to be found in the nonabiding nirvāṇa, there would be the consequence that "thus," etc., would not be stated in them, [while in fact it is.]

The third claim is also not viable. It says in the *Hevajra*, "I am the teacher and also the teaching."[215] Since it says this, "Thus have I heard" would not be shown there [according to this claim, but it is.][216]

The fourth claim is also not tenable, for if you state that it is like the *Mañjuśrīnāmasaṁgīti* in which "Thus have I heard" is not mentioned, there is also doubt in regard to that, as the point of disputation here is taken as an answer.

---

[214] The *Vajramālā* (To. 445) and the *Sandhivyākaraṇa* (To. 444) are both important explanatory Tantras for the *Guhyasamāja Tantra*, on which Tsong Khapa relied in his elucidation of the *Guhyasamāja*, and from which he draws in the elucidation of other Tantras such as the *Cakrasaṁvara*.

[215] Tsong Khapa here quotes the following famous verse HT 2.2.39: *vyākhyātāham ahaṁ dharmaḥ śrotāhaṁ suganair yutaḥ // sādhyo 'ham jagataḥ śāstā loko 'haṁ laukiko 'py ahaṁ//* (Snellgrove 1959, 2.48–50).

[216] Both the the *Guhyasamāja* and *Hevajra Tantra*s begin with the famously erotic version of the narrative context verse, as follows: "Thus have I heard: at one time the Blessed Lord was residing in the vulvae of the Adamantine Ladies, the essence of the Body, Speech, and Mind of all Tathāgatas" (*evaṁ mayā śrutam ekasmin samaye bhagavān sarvatathāgata-kāyavākcittahṛdaya-vajrayoṣidbhageṣu vijahāra*; see Matsunaga, 1978, 4, and Snellgrove, 1959, 2.2).

The arrangement of [Bhavyakīrti's] own system is also unacceptable, because he is unable to prove that there was no "thus," etc., in the teaching of buddhas earlier than Śākyamuni, and also because there are many Tantras with the statement "thus," etc., which were spoken by the ten million buddhas, and so forth. Furthermore, there are also sutras, and so forth, such as the *Prajñāpāramitā*, the *Saṁvarodaya*, and the *Abhidhāna*, which are continually practiced in the infinite buddhalands of the ten directions. "Thus," etc., would not be stated in them as well [according to his theory].

3.3.3. 2. The actual explanation of the text's meaning

This second part has three sections: (1) the first chapter's introduction to the significance of the entire Tantra, (2) the detailed exegesis of those meanings by the remaining forty-nine [chapters], and (3) the fifty-first chapter's summarization of the previous [chapters].

3.3.3. 2.1. The first chapter's introduction to the significance of the entire Tantra

This first part has two sections: (1) the actual text, and (2) showing the name of the chapter.

3.3.3. 2.1.1. The actual text

This first part has four sections: (1) the promise to explain the secret, (2) the exhortation to listen to the secret, (3) the method for making progress in the secret of the path, and (4) showing the place of practicing the secret.

3.3.3. 2.1.1. 1. The promise to explain the secret

The term **and now (1.1a)** is the equivalent to the [Sanskrit] term *atha*.[217] Nāropā explained it in terms of the four procedures [of Tantric hermeneutics].[218] Regarding its verbal meaning, it is [the term] used when,

---

[217] The text here and below provides the incorrect reading *ātha*.

[218] The "four procedures" (*tshul bzhi*) of Tantric hermeneutics involve a fourfold analysis of a word in terms of its "general meaning" (*spyi'i don*), "verbal meaning" (*yi ge'i don*), "hidden meaning" (*sbas pa'i don*), and "ultimate meaning" (*mthar thug gi don*). Tsong

(cont'd)

following the completion of the previous root Tantra, its appendix is stated. Its general meaning is the store of gnosis that is the realization of the intrinsic birthlessness of all things. "The letter *a*[219] is the source of all things," *akāro mukhaṁ sarvadharmāṇāṁ*,[220] [which is signified] by the augment *a*, while the store of merit is [signified by] its match *tha*. *A* is the lotus of wisdom, and *tha* is the vajra of art, which is the hidden [meaning]. Within the hidden [meaning] is the hidden reality of passion. *A* is perfectly pure wisdom, and *tha* is the great bliss of unobjectifying compassion—this is the ultimate [meaning].

In addition to these four meanings of *atha*, it also has the meaning of auspiciousness, of a conjunction, of a continuative, and of topicality. As for the first, this term is used as a blessing. Second, it is [used as a conjunction in contexts] such as "and now, at the very time when the Blessed Lord passed into nirvāṇa." It means here that having stated the extensive Tantra, he then stated the abbreviated one. As for the third, just as in the [context of statements such as] "and now, all doubts were immediately cut off," here just after having taught the extensive root Tantra, he taught this one. He elucidated it without interruption. As for the fourth, it shows that the entire Tantra from head to foot is about the inseparability of emptiness and compassion. Here [all] four explanations are applicable.

Since these are not disclosed to those who do not have an affiliation with this vehicle, it is a great **secret (1.1a)**. The reason it is not disclosed is that it ought to be hidden. Furthermore, there are seven types [of hidden things], as follows:

> The first secret is the realm of reality,[221] the second the conqueror's wheel; the third is hidden truth, while the

---

Khapa analyzes the term *atha* via these four categories in the passage immediately following this.

219 Here and below Tsong Khapa's text mistakenly reads *ā* rather than *a*. This is apparently due to his belief that the Sanskrit text begins with *ātha*, rather than *atha*.

220 Here I read *sarba dharma ṇaṁ* as *sarvadharmāṇāṁ*.

221 This first item is represented as *de nyid yul* in Kambala's commentary (SN D 2b, Q 174.2), and *de nyid phyogs* in the *Saṁpuṭatilaka* (D 166b; Q p. 283.3). I translate it as "realm of reality," since "realm" captures the lexical overlap of these terms.

> fourth is the secret lotus. The fifth secret is joy by means of the seeds; the sixth is total union. The final secret is uninterrupted bliss.[222]

This is quoted from Kambala's commentary, and with the exception of a few instances, they are also explained in this way in the *Saṁpuṭa Uttaratantra*.

As for their meanings, the first is the object of wisdom, reality itself. The second is the deity's wheel. As for the third, as it says in the *Uttarasaṁpuṭa*, "the secret is the hidden holy substance,"[223] it refers to the hidden supreme [substances]. In regard to the fourth, the channel wheel is explained as the lotus, the lotus of the seal. The fifth is the joy that arises from the dripping of awakening spirit from the seed syllable *haṁ* of the crown, while the sixth is the union of secrets such as the vajra and lotus. The seventh is the uninterrupted involvement in experiential unity of both subjective and objective reality. There are two explanations, namely, [the above] along with the explanation of master Koṅkaṇa, who took "the secret" as the signified, and applies it to the signifier, the four lines beginning with **Śrī Heruka (1.1.c–1.2.b)**.[224] There are also the some [Tibetan] lamas who have stated that the secrets of both the path and result are relevant to [the term] "secret" in this [verse].[225] [This explanation] and the [previous] two, [of Kambala and Jayabhadra,] are not discordant.

---

222 As Tsong Khapa indicates below, his source is Kambala's commentary (SN D 2b, Q 174.2). It can be also found in the *Saṁpuṭa Uttaratantra* called the *Mahātantrarāja śrīsaṁpuṭatilaka-nāma*, with significant variation, but with commentary (D 166b–167a).

223 *Saṁpuṭatilaka*, *gsang ba ni dam pa'i dngos po sbas pa'o* (D 166b–167a).

224 Jayabhadra discusses the term "secret" in terms of these lines. See CP 41b, and Sugiki 2001, 105–106.

225 Tsong Khapa here refers to Sachen's argument, which occurs as follows: "**The secret**, the subject of this Tantra, [concerns] the two stages. For whom are they secret? [They are secret] for those who participate in the Pāramitā vehicle. The common secrets are those of the creation stage. The secrets of the perfection stage are uncommon, since they are secret to the creation stage meditator who has received the vase consecration. These two are the secrets of the path. The secret of the result is that which is within the cognitive scope of buddhas alone, by means of the gnosisof natural reality of all ultimate things. It is not within the scope of those who have not realized this, even of [bodhisattvas] up to the tenth stage" (PG 293.4).

What sort of text states a promise such as **I will explain the secret (1.1a)** that is like this? It is a **concise** text selected from the **extensive (1.1b)** root Tantra, while its meaning is not concise, but is extensive. This explains the import of **not extensive.** From which root Tantra [was it selected]? Laṅka Jayabhadra, Vīravajra, and so forth, say that it was selected from the hundred-thousand-stanza *Khasama Tantra*.[226] In the *Saṁcāra* it says that the hundred-thousand-verse root Tantra from which this Tantra is selected and the *Khasama* are distinct.[227] Kambala stated, in agreement with the *Ḍākārṇava*, that it is abbreviated from the three hundred thousand verse root Tantra.[228]

In a certain edition it says, "And now, from that I will explain the secret," indicating that it was extracted from the extensive Tantra. Another edition has "And now, for the sake of that I will explain the secret," as if it is explained for the sake of or because of a request by an interlocutor.[229]

3.3.3. 2.1.1. 2. The exhortation to listen to the secret

The second part has two sections: (1) the secret that should be heard, and (2) the actual exhortation to listen to [the secret].

3.3.3. 2.1.1. 2.1. The secret that should be heard

The second part has two sections: (1) showing in brief the presentation of the secret, and (2) explaining the presentation [of the secret] somewhat more extensively.

3.3.3. 2.1.1. 2.1.1. Showing in brief the presentation of the secret

The second part has two sections: (1) explaining the interpretable meaning, and (2) explaining the definitive meaning.

---

226 See CP 41a and Sugiki 2001, 105, as well as PD 355b.

227. See YS 41a, and the discussion in the introductory section 2.1.1.

228 See SN 1a.

229 Tsong Khapa discusses here variant Tibetan translations of the text's opening term. The translations *de nas de las* and *de nas de phyir* appear to be overly literal translations of *athāto*, the first term in the text. The former occurs in the SM revised translation, while the latter is preserved in one of Vīravajra's commentaries (ST 157a).

3.3.3. 2.1.1. 2.1.1. 1. Explaining the interpretable meaning

The practitioner, him- or herself, is the divine couple, which is principally characterized by the divine body of Mahāmudrā, which is the **union** of **Śrī**, i.e., Glorious, **Heruka (1.1c)**, who assumes a form with face and hands, together **with** his consort Vajravārāhī. Within their perfected retinue are the **ḍākinīs**, namely the thirty-six yoginīs, the four essence yoginīs, etc. Represented by them are the twenty-four heroes; the **network** is the host of them. The *saṁ* or *śaṁ* of *saṁvara* (**1.2b**) means "bliss," and *vara* means "supreme." *Saṁvara* is so explained because that entire host is at each moment delighted with bliss. Kambala connects the latter line to the retinue, and it is good to apply it to the commentarial tradition of the previous lamas.[230] Here the secret is connected with the creation stage.

3.3.3. 2.1.1. 2.1.1. 2. Explaining the definitive meaning

First, in other commentaries of the root Tantra [that comment] on textual passages such as **union with Śrī Heruka (1.1c)**, there usually are not any explanations of the definitive meaning, which concerns the arts of inserting the life force into the central channel. Vīravajra's commentary states:

> Here I will not write on the details of the perfection stage, in order to protect both the great practice instructions and those who have not served the lama. Therefore, once you have investigated and delighted the guru, you will realize it following after the *Śrīheruka Abhidhāna*.[231]

It seems that he thought that one should learn the oral instructions on these [matters] elsewhere.

In this commentarial tradition of Nāropā, the perfection stage [import] of these passages also occurs a bit, roughly, at the occasion of the explanation of the Tantra, but it is actually given elsewhere. Here it is

---

[230] See SN 2b–3a.

[231] I did not find a statement to this effect in any of Vīravajra's commentaries. In one commentary (PD 355a) he does discuss the perfection stage in the context of commenting on this verse, but without any of the reservation that Tsong Khapa attributes to him here.

explained as in that system. Certain previous [Tibetan lamas] connected the four syllables beginning with *śrī*, [i.e., *śrī-he-ru-ka*,] to many things such as the four channel wheels, the four joys, the four yogas, the four consecrations, etc.[232] Now, in explaining the oral instructions, authoritative textual quotations are not needed in every case. However, they have explained the oral instructions in a speculative fashion by claiming that there are no textual quotations in [support of their] most important points. In [support of] all these semblant explanations, it seems that they state that: "This an oral instruction of my lineage, which is descended from the Buddha." Since it is not possible to differentiate [between them and real teachings], they should be abandoned, as they serve as conditions for the decline of the true teachings. However, even when you have quotations from the Tantras and commentaries, to the extent to which they exist, the explanations winnowed from them can have the fault of over-explanation. They should thus be explained in a measured way.

Here Lama Mardo's connection [of this verse] with the fourth stage (i.e., clear light), taking Heruka as "spring" (*vasanta*) and Vārāhī as the "drop" (*tilaka*), is good. As it says in the *Saṁpuṭatilakā* explanatory Tantra, and as is explained in the *Vasantatilakā*, Heruka is "spring," which is *vasanta*, which is the [syllable] upside-down *hūṁ* in the center of the heart channel wheel. Vārāhī is the drop, *tilaka*, which is the [syllable] *aṁ*, the fury fire (*caṇḍālī*) blood drop in the middle of the navel channel wheel. Those two exist in the aspect of kissing, the upper one upside down, and the lower one shown directed upward; they are united.[233] Having relied on the explanatory Tantra, together with this sort of explanation, one could also understand the union of the upper and lower as being the letter *oṁ* of the throat channel wheel and the letter *haṁ* of the crown channel wheel. Thus the Tantric process is revealed by the first verse.

---

[232] See PG 294.1–2.

[233] The first ten verses in the sixth chapter of Kāṇha's *Vasantatilakā* covers most but not all of the points to which Tsong Khapa refers here. These verses are edited in Samdhong and Dwivedi's edition (1990) of this text. See pp. 37–40 and pp. 65–69. They are explicated in Vanaratna's *Rahasyadīpa* commentary, in the same edition. I was not able to find this text in the *Mahātantrarāja-śrīsaṁpuṭatilaka-nāma*.

The **ḍākiṇī** are the thirty-six channels, and their **network** is the host of channels. The gnosis that arises from the descent of the awakening spirit that is impelled by the wind that moves within these channels is the supreme bliss called *saṁvara* (**1.2b**). Thus, it also says in the *Tattvaprakāśa* that "the yoginīs are the thirty-six channels, and the channels are said to arise from the head. The gnosis impelled by them is the reality of the supreme joy (*paramānanda*)."[234] Furthermore, the *he* is empty with respect to the cause of things in reality, *ru* is empty with respect to the lack of self-nature, and *ka* is nonlocality. *Śrī Heruka* also means *union*, which is the union of the gnosis of great bliss, the meaning of *śrī*, with the emptiness that is like that.

It says in the *Tattvaprakāśa* that "*he* is causeless, *ru* lacks [self-] nature, *ka* does not abide anywhere, and *śrī* exists nondually."[235] Furthermore, regarding Śrī Heruka having the meaning of *union*, it also says in the *Tattvaprakāśa* that "*śrī* signifies the vulva (*bhaga*), and Heruka the mind. *Śrī Heruka* is said to mean that very abiding in the space realm. The agent of the process is gnosis, which is said to be "born from that," and which is in the place of glory of the *Jālandhara*, which assembles the yoginīs."[236]

As for the meaning of those [terms], the vulva is the place on which one depends during the descent of the awakening spirit. *Śrī* means glory, and the "place of glory" is the vulva. *Jālandhara* is the crown [of the head], and is one of the twenty-four places within which the yoginīs, i.e., the channels, are well collected. The awakening spirit descends from the syllable *haṁ* of this place. In the beginning, at the time of descent, the awakening spirit descends from there. At the time of ascent, bliss is stabilized if the awakening spirit ascends to there. Thus it is called the "place of glory."

Relatively speaking, Heruka, taken as the awakening spirit, is like white jasmine (*kunda*). Its application is that when you fuse it in the center of the channel wheel, the joys are generated. Taken in terms of the ultimate, it is great bliss, the union of that [awakening spirit] with space-

---

234 Tsong Khapa here quotes Kāṇha's *Guhyatattvaprakāśa*. See TP 355a.

235 See TP 354b.

236 See TP 354b.

realm emptiness, which is the meaning of **union** (*saṁyoga*). The performer of this process, the agent, is the definitive meaning of Heruka, which is the natural gnosis. The meaning of *śrī* is that which arises from the vulva.

The first [, i.e., Mardo's,] and third [, i.e., the *Tattvaprakāśa*'s,] of the three explanations of the first (**1.1c**) of the two lines that are applicable to the perfection stage indicate a method for deriving the great bliss of the perfection stage, [taking] Heruka as one aspect and *śrī* [as the other]. The Heruka aspect of the second [, i.e., the *Vasantatilakā*'s,] and third explanations and the explanation of the final line (**1.2b**) indicate the indivisibility of bliss and emptiness, which is the union of emptiness with the bliss derived by that method.[237]

Everything that arises with the distinctive bodily forms of Heruka, Vārāhī, and so forth, are applicable either to the creation stage or to the resultant context. Not applying them to the perfection stage seems to indicate the fault of not distinguishing well the distinctions such as that between the mantric body of the deity created through the creation stage and the gnostic body of the deity created through the perfection stage, or that between the creation of the conceptually conceived divine body or the creation of the divine body in reality from mere wind-mind that is not conceived. Therefore, the [*Saṁvarodaya*] explanatory Tantra states the following:

> The yoga of creation is mandala visualization. This should be contemplated by dull and middling [adepts]. The sharp ones contemplate the mandala of mere mind itself by the aspect of instantaneity. One should meditate on the perfection stage with the yoga of instantaneity. The nature of the three realms is the measureless mansion, and sentient beings are mandala beings. And amidst them, [the yogī] is the lord of the mandala by the aspect of instantaneity.[238]

---

237 Tsong Khapa evidently refers to the three explanations discussed in this section, namely, that of Mardo, that in the *Vasantatilakā*, and that in the *Tattvaprakāśa*.

238 Tsong Khapa quotes here quotes the third and fourth verses of the third chapter of the *Saṁvarodaya Tantra*, which occur as follows in Tsuda's edition: *utpattiṁ mṛdumadhyo*

(cont'd)

It also states the following: "The wheel that is stamped by the seal of suchness is thus space-like emptiness. The effortless nondual integration of selflessness and suchness with the various arts and the power of compassion is the supreme essence of the mandala."[239]

The [former quote] states distinctly the two kinds of deities of the wheels of the mandalas of the creation and perfection stages. "The mandala of mere mind by the aspect of instantaneity" indicates the process of rising in a split second into the wheel of the mandala from the mere wind-mind of clear light, just as a fish leaps up from the water; it does not refer to [creation stage] instantaneous creation. Therefore, while the dull and middling ones can only go up to the limit of the creation stage, the sharp ones, having already reached that limit, are able to visualize the gnostic body of the perfection stage. However, master Abhayākara[240] and Ratnarakṣita claimed that if you take this in terms of two stages of a path for a single person, then they should be taken as separate stages [in the development] of one's faculties.

There is the wisdom of the objective clear light of the space-like emptiness, which is suchness and universal selflessness, and the art of the wheels of the deities of various body colors, who have the various powers of compassion, which is indivisible from and sealed by that wisdom. Their union is said to be the deity mandala of integration.

The magic body of the perfection stage of the phenomenal aspect[241] is of very great importance in the system of this Tantra as well. The *Ḍākārṇava* states:

---

yogī dhyāyād mandalabhāvanā / adhimātro jhaṭitākāraṁ mandalaṁ cittamātrataḥ / jhaṭitākārayogena utpannakramabhāvanā // traidhātukamayaṁ kūṭaṁ prāṇino māṇḍaleyakāḥ/ tanmadhye jhaṭitākāraṁ yogī syād maṇḍalādhipaḥ // (1974, 77).

239 Tsong Khapa quotes here quotes the eighth and the first half of the ninth verses of the third chapter of the *Saṁvarodaya Tantra*, which occur as follows in Tsuda's edition: *tathatāmudritaṁ cakraṁ kham iva śūnyatā tathā / nairātmyā tathatā viśvam upāyaḥ karuṇābalaḥ // yuganaddham anābhogaṁ mandalaṁ sāram uttamam /* (1974, 78).

240 Here I read *a bya ka ra* as Abhayākara.

241 Tsong Khapa, in his discussions of advanced deity yoga meditation practices, distinguishes two aspects of deity visualization, the "phenomenal aspect" (*snang phyogs*), which correlates to art and compassion, and the "empty aspect" (*stong phyogs*), which correlates to wisdom. These aspects of deity yoga practice need to be integrated. Tsong Khapa discusses these terms in far more detail in the creation stage section of his *sngags*

(cont'd)

> One who has mastered the yoga of divine shape (*rnam pa*) manifests instantaneously in a divine form, assuming a transformed shape (*dbyibs*) through the yoga of a cast image, etc. The yoga of emptiness is the natural form, and is the definition of self-consecration (*svādhiṣṭhāna*). As for the yogī who lacks self-consecration, know him to be like a heap of chaff. This sort of supreme characteristic is not known by men who are beasts (*paśu*, *phyugs*). Therefore, if one meditates on this magic emanation, one will attain unexcelled awakening.[242]

The yogī **who has mastered the yoga of divine form** creates a **manifestation in just an instant**. The **form** that is **natural**, i.e., that truly exists, [does so] with the **yoga of emptiness** and clear light, that is, the gnosis of clear light united indivisibly with that. This is **definition of self-consecration**. This identifies the magic body.

What is the shape (*rnam pa*) of the form (*gzugs*) that is referred to as "divine shape" and "form"? This is shown by the two lines beginning with "cast image." It is the bodylike form that is meditated upon by visualizing the deity in a shape with arms and faces, as [cast in metal or] painted on cloth, etc. Those who lack that magic body lack substance like a **heap of chaff**. And **this supreme characteristic is not known by** the **beast**like. It states that **if one meditates on this magic emanation**, i.e., magic body, **one will** quickly **attain awakening**. If you do not know how to create this body, then you do not know half of the two principles of the perfection stage.[243] As this method occurs in the perfection stages of Lūipa and Ghaṇṭapā, I have explained it [fully] in my commentaries on their [systems].[244]

Therefore, one should understand both Herukas in the perfection stage context: the empty aspect Heruka of the indivisibility of bliss and

---

rim chen mo. Regarding this, see Yarnall 2013, 6, and also his forthcoming work, *The Emptiness That Is Form*.

242 See DA 139b.

243 These are the stages of clear light and the magic body.

244 Tsong Khapa refers to his commentaries on Lūipa's *Śrībhagavad-abhisamaya* and Ghaṇṭapā's *Pañcakrama*.

emptiness, and the phenomenal aspect Heruka of the magic body of the two truths indivisible.[245] One should keep this in mind in later contexts, again and again. They are applicable to the secret perfection stage. If you explain the demonstration of the particulars of the secret path by the second and third lines in a way common to both stages, the functional distinction is that it is **the means for achieving all of the desired aims** (**1.1d**) impartially and without exception. Its profound distinction is such that it is **lofty** (**1.2a**), i.e., higher, than the *Prajñāpāramitā*, and also than the three lower classes of Tantra. It is the path of the scriptures that is lofty, high, and unexcelled. By the implication of saying that it is "the means of achieving all desired aims," it teaches the means of attaining the two accomplishments, and thus it teaches the secret of fruition. This is what the lofty ones have stated.

These scriptural passages show the aim and relevance[246] of the Tantra. The three secrets together with the branch [subjects] are the topic of this [Tantra]. Understanding that [topic] exactly in reliance on this [text] is the immediate aim. Obtaining ability in each of the two stages, depending on that [understanding], is the further aim. The ultimate aim [consists of] the accomplishments, the supreme of which is awakening, and the ordinary of which are the worldly powers. The relevance is the dependence of the immediate aim on both the text and the essential, ultimate aim.

3.3.3. 2.1.1. 2.1.2. Explaining the presentation [of the secret] somewhat more extensively

The second part has three sections: (1) the actual meaning, (2) the difficult to obtain, and (3) showing an example of the union of bliss and emptiness.

3.3.3. 2.1.1. 2.1.2. 1. The actual meaning

The second part has three sections: (1) explaining the two lines [that begin with] "the secret…supreme," (2) explaining the four lines [that

---

[245] These correspond to the clear light and magic body stages respectively.

[246] Tsong Khapa here uses the technical term *dgos-'brel*. For more on this term see Broido 1983a and 1983b and Schoening 1996.

begin with] "made of all ḍākinīs" [1.3], and (3) explaining the two lines [that begin with] "*source*."

3.3.3. 2.1.1. 2.1.2. 1.1. Explaining the two lines [that begin with] "the secret ...supreme" [1.2c–d]

The second part has two sections: (1) explaining in terms of the interpretable meaning, and (2) explaining in terms of the definitive meaning.

3.3.3. 2.1.1. 2.1.2. 1.1.1. Explaining in terms of the interpretable meaning

The second part has two sections: (1) the explanation applicable to the narrative preface "Thus have I heard...," and (2) the explanation applicable to the creation stage.

3.3.3. 2.1.1. 2.1.2. 1.1.1. 1. Explaining as applicable to the narrative preface "Thus have I heard..."

The second part has two sections: (1) stating the exact words of the narrative preface, and (2) explaining their meaning.

3.3.3. 2.1.1. 2.1.2. 1.1.1. 1.1. Stating the exact words of the narrative preface

The application of the two lines that begin with **secret** (**1.2.cd**) to the narrative preface occurs in the commentarial system of the two translators. Although it does not occur in other *Saṁvara* commentaries, it does occur in the commentaries of Kambala and Devagupta, which is very good.[247] This is because, according to the *Vajraḍāka*, [the text] "secret," etc., was stated in reference to the narrative preface in the *Saṁvara* appendix, in response to a question on the "secret," etc.[248] The *Vajraḍāka* also states that:

> [Regarding] **existing in the beginning, middle, and end** (**1.4.d**), the "beginning" is the **secret**, the awareness

---

[247] See SS 71b. Kambala addresses these lines at SN 3a–4a, but does not explicitly link them to the *nidāna* verse.

[248] See VT 89a. The expression "*Saṁvara* appendix" (*bde mchog bla ma*) could refer either to the CT or the JS, both of which include the "Yoginītantra nidāna."

> of the previous source [signified by] "thus" (*evaṁ*). The "end" is **delightful**, dependence on that which is "heard" (*śrutaṁ*). The "middle" is **supreme**, and is very holy "due to me" (*mayā*). "Existing" is the **universal nature**, which is "at one time" (*ekasmin samaye*).[249]

In regard to this, Devagupta applies the seventh "in the universal nature" to the third "by me." Therefore it is said that [his application] is not sequential. This also seems to be what Kambala stated.[250] Thus, although it seems that "by me" is implied by "universal nature" in the presently existing Tantra, one should take "existing" as the meaning of **always abides**, in the same manner as Kambala's explanation that **always abides** indicates the time [of the discourse].[251] The meaning of **universal nature** should be taken as was previously [explained]. This means that it was heard directly from the Teacher by the compiler of all of these Tantras. The place in which he resides is the place of great bliss. Who is the teacher who resides there? Kambala states that he is the **self-arisen Blessed Lord (1.3c)**.[252]

If you take it in this way, then this [*Cakrasaṁvara*] *Tantra* contains the [following] narrative preface: "Thus have I heard: at one time the Blessed Lord...." [The remainder,] from "all Tathāgatas" onward, is unclear in the explanatory Tantras, nor is it clear in the two commentaries.[253] Yet if one needs here [commentary on the narrative preface] from that onward, one can apply statements from "the body...of all tathāgatas" to "was residing in the ladies' vulvae" in the *Saṁpuṭa* or

[249] See VT 90a. This quote connects CT 1.2.cd with 1.4.d, and then connects them both with the unspoken *nidāna*, *evaṁ mayā śrutaṁ ekasmin samaye*.

[250] Kambala quotes an unidentified text that reads as follows: "The **secret** is 'thus,' **supreme** 'by me,' **delightful** 'was heard.' **In the universal nature** is the seventh with the meaning of the third, and it is not with any other" (SN 4a). With respect to the statement that *mayā* is "third" and *sarvātmani* is "seventh," this presumably refers to the cases in which these terms are declined, the third instrumental case and seventh locative case, respectively. Devagupta provides a lengthy commentary on the narrative preface, but does not directly discuss their declension.

[251] See SN 4a.

[252] See SN 3b.

[253] That is, Kambala's and Devagupta's.

Saṁvarodaya explanatory Tantras.[254] Or, you can apply statements such as the following in the *Abhidhānottara*: "the Blessed Lord was residing in the secret essences of the net of the vajraḍākas and vajraḍākinīs of all tathāgatas."[255]

The *Tattvaprakāśa* says that the perfection stage shown in the expression "Thus," etc., in the art Tantras is shown by *secret*, and so forth, in Mother Tantras.[256] This is mainly in regard to the *Cakrasaṁvara*. After explaining **Blessed Lord** there, there is an explanation of the meaning of "the ḍākas and ḍākinīs of all tathāgatas." Although there is no great distinction in meaning, the wording should be like that in the *Abhidhāna*. In the commentarial tradition of the two translators, "at one time" is like the above. It is shown to exist by the universal nature. It is said that the perfected retinue is shown by the four lines that begin with **made of all ḍākinīs (1.3)** and by the two lines beginning with **source (1.4)**.[257]

3.3.3. 2.1.1. 2.1.2. 1.1.1. 1.2. Explaining their meaning

The term **and then**, which is shown by **secret**, is a conjunction that indicates that it was heard without addition or omission, just exactly as it occurs here in the entire assembly of the Tantra, from "And then...the secret" up to "delight in each and every...."[258] It is *evaṁ* in Sanskrit, and the term **secret** is said to be a sign for the Tathāgata, a sign for the hero, and a sign for the yoginī, which is not in any of the grammatical texts or

---

[254] Regarding the *nidāna* verses of these texts, see Skorupski 1996, 216, and SU 265a.

[255] Tsong Khapa's quote is similar to, but not identical to the AU's *nidāna* verse, which reads as follows: "Thus have I heard: at one time the Blessed Lord was residing in the secret essences of the adamantine fierce dākinī of all tathāgatas" (J 2.3: *evaṁ mayā śrutam ekasmin samaye bhagavān sarvatathāgatavajrakrodhaḍākinīguhyahṛdayeṣu vijāra*; see also AU 247a).

[256] See TP chapter 2, especially DK 349b, 350a.

[257] Tsong Khapa here is referring to the SM translation, which begins with the *'byung ba*, and reads as follows: *'byung ba sgra tshul las 'byung rnams* (SM 1b). The other revised translations preserve different readings of this line (PM 213b: *sgra yi tshul las nges 'byung rnams*; SL 95b: *sgra'i tshul las ngas 'byung zhing*).

[258] Tsong Khapa here quotes the first and last lines of the Tantra, which are the same in both the Sanskrit text and the Tibetan translations.

colloquial languages, and it is called "barbaric language" (*mlecchabhāṣā*, *kla klo'i skad*), meaning it is a symbolic language. One should also know the following [esoteric meanings].

"Previously" signifies the semen and blood that previously created the aggregates, elements, and sense media. And since supreme bliss arises from them, they are the source. [*Evaṁ* thus] indicates the awareness of supreme bliss that arises from the source of semen and blood. This is the meaning of *evaṁ* and **secret**.

The [term] "by me," which is indicated by the [term] **supreme**, is *mayā*, [meaning] it was heard directly by the compiler himself from the **universal nature**, and not indirectly. "Very holy" means that it is supreme. Regarding the [term] "heard" that is indicated by **delightful**, while it is hearing by means of the wisdom of hearing, it is not the direct realization of all of the meanings of the Tantra. If this were not so, then there would be no difference in degree of superiority between the Teacher and the compiler. Furthermore, here I do not accept the context as literally explained.

That on which one should rely is the wisdom arising from learning, which is *śruta*, "heard." [The expression] **in the beginning, middle, and end** [**1.4d**] is connected to the first, middle, and final words of the expression "the secret that is supreme and delightful." The [expression] "at one time" is indicated by **always abides** and also by **existing**. "This is heard at only one time; at other times other Tantras were heard" shows the compiler's multiple hearings. [The phrase] "he heard it at one occasion, not at another" reveals that this [Tantra] is rare, and "he heard it in a instant of time" shows that the compiler had excellent wisdom. It occurs in the Tantra in Sanskrit as *ekāsmin samaye*.[259]

[The term] *bhaga* of *bhagavant*,[260] which is the equivalent term of *bcom ldan 'das*, means "fortune," while [the suffix] *-vant* means "possessed of," hence the meaning of *bhagavant* is "fortunate one." There are six types of good fortune. The *Saṁpuṭa* defines it as fortune in the six perfections, as follows: "lordship, good form, glory, fame, intuition knowledge, and diligence should be taken to be the six fortunes."[261]

---

[259] Here I read *e ka smin sa ma ya* as *ekāsmin samaye*.

[260] Here I read *bha ga wan* as *bhagavant*.

[261] Tsong Khapa quotes ST kalpa 1 ch. 4, which occur as follows: *aiśvaryasya samagrasya rūpasya yaśasaḥ śriyaḥ / jñānasyārthaprayatnasya ṣaṇṇāṁ bhaga iti smṛtaḥ /*

(cont'd)

"Possessed of" means he has those six. Etymologically, *bhaga* also means "to destroy,"[262] the destruction of the devil of the afflictions (*kleṣamāra*) and so forth. Since he possesses each of these destructive [powers], he is thus a *bhagavant*. As for *'das*, "to transcend," since [the appellation] *bhagavant* is also applied to the great worldly gods, the former translators added [the syllable *'das*] in order to show that he has transcended them.

Since they come (*āgata*) to the ultimate subjective gnosis of exact objective reality (*tathā*), they are tathāgatas. The teacher of the Tantra is the actuality of all tathāgatas, and hence is universal. Their "net" is the host of vajraḍākas, who are the heroes, and ḍākinīs, who are the heroines. Their "secret essence" has the same meaning as the vulva of a young woman. Therefore, they reside in the divine palace that is in the center of the triangle.

3.3.3. 2.1.1. 2.1.2. 1.1. 1.2. The explanation applicable to the creation stage

As it says in the *Saṁpuṭa*, and as is explained in the *Tattvaprakāśa*, "**secret** is the element of earth, and likewise water is **supreme**. Fire is **delightful**, and wind is the **universal nature.** Space **always abides**, and is the nature of great bliss."[263] Therefore, you should also know the stacking-up of the elements visualization on the occasion of creation stage visualization as shown by the *Abhidhāna*, *Saṁcāra*, and *Saṁvarodaya*. By **always abides**, the element of space is shown to be great bliss, as in the quote from *Hevajra*, "the element of space is bliss."[264] The quotation

(Skorupski 1996:242); *dbang phyug dang / gzugs dang / grags pa dang / dpal dang / ye shes dang / brtson 'grus phun sum tshogs pa ste / bha ga drug ces gsung so /* (D 82a). This seems to be a standard and long-standing interpretation of the term *bhagavant*. For example, in Haribhadra's commentary on the *nidāna* of the *Aṣṭasāhasrikā Prajñāpāramitā* he cites an almost identical passage from the *Buddhabhūmi-śāstram*, as follows: *aiśvaryasya samagrasya rūpasya yaśasaḥ śriyaḥ / jñānasyārtha prayatnasya ṣaṇṇāṁ bhaga iti śrutiḥ //* (Vaidya 1960, 272).

[262] This appears to be an interpretive alliterative etymology based upon the similarity between the terms *bhaga* and *bhagna*, "broken."

[263] See ST 117b.

[264] Tsong Khapa here quotes HT 1.10.40a, which occurs as follows in Snellgrove's edition: *saukhyam ākāśadhātuś ca* (1959, 2.40), *bde ba nam mkha' nyid kyi khams /* (1959, 2.41).

by Lama Mardo and others from the *Saṁpuṭa*[265] "**always abides** is Mt. Sumeru" does not appear to be in that text.

Great bliss indicates the deity creation from the perspective of the five manifest awakenings that signify great bliss. It is also taught that the stacked-up elements, and so forth, are to be imagined as having the nature of great bliss. Deity creation from the moon is explained in the context of the manifest enlightenment of the Yogatantras, wherein they are stated as being only white in color. Here, however, it is necessary to show that the vowels and consonants are white and red, and that the moon and sun are white and red, or, when there is just the moon, that it is white with a reddish tinge. This is for the sake of signifying the generation of great bliss from the conjunction of the red and white elements.

At the end of the explanation of the stacked-up elements in the thirty-second chapter of this [tantra] there is the statement "**one should produce...that which is made of the great conch**" (**32.11a**). This should also be taken in terms of great bliss. The equivalent term for "conch" is *śaṁkha*, and concerning the sound *śaṁ*, it says in the *Āmnāya-mañjarī* that "*śaṁ* is bliss, and since it transcends the three realms, it is supreme."[266] Therefore, since *śaṁsukha* or *saṁsukha* is bliss, [this passage] means "one should produce...that which is made of great bliss."[267] The way of doing this is as previously explained.

When explaining the stacked-up elements of the creation stage, in the elaboration of that there is the creation of the vowels and consonants on Mt. Sumeru and the lotus. This is clear in chapter fifty-one, [which states] "**on a stalk on the summit of the mountain are a universal lotus and the vowels and consonants**" (**51.14cd**). The divine palace is clear in the second chapter. As for the remainder of these [topics], they can be known relying on explanatory Tantras such as the *Abhidhānottara*.

---

265 Here I read *saṁ bhu ṭa* as *saṁpuṭa*.

266 See AM D fol. 8a.

267 The Sanskrit for this line is *mahāśaṁkhamayaṁ kuryāt*. The SM translation, which Tsong Khapa follows, is closest to this, reading *dung chen po yi rang bzhin bya* (SM 28a). Tsong Khapa's interpretation is supported by Mardo's revised translation, which is clearly interpretative, reading *bde ba chen po'i ngo bor bya* (PM 235b). Sumatikīrti's revised translation has a different and clearly defective reading, *brag chen po'i ngo bo ru* (SL 125b).

3.3.3. 2.1.1. 2.1.2. 1.1.2. Explaining in terms of the definitive meaning

The second part has three sections: (1) the definitive meaning as applied to the narrative preface, (2) the definitive meaning as applied to the creation stage, and (3) explaining the sixteen syllables in reference to alchemy.

3.3.3. 2.1.1. 2.1.2. 1.1.2. 1. The definitive meaning as applied to the narrative preface[268]

In regard to the [above] explanation of the definitive meaning of the *secret supreme* as applied to *evaṁ mayā*, etc., in the *Vajraḍāka*, the *Saṁpuṭa* states, "[the syllable] *e* should be known as earth. It is the actual seal, Locanā herself."[269] And also "in the center, in the universal lotus, lies the emanation wheel."[270] The four syllables (*e vaṁ ma yā*) are connected to many sets of four, such as the four channel wheels, the four [goddesses] such as Locanā, and so forth. Here I will briefly address the applications to the channel wheels and [the goddesses,] Locanā, etc.

Regarding the first, the two explanatory Tantras[271] show the arrangement of each one in the petals and center of each wheel, and the stages of Tantra are shown in the *Ālicatuṣṭaya*. As for adding the three remaining stages to that, they should be known from *Ālicatuṣṭaya*, namely, the art of conducting natural bliss by means of the fury fire that depends on the four wheels.

In regard to the application to the Locanā, and so forth, it says in the *Mukhāgama* that "the woman who is an illusory seal is superior to all [other] illusions. Illusions in this world are purified as Locanā, etc., whose clans are fourfold."[272] It thus states that the four [types of] seal

---

268 This entire chapter is commentary on the AU *nidāna*, as understood by Tsong Khapa. See section 3.3.3.2.1.1.2.1.2.1.1.1.1.1 above for a statement of this. Direct quotations of this *nidāna* are placed in bold in this chapter.

269 See ST 81a; the Sanskrit occurs as follows in ST *kalpa* 1, ch. 4: *ekāraḥ pṛthivījñeyā karmamudrā tu locanā* (Skorupski 1996, 240).

270 See ST 81a; the Sanskrit occurs as follows in ST *kalpa* 1, ch. 4: *sthitā nirmāṇacakre vai nābhau catuḥṣaṣṭāmbuje* (Skorupski 1996, 240).

271 In this case, the *Saṁpuṭa* and *Abhidhānottara*.

272 This quote is from Buddhaśhrījñānapāda's *Dvikramatattvabhāvana-nāma-mukhāgama*, where it occurs as follows: */bud med sgyu ma'i phyag rgya ni/ /sgyu ma kun las khyab*

(cont'd)

consorts (*phag rgya ma*) such as the *padminī* (*padma can*), etc.,[273] are purified as the four [goddesses] such as Locanā. That is the art of conducting natural joy relying on an outer seal. One should know they also indicate the four classes of gnostic seals.

The [Sanskrit] term *śruta* is the equivalent for the word "heard." In regard to its meaning, it says in the *Saṁpuṭa*, "*śru* means 'trickle,' and *ta* is the lord, great bliss."[274] Relying on the instigation by the fire of *caṇḍālī* meditation, awakening spirit trickles from the crown and through the four wheels down to the tip of the secret place. Depending on that, one gives rise to the joys of great bliss, and to the lord of those, the principal natural joy.

The definitive meaning of "at one time" (*ekasmin samaye*) is stated in the *Saṁpuṭa*.[275] In the *Tattvaprakāśa* it says:

> *Samaya* is said to be time, and time has three aspects, good time, bad time, and inconceivable time. Coming from the very orifice of the nose is good time, while going is bad time. These, propounded as one, are, as one, matchless. Inconceivable time is free of life force and effort, and abandons the inhalation and exhalation of breath. It is liberated from coming and going. That is said to be "at one time."[276]

The "nose" here is the lower tip of the central channel, known as the "human nose." The human nose is also the nose of both of the male and

---

par 'phags/ /sgyu ma de yang 'jig rten 'dir/ /spyan la sogs par rnam dag par/ /rigs ni rnam pa bzhir 'gyur te/ (D fol. 4a.3–4).

273 Tsong Khapa here refers to the well-known categorization of women into four classes, namely *padminī*, *citriṇī*, *hastinī*, and *śaṅkhinī*. They are described, for example, in the *Ratiśāstra*. See Zysk 2002, 73–75.

274 Tsong Khapa here quotes the canonical translation, which I translate here (ST 81b: */shru zhes bya ba ni 'dzag par gsungs so/ /ta zhes bya ba ni gang yang bde ba chen po'i mgon po'o/*); the Sanskrit occurs as follows in ST *kalpa* 1, ch. 4: *śruśravaṇaṁ nirdiṣṭaṁ ta yaś ca mahāsukho nāthaḥ* (Skorupski 1996, 241). Note, however, that the translation of *śravaṇa* as *'dzag* is highly interpretive. The ordinary meaning is "hearing" or "ear."

275 See ST 81b–82a and Skorupski 1996, 241.

276 See TP 351b.

female, because it is said to be the nose that starts from the root of the vajra of the male. That which "comes" in that nose is awakening spirit that is like a stream of milk. "Good time" is the time of the three joys. "Going" is the going outside of the drop. Since one is agitated like fire at that time, it is "bad time." "These, propounded as one" refers to the occasion when both of those two previous times are abandoned—in short, "inconceivable time." They are explained relying on the *Āmnāyamañjarī*.

There is another explanation of "at one time," which involves the four lines [beginning with] "life force and."[277] The meaning of the first line, explained by the second, is that it is the time free of the coming and going of wind. Relying thus on fury fire meditation, the wind, free of coming and going in the left or right channels, is injected into the central channel. This shows that the central channel is also free of coming and going.

The *Ālicatuṣṭaya* also states that "'at one time' is a time and a measure of time. It is the time of obstruction, and the time of spring. This refers to [the time when] the wind that enters the left and right nostrils is obstructed."[278] This "time of obstruction" refers to the obstruction of the in-and-out movement of wind. The "time of spring" is the time when joy is augmented, as in springtime.

As was [discussed] above, their "ladies" exist in the form of humans, etc. That is the meaning of "in [their] vulvae."[279] It is also necessary to apply that meaning to "at one time." This shows the vital points for the entry of the life force into the central channel, also relying on the outer seal. The natural joy of the perfection stage arises from the entry, abiding, and dissolving of the life force into the central channel. Since the vital points are very important, one must know well from the start all of the oral instructions on penetrating the vital points in the body.

The meaning of **blessed lord** is stated in the *Tattvaprakāśa* as "those who are the reality of supreme joy, who alone are self-arisen, are

---

[277] These are the last three sentences in my TP translation above.

[278] Kāṇha, *Ālīcatuṣṭaya*, D 358b, Q p. 229.4–5. Note that the Derge edition contains a corruption, reading *'bog pa'i dus* rather than *'gog pa'i dus*. The correct reading occurs in the Beijing edition.

[279] Tsong Khapa refers to ST and SU *nidāna* verse, discussed above in section 3.3.3. 2.1.1.2.1.2.1.1.1.1.1.

said to be **blessed lords**."[280] They are possessed of fortune in the natural gnosis of the supreme joy, and they also have the various types of power for overcoming their opponents. In regard to **all tathāgatas** it says in the *Tattvaprakāśa* that "regarding what is meant by 'all,' they are like a heap of buddhas, and so forth."[281] And also, "heap of buddhas, and so forth, designates their elements and sensory fields."[282] All buddhas means all tathāgatas. The sensory fields that are assembled from the five aggregates, and so forth, are designated as sensory fields with respect to the elements of the aggregates.

Continuing from the previous [passage, the *Tattvaprakāśa* states that] "due to the conception of women and men, thought is said to have two aspects."[283] Due to the conception that "this one is a woman, this one is a man," by that thought there are also two aspects to the object of thought. "Men" are the heros and **vajraḍākas**, while "women" are the **ḍākinīs**. Furthermore, if you explain with regard to the inner [reality], the vajraḍākas are the inner sensory fields of channels. As for the ḍākinīs, they are the thirty-six channels, just as it says in the *Tattvaprakāśa*: "Like a heap of buddhas, and so forth, these blissful ḍākinīs are the thirty-six channels."[284] The **secret** is the seal's vulva that has a triangular shape. It is in that place that they **reside**, in the place of great bliss. As for **essence** (*hṛdaya*), it is great bliss that is created relying on that. This applies to the perfection stage that is developed from the injection of the life force into the central channel in reliance upon the actual seal (*karma-mudrā*).

---

280 The text of the TP preserved in the Kangyur reads: */mchog tu dga' ba'i ngo bo ste/ /'di de bcom ldan zhes su gsungs/ /'di de rang 'byung gcig pu nyid/* (TP 355a). Tsong Khapa reverses the order of the second and third lines.

281 See TP 355a.

282 See TP 355a.

283 See TP 355a.

284 Tsong Khapa here reads: */sangs rgyas phung sogs de bzhin te/ /de yi mkha' 'gro ma de dag /rtsa ni sum cu rtsa drug nyid/*. The TP reads: */sangs rgyas phung songs de bzhin te/ /bde ba'i mkha' 'gro ma de dag /rtsa ni sum cu rtsa drug nyid/* (TP D 355a, Q p. 228.1). Note that I translate the Tengyur's reading *bde ba'i mkha' 'gro ma de dag*, rather than Tsong Khapa's *de yi mkha' 'gro ma de dag*.

3.3.3. 2.1.1. 2.1.2. 1.1.2. 2. The definitive meaning as applied to the creation stage[285]

Although there are many occasions where the perfection stage is concealed in the root Tantra, the more important ones are, it is said, at the occasion of the creation stage, such as the four words such as "secret," etc., and the four words such as "bull pen," [which are relevant to] the visualization of the stacked-up elements, the meditation on Mt. Sumeru, the visualization of Mt. Sumeru in which the vowels and consonants are created within the universal lotus atop the mountain, and the creation of Heruka from the vowels and consonants within that lotus on top of it. The explanatory Tantras clearly elucidate [some of these] hidden matters; the *Saṁpuṭa* states:

> In the sole of the foot the Herambha wind (*rtsom chen rlung*)[286] abides in the shape of a bow. In that way the triangle blazes within the loins (*trikaṭi*).[287] Water abides in the navel with a circular form. Earth itself is in the heart, it being completely square. Mt. Sumeru, king of mountains, [exists] with the form of the spinal column.[288]

And also: "the perfected mandala exists due to the gurus' lineage succession, and in accordance with the order of Herambha, and so forth."[289]

---

[285] Although this section is titled "the definitive meaning as applied to the creation stage," it actually addressed the perfection stage. I presume that this is because the perfection stage is not addressed at all in the root Tantra itself. It is thus the hidden "definitive meaning" of the passages that imply creation stage practices.

[286] The Tibetan *rtsom chen* here translates the Sanskrit *Herambha*, which is evidently an alternative name for Heruka.

[287] The Sanskrit here reads *trikaṭi*, "loins" (IABS ms. LMhj 000,017, MBB I-17, fol. 392b, ln. 3–4). Note that the Tibetan *sum mdo* is not a good translation for this term.

[288] See ST 6.3, D 113b, Q p. 261.1.

[289] This passage reads in both Tsong Khapa's text and in ST kalpa 6, ch. 3, as follows: */ji ltar rtsom chen la sogs rim/ /bla ma'i dus thabs rim nyid kyis/ /de ni rdzogs pa'i dkyil 'khor gnas/* (ST D 113b, Q p.261.1). As this seemed somewhat unclear to me, I decided to consult a Sanskrit manuscript of the ST, which here reads: *herambhādiyathākrama guruparvakrameṇaiva sampannamaṇḍalasthitaṁ* (IABS ms. LMhj 000,017, MBB I-17, fol. 392b, ln. 3–4). Note that the translation of *parva* as *dus* is incorrect in this context.

If you explain Mt. Sumeru and the stacked-up elements from an inner perspective, they are evident in the body, from head to foot. Furthermore, that is said to be the perfection stage body mandala, which is the vajra body wherein the perfection stage practitioner penetrates the vital points. As for "outer" of Kāṇha's explanation of both outer and inner in regard to the body mandala, it is like Ghaṇṭapā's application of Mt. Sumeru and the elements to the body visualized as the creation stage body mandala.

Now I will explain the inner [import]. As for the particularities of penetrating the vital points of the vajra body, since the four syllables of "*evaṁ*," etc., of the narrative preface apply to the four channel wheels, they should be known from the *Saṁpuṭa*.[290] If you take literally the two lines "atop Mt. [Sumeru]," etc., they can be applied to the simultaneous creation of habitat and inhabitants in the manner of Lūipa. If it is joined with the outer creation of Heruka from the vowels and consonants within the lotus, in the middle of the previously created measureless mansion atop Sumeru, then the body is equalized here and there, above and below. It becomes a four-doored, equal-sided palace, and therefore should show the body that is the place where you hit the vital points in the perfection stage.

Kāṇha explains the definitive meanings of the lotus, vowels, and consonants that are stated in the *Saṁpuṭa*. In the *Tattvaprakāśa* he explained, "it is said the thirty-two-petaled lotus is in the top of the head,"[291] and "in the center of that is the letter *ham*. Emanated from the vowels and consonants, the enjoyment of the state of the indestructible [drop] is said to be great bliss. In the great wheel of great bliss is the final class that takes leave of names."[292]

As for the definitive meaning of that, although there is also a moon in the emanation from the vowels and consonants, the principal point is that one must explain here the statements in the root Tantra about the creation of Heruka from both of them.

---

290 ST 1.4 links the four syllables *e-vaṁ-ma-yā* to various sets of four such as the four elements, the four channel wheels, the four mudrās, and the four yoginīs such as Locanā. See Skorupski 1996, 240, and ST 81a,b.

291 See TP 355a.

292 See TP 355a.

In regard to the meaning of the last two lines, the crown is where the wheel of great bliss exists. When you drop the letter *kṣa* from the final class of constants, you get *ha*, to which a drop is affixed. The natural state (*sahaja, lhan skyes*) that arises from the jasmine-like [drop] that descends from that letter *haṁ*, called the "indestructible," is the definitive meaning of the creation of Heruka from the vowels and consonants.

The *Saṁpuṭa* states that it is "that which trickles in the form of ambrosia abides day and night,"[293] meaning that the awakening spirit trickles from the letter *haṁ* in the crown. This is recognized as the essence of the path of natural great bliss in the systems of both Tantras.[294] The *Tattvaprakāśa* states that: "In the Yogatantras the Tathāgata said *evaṁ mayā*. In the Yoginītantras he stated this as 'union' (*saṁvara, bde ba'i mchog*). In both the so-called Yogatantras and Yoginītantras, these [statements] express the supreme gnosis of great bliss, which is called 'fire.'"[295]

In order to create that great bliss, white awakening spirit must trickle from the *haṁ* of the crown down to the tip of the secret place. And the awakening spirit must be melted by the blazing fire of *caṇḍālī*. The *Abhidhāna* states that "Equalizing the vowels and consonants, [they] should be joined as a line. The line blazing above causes flowing below; it flows in the form of semen into the form of an ambrosial drop."[296] Although this text also occurs in the *Mahāmāyā* and is explained elsewhere by Śāntipa, here it is not like that.[297] The vowels signify the left

---

293 See ST 114a.

294 That is, the *Cakrasaṁvara* and *Hevajra Tantra*s.

295 See TP D 355b.

296 Tsong Khapa quotes the fourteenth chapter of the AU (D 291b). The Sanskrit occurs as follows in Kalff's edition: *ālikālisamāṁ kṛtvā rekhāṁ tatra niyojayet // jvalitārdharekhā tvadhaḥ śravati kāriṇī // śravate śukrarūpena amṛtabindusvarūpiṇaṁ //* (1979, 327). This evidently is a cryptic account of the perfection stage process of injecting the winds into the central channel. According to Śūraṅgavajra's commentary on the *Abhidhānottara*, this passage refers to the unification of winds in the central channel, with the resulting development of heat that melts the drop at the crown, the descent of which gives rise to the four joys. See Kalff 1979, 212, n. 1.

297 Tsong Khapa here refers to the *Mahāmāyā Tantra*, and Ratnākaraśānti's *Guṇavatī-ṭīkā*, a commentary thereon. The *Mahāmāyā* does contain a passage almost identical to the passage from the AU quoted above. The passage corresponds to verses 20 and 21 in

(cont'd)

channel through which white awakening spirit descends, while the consonants signify the right channel through which red awakening spirit descends. Regarding their equalization, it is said that the winds of those two mix in the central channel at the center of the navel. By these [winds] entering there, they blaze in lines of fire up to the crown at the top. By that blazing the ambrosial fluid trickles down from the letter *haṁ*. In order for there to be trickling from the letter *haṁ* in the middle of the lotus of the crown, the blazing fire must arrive there. This explains the "vowels and consonants."

In order for the fury fire to blaze via the insertion of the life force into the central channel, it is necessary to penetrate the vital points of the body, which are places on the central channel. [These include:] the wheel of great bliss of the crown, where the majority of white awakening spirit exists; the wheel of emanation of the navel, where the majority of red awakening spirit is found; the secret place's bliss-sustaining wheel; and the reality wheel of the heart, where the white and red [awakening spirits] exist in equal proportion. And there are many [channel] apertures that are vital points to be penetrated, such as the upper and lower nostrils of the central channel, and so forth.

In regard to these, in the system of Lūipa both the drop visualization and vajra repetition are performed from the navel. According to

---

Samdhong and Dwivedi's (1992) edition, occurring as follows: *ālikālisamāṁ kṛtvā tatra rekhātrisaṁpuṭāṁ // jvalitordhvamukhī rekhā tadādhaḥ srutikāriṇī // śukrarūpena sravati amṛtaṁ bindusvarūpiṇaṁ //* (1992, 16–17). The same volume contains Ratnākaraśānti's commentary, which occurs on the same page as the passages from the *Mahāmāyā* quoted above. His comments are brief, but he does seem to differ from Tsong Khapa on at least one point. Tsong Khapa below identifies the vowels and consonants with the left and right channels respectively. Ratnākaraśānti, on the other hand, seems to imply that the vowels and consonants are what are joined at the place where the right and left channels join the central channel. Commenting on the same line, he wrote: "It is said that 'the vowels and consonants,' etc., are 'joined,' that is, united by means of restraint (*niyamana*), 'there' in the junction (*saṁpuṭa*) of the sun and the moon," *tam evāha ālikālītyādinā tatreti ravicandrasaṁpuṭe niyojiteti niyamanāya yojitā* (p. 16); / *de nyid ālikāli zhes bya la sogs pa gsungs pa ste / de la zhes bya ba ni nges par bcing ba'i phyir sbyar ba'o* / (p. 106). His commentary implies that what is being discussed here is the third and fourth stages of the *ṣaḍaṅgayoga* (*prāṇāyāma* and *dhāraṇā*), in which the winds, restrained (*niyamana*) through breath control, are unified and inserted into the central channel at the *ravicandrasaṁpuṭa*, the junction of the three vessels below the navel. A good discussion of this process in English occurs in Bentor 1997; see esp. p. 55.

Ghaṇṭapā, both self-consecrations are performed from the heart, and the two processes of the universal vajra are performed from both of the upper and lower nostrils of the central channel. The Jālandhara process is performed in the secret place, and the inconceivable process in the heart. In the system of Kāṇha it is as he states in the *Ālicatuṣṭaya*. Generally, one penetrates the vital points on the four wheels, particularly the navel.

The explanatory Tantra states that the crown channel wheel, the lotus of which is the basis of the vowel and consonant arrangement, is the place from which awakening spirit trickles.[298] In the art of conducting awakening spirit from that place you penetrate the vital points on the body, and since you need the lotuses of the other wheels, these also serve as bases for the vowel and consonants arrangements.

The definitive meaning of the creation of Heruka from the vowels and consonants is the import of the creation of Heruka from the assembly of red and white awakening spirit there, which is definitive. Furthermore, Heruka is created by penetrating [the vital points] not only on the crown but also on other parts of the body. In regard to the Heruka of definitive meaning, one should know that there are two Herukas, the phenomenal aspect and the empty aspect. Regarding the [implication of] alternate perfection stages in the meaning of the root Tantra, I will comment on this from time to time. If you know how to explain by means of the method previously discussed, you will come to know well the essential points of the personal instructions of the three great saints who explained the very secret points of the root Tantra, relying on the explanatory Tantras. If you do not know how to explain like that, although there seems to be some little explanation in Kāṇha's *Ālicatuṣṭaya*, it does not appear that one could know how to explain the hidden points of the perfection stages of Lūipa and Ghaṇṭapā [as indicated] anywhere in the root Tantra.

---

298 Tsong Khapa is here referring to a passage in AU ch. 14, a small portion of which he quoted above. See lines 89b2 to 90a3 in Kalff's edition (1979, 211–214).

3.3.3. 2.1.1. 2.1.2. 1.1.2. 3. Explaining the sixteen syllables in reference to alchemy

The *Vajraḍāka* states, in answer to the request concerning the sixteen syllables stated in the *Uttarasaṁvara*,[299] that the alchemical substances were taught corresponding to the sixteen syllables. The sixteen syllables are as follows: *ra ha sye pa ra ma ra mye sarva tma ni sa dā sthi taḥ*.[300] These are the Sanskrit equivalent to the two lines that [begin with] the **secret that is supreme** (**1.2.c,d**). The meaning of each separate syllable is stated in the *Vajraḍāka*. They occur in Kambala's commentary, as follows:

> *Ra* is the element of great vermillion. *Ha* is "that which is mountain born," that is, head born [i.e., hair]. *Sye* is receptacle of scent. It is like body odor. *Pa* is said to be wind (*pavana*), and *ra* is said to be scent. The syllable *ma* is a flower, and *ra* is salt. It is accepted that *mye* is the "great flesh." *Sa* is union, and *rva* is said to be the head. The goddess is the essence of fire. *Ni* is scented clarified butter, and *sa* is the teeth and fingernails. *Dā* is ocean born. *Sthi* is the essence of thè mouth, and *taḥ* is camphor.[301]

In regard to that, *ra* is the menstrual blood that descends periodically. *Ha* is human brain that is not rancid. *Sye* is the scent of the body. In regard to the fourth one, in another translation it says "*pa* is said to be skin." This is said to be the finely cleaned skin of a young child. *Ra* is feces that is not the product of greasy food. *Ma* is evident in the statement "the blood arising from play with an eight-year-old girl." *Ra* is urine [collected] at dawn. *Mye* is great flesh from which serum (*chu ser*) has been extracted one time. *Sa* is rendered human fat. *Rva* is hair oil and salt. *Tma* is fecal

---

299 The VT correctly attributes these syllables to the *Uttarasaṁvara*, *bde mchog phyi ma*, evidently a shorthand name for the JS, which does indeed contain these syllables. See JS 151a.

300 This is a paraphrase of a passage in chapter 42 of the VT; see esp. D fol. 89a,b; Q p. 1302.3. The syllables are as listed in Tsong Khapa's text. The Sanskrit text on which it is based reads *rahasye parame ramye sarvātmani sadā sthitaḥ*.

301 See SN 3a.

oil. *Ni* is the marrow, and *sa* is clear.[302] *Dā* is the middle urine, and *sthi* is saliva. *Taḥ* is explained as the semen of an adult man. Although in that way there are eighteen, both substances corresponding to *rva* are counted as one, as are the teeth and fingernails. Therefore, there are sixteen.

The essence of these collected is the five ambrosias. It says in the *Vajraḍāka*, "the substances of the yogin, the 'secret,' etc., are taken to be the five such as feces, urine, etc. The series of collected elements is the teaching on alchemy."[303] This applies the five words[304] from **secret** to **always abides** to the five ambrosias. It also occurs like that in the *Saṁpuṭa*. If you wish to know how to produce hair oil, fecal oil, and "middle urine," as well as how to make use of the substances, you should know it from the *Great Saṁvara Commentary*.[305]

On this path, great bliss is of principal importance. In order to augment the body's power, depending on the increase of the body's jasmine-like [semen] (*kun da lta bu*), there is the previously [discussed system of] alchemy. If you rely on the bliss that arises through dependence on the alchemy of the five ambrosias and sixteen substances, even though there is non-correspondence in parts of the sixteen with the alchemy of the outer substances, then it is said that bliss increases, and by relying on the union of that bliss with the sphere of reality, one will always be given bliss.

---

302 That is, the esoteric significance of *sa* does not need further explanation.

303 See VT D 89b.

304 The lines *rahasye parame ramye sarvātmani sadā sthitaḥ* actually contain six lexical units, but Tsong Khapa appears to read *paramaramye*, which would yield five.

305 Tsong Khapa refers here to Büton's monumental NS commentary. In commenting on this section Tsong Khapa draws heavily on this text. His quote from the VT above is actually a small portion of a much larger passage quoted by Büton, and Büton goes further, fully showing the connection between the words of this verse and the elements, the levels of interaction between the deities (laughing, gazing, hand-holding, and intercourse), and so forth. See NS 183–195. Büton also quotes the passage in the ST to which Tsong Khapa refers; this passage was previously quoted by Tsong Khapa in section 3.3.3.2.1.1.2.1.2.1.1.1.2 above.

3.3.3. 2.1.1. 2.1.2. 1.2. Explaining the four lines [that begin with] "made of all ḍākinīs" [1.3]

The second part has two sections: (1) the explanation applied to the goal, and (2) the explanation applied to the perfection stage of the path.

3.3.3. 2.1.1. 2.1.2. 1.2.1. The explanation applied to the goal

In regard to the latter of the two explanations of **made of all ḍākinīs (1.3a)**, etc., in the *Vajraḍāka*, if you explain as applied to the goal, then **all ḍākinīs** are Pracaṇḍā, and so forth.[306] "Made of" means that Heruka is the nature or actuality composed of the extremely subtle particles of those ḍākinīs. Since he is empowered in [fulfilling] the aims of sentient beings, he is a **hero** (*sattva*). Since the gnosis of Heruka destroys the mountain of ignorance, it is **adamantine** (*vajra*). The meaning of the latter [term] "hero" is not explained, as it is considered to be similar in meaning to the former "hero."[307] Here the *Vajraḍāka* states that:

> It is said that there are two types of *sattva*, the environmental and essential worlds. The essential are animate beings, and the environment is their habitat. Each of them also has two types, the fortunate and unfortunate. They exist in four aspects, in the forms of earth, water, fire, and wind.[308]

This states that the term [*sattva*] implies the 'beings' whose aims are accomplished as well as the 'heroes' who possess the capacity to [do this]. From that perspective, this term is also connected to the environment that is their abode. [Here] the term refers directly to the teacher (*'dul byed*) who has that ability. Thus, the pure environmental and essential [worlds] of the teacher are fortunate, while the impure environmental and essential [worlds] of disciples (*'dul bya*) are unfortunate. They assume forms that take the four elements as their mode and course.

---

306 Tsong Khapa is referring to the twenty-four ḍākinīs listed in chapter 4 below.

307 That is, the second *sattva* in the compound name *vajrasattva*. Tsong Khapa here is commenting on the text of 1.3ab, which reads: *sarvaḍākinīmayaḥ sattvo vajrasattvaḥ paraṁ sukham*.

308 See VD 89b.

Supreme bliss is perfection. The term *ni* of [the text] *'di ni* (*asau hi*, **1.3c**) is an emphatic [particle]. Since the **Blessed Lord** arises in the actuality of the entire purified animate and inanimate worlds in just this way, he is **self-arisen**. I have already explained "Blessed Lord." **Hero** means one who is victorious over all discordant tendencies. **Ḍākinīs** (**1.3d**) refers to the heroes and heroines. Their **network** is the host of them. As for **binding**, they are bound in the actuality of the one Heruka. This sort of Blessed Lord speaks the Tantra. The gurus claim that these four lines show the perfection of the teacher of the Tantra, which seems to be in agreement with Kambala.

3.3.3. 2.1.1. 2.1.2. 1.2.2. The explanation applied to the perfection stage of the path

Here we should explain somewhat the connection between [the line beginning] **made of all ḍākinīs** (**1.3a**) and the previous two lines.[309] Those two lines showed that by relying on the elixir one can augment one's body.

Then one depends upon the inner art of perfection stage meditation, which in turn relies on both the general vajra body shown by the stacked-up elements, and so forth, as well as the group of four channel wheels that is shown by the four syllables *e vaṁ ma yā* connected to **the secret that is supreme**. One also depends upon the outer art of the four actual seals of the clans of Locanā, etc., who are also indicated by the four syllables. One also relies upon the definitive meaning of "at one time," [namely] the injection of life force into the central channel and the cessation of breathing, and the ignition of the fury fire by wind, as previously quoted from the *Abhidhāna*. And, as I explained [in the context of my discussion of] the definitive meaning of "heard," the equivalent of *śruta*, the great bliss that arises from the flow of awakening spirit from the crown to the tip of the secret place, is stated by the terms from "Padmanarteśvara" up to "Heruka," as in the statement that "Vajrasattva Heruka is explained as the expression **all ḍākinīs**," meaning that he is made of, i.e., has the actuality of, all ḍākinīs who are the inner heroes and heroines.

---

309 That is, the lines *rahasye parame ramye sarvātmani sadā sthitaḥ*, the "sixteen syllables" commented upon in section 3.3.3.2.1.1.2.1.2.1.1.2.3 above.

The *Tattvaprakāśa* also states that "since **ḍākinīs** are the nature of everything, [he] is made of them,"[310] and it says, regarding **hero**, "[he] is also called 'hero' since he is the actuality of supreme joy in cyclic existence."[311] Here "cyclic existence" should be taken to mean great bliss, which is the art. This is also what the "hero" (*sattva*) of "Adamantine Hero" (*vajrasattva*) means. "Adamantine" [means] that that bliss is engaged indivisibly with emptiness. For that reason, in the root Tantra after [the text, it is stated] **Vajrasattva** is **supreme bliss** (**1.3ab**). Great bliss exists as the subject [apprehending] emptiness, the realm of space. Since it is superior to other [types of] bliss, and "since his awakening spirit is uninterrupted, he is called 'Vajrasattva.'" Therefore, after that, **supreme bliss** is stated in the Tantra. "Since it exists in the realm of space, it is called 'supreme bliss.'"[312]

This supreme joy is **self-arisen** (**1.3c**) because it emerges as the body of Vairocana, etc., in the actuality of each disciple. Or, it is self-arisen because it accords with reality. He is called **blessed lord** because he is endowed with a perfect destiny, and he is a **hero** because he is endowed with the power to obliterate discordant tendencies.

The **ḍākinīs** (**1.3d**) are the thirty-six channels, and the elements within them. Their **network** is the group [of them]. The gnosis that arises from the excitation of awakening spirit by the wind that moves within them is **binding**, i.e., *saṁvara*, supreme bliss. In that way, the bliss that is the import of the four lines **all ḍākinīs**, etc., refers to the two groups of four joys, descending from above and supported from below. They are the four joys that emerge from the entry, abiding, and dissolving of the winds in the central channel. In regard to them, it says in the *Mahāmudrātilaka [Tantra]* that the four joys are also four [states of] luminance, radiance, and imminence, together with clear light, "because joy is luminance, and the supreme [joy] is luminous radiance, the special [joy] is imminence, and natural [joy] is clear light."[313]

---

310 See TP 355a.

311 See TP 355a.

312 See TP 355a.

313 Tsong Khapa here quotes the MT as follows: */gang phyir dga' ba de snang ba/ /snang ba mched pa mchog tu bshad/ /khyad dga' nye bar thob par shes/ /lhan cig skyes de 'og gsal ba'o/*. It occurs as follows in the Kangyur: */dga' ba zhes bya snang ba yin/ /mchog*

(cont'd)

Furthermore, the *Abhidhānottara* states:

> The first joy is gnosis. The great achievement of joy in sexual union corresponds to the supreme joy. Natural joy is unexcelled. The stages of the rites are *yoga*, *atiyoga*, *mahāyoga*, and *jñānayoga*. One who knows the procedure of the yoga of the drop beholds the subtle yoga.[314]

The process of the four joys stated there is the process of descending from above. The meaning of the two latter lines is that by knowing the meaning of the procedure of meditation on the yoga of the drop and the meditation on the yoga that is the union of the subtle letters and drops, you will see how the four joys are produced.

The commentary explains that they refer to the gnostic rites of *yoga*, *anuyoga*, *atiyoga*, and *mahāyoga*.[315] These stages should be

---

dga' snang ba mched par bstan/ /dga' bral snang ba thob ces bya/ /lhan skyes de ni yang dag 'od/ (MT 70b).

314 The Sanskrit here occurs as follows: *ānandaprathamaṁ jñānaṁ paramānandasamanvitam / suratānandamahāsiddhi sahajānandam anuttaram //yogātiyogamahāyogajñānayogvidhikramam / binduyogavidhānajñaḥ sūkṣmayogaṁ ca dṛśyate //* (J 297.4–5). The canonical Tibetan translation occurs as follows: */dga' ba dang po ye shes te/ /mchog tu dga' ba mnyam par sbyor/ /bde bar dga' bar grub pa che/ /lhan cig skyes dga' bla med yin/ /sbyor ba dang ni shin tu sbyor/ /sbyor ba che dang ye shes sbyor/ /de dag cho ga'i rim pa'o/ /thig le'i gzhung gi sbyor shes na/ /phra ba'i sbyor bas blta bar bya/* (AU 361a). Note that the Tibetan translates *suratānanda* euphemistically as *bde bar dga' ba*. The text *thig le'i gzhung gi sbyor shes na* is a defective translation of *binduyogavidhānajñaḥ*.

315 Tsong Khapa refers here to Śūraṅgavajra's commentary on the above passage, which occurs as follows: "The stages of the gnostic rites are *yoga*, *anuyoga*, *atiyoga*, and *mahāyoga*. In that way one should know the yoga of drops in which the four joys have the meaning of the vase, secret, wisdom-gnosis, and fourth consecrations. If both from that as well as from the subtle yoga one realizes the sphere of reality of mind, the continuum that is the cause of omniscient gnosis, then one will quickly succeed" (MV 227b: */rnal 'byor dang rjes su rnal 'byor dang / shin tu rnal 'byor dang rnal 'byor chen pa'i ye shes kyi cho ga'i rim pa'o/ /de ltar dga' ba bzhi bum pa dang gsang ba dang shes rab ye shes dang dbang bzhi pa'i don thig le rnal 'byor shes pa las kyang ste/ phra ma'i rnal 'byor las kyang thams cad mkhyen pa'i ye shes kyi nye bar len pa'i rgyud sems kyi chos kyi dbying rtogs na myur du 'grub par 'gyur ro/*). These stages are found in many different systems, and are deployed differently within them. Nāgabodhi, for example, deploys them as stages in the creation stage process of creating the central deity. He wrote: "After that, create Mahāvajradhara by means of the process of *yoga*, *anuyoga*, *atiyoga* and *mahāyoga*" (Nāgabodhi, *Samājasādhanavyavasthāli*, Q p. 7.4: */de'i 'og rnal 'byor dang / rjes su rnal 'byor dang / shin tu rnal 'byor dang / rnal 'byor chen po'i rim pas rdo rje 'chang chen po'i bdag nyid du skyed de/*).

applied, respectively, to the four joys. The *Abhidhānottara* also states that:

> In the navel, in the heart lotus between the breasts, at the root of the tongue and atop the head are the joy, supreme [joy], sublime [joy], and natural [joy wheels, respectively]. The first has sixty-four petals, the second eight supreme petals. The third has sixteen petals, and the fourth thirty-two petals. Vārāhī abides at the base of the navel, and the natural [joy] is the supreme Heruka.[316]

This is the sequence of the four joys supported from below, which [as] stated [above] involves the creation of joy in the navel, supreme joy in the heart, "sublime," i.e., special joy at the root of the tongue, namely the throat, and natural joy atop the head, i.e., on the crown. The heart lotus is said to be the channel wheel in the heart center, and the other three have channel wheels as well. Vārāhī at the base of the navel refers to the short *a* (*a thung*) fury fire. As for the identification of the natural [joy] as Heruka, since he is created at the crown when the ascending awakening spirit returns upward, the letter *ham* of the crown is said to be Heruka.

3.3.3. 2.1.1. 2.1.2. 1.3. Explaining the two lines that begin with "arising" [1.4a–b]

The third part has two sections: (1) explaining the interpretable meaning, and (2) explaining the definitive meaning.

3.3.3. 2.1.1. 2.1.2. 1.3.1. Explaining the interpretable meaning

The [term] **arising** (*'byung ba*, *sambhavāt*, **1.4a**) linguistically means 'source' (*'byung gnas*). Here *nāda* means **sound**, and those that

[316] The Sanskrit here occurs as follows: *nābhihṛtpadmastanumadhye jihvāmūle śiropari / ānandaparamāṁ caiva virajaṁ sahajaṁ tathā // catuṣaṣṭhida[l]am ekaṁ dvitīyam aṣṭadalottamam / tṛtīyaṁ ṣoḍaśadalaṁ caturtha[ṁ] dvātriṁśaddalam // vārāhīnābhim[ū]lastha sahajaṁ herukottamam /* (J 243.2–3). The canonical Tibetan translation occurs as follows: */lte ba'i snying pad nu ma'i dbus/ /lce yi rtsa dang mgo steng du/ /dga' ba dang ni mchog dga' nyid/ /dam par dga' dang lhan cig skyes/ /dang po 'dab ma drug cu bzhi/ /gnyis pa brgyad pa mchog yin te/ /gsum pa 'dab ma bcu drug pa/ /bzhi pa sum cu rtsa gnyis 'dab/ /phag mo'i lte ba'i rtsar gnas pa/ /lhan cig skyes dga' khrag 'thung mchog* (AU 339b–340a).

constitute its form include vowels, consonants, and mantras. This includes syllables that are not enunciated in speech, as they are designated as words since they appear in the mind in written form. That which is **arising from** them is the deities. Therefore, they are the source of the deities. The commitments are the goddesses. And the practice of them is the practice. The scope of that practice is the heroes. There is a way of explaining **arising from the form of sound** in reference to that which arises from the **sound** of space and the union of the two organs, but this seems to be rather partial.[317] While it seems that the former interpretation occurs in the *Vajraḍāka* commentary,[318] it appears to apply largely to the procedures for creating the deities. The gurus applied these two stanzas to the previously mentioned assembly,[319] which seems to be appropriate.

3.3.3. 2.1.1. 2.1.2. 1.3.2 Explaining the definitive meaning

Here **arising from the form of sound** refers to the origin, that is the creation, of the supreme bliss from the semen and menstrual blood, which are explained as creating the aggregates, etc. As for the things **arising from** that, this Tantra teaches that the awakening spirit generates the great bliss, and this is also asserted in other Tantras. This is the definitive meaning of **arising**.

In brief, if you meditate on the perfection stage, you generate the awakening spirit from the blazing up and flowing down of the white and red awakening spirits. That very thing is that on which the yogī relies, as well as that which must be served—the **commitments**. The **scope of** their **practice** is the enjoyment of the six types of sense objects by the six sense faculties.[320] This **scope** is designated vis-à-vis the sense faculties because ultimately sense faculty and object are inseparable. These objects, by the process of their arising as the play of great bliss, are enjoyed and therefore cause the blazing of great bliss. One attains the state of natural experiential unity in which object and subject are not perceived as isolated.

---

[317] See SN 4a.

[318] Bhavabhaṭṭa interprets the term "arising" as creation from the union of the semen and menstrual blood. See VV 181b.

[319] That is, the assembly of heroes and heroines, discussed in the context of the text *ḍākinījālasamvara* in section 3.3.3.2.1.1.2.1.2.1.2.1 above.

[320] That is, sight, hearing, smell, taste, touch, and mind.

This is explained relying on the root commentary of the *Vajraḍāka*.[321] This occurs as previously explained in all occasions of meditating on the perfection stage in which one penetrates the vital points on the body, so there is no need to explain this in a partial way, in the manner of the *Āli-catuṣṭaya*.

3.3.3. 2.1.1. 2.1.2. 2. The difficult to obtain

It seems that the explanatory systems of the two translators are also not in agreement with the two lines [beginning with] **world (1.4cd)**. Three commentaries explain that "the heroes who dwell in the three wheels—of the **beginning**, which is mind; the **middle,** which is speech; and the **end**, body—are **difficult to obtain in the triple world** of the heavens, earth, and underworld."[322] In regard to this, the first explanation of the two explanatory systems is that the meaning of *beginning* [1.4d] and *secret* [1.2.c], *middle* and *supreme*, and *end* and *delighted* is the previously explained definitive meaning of "thus have I heard at one time."[323] And this is the meaning that is very **difficult to obtain**, i.e.,

---

[321] The VD glosses the term "arising" (*nges 'byung*) as "generation of awakening spirit" (VD 90a: *sems skyed*). Bhavabhaṭṭa explains this as follows: "Regarding the attainment of awakening spirit, it is the attainment of the state of natural experiential unity when subject and object are mixed. This indicates the **scope of the commitments**" (VV 181b: *byang chub kyi sems thob pa zhes bya ba ni/ yul dang yul can 'dres nas lhan cig skyes pa ro gcig pa'i gnas skabs thob pa ste de dag gis ni dam tshig spyod yul yin zhes bsnyad do*).

[322] It appears that Tsong Khapa is not directly quoting, but rather paraphrasing, Jayabhadra's commentary, which occurs as follows: CP 45a: */'jig rten gsum du rnyed dka' ba/ /zhes bya ba ni don ji bzhin nyid de/ mtho ris dang / mi yul dang / sa 'og rnams su zhes bya ba'i bar du'o/ /yang na 'jig rten gsum po dag na dpa' bo la sogs pa'i 'jig rten gang yin pa de rnams ye shes zhes bya bar sbyar ro/ /thog ma dbus mthar yang dag gnas/ /zhes bya ba ni/ thugs dang /gsung dang / sku la rnam par gnas pa'am/ /yang na lha thams cad ro gcig pa nyid kyis cho ga'i ye shes gsungs pa yin no/*; Sugiki 2001, 109–110: *durlabhaṁ triṣu lokeṣv iti yathārtham eva, svargamartyapātāleṣv iti yāvat/ athavā triṣu lokeṣv iti trayo lokā vīrādayaḥ, teṣu vidhijñānam iti vā saṁbandhaḥ// ādimadhyānta-saṁsthitam iti citttavākkāyasaṁsthitam / athavā sarvasamarasatvād vidhijñānasyoktam iti//*. This commentary is repeated, in part, by Bhavyakīrti (BC 7b) and Vīravajra (ST 168b). There are various other interpretations of this. Kambala and Durjayacandra gloss it in terms of the three realms—the desire, form, and formless realms—and states that since these are contaminated, [the yoga] is difficult to obtain therein (SN 4a, RG 249a).

[323] Tsong Khapa here refers to the explanation in the VD linking the lines in this text, 1.2.c and 1.4.d, with the traditional Buddhist *nidāna* verse. See section 3.3.3.2.1.1.2.1.2. 1.1.1.1.1 above.

difficult to realize, **in the triple world** of the three regions.[324] This is the intention of the *Vajraḍāka*.[325]

The *Vajraḍāka* states that "difficult to attain in the triple world means that it will not be found among the three contaminated things."[326] In this way, the three worlds should be taken as being joy, supreme joy, and distinctive joy. These show the location of the difficult to obtain. That which is difficult to obtain is natural gnosis. The reason it is difficult to obtain is that the three joys are contaminated. The meaning of that is that the word "world" indicates an objectified conceptualization. Furthermore, being analyzed into the [respective] portions of the beginning, middle, and end, they are truly conceptualized. This is Bhavabhaṭṭa's exegetical approach.[327] This means, in short, that so long as there is no end to the appearance of duality and to the conceptualization that is dependent on that, there will be no experience of the actual natural [gnosis]. The natural [gnosis] that is difficult to obtain is no mere natural [state].

3.3.3. 2.1.1. 2.1.2. 3. Showing an example of the union of bliss and emptiness

While it is the case that through the combination **of the churned**, i.e., the place of rubbing, and **the churner (1.5a)**, which is the fire stick, and the efforts of the hand, smoke arises and fire spreads, if you investigate this, there is no existence or emergence of fire in those three. Likewise, through **the union of the churned**—that is, the seal's vulva—**and the churner**—that is, the vajra of the art—the ambrosia-like natural gnosis that bestows buddhahood arises. And if you examine this, you will know that that it does not arise from any sort of cause or condition.[328] Kāṇha [explained that one should]:

---

324 The Tibetan *sa gsum* is a synonym of *'jig rten gsum*, referring to the regions oriented vis-à-vis the surface of the earth (*sa*), i.e., *sa bla*, *sa steng*, and *sa 'og*; i.e., celestial, terrestrial, and subterranean.

325 This is in reference to the passage in VD ch. 42 previously quoted and discussed by Tsong Khapa in section 3.3.3.2.1.1.2.1.2.1.1.1.1.1 above. Sachen also discusses this passage at PG 297.4–298.1.

326 See VD 90 a.

327 See CV 154a, Pandey 2002, 17.

328 This passage seems to be drawn from Devagupta's commentary; see SS 72a.

> Visualize a peak of flame depending upon the fire stick, the rubbing place and the effort of the hand. If you examine this, [the flame] is not found in the fire stick, and so forth. Just so are beings, movement, and so forth. Just as all beings seem to be there separately, one experiences joy when not examining the reality of bliss, and so forth. And expressions such as "Thus have I [heard]," etc., are inconceivable; also just like this.[329]

And also, [it is said that] "from the union of the churner and the churned, the reality body is likewise just so."[330] If we thoroughly examine animate and inanimate beings, we don't find them, and, in particular, if we don't examine the great bliss stated by the text of the narrative preface (*nidāna*), it exists there just as a joyous experience. It should be understood to be just like the fire [produced by] rubbing. If bliss is created from union with the seal and from the art of penetrating the vital points on the body, and one connects it with the view that realizes that [all phenomena] are empty of intrinsic reality status, one should understand that one can just enjoy the experience without examination, the illusion-like aftermath. Although there are many methods of elucidating this, I have explained here in accordance with the exegetical systems of Kāṇha and Kambala.[331]

---

329 See TP 354b.

330 Kāṇha uses the image of the churning and rubbing in many of his works, but I have not found it compared to the *dharmakāya* in any of them.

331 In addition to Kāṇha's writings quoted above, Tsong Khapa also drew upon Kambala's SN, in which there is the following commentary on 1.5a, as follows: "**Just like the union of the churned and the churner** is as follows. Although from the kindling, fire stick, and the person's hands smoke rises and fire is kindled, there is no fire in the kindling, fire stick, or the person's hands, and if we investigate them it doesn't exist in any one. And just as in the case of fire, likewise the **churned** is said to be the vulva, and the **churner** the vajra. Likewise, from their **union** arises the ambrosial gnosis, which produces manifest awakening. The gnosis that arises in the wisdom body is the sky-like (*khasama*) method and simultaneousness, and it is the sole form of great bliss; this should be known from the true consecration." */bsrub bya bsrub bya'i sbyor ba bzhin/ /de bzhin zhes bya ba 'di lta ste/ gtsub gtan dang gtsub shing dang skyes bu'i lag pa'i rtsol ba las du ba rab tu skye zhing me mngon par mched mod kyi/ me de yang gtsub shing la yang med gtsub gtan la yang med skyes bu'i lag pa dag la yang med yongs su brtag na gcig la'ang mi gnas so/ /me 'di ji lta ba bzhin du/ 'dir yang / bsrub bya'i chos 'byung rab tu gsung / bsrub pa rdo rjer brjod pa'o/ /de yang dag par sbyor ba las/ de bzhin du bdud rtsi lta bu'i ye shes 'byung ba ni/ mngon par sangs rgyas pa nyid kyi byed*

(cont'd)

3.3.3. 2.1.1. 2.2. The actual exhortation to listen

Many [topics] are explained by Kambala, etc., such as, "the Blessed Lord said to the Lord of the Secret Ones, '**Listen to what is taught in the Tantra**' (**1.5d**)," which summarizes the teachings of the extensive Unexcelled Yoginī Saṁvara root Tantra, [namely] the knowledge of procedures of the sadhāna and the ritual implementations: the **repetition** of the essence [mantras], and so forth, for the purpose of mantra repetition, vajra repetition, and so forth, and moreover the **contemplation** of both the creation and perfection stages, and those [practices] included within the drawing of the mandala, the fire sacrifices, commitments and vows, etc. And having [mastered] repetition and contemplation, there is the achievement of the four ritual applications of pacifying, enriching, etc., as well as the knowledge of procedures that go beyond those.[332]

The bodhisattva commentary explains that Vajravārāhī was the supplicant.[333] There appear to be many different teachings taught, and many different presentations of the Teacher's body with the retinues [present] at each of the teaching occasions, so it may not be necessary to insist on one position or another here.[334]

The line [starting with] "Unexcelled Yoginī" and [the text] "I will explain the Tantra" does not occur in the unrevised translation of Lochen, nor does it occur in Mal's translation, or in the Prajñākīrti-Mardo dual translation.[335] Nor is it found in the commentaries. In regard to its import, however, there doesn't seem to be any fault.

---

pa po ste/ shes rab lus 'byung ye shes ni/ /mkha' mnyam thabs dang lhan cig nyid/ /bde chen rnam pa gcig pu ni/ /yang dag dbang bskur las shes bya/ (SN 4b).

332 Tsong Khapa here is paraphrasing and expanding upon a much briefer passage in Kambala's commentary, which occurs as follows: */sngags bzlas bsam gtan la sogs ldan/ /rgyud 'di bshad kyis nyan par gyis/ /zhes bya ba ni bcom ldan 'das kyis gsang ba pa'i bdag po la gsungs pa'o/* (SN 4b).

333 See the discussion in section 2.2 above.

334 Tsong Khapa here tacitly accepts the existence of the different commentarial traditions of the CT, which often vary considerably.

335 The line *rnal 'byor bla na med pa yi* is found in both the PM and SM translations, but does not occur in the SL translation or the extant Sanskrit. The text *rgyud ni bshad kyis* occurs only in the SM, where it is an alternate (and incorrect) translation of the Sanskrit *tantre nigaditaṁ*, which is correctly translated as *rgyud las gsungs pa* in the PM and SL translations. See my editions of these texts in Gray 2012.

3.3.3. 2.1.1. 3. The method for making progress in the secret of the path

In this section there are three subsections: (1) worship of the clanswoman, (2) protecting the commitments, and (3) meditation on the four seals.

3.3.3. 2.1.1. 3.1. Worship of the clanswoman

In this section there are three subsections: (1) general worship of the clanswoman, (2) the attainment of power depending upon the clanswoman, together with worship, and (3) the benefits of worshipping the clanswoman.

3.3.3. 2.1.1. 3.1.1. General worship of the clanswoman

[This section] applies to [the sixth verse, which concludes with the text] **should be worshipped** (**1.6c**). By whom? It is by the yogī who has the Lord's yoga. At what time? [It is done] on **special occasions** (**1.6d**), namely on the tenth day of the waxing and waning fortnight of each month, or the tenth day of the waning fortnight of the mid-winter month of each year. Is it [done] on one occasion? No, it [is done] **always**, without interruption. With what offering substances? These include saliva that is "exhaled" since it emerges drawn forth by **breath** (**1.6a**), or the great flesh that gives rise to the power of breath. Since the former does not occur in the young and the latter in the aged, the **central** one that occurs in between is blood. Among the elements it is superior, which is to say it is [the red] awakening spirit.

Scented refers to the great scent, and **water** to vajra water. **With** (**1.6b**) indicates the five [ambrosias] altogether, since they are together with the second one, and so forth. The word "also" (*kyang*, *tu*) shows that this is connected with the five offering substances as well.[336]

For whom [are they]? They are for the **clanswoman** famed in the treatises, who is a member of the one of the classes famed in the world such as the warrior class, or who has the clan affiliation of Akṣobhya, etc., as indicated at the time of consecration. This occurs in the exegetical system of the two translators.

---

[336] The term *tu/kyang* was not translated in my translation. As Tsong Khapa indicates, the term "scented water" (*gandhodaka*, *dri yi chu*) can be interpreted as a reference to the five ambrosias (*pañcāmṛta*), which are also offering substances (*upacāra*, *nye bar spyod pa*).

Breath refers to the lady who is well skilled in meditation, etc., on her chosen deity. **Central** refers to one who menstruates who is between youth and old age. **Superior** or "holy" refers to a "central one" with good qualities. If we distinguish them, there are five [types of] pure seal consorts (*phyag rgya ma*) connected to the five pure gnoses. First, there is the eleven-year-old; playing in her lotus, one achieves alchemy. Second, the twelve-year-old, playing with whom one strives for the commitment; here the commitment is great bliss. Third is the sixteen-year-old; playing with her has the aim of familiarity with mantra—that is, for the sake of success. By playing with the fourth, the twenty-year-old, flight will be achieved. Fifth is the twenty-five-year-old—play with her in order to be consecrated. This seems to explain the meaning of the *Vajraḍāka*.[337]

This sort of **clanswoman** should be anointed with excellent scented substances, and by that example should be adorned with various flowers, clothes, ornaments, and so forth. And in regard to the "water" in the statement **with [scented] water**, she should be given various alcoholic drinks that clear away the wind, bile, and phlegm disorders.[338] Enjoying them yourself, make offerings to the clanswoman. **Always** indicates that one should make the offering of the meditation on reality without interruption.[339] By whom [is this done]? [It is done] by the yogī who meditates on the two stages.

What is the time for the offerings? The *Vajraḍāka* says that the **special occasion** is the morning.[340] Two commentaries state that there are six times, from among which the former is taken as an example.[341] Another commentary states that it is especially the occasion of the union

---

[337] See VD 91a. This commentary is repeated by Kambala (SN 4b–5a) and Devagupta (SS 72 a–b).

[338] Tsong Khapa here reproduces Kambala's commentary at SN 5a.

[339] See SN 5a.

[340] See VD 91a.

[341] Kambala, for example, states that there are six times, which are the six seasons of the hot season, the rainy season, fall, winter, late winter, and spring. These seasons are connected, respectively, to Hayagrīva, Heruka, Vajrasurya, Padmanarteśvara, Vajrasattva, and Vairocana. (SN 5a–b). These comments are, as usual, repeated by Devagupta (SS 73a). Büton also quotes this entire passage (NS 213–215).

of the two organs.[342] Another commentary similar to the above, which holds that the definitive meaning of the statement is that one should make offerings of reality while equipoised in the clanswoman, takes **breath** as a reference to the two winds of the left and right nostrils. The **central** refers to that which is between the right and left channels, namely being equipoised in the central channel. The **superior** is the supreme unchanging seal at the time of the injection of those two winds into the central channel at the base of the navel.[343] The meaning of this last word ["superior"] is that when one injects the two winds into the central channel relying on a seal, the seal consort (*phyag rgya ma*) herself is the **superior** method of drawing forth immutable bliss. **Scented water** is *sihlakaṁ*, i.e., blood.[344] **With** refers to the camphor, i.e., semen, which is offered to the clanswoman. These are explained in reliance on the commentaries of Kambala and Devagupta.[345]

---

342 Büton explains that "at the special occasion of the completion of menstruation, made special by the union of the vajra and the lotus, one should worship, i.e., give pleasure to, the kinswoman, the outer goddess with the nature of Vajravārāhī." / *dus te 'bab pa'i mtha'i dus khyad par te rdo rje padma 'dus byas pa'i khyad par gyi rigs ldan ma ste rdo rje phag mo'i rang bzhin gyis phyi'i lha mo la mchod pa ste dga' ba bskyed par bya'o* / (NS 216).

343 This in reference to the following passage from Devagupta's SS: "Furthermore, as for **breath**, when the two breaths of the left and right nostrils are fully joined at the base of the navel, that is the superior unchanging seal (*mudrā*)." /*yang na dbugs 'byin pas zhes pa ni sna bug gyas gyon gnyis kyi dbugs rnams lte ba'i rtsa bar de rnams kyi yang dag par phrad pa'i dus na phyag rgya mchog nyid ma 'gyur ba'o*/ (SS 72b).

344 *Sihlaka* is olibanum or frankincense; its connection to blood is no doubt due to its dark reddish color. This is from Kambala's commentary as follows: "**Scented water** is frankincense, and camphor is **with** it; the [substance] thus produced is offered to the clanswomen." /*dri'i chu ni si hla kaṁ ngo* / /*de dang bcas pa ni ga pur te*/ /*de lta bur gyur pas rigs ldan rnams la mchod par bya zhes so*/ (SN 5a). Interestingly, Kambala here makes use of the Hevajra *sandhyābhāṣa* system in "elucidating" an obscure term in the CT. In fact, his explanation may very well be a direct reference to a line in the *Hevajra Tantra* (2.2.18), which describes the female consort as "possessed of frankincense and camphor," *sihlakarpūrasaṁyuktāṁ*, *si hla ga pur yang dag ldan* (Snellgrove 1959: 2.46–47). The bodhisattva Vajragarbha explains in his Hevajra commentary that this refers to "one who has arrived at time of menstruation who takes pleasure in the bliss of awakening spirit" (Snellgrove 1959: 1.90, note 2: *khrag 'byung ba'i dus la bab pa byang chub sems kyi bde ba la dga' ba*).

345 In this section Tsong Khapa relies heavily upon Kambala and Devagupta; most of this section is a paraphrase, with comments, of passages from Kambala's (SN 4b–5b) and

(cont'd)

3.3.3. 2.1.1. 3.1.2. The attainment of power depending upon the clanswoman, together with worship

Bhavabhaṭṭa [explains] that they are **messengers**, (**1.7a**) since they are distressed over the suffering of sentient beings.[346] In addition to this literal [interpretation], the gurus say that the seal is called a "messenger," since she is like a messenger who rapidly accomplishes one's aims. This is in accordance with Kambala.[347] Here Bhavyakīrti says that as there are three [types of] messenger, the [text] **natural and accomplished** (**1.7a**) is just an illustration. In regard to them, the **lofty** (**1.7b**) is the "natural" one. The **middling** is the "seat born" one, who is the same as the "womb born" one.[348] The **lowly** type is the kind born from mantra. The **lofty**, etc., can also be understood as referring respectively to those who range in space, on earth, and in the underworld. Why is it necessary to accomplish them? It is explained that they **give rise to the achievement of pleasure with one's inwardly focused mind** (**1.7cd**).[349] The gurus indicate the **natural** with the actuality of the natural.[350] **Accomplished** means achieving a yoginī from the great spirit of the field, and achieving a yoginī by means of concentration, repetition, and so forth.

It is said that the first, the **lofty**, is the bestower of both achievements.[351] The second, the **middling**, is the bestower of worldly achievements. And the third, the **lowly** type, is unable to bestow either success,

---

Devagupta's commentaries (SS 72a–73a). The same information also occurs in Büton's commentary (the NS 213–216).

346 This text occurs in Bhavabhaṭṭa's commentary as follows: *tataś ca dūyante sattva-duḥkhena tapyanta iti* (Pandey 2002, 22); */de yang sems can sdug bsngal ba la gdung bas na pho nya'o/* (CV 158a)

347 Kambala's commentary does not contain any comments to this effect.

348 I translate *zhing skyes/kṣetraja* as "womb born," taking *kṣetra* in its more specific sense of body. This translation is supported by the fact that *kṣetraja* has a specific meaning of a type of birth in Hindu law, although here the reference is more general. See Monier-Williams 2002, 332 col. 2; see also Doniger 1996, 40.

349 Tsong Khapa closely paraphrases Bhavyakīrti's commentary here. See BC 8b–9a.

350 That is, the term "natural" (*sahajāḥ*, *lhan cig skyes*) is understood by some commentators to refer to an internal state of realization rather than any outwardly existing female messenger, as Tsong Khapa explains more fully below.

351 That is, both worldly powers and the ultimate achievement of awakening.

but accompanies the attainment of these two.[352] Although there are many different ways of identifying the three messengers, the first, the highest attainment in one's [psychosomatic] continuum of the actual orgasmic, is the transcendental ḍākinīs. Second, there are those who become yoginīs since they are born in thirty-two places, etc., and are raised by yoginīs. Third, there are yoginīs of the first stage whose psychosomatic continuums are well cultivated by means of initiation, and so forth. These latter two are mundane yoginīs.

Since one has union **with one's inwardly focused mind**, i.e., in accordance with what is called the method of union with the wisdom consort (*shes rab ma*) who gives birth to all transcendent lords, one is satisfied, so one's mind does not wander elsewhere. Thus one will attain **the achievement of pleasure**. In that way, the *Vajraḍāka* states the **lowly**, **middling, and superior** ones in the context of satisfying the messenger with offerings; [this explanation] differs from the previous explanation of **superior**, etc.[353] If we explain literally statements such as **worship the buddhas and bodhisattvas with one's own seminal drops (1.8ab)**, which arise from equipoise with the messenger, then one should outwardly satisfy the mandala deities and the heroes and yoginīs of the assembly with the ambrosia that is emitted in the vulva and taken up by

---

352 Tsong Khapa here closely paraphrases Bhavyakīrti's commentary (BC 9b). See as well Sachen's more lengthy discussion (PG 299.1–2).

353 Tsong Khapa paraphrases the VD here. The text to which Tsong Khapa refers to does indeed differ from Bhavyakīrti's explanation. Rather than taking these terms to refer to three types of seal, it takes them in terms of three types of practice, namely (1) "outer" practice with a seal, (2) inner body mandala practice, and (3) a thoroughly interiorized contemplative practice. The text in question reads as follows: "Following this worship is the **lowly, middling, and superior.** The **lowly** is the method of great passion. Moreover, the one who has the vajra (*vajrī*, *rdo rje can*) condenses everything, and the lady's vulva emits it as great bliss. This connects with [the text] **there one should draw the mandala (1.16d)**. It is taught in the manner of the reality of another. The **middling** is the reality of the self—all wheels are assembled inside of oneself by Vajradhara. Meditation on one's nature as entirely adamantine by this method is the **superior**." (VD 92a: */de ltar mchod pas tha ma mchog dang bar ma ste/ tha ma ni chags pa chen po'i tshul lo/ /de yang rdo rje can gyis thams cad bsdus nas btsun mo'i bha ga bde ba can du spros la/ der ni dkyil 'khor bri bar bya zhes bya ba dang sbyar ba ste/ gzhan gyi de kho na nyid ji lta ba bzhin du bstan pa'o/ /bar ma ni bdag gi de kho na nyid de/ rdo rje 'dzin pas 'khor lo thams cad rang gi dbus su bsdus la/ rdo rje kun gyi rang bzhin du byas pa cho ga des bsgoms pa ni mchog go/.*)

the tongue. This is like what the gurus say. If one explains in a non-literal fashion, then it has the meaning of satisfying the buddhas, i.e., the five aggregates, and the bodhisattvas, the [sense powers of] the eye, and so forth.[354] The worship of the clanswoman is extensively explained in the gurus' oral precepts in the context [commenting on the text] from the line **superior breath (1.6a)** up to this point.[355] Fearing prolixity, I will not write on it here.

3.3.3. 2.1.1. 3.1.3. The benefits of worshipping the clanswoman

The yogī who does this practice relying upon the messenger, though he might be **seen** by other people's eyes or **touched** by their bodies, or news of him might by **heard** by their ears or **thought** of by their minds **(1.8cd)**, if there is **no doubt** that this yogī is **thus liberated from all the sins (1.9ab)** of karmic obscuration, that they are washed away, and that such a **yogī** has himself gathered up **supreme** assemblies of **purifying merit**, and that his **sins** are **destroyed (1.9cd)**, i.e., overcome, what need is there to say more? One who thus relies on the messenger will quickly attain both achievements **with** the definitive and interpretable **mantra repetition** and **with** the definitive and the interpretable **meditative states**.

---

[354] A similar passage, which nonetheless differs significantly on an important point, occurs as follows in Bhavyakīrti's BC commentary: "**With one's own seminal drops** means with one's awakening spirit. The word **buddhas** is explained as the [sense powers of] the eye, and so forth, and **bodhisattvas** are the hands, feet, etc. This is as is stated in the *Śrī Guhyasamāja*: 'One of firm intelligence should eat the secret semen with eyes wide open. This is called the worship of the body, speech, and mind of all mantras, the secret of those who possess the gnostic vajra, which brings about success in mantras.'" (BC 9a: */rang rdzas thig les zhes pa ni rang gi byang chub kyi sems kyis so/ /sang rgyas kyi sgras ni mig la sogs pa la bya bar bshad la/ byang chub sems dpa' ni lag pa dang rkang pa la sogs pa'o/ /de yang dpal gsang ba 'dus pa las/ mig bzang brtan pa'i blo ldan pas/ /khu ba blang nas bza' bar bya/ /'di ni sngags rnams thams cad kyi sku gsung thugs kyi mchod pa ste/ /ye shes rdo rje can gyis gsang/ /sngags rnams rnams dngos grub byed par gsung / /zhes ji skad gsung ba lta bu'o/.*) Bhavyakīrti here quotes the *Guhyasamāja Tantra* 8.26–27, which reads as follows: *guhyaśukraṁ viśālākṣīṁ bhakṣayed dṛḍha-buddhimān // idaṁ tat sarvamantrāṇāṁ kāyavākcittapūjanam / mantrasiddhikaraṁ proktaṁ rahasyaṁ jñānavajriṇām //* (Matsunaga 1978, 25–26).

[355] Sachen, for example, devoted several pages in his *Pearl Garland* commentary to this subject; he interprets worship of the clanswoman as referring to inner body yogic meditation, in which the awakening spirit is both the object of continual worship and the substance of the offering. See PG 199.3–200.2.

The word **even** (*kyang*) shows that it is even attained by meditative states alone, which is taken as meaning inner absorption.[356]

While [the line] "will be attained even by bliss" does not occur in the Lochen and solo Mardo translations, nor in many of the commentaries, it does occur both in the translation of Mardo and Prajñākīrti and in Mal's translation.[357] It also says in the *Commentary Praising Saṁvara* that from the force of demonstrating retention (*dhāraṇā*, *'dzin pa*) by mantra repetition, it is implied that restraint of the life force (*praṇāyāma*, *srog rtsol*) is previous to that. By directly indicating the meditative states (*dhyāna*, *bsam gtan*), it implies that withdrawal (*pratyāhāra*, *sor sdud*) precedes it. By directly indicating concentration (*samādhi*, *ting nges 'dzin*) with bliss, it is shown that recollection (*anusmṛti*, *rjes dran*) precedes it.[358]

There is no contradiction in explaining the many different meanings in each of the Tantra's adamantine expressions by means of the parameters (*tshad ldan*). The adherents to Mal's exegetical tradition explain "even by bliss" in terms of practice.[359]

---

[356] The term *kyang* here occurs only in the SM translation, and has no Sanskrit equivalent. It does not occur in my translation.

[357] The line *bde bas kyang ni 'grub par 'gyur* occurs, as Tsong Khapa correctly notes, in the PM and SL translations. The SM translation omits *bde bas*.

[358] Tsong Khapa here paraphrases Vajrapāṇi's somewhat forced attempt to demonstrate that this verse indicates the *ṣaḍaṅgayoga* of the Kālacakra tradition (regarding this, see Orofino 1996). It occurs in the LT as follows: "Thus, one should know that *pratyāhāra* precedes *dhyāna*, and that *praṇāyāma* precedes mantra repetition. Here, the expression 'mantra repetition' refers to "hermaphrodite repetition," i.e., vajra repetition, or retention of the life force. Know that *anusmṛti* precedes bliss. Here the word 'bliss' means *samādhi*. In this way the the state of being a yogī, buddhahood, is achieved by means of these six branches" (Cicuzza 2001, 136: *ato dhyānapūrvaḥ pratyāhāro veditavyaḥ / mantrajāpapūrvaḥ prāṇāyāmo veditavyaḥ / atra mantrajāpaśabdena napuṁsakajāpo vajrajāpo vā prāṇadhāraṇā ucyate / sukhapūrvānusmṛtir veditavyā / atra sukhaśabdena samādhir ucyate / evaṁ ebhiḥ ṣaḍaṅgaiḥ sidhyati yogitvaṁ buddhatvaṁ iti /*; LT 130a: */de phyir bsam gtan gyi sngon du so sor sdud pa rig par bya'o/ /sngags bzlas pa'i sngon du srog rtsol rig par bya'o/ /'dir sngags bzlas pa'i sgras ma ning gi bzlas pa'am rdo rje'i bzlas pa ste srog 'dzin par brjod do/ /bde ba'i sngon du rjes su dran par rig par bya ste 'dir bde ba'i sgras ting nge 'dzin brjod do/ /de ltar yan lag drug po 'di rnams kyis rnal 'byor pas sangs rgyas nyid 'grub par 'gyur ro/*).

[359] See PG 300.1.

3.3.3. 2.1.1. 3.2. Protecting the commitments

In this section there are two subsections, (1) maintaining the commitments that are to be protected and (2) protecting the food commitments.

3.3.3. 2.1.1. 3.2.1. Maintaining the commitments that are to be protected

The **adept** of this path who is very **well equipoised (1.10d)**, that is, whose three doors are unwavering, **should always** and continually **protect** without impairment **the commitments (1.10c)** to be guarded, the root and branch commitments taught in other Tantras as well as the commitments taught in this Tantra.

In regard to the penalties of not guarding the commitments, **due to the breaking of the** root **commitments (1.11a)**, **power will not be gained in the mandala** into which one was previously **consecrated (1.11b)**, meaning one's power will be impaired. One will not be **successful with mantra repetition (1.10.ab)**, etc. Aside from that, there are the very great penalties of going into the lower realms later, and so forth. Therefore, one should endeavor from the start to not be tainted by an offense. If there is a root downfall, the vow can be restored by the guru setting up the mandala, or by self-consecration. If an excessive downfall occurs, it can be purified by the rite of renewal following confession, and so forth. However it will not work if you think that it can be remedied later.[360] Though it may be remedied, one will not rise up from a subsequent offense, as one would not be worthy of the remedy in such a case, it is also said. This is the teaching of Mardo, which is excellent.

3.3.3. 2.1.1. 3.2.2. Protecting the food commitments

In regard to the **honey** called the "great honey," Devagupta stated that it is the great butter (human fat, *mar chen po*);[361] its synonyms are great (human) suet (*tshil chen*) or the tallow (*zhag*) [derived] from that. **Vermilion**, i.e., blood, is the menstrual blood that periodically descends. **With camphor (1.11c)** is said to refer to the flower that is found along

[360] That is, if you intentionally violate the vow with this excuse as a justification.

[361] See SS 73b.

with camphor. This is the flower that is together with semen, which previously referred to blood alone. **Red sandalwood** is great (human) flesh (*sha chen*). This **mixture (1.11d)**, since it occurs with feces, and so forth, is unequaled, the alchemy of the six great savors.[362] The five nectars together with the "human fat" make six.

The text "all vajras," i.e., **universal vajra**,[363] is Heruka, who is the Lord of all deities. His **mark** is the skull bowl. As for **bearing (1.12b)** this **mark**, he grasps the skull bowl by "joining"[364] **the tips of the thumb and ring finger (1.12cd)** around it. Furthermore, it is like the ambrosia protected by the ocean that was produced, i.e., stirred up, with a "thick one" (*sbom po*), or thumb, that is Mt. Sumeru, in the ocean that rests on the earth, namely the ring finger, on the **tip** at which is the little finger.[365] By the *ha* of *oṁ ha ho hriḥ* there is color, *ho* overcomes the fault of taint, and *hriḥ* greatly augments.[366] The yogī who practices deity yoga and who repeats the mantras should always mix and **consume** it with the knowledge of the method of relying on the nectars. The method of consuming it is as was stated:

---

[362] Tsong Khapa marks the entire passage from Devagupta to here as a quote, but he is not directly quoting, but rather loosely paraphrasing Devagupta's commentary. See SS 73b.

[363] Tsong Khapa here glosses the translation of *sarvavajra-*, *rdo rje kun*, found in the SL and SM translations, as *thams cad rdo rje*, the usual translation of *viśvavajra*. The PM translation here reads *thams cad rdor*.

[364] Tsong Khapa gives the verb contained in all of the Tibetan translations, *sbyar bas*. I translated the verb contained in the Sanskrit text, *lehayed*, as "should cause to lick."

[365] Tsong Khapa here invokes the code words for the penis and vulva given in the VD, which are *sbom po*, "thick one," and *mtha' ltag*, "top end," respectively. See VD 92a.

[366] Tsong Khapa here closely paraphrases the comments given in Kambala and Devagupta's commentaries. However, there are important differences among these three sources. I have translated Tsong Khapa's text above. Kambala's comments read as follows: "*Oṁ ha hoḥ hrīḥ*: *Ha* removes defilement, the syllable *hoḥ* overcomes taint, and the syllable *hriḥ* is to some extent blazing fire, but is well known to refer to wind" (SN 6a: */oṁ ha hoḥ hrīḥ'o/ /de la/ /ha zhes bya bas snyigs ma 'phrog /yi ge hoḥ yis dri 'joms la/ /gang zhig me 'bar hrīḥ yig ste/ /pa ba ka zhes rab tu bsgrags/*). Devagupta reads: "Moreover, as for *oṁ ha hoḥ hrīḥ*, the syllable *ha* overcomes color, the syllable *hoḥ* removes taint, and the syllable *hrīḥ* kindles a blaze" (SS 73b: */de yang oṁ ha hoḥ hrīḥ zhes pa ste yi ge has ni kha dog 'joms/ yi ge hoḥs sa ni dri nyid sel/ /yi ge hrīḥs ni 'bar bar sbar/*). Note as well that Tsong Khapa's presentation of the mantra differs from Kambala's and Devagupta's.

> Taste the nectar prepared by the wise, but first make offerings to the guru, and after that offer to Heruka, since he has the vajra. Offering it to the seal, one will **consume** it, the fivefold ambrosia that is the essence of all preparations. One will be equal to Vajrasattva via this sort of preparation.[367]

Amidst the host (1.12a) means in the midst of the three wheels, or, amidst the yogīs and yoginīs who alone hold the yoga of Saṁvara. [The word] "set" is explained in another commentary as "practice."[368]

Additionally, if you explain in a way other than literally, **with camphor** could be explained as "together with the awakening spirit." That "awakening spirit" is great bliss, and "together with it" means its union with emptiness, which is the definitive meaning of the white and red elements. **Standing amidst the host** designates the coming together of the assembly of the six sense powers of the eye, and so forth, and in particular the assembly of the male and female organs. "Host" thus has the meaning of coming together. In general, it is the coming together of the six powers of art and wisdom, and in particular it is the coming together of the male and female organs.

What are those two? The "thick one" is the vajra of art, and the "top end" is the seal's lotus; as the lotus is [at] the lower part of the body, it is [at] the "end," and as it is at the "top" of that, it is high. This means that the two tips—known as the "lower nose" of the central channel, namely the tip of the father's secret place, and the tip of the mother's secret place, the "crow's face"—kiss. It says in the *Vajrapañjara* that "the vajra's place is excited by the application of the vajra finger,"[369] and

---

[367] This passage occurs in Kambala's commentary at SN 6a. Note that here I am translating *sbyor* as "preparation," since it seems to be referring to the ambrosia prepared via the procedure described above.

[368] Tsong Khapa here is commenting upon the verb used to translate the Sanskrit term *pratiṣṭhaṁ*, *bzhag*, contained in two of the three extant translations (PM and SM; SL reads *gzhag*). Jayabhadra glosses *pratiṣṭhaṁ* with *anuṣṭheyaṁ* (*nyams su len pa*), which means "to be observed, effect, put into practice," etc. See Sugiki 2001, 111, and CP 46a.

[369] Tsong Khapa quotes the *Vajrapañjara* as follows: */rdo rje sor mo'i rab sbyor gyis/ /rdo rje'i sa gzhi rab bskul te/*. It occurs in the Kangyur as follows: */rdo rje mdzub mo'i sbyor ba yis/ /rdo rje gnas ni rab bskul bya/* (DV 56a).

"after that, endowed with that bliss, Vajrasattva is inserted, and one begins the vajra worship through the union that binds the vajra."[370] The finger excites the place, i.e., the receptacle, of the vajra, the channel of the lotus. After the channel is awakened, one engages in equipose by means of the union that "binds the vajra," i.e., inseparably binds the two channels, as [the *Vajrapañjara*] stated. By doing this relying on the seal as previously explained, the two winds are injected into the central channel. This seems to be the sublime essence of worship of the clanswoman.

The *Vajraḍāka* states that "**standing amidst the host** occurs in all of the sense powers; the savor of all of those is alchemy (*rasāyana*)."[371] This indicates the alchemy that takes up the savor of all of them, the awakening spirits that arise from the union of the organs of the art and the wisdom. This sort of yogī should engage in that continually by means of the essential knowledge that applies to the restraint of the life force (*praṇāyāma*, *srog rtsol*) with seals (*mudrā*).[372]

Regarding the benefit of practicing in this manner, if one **consumes** —that is, if one relies upon—**it as if it were the beverage soma** that is like divine ambrosia as previously explained, then **success is always (1.13b)**, i.e., irreversibly, **attained**. Thus, by the alchemy of the "half-ten," i.e., **five**, "not-dead," **ambrosia**,[373] **(1.13c)**, this reliance on the seal consort (*phyag rgya ma*) of complete characteristics who has cultivated a lily-like receptacle of bliss will bring about the **origination**, i.e., achievement, **of all powers (v.13d)**, both [the mundane and ultimate].

---

370 See DV 56a.

371 See VD 91b.

372 Here the term *phyag rgya/mudrā* in the expression *phyag rgya srog rtsol* almost certainly refers to the blocking of channels with yogic seals that play an essential role in the practice.

373 Here Tsong Khapa is glossing the deliberately obscure translation *mi 'chi bcu phyed*, contained in all three extant translations (PM and SM; SL has the corrupt reading *mi 'chi bcad phyed*). This translates the thoroughly clear Sanskrit *pañcāmṛtaṁ*.

3.3.3. 2.1.1. 3.3. Meditation on the four seals

Although there are many different textual traditions with respect to [the text] **four [types of] worship (1.14a)** and so forth,[374] and also many different exegetical methods,[375] I will comment on the meditation on the four seals of Nāropā's system in accordance with my previous explanation in the context of the summary of the chapters.[376] Additionally, the four

[374] Verse fourteen appears to be corrupt in the surviving Sanskrit texts, and the Tibetan translations and commentaries preserve many variant readings. The verse reads, in my edition of the Sanskrit, *catuḥpūjā tathā yoginyo vīrāḥ/ dvayendriyasamāpatti-samāpannaṁ ca tattvadhṛk //*, although there are significant variants among the Sanskrit sources, as I document and discuss in my edition (see Gray 2012, 33–34, 52). The Tibetan translations add a fourth line, but they do not agree what this line should be. The PM and SM translations read: */mchod bzhi dpa' bo chen po ni/ /yid la 'dod pa byed pa ste/ /dbang gnyis snyoms par 'jug pa yi/ /snyoms par zhugs pa'ang de nyid 'dzin/*. These translations lack text corresponding to *yoginyo*, but seem to suggest *mahāvīra-* rather than *vīrāḥ*. The opposite is the case with the SL, which lacks an equivalent to *vīrāḥ*, but seems to suggest *māhayoginī-*. It reads as follows: */mchod bzhi rnal 'byor chen mo'i ni/ /ji ltar 'dod par bya ba ste/ /dbang gnyis snyoms par 'jug pa ni/ /dbang gnyis sgoms par 'jug pa ni/ /snyoms par 'jug pa de nyid 'dzin/*. Kambala and Vīravajra read *mchod bzhi de bzhin rnal 'byor ma* for the first line, matching the extant Sanskrit (SN 6a, SG 157a). Clearly, by the eleventh century there were alternate redactions of the text circulating. Büton (NS 222) seems to resolve the enigma. He initially cites the verse as *mchod pa bzhi dpa' bo chen po*, which would be the equivalent of **catuḥpūjā mahāvīra-*. He goes on to state, however, that there is an alternate Indian text that has *mchod bzhi de bzhin rnal 'byor rnams*, which is the exact equivalent to *catuḥ pūjā tathā yoginyo*. He also says that *dbang gnyis*, the "two organs" is the equivalent to *dpa' bo gnyis su med*, *vīrādvaya*, which occurs in some of the Sanskrit texts.

[375] Büton provides us with many of these interpretations. First, quoting Bhavabhaṭṭa, he defines the four offerings as the outer, secret, mind-made (*manomaya*, *yid kyi rang bzhin*), and direct (*sākṣāt*, *dngos po*). He then goes on to define them as the four creation stage processes, which he lists as (1) the "emptiness awakening," (2) the seed, (3) the form perfected, and (4) the placement of the syllables. Alternately, they can refer to four types of yoga, namely *yoga*, *anuyoga*, *atiyoga*, and *mahāyoga*. He goes on to say that the word *tathā* indicates the object of creation, the four skulls placed atop the vases, or the four essence yoginīs (NS 222). Vīravajra, in his SG commentary, gives a slightly different list of the four offerings, and then relates them to the four seals, as follows: "The four offerings are the outer, secret, mind-made, and the offering of reality. Moreover, they are also four seals, namely the great seal (*mahāmudrā*), symbolic seal (*samayamudrā*), reality seal (*dharmamudrā*), and actual seal (*karmamudrā*)" (SG 157a: */mchod bzhi ni phyi dang gsang ba dang yid kyi rang bzhin dang de kho na nyid kyi mchod pa'o/ /yang na phyag rgya chen po dang / dam thig dang / chos dang / las kyi phyag rgya bzhi ni mchod pa bzhi'o/*). For additional explanations of this text see Gray 2007, 161.

[376] See section 3.2.2 above.

seals—the actual, reality, great, and symbolic—are indicated in the *Saṁpuṭa* by the four syllables *e vaṁ ma yā*,[377] respectively, which correspond to [the text] **secret that is supreme**. The equivalent term of "worship" is *pūjā*,[378] etymologically explained as "that which fills the mind," since meditation on the four seals at the four occasions fills the mind with bliss.

One who has the pride of the "great **hero**," Heruka, meditates on the seal that is "desired in one's mind."[379] In regard to the **equipoise of the two organs** (**1.14b**) at that time from [the perspective] of the four [seals], in the context of the actual seal it is the physical equipoise of the two organs. In the context of the symbolic seal it is the equipoise of the two organs visualized by the mind. In the context of the reality seal it is the equipoise of the "spring" and the "drop" (*vasantatilaka*), which is merely a conventional designation for the equipoise of the two organs. In the context of the great seal, both great bliss and emptiness are equipoised, which is called the "equipoise of the two organs." Equipoised in that way, even the actual [seal] **holds reality** (**1.14d**) with natural bliss. Although this [interpretation] applies to the great seal only, natural bliss is drawn forth by meditating on [all] four, and when it is drawn forth, there is also the need to unite it with emptiness with respect to all four [seals]. This will be clearly shown below.

The **vajra** is the Divine Lord Heruka, and the one who **holds** that [vajra] (**1.14d**) is the yogi of this.[380] [Compared] to the bliss produced by him in the manner of the union of bliss and emptiness, in reliance on the four seals, **the** ordinary **happiness of gods and humans**, **if taken together**, **would not amount to** even **one sixteenth of that** (**1.15**), it is said. This is intended for those who have developed excellent ability in the perfection stage. This is the majority explanation, and it is the expla-

---

377 See Skorupski 1996, 240. Here I read Tsong Khapa's *ya* as *yā*, following the ST.

378 Here I read Tsong Khapa's *pū dza* as *pūjā*.

379 Tsong Khapa here comments on the line *yid la 'dod pa byed pa ste*, contained in the PM and SM translations but unattested elsewhere. The SL translation reads "as one desires" (*ji ltar 'dod par bya ba ste*).

380 Tsong Khapa here glosses the term *rdo rje 'dzin pa*, which is found at 1.15c in all three translations. Rather than *vajradhara*, the extant Sanskrit reads *vajrakaṇikayā*, which I translate as "adamantine particle."

nation of the scholar Mardo, and as it is in the exegetical tradition of Nāropā, it appears to be particularly good.

Although many Indian commentaries explain the four offerings in terms of the four seals, the application of the four [types of] worship to the creation stage in the *Vajraḍāka*[381] is similar to Kambala's application of the four vajras to the creation stage.[382] The remaining texts apply them to the perfection stage.

3.3.3. 2.1.1. 4. Showing the place for practicing the secret

In regard to what words refer to the places of secret practice, "thickets" are dense forests.[383] [The term] **groves (1.16a)** is not present in the translations of Lochen and Mal, but there is a substitute for that, "cave and mountain ravine."[384] **Riverbank (1.16b)** means the bank of a river.[385] **Primordially established (1.16c)** refers to previously produced **charnel grounds**.

---

381 The *Vajraḍāka* calls for worship having generated *bodhicitta* and having perfected one's form, which appears to refer to creation stage practice. See VD 92a.

382 The passage in Kambala's commentary Tsong Khapa here refers to a passage in Kambala's SN commentary that occurs as follows: "The meaning of [the line] **the four [types of] worship, thus the yoginīs** is that one should worship the four skull bowls placed atop the vases, and likewise the four yoginīs who are Ḍākinī, etc., and the Lord of the wheels their mandala, with the four vajras, which are, first of all, the awakening of emptiness; second, the concentration of the seed; third, the perfection of the reflected image; and, fourth, the arrangement of letters" (SN 6a: */mchod bzhi de bzhin rnal 'byor ma/ /zhes bya ba ni rdo rje bzhi yis te/ dang por stong pa'i byang chub po/ /gnyis pa la ni sa bon bsdu/ /gsum pa la ni gzugs brnyan rdzogs/ /bzhi pa la ni yi ge dgod/ /ces bya ba dang / bum pa'i steng gi thod pa bzhi rnams dang / de bzhin du mkha' 'gro ma la sogs pa'i rnal 'byor ma rnams te/ de dag gi dkyil 'khor gyi 'khor lo'i bdag nyid mchod par bya'o zhes bya ba'i don no/*).

383 Line 1.16a reads *girigahvarakuñjeṣu*, and the Tibetan text *tshang tshing*, "thicket," contained in all three extant translations, is a secondary meaning of *gahvara*. I translate it as "cave," the primary meaning of the term.

384 The Tibetan term *sman ljongs*, found in the PM and SM translations, is an accurate translation of the Sanskrit *kuñja*. Tsong Khapa lists two alternative translations, *phug*, "cave," which is found in the SL translation, and *ri sul*, "cave," "ravine," "valley," both of which are possible translations of *gahvara*.

385 Tsong Khapa glosses *ngogs* with its synonym, *'gram*.

If we explain symbolically, since the seal that is a woman (*bu med kyi phyag rgya*), on account of having the nature of great bliss, is unmoved by the view of the self contrived by the heretics, she is a **mountain (1.16a)**. Since inferior sentient beings are unable to penetrate [her] depths, hence "thickets." Since [her] cavity is filled with nectar, hence **cave**. Her **riverbank** is vast and profound due to the union of the art and the wisdom. **Primordially established** refers to the reality that abandons production and destruction, and she has the nature of that due to the conception of great bliss. Since she burns the awakening of the disciples and the solitary buddhas by the flames of great desire, hence **charnel ground**.[386] Since in this place, explained literally and symbolically, the essence is extracted, it is the "mandala"; *maṇḍa* is essence, and *lāti* means "to extract."[387] One should meditate on the inner and outer mandalas where the essence is extracted, which is drawn with lines, and so forth, or drawn mentally. In this way the first chapter is connected with the second, as it is relevant like the second to the contexts of the mandala meditations of the two stages.

3.3.3. 2.1.2. Showing the name of the chapter

In the *Concise* ***Śrī Herukābhidhāna Tantra***, [this] is the **descent of the mandala**, because in this **chapter** there is the entry into the mandala, namely the body mandala that applies to the previous four elements, etc., the vulva mandala [indicated] by the "resided in the vulva" [line] of the context, and also the mandala of the awakening spirit. As for [the term] **chapter**, *pariccheda*[388] or "discernment," there are both the discernment of the meaning of the subject matter and the discernment of the text of the discourse. As for it being **first**, it is the first of fifty-one.

---

386 This interpretation of the consort as the "place" for drawing the mandala is found in many of the Indian commentaries. See my translation of Kambala's and Indrabhūti's comments (Gray 2007, 162–163). See also Devagupta's comments (SS 64b–65a).

387 Tsong Khapa here cites a well-known alliterative etymology that connects the syllable *la* in *maṇḍala* with the verb √*lā*, to take, grasp, hold, protect, the third-person singular present indicative of which is *lāti*.

388 Actually, the Tibetan term *le'u*, here and elsewhere in this text, translates the Sanskrit term *paṭala*, and not *pariccheda*. Note that I read Tsong Khapa's *pa ri tshe da* as *pariccheda*.

This is the explanation of the first chapter from the *Illumination of the Hidden Meaning, A Detailed Exegesis of the Concise Saṁvara Tantra Called the "Cakrasaṁvara."*

CHAPTER 2

Chapter 2 Outline

3.3.3. 2.2. The detailed exegesis of the meaning by the remaining forty-nine [chapters]

The second part has two sections: (1) becoming a suitable vessel for meditating on the two stages, and so forth, and (2) detailed exegesis of the secret for suitable vessels.

3.3.3. 2.2.1. Becoming a suitable vessel for meditating on the two stages, and so forth

The first section has two subsections: (1) drawing the mandala, and its worship upon completion, and (2) bestowing consecration in the completed mandala.

3.3.3. 2.2.1. 1. Drawing the mandala, and its worship upon completion

The first section has three subsections: (1) the characteristics of the master, (2) how he performs the rite, and (3) showing the name of the chapter.

3.3.3. 2.2.1. 1.1. The characteristics of the master

It is said that the text in this root Tantra is scrambled in order to hinder those who have not served a guru from entering this Tantra on their own impulse. I will explain it, resolving this scrambling. Just what sort of characteristics should a master who performs the mandala rite possess? It is generally taught that the **master** of the mandala **has all of the good qualities** (**2.3d**) expounded in the Tantra. In particular, [he has] **knowledge** by means of great bliss of the **proper** meaning of reality, and [he] **understands** the adamantine expressions of **the Tantras** (**2.4a**), the *Saṁvara*, and so forth. Having well understood **the mantra of** the blood drinker, **Śrī Heruka** (**2.4b**), he is one who has completed the preliminary practice of mantra repetition. As it says in the *Saṁvarodaya*, "One who is solicited or desires merit for himself should first perform the preparatory service as a deity abiding in one's own wheel."[389] The number of repetitions is one hundred thousand for the mantra of either the principal or one's own deity, and ten thousand for those of the other [deities], as it says in the *Abhidhānottara*.[390]

Not angry (**1.4c**) means that he should not be disturbed when someone causes him temporary harm. **Pure** means that he is not besmirched by the root downfalls, and so forth, and is free of the fault of a perverse mind. Regarding **competent**, the *Saṁvarodaya* states that "he is perfected in consecration and offering cakes, understands the reality of fire sacrifice and mandalas, and is learned in all fields of knowledge."[391]

---

389 This passage occurs at SU 17.1c–2b, in Tsuda's edition: *evaṁ kaścid adhyeṣya svayaṁ vā puṇyakāmataḥ // pūrvasevā svacakrasthaṁ prathamaṁ devatātmakam /* (1974:119); */'di ltar 'ga' shig gsol 'debs pa'am/ /rang nyid bsod nams 'dod pa yis/ /dang por rang lha'i bdag nyid kyi/ /'khor lo la gnas sngon bsnyen bya/* (1974: 202).

390 The AU indicates that the number of repetitions should be one hundred thousand or ten thousand (AU 258b), but does not specify under what conditions one or the other should be made. Śūraṅgavajra comments that one should make ten thousand repetitions for the retinue and one hundred thousand for the principal deity, confirming Tsong Khapa's claim. See MV 145b.

391 This passage occurs at SU 17.3b–d, in Tsuda's edition: *pratiṣṭhābalipāragaḥ / homamaṇḍalatattvajñaḥ sarvavidyāsu kovidaḥ //* (1974:119); */rab gnas gtor ma'i pha rol son/ /sbyin sreg dkyil 'khor de nyid shes/ /rig pa'i gnas ni thams cad rig/* (1974:202). / The first line of this verse, not quoted by Tsong Khapa, includes as his qualifications the following: "He is steadfast and knows the profound Dharma" (*dhīro gambhīradharmajñaḥ, /brtan shing zab mo'i chos shes pa/*).

Understands yoga (1.4d) refers to one who knows the ritual applications such as pacifying, and so forth. **Perfected in knowledge** means that he has gone to the other side of knowledge. One who is endowed with characteristics such as these should perform the mandala rite.

3.3.3. 2.2.1. 1.2. How he performs the rite

The second part has four sections: (1) the rites of the ground, (2) the rites of drawing and completing the mandala, (3) making and placing the vases, and (4) the rite of mandala worship.

3.3.3. 2.2.1. 1.2.1. The rites of the ground

The first section has two subsections: (1) purifying the ground and (2) occupying the ground.

3.3.3. 2.2.1. 1.2.1. 1. Purifying the ground

The *Vajraḍāka* explains the purification done once one has examined and dug the ground.[392] As purification [prior to] digging the ground, etc., is not necessary, one should purify as stated there and in the *Saṁvarodaya*.[393] In regard to the drawing of the mandala, the **ground** on which the **mandala** is **made should be anointed (2.1b) there with cow dung** that is "suspended," i.e., **unfallen (2.1a)** onto the ground. As this also indicates the remaining cow products, it is anointed with [all of] the five cow products.[394]

Are these alone sufficient? One must also have the **ash** of a corpse burnt in a **charnel ground (2.1c)**. The mandala ground is anointed not only with that but also **with** the "half of ten not-deads," that is, **the five ambrosias (2.1d)**.[395] It is taught that the ground is purified with these.

---

392 See chapter 46 of the VD, which covers the preparation and drawing of the mandala.

393 This is covered in chapter 17 of the SU, which is edited and translated in Tsuda (1974).

394 These are dung, urine, milk, butter, and yogurt. The Sanskrit here more generally indicates "cow products," *gomayena*. The Tibetan translation, however, specifies cow dung, *lci ba*.

395 Here Tsong Khapa follows the more obscure translation for *pañcāmṛta-samanvitaṁ*, *mi 'chi bcu phyed bcas pa yis*, contained in the SL and SM translations. The PM translation gives the more straightforward translation *bdud rtsi lnga dang bcas pa yis*.

There, on the **anointed ground (2.2a)**, the drawing of **the mandala should be undertaken (2.2b)**. The basis for this endeavor, moreover, is **accomplished** in a **charnel ground (2.2c)**. If it is not in the charnel ground, then imagine that place as a charnel ground and undertake the mandala. The second line [of the second half verse] does not occur in Mal's translation.[396] Although it appears in the translations of both Lochen and Mardo, there appear to be differences among the Indian texts. Just because it does not appear in a single Indian text, one should not [state] that "it does occur in the Indian texts."[397]

3.3.3. 2.2.1. 1.2.1. 2. Occupying the ground

The system of Lama Mal claims that [the lines] from **hair...with skulls (2.5a)** up until **armored (2.9b)** [indicate] the occupying of the ground.[398] This is good, since it is in accordance with the two explanatory Tantras. The *Saṁvarodaya* says that the ground is occupied by the expulsion of the demons by the master, who invokes [himself] as the deity himself, holding the vajra and bell.[399] The *Vajraḍāka* also says that,

---

[396] Mal's translation contains three lines for this verse, just like the extant Sanskrit, and the third line, *dur khrod du ni kun spyod cing*, corresponds exactly to the Sanskrit, *śmaśānaṁ tu samācaret*. The PM and SM translations read two lines here, namely */gnas de ru ni bsgoms pa yis/ /dur khrod du ni kun tu brtag* (PM) and */dur khrod du ni kun spyod cing / /gnas de ru ni bsam byas nas/* (SM). Tsong Khapa is referring to the line *gnas de ru ni bsam byas nas*, the second in the SM translation.

[397] Tsong Khapa here refers to Büton's observation that the line *gnas de ru ni bsgom pa yi* does not occur in the Indian texts and commentaries (NS 233). Büton is correct in stating that this line is not attested in any of the extant Indian texts or translations thereof, but naturally Tsong Khapa is also correct in asserting that absence of evidence is not evidence of absence. That is, it is certainly possible that the PM and SM translations are based upon a now lost alternate Sanskrit redaction.

[398] Indeed, Sachen comments on these verses in his subsection "Occupying the Ground," PG 302.1–4.

[399] SU ch. 17 reads as follows: "The master who has the nature of the deity, with the forms of all Buddhas, the hero who holds the vajra and the bell, should be supplicated together with the ḍākinīs. Brandishing the vajra and ringing the bell, the wise one should expel the evil ones, the gods, titans, and secret ones" (Tsuda 1974, 120: */ devatātmaka ācāryaḥ sarvabuddhātmamūrtibhiḥ / vajraghaṇṭādharo vīro adhyeṣyo ḍākinīsaha // vajram ullālayan dhīmān ghaṇṭāvādanatatparaḥ / utsādayet praduṣṭaughān sadevāsuraguhyakān //*; p. 203: */slob dpon sangs rgyas kun rang bzhin/ /lha yi sku yi bdag nyid can/ /dpa' bo rdo rje dril 'chang ba/ /mkha' 'gro bcas la gsol ba gdab/ /blo ldan rdo rje gsor byed cing*

(cont'd)

in the context of the ground rites, having visualized oneself as a great fierce deity, after driving in the stakes, one should construct the vajra foundation, the vajra wall, and the net of arrows. These seem to be the meaning of the text of the root Tantra.[400]

Regarding the apparel that the master should have previously donned, his "crown,"[401] i.e., his crest of dreadlocks that grows upon his head, is **marked with** a row of **skulls (2.5a)** on which are drawn the forms of the five buddha clans. All of **his limbs are smeared with** the **ash (2.5b)** of burnt corpses and with the five ambrosias, and **his body** should be **decorated with (2.5c)** the insignia of earrings, necklaces, and so forth.[402] Although some translations have "**his body is decorated with ornaments"** (*gug skyed*), it is better translated as "insignia" (*phyag rgya*).[403]

Lochen translated the **bone garland** [line] **(2.5d)** as [his] "**bone garland has bone**."[404] It is said that this means that he is ornamented by

---

/ /dril bu 'khrol bar brtson pa yis/ /lha dang lha min gsang ba dang / /rab tu gdug pa'i bgegs tshogs bskrad/).

400 See VD 98a.

401 Tsong Khapa is glossing the Tibetan term *spyi bor*, "on the crown," which is an inaccurate translation of the Sanskrit *mūrdhaja*, literally "that which grows on the head," i.e., the hair. Although the translation is faulty, Tsong Khapa's comment is correct.

402 Here Tsong Khapa is glossing the SM translation, which reads */phyag rgya dag gis lus brgyan cing /*.

403 The term *phyag rgya/mudrā* here means "insignia," a derivative of its root meaning as seal. This is a plausible translation, given the *pañcamudrā*, "five insignia," that a Cakra-saṁvara yogī must pledge to wear, such as the earring, necklace, and so forth, as indicated in chapter 27. The only problem is the fact that the Sanskrit here reads not *mudrā* but *mātra*, "ornament," so *mudrā* qua insignia is probably not appropriate. However, the term *phyag rgya* can also designate a bone ornament, which appears to be what is intended here. This appears to be the import of the rather unusual term found in the other translations, *gug skyed* (PM) and *gug bskyed* (SL). Sachen explains *gug skyed* as follows: "His body is ornamented with the *gug skyed*, that is, with the six bone ornaments that have the mantras *namahi*, etc." (PG 302.2). This implies a set of six bone ornaments inscribed with the six armor mantras of Śrī Heruka. These may be the six insignia mentioned by Dārika in his *Śrīcakrasaṁvarastotra Sarvārthasiddhiviśuddhacūḍāmaṇi*, in which Heruka is described as "beautified by the six insignia of the six perfections" (fol. 193a: *pha rol phyin drug phyag rgya drug gis mdzes*).

404 The "Lochen" translation quoted by Tsong Khapa as *rus 'phreng rus par yang dag gnas* is almost identical to the SL translation, which reads *rus phreng rus pas yang dag*

(cont'd)

bone ornaments; evidently it refers to a sacred thread of bone. His "crown" is **marked** by a disk made from a "single piece" of skull (**2.6a**).[405] "**Wears a bone garland**" (**2.6b**) refers to a necklace that is a garland of fifty heads.

With a khatvanga staff placed (**1.6c**) in the crook of his left arm, the master himself assumes the appearance of the blood drinker **Śrī Heruka** (**2.6d**) in the middle of the mandala. Having done that, **think of Śrī Heruka** (**2.7a**) refers to his *sadhāna* meditation. Bhavyakīrti explains that **taking oneself to be Heruka** (**2.6d**) refers to the creation of the commitment hero, and "thinking of him" is thinking of the gnosis hero.[406]

---

ldan, both of which closely approximate the Sanskrit, *asthimālāsaṁsthitaś ca*, provided that one ignores the superfluous *rus par*. The PM and SM translations are quite different, reading "[He] is decorated with a bone ornament, and so forth" (PM: *rus pa'i phreng la sogs pas brgyan*; SM: *rus pa'i phreng la tsogs pas brgyan*).

[405] This line, *ekakhaṇḍīkṛtamūrdhajaḥ*, is particularly challenging. Once again the Tibetan translations read *spyi bor*, "crown," rather than hair. The term for hair, *mūrdhajaḥ*, is modified by *ekakhaṇḍīkṛta*, literally "formed into a single piece." Bhavabhaṭṭa interprets this as a reference to the paradigmatic hairstyle of a *yogī*, in which his dreadlocks are formed into a crest on the top of the head. He glosses this line as "crest made of hair," *keśakṛtamukuṭa* (Pandey 2002, 30). As this made excellent sense, I translated the line as "his hair is formed into one plait." However, there is another interpretation advanced by the majority of commentators, including Tsong Khapa. This is the Indian commentarial tradition, which interprets it as a disk made from a seamless skull. Bhavyakīrti explains: "Regarding 'his head ornamented with a seamless [skull],' it means that a human skull with a universal vajra is set on his head" (BC 12b–13a: */dum gcig spyi bor brgyan pa dang / zhes bya ba ni spyi bo mi'i thod pa la sna tshogs rdo rje yod 'jog pa'o/*). This is also cited by Büton (NS 234). Laṅka Jayabhadra provides an even clearer explanation, writing: "Regarding **his hair** 'has a one-piece,' it is said that this refers to a skull garland on the forehead, and it is also said that a skull that is seamless is the very best" (Sugiki 2001, 112: *ekakhaṇḍakṛtamūrdhaja ity anena lalāṭopari kapālamāloktā/ anenaivaikakhaṇḍaṁ padmabhājanam uttamam uktam/*; CP 46b: */dum cig spyi bor brgyan pa dang / /zhes bya ba 'dis thod pa'i phreng ba yod par ston to/ /'di nyid kyis ni dum bu gcig pa'i thod pa mchog nyid du bshad do/*).

[406] Tsong Khapa here loosely paraphrases Bhavyakīrti's explanation of these two lines in his BC commentary, which occurs as follows: "**Taking oneself to be Heruka** means, according to the oral instructions, that one undertakes the yoga of Śrī Heruka. After that, **think of Śrī Heruka** means that one should invite the gnosis wheel (*jñānacakra*)" (BC 13a: */bdag nyid śrī he ru kar byas nas zhes bya ba ni man ngag ji lta bas dpal he ru ka'i rnal 'byor du byas pa'o/ /de 'og tu ni/ dpal ldan he ru ka dran bya/ /zhes bya ba ni ye shes kyi 'khor lo spyan drang bar bya'o/*)

The meditation on Heruka is shown to be a body mandala meditation by the text **place the wheel (2.7b)** of the thirty-seven goddesses in the points of the body mandala that are illustrated by the [text] "his heart."[407] **Having thus armored oneself (2.7c)** with the visualization of the inner and outer mandalas, at the end of the meditation the demons will be vanquished, and so forth. Once demons that were previously there are vanquished, one should **place** the vajra **fences** in the cardinal and ordinal **directions (2.7d)** so that they will not re-enter later. Not only in the directions, but also **below** the ground, **place weapons (2.8b)** reaching down to the golden earth.[408] The universal vajra should serve as the foundation.

The solo Mardo translation reads "the essence of the wheel is like a weapon." The translation of the two translators together reads "the wheels are garlands of swords." "Having placed the essence of the wheel" in Lochen's translation should be taken as occurs above.[409] This [line] should be taken to mean: "Having placed the essence of the wheel" (**2.8c**) that protects below and in the directions, **make a net of arrows above (2.8d)**."

Having produced the net of arrows above, then make the vajra **enclosure** that is **floating (2.9a)**, i.e., above, "one has the armor" that

[407] Tsong Khapa here takes "wheel" (*'khor lo*) to be the object of the verb to place (*dgod*) and take the locus of this placement to be his heart (*'di'i snying ga*). This analysis is supported by the Tibetan translation, e.g., *'khor lo 'di yi snying gar dgod* (SM). However, the Sanskrit is quite different, reading *cakrasya hṛdaye nyaset*, the object of which is the *herukaṁ* of the preceding line. I thus read "Place [him] in the center of the wheel."

[408] This is the level of the earth element in the stacked-up elements model of the cosmos. It is the disc of golden earth that arose from the churning of the mass of waters by wind. See Jamgön Kongtrul 1995, 109, and Sadakata 1997, 25–26.

[409] There are numerous variant readings for this line. The reading that Tsong Khapa reports as belonging to the solo Mardo translation, *'khor lo'i bdag nyid mtshon cha mnyam*, occurs in the Kumbum redaction of the SM translation. The translation that he attributes to Rinchen Zangpo's original translation, *'khor lo'i bdag nyid bkod nas ni*, is preserved in the Dharamsala redaction of the SM tradition. Moreover, the version he attributes to the dual revised translation, *'khor lo mtshon cha'i 'phreng ba dag*, occurs as we would expect in the canonical PM revised translation. Another reading, unmentioned by Tsong Khapa, is that preserved in the SL revised translation, *'khor gnas pa yi bdag nyid mnyam*.

cannot be harmed by demons.[410] A certain commentary explains that one should produce the enclosure above after inviting the gnosis hero from above, and after it is absorbed into the commitment hero.[411] But as the production of the enclosure does not occur before this, it is not acceptable.[412] When you are **thus armed** (**2.9c**) in the manner previously explained, as one is **unbreakable** (**2.9d**), i.e., indestructible, **even by the** Lord of the **Thirty-three** deities, then what need is there to speak of the other demons? This shows the greatness of this divine yoga and protective wheel.

3.3.3. 2.2.1. 1.2.2. The rites of drawing and completing the mandala

The second part has two sections: (1) drawing the mandala and (2) completing the mandala.

3.3.3. 2.2.1. 1.2.2. 1. Drawing the mandala

It is taught in brief that **well-protecting oneself thus** (**2.10a**) as previously explained, and being **ornamented with the mudrā** of Vajravārāhī, **and with** the root **mantra** (**2.10b**), etc., one should **draw the terrifying**, i.e., fierce, **mandala** (**2.10c**) **which bestows** all the **power**s (**2.10d**).

The statement in the root Tantra that one first draws by color and then by marking string is jumbled. The explanatory Tantra resolves the confusion, explaining in accordance with the explanation on drawing.

---

[410] Tsong Khapa here comments upon a portion of line 2.9b, *go char 'gyur*, found in all three translations. The Sanskrit preserves an alternate reading, *kṛtvātmānaṁ susamāhitaḥ*, "one is well positioned."

[411] It appears that Tsong Khapa is referring to Jayabhadra's comments, which read: "Again, regarding **one**, after the entry of the gnosis hero, and its placement inside the palace, then the **enclosure**, etc., are set up" (Sugiki 2001, 112: *punar ātmānam iti jñānasattvapraveśottarakālaṁ kūṭāgāram abhyantarīkṛtya pañjarādikam upakalpayed iti bhāvaḥ*; CP 47a: */yang bdag nyid ces bya ba ni ye shes sems dpa' zhugs pa'i 'og tu gzhal yas khang nang du bzhag la dra ba la sogs pa nye bar bstan par bya'o zhes bya bar dgongs so/*).

[412] Tsong Khapa's comments here do not seem to make sense. If he holds that production of the enclosure does not occur prior to the entry of the gnosis hero, then it seems that he is in agreement with this point of view.

This part has two sections: (1) drawing with marking string and (2) drawing with color.

3.3.3. 2.2.1. 1.2.2. 1.1. Drawing with marking string

Then, after the ground rites, one marks the lines. The thread is "mindless," meaning a **corpse thread (2.11a)**.[413] That is explained as being string that was carried to the charnel ground together with a human corpse, and that has not fallen to the ground, or string made of the sinew of a human corpse. **Or** indicates that if there is none of that, then, with thread **colored with the great blood (2.11b)**, i.e., human blood, together with the five ambrosias, **lay out the terrifying mandala (2.11c)** of Śrī **Heruka's supreme mansion (2.11d)**. There are also explanations that omit [the term] "or." Among the [strings], there is the action line, which is a moistened string. The gnosis line is stated in the two explanatory Tantras as being the five-colored string of twenty-five [threads].[414]

In regard to the size of the mandala, the root line can be of **a single cubit, four, or eight (2.12a)**. It also says in the *Saṁvarodaya*, "Starting from half a cubit, and so forth, up to as much as a hundred cubits."[415] [The size is thus] uncertain, being limited by the extent of the disciple's wealth, etc. In regard to the size of that root line, the mandala should be

---

413 Tsong Khapa here glosses *sems med*, an obscure translation of *mṛtaka*, "corpse."

414 Tsong Khapa here writes *ye thig* as an abbreviation of *ye shes thig skud*, which is described in the SU 17.19, as consisting of 25 threads twisted together, representing the five gnoses. The first half of verse 20 states that it should be anointed with the five ambrosias while one recites the syllable *hūṁ*, thus linking the five gnoses, nectars, and colors. The verses occur in Tsuda's edition as follows: *pañcajñānānvitaṁ sūtraṁ pañca-viṁśatibheditam / valayet sūtram anyonyaṁ sarvadharmasvabhāvataḥ // hūṁkāroccāra-yed yogī pañcāmṛtena lepitam /* (1974, 121); */srad bu ye shes lnga ldan shing/ /nyi shu rtsa lngar rnam dbye bas/ /chos kun ngo bo nyid kyis ni/ /sras bu phang tshun bsgril bar bya/ /sgrub pos yi ge hūṁ brjod de/ /bdud rtsi lngas ni byug par bya/* (1974, 204). Pema Losang Chögyen (1953–1996) a monk from Namgyal monastery trained in mandala construction, and a Ph.D. candidate at Columbia University prior to his untimely death, explained to me that this line is only visualized; the action line is the actual marking line used to lay out the mandala. The gnosis line is visualized as a multicolored line that enters the mark just as it is being made.

415 This text occurs at SU 17.23. It occurs as follows in Tsuda's edition: *ardhahastādi-kaṁ samārabhya śatahastaṁ tu yāvat /* (1974, 121); */khru phyed la sogs nas brtsams nas/ /ji srid khru ni brgya yi bar/* (1974, 204).

bedecked with four doors, four corners, i.e., should be square, **and four arches (2.12b–d)**.

[The term] **all around (2.12b)** means that they should be equidistant from the root line.[416] The adept drawing the mandala "measures" or examines the length of the line thread as "twice" that of [the radius of] the mandala (**v.13.a**).[417] It says in the *Saṁvarodaya* that "the length is twice that of the mandala, and the door is one twentieth [as long as that]."[418] The *Vajramālā* explains that the marking string is twice [the distance] from root line to root line with respect to the sixty-fourth small measure, and twice the distance from parapet to parapet with respect to the ninety-sixth smaller portion.[419] I have already explained at length the

---

416 Tsong Khapa is being a bit laconic here, no doubt because he assumed his readers would be familiar with the basics of mandala construction. He is commenting on the term *kun nas*, which translates *samantataḥ*, from lines 2.12b–d: *caturasraṁ tu samantataḥ / caturdvārasamākīrṇaṁ catustoraṇabhūṣitam //* "[with] four corners all around, bedecked with four doors, adorned with four arches." The root lines are the two lines that bisect the mandala at right angles. Büton is a little clearer in writing: "The four sides that join at the end of the two root lines all around," meaning that it is at the sides of the square where the two root lines begin and end (NS 238: *kun nas rtsa thig gnyis kyi rtse mo phrad pa'i zur bzhi pa*).

417 Tsong Khapa here glosses the text *nyis 'gyur rnam par spyad*, which translates *vicared dviguṇaṁ*. I translate this as "should double," but Tsong Khapa glosses each word individually.

418 This passage corresponds to SU 17.20cd, which Tsuda mysteriously omits from his translation, but fortunately not from his edition, where it occurs as follows: *cakraṁ dviguṇato dīrghaṁ dvāraviṁśatibhāgikam //* (1974, 121); */ dkyus su 'khor lo'i nyis 'gyur la // sbom su sgo yi nyi shu cha /* (p. 204). Tsong Khapa quotes a somewhat less clear version of the text as follows: */ ring ba 'khor lo'i nyis 'gyur te // sgo yi nyi shu cha dag go /*.

419 Chapter 54 of the *Vajramālā* deals with the drawing of the mandala, and fols. 254 and 255 therein deal with the threads, but they do not really clarify Tsong Khapa's esoteric description here, which deals with the grid work of lines laid down as the first step in the drawing of the mandala. This grid is laid down in a precise way, in which the position and length of smaller lines that represent features of the mandala are calculated as fractions of the original root line. Geshe Yama Tseden of Namgyal monastery in Dharamsala, India, explained to me that the "root line," *rtsa thig*, is divided into four "greater measures," *cha chen*, which in turn divide into twelve "smaller portions," *cha chung*. These are used to measure the details within the mandala, such as the size of the doors, which together make up the innermost square of the mandala, or the balconies (*mda' yab*), which make up the outermost ring of the mandala excluding the arches (*toraṇa*, *rta babs*). See appendix I in George 1974, 86–87, which consists of a useful diagram of the mandala, with its major parts identified. As before, Büton is clearer,

(cont'd)

arrangement of these in my commentary on Lūipa's *sādhana*.[420] The statement in Kambala's commentary that "the intelligent one should lay out the mandala by the process of increasing the proportion" is explained in another text.[421]

The **ḍākinīs** are the heroes and heroines. The **network** is the host of them. Cakra**saṁvara** is the principal deity.[422] As for the statement about **worship**ping them (**2.13b**), although it is explained in connection to what follows, it has the meaning of worshipping the mandala of the preparatory deity rite, after having made the action lines. Thus, there is no need to order the disorder of the text. Since I have clearly explained elsewhere the means of knowing them, I will not elaborate here. Thus, the root Tantra speaks of the preliminary rites for both the deities and the vases. As the remaining preparations are discussed in the explanatory Tantra, the gap is filled.

3.3.3. 2.2.1. 1.2.2. 1.2. Drawing with color

With what sort of colors is the mandala drawn? It should be made with the five types of pigments that occur in the charnel ground. [Dark]

---

saying that that the line thread is twice the length of the root line, so that if one needs a line thread eight cubits long for a mandala four cubits in size, this makes sense, given the fact that the lines are placed on the ground and snapped to leave a mark (NS 238: *dkyil 'khor ni rtsa thig nas rtsa thig gi bar yin la/ de'i nyis 'gyur gyi thig skud ring thung ste / dkyil 'khor khru bzhi pa la thig skud brgyad pa la sogs pa'o/*). Bhavabhaṭṭa also is to the point in commenting, "Regarding 'double measure,' [one cubit is measured as] two cubits, and eight cubits as sixteen: this is a characteristic of the string, which should be made twice [as long] as the circumference [of the mandala]" (Pandey 2002, 32: *vicared dviguṇam iti dvihastam aṣṭahastaṁ ṣoḍaśahastaṁ ceti / sūtrasya viśeṣaṇam idam / cakradviguṇatvaṁ sūtrasyeti pratipāditam /*; CV 163b: */nyis 'gyur rnams dpyad cing zhes pa ni/ khru gnyis dang ni khru brgyad dang / /khru ni bcu drug ces pa ni/ thig skud 'di yi khyad par ro/ /'khor lo nyis 'gyur thig skud bya'o/*).

420 This text is entitled *bcom ldan 'das dpal 'khor lo bde mchog gi mngon par rtogs pa'i rgya cher bshad pa 'dod pa 'jo ba*, in vol. ta of the Tashi Lhunpo print of his *gsung-'bum*. See above, p. 46n95.

421 This text reads as follows in the Tengyur: */cha 'phen pa yi rim nyid kyis/ /blo bzang dkyil 'khor thig gdab bya/* (SN D 8a, Q p. 177.1). Tsong Khapa's text has the correct reading *cha 'phel*, rather than the incorrect *cha 'phen*.

422 Tsong Khapa comments here on the compound *ḍākinījālasamvaraṁ*, which I translate here as "the binding of the ḍākinīs' network."

blue pigment is made from the charcoal powder of burnt corpses. Red pigment is made with the bricks of the charnel ground. White pigment is made from human bone powder. Yellow pigment is made from turmeric mixed with human bone powder. Green pigment is human bone powder together with leaf powder. One possessed of these should draw an excellent mandala. It also says in the *Saṁvarodaya* that [it is made] "with powder made of the five types of jewels, or with rice, and so forth."[423] Therefore, the colors that are made from the charnel ground substances are intended for a few particular mandalas.

The colored paints are consecrated, and with those pigments one should **place**, that is, draw, **in the middle of that a** multicolored **lotus (2.13c)** mandala **with a center and** eight **petals**, "blazing" **(2.13d)** with the aspect of blazing light rays.[424] **Endowed with filaments (2.13e)** refers to both the anthers and the filaments. The former are in the center [of the lotus]. The latter should be between the center and the petals, encircled by orange lines. The body, speech, and mind wheels should also be drawn as illustrated by that. This I have exhaustively explained elsewhere.[425]

In regard to the method of drawing the inhabitant mandala upon the thus drawn habitat mandala, the *Abhidhānottara* describes the syllable —i.e., the seed syllable—of each deity, their hand implements, the gesture that each deity forms with the hand, the image of each deity, and the placement of bunches of flowers.[426] It is also said that [the text] **place in the center the hero (2.14a)**, and so forth, indicates the drawing of the deities' forms in the mandala. Since it is also clear that [this text] refers to the mental placement of the commitment hero in the mandala, in accordance with the text **who makes the tremendous noise of very loud**

---

[423] This text occurs at SU 17.30 in Tsuda's edition as follows: *pañcaratnamayaiś cūrṇair atha vā taṇḍulādibhiḥ* / (1974, 122); */rin chen lnga yi phye ma'am/ /yang na 'bras la sogs pa ste/* (1974, 205).

[424] The Tibetan translation here reads *lte ba 'bar dang bcas*, translating the compound *karṇikojjvalam*, which I translate as "fully opened center." Tsong Khapa appears to take *lte ba* and *'bar* as separate terms, and comments accordingly.

[425] In his *sngags rim chen mo*.

[426] These additional details are provided in the much more elaborate description of the mandala in AU ch. 14, which is edited and translated in Kalff 1979.

laughter (2.14d), in general it is suitable to explain it in both ways, but [here we are] primarily [concerned with] the construction of the mandala.[427]

3.3.3. 2.2.1. 1.2.2. 2. Completing the mandala

Then, once one has drawn suitably the characteristics of the habitat and inhabitant mandalas, one simultaneously creates the habitat and the inhabitants in order to complete the mandala, in accordance with the system of Lūipa, which is the intention of the *Saṁcāra* and the *Saṁvarodaya*. This accords with what is said in the fifty-first chapter, ending with the creation from the wind [sphere] up until Mt. Sumeru and the lotus.[428] After creating the habitat and inhabitants from the manifest awakening of the vowels and consonants, and so forth, visualize the palace. The deities are visualized as explained. If one first creates the habitat and afterwards creates the inhabitants as in the *Abhidhānottara*, they are created as before up to Mt. Sumeru, each from his or her own seed syllable. After the creation of the palace from Vairocana, the deities should be created from the manifest awakening in the middle of the central lotus.

Furthermore, the **hero** Heruka who should be **placed in the center of the lotus (2.14a) is the terror of** even **Mahābhairava (2.14b)**, i.e., Īśvara, who is famed as a great power in the world. He has great **brightness and is brilliant (2.14c)**. He **laughs**, pervading space with its **tremendous noise (2.14d)**, and he **wears a rosary** of five dried **skulls** on each head **(2.15a)**. He is **divine**[429] because he is the essence of great bliss. Each of his **four faces** has **three eyes (2.15b)**. He is **covered with** a moist white **elephant hide (2.15c)** on his back, with its head and hair

---

[427] That is, this verse can be interpreted as referring to either the physical construction of the mandala or its mental visualization.

[428] This is in reference to 51.14cd, "On a stalk on the summit of the mountain are a universal lotus and the vowels and consonants" (*girimastakakiñjalke viśvapadmālikālyaṁ ca*; PM: */ri steng sna tshogs padma yi/ /lte bar ā li kā li skyes/*).

[429] My translation here, "divine," follows the Sanskrit, *divyaṁ*. Tsong Khapa, however, follows the Tibetan translation, *bzang po*, which can translate *divya* in its sense of "lovely," "agreeable." In this context, however, *bzang po* arguably is not a very good translation, given Heruka's fiece demeanor.

showing. His **excellent eyebrows** are **split**,[430] i.e., separated, all the way up to the **vajra (2.15d)** garland on his forehead.[431] **He wields a khatvanga staff** and a human skull in his left **hand (2.16a)**.[432] His neck **is ornamented with a garland of half a hundred (2.16b)**, i.e., fifty, wet human heads strung with wet intestines.

---

430 Here I give my translation of the Sanskrit, *sambhinna*. Tsong Khapa reads *'byes*, a reading that is also found in the Kumbum print of the SM translation. The PM and SL translations, and the Dharamsala SM print, read *dbyes*.

431 This explanation is ultimately drawn from Jayabhadra's commentary, likely by way of Büton's, which quotes it at length. Büton's comments occur as follows: "The equivalent term of *'byes* is *bhinna*, which can be applied to 'destroy' (*bcom*), so his eyebrows that are **split by a vajra**—i.e., are the variety that seem to be shattered as if by a vajra—are **excellent**, i.e., uniform. The eyebrows in the middle and the eyes below form a three-pronged vajra. Furthermore, his eyebrows are split or cleft all the way up to the vajra garland on his forehead. Someone claimed that "regarding 'split by a vajra,' it indicates the vajra and bell, namely, that the beautiful eyebrows that are completely split by a vajra are the eyebrows of the fortunate one" (NS 240: */'byes pa'i skad dod bhinna ni bcom pa la 'jug pas/ rdo rje lta bus sna tshogs yang dag par bcom pas na rdo rje 'byes pa'i smin ma bzang zhing mnyam pa nyid kyi dbus lte ba smin ma dang mig dag gi 'og tu rdo rje rtse gsum pa nyid du grub pa'o/ /yang na dpral ba'i rdo rje phreng ba'i mthar thug pa'i bar du smin ma 'byes shing gyes pa'o/ /kha cig/ rdo rje dang dril bu ste/ do rje nyid kyis yang dag par 'byes shing brgyan pa/ smin ma bzang po ni skal pa dang ldan pa'i smin ma'o zhes bzhed do/*). The text up until "someone," *kha cig*, is drawn from Jayabhadra's commentary, which reads as follows: "Regarding **excellent eyebrows split by a vajra**, as the eyebrows are uniform they are excellent eyebrows. The compound [refers to him] whose eyebrows are truly split as if by a vajra. Furthermore, it means that his eyebrows are split all the way up to the vajra garland on his forehead" (Sugiki 2001, 112–113: *vajrasaṁbhinnasabhruvam iti, samāne bhruvau sabruvau, vajravat samyak bhinne sabhruvau yasyeti samāsaḥ / athavā lalāṭopari vajramālāparyantaṁ bhinnaṁ sabhruvaṁ ity arthaḥ //*; CP 47b: */smin ma bzang po rdo rje dbyes/ zhes bya ba la/ smin ma bzang zhing mnyam pa ni smin ma bzang po ste/ rdo rje ltar dbyes pa gang la mnga' ba de la skad ces bya'o zhes bya bar sbyar ro/ /yang na dpral ba'i rdo rje phreng ba'i mthar thug pa'i bar du smin ma 'byes shing gyes pa mnga' ba zhes bya ba'i don to/*).

432 Tsong Khapa here is following the standard translation (PM: *phyag na kha ṭvāṁ mi thod bsnams*, SM: *phyag na kha ṭvaṁ mi thod bsnams*; the Sanskrit of this line, *khaṭvāṅgakṛtahastaṁ tu*, lacks anything corresponding to *mi thod*, as does the SL translation (*phyag na kha traṁ kha bsnams shing*). Regarding this discrepancy, Büton, who evidently had access to a Sanskrit manuscript (and could read it!), commented that "since there is no Sanskrit equivalent to 'human skull,' and as the commentaries do not elucidate it, it should be understood to be a nonliteral translation" (NS 240–241: */mi thod ces pa skad dod la med cing 'grel pa rnams kyis kyang ma bkral bas don 'gyur du shes par bya'o/*).

The **goddess who stands before him** (**2.16c**), i.e., Heruka, in the mode of being embraced **is Vajravārāhī**, who is **truly awesome** (**2.16d**) since she menaces the malicious and stands **facing Śrī Heruka** (**2.17a**). She has **three eyes and a fierce form** (**2.17b**). She holds with her left hand a **skull bowl filled** (**v.17.c**) **with** the **entrails** (*antra*) and blood of demons. **Blood** (*rudhira*) **trickles from her mouth** (**2.17d**). With her right hand **she threatens the gods, titans, and humans** in **all of the quarters** (**2.18ab**).

The principal couple's implements are not clearly stated. Since the import of the root Tantra is explained in many different ways by the explanatory Tantras, the complete meaning of the root Tantra is not found in any single [text]. However, in regard to the practice of the ritual procedures of Lūipa, Kāṇha, Ghaṇṭapā, and so forth, I will compare their systems and explain their significance when the opportunity arises. For example, either Lūipa's explanation that Vārāhī holds a vajra in her right hand or Ghaṇṭapā's explanation that she holds a chopper may be the import of the root Tantra. And as Heruka's remaining implements are also explained in many different ways in the explanatory Tantras, I will explain them when the occasion arises. But since these matters must be known from the *sādhana*s of the respective traditions, I will not explain them here. The remaining [details] should also be known in this way.

The **twenty-four ḍākinīs**, Pracaṇḍā, and so forth, **arising from Vajravārāhī's clan** (**2.18cd**)[433] **should be worshipped**, visualizing them **in the directions**, counterclockwise starting from the east, **and in the quarters**, clockwise from the southeast. **Amidst the wheels** (**2.19ab**) means within the palace or within the spokes of the wheel. Are there only the twenty-four heroines? In the same way that one must visualize and worship the twenty-four heroines, one should visualize and **worship the** twenty-four **heroes as well here** in the palace. **Positioned in the wheel** (**2.19cd**) means being placed amidst the spokes of the wheel. **If the adept desires power, he should worship the hero** who is **nondual**

433 Sachen has an interesting comment on this line, which is not repeated by Büton or Tsong Khapa. He wrote that "The ḍākinīs are the twenty-four ḍākinīs of the three wheels. What is their clan? Vārāhī is the openness of quiescence (*śamatha*), and those who arise from that are of Vārāhī's clan" (PG 303.4: */mkha' 'gro ma ni nyi shu bzhi ni 'khor lo gsum gyi mkha' 'gro ma rnams yin la/ de rnams gang gi rigs yin zhe na/ phag mo ni zhi gnas stong pa yin la/ de las byung bas phag mo'i rigs so/*).

(**2.20ab**) with the heroine, that is, with the principal goddess, but not separate [from her].

The previous gurus claim that the two lines concerning the underworld mothers show the placement of the twelve mothers, which is good.[434] One should place, that is, visualize from amongst **all** twelve **mothers**, the four [essence yoginīs] such as Ḍākinī **in the** four **directions** at the center of the lotus, the four [gatekeepers] such as Kākāsyā at the gates in the four directions, and the four [quarter guardians] such as Yamadāhī[435] in the four **quarters** (**2.27cd**). Likewise, the four skull bowls or four vases with skull bowls are placed in the four quarters on the petals of the lotus. This is the creation of the commitment heroes. Concerning the deities of the retinue, there is also no statement with any degree of clarity in one place in the root Tantra, and it seems that the deities' body colors, numbers, implements, and so forth, are explained in many different ways in the explanatory Tantras. In order to actually put into practice now [the traditions of] Lūipa, Ghaṇṭapā, and so forth, it is necessary to apply this information to that included in each of their *sādhana*s, but I will not discuss that here. Instead I am happy to explain connecting the explanatory Tantras to the general lack of clear information, but here I will not comment on each and every point. These should be known in other instances as well in accordance with [the above method].[436]

---

434 Tsong Khapa here is commenting on the lines 2.27cd, which deal with the twelve *mātṛ*, skipping over the intervening verses concerning the vases. The root Tantra itself only identifies them as "all the Mothers" (*mātarāḥ sarvā*, *ma mo thams cad*). Tsong Khapa is evidently praising Büton's enumeration of them as twelve. Büton identifies them as consisting of the four essence yoginīs and the eight gate and quarter goddesses. See NS 253–254.

435 In the CT, the four essence yoginīs, who correspond to the four elements, are Ḍākinī, Lāmā, Khaṇḍarohā, and Rūpiṇī. The four gatekeepers are Kākāsyā, "Crowface," Ulūkāsyā, "Owlface"; Śvānāsyā, "Dogface"; and Śūkarāsyā: "Sowface." The four quarter guardians are Yamadāhī, Yamadūtī, Yamadaṁṣṭrī, and Yamamathanī.

436 One might expect that such details would be included in a commentary that purports to "illuminate the hidden meaning" of the root text. But as Tsong Khapa states, he deals with these details in his commentaries on the Indian *sādhanas*. Some of the Indian commentators, such as Kambala and Durjayacandra, describe at some length the various deities. And Büton, in his NS commentary, does what Tsong Khapa did not do in his commentary, which is to painstakingly describe the deities in reliance upon the Indic commentaries and *sādhanas*. See NS 240–249.

Regarding the entry of the gnosis hero, the **ḍākinīs in space**, namely, the gnosis heroines of the mind wheel, are **all placed above** (**2.26ab**), i.e., inserted into each mind wheel commitment heroine who ranges in space. The gnosis heroines who are the **ḍākinīs on earth**, that is, of the speech wheel, are **placed**, i.e., inserted, into the commitment beings of the speech ḍākinīs of **the mandala** (**2.26cd**). **Any ḍākinīs in the underworld**, that is, the gnosis heroine ḍākinīs of the body wheel, are **placed in the underworld** (**2.27ab**), namely, in the commitment beings of the body wheel. The expression **in the mandala** (**2.26d**) is applicable to the preceding and following [verses] as well.[437] In addition, placement "in the middle" should be understood by virtue of the terms **above** (**2.26b**) and **under** (**2.27ab**). The gurus have explained in this way, and it seems to be the intention of Kambala and Devagupta as well.[438]

That illustrates as well the entry of the gnosis heroes into the remaining commitment heroes, and the remaining ritual procedures should be known from the mandala ritual [texts]. It is the placement of the sixty-two deities into the mandala of consecration that is taught here, and any uncertainty is in regard to that alone; and since the explanatory Tantras also elucidate the mandalas of the five, thirteen, and thirty deities along with that of the solitary hero, one should also understand about consecration, and so forth, in those mandalas.

3.3.3. 2.2.1. 1.2.3. Making and placing the vases

Having explained the making of the mandala, **then**, I will explain the way in which one should **make the vases** (**2.20c**). The vases should have no **base** or stand, and should be free of faults such as **black** color, and, by virtue of the expression **and so forth** (**2.20d**), ugliness, cracks, etc.

---

437 That is, it should be understood that the **ḍākinīs in space** (**2.26a**) and the **ḍākinīs in the underworld** (**2.27a**) are also placed **in the mandala** (**2.26d**).

438 Kambala, in his SN commentary, gives a general overview of the meditative process indicated by these verses, but does not give a word-by-word commentary here. The relevant passage reads as follows: "The [lines] **space**, etc., should be taken in terms of the invitation, entry, and binding of the of the gnosis wheel to the commitment wheel, in accordance with the stages of the three realms" (SN 11ab: */nam mkha'i zhe bya ba la sogs pa la khams gsum pa go rim bzhin du ye shes kyi 'khor lo dam tshig gi 'khor lo la dgug pa dang gzhug pa dang bcing ba dang dbang du bya ba ste/*). He then goes on to describe the meditation by which this is accomplished.

The substances inside the vases include the five treasures, namely **pearls, gold, and jewels**, i.e., beryl, **coral, silver**, and also **copper (2.21ab)**, since in the *Pearl Garland* it is reckoned amongst the five treasures.[439] The **foods** [inside them] are the five ambrosias. The term **all** extends as well to the five grains, the five medicinal substances, and so forth. **They are filled with (2.21c)** water together with those [substances]. The vessels filled with scented water along with the five nectars are **skull bowls** that should be **placed upon (2.21d)** the vases.

The **neck**s of the vases are **wound with thread**, and their **tips are adorned with** "leaves" **(2.22ab)**, that is, fresh leafy twigs.[440] Their necks should be **well wound with a pair of** new cotton **cloths (v.22d)**. The production of the vases entails fumigation and purification (*bsang sbyangs*), that is, the [meditative] creation of the vases, the creation of the deities therein, mantra repetition, and so forth.

Then, regarding the placement of the vases, **eight** vases [in total] are **placed** in pairs **at** [each of] **the** four **doors (2.22c)** in the east, etc. Kambala explains that **the ninth vase** is placed in front, which is explained as placement in the east. The apparent fact that the ninth is placed in the **center (2.23a)** seems to be intended for the time of initial preparation.[441]

---

[439] I presume that by *phreng ba* Tsong Khapa refers to Sachen's *Pearl Garland* commentary, but this assumption may not be correct, as his comments do not exactly match Tsong Khapa's description. The PG reads as follows here: "What is placed inside of the vases? The five treasures, and so forth, are placed inside, illustrated by **pearls, gold, jewels, and coral**. From what are the vases made? They are made of precious things, as illustrated by **silver** and **copper**" (PG 304.3: */bum pa de dag gi nang du bcud gang gzhug ce na/ mu tig gser dang rin chen dang / /byu ru zhes pas mtshon pa'i rin po che lnga la sogs pa gzhug/ bum pa'i rgyu gang zhe na/ dngul dang zangs ma can zhes pa ni mtshon pa ste/ rin po che'am sa la sogs pa las byas pa'o/*).

[440] The Tibetan here reads *'dab ma*, "leaf, petal," which Tsong Khapa glosses as *shing lo*, "tree leaves."

[441] Tsong Khapa is referring to the following passage in Kambala's SN commentary: "The ninth, which is the victory of all powers, should be placed in front" (SN 9b: *dgu pa ni dngos grub thams cad rnam par rgyal ba ste mdun du dgod par bya'o*). Tsong Khapa's interpretation that "in front" means in the east makes sense, since typically one views and enters the mandala from the east. Both Sachen and Büton, however, have a different interpretations. Sachen commented: "That which is **wound with a pair of cloths** is, as previously explained, **the ninth vase**, the vase of the victory of all powers, should be placed in the center of the mandala" (PG 304.4: */gos zung gis ni dkris pa ni/ sngar bshad la bum pa dgu pa ni dngos grub thams cad rnam par rgyal ba'i bum pa ste/ /de ni dkyil*

(cont'd)

3.3.3. 2.2.1. 1.2.4. The rite of mandala worship

The second part has two sections: (1) ornamenting the mandala and (2) worshipping the mandala.

3.3.3. 2.2.1. 1.2.4. 1. Ornamenting the mandala

[The mandala] should be **decorated with gold, silver, pearls, or jewels (2.23cd)** other than those. In Lochen's translation there is no "or." Regarding the method of decoration, one **should scatter jewels and gold**, etc., as previously explained on the outer periphery of the **mandala**'s ground (**2.24.ab**) to beautify it.

3.3.3. 2.2.1. 1.2.4. 2. Worshipping the mandala

Were one to worship the delightful supreme abode (2.24c), i.e., mandala, worship **without doubt** concerning the attainment of the **power (2.24d)**. The master should **sprinkle himself with scented water**. "Head" refers to the **face**. **Everywhere (2.25ab)** refers to one who has four faces in all directions; hence it is oneself as four-faced Heruka who is satisfied.[442] As the drawing of the mandala with colored powders is completed, this is stated on the occasion of beginning to engage in practice.

Should one desire the ultimate power, offer one hundred lamps (2.25cd). That is, **if** one **desires** the ultimate **power (2.28c)**, in addition to offering **one hundred lamps, offer (2.28b)** as well one hundred **scents**, one hundred **flowers**, and one hundred **incense (2.28a)** sticks. The line

---

'khor gyi dbus su dgod par bya la/). Büton wrote that "**the ninth vase** that is **well wound with a pair of cloths,** the victory of all powers, should be placed in the **center**, that is, atop the lotus" (NS 251: */gos zung gis legs par dkris pa'i bum pa dgu pa dngos grub thams cad rnam par rgyal ba dbus su ste lte ba'i steng du dgod par bya'o/*). Of interest as well is the apparent fact that each of the vases was individually named; the name of the ninth vase seems to have been **sarvasiddhivijaya*.

442 Tsong Khapa here is commenting on the Tibetan translation *kun nas sgo*, the SL and SM translation for the Sanskrit compound *sarvatomukham*, "facing everywhere." Tsong Khapa does not seem to recognize that this is a translation of a compound, although his comment on *kun nas* correctly explains this text.

[beginning with] "rite" is not in the translations of Lochen or Mal.[443] The first of the two statements concerning the hundred lamps (**2.25c**) refers to lamps of sesame oil. The second (**2.28c**) emphasizes the need for their placement, and, according to Bhavyakīrti, "shows the central importance of the hundred lamps."[444] Someone also explains the latter literally, and the former in reference to the five fleshes.[445] Bhavabhaṭṭa also seems to explain that the former are ordinary lamps and the latter are lamps of the "great oil."[446]

Whom should one **worship**? This is shown by the two lines [beginning with] **Heruka**. The worship with the five **banners** is also for the mandala (**2.29**). If one does not have at one's disposal **cloths** of **sundry** colors, one for each deity, then one in common [will do]. They should be **adorned** with many **various** flower **wreaths** above, **canopies** above, and **curtains** (**2.30**) to the side. Likewise, **make offerings well equipoised**, that is, with a one-pointed mind, **with** delicious **food and drink** (**2.31**).

---

443 Tsong Khapa refers to the line *cho ga bzhin du de bzhin mchod*, "offer in accordance with the rite." This is found in the PM and SM translations, but is not found in SL or the extant Sanskrit.

444 Tsong Khapa quotes from the following passage in Bhavyakīrti's commentary: "The [passage] **offer one hundred lamps**, etc., refers to lamps of sesame oil. It is repeated to emphasize the definite need for their placement, in order to show the central importance of the lamps" (BC 13a: */mar me brgya ni dbul bar bya/ /zhes bya ba la sogs pa ni til mar gyi mar me'o/ /yang smos pa ni nge par gzhag dgos pa'i phyir te/ mar me brgya ni gtso bo yin pa bstan pa'i phyir ro/*).

445 This "someone" was Vīravajra, who wrote: "**Offer the hundred lamps** refers to one hundred vessels of the fleshes of the five heroes, which are created and offered to the Goddess" (PD 368a: */mar me brgya ni dbul bar bya/ /zhes bya ba ni dpa' bo lnga'i sha'i snod brgya lha mor bskyed cing dbul ba'o/*).

446 Tsong Khapa here refers to the following passage in Bhavabhaṭṭa's commentary: "It is said that the former **lamps** are one hundred ordinary lamps, while the [other] **hundred lamps** are of the great oil" (Pandey 2002, 36: *prāgdīpānām iti sāmānyena tailadīpaśatam uktaṁ dīpānām tu śatam iti/ mahātailabhavam/*; 2002, 231: */gong gi mar me zhes pa ni thun mong gi mar me brgya bya bar gsungs so/ /mar me brgya yang zhes pa ni mar khu chen po gyur pa'o/*). The "great oil," like the "great flesh" or "great fat," would appear to be rendered human fat.

3.3.3. 2.2.1. 1.3. Showing the name of the chapter

In the *Concise* ***Śrī Herukābhidhāna Tantra***, [this] is the **second chapter** on the placement of the mandala's **wheel**s and **the procedure of** their **worship**. This is the explanation of the second chapter in the *Illumination of the Hidden Meaning, A Detailed Exegesis of the Concise Saṁvara Tantra Called "The Cakrasaṁvara."*

Chapter 3

Chapter 3 Outline

3.3.3. 2.2.1. 2. Bestowing consecration in the completed mandala

The second part has six sections: (1) pleasing the guru and the deities in the beginning, (2) entering the mandala and bestowing consecration, (3) offering the fee, and its benefit, (4) showing the definite need for consecration, (5) showing the significance of consecration, and (6) showing the name of the chapter.

3.3.3. 2.2.1. 2.1. Pleasing the guru and the deities in the beginning

[The word] **thence**, namely, after having stated the second chapter, brings us to the statement of the third. The **adept**, the disciple to be initiated, **should first**, that is, before the consecration, well **please the master**. With what? [One should do so] **with all things (3.1ab)** of body, speech, and mind. Furthermore, **one who desires power**, who is **well equipoised**, i.e., devoted one-pointedly, **should worship the guru to the extent of his ability (3.1cd)**, and should beseech him to the extent of his ability.

Having hung sounding bells (3.2a) from above, and being **decorated with flowers and incense (3.2b)**, **the adept should sound a melodious bell and** beat **a drum (3.2cd)**, i.e., a hand drum (*ḍamaru*),

and should make the sound "*ha ha*" (3.2e). If we explain symbolically, Kambala states that "it is said that the bell is a girl sixteen years old, and the drum a girl of twelve years."[447] It is said that the [term] "adept" (*sgrub pa po*, *sādhaka*)—in [the following instances of its usage:] **the adept (3.2d)**, **the well-equipoised adept (3.4d)** and **the adept will always (3.18ab)**—refers to the disciple. Therefore, it is the disciple who is the drumbeater, and who should thus be taken as the bell ringer as well.

Melodious refers to a woman who has the distinction of being perceived as having a pleasant voice and a beautiful body. **Sounding** means that one should adore [her], it is said. [Words] like **sounding**, etc., mean that the disciple should be equipoised in those spell consorts (*rig ma de dag*).

On what occasion does this occur? It must be done on the occasion of the bestowal of the wisdom-gnosis consecration upon the disciple. This thus indicates the bestowal of the third consecration, which shows that [the text] strays from the order of the consecrations. Bhavabhaṭṭa explains that the "bell ringing" also indicates the bell consecration.[448]

3.3.3. 2.2.1. 2.2. Entering the mandala and bestowing consecration

The second part has two sections: (1) entering the mandala and (2) bestowing consecration upon the entrant.

3.3.3. 2.2.1. 2.2.1. Entering the mandala

Applicable here is the statement that **worshipping in accordance with the rites (3.3a)** of worshipping the previously described **mandala**, one should enter into the mandala of colored powder or images on

---

[447] Kambala commented here as follows: "Now, it is said that the **bell** is a girl sixteen years old, and the **drum** a girl of twelve years. **Melodious** means that she has a pleasant voice, a beautiful body, and a comely complexion. **Sounding** means that one should adore [her]" (SN 12a: */de nas dril bu ni lo grangs bcu drug pa'i bu mor gsungs la/ lnga ni lo grangs bcu gnyis ma'o/ /shin tu sgra snyan zhes bya ba ni ngag snyan zhing gzugs mdzes pa la mdog sdug pa'o/ /rdul zhes bya ba ni rjes su chags par bya'o/*).

[448] He states this in his CV commentary as follows: "**Sounding bells,** etc., indicates the bell consecration" (Pandey 2002, 37: *ghaṇṭānādam ityādinā ghaṇṭābhiṣekaḥ pratipādyate/*); see also CV 166b.

cloth.[449] And, just as in the case of the symbolic explanation of "bell ringing," etc., we can apply here as well the assertion that one should enter into the vulva mandala having worshipped from the perspective of being equipoised in the body mandala of the wisdom consort (*shes rab ma*), that is, in the woman who has all of the desired virtues, who has a beautiful body, pleasant voice, delicious scent, the supreme taste, and who is soft to the touch, in accordance with the rite of being equipoised through the blessings of the vajra and lotus.[450]

The **lads** who are taken as such at the occasion of preparatory rituals in accordance with the first of those two [explanations above][451] are attractive and pleasing,[452] and are set outside the curtain, their **faces covered with** silk or cotton **cloth (3.3cd)**. In regard to that, "the **cloth** illustrates nonclarity, and thus **covering** illustrates the extremely secret;

---

[449] Tsong Khapa here summarizes Büton's commentary, as follows: "The one who has done preliminary worship with flowers, and so forth, as previously explained should worship and enter into the **mandala** of colored powder or drawn on cloth **in accordance with the rite**. That is the oral transmission of Kambala" (NS 259: */sngar bshad pa de ltar/ me tog la sogs pa'i mchod pa sngon du 'gro bas cho ga bzhin bris pa'i ras bris sam rdul tshon gyi dkyil 'khor yang dag par mchod la gzhug par bya'o/ /zhes pa lva wa pa'i man ngag go/*).

[450] This is drawn from a passage in Büton's commentary, attributed in this case to Durjayacandra, which occurs as follows: "The secret consecration should be bestowed once one has worshipped by means of the worship (*pūjā*) of being equipoised in the body mandala of the young lady (*gzhon nu ma*, *kumarī*), that is, in the woman who has all of the desired virtues, who has a beautiful body, pleasant voice, delicious scent, the supreme taste, and who is soft to the touch, in accordance with the rite of being equipoised through the blessings of the vajra and lotus. That is the explanation of Durjayacandra that is not literal, or that hides the reality of passion" (NS 258: */de ltar rdo rje dang padma byin gyis brlabs nas snyoms par 'jug pa'i cho ga bzhin du gzhon nu ma'i lus kyi dkyil 'khor gzugs sdug sgra snyan dri zhim ro mchog reg bya 'jam ste 'dod pa'i yon tan kun ldan pa la snyoms 'jug gi mchod pas mchod nas gsang ba'i dbang bskur bar bya'o/ /mi thub zla ba'i bshad pa ste sgra ji bzhin pa ma yin pa'am 'dod chags chos kyi sbas pa'o/*).

[451] That is, the first of the explanations drawn from Büton's commentary, attributed to Kambala. This is the literal interpretation that this passage refers to entry into a mandala drawn on the ground or painted on cloth.

[452] Tsong Khapa is here commenting on the word "attractive," *sdug*, in the expression "attractive boy" (*bu sdug*), which is the Tibetan translation of *putraka*. This translation seems to have been interpretative, as *bu*, "boy" would have translated *putraka* well enough. The extra syllable might have been added for metrical reasons.

just so the cloth is a symbol of nonclarity, and **covering** a symbol of the secret."[453]

When their eyes are covered in this way, **place them with their palms full of flowers (3.4a)**, i.e., cause them to hold a flower garland between their palms. They should be caused to enter, i.e., placed,[454] inside of the curtain. **Then the adept**, that is, the disciple,[455] who is **well equipoised**, that is, composed, **circumambulating (3.4bc)** the mandala, **should enter** Heruka's **pleasing palace (3.5a)**, meaning that one should visualize oneself mentally entering the mandala. The line [beginning with] "intelligent" is not in the translations of Lochen or Mal, and hence appears to be superfluous.[456]

Regarding **resting his body to the south (3.5b)**, someone explains that since Saṁvara's face gazes to the south, one enters on that side.[457] Kambala, taking **resting to the south** as an illustration of the flower casting, explains that there is also flower casting from the other three

---

453 Tsong Khapa's source for this somewhat redundant passage was evidently Büton, who also quotes it without identifying the source, as follows: */dar gyis mi gsal ba mtshon la des bkab pas shin tu gsang ba mtshon te/ ji skad du/ dar ni mi gsal mtshon pa te/ bkab pa gsang ba mtshon pa'o/* (NS 260). My translation follows Büton, as his version of the passage is slightly less redundant.

454 Tsong Khapa corrected the faulty translation *zhugs pa* to *gzhug par bya*. The latter is a correct translation of the Sanskrit *prakṣipet*.

455 As Tsong Khapa explained above, he takes the term *adept* (*sādhaka*) here and in other instances in this chapter as referring to the disciple. However, in verse 4 *sādhakaḥ susamāhitaḥ* is the grammatical subject while the disciples, the *putraka*, are the implicit object (of *prakṣipet*), while their faces are the object of *saṁchādya*. This calls into question Tsong Khapa's interpretation here. It would be valid, however, if we take *sādhakaḥ susamāhitaḥ* in reference to the following verse, which he seems to do.

456 Tsong Khapa is referring to the line *slo bzang yid ni mnyam bzhag pa*, "the intelligent, equipoised one," which occurs in the PM and SM translations, but not elsewhere.

457 Here again the "someone" seems to be Büton, although he talks about not "entry to" (*zhugs*) but "being positioned in" (*gnas*) the south. He reported that "Since Saṁvara's face is seen to the south, it says 'abide in the south.' This means that one abides on the side of Ḍākinī in front of the Blessed Lord, since Ḍākinī arises as a mantra of his implement from the south" (NS 262: */bde mchog zhal lho bstan du yod pas/ lho phyogs gnas zhes gsungs te/ don la bcom ldan 'das kyi mdun mkha' 'gro ma'i ngos su gnas pa yin te/ lho phyogs nas phyag 'tshal ba'i sngags la mkha' 'gro ma byung ba'i phyir ro/*).

doors, and that by casting in that manner one will attain different powers.[458]

Then the flower previously held between the **palms (3.5c) should be cast above the mandala (3.5d)**. Then [the disciple's] eyes are opened, and the deity on which that **flower fell** upon the mandala is the deity of the **clan** to which the disciple is **assigned (3.6ab)**. **He may be shown the seat**, the palace, **of Śrī Heruka, and so forth (3.6c)**, that is, the other deities. Here Kambala says that he should be shown just the mandala, and should not be shown the reality of the mandala.[459]

However, how is it that Āryadeva, Nāgabodhi, and so forth, say that on this occasion the mandala reality is shown?[460] Here someone said, regarding the nonshowing of reality, that it is in regard to disciples who do not uphold the vows of the five clans and who have not requested the vajra master consecration. He explains that reality is shown on this occasion

---

458 Kambala comments as follows: "Regarding **resting to the south**, [cast the flower] from the eastern door of the mandala for the sake of attaining a kingdom as a king, the powers of the sword and subterranean [travel], freedom from disease, gnosis, and liberation. [Cast] from the southern door of the mandala for the sake of gold transmuting elixir, alchemy, freedom from disease, gifts of wealth and grain, glory, good fortune, and eternal peace. [Cast] from the western door of the mandala for the sake of [the powers of] controlling, summoning, perfecting, pacifying, augmenting, enticing people, and increasing sons, grandsons, etc. [Cast] from the northern door of the mandala for the sake of cutting off the life of the malicious to preserve the Teaching, and for averting and defeating enemies" (SN 12a: */lho'i phyogs su brten ba ni zhes bya ba la/ sa'i bdag po yul 'khor rnyed pa dang / ral gri dang sa 'og gi dngos grub rnams dang / nad med pa dang ye shes dang thar pa'i don du ni dkyil 'khor gyi shar sgor ro/ /gser 'gyur rtsi dang bcud kyi len pa dang / nad med pa dang / nor dang 'bru rab tu sbyin pa dang / dpal dang bkra shis dang rtag tu zhi ba'i don du ni dkyil 'khor gyi lho sgor ro/ /dbang dang dgug pa dang phun sum tshogs pa dang / /zhi ba dang rgyas pa dang / skye bo rnams kyi yid du 'ong ba dang / bu dang tsha bo la sogs 'phel ba'i don du ni dkyil 'khor gyi nub nas so/ /bstan pa bsrung ba'i don du gdug pa can rnams tsher bcad pa dang / dgra rnams bzlog cing pham par bya ba'i don du ni dkyil 'khor gyi byang sgor ro/*).

459 See SN 12b.

460 Āryadeva comments thus in his *Śrīcatuṣpīṭhatantrarāja-maṇḍala-vidhisāra-samuccaya*, in ch. 26, which is entitled "The procedure for instructing all of the initiates." In particular he wrote that "reality is shown to all disciples and all sentient beings" (D 136b: */slob ma dag ni thams cad dang / /sems can kun la de nyid bstan/*). Nāgabodhi, in his *Śrīguhyasamājamandalaviṁśatividhi*, makes no specific reference to *mandalatattva*, but he does state that the disciple is taught the stages of the mandala rite as well as the nature of the mandala deities. See fol. 140b.

to one who has previously upheld the vows and who has resolutely requested the master and disciple consecrations.[461] However, Kambala says that after the secret consecration the mandala is shown, which means that everything is apprehended, that everything such as the mandala reality, and so forth, is completely revealed.[462]

Since it seems that [Kambala] thinks that the third consecration is indicated by "bell ringing," and so forth, and since reality is completely revealed once one has received the higher consecrations, it should not be accepted that the mandala reality is only shown after one has received the master consecration, but rather that "reality," taken in terms of the two stages, is shown. In this way, there is no contradiction in taking it as both showing the reality of the mandala, understood in terms of the creation stage on the occasion of showing the face of the deity, and completely showing reality that is the completion of the consecration.

3.3.3. 2.2.1. 2.2.2. Bestowing consecration upon the entrant

The second part has two sections: (1) the actual consecration bestowal and (2) the salutation at the end of that.

3.3.3. 2.2.1. 2.2.2. 1. The actual consecration bestowal

The first section has two subsections: (1) bestowing the vase consecration and (2) bestowing the higher consecrations.

---

461 This quote is taken from a passage in Büton's commentary that occurs as follows: "Here it is said that that reality is not shown to disciples who do not uphold the vows and who have not requested the the Vajrācārya consecration. For a person who upholds the vows and who requests in verse the disciple and master consecrations, gnosis descends and he enters into the secret mandala. It is necessary to reveal to him the secret mandala, and since showing the secret mandala is showing reality, concluding from that it is said that reality is shown to him" (NS 263: */des na slob ma sdom pa ma bzung zhing rdo rje slob dpon gyi dbang mi zhu ba rnams la 'dir de nyid mi bshad pa yin la/ sdom pa bzung slob ma'i dbang dang slob dpon gyi dbang chig chod du zhu ba'i gang zag ye shes babs pa ni/ gsang ba'i dkyil 'khor du zhugs pa yin/ de la gsang ba'i dkyil 'khor bstan dgos shing / gsang ba'i dkyil 'khor bstan pa ni de nyid bstan pa yin pas/ de la dgongs nas de nyid bstan par gsung pa yin no/*).

462 Kambala comments as follows: */de nas gdong phye dkyil 'khor dstan/ /zhes bya ba ni thams cad zin nas dkyil 'khor gyi de kho na nyid la sogs pa thams cad rdzogs par bstan par bya'o/* (SN 12b).

3.3.3. 2.2.1. 2.2.2. 1.1. Bestowing the vase consecration

The disciple who casts the flower comes to have the name of the deity on which the flower lands, so from the perspective of the name, i.e., secret name revealed by the master at the time of the bestowal of the name consecration, this is the name consecration.[463] In regard to this, the *Saṁvarodaya* states the following: "[The master] should bestow the five consecrations that are the nature of the [five] Tathāgatas, the water, crown, vajra, bell, and name consecrations, and also the observance (*vrata*), prediction (*vyākaraṇa*), permission (*anujñā*), inspiration (*āśvāsa*), and non-retrogression (*avaivartya*) [rites] that arise from the vase [consecration]."[464] This is stated here on the occasion of the name consecration in order to state the ten [consecrations] in the vase consecration.

If one explains **sound a melodious bell (3.2a)** literally, it shows the bell consecration since it is the ringing of the bell by the disciple. The text concerning the placement of the remaining vases in chapter two shows the water consecration, since it is for the purpose of bestowing the water consecration. In other words, three consecrations are shown [in this

---

463 Tsong Khapa is commenting here upon two lines in the PM and SM translations, which occur as follows: "S/he gains the name of that clan, the name revealed by the master" (*/de ni rigs de'i ming 'gyur bar/ /slon dpon gyis ni ming bstan to/*). There is no equivalent to this, however, in the Sanskrit, or in the SL translation. Regarding these lines Büton wrote: "Although this [text] is not in two of the Tantra's commentaries or in the majority of Indic texts, it occurs in [Tathāgatarakṣita's] *Ubhayanibandha*" (NS 263–264: */'di rgyud kyi 'grel pa gnyis dang / rgya dpe phal che la med kyang gnyis ka'i bshad sbyar las byung ngo /*).

464 This passage occurs at SU 18.26a–27b in Tsuda's edition, as follows: *udakamakuṭa-vajraghaṇṭānāmābhiṣekam / pañcatathāgatātmakaṁ sekaṁ vrata vyākaraṇam eva ca // anujñāśvāsāvaivartyān dadyāt kalaśasaṁbhavān //* (1974, 127); */chu dang cod pan rdo rje dang / /dril bu dang ni ming dbang bskur/ /de bshin gsegs lnga'i bdag nyid dbang / /brtul shugs dang ni lung bstan nyid/ /rjes gnang dang ni dbugs dbyung dang / /phyir mi ldog pa'ang sbyin bya ste/.../bum pa las ni byung ba'o/* (1974, 209). This text is also quoted by Büton (NS 264). Tsuda, in pp. 297–298 n. 5, clarifies this passage based on Büton's *Maṇḍalavidhi*. There are ten consecrations, and the first five (water, crown, vajra, bell, and name) are called the *vidyā* consecrations, and correspond respectively to the *pañcajina* (Akṣobhya, Ratnasambhava, Amitābha, Amoghasiddhi, Vairocana) and their wisdoms. The *avaivartya* consecration is another name for the *ācārya* consecration, and it includes the *vrata*, *vyākaraṇa*, *anujñā*, and *āśvāsa*. The vase consecration includes both the five *vidyā* and the *ācārya* consecrations, but as the former are a prerequisite of the latter, it is considered to be equivalent to the *ācārya* consecration. These consecrations, although overlapping, constitute the ten consecrations, which is one of many enumerations.

Tantra]. Regarding the [other] seven such as the crown and vajra consecrations, the non-retrogression, and so forth, the explanatory Tantra fills the gap, but those things that are not explained there must be known from the mandala rite texts.

3.3.3. 2.2.1. 2.2.2. 1.2. Bestowing the higher consecrations

Then, after bestowing the vase consecration, **the master,** in order to give the secret consecration to the disciple, **well equipoised** in the Heruka concentration, **should** perform the **worship** of contemplative union with **the consort (3.7ab)**—transformed into Vajravārāhī—who is qualified as a spell consort (*rig ma*) and offered by the disciple. After being united, the master "should perform the ritual actions" of the secret consecration bestowal.[465] At what time is [this done]? It is said that the consecration is bestowed **on the second day (3.7c)**, that is, [after] midnight. Since many commentaries explain that it occurs on the second day, it should be done at midnight on the second day, once one has attended to the preparatory rituals.[466]

The statement by the gurus that the four lines beginning with "then" (**3.7**) describe the secret consecration accords with many of the commentaries. Regarding the "great vermilion," it is the "great **blood**."[467] The equivalent term of "blood" is *rakta*, which can also be taken as meaning "passion"; hence it is explained as being that which "arises from the passion of the body, speech, and mind" of the divine couple.[468] It is the

465 Tsong Khapa here is commenting upon a line that is found in the SM translation, *las 'di yang dag spyad par bya*, a close variant of which is also found in the PM translation, *las ni yang dag spyad par bya*. It does not occur in the extant Sanskrit or in the SL translation. Büton reports, accurately, that it does not occur in the Indic texts or in the commentaries (NS 264: */'di yang dag spyad par bya/ /zhes pa rgya dpe dang / 'grel pa rnams la med/*).

466 Kambala, for example, simply states that it is done at midnight of the next day (SN 12b: */phyi de nyin par zhes bya ba ni nam phyed na'o/*). Devagupta similarly commented that it occurs "on the second day, which means at midnight" (SS 80b: */nyin gnyis par zhes pa ni mtshan phyed na zhes pa'i don to/*).

467 "Great vermilion" (PM, SM: *mtshal chen*; SL: *'tshal chen*) is a euphemistic translation for *rakta*, which can mean vermilion, but more commonly means blood, which it clearly means here.

468 This is a quote from a longer passage in Büton's NS commentary, which unabashedly explains the secret consecration alluded to in the root Tantra. It occurs as follows: "Then,

(cont'd)

drop that arises from the equipoise of the divine couple of the guru. It is explained that by being **thrice enchanted** with the three seed syllables, the mantrin **should make the drop (3.7d)** on the heart, between the eyebrows, and on the throat and crown of the **disciple (3.7c)**.[469] Another commentary explains that the disciple is blindfolded at the occasion of the guru couple's union, and that the secret substance is given unto his mouth and two eyes along with the four places previously stated, as a drop over which was repeated the essence, quintessence, and root mantras, and that it should be done at the time of bestowing the secret consecration. The disciple should taste that which is given as if it were

---

equipoised by means of the art of the union of the moving vajra and lotus, etc., by the application of passionate love, invite the Tathāgatas with the light rays of the heart center's seed syllable; they enter through one's crown and are melted by the fire of passionate love. The [resulting] natural bliss is stabilized at the vajra's jewel tip; worship the buddha with that bliss. Achieving the benefit of sentient beings, take on the divine pride with the mantra of passionate love. *Oṁ āḥ hūṁ ha ho hrīḥ* is repeated three times over the "great vermilion," i.e., blood, which arises from that, which is blood—namely, menstrual blood, since it arises from the passion of body, speech, and mind—and also over the semen, which is illustrated by that. Alternately, repeat the root, essence, and quintessence mantras three times. With [this consecrated substance] form a drop on the four places, i.e., on the crown, between the eyebrows, at the throat, and at the heart, or on the seven places, namely, on the head, brow, the two eyes, the mouth, throat, and heart. In particular, it should be given unto the mouth with the thumb and ring finger, and the disciple should taste it as if it were ambrosia, saying, 'Oh, what bliss!' Then the wisdom consort also gives him the honey that exists in her lotus in the same way" (NS 264–265: */de nas rjes su chags pa'i sbyor bas rdo rje padma bskyod pa la sogs pa'i sbyor thabs kyis snyoms par zhugs pas thugs ka'i sa bon gyi 'od zer kyis de bzhin gshegs pa rnams spyan drangs sphyi bo nas zhugs te chags kyi mes zhu/ rdo rje nor bu'i rtse mor lhan cig skyes pa'i bde ba brtan par byas/ de'i bde bas sangs rgyas mchod / sems can gyi don byas nas rjes chags kyi sngags kyis nga rgyal bzung la/ de las byung ba'i mtsal chen te khrag/ lus dang ngag dang sems chags pa las byung ba'i phyir khrag ste zla mtshan dang des mtshon nas khu ba la/ oṁ āḥ hūṁ ha ho hrīḥ las gsum bzlas ba'am/ yang na rtsa sngags dang snying po dang nye snying las gsum bzlas bas spyi gtsugs dang smin ma tshams dang mgrin pa dang snying ga ste/ gnas bzhi'am/ mgo bo dang dpral ba dang mig gnyis dang kha dang mgrin dang snying ga ste/ gnas 'dun du thig le bya'o/ /khyad par khar mthe bo srin gyis sbyin zhing / slob mas kyang bdud rtsi bzhin du myangs te/ aho sukha zhes brjod par bya'o/ /de nas shes rab mas kyang de'i padma na gnas pa'i sprang rtsi de bzhin du sbyin no/*). A good portion of this passage, including the portion quoted by Tsong Khapa, is drawn from the commentaries of Kambala (SN 12b–13a) and Devagupta (SS 80b).

469 Tsong Khapa again refers to Büton's explanation quoted in the previous note above.

ambrosia.[470] It would be excellent to add this explanation to the previous one.

Having unveiled the disciple's face (**3.8a**) is here relevant before the **showing of the mandala** (**3.8b**) and after the bestowal of the secret consecration. Regarding the bestowal of the third consecration after the blindfold has thus been removed, I have already discussed that.[471] And I will comment on the bestowal of the fourth consecration by showing the way in which reality is shown.[472]

Then, the one who has completed all of the consecrations **should be** completely **shown** the reality of **the** two **mandala**s (**3.8b**), taken in terms of the two stages, that of the **deity**, i.e., the inhabitants, and that of the habitat, which is **the place** (**3.8cd**) where they reside. The previous gurus claim that the three lines [beginning with] **then...the mandala** (**3.8bcd**) show the secret consecration. Having entrusted the wisdom consort (*shes rab ma*) into the hands of the disciple, he makes known [to him] the body mandala that is shown with respect to the veins of the seal's body, such as *Pracaṇḍā*, etc.; the vulva (*bhaga*) mandala shown by seeking out the channels that exist within the vulva; and the awakening spirit mandala shown in reference to the four joys in this context. It is said that this is the bestowal of the actual basis of the wisdom-gnosis consecration. This is explained in the [oral transmission] of personal instruction.

3.3.3. 2.2.1. 2.2.2. 2. The salutation at the end of that

Then, after finishing the consecration, **one bows correctly,** that is, with great devotion, to **the palace**, i.e., mandala, **as well as the master** (**3.9ab**), **circumambulates** the mandala, then circumambulates the guru and the mandala **once again** (**3.9c**), **beginning from the left**

---

470 Tsong Khapa here refers to a passage in Jayabhadra's commentary. See my translation of this in Gray 2007, 174 n. 8.

471 Following commentators such as Kambala, Tsong Khapa interprets line 3.2a ("should sound a melodious bell," *ghaṇṭāṁ vādayet susvarāṁ*) as a reference to the wisdom-gnosis consecration, in which the disciple is united with a consort; see section 3.3.3.2.2.1.2.1 above.

472 He discusses this in his commentary on the fourth chapter below, which focuses on the four *tattva* of the creation and perfection stages, the disclosure of which constitutes the fourth consecration, and which are the alleged import of the chapter.

[i.e., counterclockwise] (**3.9d**). Once one has done that, **salute the mandala and guru in accordance with the rite (3.10ab)**, i.e., ritual procedure, of salutation.

3.3.3. 2.2.1. 2.3. Offering the fee, and its benefit

The third part has two sections: (1) offering the fee and (2) the benefit of offering.

3.3.3. 2.2.1. 2.3.1. Offering the fee

[The fee] **declared by the Tathāgata (3.10d)** is that which is stated in the Tantras. **A hundred thousand gold (3.11a)** means one hundred thousand ounces of gold. "As stated" means in accordance with what other Tantras state regarding what one should give.[473] **All things (3.13c)** refers to all things of one's three doors. "In that way" means that they are offered in the same way that gold, and so forth, are offered.[474] The method by which they are offered is shown by the two lines [beginning with] **henceforward (3.14ab)**. The rest is easily understood.

3.3.3. 2.2.1. 2.3.2. The benefit of offering

In regard to the two [lines beginning with] **thus (3.14cd)**, they clearly occur as "settling thus, [things] are well settled by the adept" in Lochen's translation.[475] It is the offering of gifts that must be settled. The

---

473 Tsong Khapa here is commenting on a line in the SM translation, *slob mas ji skad gsungs pa bzhin*, "by the disciple, as stated," which occurs in the context of verse 13 at the conclusion of the statement of the fee. A close variant occurs in the PM translation, *ji skad gsungs bzhin slob ma ni*. This line is not attested in the Sanskrit or present in the SL translation.

474 Tsong Khapa here comments on the expression *de bzhin du* in the line *de bzhin du ni dbul bar bya* (3.13d) in the PM and SM translations. This term is not attested in the Sanskrit or present in the SL translation.

475 Tsong Khapa reports that Lochen's translation here reads */de ltar nges par bya ba ni/ /sgrub pa po yis rab nges bya/*, which is the reading preserved in the SL translation (*/de ltar nges par bya ba ni/ /bsgrub pa po yi nges par bya/*). The PM and SM translations contain the alternate translation */de nas sgrub pos rab nges par/ /de ltar cho ga byas na ni/*, which corresponds much more closely to the extant Sanskrit, *evaṁ vidhis tataḥ kṛtvā sādhakena suniścitaḥ*, and which I have translated as "Doing thus the ritual procedure [things] are well settled by the adept."

adept should well settle that which must be settled thus, i.e., as previously explained.

On account of having done **that**, i.e., from that cause, the twelve **ḍākinīs** and the twenty-four yoginīs **are pleased with him (3.15ab)**, that is, the disciple. And being pleased with him, **Ḍākinī, Lāmā, Khaṇḍarohā, and Rūpiṇī (3.15cd)**, that is, the **ḍākinīs** of their clans and **the adept should wander (3.16ab)**, i.e., go everywhere together. By thus going [with them], **there is no doubt regarding anything done by the adept (3.16cd)**, i.e., in those ḍākinīs doing all that one commands.

Were he to be accomplished in this yoga (3.17a), **the adept will always, without fail give rise, as he wills (3.18.ab)**, to the power of **being unhindered** by anyone **in the three worlds (3.17b)**, the **invisibility** of not being seen by others, the power of **the underworld** of moving in caves or in underworld cavities, **flight**, i.e., traveling in the sky, the **foot unguent** by which one arrives at whatever place one desires through the application of a medical preparation to the foot, and the **alchemy (3.17cd)** of achieving an eon-long lifespan through the consumption of various substances produced from mercury, and so forth.

He **will produce** emanations **of many** different **forms**, and **will** magically **travel** in **space (3.18cd)**. And he **destroys above all the** evil **dākinīs (3.19a)**. Lochen's translation has "destroys all beings, especially the ḍākinīs."[476] Not only the ḍākinīs, but other beings as well are destroyed **through** just **a single glance (3.19c)**. That sort of yogī **gives rise to the state of** inseparable "union"[477] of art and wisdom **in an instant (3.19d)**.

3.3.3. 2.2.1. 2.4. Showing the definite need for consecration

If one wonders whether or not one will achieve results through meditation on this path even if one has not obtained consecration into the

---

[476] Tsong Khapa reports Lochen's translation as reading */mkha' 'gro rnams kyang khyad par du/ /nges gnon 'gro ba thams cad kyang /*, which is almost identical to the SL translation, which reads */mkha' 'gro rnams dang khyad par du/ /des gnod 'gro ba thams cad dang /*. The SM translation has the similar reading */mkha' 'gro rnams kyang khyad par du/ /'gro ba rnams kyang nges gnon par/*. The PM translation has the same reading, but separates the two lines with an intervening line.

[477] Tsong Khapa interprets the SM translation *sbyor nyid* as "state of union." I follow the Sanskrit *yogitvaṁ* in reading it as "the state of being a yogī."

mandala, the **yogī who has not seen the mandala (3.20a)**, i.e., who has not entered and been consecrated in the mandala, **and who longs for the state of being a yogī (3.20b)** and the attainment of powers, is like one who, though he **punches at the sky (3.20c)**, does not strike it, and who, though he wishes to **drink the water of a mirage (3.20d)**, is unable to do so. That is, his effort is fruitless. It is most commonly said that a consequence of engaging [in this practice], without having been consecrated, is going to hell, and so forth. Therefore, it is taught that it is a pointless effort for those who have embarked upon the path of mantra without properly attaining consecration, or for those who have embarked upon the path having entered into and seen the mandala, but who have received only a few aspects of consecration without having undergone the bestowal of the successive consecrations.

3.3.3. 2.2.1. 2.5. Showing the significance of consecration

The fifth part has two sections: (1) showing the supremacy of this consecration and (2) addendum on the difficulty of obtaining this consecration.

3.3.3. 2.2.1. 2.5.1. Showing the supremacy of this consecration

The yogī who has been consecrated in the *Saṁvara* mandala and **this yoga** of this Tantra **is excellent (3.21a)** since he is superior to the others, and is **the highest**, i.e., the supreme, **among** the other [yogīs and] **yogas (3.21b)**. One **will go forth conquering (3.22a) anyone one desires (3.21c)** in one's mind, **gods, titans, and men (3.21d)**.[478] In Lochen's translation it occurs as "anyone one desires."[479]

---

[478] Note that I mistranslated this verse in my translation of the root Tantra, due to a mistaken reading of the Sanskrit verb *kāṅkṣiṣyate*, "desires," as *kāṁ kṣipyate*. I am indebted to Prof. Harunaga Isaacson for correcting my misreading of this term. Originally I translated 3.21–22 as follows: "This yoga is the most excellent, the highest among all yogas, which can kill anyone, gods, titans or men. The adept who has been taught all Tantras, and who has been initiated in the mandala, will go forth, conquering" (2007, 176). I would revise this to the following: "This yoga is the most excellent, the highest among all yogas. The adept who has been consecrated in the mandala, and who has been taught all Tantras, will go forth, conquering whomever he desires, gods, titans, or men."

[479] Tsong Khapa here quotes Lochen's translation as *gang zhig cung zad 'dod gyur pa*, which closely matches the extant Sanskrit, *yaḥ kāṅkṣiṣyate kaścit*. The surviving Tibetan

(cont'd)

The person **who has been consecrated in the mandala (3.22b)** of this *Saṁvara Tantra* is said to be **the adept who has been taught all** of the four [classes] of **Tantras (3.22c)**, such as the action [Tantra], etc. If one is **consecrated (3.23c)** into **looking**, i.e., action Tantra; **laughing**, i.e., performance Tantra; **hand-holding**, i.e., Yoga Tantra; and **coupling (3.23ab)**, i.e., Unexcelled Tantra, then, as this Tantra is the **supreme of all Tantras (3.23d)**, the yogī of this [tradition] **will go forth overpowering** all **gods and men**. Mal's translation seems to have "laughing, looking, hand-holding, coupling, and so forth," which is good.[480] Although someone claims that the expression **and so forth** here indicates the further Unexcelled Mother *Saṁvara Tantra*,[481] since the *Saṁvara Tantra* is also a Tantra of coupling, there is nothing aside from that. Since it is said that an alternate meaning of the expression **and so forth** (*ādikam*) is "supreme," it means that it is the supreme of the coupling Tantras.

The statement that if one attains consecration in this [Tantra], one is adept in all Tantras means, I think, that collected into this path are the imports of all Tantras, the primary of which is the indispensability of all Tantras. It is said here that if you are consecrated in this [tradition] you are consecrated in the four [classes of] Tantra. While this does not mean that if you have attained this [consecration] there is no need to seek elsewhere

---

translations all read *gang zhig rtag tu 'dod gyur pa*. The term "always," *rtag tu*, is not attested elsewhere, and does not make much sense in this context.

480 Tsong Khapa's quotation of Mal's translation, */rgod dang bltas dang lag bcangs dang / /gnyis gnyis 'khyud pa la sogs/*, is, as we would expect, quite close to the reading preserved in the Phug-brag ms. Kangyur, */rgod dang lta dang lag bcangs dang / /gnyis gnyis 'khyud pa la sogs dag* (SL). It is the closest translation to the extant Sanskrit, *gopya īkṣaṇa pāṇiṁ tu āliṅga dvandvam ādikam*.

481 Tsong Khapa here refers to the following comment by Sachen: "The expression **and so forth** brings in the Mother Unexcelled [Tantras], and this Tantra is the chief of them all" (PG 308.1: */sogs kyis ma bla na med pa bsdus te/ de thams cad kyi bdag po rgyud 'di yin pas so/*). Earlier in his commentary, he classifies the Tantras into the following six categories: "Action Tantras, Performance Tantras, Yoga Tantras, Unexcelled Yoga Tantras, Unexcelled Yoginī Tantras, and the Yoginī Further Unexcelled Mother Tantras" (PG 289.4: *de yang bya ba'i rgyud dang / spyod pa'i rgyud dang / rnal 'byor gyi rgyud dang / rnal 'byor bla na med pa'i rgyud rgyud dang / rnal 'byor ma bla na med pa'i rgyud dang / rnal 'byor ma'i yang ma bla na med pa'i rgyud do/*). He places the *Hevajra* in the "Unexcelled Yoginī Tantra" category, and places the *Cakrasaṁvara Tantra* in the "Yoginī Further Unexcelled Mother Tantra" class. See PG 290.1.

the consecrations of the other [Tantras], through the etymological explanation of the term *abhiṣeka* (consecration) it is shown that gathered within the term "consecration" are the implications of both being "cleansed of the taint of sin" and "empowered."

3.3.3. 2.2.1. 2.5.2. Addendum on the difficulty of obtaining this consecration

It has been said that [the name *Saṁvara* in] the root Tantra, **in the *Tattvasaṁgraha*, *Saṁvara* (3.24a)**, refers to the *Khasama Tantra*.[482] This, however, contradicts the claim that it is the extensive Tantra of this. It says in the *Saṁcāra* that it "is said to be from within the *Khasama Tantra* of one hundred thousand [stanzas]."[483] Therefore, it is not the case that the mandala of this Tantra is not taught in that Tantra. Mardo claims that [the term *Saṁvara* in the root Tantra] refers to the *Jālasaṁvara* known as the *Buddhasamāyoga*, which is excellent.[484] The ***guhya*** is the *Guhyasamāja*, and the *Vajrabhairava* (**3.24b**) is evidently the *mahātantra* of that name. **This king of mandalas (3.24c)** previously did **not occur, nor will it occur (3.24d)** later in those [other Tantras]. While it is not the case that this mandala is superior to the mandalas of those other ones,[485] it does mean that it is very difficult to find since it does not occur even in

---

[482] This is the claim of Sachen, who wrote "The *Cakrasaṁvara*, that is, the *Śrīkhasama*" (PG 308.1: */'khor lo sdom ste dpal nam mkha' dang mnyam pa dang /*). Büton repeats this attribution, reading *Cakrasaṁvara* (*'khor lo sdom pa*), although he, like Tsong Khapa, identifies it with the JS (NS 276: */'khor lo sdom pa ste nam mkha' dang mnyam pa'o/*). Now, the extant Sanskrit reads *saṁvare*, not *cakrasaṁvare*, which makes little sense, since it is a list of texts to which this is superior. A parallel passage in the AU does read *cakrasaṁvare*, where such a reading makes sense (see Gray 2007, 20 n. 67). However, the SL translation, on which Sachen relied, actually does read *'khor sdom 'am*, apparently translating *cakrasaṁvare*.

[483] Tsong Khapa quotes and discusses this passage in the introductory section 2.1.1 above.

[484] Tsong Khapa is here talking about the *Sarvabuddhasamāyoga-ḍākinījālasamvara Tantra* (JS), and this identification is no doubt correct, as the JS is an earlier text to which the CT is indebted. It is the source, among other things, of the famous *nidāna* verses of this text.

[485] Tsong Khapa again takes issue with Sachen, who at this point in his PG commentary made this claim. He wrote, "It is superior to the mandalas of the *Vajrabhairava*, etc." (PG 308.1: *rdo rje 'jigs byed la sogs pa las dkyil 'khor rnams kyi mchog*).

those other Tantras that are both profound and vast. If this were not so, then they would be superior to this Tantra as well, since their mandalas likewise do not occur in this [tantra].

Everything, i.e., every power, **whatsoever**, either **spoken** in this Tantra **or unspoken** in this Tantra but spoken in other Tantras, **exists in** this yoga of the two stages of **Śrī Heruka** (**3.25**), the glorious blood drinker, and will be attained in reliance on this. This shows that this consecration is greater than those previous ones, and that having attained consecration into this Tantra, its path of meditation is greater as well.

3.3.3. 2.2.1. 2.6. Showing the name of the chapter

In the *Concise* ***Śrī Herukābhidhāna Tantra***, this is the **third chapter** on the **procedure of consecration** together with offering the **fee** to the guru. This is the explanation of the third chapter in the *Illumination of the Hidden Meaning, A Detailed Exegesis of the Concise Saṁvara Tantra Called "The Cakrasaṁvara."*

CHAPTER 4

Chapter 4 Outline

3.3.3. 2.2.2. The detailed exegesis of the secret for suitable vessels
3.3.3. 2.2.2. 1. The detailed exegesis of the secret of the path
3.3.3. 2.2.2. 1.1. The four realities of the creation stage
3.3.3. 2.2.2. 1.2. The four realities of the perfection stage
3.3.3. 2.2.2. 1.3. Showing the name of the chapter

3.3.3. 2.2.2. The detailed exegesis of the secret for suitable vessels

The second part has eleven sections: (1) the detailed exegesis of the secret of the path, (2) the detailed exegesis of attainment by means of mantra and meditation, (3) the detailed exegesis of worship of the clans-woman, (4) showing the root mantra and the detailed explanation of the commitments to be kept, (5) the detailed exegesis of the conceptually elaborate practices, (6) selecting the protective mantra that removes obstacles, (7) the detailed exegesis of the food commitments, (8) the detailed exegesis of the secret of the four [types of] worship, (9) the detailed exegesis of the two remaining [modes of] conduct, (10) examining the signs of the attainment of power, and (11) showing other methods for the attainment of mundane powers.

3.3.3. 2.2.2. 1. The detailed exegesis of the secret of the path

The [*Saṁvarodaya*] *Explanatory Tantra* states: "As instructed, afterwards one is devoted to the practice of the commitments. In the continuum of one who has become a suitable vessel there will be success perfected with the true esoteric instructions, through the stages of meditation on the wheels, and so forth, but not otherwise."[486] In accordance with the promise at the time of initiation, one who afterwards is devoted to the practice of the commitments and who has become a suitable vessel

[486] Tsong Khapa here quotes a passage from SU 18.36c–37d, where it occurs as follows: *yathopadeśataḥ paścāt samayācāratatparaḥ // bhājanīkṛtasaṁtāne cakrādibhāvanā-kramaiḥ / samyagāmnāyasampannā siddhir bhavati nānyathā //* (Tsuda 1974, 128), and */phyi nas man ngag ji bzhin du/ /dam tshig spyod pa la brtson pas/ /snod du byas pa'i rgyun gyis ni/ /'khor lo la sogs bsgom pa'i rim/ /yang dag man ngag phun tshogs pas/ /dngos grub 'gyur gyi gzhan du min/* (1974, 210).

will attain the true esoteric instructions by means of the stages of meditation on the wheels, etc. It says that if one does not act in this manner, there will be no success. Thus, one who has attained consecration should from the beginning understand and protect well the commitments.

Regarding the necessity of meditation on the path of the two stages, this is shown in this chapter by the two sets of four realities of the two stages. In this part there are three sections: (1) the four realities of the creation stage, (2) the four realities of the perfection stage, and (3) showing the name of the chapter.

3.3.3. 2.2.2. 1.1. The four realities of the creation stage

Thence, after stating the third chapter, implies that the fourth will be explained. **The ḍākinīs pervade**, that is, play in, their own "place,"[487] (**4.1ab**) which in general refers to the palace, and in particular the three wheels. This indicates the reality of the habitat mandala. This supports both the outer mandala and the body mandala. Since the characteristics of the mandala were clearly shown in chapter two, here it only summarizes with "in the place."

With respect to **Mahāvīryā**, etc., it says in the *Saṁcāra* that "one will achieve everything essential through the reverse placement of the deities, the reversal of the mantric distinctions, and the reversal of the secret meditation."[488] In this way, it talks about not only reversing the arrangement of the deities but also reversing the mantras and reversing the arrangement of the secret meditation, in order to demonstrate [the necessity of] depending upon the guru's oral instructions.

If one explains to order this disorder, regarding those that come before Pracaṇḍā and after Mahāvīryā (**4.1c–4.4a**),[489] the following four,

---

[487] Tsong Khapa gives here the translation *gnas*, "place," found in the PM and SM translations, which is a secondary meaning of the Sanskrit *bhuvanāni*, which I translate as "worlds."

[488] Tsong Khapa here quotes YS 11.12c–13b, which occurs as follows: *viparītadevatā-nyāsaṁ viparītamantrabhedanam // viparītabhāvanāgopyaṁ sarvasāra-prasādhakam /* (Pandey 1998, 106–107). See also YS 39b.

[489] The goddesses are listed in reverse order in this text, beginning at 4.1c and ending at 4.4a. Tsong Khapa lists them in the correct order, rather than the order that they are listed in the text.

Pracaṇḍā (Furious, *rab gtum ma*), **Caṇḍākṣī** (Fierce Eye, *gtum mig ma*), **Prabhāvatī** (Luminous, *'od ldan ma*), and **Mahānāsā** (Big Nose, *sna chen ma*) are arranged in the four directions of the mind wheel, counterclockwise starting from the east. Likewise, **Vīramatī** (Hero's Resolve, *dpa' bo'i blo gros ma*), **Kharvarī** (Dwarfess, *mi'u thung ma*), **Laṅkeśvarī** (Lady of Laṅka, *lang ka'i dbang phyug ma*), and **Drumacchāyā** (Tree Shade, *shing grib ma*) are placed in the four quarters of the mind wheel, clockwise, starting from the southeast. The following four, **Airāvatī** (Earth Guard, *sa srungs ma*),[490] **Mahābhairavā** (Great Terrifier, *'jigs byed chen mo*), **Vāyuvegā** (Wind's Velocity, *rlung shugs ma*) and **Surābhakṣī** (Lush, *chang 'thung ma*), are placed in the four directions of the speech wheel, counterclockwise, starting from the east. Taking *śyāma*[491] as "turquoise" or "green," the four, **Śyāmādevī** (Turquoise Goddess or Green Goddess),[492] **Subhadrā** (Extremely Good, *shin tu bzang mo*), **Hayakarṇī** (Horse Ears, *rta rna ma*), and **Khagānanā** (Bird Face, *bya gdong ma*)[493] are placed in the four quarters of the speech wheel, clockwise starting from the southeast. The following four, **Cakravegā** (Wheel Force, *'khor lo'i shugs ma*), **Khaṇḍarohā** (*dum skyes ma*), **Śauṇḍinī** (Barmaid, *chang 'tshong ma*) or Nosy, or Elephant Snout (*glangs sna ma*),[494] and **Cakravarmiṇī** (Wheel Armored, *'khor lo'i go cha ma*), are arranged in the four directions of the body wheel, counterclockwise starting from the east. The next four, **Suvīrā** (Excellent Heroine, *rab dpa' mo*), **Mahābalā** (Great Strength, *stobs chen ma*), **Cakravartinī**

---

490 The name *Airāvatī* was the name for the wife of Indra's elephant, *Airāvata*. If literally translated, the result would be "She who possesses refreshment." The Tibetan translations *sa srungs ma* and *sa srung ma*, "Earth Protectress," are not literal.

491 Here I read *shye ma* as *śyāma*.

492 Tsong Khapa here cites two translations for *śyāmādevī*, *sngo bsangs lha mo* and *ljang lha mo*. The latter occurs in all three of the extant translations.

493 Tsong Khapa here cites two translations for *khagānanā*, *mkha' 'gro gdong ma* and *bya gdong ma*. The former occurs in the SM translation and the latter in the PM and SL translations.

494 The Sanskrit here reads *śauṇḍinī*, and this is translated in both the PM (*chang 'tshong ma*) and SL (*chang tshong ma*) translations. The first translation he cites, *sna can ma*, occurs in the SM translation. The second, *glang sna ma*, presumably occurs in some other source.

(Wheel Turner, *'khor lo sgyur ma*) and **Mahāvīryā** (Great Energy, *brtson chen ma*), are arranged in the four quarters of Body Wheel, clockwise, starting from the southeast.

Regarding the statement that **Achiever** (**4.4a**) is not in the Indian texts, just because you do not see it in a single Indic text does not mean that it is not in the Indian texts.[495] It does occur in the translations of all three translators. Thus, it is said that these ḍākinīs achieve the adept's success. On this occasion the following occurs in Mal's translation: "As it is outwardly, so should it be inwardly in body, speech, and mind." As this also occurs in a certain manuscript of Mardo's translation, as well as in the commentaries of Kambala, and so forth, it is good.[496] In that way, just as the Pracaṇḍā, etc., are placed amidst the spokes of the body, speech, and mind wheels of the outer mandala, so too should the twenty-four [goddesses] be placed in the body mandala from the head down to the knees. This shows the body mandala.

The name of this chapter is stated as "The Placement of the Nondual Heroes and Yoginīs,"[497] and Kambala also says that the name of this chapter is "The Placement of the Nondual Heroes and Heroines."[498] Since they are also like this in the outer mandala, one should know that the remaining deities are illustrated by them. Concerning these **twenty-four ḍākinīs** (**4.4c**), Kambala explains that "**previously established** (**4.4b**) refers principally to the twenty-four, who are gathered from those who are held to number no fewer than the atoms of Mt. Sumeru."[499] This

---

495 Tsong Khapa here takes issue with Büton, quite rightly it turns out, as the word in question, *sādhakaḥ/sgrub byed*, does occur in the extant Sanskrit manuscripts as well as all three translations. Büton wrote that "the word **achiever** does not occur in the Indic text or commentaries" (NS 279: */sgrub byed yin zhes pa rgya dpe dang / 'grel pa rnams las mi byung ste/*).

496 Tsong Khapa attributed the following two lines to Mal's translation: */sku gsung thugs kyi dbus su ni/ /ji ltar phyi rol nang de bzhin/*. They occur in the PM and SM translations, with which Mardo was involved, but not in the SL translation, in which Malgyo played a direct role. They are also found in Kambala's commentary (SN 13b), as Tsong Khapa reports.

497 Tsong Khapa here quotes the title as it occurs in the PM and SM translations.

498 Kambala does not quote the name of the chapter in the edition of his SN commentary preserved in the Tengyur, so I am not sure of the source of this reference.

499 See SN 14a.

is the meaning of the statement that they are the principal ones of those **previously established**, i.e., in the beginning.[500]

Having shown the reality of the deities, with respect to the reality of the mantras [the root text shows] that one should **affix the syllable *oṁ***—which **is a lamp**, i.e., which beautifies, **everywhere (4.6a)**—at the beginning, and ***hūṁ hūṁ phaṭ*** at **the end to the mantras** in the center of **which are utterances of each one** of the sixty deities' **names (4.5ab)**. For example, there are mantras such as *oṁ ḍākinīye hūṁ hūṁ phaṭ*, *oṁ kara kara khaṇḍakapāla pracaṇḍe hūṁ hūṁ phaṭ*, and *oṁ kākāsyā hūṁ hūṁ phaṭ*, etc.[501]

If you **see** this **excellent**, i.e., extremely **supreme (4.5c)** meditation on Heruka's mandala and the mantra repetition that exhorts his mental continuum, it is like "fire," while **the others**, that is, the deity meditations and mantra repetitions of the three other classes of Tantra, **are like straw (4.5d)**, the exposed pith of which has been eaten, meaning that their power is lesser. Lochen's translation has "the others are pith-less like grass."[502] The reason is that the **yoga (4.5c)** of this is **the giver of all desired powers (4.6b)**.

Is the reality of gnosis only stated with respect to the previously [described] twenty-four heroines? One should be **realized**, i.e., perfected, in **the state of being a hero (4.6c)**. This is relevant in the context of the reality of the deities. **In the house** means being inside of the seal's lotus

---

500 Sachen gives a bit more information concerning the mythological significance of this passage. He wrote that "As for **previously established**, it means that the twenty-four regions were established when Jambudvīpa was established, and that at that time the ḍākinīs were established" (PG 308.4: */'di dag sngon nyid grub pa yin ni/ 'dzam bu gling grub pa'i dus su yul nyi shu rtsa bzhi grub ste/ grub pa'i tshe mkha' 'gro ma rnams grub pa yin no/*).

501 Tsong Khapa seems to have taken these examples from a more detailed presentation in Büton's commentary (NS 280), in which Büton lists examples taken from various sources, such as Lūipa's *Śrībhagavad-abhisamaya*, and Bhavabhaṭṭa's and Durjayacandra's commentaries.

502 Tsong Khapa reports Lochen's translation as having here *gzhan dag snying po med rtsva mtshung*. The PM and SM translations read *me ste gzhan dag sog mar mtshung*, "like fire, and the others are like straw." The SL translation reads *me ste gzhan dag rtsa dang mtshung*, "like fire, and the others are like straw." The extant Sanskrit reads *ghuṇam anyat palālavat*, "the others are like worm[-infested] straw." The comparison with fire appears to be a later addition.

(*phyag rgya'i padma'i nang*). **Having seen the mandala (4.6d)** is explained as worshipping the mandala by means of bliss with her at the time of being equipoised. It is good to ensure that one sees the awakening spirit mandala at that time. **Knowing** this method, **one should always meditate (4.7a)**. If you meditate in this way you will achieve **the powers taught by the Tathāgata (4.7b)**.

The explanation thus applied to the four realities of the creation stage shows (1) the deities of the outer mandala within the meditation together with the four elements, Mt. Sumeru, and the measureless mansion. It also shows (2) the meditation on the inner body mandala, (3) the repetition that exhorts the mental continua of the outer and inner deities thus meditated upon, and (4) the meditation in which one creates the great bliss of the creation stage in the equipoise of the divine couple. These show the complete [set of] key points of the creation stage.

3.3.3. 2.2.2. 1.2. The four realities of the perfection stage

The texts can also be explained in a way applicable to the four realities of the perfection stage. The reality of the habitat mandala is the application of the four elements and Mt. Sumeru, along with the palace, to the inner body. This is not taken in terms of the creation stage body mandala; it is explained as being the adamantine body on which the vital points are penetrated by means of the art of penetrating the vital points of the body, as I explained in the first chapter, from the perspective of the perfection stage.

In regard to the reality of the inhabitant deities, it is not acceptable to connect the application of the inner Pracaṇḍā to the body's channels, such as the head channel, etc., because in the creation stage as well they are applied to the channels due to the necessity of creating the deities in the channels in the context of the creation stage's body mandala. Therefore, regarding these thirty-seven deities who have faces and hands, there are both the mantric body of the creation stage and the gnosis body of the perfection stage. The latter is said to be the magic body. The yogī who lacks that is without essence, like a heap of chaff, as I explained previously with the passage from the *Ḍākārṇava*.[503]

[503] See his discussion of this passage in section 3.3.3.2.1.1.2.1.1.2 in chapter 1.

It also says in Atiśa's Lūipa commentary that "conventionally, however, see the thirty-seven deities from mere wind-mind clear and complete like a reflected image, colored like a rainbow, and distorted like [the image of] the moon in water. They are conventional since they arise from causes and conditions."[504] This very clearly shows the mandala of the magic body as it occurs in the *Saṁvara* tradition.

As for the reality of mantra, the definitive meaning of mantra repetition is the perfection stage of penetrating the vital points on the body, [the stage of] vajra repetition, and so forth.

The reality of gnosis is the natural great bliss that arises from the entry, abiding, and dissolving of the life force into the central channel in reliance upon the inner arts of vajra repetition, etc., and the outer arts of being **in the house (4.6d)**.[505] It is the gnosis of clear light that is inseparably engaged with the meaning of reality.

The four realities are explained as applicable to the perfection stage in this way. The first of these shows the vajra body that is the place where the vital points are penetrated. The third shows the art of penetrating the vital points on it. The fourth shows the gnosis of the natural joy, which is drawn forth by the two arts. The second shows the gnostic body, that is, the magic body, which is created from the mere wind-mind of natural joy and clear light. [Together these] show the complete [set of] key points of the perfection stage.

In this way, at the time of bestowing the fourth consecration, this import of the inseparability of reality of gnosis and the reality of the deities, the very precious word consecration is attained insofar as one is well-informed with words. Thus, Kambala The Blanketed stated that:

> The fourth consecration should be known from the guru's mouth, as follows: "Reality can be bestowed with the

---

504 This text occurs as follows in the Tengyur: */'on kyang kun rdzob tu rlung dang sems tsam las lha sum cu rtsa bdun me long gi gzugs brnyan ltar gsal la rdzogs pa/ 'ja' tshon ltar kha dog dang bcas pa/ chu zla ltar sgro skur dang bral bar ltos shig/ de ni rgyu rkyen la ltos nas skyes pas kun rdzob bo/* (AV 197b). This varies from Tsong Khapa's text only in the last line, which occurs as follows: */de ni rgyu dang rkyen las skye bas kun rdzob bo/*. My translation here follows Tsong Khapa's text.

505 That is, practice with an actual seal, *karmamudrā*, as Tsong Khapa explains above.

> word that is[506] the very essence of indicating reality, which is perfected for the sake of all beings, which is nondifferent from unexcelled, true awareness due to being bereft of the turbidity of discursive thought, which is the nature of the mandala's wheels that radiate the light rays of immeasurable hosts of sages, and which can be imparted by means of the word of actuality itself, and which is like the wish-fulfilling jewel." [This is] that which is stated.[507]

This identification is similar to my previous explanation. That which is nondifferent from true awareness since it is untroubled by discursive thought is the gnosis of clear light, and the nature of the mandala that radiates light rays is the previously explained mandala of the magic body.

In his Lūipa commentary, Atiśa wrote that "the integration that is the two truths indivisible, the great awakening spirit, is the fourth," clearly meaning that the fourth consecration concerns integration.[508] Thus,

---

[506] The Tibetan, *tshig gis*, though grammaticaly singular, is a bit ambiguous, and does not indicate definitively whether one or many words are expressed. The word "initiation" bestows "the word" of perfect union on the disciple, expressed in one or many words.

[507] This quote is not, as we might expect from Tsong Khapa's attribution, drawn from Kambalāmbara's commentary on Lūipa's *Śrībhagavad-abhisamaya*, entitled *Śrīcakra-saṁvarābhisamayaṭīkā*. Rather, it is from a work attributed to Kambala called the *Śrīcakrasaṁvaramaṇḍalopāyikā-ratnapradīpodyota*, which makes sense, since this latter work deals with the rites concerning the mandala and consecration therein. The quote occurs as follows: */dbang bskur ba bzhi po bla ma'i zhal nas shes par bya ba ni/ 'di skad du/ de nyid 'gro ba ma lus pa'i don phun sum tshogs par byed pa/ rtog pa'i rnyog pa dang bral ba nyid kyis bla na med pa yang dag par rig pa tha mi dad pa/ thub pa'i tshogs dpag tu med pa'i 'od zer 'phro ba'i dkyil 'khor gyi 'khor lo'i bdag nyid yid bzhin nor bu lta bu bstan pa'i ngo bo nyid kyi tshig gis sbyin par bya'o zhes gsungs pa gang yin pa ste/* (D fol. 271b). This differs from Tsong Khapa's text only in having *de nyid 'gro ba ma lus pa'i don du phun sum tshogs par byed pa*, "it assembles the perfected for the sake of all beings"; while Tsong Khapa's text here reads *de nyid ma lus pa'i don phun sum tshogs par byed pa*, omitting *'gro ba*. My translation follows the former, as it seems to make more sense.

[508] This passage immediately follows the passage quoted above, as follows: */de ltar bden pa gnyis mi phyed pa zung du 'jug pa ni byang chub kyi sems chen po ste bzhi pa'o/* (AV 197b).

the identification of the word "consecration" with the [stage of] integration is a key point in this tradition. This explanation applicable to the two sets of four realities is based upon the exegetical traditions of the two translators. While this is not as extensive as the explanation of the import of the first chapter of the root Tantra by the explanatory Tantras, if you look into the root Tantra itself, I have extensively explained this [in my commentary on the lines] **And now...the secret** (**1.1a**) up until **Listen...** (**1.5d**).

3.3.3. 2.2.2. 1.3. Showing the name of the chapter

In the *Concise* ***Śrī Herukābhidhāna Tantra***, this is the **fourth chapter** on the **nondual** arrangement **of the heroes and yoginīs** of the outer and body mandalas. This is the explanation of the fourth chapter in the *Illumination of the Hidden Meaning, A Detailed Exegesis of the Concise Saṁvara Tantra called "The Cakrasaṁvara."*

CHAPTER 5

Chapter 5 Outline

3.3.3. 2.2.2. 2. The detailed exegesis of attainment by means of mantra and meditation

The second part, detailed exegesis of attainment by means of mantra and meditation, has two sections: (1) selecting the mantra to be repeated and (2) the way of achieving the powers through mantra repetition.

3.3.3. 2.2.2. 2.1. Selecting the mantra to be repeated

The first part has four sections: (1) selecting the root mantra's consonants, (2) selecting the hero's armor mantra, (3) selecting the root mantra's vowels, and (4) selecting the reversed order essence mantra and the heroine's armor mantra.

3.3.3. 2.2.2. 2.1.1. Selecting the root mantra's consonants

The first part has two sections: (1) actual text and (2) showing the name of the chapter.

3.3.3. 2.2.2. 2.1.1. 1. The actual text

The first part has three sections: (1) preparing the basis for mantra selection, (2) selecting the mantra from that [basis], and (3) showing the greatness of the selected mantra.

3.3.3. 2.2.2. 2.1.1. 1.1. Preparing the basis for mantra selection

The first part has two sections: (1) the interpretable explanation and (2) the definitive explanation.

3.3.3. 2.2.2. 2.1.1. 1.1.1. The interpretable explanation

Since this follows the fourth chapter, **thence** is applied. The origin of things, that is, **the origin of all things** such as the ten powers,[509] should be taken as a triangle that illustrates the three doors of liberation.[510] Regarding that, the nature of the animate and inanimate beings, **the universe (5.1a)**, abides in that which is the essence of everything, the emptiness of the three [doors of] liberation. **In the corolla** means in the center of the origin of things. The **indestructible** is the unsundered vajra, and it is **propitious (5.1b)**. It is Vajradhara who holds this.

---

[509] There are two sets of ten powers, those of a fully awakened buddha and those of a bodhisattva. The ten powers of a buddha are: (1) *sthānāsthānajñānabala*, power of knowing right from wrong; (2) *karmavipākajñānabala*, power of knowing the consequences of actions; (3) *nānādhimuktijñānabala*, power of knowing the inclinations (of sentient beings); (4) *nānādhātujñānabala*, power of knowing the nature (of sentient beings); (5) *indriyavarāvarajñānabala*, power of knowing the mental capacity (of sentient beings); (6) *sarvatragāminīpratipatjñānabala*, power of knowing paths that go everywhere; (7) *sarvadhyānavimokṣasamādhisamāpattisaṁkleśavyavadāna-vyutthāna-jñānabala*, power of knowing the affliction, obscuration, and purification of all meditations, liberations, concentrations, and states of equipoise; (8) *pūrvanivāsānusmṛti-jñānabala*, power of knowing past lives; (9) *cyutyutpattijñānabala*, power of knowing future deaths and births; and (10) *āsravakṣayajñānabala*, power of knowing how to exhaust the outflows. The ten powers of a bodhisattva are: (1) *āśayabala*, power of resolve; (2) *adhyāśayabala*, power of resolve; (3) *prayogabala*, power of application; (4) *prajñābala*, power of wisdom; (5) *praṇidhānabala*, power of prayer; (6) *yānabala*, power of the vehicle; (7) *caryābala*, power of practice; (8) *vikurvaṇabala*, power of transformation; (9) *bodhibala*, power of awakening; and (10) *dharmacakra-pravartaṇabala*, power of turning the wheel of the Dharma (Thurman 1976, 154).

[510] The *dharmodaya* refers to a triangular shape, which is identified with the vulva. The three doors of liberation are: (1) *śūṇyatā*, emptiness; (2) *animittatā*, signlessness; and (3) *apraṇihitatā*, wishlessness.

Those that **the mantrin should write in accordance with the rite** (**5.1c**) are the letters that are the nature of Vajrasattva. This indicates that one should write in such a way that one **gathers into one all things** (**5.1d**) that are enunciated in speech. It is **the mantra's syllables** that should be written **here**, in the origin of things. The **classes** that **complete the equalized vowels and consonants** (**5.ab**) must be "gathered," that is, grouped together.[511] As for the meaning of the term "equal" (*samāṁ*, *mnyam pa*), it is explained as "complete" and "completed."[512]

Into how many classes are they grouped?[513] They **should be discerned as being four and four** (**5.2c**). That is, one is the class of vowels, and there are five classes of consonants, the velars, palatals, retroflex, dentals, and labials, which together with the classes of semi-vowels and sibilants make a total of eight. A commentary explains that twice four is eight, hence there are eight verse feet [in the root mantra].[514]

With regard to the [word] "sage" of **the supreme sage** (**5.3d**), since it is a designation for the number seven,[515] it refers to the arrangement of

---

511 Tsong Khapa here comments on the SM text of 5.2b, *sde tshan dag ni bsdu bar bya*, which corresponds to the Sanskrit *vargebhyaḥ pariṇāmitam*. I translate *pariṇāmitam* here as "completed," which interestingly is how Tsong Khapa interprets the previous line.

512 Tsong Khapa is referring here to 5.2a, *ālikālisamāṁ kṛtvā*, translated as *ā li kā li mnyam byas nas* (PM; SL: *a li ka li mnyam byas nas*) and *ā li kā li mnyam byas pa'i* (SM). While this would be literally translated as "having equalized the vowels and consonants," on the basis of commentary such as Tsong Khapa's I translate it as "having prepared the vowels and consonants."

513 Here I read *sde tshan dur byed pa* as *sde tshan du byed pa*. The former reading, which is contained in all six prints that I consulted, appears to be corrupt, but makes sense if one read *dur* as *du*.

514 This is an alternative explanation of this verse, which takes eight as referring to the number of verse-feet of the root mantra, which are, like the phonetic classification system, also eight in number. This is explained in several of the Indian commentaries. For example, Jayabhadra wrote that "**should be discerned as being four and four** refers to the mantra's eight lines" (Sugiki 2001, 115: *catuścaturvijñeyam iti mantrapadāny aṣṭau bhavantīty arthaḥ*; CP 50a: */bzhi bzhi ru ni shes bya la/ /zhes bya ba ni sngags kyi tshig rkang pa brgyad du 'gyur ba'o/*.

515 Tsong Khapa here briefly refers to a matter discussed at greater length in other commentaries, which is the exegesis of the term *muni*, which is taken as a reference to the fact that this chapter selects only the vowels of the root mantra, and thus deals only with the seven classes of consonants. According to Sachen, the "seven munis" designate the seven great buddhas of the past (PG 310.3: */yang na thub pa 'dun ni 'das pa'i sangs rgyas rab 'dun yin la/ /des mtshon pa'i kā li'i sde tshan 'dun no/*). The buddhas of the

(cont'd)

the seven classes of consonants. The system here is that after the body of the mantra is selected, the vowels particular to [each syllable] are applied to it. Prior to this, the consonants are selected.

Although the production of the lotus in the midst of the origin of things is unclear here, the *Saṁpuṭa* states that "Having made Māmakī's secret eight-petaled lotus in the delightful triangular mandala, all desired aims are achieved within the scope of the hidden corolla. The hero should draw from there, achieving all desired aims."[516] Here as well we should take it as an explanation of the production of the eight-petaled lotus within the origin of things. The *Saṁpuṭa* accords with the adherents of Mal's tradition in the placement of letters, in placing the eight classes of vowels, velars, palatals, retroflex, dentals, labials, semivowels, and sibilants on the petals, clockwise starting from the east, and the letter *a* in the center.[517] Mardo claims that one should create a **chart (5.2d)** of forty-nine squares in the origin of things without making the lotus, and that one should place the forty-nine vowels and consonants, exempting the letter *kṣ*. Although it is explained thus in the context of chapter thirty, in this context I think it is better to do so in the manner of Mal's tradition. Bhavabhaṭṭa would have one make a grid of forty-nine squares on the universal lotus within the origin of things, placing therein the forty-nine letters with the exception of *kṣ*.[518] Thus it is essential to produce the forty-nine-square chart on the corolla of the lotus.

---

past are, according to the ancient Buddhist schema, Vipaśyin, Śikhin, Viśvabhū, Krakucchanda, Kanakamuni, Kāśyapa, and Śākyamuni. See Nattier 1991, 19–20.

516 This passage occurs in ST kalpa 7, as follows: */gru gsum dkyil 'khor nyams dga' bar/ /gsang ba'i padma mā ma kī/ /padma 'dab ma bryad byas nas/ /lte ba sbas pa'i sbyod yul du/ /'dod pa kun sgrub byed pa/ /der gnas dpa' bo btu bar bya/* (ST 128b). Tsong Khapa's quote differs only in the last line, as follows: */der gnas dpa' bo kun las btu/.*

517 The foremost "adherent of Mal's tradition," Sachen, wrote the following: "As for that which is **indestructible and propitious in the corolla** in which is drawn the eight variegated petals, it is the letter *a*. Having written that, **the mantrin should draw in accordance with the rite** the sixteen vowels on the easternmost of the eight petals of the lotus, and then, on the [other] seven, draw the seven classes of consonants in a clockwise fashion" (PG 310.2: */sna tshogs padma 'dab brgyad pa bris pa'i lte ba'i dbus su mi shigs dge ni/ yi ge a ste de bris nas cho ga bzhin du sngags zhes pa ni/ padma 'dab ma brgyad kyi shar gyi 'dab ma la ā li bcu drug bri/ 'dab ma bdun po la chos skor du rim pa bzhin du kā li'i sde tshan bdun po so sor bris la/*).

518 See Pandey 2001, 48–49 (Sanskrit) and 263–264 (Tibetan); cf. CV 170b.

From the vowels and consonants that **reside there** within the origin of things one **should draw forth the hero who achieves all desired aims (5.3ab)**, that is, the root mantra. [This identification of] the hero with the mantra [demonstrates] the inseparable reality of the deity and the mantra. In order to achieve success through repetition it is necessary to have a pure mantra. [The word] "pure" indicates that the mantra is selected with dependence upon [the process of] mantra selection. The process of undertaking this is as follows.

The yogī who is adorned with the six insignia (*ṣaṇmudrā*, *phyag rgya drug*), who has a seal (*mudrā*, *phyag rgya*),[519] and who is sky-clad (*digambara*, *phyogs kyi gos can*) anoints the ground and directions of the mandala house with the five nectars, makes it captivating with flowers, fumigates it with the smoke of the "great flesh," and illuminates it with lamps of "great fat." Outside he undertakes the preliminaries such as song and dance, sounds the *ḍamaru* drum and bell, and offers sacrificial cakes. Then he draws the eight-petaled lotus with colored powders made from charnel ground bricks, and so forth, and draws "the indestructible" within the corolla and the eight classes [of vowels and consonants] on the petals, as is explained in the *Āmnāyamañjarī*.[520] The gurus also say that it is drawn after one has visualized the perfection of the clear realization (*abhisamaya*, *mngon rtogs*), performed the worship of the host (*gaṇa-pūjā*), and offered the sacrificial cakes.

3.3.3. 2.2.2. 2.1.1. 1.1.2. The definitive explanation

The text in the *Saṁpuṭa* from "in the delightful triangular mandala" up until "the seed syllables of the supreme lord's mantra"[521] is construed in the *Vasantatilakā* as referring to mantra selection,[522] and is

---

[519] Here *mudrā* presumably refers to an "actual seal" *karmamudrā* consort.

[520] Tsong Khapa here paraphrases a very similar description by Abhayākaragupta. See AM 240b.

[521] Tsong Khapa is referring to the passage quoted from ST kalpa seven in the previous section, with the addition of the following two lines at the end: "through the divisions of [the letters] *a*, and so forth, there are the [phonetic] classes of the supreme lord's mantra" (ST 128b: */a la sogs pa'i rab dbyed bas/ /sngags kyi sde tshan dbang phyug mchog /*). Tsong Khapa reads the last line as: *sngags ni yig 'bru'i dbang phyug mchog*.

[522] This is indeed discussed at length in VT ch. 9. See Samdhong and Dwivedi 1990, 61 ff. (Sanskrit) and 125 ff. (Tibetan).

an explanation of the definitive meaning of the basis of mantra selection. In the *Āmnāyamañjarī* there is an explanation of the definitive meaning of this text in the *Saṁpuṭa* that shows the basis for mantra selection.[523] Here as well, if we were to explain the definitive meaning of these matters,[524] the "mandala" of the triangular mandala is the seal's vulva. It is "delightful" because it is the cause of superlative bliss. "Māmakī" is an appellation of Mānavajriṇī (*rdo rje bsnyems ma*). The eight-petaled lotus of the seal's secret place are the eight channels in the vulva. The channel in the "corolla," i.e., middle [of that] is the channel called "Crow's Face" (*kākāsyā*). It is secret because it is "bound," i.e., located amidst the eight channels. The "scope" is the basis, the central cavity there. The "hero" is the awakening spirit of inseparable bliss and emptiness. It is he alone who is to be "drawn forth," i.e., accomplished; it is he who achieves all desired aims. Thus the seal's vulva is indicated by the "triangular" mandala that is the basis of selection, the eight channels by the eight-petaled lotus, and the lower opening of the central channel by the "corolla" of the lotus. The "drawing forth of the hero" indicates the drawing forth of natural gnosis through the union of the two tips of the channels of the male and female couple, as explained in chapter one. This is explained within the text of the seventh *kalpa* of the *Saṁpuṭa*. Moreover, the first *kalpa* of the *Saṁpuṭa* [states the following]:

> In the middle of the pure triangle, with the shape of the syllable *e*, is the lovely *evaṁ*. The delightful triangular mandala is said to be the vajra's abode (*vajrārali*),[525] which is called the "origin of things" (*dharmodaya*) and also the ladies' vulva[e] (*yoṣitāṁ bhage[ṣu]*). The lotus that goes within that has eight petals and a corolla. In it

523 Tsong Khapa here closely follows Abhayākaragupta's explanation in AM ch. 27, fol. 240a.

524 In what follows Tsong Khapa explicates the ST passage quoted above, largely following the VT and AM commentaries previously indicated.

525 Note that I am also taking *vajrārali* as a variant of *vajroli*, and am following David White's suggestion that this may in turn be a middle Indo-Aryan shortening of *vajrālaya* (1996, 454–455, n. 98), hence "vajra's abode." If this is correct, then *vajrārali* is almost certainly an intermediate form between *vajrālaya* and *vajroli*. This is a highly speculative interpretation, but seems to be appropriate in this context at least.

> the vowels and consonants mix, positioned in the eight classes.[526]

It also states that "the supreme lord is in the middle on the filament, and the supreme syllable, *A*, the foremost of all syllables, is surrounded by the eight classes."[527]

With regard to "the lotus of the navel, and so forth," the *Āmnāyamañjarī* explains that the [statement] "the shape of the letter *e*" indicates the channel wheels of the navel, and so forth.[528] It is held that there are four [channel] wheels, the other three being indicated by the expression *and so forth*. Furthermore, it seems to say in the explanatory Tantra that the navel and throat channel wheels have the triangular shape of the letter *e*, and the heart and crown channel wheels have the round shape of the letter *vaṁ*.[529] Thus two of the channel wheels are indicated by the inner

---

[526] This passage occurs at ST 1.4 as follows: *trikoṇake śuddhe // ekārākṛtimadhye rasayaivaṁ yathā bhavati // trikoṇe maṇḍale ramye vajrārali vinisṁṛtaṁ // dharmodayeti vikhyātaṁ yoṣitāṁ bhaga ity api // tasya madhye gataṁ padmaṁ aṣṭapatraṁ sakarṇikam // tatrālikālisammiśrā aṣṭau varṇavyavasthitāḥ //*; */gru gsum dag pa e yi dbyibs/ /dbus su dgyes pa'i evaṁ yin/ /gru gsum dkyil 'khor nyams dga' bar/ /rdo rje ra li rnam par byung / /btsun mo'i bhaga zhes kyang bya/ /chos kyi 'byung gnas zhes byar bshad/ /de yi nang song padma ni/ /'dab ma brgyad pa snying por bcas/ /de la ā li kā li 'dres/ /sde tshan brgyad ni rnam par gnas/* (Skorupski 1996, 238); cf. ST 80b.

[527] This passage, also from ST ch. 1.4, occurs as follows: *eṣaṁ madhye tu kiñjalke vidyate parameśvaraḥ // aṣṭabhir vargakaiś caiva veṣṭitaḥ paramākṣaraḥ // akāraḥ sarvavarṇāgro* (Skorupski 1996, 239); */de rnams dbus su ze 'bru la/ /dam pa'i dbang phug ma yod do/ /sde tshan brgyad po rnams kyis ni/ /yi ge dam pa yongs su bskor/ /a ni yig 'bru kun gyi mchog/* (1996, 238); cf. ST 80b–81a.

[528] In his commentary on ST ch. 1.4, Abhayākaragupta explains that the syllable *e* of *evaṁ* indicates both the navel and crown channel wheels. He wrote that: "It should be understood that the syllable *e*, etc., [indicates] the upward-facing lotus of the navel and the downward-facing lotus of the crown are the letter *e*, meaning that they have the triangular shape of the syllable *e* and that they have the nature of wisdom. The downward-facing lotus of the heart and the upward facing lotus of the throat are the syllable *vaṁ*, meaning they have the round shape of the syllable *vaṁ* as well as the nature of art." */e yig gis ni zhes pa la sogs pa'o/ /gyen du lta ba'i lte ba'i chu skyes dang 'og du phyogs pa'i spyi bo'i mtsho skyes ni e yig ni e yig gi dbyibs can gru gsum shes rab kyi rang bzhin du mos par bya'o/ /thur du ltas pa'i snying ga'i chu skyes dang gyen du ltas pa'i mgrin pa'i chu skyes ni vaṁ yig ste vaṁ yig gi dbyibs can zlum po thabs kyi rang bzhin du'o/* (AM 56a).

[529] This is *not* the system of the *Saṁpuṭa Tantra*, the explanatory Tantra that is being commented upon here. Abhayākaragupta follows up the passage translated in the previous note with the following, which quotes a verse from ST ch. 6.3 (fol. 114b): "Where is

(cont'd)

explanation of the of the triangular origin of things, while the other two are indicated by the lotus within it, which has a round shape. The "triangular mandala" is taken to be both the seal's vulva and the navel and throat channel wheels.

"Vajra" is the secret place of the vajra as well as the jasmine-like awakening spirit. The meaning of "rali" is the sport called *arali*, which gives an indication of the joy of bliss through the sport of Vajrasattva, who is the very embodiment of great bliss. Regarding the meaning of both the "going within" that and the "classes," it appears to refer to the visualization of the eight classes within the triangular *e* of the channel wheel in the navel, as explained in the *Ālicatuṣṭaya*.[530] From this illustration, the visualization of the syllables in the other channel wheels should also be understood.

These [matters], applied within the context of the basis of mantra selection, indicate the fury fire meditation that relies upon the four wheels.[531] In regard to this, "mixing the vowels and consonants" indicates

---

this stated? 'The wheels that apply to the crown and navel exist in the aspect of the letter *e*. Those that exist in the heart and throat are described as being similar to the letter *vaṁ*.' Both this correspondence and [the correspondence of] the navel and heart lotuses and the throat and crown lotuses are integrated through experiential unity (*ekarasa*) in bliss at the times of the going and coming of the fury fire (*cāṇḍalī*), which is excellent" (AM 56a: */gang gsung bar 'gyur ba/ /spyi bo lte bar son 'khor lo/ /e yig rnam par yang dag gnas/ /snying ga mgrin par yang dag gnas/ /vaṁ gyi yi ge 'dra bar 'dod/ /ces so/ /lte ba dang snying ga'i chu skyes dag dang mgrin pa dang spyi bo'i mtsho skyes dag gi dang de'i rje su zung gnyis kyi yang gtu mo 'gro ba dang 'ong ba'i dus su bde bar ro gcig pa nyid kyis snyoms par 'jug pas mdzes so/*).

530 This is not discussed in the AC itself, but in Kāṇha's autocommentary, the *Ālicatuṣṭaya-vibhaṅga*, at D fols. 58b–64a.

531 Needless to say, it is by no means obvious how *caṇḍālī* meditation is esoterically indicated by a chapter on mantra selection. Tsong Khapa here follows Kāṇha, who, in his *Ālicatuṣṭaya-vibhaṅga*, considers his "stage of Tantra"—which deals with the visualization of the letters in the lotuses, as nondifferent from his "stage of mantra"—which deals with *caṇḍālī* meditation. He writes that in "the 'stage of mantra' [things] occur as in the [stage of] Tantra, because the syllables that exist in the four wheels are not different from the vowels and consonants, and also because the ascent [of the *caṇḍālī*] ascends possessed of the consonants, and the descent descends possessed of the vowels" (D fol. 64b: */sngags kyi rim pa'o zhes bya ba ni/ de ltar rgyud la gnas pa ste/ 'khor lo bzhi gnas pa'i yi ge rnams ā li kā li las gzhan ma yin pa'am/ yang na yar 'gro ba ni kā li'i sgra dang ldan par 'gro la/ mar 'ong ba ni āli'i sgra dang ldan par 'ong ba'i phyir ro/*). Apparently, Kāṇha associates the ascent and descent of the *caṇḍālī* with the consonants and vowels, respectively.

that there is another explanation for the vowels and consonants that are the basis of selection. Since [the *Saṁpuṭa*] has it that they are "positioned" in a "mixture," this means that they exist in an unclear state. When the vowels and consonants are enunciated, they arise in an indistinct manner from the wind that previously moved in the space within the vulva, and then are clearly created at [sites of] production such as the palate, and so forth. It is just as it is said, "Sound is produced in the mouth arising in a form issuing from the wind of space. Sound becomes syllables when they originate in the various places."[532]

Regarding the syllable *a* in the middle, since it is naturally unproduced, it is the "foremost" lord "of all the sounds" of the mantra. This illustrates emptiness that is naturally unproduced. If taken in this manner, the inner explanation of the letters on the petals, the lotus, and the origin of things illustrates the art of drawing forth great bliss. The union of emptiness and great bliss drawn forth via the two methods is exemplified by the syllable *a* that is in their midst. Just as, conventionally, the syllable *A* is the source of all speech sounds in general and all mantras in particular, ultimately it gives rise to all of the powers as stated in the explanatory Tantra.[533] As for the syllable *A*'s illustration of emptiness, since one's efforts are fruitless if one is devoid of the view [resulting from] the realization of emptiness, it means that there is a definite need for this. This is because, as it says in the *Vairocana Abhisaṁbodhi*, "Lord of the Secret Ones, the bodhisattva will accomplish all deeds by abiding in the syllable *A*."[534] It is also as is stated in the *Acala Kalpa*, namely that:

---

[532] Tsong Khapa did not indicate the source of this passage, which is apparently from a translation of a Sanskrit text. It does not appear to be from the texts he has been citing elsewhere in this chapter.

[533] The powers achieved through the syllable *A* are listed in ST ch. 1.4, immediately following the passage on which Tsong Khapa is currently commenting. See Skorupski 1996, 239, and D fol. 81a.

[534] This passage occurs in ch. 12 of the Tibetan translation and ch. 10 of the Chinese translation of the *Mahāvairocanābhisaṁbodhi*. It occurs in the former as follows: */gsang ba bdag po de la byang chub sems dpas a zhes bya ba la gnas te / dgos pa thams cad bsgrub par bya'o/* (203a). Tsong Khapa's source for both this and the following quote is Abhayākaragupta, in whose text it occurs as follows: */de la gsang ba bdag po byang chub sems dpas a yig la gnas pas bya ba thams cad bsgrub par bya'o/* (AM 54b). Tsong Khapa's text differs from Abhayākara's only in omitting *de la*. See TL fol. 70b, LH 66a.

> Once the spirit of awakening is stabilized, then one may speak of the powers of mantra. Otherwise the rites for accomplishing the powers of mantra are all fruitless. In short, the spirit of awakening is attained from considering all things as lacking intrinsic reality, otherwise it is not [attained].[535]

These are quoted in this context in the *Āmnāyamañjarī*. One should understand the very great importance of the view of emptiness illustrated by the syllable *a*.

3.3.3. 2.2.2. 2.1.1. 1.2. Selecting the mantra from that [basis]

The second part has two sections: (1) selecting the eight-line root mantra and (2) selecting the *kara kara* root mantra.

3.3.3. 2.2.2. 2.1.1. 1.2.1. Selecting the eight-line root mantra

The first part has two sections: (1) selecting the first four lines and (2) selecting the latter four [lines].

---

[535] These two verses occur in the *Āryācalamahākrodharājasya-sarvatathāgatasya-balāparimitavīravinayasvākhyāta-nāma-kalpa*. Tsong Khapa follows Abhayākaragupta in omitting two intervening verses. The full passage occurs as follows: "Once the spirit of awakening is stabilized, then one may speak of the powers of mantra. Otherwise the rites for accomplishing the powers of mantra are all fruitless. Just as if a tree fails to produce a root it will not have flowers or fruits, likewise, the mantra is the fruit and the spirit of awakening is the root. Once one has produced the awakening spirit, one can then attain the supreme state. All things exist through generation and abiding. In short, the spirit of awakening is attained from considering all things as lacking intrinsic reality, otherwise it is not [attained]" (D fol. 267b: */byang chub sems ni brtan byas nas/ /sngags kyi dngos grub brjod par bya/ /sngags kyi dngos grub bya'i cho ga /gzhan du thams cad 'bras bu med/ /ji ltar rtsa ba bskyed min na/ /shing gi me tog 'bras bu med/ /de ltar gsang sngags 'bras bu shes/ /byang chub sems ni rtsa ba yin/ /byang chub sems ni bskyed nas su/ /bla na med pa'i go 'phang 'thob/ /'di la gnas pa'i chos kun ni/ /skye dang gnas pas 'byung ba ste/ /dngos po thams cad mdor bsdus nas/ /rang bzhin med cing bsam du med/ /byang chub sems ni nges par 'thob/ /gzhan du 'ba' zhig par 'gyur ro /*). The text as it occurs in Abhayākaragupta's text actually seems more reliable, and hence I followed it closely in my translation. It occurs as follows: (AM 54b: */byang chub sems ni brtan byas nas/ /sngags kyi dngos grub gsungs ba ste/ /gzhan du sngags grub cho ga yi/ /bya ba thams cad 'bras bu med/ /dngos po thams cad mdor bsdus pas/ /rang bzhin med nyid bsam pa las/ /byang chub sems ni nges par 'thob/ /gzhan du 'ba' zhig 'gyur ba min /*).

3.3.3. 2.2.2. 2.1.1. 1.2.1. 1. Selecting the first four lines

Place in the empty space in the beginning [the syllable] *oṁ* as a pure shield. Then, it is said, write the letters in accordance with the stages. Since the vowels are not selected here, selecting then from the consonants, **that which is the fifth of the fourth (5.3c)** dental class is *n*. Immediately after that, **also that which is the fifth of the fifth (5.3d)** labial class is *m*, and **that which is the fourth of fifth (5.4a)** class is *bh*. **That which is the third of the first (5.4b)** velar class is *g*, and **thus as well the twenty-ninth (5.4c)** counting from *k* is *v*. **That which is the first of the fourth (5.4d)** dental class is *t*. **The fourth of the semivowels (5.5a)** is *v*, **and the second of them (5.5b)**, i.e., of the semivowels, is *r*. **Taking the thirtieth (5.5c)** counting from *k* yields *ś*. **Likewise the twenty-sixth (5.5d)** is *y*. **Drawing out all (5.6a)** of the above letters [yields] the body of the first line.

The second line is selected in the same manner as the first. **Half** of **a hundred** is fifty, and **half (5.6d)** of that, the twenty-fifth, is *m*. **Then** after *m* one should **take the thirty-third (5.7a)**, *h*, **the first of the first (5.7b)** class that is *k*, and **the third semivowel (5.7c)** which is *l*. Regarding the nonoccurrence of the *p* that is affixed to *l* here, the selection [here] does not take into account the affixed letter.[536] **The third of the first (5.7d)** class is *g*. **The thirty-second (5.8a)** counting from *k* is *s*, **and that which is the fifth of the fourth (5.8b)** class is *n*. **That which is fourth of the fifth (5.8c)** is *bh*, **and the first of the semivowels (5.8d)** is *y*, [which yields] the body of the second line.

The **third of the second (5.9a)** palatal class is *j*, **the first of the third (5.9b)** retroflex class is *ṭ*, **the fifth of the fifth (5.9c)** class is also *m*, **and the first of the first (5.9d)** velar class is *k*. **Likewise the eleventh (5.10a)** counting from *k* is *ṭ*. **The sixteenth**, counting from *k*, *t* **is also** taken **by** those **skilled (5.10b)** in mantra selection. [The letter] *k* does not occur after it due to the fact that it is subjoined to *t*.[537] **The first of the third (5.10c)** retroflex class is *ṭ*, and **the twenty-sixth** is **likewise (5.10d)** *y*, [which yields] the body of the third line.

---

[536] At issue here is the letter *p* in *kalpa*. This letter is selected with the vowels in chapter 7.

[537] As before, the second letter in the consonant cluster *-tka* is selected in chapter 7.

That which is third of the fourth (**5.11a**) dental class is *d*, and **the second sibilant** (**5.11b**) is *ṣ*. The nonoccurrence of *ṭ* is as previously [discussed]. **That which is first of the first** (**5.11c**) velar class is *k*. **Thus the twenty-seventh** (**5.11d**) is *r*, **and again the twenty-eighth** (**5.12a**) is held to be *l*. One should know that these are counted from *k*, as is also the case elsewhere. **The third of the first** (**5.12b**) velar class is *g*, **and the fourth of the fifth** labial class is *bh* **as well** (**5.12c**). **Take then the thirty-first** (**5.12d**), which is *ṣ*, **and the fifteenth** (**5.13a**), *ṇ*. **Likewise the twenty-fifth** (**5.13b**) is *m*, **and the second of the first** (**5.13c**) velar class is *kh*. **Likewise the twenty-sixth** (**5.13d**) is *y*, [which concludes] the body of the fourth line.

3.3.3. 2.2.2. 2.1.1. 1.2.1. 2. Selecting the latter four [lines]

The thirty-second letter (**5.14a**) from *k* is *s*, and **the last of the sibilants** (**5.14b**) is *h*. **The thirty-second** (**5.14c**) is *s*. **The fourth of the fifth** (**5. 14d**) labial class is *bh*, **and the third of the second** (**5.15a**) palatal class is *j*. **The fourth of the fifth** (**5.15b**) labial class is *bh*, **and the third sibilant** (**5.15c**) is *s*. In addition to these, **the twenty-seventh** (**5.15d**) is *r*, **and the first semivowel** (**5.16a**) is *y*, [which completes] the body of the fifth line.

The sixth line is selected in the same manner as the fifth. **The twenty-first** (**5.16b**) from *k* is *p*, **and the second semivowel** (**5.16c**) is *r*. As in the case of the previous selection of the letter *ś*, **thus once more the thirtieth** (**5.16d**) is *ś*. **The first of the fifth** (**5.17a**) labial class is *p*, **the first of the sibilants** (**5.17b**) is *ś*, **and thus the syllable** ***dya*** (**5.17c**).[538] **That which is the first of the fourth** (**5.17d**) dental class is *t*, **and that which is the first sibilant** (**5.18a**) is *ś*. **Likewise the twenty-eighth** (**5.18b**) is *l*, **and the second of the first** (**5.18c**) velar class is *kh*. **The first of the third** (**5.18d**) retroflex class is *ṭ*, **and that which is the third of the first** (**5.19a**) velar class is *g*. **The fourth of the fourth** (**5.19b**) dental class is *dh*, **and the second semivowel** (**5.19c**) is *r*. **The fifth of the third** retroflex class **as well** (**5.19d**), *ṇ*, [concludes] the body of the sixth line.

---

538 The correct reading here, *dya* (i.e., the *-dya-* in *paraśupāśodyataśūla-khaṭvāṅga-dhāriṇe*), is the reading given in the Sanskrit as well as the PM and SM translations (SL read *dhya*). Among the KS prints I consulted, only Q reads *dya*; the rest read *dyā*.

Following the selection of the sixth line, take **the syllable *vyā* (5.20a)**. It is claimed that both this and the syllable *dya* refer, respectively, to the blessings of the vajra and lotus; they are thus selected together with the limbs.[539] However, while both syllables are included in the sequence of the eight lines, it is not the case that the semivowels are selected with the "limbs" that are the vowels. Although [the semivowels] are consonants with respect to the other consonants in the sequence, those that are subjoined to or conjoined with other consonants are not selected here. [The cases in which] *p* is attached to *l* or *n* to *g* [to form the consonant conjuncts in *kalpa* and *agni*] are dissimilar to [the cases in which] *h* is added to *d* and *b* [to represent the aspirate letters *dh* and *bh*], which in each case represent [simple] consonant letters.[540]

That which is the fourth of the first (5.20b) velar class is *gh*, **and** after that **the eighth (5.20c)** from *k* is *j*. **That which is the fifth of the fourth (5.20d)** dental class is *n*, **and the fifth of the fifth** labial class **as well (5.21a)** is *m*. I believe that the nonoccurrence of *b* after this indicates that they are conjoined. **Likewise the twenty-seventh (5.21b)** is *r*, **and the fourth of the fourth (5.21c)** is *dh*. **The twenty-seventh once again (5.21d)** is *r*, **and likewise the twenty-sixth (5.22a)** is *y*, which [concludes] the body of the seventh line.

Take the twenty-fifth (5.22b), *m*, **and the thirty-third (5.22c)**, *h*. **The fourth of the fourth (5.22d)** is *dh*, **and the fifth of the fifth (5.23a)** *m*. **The fifth of the fourth (5.23b)** dental class is *n*, **and the first of the first** *k* **(5.23c)**. **Likewise the twenty-seventh** is *r* **(5.23d)**, **and the fourth semivowel** is *v* **(5.24a)**. **Thus the twenty-first** is *p* **(5.24b)**, **the second sibilant** *ṣ* **(5.24c)**, **and likewise the twenty-sixth** *y* **(5.24d)**, [which completes] the selection of the eighth line.

---

539 It is Büton who links these syllables to the blessings, although he says nothing about these syllables being selected with the vowels, so I am not sure what is the basis of Tsong Khapa's criticism here. See NS 302.

540 Unlike Sanskrit but like English, Tibetan lacks letters in its alphabet representing the aspirate sounds, and thus represents them (as we do here in English) by adding an *h* to the corresponding letter representing the unaspirated sound. In this chapter only the basic consonants are selected, and the conjunct consonants are delineated below. The aspirated consonants are represented by a single letter in Sanskrit, and are thus selected here with all of the other consonants, despite the fact that they appear to be conjunct consonants when represented in Tibetan orthography.

In the translations of Lochen and Mal there is no further mantra selection after the selection of the eight-line [mantra] with the exception of the presentation of the *kara kara* root mantra. In the *Pearl Garland* there is [the following text]: "The selection of the *kara kara*, etc., mantra was inserted in the text of Lo-chung[541] by him himself; it is said that it does not occur in the root Tantra in any of the Sanskrit texts."[542] Thus a fabricator inserted a spurious selection of the *kara kara*, etc., [mantra] into Mal's translation, and also inserted it into the translation of Mardo alone.[543] I will not write about this sort of fabrication.

Excepting the selection of the eight-line mantra, there is no selection of the *kara kara* mantra in the translation of Lochen as refined by Gö,[544] nor in the revision of Paṇḍita Sumatikīrti and Mardo, and in this

---

541 The title *lo chung*, "Lesser Translator," usually refers to Ngok Lochung Legpay Sherab, one of Rinchen Zangpo's disciples, but he is not associated with any known translation of the CT. Rather, as Tsong Khapa points out, Sachen almost certainly refers here to the translator Mardo, whose PM revised translation is the only extant translation that contains the selection for the *kara kara* mantra. The other two, and, as Tsong Khapa informs us, Rinchen Zangpo's original translation, do not contain this. Rather, like the extant Sanskrit text, they simply state this mantra outright. This is probably the reason for Sachen's claim that this text was inserted into the translation by Mardo.

542 Tsong Khapa here quotes directly from Sachen's commentary, where the text occurs as follows: */de yang kara kara la sogs pa btu ba lo chung gi dpe la khong nyid kyis bcug nas yod de/ /de ni rgya gar gyi rgya dpe thams cad la rtsa rgyud la 'di na med gsung /* (PG 312.2–3).

543 Neither Mal's translation (in both the text preserved in the Phug-brag Kangyur as well as the text commented upon by Sachen) nor Mardo's solo translation (SM) contains the selection for the *kara kara* mantra. Sachen hence does not comment on it in his PG commentary, and merely says, following the statement quoted above, that "As for the selection of that [mantra], it is explained in the *Vajraḍāka* and in the *Abhidhānottara*, and it should be known as it occurs in those explanatory Tantras" (PG 312.3: */de'i btu ba ni rdo rje mkha' 'gro dang nges brjod bla ma gnyis nas btu ba bshad pa ni bshad rgyud nyid de shes par bya'o/*). Tsong Khapa surely knew this, and I thus suspect that he wrote this comment to deflect criticism from the PM translation (which does contain the *kara kara* mantra selection) by directing the reader's attention to (apparently nonexistent) spurious versions of the SL and SM translations.

544 The original Lochen translation was revised during the eleventh century by Sūryagupta and Gö Hlaytsay on the basis of a Sanskrit text of Kambala's commentary. This translation apparently was available to Tsong Khapa, but is now lost. It was, however, the basis of the SM commentary preferred by Tsong Khapa. For more information on the history of this text see Gray 2012, 28–32.

context there is not even the presentation of the *kara kara* mantra.[545] The translation of Lochen as revised by both the translator Prajñākīrti and Mardo does contain the *kara kara* mantra selection.

Moreover, the "Kīrti" in whose presence [the revisions] were conducted with reference to a text from Magadha seems to have been Sumatikīrti, who evidently had several different Sanskrit texts.[546] The paṇḍita who produced Mal's tradition was also Sumatikīrti. In this way, the Nepali Bhatanta consulted the text of Prajñārakṣita, who was an actual disciple of Nāropā, for the sake of the Tibetan scholars, and it appears that this was [a text] reputed to have had the mantra selection of the complete root mantra. Although there is no mention of anything other than the selection of the eight-line mantra in the commentaries of the Tibetan scholars,[547] Kambala's commentary refers to the selection of the entire root mantra in the root Tantra, saying "[Through text such as] **the fifth of the fourth**, etc., there is selection of the root mantra, the Blessed Lord's mantra in eight lines, together with the *kara kara*, etc., [mantra]."[548]

---

545 As Tsong Khapa correctly points out, the SM translation does not even include the transcription of the *kara kara* mantra.

546 Tsong Khapa seems to be referring to the colophon of the PM translation, the end of which reads: "In order to infuse it with the scent of superior moral discipline and have it concord with the import of stainless teachings, it was [revised] in the presence of one famed as being realized by the translator-monk Prajñākīrti and the translator Marpa Chökyi Wangchuk, relying on a text from Magadha, the source of the scholars" (Gray 2012, 413–414: */lhag pa'i tshul khrims dri yis bsgos gyur cing / /dri med bka' don 'thad pa dang bcas par /rtogs pa dang ldan grags pa'i zhal sngar ni/ /sgra bsgyur dge slong prajñā kīrti dang / /mar pa sgra bsgyur chos kyi dbang phyug gis/ /mkhas pa'i 'byung gnas yul dbus dpe dang gtugs//*). On the basis of this text, it is clearly that the "Kīrti" involved with this revision was Prajñākīrti, not Sumatikīrti. Tsong Khapa's claim, that Sumatikīrti was involved with all three revised translations, seems far-fetched.

547 Sachen does not comment on its selection, but Büton does, as Tsong Khapa was surely aware, as his previous comment about the "Nepali Bhatanta" was drawn directly from his commentary. See NS 303.

548 Kambala's comments here seem ambiguous; while he mentions the *kara kara* mantra, it is not clear to me if he is referring to its selection, or simply its presentation, as occurs in the extant Sanskrit. It occurs as follows: */bzhi pa yi ni lnga pa dang zhes bya ba la sogs pa rnams kyis bcom ldan 'das kyi sngags kyi tshigs bcad brgyad pa dang / ka ra ka ra zhes bya ba la sogs pa dang bcas pas rtsa ba'i sngags btu ba'o/* (SN 14b).

Therefore, as there are many differences among the Indian texts, there would likely have been a selection of the complete mantra.[549]

3.3.3. 2.2.2. 2.1.1. 1.2.2. Selecting the *kara kara* root mantra

The second part has three sections: (1) selecting the mantra's first set of eight [lines], (2) selecting the mantra's middle set of eight [lines], and (3) selecting the mantra's final set of eight [lines].

3.3.3. 2.2.2. 2.1.1. 1.2.2. 1. Selecting the mantra's first set of eight [lines]

The first of the first velar class of consonants is *k*, and **the second semivowel** is *r*. **The first of the** velar class, which is **second** if you take the first to be the vowel class, is *k*, and **the second of the sixth (5.A1)**[550] class of semivowels is also *r*.[551] **The first of the first** guttural class of consonants is *k*, and **the second semivowel** is *r* as previously explained. **The first of the second** is *k* as was previously the case, and **the second of the seventh (5.A2)** class, taking the vowels as the first, is *r*. The "fourth of the sixth" class counting from the vowel class is *bh* as well.

---

[549] Tsong Khapa may of course be right about this, but it should be noted that none of the Indian commentaries actually comments on the coding of the *kara kara* mantra. Many skip over the mantra selection, evidently because this was considered easy and thus not in need of commentary. Both Bhavabhaṭṭa and Durjayacandra are exceptions in that they do comment upon the mantra selection. Interestingly, they only comment on the selection of the eight-line mantra, which Bhavabhaṭṭa calls the *mūlamantra*. Following this, however, Bhavabhaṭṭa lists the entire *kara kara* mantra, commenting only that one needs to add the syllables *phaṭ phaṭ* to the end, which are left out in the Tantra (Pandey 2002, 58; CV fol. 173b), while Durjayacandra makes the same comment without presenting the mantra (RG 273a). If the *kara kara* mantra was inserted into a Sanskrit text of this Tantra, it was probably a very late redaction.

[550] Since the selection of the mantra occurs only in the PM translation, I have assigned it the alternate verse numbers A1–A34, to clearly indicate its anomalous status. I indicate the verse number at the conclusion of the verse. See my (2012) edition of the PM revised translation for a full presentation of the text, and the verse numbers that I assign to it.

[551] The hypothesis that the *kara kara* mantra section is a distinct microform, produced by different author(s) and drawn from a different text (almost certainly the AU), is supported by the differences in the selection process between the previous eight-line mantra section and this one. These include the alternate system found here of counting from both the vowels and the consonants. This section also differs in referring to semivowels as the "sixth class." Other innovations include selecting the subjoined semivowels, as well as a number of other inconsistencies that are noted below as they occur.

Here [the text] "**the third of the sixth**" is corrupt, as it is essential to select *bh*.[552] The explanatory Tantra, moreover, states that it is the "fourth."[553] **The fifth of the fourth** dental class is *n*, and one should affix to that *dh*, the fourth of that class, which is subjoined to it. Although [the text next] calls for *v*, **the fourth of the semivowels (5.A3)**, here it is essential to select *bh*;[554] it seems that it might be the case that *bh* is the fourth [of the labial class of consonants] which "reside at the end,"[555] i.e., after the velar, palatal, retroflex, and dental classes. The **fifth of the fifth** dental class is *n*, and it **is seated by the fourth** of that [class], ***dh***, meaning it is joined to it.

The first of the fifth dental class is *t*, which **has below a seat of fire (5.A4)**, i.e., a subjoined letter *r*. **Likewise, the third sibilant** is *s*, and **the first semivowel** *y*. In the same way, **the first of** the dental class, **the fourth** counting from the vowels,[556] is *t*, which **is seated by fire (5.A5)**, i.e., a subjoined *r*. **The third of the seventh** class, the sibilant class counting from the velar class, is *s*, and **the first of** the semivowels, **the sixth** class counting from the velars, is *y*.

By attaching below or stacking *ṣ* with the **first,** *k*, one **takes up** that which **should be called** *kṣ*. The **fourth of the fifth (5.A6)** labial class is *bh*, and **the first semivowel** is *y*. In the same manner as that previously held to be *kṣ*, **once again** one **takes up** *k* and *ṣ* as **a mass. The**

---

552 Actually, Tsong Khapa is incorrect here. The Sanskrit here reads, correctly, *bandha*, not **bhandha*, as Tsong Khapa seems to believe.

553 As Tsong Khapa reports, the AU here reads, incorrectly, "the fourth of the sixth as well" (H 167a.5, I 609a.6, J 271.5: *ṣaṣṭhasyāpi caturthaṁ tu*). I am not sure how Tsong Khapa knew this, since the canonical AU translation, like the PM text, both give the correct reading "the third of the sixth" (AU 351a: *drug pa yi ni gsum pa dang*). This may represent a case in which the translators corrected an error in the Sanskrit.

554 Again, the text should read *ba* here, not *bha*. The confusion of the letters *va* and *ba* is quite common in this literature.

555 This seems like a rather fanciful attempt to arrive at the reading that Tsong Khapa believes (mistakenly) is correct. Here he plays with the Tibetan translation *mthar gnas pa*, literally "positioned at the end." This is actually a mistranslation of the Sanskrit term *antaḥstha*, which literally means "positioned between." This mistranslation is based upon the fact that the term is often written *antastha*, with the *visarga* dropped.

556 Actually, the dental class is the *fifth*, counting from *and including* the vowels. It is the fourth counting from the velar class, excluding the vowels.

fourth of the fifth labial class is *bh*, and **the first of the seventh (5.A7)**, the semivowels, is *y*. **The fourth sibilant** is held to be *h*, the **fourth of the seventh** sibilant class is *h*. Regarding **split by Vajrasattva**, someone commented that it is the drop above the *h*,[557] but this is not its meaning, since the drops are stated in the context of the selection of the vowels in chapter seven, and also because "split by Vajrasattva" is explained as meaning split by the letter *r*. Thus "split by Vajrasattva" means that the *r* is affixed to both of the [letters] *h*.

The fourth sibilant (5.A8) is *h*, and **seated by the sun** indicates that an *r* is affixed to it. **The fourth of** the sibilant class, **the seventh** counting from the velars, is *h*. This yields *hra*. The **seat of fire below** it indicates a subjoined *r*. Both of these *hra* [syllables] are **endowed with *visarga* (5.A9)** at their ends. **The second of the** labial class, t**he fifth** counting from the velars, is *ph*, and **likewise the twenty-second** counting from *k* is *ph*. These are the two that will go on to form *pheṁ pheṁ*.

3.3.3. 2.2.2. 2.1.1. 1.2.2. 2. Selecting the mantra's middle set of eight [lines]

Join to the end of **the second of** the labial class, **the sixth** class starting with the vowels, *ph*, **the eleventh (5.A10)** letter starting from *k*, *ṭ*. Once again, **taking the twenty-second**, *ph*, join to it *ṭ*, **the first of** the retroflex class that is **the third** counting from the velars. **The third of the fourth** dental class is *d*, and **the fourth sibilant** is *h* **(5.A11)**. **The third of the fifth** dental class is *d*, and **the fourth of the seventh**, the sibilant class, is *h*. **Then select** *p* as **the twenty-first**, and **the first of the second** palatal class is *c* **(5.A12)**.[558] **The first of the fifth** labial class is *p*, and select *c*, **the sixth letter** counting **from** *k* of the velar class, which is **the second** if the vowel class is taken to be first. **The fourth of the fifth** labial class is *bh*, and likewise *kṣ*, **which should be called *ka* and *ṣa* (5.A13)**. **Then select the twenty-fourth** counting from *k*, *bh*, and **again the mass**, i.e., the previously selected *kṣ*.

The third of the fifth labial class is *b*, and **the third sibilant** is *s* **(5.A14)**. **The second semivowel** is *r*, **the fourth of the fifth** dental class

---

557 This "someone" is Büton. See NS 304.

558 While the Tibetans represent the Sanskrit palatal consonants as *tsa*, *tsha*, *dza*, and *dzha*, here I represent them as *ca*, *cha*, *ja*, and *jha*, the actual Sanskrit palatal consonants.

dh, and **again the sun**, the letter *r*, **is bestowed**. **The twentieth letter** counting from *k* is *n*, **underneath (5.A15)** it **is** its **seat**, i.e., a subjoined **sixteenth** [letter], *t*. **Underneath** *t* it **is illumined by fire**, which means it has a subjoined *r*. The **fifth of the fifth** labial class is *m*, and **the third semivowel** is *l* **(5.A16)**. **The third of the fifth** labial class is *b*, **the third of the sixth**, the semivowels, is *l*, and **the fourth semivowel** is *v*. Someone said that in the Sanskrit text *b* and *v* are similar.[559] It is **distinguished by the twenty-fifth (5.A17)**, which means that it is affixed to *m*. The **fifth of the fourth** dental class is *n*.

The third of the velar class, which is **the second** counting the vowels, is *g*, and it is **split by the son of the sun**, which indicates a subjoined *r*. **The fourth sibilant** is *h* **(5.A18)**, and **the fifteenth**, *ṇ*, serves as its **seat below** the *h*. **The third of the first** velar class is *g*, and it is **seated by fire**, i.e., affixed with *r*. **The fourth of the seventh (5.A19)**, the sibilants, is *h*, and **below** it is **the seat of the fifteenth**, *ṇ*.

The third sibilant is *s*, and **the first of the fifth** labial class is *p*, which **is seated by the sixteenth**, *t* **(5.A20)**. **Take the twenty-first**, *p*. **The first of the fourth** dental class is *t*. **The third semivowel** is *l*. **The third of** the velar class, which is **the second (5.A21)** [class] counting the vowels [as the first class], is *g*, and **the first of the fourth** dental class is *t*. **The fourth of the fifth** is *bh*, and **the third of** the palatal class, which is **the third** counting the vowels, is *j*. **The third of the first** velar class is *g* **(5.A22)**, and **the third sibilant** is *s*. **Likewise the twenty-first** is *p*, and both letters are **trodden by the sun**, i.e., superscribed [letters] *r*.[560] The **third of the fifth** labial class is *b* **(5.A23)**.

The first of the fourth dental class is *t*, **the third of the third** class taking the vowels to be first is *j*, and it is **illuminated from above by fire**, i.e., adorned by the letter *r*. *Y* is that which **is said to be the first semivowel (5.A24)**. **Then** again following that is **the sixteenth**, *t*. **The**

---

559 This of course is true, but this still does not excuse the errors of this text. The letters *b* and *v* are chronically confused here, sometimes yielding amusing results as, in this case, **abalamvini* in the place of *avalambini*. This suggests that this passage is the result of a misreading, either unintentional or deliberate, of the Sanskrit.

560 By the expression "both letters" Tsong Khapa may be alluding to the doubling of the consonants preceded by a superscribed letter *r* in Sanskrit orthography, which does indeed occur in the extant manuscript at this point.

third of the third palatial class is *j*, which is **marked on the crown by the letter of fire**, *r*, and **furthermore the twenty-sixth** counting from *k* is *y* (**5.A25**).

The first of the first vowel class is *a*. Although the accessory vowels are not selected here, it is not erroneous to select a freestanding vowel. **The first of the second** velar class, taking the vowels as the first, is *k*. **The fourth of** the retroflex class, **the third** counting from *k*, is *ḍh*, which is **surmounted by** *ḍ*, **the thirteenth** counting from *k* (**5.A26**). Furthermore, **the first of** the vowel class is *a*, **the first of the second** velar class is *k*, and **the fourth of the third** retroflex class is *ḍh*, which is **surmounted by the thirteenth** (**5.A27**), *ḍ*.

The fourth sibilant, *h*, is **seated by the twenty-seventh**, *r*, to yield *hr*. **The seed that is the eighth** counting **from the letter *y*** is *h*, and it is **illuminated by the sun**, *r* (**5.A28**). **The third of the second** palatal class is *j*, and it is **seated by the fifteenth**, i.e., *ṇ* is affixed to it. Also **the third of the second** palatal class, *j*, **rides upon the fifth of the third**, *ṇ* (**5.A29**). Here the Tibetan scholars say that *ṇ* as written conjoined to *j* is not particularly distinct from *ñ* in most of the Sanskrit texts, and in one Sanskrit text it appears completely fixed in the form of *ñ*,[561] and appears thus in all of the Tibetan texts. It does not occur thus, however, in the mantra selection.[562]

3.3.3. 2.2.2. 2.1.1. 1.2.2. 3. Selecting the mantra's final set of eight [lines]

Having selected the seed of *ka* and *ṣa*, *kṣ* is **seated by the twenty-fifth**, *m*. **Selecting the distinguished mass** made of *k* and *ṣ*, *kṣ* is **seated with the letter *ma*** (**5.A30**). **The fourth sibilant** is *h*, and **the fourth of the seventh** sibilant class is also *h*. **The seed that is the eighth** counting **from the semivowels**, i.e., from *ya*, is *h*. **Likewise, the thirty-third** is *h* (**5.A31**). **Selecting the nature of the fifth** wisdom, *hūṁ*, **one should be certain that that *hūṁ* has a second. The first of the second**

561 Tsong Khapa here paraphrases Büton; see NS 307. All of the extant Sanskrit manuscripts read *jñ* here, rather than *jṇ*. Moreover, the Tibetan texts do not unanimously support the *jṇ* reading; the SL translation reads *dznyoṁ* here, representing the Sanskrit *jñoṁ*.

562 With respect to the mantra selection, "the fifteenth" unambiguously refers to *ṇ*, but the "fifth of the third" is ambiguous, and could code either *ñ* or *ṇ*, depending on whether one is counting the vowel class or not.

velar class is *k*, and **the third semivowel** is *l* (**5.A32**). **Likewise, the thirty-second** letter is *s*, and **the third of the seventh** semivowel class is *l*. **The fourth of the seventh** sibilant class is "**h**," and **the third of the sixth** semivowel class is *l* (**5.A33**). **The fourth of the fifth** dental class is *dh*, and **the third of the sixth** semivowel class is *l*. These **four** lines are recited **twice**.

These thirty-three stanzas and three lines [beginning with] "the first of the first, and the second semivowel" occur in the translation of the root Tantra of the two translators combined, and are absent in the solo Mardo translation, which was written in accordance with what is stated in that.[563] They should not be taken to be spurious insertions on account of that. It seems that both this [translation] and the *Abhidhānottara* are exceptions.

3.3.3. 2.2.2. 2.1.1. 1.3. Showing the greatness of the selected mantra

The [term] **spell** (*vidyā*, *rig pa*) refers to the ḍākinīs of the three wheels, and their **king** is Heruka. His **mantra** (**5.25a**) is the selected root mantra, which **achieves all ritual actions that are to be achieved** (**5.25b**).[564] **Other than this** root mantra **there is no** other mantra **greater within the three worlds** (**5.25cd**), the supernal, terrestrial, and infernal. **Knowing Śrī Heruka's mantra** (**5.26a**), its repetition is like fire, and **the other** mantras **are like straw** (**5.26b**), which indicates the singular greatness of the extent of its power. Since it is a mantra that is the root of all success, **it is famed as the root mantra** (**5.26c**).[565]

Regarding "all actions," Koṅkaṇa wrote that "**obviates all means of achievement** (**5.26b**) means that it is accomplished through recitation

---

563 I presume that by the "translation of the two translators" Tsong Khapa refers here to the Mardo/Prajñākīrti (PM) translation, which is in fact the only translation that contains the *kara kara* mantra selection. It certainly does not occur in the Sumatikīrti/Mardo (SM) translation.

564 There is considerable variance with respect to this line. Tsong Khapa here glosses the PM and SM readings (PM: *bya ba thams cad rab sgrub pa'o*; SM: *bya ba thams cad sgrub pa po*). The SL translation has a less coherent reading, *bsgrub pa thams cad rnam pa'o*, while the Sanskrit reads "obviates all [other] means of achievement" (*sarva-sādhanavarjitaḥ*).

565 I failed to translate this line in my published translation of the root Tantra.

only."[566] Bhavabhaṭṭa and Vīravajra also explain it in this fashion.[567] This means that one will succeed through repetition only without regard for other means of achievement such as fire sacrifice, and so forth.[568] Therefore, since it is essential to repeat it, the root mantra itself should be taken to be principally important.

3.3.3. 2.2.2. 2.1.1. 2. Showing the name of the chapter

In the *Concise* ***Śrī Herukābhidhāna Tantra***, this is the **fifth chapter** on **the procedure of selecting the letters of the root mantra**. This is the explanation of the fifth chapter in the *Illumination of the Hidden Meaning, A Detailed Exegesis of the Concise Saṁvara Tantra Called "The Cakrasaṁvara."*

---

[566] This passage occurs as follows in Jayabhadra's commentary: *sarvasādhanavarjita iti paṭhitamātreṇa siddha ity arthaḥ* (Sugiki 2001, 117); */sgrub pa thams cad spangs pa'o/ /zhes bya ba ni bklags pa tsam gyis 'grub par 'gyur ro zhes bya ba'i don to/* (CP 50b).

[567] See Pandey 2002, 58, CV 174a, and also SG 179b.

[568] Tsong Khapa here paraphrases the comments of Bhavabhaṭṭa, who wrote: "**obviates all means of achievement** refers to means of achievement such as fire sacrifice, and so forth, because one will succeed by means of repetition alone" (Pandey 2002, 58: *sarvasādhanavarjita iti / homādisādhanavarjitaḥ / japamātreṇa sādhyatvāt*; cf. CV 174a).

Chapter 6

Chapter 6 Outline

3.3.3. 2.2.2. 2.1.2. Selecting the hero's armor mantra

The second part has two sections: (1) the actual text and (2) the name of the chapter.

3.3.3. 2.2.2. 2.1.2. 1. The actual text

The second part has two sections: (1) the enumeration of the two mantras' syllables together with the selection of the armor mantra and (2) showing the places on which the armor [mantras] are set down.

3.3.3. 2.2.2. 2.1.2. 1.1. The enumeration of the two mantras' syllables together with the selection of the armor mantra

Aside from the root mantra, **there are the twenty-two syllables (6.1a)** in the **essence** mantra that will be explained below. In the essence and **quintessence** mantras there are **seven syllables (6.1b)**.[569] There are three [variants for the next word], "the *ya* host" (*ya tshogs*), "*ya*, etc." (*ya sogs*), and "**the ya class**" (*ya sde*). The first is a bad translation. While the latter seems simply to accord with the explanations, the middle one is best.[570] **The seed** of the **eighth (6.1c)** syllable *from ya*, etc., is *h*. **The ornaments** are the vowels or terminations [of the syllables]. **Twelve**

---

[569] I am not sure why Tsong Khapa adds the essence mantra here, as only the quintessence mantra has seven syllables. The root Tantra is quite clear that the essence has twenty-two syllables, and the quintessence seven.

[570] Tsong Khapa's favored translation, *ya sogs*, is probably the worst translation of *yavargāt*. Tsong Khapa likely favors this since it is the SM reading. PM and SL both read *ya tshogs*.

remain after the four retroflex and dental vowels are excluded. They are *a ā* through *aṁ aḥ*. **Thus**, adding these **twelve (6.1d)** to the letter *h* yields *ha hā hi hī hu hū he hai ho hau haṁ haḥ*. [Of these] the five long **syllables** that **intervene** between two short syllables and the final [syllable] should be **omitted (6.2a)**. Another translation has "omitting the final syllables," which means omitting the long syllables that are the final of each pair [of syllables].[571] Having omitted these, there are six short syllables such as *ha*, etc., which are said to be the **six limbs** of **Śrī Heruka**'s heart, and so forth **(6.2b)**. Since the habitat, i.e., the heart, and so forth, and the inhabitant, the syllables *ha*, etc., are essentially or ultimately inseparable, they are known as the six limbs.[572] One should form the **unification** of, i.e., apply, the [syllables] *oṁ*, and so forth, that are the **six heroes (6.2c)** such as Vajrasattva.

What are the syllables that accompany them? **Each syllable** such as *ha* **is positioned (6.2d)** with them, such that *oṁ* is placed before *ha*. Likewise are joined *nama hi*, *svāhā hu*, *vauṣaṭ he*, *huṁ hūṁ ho*, and *phaṭ haṁ* **(6.3ab)**. **The essence** of the six heroes **should be known by the adept (6.3c)**.

3.3.3. 2.2.2. 2.1.2. 1.2. Showing the places on which the armor [mantras] are set down

The first armor mantra, *oṁ ha*, is placed in **the heart (6.4a)**. One should **know that the second** mantra is placed on **the head (6.4b)**. **The third** mantra is applied to **the crown (6.4c)**. **Let the fourth be the armor (6.4d)** [means], as is stated in the *Saṁcāra*, that it is placed on the shoulder.[573] **Let the fifth** mantra **be the eye (6.5a)**, meaning it is placed on both eyes. **The sixth is said to be the weapon (6.5b)** means, as is stated in the *Saṁvarodaya*, "*phaṭ haṁ* is the weapon for all of the

---

[571] All of the extant translations here read *bar ma*, rather than *tha ma*.

[572] Tsong Khapa here paraphrases Jayabhadra's commentary, which is: "**The six limbs spoken by Śrī Heruka** refer to Heruka's six limbs, on account of being a metaphor via the nondifference of the container, or on account of the ultimate meaning" (Sugiki 2001, 117: *ṣaḍaṅgaḥ śrīherukocyata iti herukaṣaḍaṅgaṁ ity arthaḥ, ādhārādheyayor abhedenopacārātparamārthato vā //*; see also CP 51a).

[573] The seventh chapter of the YS indicates that the shoulder (*skandha*) is the locus for the fourth armor mantra. See Pandey 1998, 70, and YS 37b.

limbs."[574] Regarding "all of the limbs,"[575] they are as was stated by Kambala and also explained by Prajñārakṣita, namely, "They are the atoms that exist in the skin that are the nature and color of the [respective deities]."[576] One should thus venerate all of the atoms of the physical faculty, as [for example], green [syllables] *phaṭ haṁ*, which are the actuality of Paramāśva. Regarding the placement of [this] mantra, it should be placed on the brow as stated by Kambala.[577] In placing the deities one should also venerate the atoms of the physical faculty as their actuality.

Someone [claims that] since it is said that they are "on all of the limbs," it is unacceptable to not place one on the brow.[578] This is indeed the case, since many other things would become unacceptable, such as the statements "the form aggregate is Vairocana" and "Īrṣyāvajrā is in the body," and the visualizations of these deities on the crown and brow.[579]

---

574 This text occurs at SU 13.35 in Tsuda's edition as follows: *phaṭ haṁ sarvāṅgeṣv astram* (1974, 118); */phaṭ haṁ yan lag thams cad la ste mtshan cha'o/* (SU 281b).

575 This text, *sarvāṅgeṣu/yan lag thams cad la*, does not occur in the root text itself, but is found in the explanatory Tantras, as Tsong Khapa just noted. It does, however, appear in Vajraghaṇṭa's *Śrīcakrasaṁvara-sādhana* (D fol. 224a) and Kāṇha/Kṛṣṇācārya's *Śrīcakrasaṁvara-sādhana* (D fol. 273b), which along with Lūipa's BA are the bases of major CT meditation traditions.

576 Kambala correlates the armor mantras with their respective deities and colors in his *Śrīcakrasaṁvarābhisamayaṭīkā*, Q p. 97.2–3. There is no statement there, however, which corresponds to Tsong Khapa's quote. An almost identical passage does occur, however, in Prajñārakṣita, in his *Śrī-abhisamaya-nāma-pañjikā*, where it occurs as follows: *pags pa'i nang du son pa'i rdul phra rab kyi rang bzhin de'i kha dog can no/* (D fol. 42a.)

577 See SN 15a.

578 Tsong Khapa is disagreeing with an unknown commentator here, possibly Mardo, who apparently was objecting to a common idea of where the sixth armor should be placed. Jayabhadra, in a manner similar to the SU, comments that the sixth armor mantra, identified laconically as "the weapon," refers to "the weapons of all limbs," *sarvāṅgasyāstram* (Sugiki 2001, 118). Sachen comments here that "**the sixth**, *phaṭ haṁ*, **is the weapon**, which should be taken as Hayagrīva placed on five [spots], both shoulders, both thighs, and the forehead" (PG 313.2: *drug pa ste phaṭ haṁ mtshon cha ni dpung pa gnyis brla gnyis dpral ba dang lngar bkod la rta mchog tu bya'o/*). Tsong Khapa here follows Büton closely (NS 312), but this objection is neither quoted not refuted by Büton.

579 These statements occur in Lūipa's *Śrībhagavad-abhisamaya*. The passages occur as follows at BA 186b: */gzugs gi phung po ni rnam par snang mdzad do/*, and */reg la ni phrag dog rdo rje'o/*. Note that in the second quote Tsong Khapa has *lus la* instead of *reg*

(cont'd)

The statement "on the skin" [indicates that] the armors of the remaining deities are also placed on the body. However, on how many deities are these armors placed? Although it is stated in the body mandalas of Lūipa and Ghaṇṭapā that twelve armors are placed, it is not clear on which deities they are placed.[580] In Ghaṇṭapā's five-deity system, the armor is placed after the creation of the principal couple but before the creation of the retinue; they are thus placed on the principal couple.

In Kṛṣṇācārya's *sādhana* they are placed on just the principal couple and not on the others.[581] Furthermore, at the end of the explanation of the heroine's six armors, the *Saṁcāra* states that "the six armors are themselves Vārāhī."[582] Hence it is clear that the six [hero's armors], *oṁ ha*, and so forth, are placed on the principal deity as well in agreement with that. In general, many scholars explain that the armors are placed on the principal deity couple. While a few others explain that they are placed on all of the deities, in the context of the *sādhana*s of Lūipa, Kāṇha, and Ghaṇṭapā there is adherence to the principle of placing the armors on the principal deity couple only. I have given a more extensive argument [about this] in my commentary on Lūipa's *sādhana*.[583]

How are the armors placed on them? Kambala explains that there are two methods, namely placing the mantras themselves that are understood as being nondifferent from the deities, and placing the deities

---

la, which actually makes more sense, as the previous lines relate the goddesses to the organs of sense and not the sense powers.

[580] For Lūipa there are evidently twelve armor mantras corresponding to six deity couples, the six heroes and their "seal" consorts (*mudrā*). See BA 192a. Lūipa does not mention the deities in the mandala on which these armors are placed, as Tsong Khapa notes. This information is also not provided by Vajraghaṇṭa in either his *Śrīcakrasaṁvara-sādhana* or his *Abhisamaya* (To. 1434).

[581] See Kāṇha/Kṛṣṇācārya's *Śrīcakrasaṁvara-sādhana*, D fol. 273 ff.

[582] The text Tsong Khapa is referring to occurs at YS 7.7cd, as follows: *ṣaḍbhiḥ kavacaṁ vajravārāhyā vīrādvayayoginī* (Pandey 1998, 74); */go cha drug nyid phag mo dang / /dpa' bo ngnyis med rnal 'byor ma'o/* (YS 37b). Note that the Tibetan translation does not accurately reflect the Sanskrit grammar here.

[583] See Tsong Khapa's *bcom ldan 'das dpal 'khor lo bde mchog gi mngon par rtogs pa'i rgya cher bshad pa 'dod pa 'jo ba* (Tashi Lhunpo print, vol. ta, pp. 72–460).

having created them from the mantras. Prajñārakṣita also explains in this manner.[584]

The body colors and hand implements of the armor deities should be known from the *sādhanas*. The armor mantras of the root Tantra are stated in the same fashion in the *Saṁcāra* and the *Saṁvarodaya*, and likewise occur in the texts of both Lūipa and Ghaṇṭapā. Kāṇha relies on the *Vajraḍāka* in adding the syllable *oṁ* to the beginning of each of the twelve [mantras].[585] The *Abhidhānottara* explains the mantras in regard to each of the *Saṁvara* clans such as body, speech, mind, and commitment [wheels], etc., such that there many similarities and differences [between it] and the root Tantra.[586]

3.3.3. 2.2.2. 2.1.2. 2. The name of the chapter

In the *Concise* ***Śrī Herukābhidhāna Tantra***, this is the **sixth chapter** on **selecting the hero's six armor** mantras. This is the explanation of the sixth chapter in the *Illumination of the Hidden Meaning, A Detailed Exegesis of the Concise Saṁvara Tantra Called "The Cakrasaṁvara."*

---

584 As before this is not stated directly but seems to be implied by Kambala in his *Śrīcakrasaṁvarābhisamayaṭīkā*, p. 97.3. Prajñārakṣita's comments in his *Śrī-abhisamaya-nāma-pañjikā* are more directly relevant. While he does not explicitly articulate two methods of placing the mantra, he does comment that the mantras are nondifferent from the deities, as Tsong Khapa notes above. Following this assertion he continues with the statement that "one should visualize [the deities] Vajrasattva, and so forth, in the places perfected from their respective mantras" (D fol. 42a: */yang na de dang de'i sngags las rdzogs pa'i gnas de ru rdo rje sems dpa' la sogs pa sgom par bya ste/*). This could be interpreted as conforming to Tsong Khapa's second option, although it seems that it more likely refers to the placement on the body of the mantras, which are understood to be nondifferent from the deities, and the creation of the deities on the body following this placement. Tsong Khapa could thus be interpreting a description of a single procedure as a listing of two alternatives.

585 Kāṇha does indeed affix *oṁ* to each of the twelve armor mantras. See his *Śrīcakrasaṁvara-sādhana*, D fol. 273b. The armor mantras appear in ch. 33 of the VD, but *oṁ* is affixed to them neither in the root text nor in Bhavabhaṭṭa's commentary.

586 See the *kośa-prastāva-pīṭha-sampradāya* chapter of the AU, which is ch. 13 in the Tibetan translation, for a discussion of the wheels in relation to the armors.

CHAPTER 7

Chapter 7 Outline

3.3.3. 2.2.2. 2.1.3. Selecting the root mantra's vowels

The third part, selecting the root mantra's vowels, has four sections: (1) the actual selection of the auxiliary vowels, (2) the greatness of the selected mantra, (3) selecting the root mantra's first and last syllables, and (4) showing the name of the chapter.

3.3.3. 2.2.2. 2.1.3. 1. The actual selection of the auxiliary vowels

The second part has two sections: (1) selecting the vowels of the eight-line [mantra] and (2) selecting the vowels of the *kara*, etc., [mantra].

3.3.3. 2.2.2. 2.1.3. 1.1. Selecting the vowels of the eight-line [mantra]

The second part has two sections: (1) selecting the vowels of the first four lines and (2) selecting the vowels of the last four [lines].

3.3.3. 2.2.2. 2.1.3. 1.1.1. Selecting the vowels of the first four lines

[Line One]

Having selected the body of the root mantra, **next, the second letter**[587] of the selected body, *m*, **is endowed with the second thirteenth vowel**, *o*, [yielding] *mo*. **The sixth** selected **letter**, *t*, **should be** ornamented by being **graced** or furnished **with the eleventh vowel**, *e* **(7.1)**. **The seventh letter**, *v*, **is furnished with the fourth vowel**, *ī*. **The wise provide the eighth letter**, *r*, **with the eleventh vowel**, *e* **(7.2)**. **The ninth letter,** *ś*, should be ornamented with **the second vowel**, *ā*.[588]

[Line Two]

The second vowel, *ā*, **is joined** to **the twelfth letter**, *h* **(7.3)**. **Taking the twenty-first** letter counting from *k*, i.e, *p*, **it is joined with the second vowel**, *ā*, **and** subjoined to **the fourteenth** letter, *l*. **The twentieth (7.4)**, *n*, is **joined to the third vowel**, *i*. The resulting **ni** is linked, i.e., subjoined to, **the fifteenth letter**, *g*. **The fifteenth of the vowels**, *aṁ*, **distinguishes the sixteenth letter**, *s* **(7.5)**. Furthermore, since this also implies that the *a* vowel is vocalized, afterwards a nasal sign (*anusvāra*)[589] is given to the *sa*.[590] It is established that **the seventeenth letter**, *n*, is possessed of **the third vowel**, short *i*. **The second of the vowels**, long *ā*, is joined to **the eighteenth letter**, *bh* **(7.6)**.

---

587 The reader may be aware that I translated the Sanskrit and Tibetan terms *akṣara* and *yi ge* in this chapter as "syllable" in my (2007) translation, and "letter" here. Both terms are in fact ambiguous, and can have either meaning. In my earlier translation, I took the numbers to refer to a syllable count. That is, the text gives the number of syllables that contain vowels other than short *a*, which is the default vowel in both languages. However, as Tsong Khapa in his explanation indicates which consonant is attached to which vowel, using the term *yi ge* in its sense as "letter," I use the translation "letter" here to avoid confusion.

588 Tsong Khapa here follows the Tibetan translations. The extant Sanskrit gives a different reading, namely "Taking the ninth syllable, it is likewise furnished with the second vowel" (*navamaṁ tato gṛhyākṣaraṁ dvitīyasvarasaṁyuktaṁ*).

589 Here the Tibetan term *thig le*, "drop," translates *anusvāra*; this is made clear in Bhavabhaṭṭa's commentary, where *anusvāraḥ* is translated thus (Pandey 2002, 63).

590 I presume that *phyis la* here refers to time rather than location, since the *anusvāra* is vocalized as a nasal *after* pronouncing the short *a* vowel. This usage may reflect a cognizance of the literal meaning of the term *anusvāra*, "after-sound."

[Line Three]

The second vowel, long *ā*, **is linked with the twenty-first letter**, *ṭ*. **The fifth vowel**, short *u*, **is linked with the twenty-third letter**, *k* (**7.7**). **The thirteenth of the vowels**, *o*, **is linked with** *ṭ*, **the twenty-fourth letter**. **Taking the first of the first**, i.e., velar class, *k*, **it is conjoined with**, i.e., attached to, **the twenty-fifth letter**, *t* (**7.8**). **The twenty-sixth letter**, *ṭ*, **should be** possessed of **the second vowel**, long *ā*.

[Line Four]

The twenty-eighth, *d*, is joined with **the fifteenth** vowel, *aṁ*, meaning that in addition to the *a* the nasal sign (*anusvāra*) is given to the *d*. (**7.9**) **The twenty-ninth letter**, *ṣ*, **is endowed with the first of the third** retroflex class, *ṭ*, and has **a portion below**, namely **fire** (**7.10**), the *r* affix. That is, it is linked with the second vowel, ā, with *ṭ* subjoined together with *r*. **The thirty-first letter**, *r*, **is supplied with the second vowel**, long *ā*. **The thirty-second letter**, *l*, **is endowed with the thirteenth vowel**, *o* (**7.11**). **The thirty-third letter**, *g*, should be **endowed with the sun**, the *r* affix. **The fourth of the vowels**, long *ī*, should be in the possession of the **thirty-fourth** letter, *bh* (**7.12**). As for that, **it is the means of achieving all desired aims. The fifth vowel,** short *u*, is possessed by **the thirty-seventh** letter, *m*. Since with this one can exhort the mind-stream of the **ḍākinīs**, it is the **means of achieving** the powers (**7.13**). This *kh*, **the thirty-eighth, is provided with the second vowel**, long *ā*. **Have no doubt that this very** syllable of the mantra is the cause of **achieving the deities** (**7.14**), namely, the heroes and heroines.

3.3.3. 2.2.2. 2.1.3. 1.1.2. Selecting the vowels of the last four [lines]

[Line Five]

Fire, i.e., *r*, is joined, i.e., affixed, to **the portion below the** previously selected **forty-second** letter, *s*, **by the adept** (**7.15**). **The forty-third letter**, *bh*, **is supplied with the fifth vowel**, short *u*. **The forty-fifth** letter, *bh*, **is supplied with the second vowel**, long *ā* (**7.16**). **The forty-sixth**, *s*, should be **connected with the fifth vowel**, short *u*. **It is worshipped by all heroes** (**7.17**). **The forty-seventh**, *r*, **is provided with the second vowel**, long *ā*. These mantras are the essence of **the**

supreme Vajrasattva (**7.18**), because the mantra and the deity are non-different.

[Line Six]

The fifty-first letter, *ś*, **is thought to be most splendid through the fifth vowel**, short *u* (**7.19**). **The fifty-second**, *p*, **is provided with the second vowel**, long *ā*. **All deities**, etc. (**7.20**), are as previously explained. **The fifty-third**, *ś*, **is supplied with the thirteenth vowel** (**7.21**), *o*. **The fifty-sixth letter**, *ś*, **is provided with the sixth vowel**, long *ū*. **It destroys enemies**. **The fourth semivowel** (**7.22**), *v*, **is supplied with the second vowel**, yielding long *vā*. It is **likewise endowed with the fifteenth**, *aṁ*, as previously [explained]. It is **the means of achieving all powers**. **The fifty-ninth syllable** (**7.23**) is *ṭ*, after which is affixed the long *vā*. Giving a nasal mark on the top of the *ṭ* yields *ṭvāṁ*. **The sixty-first letter**, *dh*, **is endowed with the second vowel**, *ā*. **This very** mantra **is said to be supreme**[591] (**7.24**). **The sixty-second** letter, *r*, **is supplied with the third vowel**, short *i*. **It is considered to be the supreme** spell **of the ḍākinī**s (**7.25**). **The most splendid syllable** consists of the **sixty-third** letter, *ṇ*, **endowed with the eleventh vowel**, *e* (**7.26**).

[Line Seven]

The sixty-fifth, *gh*, **as well, is split by Vajrasattva**, i.e., has a subjoined *r*. **This seed syllable is the supreme divine substance,** i.e., ambrosia, **and it bestows** worldly **powers and it bestows great liberation** (**7.27**).[592] Here in Lochen's translation there is the following: "The sixty-fourth as well, split by Vajrasattva, is provided with the second vowel."[593] Mal's translation reads "The sixty-fourth is provided with the

[591] Tsong Khapa here follows the Tibetan translations of this line, *'di nyid mchog ni yin par bshad*. The extant Sanskrit reads "The wise know thus," *evam eva vidur budhāḥ*.

[592] Tsong Khapa here comments upon the text contained in the PM and SM translations: */de bzhin drug curtsa lnga pa/ /rdo rje sems dpas phye ba dag /sa bon 'di ni lha rdzas mchog /grub sbyin thar pa sbyin chen po/*.

[593] Lochen's translation corresponds exactly to the extant Sanskrit mss. It is incorrect, as it is the sixty-fifth syllable selected in the fifth chapter, *gh*, that needs to be "split by Vajrasattva," i.e., augmented with a subjoined *r*. The correct Sanskrit reading is preserved in the AU. For a lengthy discussion of the Sanskrit text see Gray 2007, 191 n. 16.

second vowel, and is not split by Vajrasattva."[594] There is nothing stated regarding the sixty-fourth in either of Mardo's two translations.[595] Although it does not agree with these, Mal's translation seems to be best. [The text] in the *Abhidhānottaras*[596] and in Lochen's translation, that the sixty-fourth is split by Vajrasattva and the sixty-fifth is joined to the third vowel, is corrupt.[597] [The text stating that] the sixty-fourth is joined to the second vowel appears to be correct.[598]

The sixty-sixth, *j*, **is equipped with the third vowel**, *i*. These mantras **bestow success in all affairs, [as] the Tathāgata stated (7.28). The sixty-seventh letter**, *n*, **is endowed with the second vowel**, long *ā*. **Have no doubt** that it thus fulfills **all of the yoginīs'** aims **(7.29). The sixty-eighth** is *m*; **attach a *b* to it. Put**, i.e., subjoin, **it in the portion below** the seed letter *m* **(7.30). The second vowel**, *ā*, is joined to the

---

594 Tsong Khapa apparently is utilizing a version of Mal's translation that is no longer extant. His reading is not supported by Sachen's commentary, which relies upon it. Sachen simply gives the correct reading without commenting on the textual problems here. It reads: "**The sixty-fifth** letter of the [mantra's] body, *gh*, **is split by Vajrasattva**, linked to *ra*, hence *ghra*" (PG 311.4). The text quoted by Tsong Khapa here is not incorrect, as the sixty-fourth syllable selected in the fifth chapter is *vyā*, but it is superfluous, as this is one of two syllables for which the vowel was selected in fifth chapter. This may represent an attempt to correct the erroneous text faithfully translated by Lochen. The SL preserves a different yet still redundant attempt to correct the old text, reading: "The sixty-fourth is also endowed with the second vowel. It is the great eye of liberation on account of the powers. The sixty-fifth syllable is split by Vajrasattva" (*/drug cu rtsa bzhi pa nyid ni/ /dbyangs yig gnyis par yang dag ldan/ /grub phyir thar pa'i spyan chen po/ /yi ge drug bcu rtsa lnga pa/ /rdo rje sems dpa' phye ba dag*).

595 As noted above, both the PM and SM translations, in which Mardo played central roles, read "sixty-fifth" rather than "sixty-forth."

596 Tsong Khapa here wrote *mngon brjod rnams*, *Abhidhānottaras*. Perhaps he was referring to multiple translations of the text.

597 Tsong Khapa is correct here with regard to the Tibetan translation of the *Abhidhānottara*, which corresponds to his text here (see AD fol. 353a,b). However, this translation differs from the extant Sanskrit AU mss., which in fact preserve the correct reading here, as follows: "The sixty-fifth, moreover, is split by Vajrasattva, and the sixty-sixth letter is linked to the third vowel" (H 170a.3–4, I 610b.1–2: *pañcaṣaṣṭi tathā caiva vajrasattvena bheditaḥ / ṣaṭṣaṣṭir akṣaraṁ tu tṛtīyasvarayojitaṁ /*; J 277.7: *pañcaṣaṣṭi tathā caiva vajrasattvena bheditaṁ / ṣaṭṣaṣṭi akṣaraṁ tu tṛtīyasvarayojitaṁ /*).

598 As noted above, this text is both correct and superfluous.

seventy-first letter, *r*. **Have no doubt that it is the splendor of all syllables (7.31)**.

[Line Eight]

The seventy-fourth, *h*, **is equipped with the second vowel**. It causes one to achieve **the primal power** spoken **from the mouth of the Tathāgata (7.32)**. **The seventy-fifth**, *dh*, is endowed with **the sixth** of the vowels, *ū*. **It is the** excellent, **supreme yoga (7.33)** for the achievement of all ritual actions. **The seventy-sixth** is *m*. **The letter** ***v***[599] is subjoined **to that** *m*. It is **split by the sun (7.34)**, i.e., an *r* is attached to that *v*. There is no other more splendid than that "seed of fire," which is **endowed with the second vowel**, long *ā*. In Mardo's other translation there occurs "attach the letter *v* there."[600] **The seventy-seventh** is *n*. One should **attach**—i.e., subjoin—the [letter] ***dh*** **there**, to the *n*. The mantra of this seed syllable **is held to be splendid by the ḍākinīs (7.35)**. **The seventy-eighth** letter, *k*, **is endowed with the second vowel**. This seed syllable **is believed to be** the supreme good and **the ultimate cause** of the powers **(7.36)**. **The eighty-first letter** is *p*. **The fourth** vowel is *ī*. **That which follows** it is *u*. Since it is **distinguished by** that, [the resulting syllable] is *pu*. This **is that which produces the primal power and promotes all powers (7.37)**. **The eighty-second letter**, *ṣ*, **is endowed with the second vowel (7.38ab)**, long *ā*, yielding *ṣā*.

Although there is no [further] selection of vowels following this in other translations, since there is further selection of vowels of the *kara*, etc., [mantra] in the dual translation as well as in the *Abhidhānottara*, I will therefore comment upon this here.[601]

---

[599] Here I read the Tibetan *ba* as referring to the Sanskrit *va*.

[600] Tsong Khapa here quotes the SM translation exactly, as *yi ge ba la de sbyar bya*. This differs only slightly from the PM translation, which reads as follows: *yi ge ba ni der sbyar bya*.

[601] As noted above in chapter 5, section 3.3.3.2.2.2.2.1.1.1.2.1.2, only the PM revised translation contains the selection for the consonants and vowels of the *kara kara* mantra.

3.3.3. 2.2.2. 2.1.3. 1.2. Selecting the vowels of the *kara*, etc., [mantra]

The second part has three sections: (1) selecting the vowels of the first set of eight [lines], (2) selecting the vowels of the middle set of eight [lines], and (3) selecting the vowels of the final set of eight [lines].

3.3.3. 2.2.2. 2.1.3. 1.2.1. Selecting the vowels of the first set of eight [lines]

In the same way that the vowels were joined to the selected body of the eight-line [mantra], the vowels are applied to the selected body of the *kara*, etc., [mantra]. Joining **the fifth among the** "mothers" (*ma mo*, *mātṛkā*) or **vowels**, short *u*, to **the eighty-eighth** of the selected letters, *k*, yields *ku*. Here the "mothers" should be taken to be vowels. It is said that here "eighty-eighth" takes into account the addition of the *kara kara* [letters] on top of the letters selected for the body of the eight-line [mantra]. **The fifth among the vowels**, *u*, is joined to **the eighty-ninth letter**, *r* (**7.A1**). **Likewise, the fifth among the vowels**, *u*, is joined to **the ninetieth letter**, *k*. **The fifth among the vowels**, *u*, is joined to **the ninety-first letter**, *r* (**7.A2**). **The second among the vowels**, *ā*, is affixed **to the ninety-sixth letter**, *tr*. *Trāsaya*, which [also results from] **the second vowel** being affixed the second *tr*, **the ninety-ninth letter** (**7.A3**), **terrifies the malicious ones** and **gives rise to bliss for the *mantrins***. In the *Abhidhānottara* there occurs [here] "[it] is the state of bliss of all Mothers."[602]

Thus the *s* of the latter *trāsa[ya]* is the hundredth letter. Having reached the hundredth letter, the *y* [of the second *trāsaya*] should be taken to be one, in order to count again from one. **The thirteenth vowel**, *o*, should be **possessed of the second letter** counting from the *y* [of the second *trāsaya*], namely *kṣ* (**7.A4**). **The thirteenth vowel**, *o*, **has the fifth letter** counting from *y*, namely, the latter *kṣ*. The syllable[603] *kṣa* also

602 Tsong Khapa here correctly reproduces the Tibetan translation of this line of the AU, which occurs as follows at AU fol. 353b: *ma mo kun gyi bde ba'i gnas*. The Sanskrit, however, differs somewhat from the Tibetan translation, as follows: *mātṛkāṇāṁ ca sukhāvahāṁ* (H 170b.6, I 610b.8, J 279.1–2). Interestingly, there is a better translation of *sukhāvahāṁ* in the PM translation, *bde 'byung byed* (D fol. 220a). While my translation follows the Tibetan text, from the Sanskrit this line should read "[it] is that which conveys the bliss of the Mothers."

603 Here I read *ka ra* as *kāra*.

destroys the malicious ones, and it is the place on which **the bliss of the ḍākinīs alights**[604] (**7.A5**). This is also like the "bliss of the Mothers."

The fourteenth vowel is *au*. It should be **endowed with the eighth letter**, *hr*. That **serves as the seat for** *anusvāra*, **the fifteenth** vowel. Regarding *au*, **the fourteenth among the vowels** (**7.A6**), it **has the ninth letter**, *hr*, and **its crown is adorned with a drop** [i.e., *anusvāra*]. **It particularly delights the ḍākinīs for the adept** (**7.A7**). **The eleventh among the vowels** is *e*. **It has the twelfth letter and its crown is adorned with a drop**, yielding *pheṁ*[605] (**7.A8a–c**). The second *pheṁ* is also thus [derived].[606]

3.3.3. 2.2.2. 2.1.3. 1.2.2. Selecting the vowels of the middle set of eight [lines]

The fifth among the vowels, *u*, has **the thirty-second letter**, *r* (**7.A10cd**). It is said that the assignment of *r* as the thirty-second implies that the [letters] *ph* and *ṭ* of both *phaṭ* [syllables] are counted separately.[607] **The third vowel**, *i*, **has the thirty-third letter**, *dh*, hence *dhi*. **The second vowel**, *ā*, **has the thirty-fourth letter**, *r* (**7.A11**). **The second vowel has the thirty-sixth**, *m*. **The thirty-seventh letter**, *l*, **has the second** counting **from the beginning**, the vowel class (**7.A12**). **The fortieth letter**, *b*, **is endowed with the third of the vowels**, *i*. **The forty-first**, *n*, **is endowed with the eleventh vowel**, *e* (**7.A13**).

---

604 This encomium is a variant of that attributed above to the syllable *trā*. It illustrates well the vagaries of Tibetan translations of Sanskrit. Tsong Khapa reproduces it in an expanded commentary style as follows: *gdug pa rnams ni zad par byed cing / mkha' 'gro ma rnams kyi bde ba 'bab pa'i gnas so/*. Mardo's translation reads: */gdug pa rnams ni zad byed cing / /mkha' 'gro ma rnams kyi bde ba 'bab pa'o/*. It occurs in the *Abhidhānottara* trans. as follows: */gdug pa thams cad 'khrug byed de/ /mkha' 'gro ma yi bde ba'i gnas/*. The Sanskrit reads as follows: "[it] is the disruption of all wicked ones and that which conveys the bliss of the ḍākinīs," *kṣobhaṇaṁ sarvaduṣṭānāṁ ḍākinīnāṁ sukhāvahaṁ* (H 171a.2; I 610b.8–9: *kṣobhanaṁ*...; J 279.2–3: *sobhanaṁ*...). Note that *bde ba 'bab pa* is a much better translation of *sukhāvahaṁ* than *bde ba'i gnas*.

605 Tsong Khapa correctly identifies the vowel as *e*, but the texts that I consulted all incorrectly give *phaiṁ* rather than *pheṁ* here.

606 Tsong Khapa here skips over the coding from 7.A8d–10b.

607 This is argued by Büton at NS 321.

"The third vowel, *i*, is possessed of the forty-second letter, *gr*," and "the third vowel, *i*, is endowed with the forty-fourth" (7.A14). It has been stated that both of these [syllable codings] are:

> ...translated from corrupt Sanskrit texts. The *Abhidhānottara* has "the seventh letter of the vowels is linked to the forty-second, and the seventh of the vowels is joined to the forty-fourth letter," which is correct. In other words, the seventh vowel, *ṛ*, is connected to the forty-second letter, *g*, which after the *r* yields *gṛ*, which is correct,[608] since [it] also is selected thus in the *Saṁvarodaya*, etc.[609]

This is contradicted by our previous subjoining of the letter *r* at the occasion of selecting the body of the mantra.[610] Even in the many [texts

[608] Both the source of this quote, Büton's commentary, and Tsong Khapa's quotation from it are slightly garbled here. Note that I am using the same symbol that represents the Sanskrit retroflex vowel, *ṛ*, to transliterate the Tibetan representation of the retroflex vowel, which is the consonant *r* (or subscribed *r*) with a reversed "i" *gi-gu* vowel sign. Büton's text reads *dbyangs kyi bdun pa ṛ yi ge bzhi bcu gnyis pa gra la sbyar la ra phyis gṛ zhes pa dag ste* (NS 322). Note that the *gra* here is technically incorrect, but this is corrected (or more faithfully reproduced) in Tsong Khapa's quote: *dbyangs kyi bdun pa ṛ yi ge bzhi bcu pa ga la sbyar la ra phyi gṛ zhes pa dag ste*. Note that Tsong Khapa's text omits *gnyis*, which I have corrected in my translation. I am not exactly sure what Büton means by "behind/after the *r*," (*ra phyi/phyis*). Clearly, if the text is coding the retroflex vowel *ṛ* there should be no selection of the *r* semivowel.

[609] This unattributed quote is from Büton. Tsong Khapa begins the quote abruptly, dropping the initial topic, represented here by the ellipsis. He also severely abridges the last line, which is represented by the bracketed pronoun "[it]" in my translation. The full text of this passage occurs as follows in Büton's commentary, with text omitted by Tsong Khapa in bold: ***dbyangs las gsum pa i/ nyid yi ge bzhi bcu gnyis pa gra la sbyar zer ba ni/*** *rgya gar gyi dpe ma dag pa la bsgyur ba ste/ nges brjod bla mar/ dbyangs kyi yi ge bdun pa ni/ /yi ge bzhi bcu gnyis par sbyar/ /dbyangs kyi bdun pa nyid dang ni/ /yi ge bzhi bcu bzhi par sbyar/ /zhes pa dag ste dbyangs kyi bdun pa ṛ yi ge bzhi bcu pa ga la sbyar la ra phyis gṛ zhes pa dag ste/* ***gṛhna btu ba*** *sdom 'byung sogs las kyang* ***ga la dbyangs yig ṛ bcug par*** *btus pa'i phyir ro/* (NS 322).

[610] Tsong Khapa is correct in pointing out that the text here clearly selects *gri* rather than *gṛ*, which may reflect the common conflation of the retroflex vowel with other vowels (usually *i*) following the *r* semivowel. This may reflect the usual substitutions of other vowels for *ṛ* in the Prakrits and later languages, and perhaps confusion concerning the spelling of the word, either on the part of Indians, who no longer pronounced the vowel *ṛ*, or Tibetans, who likewise had no equivalent sound in their languages.

of the] *Abhidhānottara*, such as the translations by Drogmi and Kyungpo, it seems that the [semivowel] *r* is affixed to both letters *g* in the context of selecting the body.[611] Moreover, in chapter thirty of the root Tantra [i.e., this text] as well, [the letters] *g* and *r* are joined and then given the vowel *i*.[612] Since the commentaries also explain in accordance with this, in the root Tantra, while it is correct to affix the [vowel] *i* to the two *gr*, it is not correct to affix the [vowel] *ṛ*.[613]

Therefore, if there are [passages] such as "the seventh letter of the vowels" in the *Abhidhānottara*, it is essential that one investigate their relevance in the context of selecting the body [of the mantra] in that Tantra. Many [texts of] the *Abhidhānottara* have "Join the second vowel, [*ā*],[614] with the forty-second letter," while the dual translation has the third vowel, [*i*].[615] In general, since *g* and *ṛ* are also selected in the *Saṁvarodaya*,[616] one should know that there are two methods [for coding this syllable].

The second among the vowels is endowed with the forty-eighth letter, *p*. **The second vowel is endowed with the forty-ninth letter**, *t*

---

[611] I only have access to one Tibetan translation of the *Abhidhānottara*, the canonical Kyungpo revision of the translation by Atiśa Dīpaṅkaraśrījñāna and Rinchen Zangpo (AU). It does confirm Tsong Khapa's comment here. In ch. 57, where the body of the mantra is selected, it does select, twice here, the letter *g* with a subjoined *r* semivowel. See AU fol. 351a.

[612] This is in fact the case; they are selected thus in the context of selecting the first syllable of the very same word, *gṛhṇa*. See Gray 2007, 294.

[613] Here Tsong Khapa is correct from a textual/traditional point of view, but incorrect from a philological point of view.

[614] The Kyungpo revision preserved in the Kangyur (at AU 354a) inexplicably codes for the second vowel, *ā*, for the forty-second letter, and the third vowel, *i*, for the forty-fourth letter. The Sanskrit text is more consistent, as follows: "The forty-second letter is endowed with the third of the vowels, and the forty-fourth letter is endowed with the third of the vowels" (H 171a.6; I 611a.3–4; J 280.1: *svarāṇāṁ tṛtīyena saṁyuktaṁ dvācālīśākṣaraṁ / svarāṇāṁ tṛtīyena saṁyuktaṁ catuḥcālīśākṣaraṁ*). This corresponds with the Mardo translation of the CT, and may very well be its source.

[615] See PM 220b.

[616] Chapter 32 of the *Saṁvarodaya* reproduces this mantra, correctly giving *gṛhṇa gṛhṇa* (SU 308b.) Chapter 27 codes a mantra, and while I have not taken the time to decode it, it does call for the "seventh vowel," which is presumably *ṛ* (SU 301b).

(**7.A15**). **The fifth of the vowels**, *u*, is possessed of the fifty-third letter, *bh*. **The fifty-fourth letter**, *j*, **is also ornamented by a drop** (**7.A16**). **The fifty-fifth letter**, *g*, **is ornamented on its crown with a drop**, **and endowed with the second vowel**, *ā*. **The fifty-seventh letter** is *rv* (**7.A17**). **It is surmounted by a drop**, and endowed with **the second vowel**. **The fifty-eighth letter**, *b*, is endowed with **the second vowel** (**7.A18**). **The second vowel**, *ā*, is possessed of **the sixty-fifth**, *a*.[617] **The sixty-eighth**, *a*, **is endowed with the second vowel**. These **summon all powers** (**7.A19**) and **bestow glory**, i.e., perfection, **upon adepts**.

The fourth vowel, *ī*, **is possessed of the seventy-first letter**, *hr*, and **ornamented with a drop** (**7.A20**). **The fourth vowel**, *ī*, **has the seventy-second letter**, *hr*, the head of which is **surmounted by a drop**. These **dominate all beings** (**7.A21**). **The seventy-third letter is endowed with the fourteenth vowel**, *au*, yielding *jñau*. **The fourteenth vowel**, *au*, **is possessed of**, i.e., affixed to, **the seventy-fourth letter**, *jñ*, yielding *jñau* (**7.A22**). Just as *hri hri* is adorned by drops, both *jñau* are **likewise ornamented with drops** (**7.A23a**).

3.3.3. 2.2.2. 2.1.3. 1.2.3. Selecting the vowels of the final set of eight [lines]

The second vowel, *ā*, **has the seventy-fifth letter** (**7.A23bc**), *kṣm*, yielding *kṣmā*. The dual translation omits *kṣmā*'s *anusvāra*, the seventy-sixth and the seventy-seventh, and has "the second among the vowels is possessed of the seventy-eighth letter, the top of which is adorned with a drop."[618] Drogmi's translation of the *Abhidhānottara* reads:

> ...is affixed to the seventy-fifth, and ornamented with a drop. The second of the vowels[619] is also joined to the seventy-sixth letter, and adorned with two drops. The second of the vowels is also affixed to the seventy-seventh. The fourth of the vowels is joined to the seventy-eighth. Its head should be surmounted by a drop. The

[617] This syllable is the *ā* of *ākaḍḍha*. This syllable lacks a consonant, but the vowel *a* was selected in chapter 5, probably because this sound is considered to be implicit in all others.

[618] See PM 220b.

[619] Drogmi mistranslates the Sanskrit *mātṛkā* as *phyi mo*, "grandmother," which is one of the meanings of *mātṛkā* but clearly not the meaning intended here.

> fourth vowel is also affixed to the seventy-ninth. It is produced with the sound of the drop, i.e., is also ornamented with a drop.[620]

The second line of this [passage] shows that the first *kṣ* has a drop. [The statement] "the second vowel is joined to the seventy-sixth" indicates the second *kṣ*. The word "also" shows that the latter is also adorned by a drop. "The second of the vowels is affixed to the seventy-seventh" indicates [the syllable] *hā*. Since it states that it should be adorned by two drops, there should be two *hāṁ*.

The former of the two, **the seventy-eighth** and **seventy-ninth (7.A24a,d)**, which are joined to **the fourth vowel (7.A24c)**, is **surmounted by a drop (7.A25a)**, yielding the first *hīṁ*. The latter is **ornamented with a drop (7.A24b)**, resulting in the second *hīṁ*. "Produced with the sound of the drop" means that sound, *nāda*, is produced with the drop, i.e., that it should have the sound of the drop.

The **sixth among the vowels** is *ū*. There are many explanations of the import of **king of horses**. Some explain that it is [the letter] *h*, and **produced** refers to the seed that is joined to it. Since it **is ornamented** above **with a drop-sound (7.A25b–d)**, the result is *hūṁ*. Since this is doubled, it [corresponds to] the eightieth and eighty-first [syllables]. Previously, in the context of selecting the body of this mantra, the selection method was unclear [in stating] "selecting the nature of the fifth [wisdom]." Here it is made clear. And the statement that "again, the second here, too, indeed" shows that here the *hūṁ* must be doubled.[621]

---

620 Tsong Khapa is correct that Mardo's PM translation as well Kyungpo's canonical AU translation both inexplicably leave out the coding for the hundred seventy-fifth and -sixth syllables here. See AU 354b. Drogmi's translation contains the missing lines, as does the Sanskrit mss. for the AU. See H 172a.1–3, I 611a.8–b.1, J 280.6–281.1.

621 Tsong Khapa here quotes two lines from ch. 5, discussed in section 3.3.3.2.2.2.2.1.1.1.2.2.3 of his ch. 5 commentary above, which correspond to the following line in the AU: *pañcātmakaṁ samuddhṛtya punaḥ dvitīyaṁ tu atra vai* (H 168b.4, I 610a. 1, J 274.3) There is no coding of the vowels for *hūṁ* in the corresponding section of the AU, which makes sense, as this passage codes both syllables in their entirety, as the *pañca* of *pañcātmakaṁ* is understood as referring to the fifth wisdom, the seed syllable of which is *hūṁ*. The fact that the Mardo translation nonetheless codes the vowel is yet another inconsistency in this text.

Although the *Abhidhānottara* [translations] omit the selection of the *hūṁ* here, its occurrence in the dual translation is excellent.

The third of the vowels, *i*, **is endowed with**, i.e., affixed to, **the sixteen letters** from *k* and *l* to *dh* and *l*, yielding *kili*, etc.[622] Thus, **the count of syllables** of the [mantra's] body is **ninety-eight on top of one hundred** (**7.A26**) in the dual translation. While in the *Abhidhānottara* [the number] appears to be ninety-seven, since it omits one of the *hāṁ* [syllables], it should be taken to be ninety-eight.[623] Since there is no second *hāṁ* either before or after the seventy-seventh [syllable], it is clearly necessary that there should be both *hāṁ* at the occasion of the seventy-seventh, as was previously explained.

Regarding the occurrence of [this selection of the *kara kara*, etc., mantra], from [the line] "the fifth of the vowels" up to "is ninety-eight," in the dual translation, it should not be taken as an entry into error in the solo translation of Mardo, who wrote here for the purpose of elucidation.[624]

Regarding this selection from the perspective of the vowels and consonants, one should **know** that it is the supreme **root mantra** (**7.38c**) **of Lord Śrī Heruka that is selected from the chart** (**7.A27**). Since it is said that an equivalent term for "chart" (*re'u mig*, *prastāra*) is a pattern, this means that it is selected from the pattern of vowels and consonants that is the basis of the selection [process].

3.3.3. 2.2.2. 2.1.3. 2. The greatness of the selected mantra

This extensive root mantra is **the abode** or basis **of all powers**, the mundane and supramundane. Just by reciting it, **the hearts of** all of **the** terrible **ḍākinīs** and also the fears [themselves] are **pulverized**, i.e., they are terrified. It has been argued that "I, Bhavyakīrti, hold that **pulverizes**

---

622 The "sixteen letters" here refer to the sixteen syllables, all of which have the same vowel, of the following segment of the mantra: *kili kili sili sili cili cili dhili dhili*. This is another segment that violates the coding rules that governed the previous section. It is not in fact a genuine coding, in that the mantra could not possibly be derived from the information given.

623 This is true, but it is also the case that the PM translation omitted one of the *hāṁ* syllables. The *Abhidhānottara* is at least consistent. See AU 354b.

624 Tsong Khapa appears to acknowledge here that this section was in fact a spurious addition, although he defends it as a useful addition to the text.

the hearts means summoning their hearts and bringing them under one's control."[625] **The power from reciting** his mantra, which is the **king of spells of the deity Śrī Heruka (7.39)**, fulfills one's desired aims.

3.3.3. 2.2.2. 2.1.3. 3. Selecting the root mantra's first and last syllables

The syllable *oṁ* is applied **at the beginning** of the root mantra, **and *hūṁ hūṁ phaṭ* is joined at the end. The root mantra,** i.e., this mantra, **achieves all powers (7.40)**. It is explained that the two *hūṁ* are long [i.e., have long vowels].

3.3.3. 2.2.2. 2.1.3. 4. Showing the name of the chapter

In the *Concise* ***Śrī Herukābhidhāna Tantra***, this is **the seventh chapter** on **the procedure**, i.e., the method, **of selecting the** root **mantra**'s vowels. This is the explanation of the seventh chapter in the *Illumination of the Hidden Meaning, A Detailed Exegesis of the Concise Saṁvara Tantra Called "The Cakrasaṁvara."*

---

[625] Tsong Khapa here not only directly quotes Bhavyakīrti but also closely paraphrases Bhavakīrti's quotation of a passage from Jayabhadra's commentary, which immediately precedes his comments. Bhavyakīrti's text reads as follows: "The master states that **pulverizes the hearts of the ḍākinīs** [means that] just by reciting this mantra the terrors, that is, all of the terrible yoginīs, are terrified. I, Bhavyakīrti, hold that **pulverizes the hearts** means summoning their hearts and completely subjugating them" (BC 16b: */mkha' 'gro ma'i snying 'joms pa yin/ /zhes bya ba ni sngags 'di brjod pa tsam gyis 'jigs pa rnams kyang 'jigs par byed pa'i rnal 'byor ma thams cad kyang rnam par skrag par 'gyur ro zhes slob dpon bzhes do/ /skal ldan grags pa ni snying 'joms pa ni snying 'dren zhing mchog tu dbang byed par sgrub pa yin no zhes 'dod do/*). The "master" here is Jayabhadra, who wrote: "**Pulverizing the hearts of the ḍākinīs** means that just by repeating this mantra, all of the terrible ḍākinīs, and so forth, are terrified" (Sugiki 2001, 119: *ḍākinīnāṁ hṛdayam ardanam ity ayaṁ mantra uccāritamātreṇa sarvā bhayaṁkarā ḍākinyādayas trāsam āpadyante*; CP 52a: */mkha' 'gro ma'i snying ni 'joms pa yin/ /zhes bya ba ni sngags 'di bzlas pa tsam gyis thams cad 'jigs par byed cing mkha' 'gro ma la sogs pa skrag par byed pa yin no/*).

CHAPTER 8

Chapter 8 Outline

3.3.3. 2.2.2. 2.1.4. Selecting the reversed order essence mantra and the heroine's armor mantra

The fourth part, selecting the reversed order essence mantra and the heroine's armor mantra, has four sections: (1) the essence mantra, (2) the armor mantras together with the four treasures, (3) the method of performing the mantra authorization, and (4) the name of the chapter.

3.3.3. 2.2.2. 2.1.4. 1. The essence mantra

Having selected the root mantra's vowels, **thence** the essence and armor mantras are taught. The mantras that are Heruka's **own nature** are the self-nature of the **network**, i.e., host, **of** the twenty-four **ḍākinīs**, who **are united with all** of the twenty-four **heroes**. As for the **binding** of all of them, it is said that this is the *Cakrasaṁvara* (**8.1**).[626] This is the meaning of *ḍākinījālasaṁvara* and *herukaṁ*.

Regarding these types of mantras, they can be stated in accordance with the [reversed] order of *svāhā*, etc. It is also said to be the selection of this mantra.[627] It is "*oṁ śrīvajraheherurukaṁ hūṁ hūṁ phaṭ ḍākinījāla-saṁvaraṁ svāhā*." There is a tradition that this [mantra] has twenty-two

[626] Tsong Khapa here translates the line */'khor lo bde mchog yin par 'dod/*, which occurs not only in all three revised translations (see Gray 2012) but also in in two of the Tibetan translations of Sanskrit commentaries, by Indrabhūti (IC 243b) and Vīravajra (PD 377b). Interestingly, it also occurs in the *translations* of Jayabhadra's commentary (CP 52a) and in the corresponding passage of Kyungpo's AU trans. (AU 354b), but *not* in any of the Sanskrit mss. of these texts. It is replaced in the CT mss. by the alternative line "the producer of all powers," *sarvasiddhisamāvahaṁ*, which is not attested in any of the commentaries. This may represent a case where there were at least two textual variants, and three if we include the absence of either line.

[627] That is, stating a mantra in reversed order is the simplest method of "coding" it.

syllables. Someone says that *va* and *jra* should be counted as two, while someone else takes *pha* and *ṭ* as two.[628]

"Now I will relate this mantra, the **king of spell's essence**, which **has not arisen** previously; nor will it later **arise (8.2)** in other Tantras." This demonstrates the mantra's great rarity.[629]

3.3.3. 2.2.2. 2.1.4. 2. The armor mantras together with the four treasures

The seeds of the six yoginīs are the six [syllables] from *ṭaph* [i.e., *phaṭ* reversed] until *oṁ*. Selecting the mantra without inverting the order, it is: ***oṁ haṁ hriṁ***[630] ***hreṁ hūṁ phaṭ*** **(8.3)**. These are joined with **the syllables *vaṁ*, *yoṁ*, *moṁ*, *hreṁ*,**[631] ***hūṁ***, and ***phaṭ*** **(8.4)**, yielding *oṁ vaṁ haṁ yoṁ hriṁ moṁ hreṁ hrīṁ hūṁ hūṁ phaṭ phaṭ*.

These six mantras are correlated to the six armor yoginīs, since mantras and deities are nondifferent. As is stated in the *Saṁvarodaya*, "The mantra itself is the form of the yoginī, and the yoginī has the mantra's form. If one desires the supreme state, you should not investigate their difference."[632]

---

628 Bhavabhaṭṭa wrote that "this is the twenty-two-syllable essence mantra" (Pandey 2002, 73: *hṛdayamantro dvāviṁśatyakṣaro 'yaṁ*). The former position, that *vajra* has two syllables, is of course the correct one, although this is many not have been apparent to Tibetans relying on the Tibetan transliteration, which appears to be one syllable in length.

629 Tsong Khapa may here be elaborating on Büton, who simply quoted the two lines and then commented that it "shows the mantra's greatness" (NS 327). Tsong Khapa may also perhaps have been paraphrasing Bhavabhaṭṭa's commentary, as follows: "the import of *has not arisen*, etc., is that 'I will relate this mantra which has not been related by me in past or future times'" (Pandey 2002, 73: *na bhūta ityādi / atītānāgatayoḥ kālayor na mayā kasmaicid ayaṁ mantraḥ kathitaḥ kathayiṣyate ceti bhāvaḥ /*).

630 Tsong Khapa has *haṁ hriṁ* here, but the Sanskrit mss. all have long vowels, i.e., *hāṁ hrīṁ*. The SL and SM translations also read *haṁ hriṁ*. This mantra is omitted in the majority of prints and manuscripts of the PM translation, but the Lhasa edition reads *haṁ hriṁ*, while the Derge and Urga editions read *haṁ hrīṁ*. See my edition of these texts in Gray 2012.

631 The majority of sources read *hrīṁ* here. These include the CT mss., Bhavabhaṭṭa's and Jayabhadra's commentaries, and the PM translations, while the SL and SM translations read *hriṁ*. The AU mss., however, attest both *hreṁ* and *hrīṁ* here. See Gray 2012 for detailed information about variant readings found here.

632 This passage occurs in the translation preserved in the sDe-dge canon in a form somewhat different than quoted by Tsong Khapa. The SU reads here as follows: */sngags nyid rnal 'byor ma yi gzugs/ /rnal 'byor ma nyid sngags kyi gzugs/ /ci ste gal te go 'phang mchog thob na/ /de dag dbye bar mi bya/* (SU 302a).

In this context, ***oṁ vajravairocanīye huṁ huṁ phaṭ svāhā*** occurs in the translations of Lochen and Mal. Mardo's translation has *oṁ vajravairocanīye svāhā*.[633] The translations in Bhavyakīrti's[634] and Vīravajra's[635] commentaries accord with the former, while those in Laṅka [Jayabhadra]'s[636] and Bhavabhaṭṭa's[637] accord with the latter. Bhavyakīrti,[638] Laṅka,[639] Vīravajra,[640] and Bhavabhaṭṭa[641] explain that it is the Mother's quintessence [mantra], while Durjayacandra states that it is the essence [mantra].[642]

These mantras are **the great spell of the ḍākinīs**. They **have not arisen (8.5)**, etc., as was [explained] previously. Regarding the places on

---

633 Actually, the PM and SL translations both include *hūṁ hūṁ phat* within the mantra, while the SM translation omits the mantra entirely. However, the extant Sanskrit mss. accord with this reading in omitting *hūṁ hūṁ phaṭ*.

634 Bhavyakīrti's text almost accords with the former, with *oṁ vajravairocanīye hūṁ hūṁ phat phaṭ svāhā* (BC 17a).

635 Vīravajra cites this mantra as: *oṁ vajravairocanīye hu hūṁ phaṭ svāhā* (SG 183a).

636 Jayabhadra's commentary here reads *oṁ oṁ vajravairocanīye svāhā* (Sugiki 2001, 119; see also CP 52a).

637 Bhavabhaṭṭa's commentary also omits the *hūṁ hūṁ phaṭ*, but provides an interesting comment concerning this. He wrote: "This quintessence mantra of Vajravārāhī, *oṁ vajravairocanīye svāhā*, is selected in a secret fashion, in that syllables *hūṁ hūṁ phaṭ* are secreted in [the mantra] before the syllables *svāhā*" (Pandey 2002, 74: *oṁ vajravairocanīye svāheti / vajravārāhyā upahṛdayamantro 'yaṁ gopād uddhṛtaḥ / yata oṁ vajravairocanīye svāheti sthite hūṁ hūṁ phāt-kārau gopitau tau ca svāhākārātprāk*; see also CV 179b).

638 He identifies it as "the quintessence mantra of Vajravārāhī" (BC 17a: *rdo rje phag mo'i nye ba'i snying po'i sngags so*).

639 Laṅka Jayabhadra identifies it as "the quintessence of the Blessed Lady" (Sugiki 2001, 119: *bhagavatyā upahṛdayaṁ*; CP 52a: *bcom ldan 'das yum gyi nye ba'i snying po'o*).

640 Vīravajra likewise identifies it as the "Blessed Lady's quintessence" (PD 378a: *yum gyi nye ba'i snying po*).

641 Bhavabhaṭṭa also identifies it as the "quintessence mantra of Vajravārāhī," as noted above (note 637).

642 He identifies it as the "essence of the Blessed Lady Vajravārāhī" (RG 275a: *bcom ldan 'das ma rdo rje phag mo'i snying po*).

which those armor [mantras] are placed and the yoginīs [correlated to them], they are as is stated in the *Saṁcāra*:

> On the navel, the heart, and likewise in the mouth, the head, and the crown, and the armor[643] itself. First, Vajravārāhī, and the second is said to be Yāminī. The third is Mohanī, and the fourth is said to be Saṁcālanī. The fifth is known as Saṁtrāsanī, and the sixth is said to be Caṇḍikā.[644]

These are linked, respectively, to *oṁ vaṁ*, etc. The "armor" is explained as refering to the weapons in all of the limbs. The referents of these and the places of placement are as explained previously in chapter six. The six yoginīs' colors, implements, and so forth, should be known via the *sādhana*s.

Regarding **on the earth there are four treasures**, while there are several different commentaries on this, the explanation that they are the "mantra garland" (*mantramālā*) and the essence, quintessence, and armor mantras is best.[645] There are two sets of each of these if you differentiate them from the perspective of both the Lord and Lady. The **supreme**, i.e., best of these, is **the mantra garland**s of the Lord and Lady. Since these are rare, increase happiness, and bestow all desired aims like a wish-fulfilling jewel, they are treasures. **The great spell of the ḍākinīs** is the

---

643 The Sanskrit here reads *astra*, weapon, while the Tibetan translation reads *go cha*, armor. The commentaries agree with the former reading, as Tsong Khapa notes below.

644 This passage occurs as follows in YS 7.5c–7c, as follows: *nābhau hṛdaye tathā vaktre śiraḥ śikhāstram eva ca // prathaṁ vajravārāhī dvitīyā yāmanī smṛtā / tṛtīyā mohanī caiva caturthe saṁcāriṇī sthitaṁ // pañcamaṁ saṁtrāsinī khyātā ṣaṣṭhamaṁ caṇḍikā matā / ṣaḍbhiḥ kavacaṁ* (Pandey 1998, 72–74). The Kangyur preserves a somewhat different translation than that quoted by Tsong Khapa. It reads as follows in the Derge edition: */lte ba snying kha de bzhin kha/ /spyi bo spyi gtsug go cha nyid/ /dang po rdo rje phag mo'o/ /gnyis pa ya mi nī ru brjod/ /gsum pa rmongs byed ma nyid de/ /bzhi pa sbyin ma yin par bshad/ /lnga pa kun tu skrag par grags/ /drug pa gtum mo yin par bshad/* (YS 37b).

645 This is argued succinctly by Jayabhadra as follows: "The four mantras, which are the jewels, are the mantra garland, and the essence, quintessence, and armor mantras of the Blessed Lord and Blessed Lady" (Sugiki 2001, 120: *caturo mantrāś catvāro mantrā eva ratnānīti / bhagavato bhagavatyāś ca mantramālā hṛdayopahṛdaye kavacamantraś ca /*; see also CP 52b).

mantra of Vajravārāhī, etc.[646] **The King of Spells, Heruka (8.6)**, is the Lord's root mantra. It is explained that this is the garland mantra that is the supreme garland mantra.

3.3.3. 2.2.2. 2.1.4. 3. The method of performing the mantra authorization

First, one writes out the selection of the root mantra's body in the manner of chapter five, and then, as in chapter seven, applies to the body the selection of the root mantra's vowels.[647] Then the written [text] of both the Blessed Lord and Lady's essence and quintessence [mantras], and both [sets of] armor mantras, are placed upon a throne, and so forth. These mantras should be worshipped and praised as the self-nature of the deities. Following enjoyment among the host (*gaṇa*, *tshogs*), the master and disciple should exhibit the pride of the twelve-armed deity couple.

Both of them [i.e., master and disciple] should visualize that in the master's forehead, the root mantra is circling a white [syllable] *oṁ* on a lunar disk. In his throat, a red *āḥ* on a lunar disk is circled by the two essence [mantras]. And in his heart, a black *hūṁ* on a lunar disk is circled by the two quintessence [mantras]. Both should also likewise visualize in the disciple's three places. Then [they] should repeat the root mantra three times. Each time, a simulacrum separates from the mantra garland, together with *oṁ*, of the master's forehead and dissolves into the mantra garland in the disciple's forehead, until these have been thrice mixed. The disciples repeat the root mantra three or seven times while visualizing the white mantra garland in their own foreheads.

Likewise, during each of the three repetitions of the two essence [mantras], a simulacrum separates from the mantra garland, together with *āḥ* in the master's throat, and dissolves into the mantra garland, together with *āḥ* in the disciple's throat, and should be mixed thrice with the essence [mantra there]. Then the disciples repeat the two essence [mantras] three or twenty-one times while visualizing the red mantra garland in their own throats.

---

646 This line is a direct quote from Bhavabhaṭṭa's commentary, where it occurs as follows: *ḍākinīnāṁ mahāvidyeti vajravārāhyādimantraḥ* (Pandey 2002, 74); */mkha' 'gro ma yi rig pa che/ /zhes pa ni rdo rje phag mo la sogs pa'i sngags so/* (CV 179b).

647 This section is a close paraphrase of a section in Sachen's *Pearl Garland* commentary, PG 313.2–314.1. There is also a similar section in Büton's commentary at NS 95a.

Furthermore, during each of the three repetitions of the two quintessence [mantras], a simulacrum separates from the mantra garland, together with *hūṁ*, in the master's heart, and dissolves into the mantra garland, together with *āḥ* in the disciple's throat, until these mix thrice with the quintessence [mantras]. The disciples repeat the two quintessences twenty-one or one hundred and eight times while visualizing the blue mantra garland in their own hearts.

In the authorizations for the armor [mantras] it is not necessary to assign them in one's own places. The authorization should be performed three times, and one visualizes that these mantras enter into all of the pores of one's body.

Next, the guru rubs his hand on the arrangement of vowels and consonants that was originally the basis of selection, and places it on the disciple's head.[648] [They] visualize that all of the hosts of tathāgatas enter his body through the head in the aspect of the vowels and consonants. Likewise he rubs the root mantra and touches [the disciple's] head with its powder. He rubs the two essence [mantras] and touches the throat, and rubs the two quintessences and touches the breast. Since thereby the hosts of tathāgatas enter the body, one contemplates that one's psycho-physical continuum is blessed. When he rubs the armor mantras and touches one's head, visualize that one's armor is firm and blessed.

Next, offer flowers to the guru, saying thrice, "Blessed Lord, purify me! Blessed Lord, bless me!" The guru accepts them, places them on the disciple's head, and says, "Blessed Lord, purify him! Blessed Lord, bless him!," as well as "May the blessings of the body, speech, and mind of the Blessed Lord Cakrasaṁvara enter him."

Next, the letters are washed with a mixture of beer and ambrosia. The guru himself drinks it and rubs it on his body, and rubs it as well on the disciple's crown, throat, and breast. Drinking what is given into the palm of one's hand and rubbing it on one's body, contemplate that the hosts of tathāgatas dissolve into one's body parts. Lastly, perform a [rite of protection] with a terrifying mantra, as well as with the three armors. I have written this as it occurs in the statements of previous gurus.

---

648 The alphabetical grid used to select the mantra would be composed of colored powder, which the guru now uses to anoint the disciple's head.

3.3.3. 2.2.2. 2.1.4. 4. Showing the name of the chapter

In the *Concise* ***Śrī Herukābhidhāna Tantra***, this is **the eighth chapter** on **the procedure of selecting the reversed** essence and armor **mantras** of the six **yoginīs**. This is the explanation of the eighth chapter in the *Illumination of the Hidden Meaning, A Detailed Exegesis of the Concise Saṁvara Tantra Called "The Cakrasaṁvara."*

CHAPTER 9

Chapter 9 Outline

3.3.3. 2.2.2. 2.2. The way of achieving the powers through mantra repetition

The second part, the way of achieving the powers through mantra repetition, has five sections: (1) ritual success with the root mantra, (2) ritual success with the essence [mantra], (3) ritual success with the quintessence [mantra], (4) ritual success with the armor mantras, and (5) showing other rites accomplished with the essence.

3.3.3. 2.2.2. 2.2.1. Accomplishing ritual actions with the root mantra

The first part has four sections: (1) the promise to explain, and its greatness, (2) detailed explanation of the actual host of ritual actions, (3) showing the necessity of understanding the reality of mantra for those [rites], and (4) showing the name of the chapter.

3.3.3. 2.2.2. 2.2.1. 1. The promise to explain, and its greatness

Following chapter eight, **next I will explain the supreme ritual actions** that achieve the powers through the gateway of the **root mantra, in successive order** as was previously stated, i.e., each one sequentially. This mantra **achieves in an instant**, i.e., without long delay, **all actions**, namely **all of those** powers such as pacifying, etc., that **exist in the triple world (9.1)**, the celestial, terrestrial, and subterranean.

3.3.3. 2.2.2. 2.2.1. 2. Detailed exegesis of the actual host of ritual actions

The second part has two sections: (1) the general principles of the methods for performing the ritual actions and (2) showing each of the methods for performing ritual actions.

3.3.3. 2.2.2. 2.2.1. 2.1. The general principles of the methods for performing the ritual actions

Although there are many inferior ritual actions, those attained over a long time, and also those attained without practice, it is necessary to practice in order to quickly achieve all ritual actions in the manner to be explained, and to quickly attain the mundane powers as well as the great powers, which do not occur in the lower classes of Tantras. Therefore, practice by means of the creation stage is taught in the *Concise Root Tantra* and *Appendix*. With regard to this, through previously becoming very firm in the creation stage, perfection [mantra] repetition, and performing one-tenth as many fire sacrifices, one undertakes accordingly the three practices.[649] Thus through mantra repetition, and so forth, the ritual actions are achieved.

The creation stage also requires reliance upon a single wheel of the mandala, but it is not the case that [mastery of] just a single deity [is sufficient]. As for the mantra, while the root mantra's power is great, it is not necessary to apprehend it alone.

---

[649] Tsong Khapa here appears to be summarizing the opening section of SU ch. 11, which outlines these preliminaries in very similar language. It occurs as follows in my translation from the Sanskrit: "And now I will explain the secret, the characteristics of mantra repetition. First, on mountains, in caves, in groves, on riverbanks, at a crossroad, meeting place, or in a pleasing charnel ground, one must employ the mandala. Then, with one's self as the deity, undertake the correct preliminary service by means of the previously stated rites. Also in mountainous places one should repeat the essence mantra, *oṁ śrīvajraherukaṁ hūṁ hūṁ phaṭ svāhā*. Repeating one hundred thousand times, one should make fire sacrifices one tenth [of that in number]. Then there will quickly be powers, worldly and ultimate, but not otherwise" (IASWR ms. # MBB II-89 fols. 23b.3–24a.1: *athāto rahasyam vakṣye mantrajāpasya lakṣaṇam / maṇḍalaṁ vartayet pūrvaṁ pāścāt devatātmakaṁ / girigahvarakuñjeṣu mahodadhitaṭeṣu ca / catuṣpathe maṇḍape sthāne śmaśāne ca manoramye / pūrvoktavidhanā samyakpūrvasevāṁ ca kārayet / parvatagiristhāne 'pi japet hṛdayamantrataḥ / oṁ śrīvajraherukaṁ hūṁ hūṁ phaṭ svāhā / lakṣam eka japayitvā tu daśāṁśena tu homayet / laukikalokottarāsiddhi śigram bhavati nānyathā /*). The Tibetan translation has these lines in a different order, which makes more sense. My translation follows the Tibetan order. See SU 278b–279a.

Regarding the number of repetitions, it is required that one do as is stated in the *Saṁvarodaya*, namely: "In the *kṛta* age one would repeat once, in the *tretā* twice. In the *dvāpara* it is said to be thrice, and in the *kali* [age] one must repeat fourfold."[650] As for the method of repetition, Kambala explains that it is attained by meditation (*dhyāna*) alone, both that and repetition, or magical diagrams (*yantra*) as well in addition to them.[651] These refer to the three types of person, the superior, middling, and inferior. This [is relevant] at the time of ritual application, which does not [apply to] the first [type of person].[652]

The *Saṁvarodaya* states many times that at the time of ritual application, one succeeds by means of mantra and oblation.[653] Regarding the direction in which one faces [while engaged in ritual applications], the *Saṁvarodaya* explains that one faces east for pacifying, north for enriching, west for subduing and summoning, and south for paralyzing and killing.[654] And there is stupefying, which is like paralyzing.[655] The

---

650 This occurs as follows in SU ch. 12: *kṛtayuge japed ekaḥ / tretāyāṁ dviguṇaṁ japet / dvāpare triguṇaṁ proktaṁ / kalau caturguṇāṁ japet /* (IASWR ms. # MBB II-89 fols. 26a.5–26b.1; see also SU 280a).

651 Kambala comments as follows: "Regarding **supreme ritual actions, in successive order**, they are attained by mediation alone. Some attain them via meditation and mantra, and others by means of meditation, mantra, and the production of magical diagrams" (SN 19a: *las mchog go rims ji bzhin tu / zhes bya ba la bsam gtan tsam gyis grub par 'gyur ba dang / kha cig ni bsam gtan dang sngags kyis grub par 'gyur ba dang / la las ni bsam gtan dang sngags dang 'khrul 'khor gyi bya bas grub pa ste /*).

652 That is, since the superior person succeeds through meditation alone, she or he has no need for ritual practices.

653 These statements are made throughout SU chs. 11 and 12, including the passage from ch. 11 quoted above.

654 This passage occurs in chapter 23 in Tsuda's translation and edition (1974) as follows: "In [the rite of] pacifying, [the hearth] is of round shape, white, and faces east; the square [hearth] is [used in the rite of] increasing welfare, and is yellow and faces north. [The hearth in the shape of] a half moon and facing west is [used in the rites of] expelling and exorcising; [the hearth] facing south and of triangular shape is [used in] the rites of causing hostility and killing" (p. 307). The Sanskrit occurs as follows: *śāntike vartukākaraṁ śukraṁ pūrvānanaṁ bhavet / caturasraṁ pauṣṭikaṁ pītaṁ uttarānanaṁ bhavet // uccāṭanam abhicārāṁ ca ardhacandraṁ paścimānanam / vidveṣamāraṇaṁ karma dakṣiṇānanatrikoṇakam //* (p. 138). See also SU 292b. Note that this differs significantly from what is reported by Tsong Khapa, in that it correlates to the west "ruining and destroying" (*uccāṭanam abhicārāṁ*) rather than "subduing and summoning." The next

(cont'd)

Vajraḍāka explains that one faces the wind [i.e., northwestern direction] in order to expel. It also explains that one faces south for both expelling and separating.[656]

It is said that for pacifying the deity's color is white and the flower is white. For enriching the color and flower are yellow. For subduing the color and flower are red. For paralyzing the color and flower are yellow, and stupefying is also like that. Visualize the color black for killing, expelling, and separating. By these one should also know the colors of the mantras and other offering substances. As it says in the *Saṁvarodaya*, "the colors, and so forth, are indicated by the characteristic of the ritual action, and likewise the place, the appearance of the deity, the mantra, and the flower, in accordance with the rite."[657] It also repeatedly explains that one should perform one-tenth as many fire sacrifices as mantra repetitions at the time of the ritual application.[658] Fearing prolixity, I will not write on any remaining issues.

3.3.3. 2.2.2. 2.2.1. 2.2. Showing each of the methods for performing ritual actions

The second part has five sections: (1) the rites that largely destroy and incidentally benefit, (2) the host of destructive rites, (3) showing the way to perform rites that incidentally benefit, (4) the destructive rites of killing and restoring life, and (5) showing other beneficial rites.

---

verse lists these (*vaśyākṛṣṭi*) but does not clearly correlate them to a direction. Likewise, the southern direction correlates to exciting hostility and killing (*vidveṣamāraṇaṁ*), not "paralyzing and killing" as Tsong Khapa reports.

655 Both of these are correlated to the southwest direction, as follows: *stambhanamohanaṁ karma nairṛtyānanaṁ bhavet* (Tsuda 1974, 138).

656 See VD 94b.

657 This occurs as follows in SU ch. 11: *yasya karmaviśeṣeṇa tasya varṇādi lakṣayet / āsanaṁ devatābhāvaṁ mantrapuṣpaṁ yathāvidhiṁ //* (IASWR ms. # MBB II-89 fols. 25a.4–5). Interestingly, Tsong Khapa cites a correct translation of this passage, in contradistinction to the translation preserved in the Kangyur, which contains several errors and omissions here. See SU 279b.

658 This is stated throughout SU chs. 11 and 12, including the passage from ch. 11 quoted above.

3.3.3. 2.2.2. 2.2.1. 2.2.1. The rites that largely destroy and incidentally benefit

One causes all races of **all gods**, such as Hari, Hara, and Hiraṇyagarbha, **all serpent deities**, such as Dṛṣṭiviṣa (Poison Glance), **all yakṣa**, such as Ojohāra (Vitality Thief), and all celestial musicians **to die** just **through recollecting** one time. Why does it state "all races," having already stated "all gods," etc.? Koṅkaṇa, and so forth, state that "since [this] is clear there is no fault of repetition."[659] Bhavyakīrti states that regarding gods, serpent deities, and *yakṣa*s, etc., as referring to other sentient beings is extremely pernicious. [The destruction of] them is also "achieved in an instant." This is stated again in order to demonstrate its own greatness.[660] It is also said that this power is for [use against] the pernicious ones who exist among the gods, and so forth, and furthermore explained that it should [only] be performed by one who also has the power of reviving them.[661]

Those who [can do] this just through recollection are the [superior types] who are absorbed in the creation stage that achieves ritual actions by means of meditation without regard for mantra repetition, and so forth.

[659] Tsong Khapa here does not quote exactly but rather abbreviates a longer comment in Jayabhadra's commentary, where it occurs as follows: "Races of all gods has a clear and obvious meaning. While this is a restatement, it is not the case that there is the fault of superfluous repetition in any Tantra" (Sugiki 2001, 120: *sarvadevayonaya iti siddhivispaṣṭārthaṁ / punarvacanāni sarvatantre punaruktadoṣābhāvāt /*; see also CP 52b). Note that Jayabhadra glosses *sarvayonayaḥ* as *sarvadevayonayaḥ*. This gloss necessitates his defense against the charge of repetitiveness, since *sarvadevān* was already listed.

[660] Tsong Khapa condenses slightly the following passage in Bhavyakīrti's commentary: "I, Bhavyakīrti, hold that [just by] regarding gods, serpent deities, and yakṣas, etc., as being extremely pernicious in comparison with other sentient beings, [their destruction] is also 'achieved in an instant.'" The second repetition [of this] has the purpose of demonstrating its greatness. Thus, the gods, and so forth, are stated" (BC 17b–18a: */skal ldan grags pa ni lha dang klu dang gnod sbyin la sogs pa rnams ni sems can gzhan la ltos nas shin tu ma rungs pa yin na de rnams kyang skad cig gis 'grub par byed do zhes gnyis ka yang bdag nyid che bar bstan pa'i don yin pas kyang lha la sogs pa smos pa yin no zhes 'dod do/*). These comments follow his quotation of Jayabhadra's comment, which is likewise quoted by Tsong Khapa.

[661] Tsong Khapa here cites Bhavabhaṭṭa, who wrote: "It is said that it is power against the fierce ones among [the gods, etc.]. It should also be inferred that one has the power of reviving [them]" (Pandey 2002, 76: *madhyasthānakrūrāṁś ca prati sāmarthyam uktam / punarutpādanasāmarthyam apy unneyam //*).

Those who are absorbed in mantra affix their names [i.e., the names of their victims] to the end of the root mantra, and adding "Kill, *phaṭ*!" (*māraya phaṭ*) cause them to be scorched and shattered by its repetition.

Kambala states that [one should] "lift a flower in offering to the crown of Vajradhara, pronouncing seven times the root mantra. If one fumigates the cloud [with incense], then one turns back the rain falling from the sky."[662] It is explained in the oral instructions of previous gurus that "if one, gazing at the host of clouds, repeats fiercely, at the end of the root mantra, *sarvemeghavikiraṇavaya hūṁ phaṭ*, and visualizes red wind emerging from one's mouth, then the clouds will be dispersed."[663]

With regard to **causing rain to fall**, Kambala explains in his commentary the two [methods] in the manner of the *Abhidhānottara*. [First,] rain falls in dependence upon the body of writing of the Vajragaruḍa.[664] [Second,] one requests that a [buddha] image be bathed, and mixing together [the clay from] two banks of a river one forms an image of a nine-headed serpent deity. Bathing and worshipping it, one casts it into the main channel of a river. Thus rain falls.[665] In accordance with what is stated in the *Vajraḍāka*, he explains the four [methods] of rainfall, and

---

662 The text of Kambala's commentary differs somewhat from Tsong Khapa's quote, as follows: "Lift a flower in offering to the crown of Vajradhara, pronouncing seven times the root mantra. If one fumigates [one's] ring finger, then one turns back rain in the sky" (SN 21a: */yang na rdo rje 'dzin pa'i spyi bor phul ba'i me tog blang la rtsa ba'i sngags lan 'dun btab ste srin lag la bdugs na 'dis nam mkha' la char bzlog par 'gyur ro/*). The reading *sprin la* in place of *sring lag la* also occurs in Büton's commentary (NS 338), which is likely Tsong Khapa's source here; this may represent a correction of an error in this translation, or simply an alternate reading.

663 This rite is not mentioned in any of the Indian or Tibetan commentaries that I have consulted, and thus appears to be a genuine oral instruction.

664 This appears to be a method involving the invocation of Varuṇa and the eight *nāga* kings. See SN 19b–20a, and AU 322a,b.

665 Tsong Khapa gives an extremely elliptical account of a ritual, based on the description in Kambala's commentary (SN fol. 20a), which is in turn based on the *Abhidhānottara*'s account, which follows: "Wash a relic-containing buddha image with a mixture of scented water and milk, and make an image of a serpent deity with the mud of the bank where two rivers converge. Facing west, besprinkle the nine heads, and cast it into the river. From that moment on, torrents of rain will be unleashed upon all of Jambudvīpa" (I 588a.5–6; J 199.5–7: *buddhapratimāṁ sadhātukaṁ gandhodakaṁ kṣīramiśraṁ snānaṁ kṛtvā nāgapratikṛtiṁ kṛtvā naḍyobhayataṭamṛttikāyātena kṛtvā paścimābhimukhe navaśīrṣaṁ siñcet tataḥ naḍyāṁ pravāhayet tatkṣaṇād eva varṣadhārāṁ sakalajāmbudvīpaṁ utsṛjyati*).

so forth, relying upon the drawing of the magical diagram (*yantra*) of Phaṇīndra.[666]

In explanation of the fourth of these, draw in an earthenware vessel into which *soma* has been discharged the three wheels [of the mandala] with poison, salt, and black mustard seeds, with an eight-petaled lotus in its center. In its center write [the syllables] *hūṁ vaṁ hūṁ*, and on the petals write the essence [mantras] of the [eight] serpent deities, pressed by two *hūṁ* seed syllables. On the rim of the wheels and the edge of the lotus write *oṁ vajrakrodhamahābala hana hana paca paca vidhvansaya uccāṭaya*[667] *sarvanāgānāṁ*[668] *māraya hūṁ phaṭ*.[669] Having summoned [them], and so forth, worship [them]. Cover [the vessel] with a lid, and put it in a place where serpent deities dwell. Rain will fall when one offers burning incense made of bdellium and the sap of the Sarja [tree],[670] i.e., "white incense," along with white garlic, and repeats the mantra.[671]

Regarding averting a great rainfall, fumigate a cotton figure of a serpent deity with incense [made] of the three substances previously explained. It will be averted by repeating the root mantra with the words "*varṣa nivarṣaya*"[672] inserted or by performing the rite of cloud dispersing. Konkana provides explanations of both the definitive and interpretable [meanings] of the three expressions, "dispel clouds," etc.[673]

---

666 *Phaṇīndra* and *Phaṇīśvara* (Tib. *gdengs ka'i dbang phyug*) are names of a *nāga* king.

667 Tsong Khapa's text, following Büton's, reads *ucchataya* here, and Kambala's *ucchaṭaya*.

668 Tsong Khapa's text reads *sarvanāgānān*; Büton has *sarvanāganāṁ*.

669 This might be translated as: "Oṁ Great Power of Adamantine Ferocity, strike! strike! cook! cook! pulverize! expel! slay all *nāgas*! hūṁ phaṭ."

670 *Sarjarasa* is the resin derived from the sap of the Sarja tree, *Vatica robusta*.

671 Tsong Khapa here follows Büton's version of the rite (NS 337), which in turn is based upon Kambala's explanation at SN 20b, as well as a section of ch. 3 of the *Vajraḍāka*, at VD 10a.

672 I haven't found a description of this rite in the extant Sanskrit sources, but it probably should read *varṣaṁ nivāraya*, "avert the rain!"

673 Jayabhadra, while acknowledging the literal meaning, comments only on the "definitive meaning," as follows: "With regard to **dispelling clouds**, and so forth, first the literal meaning is apprehended, and later there is the following meaning. **Dispelling clouds** in the state of the vajra and lotus subdues the ḍākinīs. **Causing rain to fall** [occurs] via the flow of awakening spirit. **Holding it back** is immobilizing it with seals (*mudrā*) in

(cont'd)

With regard to these three, Bhavyakīrti states that "those who have not recited one hundred thousand times, even though they have the ability to do so, can only apprehend the literal meaning."[674] If one goes into the ocean and repeats the root mantra fiercely one hundred thousand times, one can **dry up the ocean**.

With regard to reversing and releasing a river's flow, make a trident of any of the seven classes of lodestone, and repeat the root mantra [over it] seven times. If one thrusts it with one's left hand into the river, it will [reverse course] as stated [in the Tantra]. What will happen if one does this? Since he is the lord of the sentient and insentient, he is [an] Indra. He is diverted from those deeds that are not to be done.[675] In a translation there also occurs "holds back lightning/hail," about which previous gurus also wrote.[676] **Through one hundred thousand repetitions of this** root **mantra**, via the method of repeating while fiercely brandishing one's index finger, and being in the *ālīḍha* pose[677] and with enthusiasm like a dancer, one delights the retinue of ḍākinīs,[678] and thereby, **causes the earth to quake**, i.e., pleases them. And **climbing a tree,** one can cause them to **go to wherever one desires (9.2.1)**, such as the [sacred] seats (*pītha*) and secondary [sacred] seats (*upapītha*), and to return and assemble again.

If the root mantra is repeated with augments such as **steal all** powers of others' **mantras**, or **steal all powers**, then one will steal all

---

intercourse with women" (Sugiki 2001, 120: *meghān trāsayatītyādi prathamaṁ yathārtho gṛhyate paścād ayam arthaḥ—vajrapadmasaṁsthāyāṁ meghān trāsayati ḍākinīr vaśīkaroti / varṣāpayati bodhicittadhārayā / nivārayati sthāpayati saha mudrābhir aṅganābhir vartante*).

674 See BC 18a.

675 Tsong Khapa here paraphrases Bhavabhaṭṭa's commentary. The Sanskrit for this occurs as follows: *indraṁ nivārayatīti / indraṁ jātyaikavacanam indrantītīndrāḥ / cetanācetanādhipatīn akāryakāraṇān niṣedhayatītyarthaḥ* (Pandey 2002, 76).

676 This variant, *thog zlog par byed*, with *thog* meaning either a thunderbolt (the weapon of Indra) or hail, does not occur in the surviving translations or Sanskrit texts. However, it is attested in Kambala's commentary; see SN 21a. Sachen, in his commentary, remarks that *indra* refers to lightning/hail (*thog*). See PG 315.3.

677 That is, in the archer's pose with right leg forward and left leg drawn back.

678 This explanation follows closely that given by Kambala at SN 21a.

powers of mantra, and steal powers such as pacifying, and so forth, and steal all power substances that achieve alchemy, and so forth. If, in order to prevent injury to the [Buddhist] teaching, one repeats fiercely adding to the end of the root mantra "draw the blood [of so-and-so], *jaḥ*,"[679] then that other one's blood is drawn forth. And if one respectfully bows down to the victim and repeats with the augment, "Blood return!,"[680] the blood is summoned and sent again, i.e., is put back in its previous place.

Regarding **assuming many thousands of forms**, one who abides in the state of the great seal (*mahāmudra*) can, through the power of compassion and aspiration, assume those forms that accord with the thinking of whichever disciples are to be trained. Those of inferior effort who are not like that can achieve various forms with seeds by means of mantra and medicines. Kambala's commentary relates four [methods], one [of which] is as follows. Twenty-nine seeds of the castor-oil plant[681] and datura plant are rubbed with flowers of the vile category, stained with the five ambrosias, and dried day and night. Fill the skull of a black dog with earth from a charnel ground, and creating [the mandala] in a place [sacred to] the mothers on the eighth or fourteenth day of the waning moon, take the prepared seeds and worship with the mantras Heruka and one's lord guru especially. Offer sacrificial cakes in a charnel ground, and enchant them. If one ties a cord around one's neck while visualizing the desired form, one will assume that form. When it is untied, one assumes one's own form again.[682]

Furthermore, there is the seed prepared by means of the commitment practiced in accordance with the rite. If one desires to appear in various forms, one casts it from one's mouth and appears however one

---

679 That is, [*che ge mo'i*, which equals the Sanskrit *amukasya*] *rakta-ākarṣaya jaḥ*.

680 Tsong Khapa does not give the Sanskrit here, but Sachen gives a garbled attempt: *amukashya rāgata ghachantu*, which probably should read *amukasya rakto gacchatu*. See PG 316.1.

681 This is *eraṇḍa*, the castor-oil plant, *Ricinus communis*.

682 This is a summary of the first of the four rites described by Kambala in his commentary, occurring at SN 21b–22a. The description of the others continues through fol. 22b.

wishes. If one desires to become invisible, one inserts it in one's mouth and disappears. I will not write extensively on this.[683]

As for **one can reduce palaces, trees, spires, and so forth, to dust (9.2.2)**, it is said that "they are chopped by the king of mantras as if by a blazing axe."[684] Visualize that fire blazes from the root mantra, and that [with it one] cuts [such things] to pieces.

Place the stainless moonlight-like wheel on one's left hand, and just by showing the palm of one's hand the **poison**s that are produced from static or animate [sources], or that are compounded, are **turned into ambrosia**. As for turning **ambrosia into poison**, [it is done] by producing a black mantra on one's palm, and displaying it.[685]

By simply visualizing that **soma**, i.e., liquor, is as stainless as moonbeams, it is **turned into milk**, i.e., water. This is called "The brahmin's jewel made by the vajra." Soak the powder of dried saffron (*kusumbha*) flowers in "cow water," and knead [this mixture] many

---

683 Kambala gives a slightly expanded instruction here. His instruction seems to imply that the yogī himself take the seeds prepared in the previous rite, which there were used on another person. He wrote: "As for the third [procedure], [here the seeds] are taken by oneself. If you place them in your mouth while positioned in the middle of the mandala of the Mothers (*mātṛkā*) who are mistresses of yoga, such as Kākāsyā, etc., one will appear in accordance with the appearance of various yogīs. In accordance with the rite, one will truly be seen in a form similar to theirs. A person who has the power of yoga will become invisible to all. Just on account of a mere portion of the seeds prepared by the commitments one will not be seen by owls, and so forth; what need is there to talk about men on earth? If the intelligent one is equipoised to the extent he desires, he will take pleasure with daughters of the gods. If one desires, cast it from one's mouth and one will be visible. If one does not desire this, one will [remain] invisible. One will be regarded as a master of invisibility" (SN 22a,b: */gsum pa ni bdag nyid kyis bzung la/ khva'i gdong pa la sogs pa'i rnal 'byor 'byung po'i ma mo'i dkyil 'khor gyi dbus su gnas te khar bcug na rnal 'byor pa sna tshogs kyi rnam pa dang mtshungs par snang ste/ cho ga ji lta ba bzhin tu nges par de 'dra ba'i gzugs su mthong bar 'gyur ro/ /sbyor ba'i nus pa skyes bu thams cad tu mi snang bar 'grub par 'gyur te/ sa bon gyi dam tshig 'grub pa'i cha tsam yang 'ug pa la sogs pa rnams kyis mi mthong na sa la skyes pa rnams kyis lta smos kyang ci dgos te/ blo dang ldan pas ji srid 'dod pa'i bar du mnyam par gzhag na lha'i bu mo rnams dang lhan cig tu rtse bar 'gyur ro/ /'dod na kha nas bton na mthong zhing mi 'dod na mi mthong bar 'gyur te/ mi snang ba'i dbang phyug tu 'dod par 'gyur ro/*).

684 This comment occurs in Kambala's commentary as follows: */khang bzangs dang shing gi rtse mo la sogs phye mar byed do zhes bya ba ni/ /sngags kyi rgyal pos me 'bar ba'i / sta gri bzhin du gtub par bya'o/* (SN 22b).

685 This is a summary of Kambala's comments at SN 22b.

times with the juice of the citron fruit.[686] If one pours this into a lotus vessel, water, that is, *milk*, will seemingly be turned into *soma*, i.e., liquor. If one rubs one's hands, and so forth, with a mixture of powdered Karaṇḍa fruit[687] together with its thorns and the bark of the Nāgara tree,[688] then one will **steal all scents (9.2.3)**, i.e., steal all scents of flowers, fruit, and so forth. Likewise, if you burn that [mixture] with the flowers and incense, their scent will move hither and thither.

As for **eagle** (*garuḍa*), etc., many other commentaries explain that "just as the *garuḍa* flies in the sky moving its two wings, in intercourse with the seal one extends both arms, and at the end having been equipoised, one takes up the awakening spirit with the tongue, and having offered it up into the seal's mouth, one drinks the remainder."[689] Kambala's commentary has the following: "Making an emission that goes by means of the eagle's mouth, one consorts with women."[690] This

---

686 Tsong Khapa's text reads here *dzambu'i 'bras bu*, presumably the fruit of the Indian rose apple. Kambala's commentary, on which Tsong Khapa's text here is based, reads *dzam bi ri 'bras bu* (SN 23a), which appears to be the fruit of the *jambīra* or citron tree. Both readings are plausible, especially given the fact that both fruits are yellow in color, like the saffron that is also included in this recipe. However, I follow here Kambala's reading, since he is clearly the source for Tsong Khapa's ritual summaries.

687 That is, the "elephant apple," *Feronia elephantum*, an Indian citrus fruit with a hard, spiny rind and edible pulp.

688 Evidently this denotes the *Euphorbia antiquorum*, an often large, leafless spiny tree native to India, particularly the Deccan region.

689 Tsong Khapa here summarizes Bhavabhaṭṭa's comments, which occur as follows: "As for **eagle**, he is like an eagle because there is movement of his two arms that are like wings. It is the *yogī* who **emits in the course**, i.e., produces an emission that moves along the course. He **consorts** with those **who gather** the **soma** that is the two awakening spirits produced in [the union of] wisdom and art. He is a **man** who is discriminating on account of the flowerlike **women** [with whom he consorts]. He is **superior** because he is uncommon. He takes up this awakening spirit with his mouth, and moving his limbs like a *garuḍa*, he offers it up into the wisdom's mouth, and eats the remainder" (Pandey 2002 p. 78: *garuḍo garuḍavad bāhudvayasya pakṣavac cālanāt / yānasya gamanasya sṛṣṭir niṣpādanaṁ karotīti yānasṛṣṭikṛd yogī / somayoḥ prajñopāyasambhavayor bodhicittayoḥ saṁgamas taṁ samācarati / yaḥ strīṇāṁ puṣpavatīnāṁ naro vivekitvāt / śreṣṭho 'sādhāraṇaḥ / etena tadbodhicittaṁ mukhenādāya garuḍavat pakṣadvayam uccālayan prajñāmukhe dattva śeṣaṁ svayam abhyavaharet /*; see also CV 181b.

690 Both this quotation and Tsong Khapa's comments on it below derive from Kambala's commentary, except where otherwise noted. See SN 23a.

means that one abandons the *nāgas* of Phaṇīndra's wheel, and when the moon is in the constellation *Puṣyā* write the [root mantra][691] with cow concretion on birch bark, inserting the names of the woman and good man, and worship this. Visualizing oneself as Heruka and one's seal as Vajravārāhī, repeat the root mantra for an entire night while equipoised by means of nondual union. When the wheel is held within the woman's body, the King of Spells (*vidyārāja*) himself comes to, i.e., consorts with, the woman. This is the meaning of **consorting with women** and also **gathering soma.** It is said that "woman" is an equivalent term of "goddess."[692] **Moutheagle** is a reversed manner of sitting, which, by lifting both knees, opens the channel that has the blood that is within the expanded lotus. "Going" there means consorting by means of intercourse, which is similar to the statement "going into the mouth" in Devagupta's commentary.[693]

Any practitioner who is a child born from the emission of the drop of awakening spirit in that opened channel in the context of the "consorting" (*samācāra*) previously explained is a **superior man** on account of being in the clan of all tathāgatas. He is glorious and has a stainless name,

---

691 Neither Tsong Khapa nor Kambala specifies which mantra one writes, but it is likely the root mantra, given the fact that this chapter deals with its ritual applications.

692 This is stated by Devagupta, who restates Kambala's comments and then adds some of his own. He writes here, following Kambala's comments that one visualizes oneself as Śrī Heruka and one's consort as Vajravārāhī, that "It is said that this means that it is the goddess who gathers *soma*" (SS 91b: */des ni zla ba'i 'dus pa'i lha mo dang zhes pa'i don bshad do/*). Sachen expands on this, writing, "the 'goddess' is the distinguished seal with whom the adept 'consorts,' i.e., with whom he is equipoised, at which time they experience bliss through the practice of intercourse in which there is the *yoga* of lifting the knees and extending them like wings" (PG 316.3: *lha mo ste mtshan dang ldan pa'i phyag rgya dang kun du spyod pa ni de dang sgrub pa po snyoms 'jug byed pa'i tshe/ pus mo bsgreng ba'i sbyor ba pus mo gnyis gshog pa ltar brkyang la 'khrig pa spyad pas bde ba myong ba des/*).

693 Devagupta here restates Kambala's comments somewhat differently. He writes, "As for **going into the mouth of the eagle**, one gathers [the soma] by going into the mouth by means of opening the orifice of the perfected red channel in the lotus that is expanded by raising the knees of both of the legs" (SS 91b, 92a: */nam mkha' lding gi gdong du 'gro bas zhes pa ni rkang pa gnyis pus gong du blangs pas padma rgyas par byas pa'i dbus na rdzogs pa'i rtsa dmar pa kha grol ba las gdong du 'gro bas 'du bar byed do/*). "Mouth" thus appears to have two interpretations here. It can refer to the actual mouth that takes the sexual fluids from the vulva, or the vulva itself, the place whence these fluids are taken.

and **no one can steal the splendor that he has in** the palm of **his hand**. Since he is an object of reverence for all beings, he is glorious like a universal monarch, and characterized by perfection in longevity and health. Thus is the production of lineage heirs explained in the commentaries of Kambala and Devagupta.[694] **Being thus endowed with the rite**,

---

[694] It should be noted that in neither of these commentaries is there any direct or obvious reference to the notion that the conception of extraordinary children is being described here. This interpretation is, in fact, at variance with the root text, where the "superior man" (*naraḥ śreṣṭhaḥ*) is clearly the one who "consorts" (*samācarati*) with women (*strīṇāṁ*), not the product of this sexual intercourse. Kambala's commentary is ambiguous, and does not articulate the relationship between the "superior man" and the "course of the moutheagle" posture. It appears to follow the root text, as does Devagupta, who follows him. It might be useful to quote his entire commentary here, which Tsong Khapa follows closely, except at the two points where he refers to Devagupta's glosses. Kambala's text occurs as follows: "**The course of the moutheagle** (*nam mkha' lding gi gdong gis 'gro ba*, literally "going with the moutheagle," which appears to be an alternative translation of *mukhagaruḍayāna*) is a reversed manner of sitting, which, by lifting both knees, opens the channel that has the blood that is within the expanded lotus, so that there is emission. The **superior man** is glorious and has a stainless name, on account of being in the clan that is the essence of all tathāgatas. **No one can steal the splendor that he has in** the palm of **his hand**. Since he is an object of reverence for all beings, he is glorious like a universal sovereign (*cakravartin*) and characterized by perfection in longevity and health" (SN CT fol. 23a,b: */nam mkha' lding gi gdong gis 'gro ba zhes bya ba ni/ go bzlog 'dug stang kyis shin tu rgyas pa'i padma'i nang du chud pa'i khrag dang bcas pa'i rtsa kha bye ba las 'byin par byed pa ni de bzhin gshegs pa thams cad kyi rang bzhin gyi rigs su 'gyur mi mchog ste dpal dang ldan zhing mtshan dri ma med par 'gyur ro/ /de'i lag mthil na yod pa'i dpal gang gis kyang 'phrogs mi nus te 'byung po thams cad kyi mchod gnas su 'gyur bas 'khor los sgyur ba dang mnyam par dpal dang ldan zhing tshe dang nad med par phun sum tshogs pa la mtshan pa'o/*). Kambala is ambiguous precisely on the relation between the "emission" and the "superior man," which probably is what gave rise to the alternate interpretation. In the root Tantra, however, these are not equated. Rather, he is the one who "emits" or "makes emission" (*sṛṣṭikṛt*). This is supported by Jayabhadra, who commented that "as for **superior man**, he is one who, on account of practicing thus, becomes the very best in the triple world" (Sugiki 2001, 121: *naraḥ śreṣṭha iti yo nara evam ācarati sa śreṣṭo bhavati triṣu lokeṣv ity arthaḥ /*). Tsong Khapa may have depended here on Büton, who likewise speaks of a son born of this sort of union. But Büton first speaks of a different sort of "birth" or generation, which appears more credible to me. Following the same quote from Kambala concerning the opening of the Lotus's channel, and influenced by Devagupta's comments here, Büton writes: "the opening of the channel that has the blood that is in the lotus expanded by raising both knees of the legs is the **mouth** of the **eagle**. 'Going' there means that one creates oneself as the King of Spells, the emission of the moving seed." This appears to be the sense in which this emission gives rise or birth to something, i.e., the "rebirth" of oneself as the deity (NS 343–344: */rkang pa gnyis pus gong du blangs te*

(cont'd)

the aspects of which have been explained above, one will have **the fruition of all the powers (9.2.4)**.

A previous guru states that the expressions "mouth eagle" and "going with the mouth eagle" designate a medicine that is the fluid from lovemaking, which is drunk having been enchanted one hundred and eight times. If one consumes the semen (*śukra*) [resulting from] the practice of erotic love (*kāmācāra*), then one will have radiance and glory as if one had splendor in the palm of one's hand.[695]

3.3.3. 2.2.2. 2.2.1. 2.2.2. The host of destructive rites

Regarding **through recollection one can cause death**, enter into the mandala of the solar circle, and draw with poison, salt, and black mustard seeds, and make an image [of the victim] with the ash and charcoal of the charnel ground. Placing it in the heart of the wheel, one summons there the consciousness of the victim. Hiding it in the charnel ground, one drives a stake made of human bone into its heart. If you pour hot water on it and repeat the mantra fiercely, he will die within seven days.[696]

If one abides in the concentration of the ignition and blazing of fury fire, and visualizes fire blazing, driven by a southern wind, one will **cause fire to flare up** wherever one desires. If one brandishes a one-pronged vajra and drives it into the ground repeating the mantra, one will **cause the underworld to split open**, i.e., be rent asunder. If one enchants the palm of one's hand and strikes with it following the wind, one causes hail to fall wherever one desires. Kambala's commentary has

---

padma rgyas par byas pa'i nang du chud pa'i khrag dang bcas pa'i rtsa kha phye ba ni nam mkha' lding gi gdong ste/ der 'gro pa ste/ bgrod ba'i thig le 'byin par byed pa las rig pa'i rgyal po rang skye bar 'gyur te/).

695 These comments attributed to "a previous guru" do not occur in any of the Indian commentaries or those by Sachen and Büton. The notion, however, that the sexual fluids are consumed and yield benefits is found in most of them. Sachen refers to *mukhagaruḍa* as a type of medicine, but one that is so called because it contains a fruit that looks like the beak of a crow or *garuḍa*. See PG 316.2: *nam mkha' lding gi gdong dang zhes pa ni / nam mkha' lding lding gi gdong dang 'dra ba'i phyir nam mkha' lding ste / sman gyi bye brag shing gi 'bras bu khva'am nam mkha' lding lding gi mchu 'dra ba zhig yod /*.

696 Tsong Khapa here and in the following descriptions of ritual actions quotes or paraphrases Kambala's commentary at SN 23b.

cause a thunderbolt to be cast down.[697] With regard to stopping hail, it is explained that if one sets up parasols, banners, and flags, the tips of which are bound with magical diagrams (*yantra*), then hail is prevented in all of the regions of the land in which the magical diagram is found.[698]

Regarding **through recollection one can cause lightning to flash**, it is said that if one writes *yabha-buddhaya-yata hūm* on red oleander with terrible ink, enchants it, and brandishing toward the sky casts it away, lightning will flash.[699] As for [one being able to] **cause the images of all deities to dance**, it is said that if one binds written magical diagrams to charnel ground cloth, burns it in a skull with great flesh and bdellium resin in a fire of charnel ground charcoal or some other fire, and fumigates [in the smoke] images of Gu-lang,[700] and so forth, one will cause their forms to dance.

If the adept, in order to accomplish the ritual action of murder, **holds the name of the victim and repeats the root mantra once**, that victim **will die in an instant (9.2.5)**.

---

697 The Sanskrit text reads *aśaniṁ*, which technically means a thunderbolt rather than hail. It is followed in the next line, however, by *vidyut*, which means lightning. The Tibetan translators appear to have sought to distinguish these by translating the former as *ser ba*, "hail." The extant translation of Kambala's commentary reads *ser ba*, "hail," rather than *thog*, "thunderbolt," as Tsong Khapa reports (SN 23b). Devagupta's commentary, which follows Kambala's closely, has the *thog* reading, which probably reflects a more literal translation of the Sanskrit. See SS 92a. This translation discrepancy is noted by Büton at NS 344–345.

698 The Sanskrit text makes no reference to turning back hail or thunderbolts, and this is in fact found only in Mardo's revised translations (PM and SM). There is no ritual for achieving this described in any of the commentaries that I have consulted, with one exception. This occurs in Vīravajra's *Samantaguṇaśālina*, as follows: "If one repeats [the root mantra] 1,008 times over a trident and twirls it around one's head, hail will be turned back" (SG 381a: *mdung rtsa gsum pa la stong rtsa brgyad bzlas nas spyi bo la bskor na ser bzlog par byed do/*). But this is a different rite than that given by Tsong Khapa here.

699 Sachen describes a similar rite as follows: "As for **through recollection one can cause lightning to flash**, if one repeats the mantra over red oleander powder and casts it into the atmosphere, one will cause lightning to flash" (PG 316.3–4: */dran pa tsam gyis glog bskyed pa ni ka ra bī ra dmar po'i phye ma la sngags bzlas nas bar snang la gtor na glog skyed par byed do/*). This is both simpler and clearer than Tsong Khapa's account, which is vague on several points.

700 According to the *bhoṭasaṁskritakośa* (Varanasi 1993, vol. 2 p. 487 col. 1), the Tibetan term *gu-lang* has been used to translate the names of several Hindu deities, namely Maheśvara, Śiva, and Rudra.

3.3.3. 2.2.2. 2.2.1. 2.2.3. Showing the way to perform rites that incidentally benefit

If one offers with the root mantra one thousand and eight bull-flesh fire sacrifices, one will obtain a kingdom of enjoyment throughout the world. If one desires to be free of sorrow by means of the desired enjoyment, you will gather the pleasures of a kingdom with the peaceful fire oblation. Due to the nondifference of the deity and mantra, with this **Blessed Lord** or garland mantra one does not need an **observance** of [wearing] a special costume in order to attain success. There is no need for practices such as bathing or ablutions, and no need for persisting in **fasting**, i.e., cutting off food [intake]. One should **undertake the ritual actions** that achieve the **desired** power **by means of this method** of doing the **ritual (9.3)** for achieving the ritual action.

3.3.3. 2.2.2. 2.2.1. 2.2.4. The destructive rites of killing and restoring life

A yogī who has completed [the requisite mantra] repetition [should] visualize with a **fervent** mental state [as follows]: a blazing blue mantra enters the victim's left nostril from [his own] right nostril, and its blazing light troubles the victim's entire body. It emerges again from his right nostril, and enters into one's own left nostril. If [one does this], one will thus **kill a hundred million** with a mere repetition. If one **repeats** it with a **peaceful** mental state, with the intention of cooling and benefiting the victim's body with white light as [visualized] previously, it is said that he or she **will be revived.** [Repeating] the mantra once means [repeating] the root mantra once.

If one cuts with a caṇḍāla's axe a branch on the southern side of a vibhītaka tree,[701] burns it in the charnel ground on the twenty-ninth night [of the lunar month], takes up the ash from the fire extinguished with

[701] Tsong Khapa here reads *ba ru ra'i shing*, which he derived from the source of this explanation, the Tibetan translation of Jayabhadra's commentary (CP 53b). However, the Sanskrit here reads *vibhītakivṛkṣa* (Sugiki 2001, 21), referring to the vibhītaka tree, *Terminalia bellerica*, the fruit of which is employed medically, like its close relative, the myrobalan. Bhavabhaṭṭa reproduces a version of this commentary. He, however, reads *ariṣṭavṛkṣa*, the soapberry tree, Sapindus detergens (Pandey 2002, 80).

donkey urine, and repeats once the root mantra, whichever victim **it strikes will immediately fall down**.[702]

Draw a magical circle on the heart of a goblin (*piśāca*), and **enchant** the previously explained **charnel ground ash** with the mantra augmented by [the victim's] name. Whichever victim **is struck by** it **will be immediately seized by a goblin**.

Repeat the root mantra once over **charnel ground char** as previously explained, and draw, on a stack of moldering boards[703] in an isolated place on the **night** of the twenty-ninth [lunar day], the previously [mentioned] magical diagram in the center of which is the name of a planetary spirit. In the center of that **write** the mantra augmented by the victim's **name**. If one fumigates it with bdellium,[704] he **will be seized by an astral spirit (9.4.1)**. All of these [victims] will live again if one washes the wheel with milk and repeats [the mantra] with a peaceful mental state.

Sit on a seat of ***atimukta* creeper**,[705] and having rolled up three threads spun by a girl, dye it with turmeric, and bind it to a branch [of creeper] on the western side. One who is naked and with hair unfurled during a lunar eclipse should hold the end of the thread with his left hand, repeating the root mantra unceasingly until [the moon] is released. Then, holding that, he who is **struck with** its tip **will come at once with**

---

702 Tsong Khapa's comments are derived from Jayabhadra's commentary, as follows: "Here the oral instruction on **charnel ground char** is stated [as follows]: Cutting a branch on the southern side of a vibhītaka tree with a caṇḍāla's axe, incinerate in a charnel ground at night on the fourteenth day of the waning fortnight. Extinguish it with donkey urine, and taking its char and ash, place it correctly. Then, doing the procedures taught in the Tantra, its effect is not hindered" (Sugiki 2001, 21: *śmaśānāṅgāreṇety atropadeśa ucyate / vibhītakivṛkṣasya dakṣiṇadiggatāṁ śākhāṁ caṇḍālakuṭharādinā-cchidya kṛṣṇa-caturdaśyāṁ rātrau śmaśāne saṁdahya kharamūtreṇa nirvāpya tadaṅgārāṇi bhasma ca gṛhītvā saṁyak sthāpayet / taduttaraṁ tantroktā vidhayaḥ kāryāḥ, tatphalam anivārtitaṁ bhavati //*).

703 This translates *sbang leb bam rtsig pa*. The Tibetan *sbang leb* translates the Sanskrit *phalaka*, "board," "tablet."

704 That is, *guggula*, the fragrant resin from trees and shrubs of the *Balsamodendron* genus.

705 *Gaertnera racemosa*, a creeper with white fragrant flowers.

the speed of the wind. And if you strike again with the intention of reversing this, he will go back to his own place.[706]

Draw a magical circle augmented with [the victim's] name in the center of a solar mandala with yellow earth and turmeric on a piece of human skull. Bury it upside down in a charnel ground or at a crossroad. Repeating [the mantra] **once** over a **pebble**, he who it touches **will be immobilized** as long as he lives. If one unearths[707] it and washes it with milk, he will be released.

Write [this mantra][708] augmented with [the victim's] name on a leaf carried by a storm with a crow quill tipped pen [dipped] in spittle and crow's blood. If one sends it rising up on the wind, [the victim] **will go**, i.e., be expelled, to **wherever one wishes**.

Mix equal portions of the five limbs of a black goat, great fat, and great **bdellium** with alcohol. If one prepares this at the time of worship and **uses it as incense** while repeating the root mantra once, the moment that its smoke enters their noses, **all beings will become entranced (9.4.2)**.

3.3.3. 2.2.2. 2.2.1. 2.2.5. Showing other beneficial rites

Write the name of the victim in a wheel on one's left hand, and summon his consciousness there. If you repeat the root mantra once over one's right hand, and cover [the left hand with it],[709] you will alleviate the poison of the black snake.[710] If you sprinkle water once enchanted

---

[706] The source of this explanation is Bhavabhaṭṭa's commentary, to which Tsong Khapa (following Büton; see NS 351) adds the important information that one holds the end of the string, a detail omitted by Bhavabhaṭṭa (see Pandey 2002, 80).

[707] Tsong Khapa's text reads *phyungs* here. Büton gives the correct past form, *phyung* (NS 353). Kambala is the source of this and subsequent explanations (SN 24a).

[708] Neither Tsong Khapa nor Büton specifies exactly what is augmented with the name. I presume it is the mantra, as it is typically mantras that are so augmented.

[709] The text is vague here regarding what is covered by what, and it is also vague in Büton's commentary, which Tsong Khapa reproduces here (NS 353). In the root text it is clear that one covers one's mouth with the enchanted hand.

[710] This may refer to the Indian cobra, *Naja naja*, which can be black in color, or one of its black-colored subspecies, such as *Naja naja karachiensis*.

with the root mantra over one who has been sealed, i.e., taken, by a ḍākinī, he will be released.[711]

Write a name-augmented wheel on an *amlaka*[712] petal with a ***karavīra***[713] **creeper** pen, and **enchant** it once with the root mantra. Thus **one can transfer** [someone's consciousness] into whichever pregnant **womb one wishes (9.4.3)**.

3.3.3. 2.2.2. 2.2.1. 3. Showing the necessity of understanding the reality of mantra for those [rites]

One who longs for all **powers** relying on this mantra **without knowing the gnosis**, i.e., the definitive meaning, **of Śrī Heruka** is like the fool who, desiring grain, **threshes chaff**. The dual translation reads "without knowing the gnosis of Śrī Heruka."[714] Being **bereft of** knowledge of the reality of **mantra (9.5)**, **this man**, i.e., adept, **will not obtain the happiness** of the ultimate and worldly **powers**. As Bhavabhaṭṭa explains, "there is no power without the mantra of selflessness."[715] In the four classes of Tantra one will not obtain the special powers from mantra repetition without firmness in the concentration of the reality of selflessness. In the Unexcelled [Yogatantra class], if one excels in the concentration of emptiness but is not steadfast in the concentration of the union of

[711] This commentary, also from Büton's text (NS 353), appears to derive from the Tibetan translation of Jayabhadra's commentary (CP 277a), although it does not occur in the extant Sanskrit mss. It varies considerably from the Sanskrit root text, which reads *stambhayati*, "to immobilize, arrest," while Büton and Tsong Khapa read *gtong*, to "send," "dismiss," following Mardo's translation (PM 222a). However, Sumatikīrti's text reads "released from transfixion" (SL 105b: *reng pa grol bar byed*). Jayabhadra's commentary supports this, reading *grol* "release," which I translate here. Apparently this ritual is for one who has been afflicted by some kind of evil spirit. The above commentary seems to indicate that the ḍākinī is the perpetrator. Vīravajra uses the more generic term "evil spirit," which according to him is the object of the act of transfixion here. See PD 382a.

[712] The tamarind tree, *Artocarpus lakuca*.

[713] The sweet oleander, *Nerium odorum*.

[714] Tsong Khapa cites here the PM translation. The other two translations read "mantra" (*gsang sngags*) in place of "gnosis" (*ye shes*). The former reading accords with the extant Sanskrit, *na jñātvā śrīherukaṁ jñānaṁ*.

[715] This commentary occurs as follows in Tibetan translation: *bdag med pa'i sngags med pas dngos grub mi 'grub po zhes bstan pa'i phyir* (CV 183b).

bliss and emptiness, although one [will attain] worldly powers, one will not obtain the special ones that incline toward bliss. Therefore, it is essential to practice this.

If one **desires the state of being a yogī** in this supreme vehicle **without knowing this** definitive meaning of **mantra (9.6)**, his **efforts are in vain**. Due to this necessity, the fruits of his labor **will not be attained**. The above shows the fruitlessness of desiring the special powers of [mantra] repetition without knowing the definitive meaning of mantra. And since the fruitlessness of desiring the special yoga without knowing the definitive meaning of mantra will be shown below, I will not repeat it [here].

Regarding being **given all powers** through mantra such as [this root] mantra, and so forth, this means relying upon the method of practice from the perspective of knowing the nature in the desired object. There are two reliances; the adept relies on the definitive meaning of mantra and the principal seal in the **practice of love** (*kāmācāra*). **Knowing** well **that which was extolled by the Sugata**, **enjoy** the savor, form, sound, scent, and touch of **foods** such as meat and **drinks** such as beer. Making such excellent offerings to yourself, you will attain all the powers. As for **the *caru* oblations**, although [someone] understands it as being a "ritual remainder," here this is not suitable. As it is explained as *cāru*, "pleasing," it refers to enjoying extremely pleasing objects.[716] Furthermore, one must increase bliss in order to produce the union of bliss and emptiness. In order to augment the "jasmine-like" [semen] on which one depends, since it is the support of bliss, it is necessary to expand the sense powers together with their supports by enjoying special desired objects. As it

---

716 Tsong Khapa refers here to Bhavabhaṭṭa's commentary, "*caru* is 'poured forth' " (Pandey 2002, 81: *carur utsṛṣṭam*), which is quoted by Büton at NS 356. In the Vedic context, *caru* is a porridge made of rice and other grains, used as an oblation in some Vedic rituals. Here, however, it appears to refer to the consecrated offerings consumed in the context of the *gaṇacakra* Tantric feast, as Vīravajra and Bhavabhaṭṭa explain in the contexts of chs. 28 and 31, respectively. Tsong Khapa reads the term as *cāru,* "pleasing," rather than *caru*, which is the spelling that occurs in the Sanskrit mss. as well as most of the Tibetan translations, in transliteration. While this may have been a mistake, it is also possible that it was an intentional reading; his interpretation is sound in that this feast is intended to augment sensual pleasure, as he states. As Bhavyakīrti explains the term *kāmācāra*, it means "the enjoyment of all objects of desire" (SM 18b).

says in the *Dvikalpa*, "Since camphor is the cause, eat meat and especially drink wine."[717]

3.3.3. 2.2.2. 2.2.1. 4. Showing the name of the chapter

In the *Concise* ***Śrī Herukābhidhāna Tantra***, [this] is **the ninth chapter** on **the procedure of the** host of **ritual actions of the root mantra**. This is the explanation of the ninth chapter in the *Illumination of the Hidden Meaning, A Detailed Exegesis of the Concise Saṁvara Tantra Called "The Cakrasaṁvara."*

---

[717] Tsong Khapa here quotes three *pāda*s from the HT 2.11.15, which occurs in Snellgrove's edition as follows: *karpūraṁ pīyate tatra madanaṁ caiva viśeṣataḥ / balasya bhakṣaṇan tatra kuryāt karpūrahetunā //*; */de la ga pur btung bar bya/ /de la ga pur rgyu yi phyir/ /sha ni bza' ba nyid du 'gyur/ /khyad par du yang chang nyid do/* (1959: 2.98–99). This is one of the verses that Snellgrove does not translate.

CHAPTER 10

Chapter 10 Outline

3.3.3. 2.2.2. 2.2.2. Ritual success with the essence [mantra]
3.3.3. 2.2.2. 2.2.2. 1. Chapter ten
3.3.3. 2.2.2. 2.2.2. 1.1. Accomplishing the triple body
3.3.3. 2.2.2. 2.2.2. 1.1.1. The promise to explain
3.3.3. 2.2.2. 2.2.2. 1.1.2. Showing the adept's accomplishment of the triple body
3.3.3. 2.2.2. 2.2.2. 1.1.2. 1. The general meaning
3.3.3. 2.2.2. 2.2.2. 1.1.2. 2. The auxiliary meaning
3.3.3. 2.2.2. 2.2.2. 1.2. The collection of rites of the essence [mantra]
3.3.3. 2.2.2. 2.2.2. 1.2.1. The promise to explain
3.3.3. 2.2.2. 2.2.2. 1.2.2. The actual collection of rites
3.3.3. 2.2.2. 2.2.2. 1.3. Showing the name of the chapter

3.3.3. 2.2.2. 2.2.2. Accomplishing ritual actions with the essence [mantra]

The second part, ritual success with the essence [mantra], has two sections: (1) chapter ten and (2) chapter eleven.

3.3.3. 2.2.2. 2.2.2. 1. Chapter ten

The first part has three sections: (1) accomplishing the triple body, (2) the collection of rites of the essence [mantra], and (3) showing the name of the chapter.

3.3.3. 2.2.2. 2.2.2. 1.1. Accomplishing the triple body

The first part has two sections: (1) the promise to explain and (2) showing the adept's accomplishment of the triple body.

3.3.3. 2.2.2. 2.2.2. 1.1.1. The promise to explain

Next, after chapter nine, **I will explain the triple body** that is free of doubt, and that is **nondual union with Śrī Heruka**, **through which** the adept **succeeds by means of consciousness only**. **Have no doubt regarding this (10.1)**. In Mal's translation this occurs as: "Next I will explain the triple body that is free of doubt, [and that is] nondual union with Śrī Heruka, through which one succeeds by means of consciousness only, have no doubt,"[718] which is felicitous.

3.3.3. 2.2.2. 2.2.2. 1.1.2. Showing the adept's accomplishment of the triple body

The second part has two sections: (1) the general meaning and (2) the auxiliary meaning.

3.3.3. 2.2.2. 2.2.2. 1.1.2. 1. The general meaning

[The text] states that the triple body is attained by means of nondual union of oneself and Śrī Heruka. What is this method? With regard to this, Kambala has previously explained that it refers to the thirty-three-deity Śaṁvara mandala explained in the fourth, fifth, and sixth chapters of the *Abhidhānottara*.[719] Thus he explains the attainment, respectively, of the body as the manifestation body (*nirmāṇakāya*), speech as the communal enjoyment body (*sambhogakāya*), and mind as the reality body (*dharmakāya*). This is the nondual union of oneself with the Heruka of body, speech, and mind. Regarding this, the triple body of body, speech, and mind is attained by means of their respective mandalas. As Koṅkaṇapa [Jayabhadra] stated:

> The state of [abiding in] the triple wheel that is created from a single syllable *hūṁ* is the [reality body]. The state of assembling [all three wheels][720] within a single body,

---

718 This translation is very close to the "standard" PM translation preserved in the Kangyur, with two exceptions. First, it lacks the instrumental termination on *sbyor ba*, corresponding to the Sanskrit *-yogataḥ*, which leaves in doubt the relationship between "nondual union with Śrī Heruka" and the rest of the sentence. Also, it adds the connecting particle *yi* at the end of *the tshom med*, which incorrectly leads the reader to assume that this modifies *sku gsum*. Rather, as in the Sanskrit *nātra saṁśayaḥ*, one is not to harbor doubt regarding the verse's claim to efficacy in general, not specifically with regard to the *kāyatrayaṁ*.

719 At this point in his commentary, Kambala provides a detailed visualization beginning at SN 25a. He does not explicitly identify this as deriving from the AU chapters noted by Tsong Khapa.

720 Jayabhadra's commentary reads here simply *sarvān*, "all, every," while Tsong Khapa reads *'khor lo gsum*, "three wheels."

> armoring [oneself] by means of the great armor,[721] and repeating [mantra] is the communal enjoyment body. After that, the state of emanating and recollecting from the vowels and consonants on a lunar [disk] in the heart is the [emanation] body.[722]

This is also stated thus by Laṅka[723] and Vīra[vajra].[724] As for perfecting the triple wheel from a single *hūṁ*, this is creating the mandala in the manner of Lūipa.[725] It is not just the triple wheel [that one creates, as] Vīravajra indicated [when he wrote] "the triple wheel, etc."[726] Since

---

721 This translates the Sanskrit, *mahākavacaiḥ kavacayitvā*. Tsong Khapa's text reads "donning armor through the ritual procedure," *cho gas go bskon pa*.

722 Tsong Khapa, apparently following Büton (NS 357), attributes the first description, "the state of [abiding in] the triple wheel that is created from a single syllable *hūṁ*," to the emanation body, and the last, "states of emanating and recollecting," to the reality body. This is inaccurate, as it reverses the actual description that occurs in Jayabhadra's text, and also seems to make much less sense. I have thus followed Jayabhadra's commentary here. It occurs as follows in Sugiki's edition: *ekahūṁkārotpanna-tricakravyavasthitāvasthā dharmakāyaḥ / sarvān ekakāya upasaṁhṛtya mahākavacaiḥ kavacayitvā jāpāvasthā saṁbhogakāyaḥ / tadanantaraṁ hṛdaye sacandra ālikāli spharaṇasaṁharaṇāvasthā nirmāṇakāya iti //* (2001, 122; see also CP 54a). Jayabhadra's comments are reproduced by other commentators, such Vīravajra (SG 185a,b) and Büton. His reading makes much more sense, as it is much more appropriate to attribute to the emanation body the visualization of emanating and recollecting light. The reversal of Jayabhadra's original correlation appears to have been undertaken by his successor Bhavyakīrti, who quotes him in this fashion (BC 18a). This reversed text was also reproduced by other commentators such as Vīravajra (SG 185a,b). Büton seems to have relied on Bhavyakīrti here, and was followed by Tsong Khapa.

723 Tsong Khapa appears to believe that Koṅkaṇapa and Laṅka are different people. Actually, both monikers were used for Jayabhadra, who was born in Śrī Laṅka (as the colophon of his commentary indicates at Sugiki 2001, 141, and CP 69a), but who lived for some time in Koṅkaṇapa on the west coast of India, according to Tāranātha (see Chimpa and Chattopadhyaya 1970, 325). Tsong Khapa likely follows Büton in attributing this quote to Koṅkaṇapa, and likely did so through his reading of Bhavyakīrti, who quotes this text and attributes it to Koṅkaṇapa (a.k.a. Jayabhadra), his predecessor as Tantric preceptor at Vikramaśīla. Tsong Khapa likely independently discovered this passage in Jayabhadra's and Vīravajra's commentaries, without realizing that Koṅkaṇapa and Laṅka Jayabhadra are one and the same.

724 See SG 185a,b.

725 Regarding this visualization see BA 187b ff.

726 See SG 185a.

Laṅka and Vīravajra both state, "emanate and recollect from the vowels and consonants on a moon [disk] in the heart's lotus,"[727] their system, like Lūipa's, takes place in the heart rather than in the navel. The [oral] personal instructions state that their system advocates a first stage of visualization that accords with the two form bodies, and a visualization that accords with the reality body, which is the perfection stage Mahāyoga visualization.

Dārika states that the visualization of the outer deity mandala, meditation on the thirty-seven elements associated with awakening, and body mandala meditation, are, respectively, the *sādhana*s for the emanation body, reality body, and communal enjoyment body.[728] The first, taught for the sake of ordinary disciples, is [correlated to] the emanation body since it is characterized in terms of the very coarse body. The second is [correlated to] the reality body since it is characterized by engagement in the aim of reality itself by means of the gnosis of great bliss. The third, taught for the sake of superior disciples, correlates to the communal enjoyment body, in which bliss is completely enjoyed by means of the empowerment of the channels and elements, since it is characterized in terms of the form body from the perspective of the extremely subtle channels and elements. [This interpretation] is excellent.

The *Saṁcāra* states that "There should be the thirty-seven [elements] associated with awakening through the manifestation of the triple wheel of reality, communal enjoyment, and manifestation. These should be permanently connected."[729] With regard to this, from the perspective of the union of bliss and emptiness, there is the reality body meditation on the thirty-seven elements associated with awakening, the communal enjoyment body meditation that associates the subtle thirty-seven [elements] to the body mandala, and the emanation body meditation that associates the

[727] The text "on a moon [disk] in the heart" does occur in both Jayabhadra's and Vīravajra's commentary, but it is omitted in Bhavyakīrti's commentary, which was the source used by both Büton and Tsong Khapa.

[728] Dārika describes all three of these meditation methods in his *Śrīsamvarasādhanatattvasaṁgraha-nāma*, and also explicitly connects this to the *trikāya*.

[729] This text occurs in YS 9.9c–10b, as follows: *dharmasambhoganirmāṇa-kāyatraya-vibhāvanāt // saptatriṁśat tu bodhiḥ syāt tatra saṁbhāvyate dhruvam /* (Pandey 1998, 88–89).

coarse thirty-seven [elements] to the outer mandala. Thus [the above quote] accords with that [i.e., Dārika's system].

The entry into clear light is the reality body. The basis for that entry is the magic body. The body of subtle integration that arises from clear light is the communal enjoyment body. The emanation—that is, visualization of the coarse mandala by that body—is the emanation body. I have explained this clearly in my commentary on the perfection stage of both Lūipa and Ghaṇṭapā. Thus the necessity of applying the triple body to the two stages is due to the essential point of meditation on both stages of the path in accordance with the resultant triple body. Here one applies the triple body that is the basis for correlation for the meditation that accords with the three—birth, death, and the between states—that are stated in chapter two of the *Saṁvarodaya*.[730] If one applies this to the triple body of the two stages of meditation that accord with that, it is excellent.

3.3.3. 2.2.2. 2.2.2. 1.1.2. 2. The auxiliary meaning

Here I will comment on the [text's] previous [promise to] explain the attainment of the **triple body in accordance with nondual union with Śrī Heruka**. Now, since it is necessary to visualize oneself as Heruka in all of the triple body meditations in the creation stage, thus there is "nondual union with Śrī Heruka." This ripens the continuum that gives rise to the triple body of the path of the perfection stage. Relying on this sort of visualization, there is the supreme meditation on the triple body of the path, which is the perfection stage's meditation on the phenomenal aspect Heruka and the empty aspect Heruka.

[The text] states that **I proclaim** the **gnosis** (*jñāna*) of the path, which is the reality body, **when one becomes adept in the bodies of the reality body** of the perfection stage, i.e., when **one's mind is thus well** placed[731] for entry into the natural clear light of bliss-void inseparable (**10.2**). That is, the adept becomes nondual with the empty aspect Heruka. [The text] states that **I proclaim** the **communal enjoyment** body of the

[730] See the edition and translation of SU ch. 2 in Tsuda 1974.

[731] Tsong Khapa here rephrases as *de ltar sems legs par gnas par gyur pa* a line that occurs in Mardo's PM and SM translations, *de ltar legs sems gyur pa la*, but is not attested elsewhere.

perfection stage **when one becomes adept in the bodies of the communal enjoyment body**, i.e., when one becomes [adept] in the body of Heruka produced from mere wind-mind, and then **abides in** the **equipoise**[732] of that magic body (**10.3**). That is, the adept becomes nondual with Heruka, who is the phenomenal aspect communal enjoyment body. **I teach the emanation body when one becomes adept in the bodies of the emanation body**, i.e., when one becomes [adept] in the coarse mandala of integration, and **one's mind** abides **one-pointedly in that**[733] (**10.4**). That is, the adept becomes nondual with Heruka, who is the phenomenal aspect coarse body. Although the three lines [containing] "mind...well [placed]," "equipoise," and "mind...one-pointed" are absent in Lochen's and Mal's translations, they do occur in Mardo's solo and dual translations, which is excellent.

It is not skillful to explain the three [lines], "become [adept] in... the reality body," etc., as referring to the context of the result, for if you explain these in terms of the result, then the previous promise, "I will explain the attainment of triple body in accordance with nondual union with Śrī Heruka," is meaningless. This is because [the text] states no other method aside from those, nor is there an explanation for a method for attaining the triple body aside from them. [This interpretation] would also be in opposition to the two lines beginning with "gnosis."[734] Although it seems just as appropriate to interpret this text in terms of the creation stage, it is primarily applicable to the perfection stage.

If one becomes accustomed to meditation on the three bodies in a path context like that [in the creation stage], then in the resultant context

---

732 Tsong Khapa here rephrases as *de nas sgyu ma'i sku de la mnyam par bzhag pa la gnas pa* a line that occurs in Mardo's PM and SM translations, *de nas mnyam par bzhag pa la*, but is not attested elsewhere.

733 Tsong Khapa here rephrases as *de la sems rtse gcig tu gnas pa* a line that occurs in Mardo's PM and SM translations, *de tshe sems de rtse gcig la*, but is not attested elsewhere.

734 He refers here to the text of CT 10.5ab, "Have no doubt that gnosis, communal enjoyment, and manifestation will be attained." While Tsong Khapa's explanation makes sense in that he understands the triple body as referring here to three distinct practice methodologies, this line does blur the distinction between path and goal, since it seems to refer to them as the result to be attained via a course of practice. No doubt the tension between path and goal, which is quite notable in Tantric traditions, underlies this ambiguity.

have no doubt that one **will attain** the **gnosis** reality body, the **communal enjoyment** body, and the **emanation** body. **Do not doubt that** the yogī himself will become the resultant **Śrī Heruka (10.5)**. These last two lines show that the triple body is also not a different continuum from the self that is one with Heruka. Here as well [as in the text at the end of chapter nine], "the means of achieving all powers" [indicates] that achieving the triple body is the ultimate achievement.

3.3.3. 2.2.2. 2.2.2. 1.2. The collection of rites of the essence [mantra]

The second part has two sections, (1) the promise to explain and (2) the actual collection of rites.

3.3.3. 2.2.2. 2.2.2. 1.2.1. The promise to explain

The questioner is implored to listen, [as follows:] "**Listen, adept, and I will explain** the secret, i.e., the attainment, of **this mantra** is the twenty-two-syllable **essence**."[735]

3.3.3. 2.2.2. 2.2.2. 1.2.2. The actual collection of rites

When, while performing the invocation of a zombie into an abandoned corpse,[736] one states, "Give the power of flight to me!" One fills a vessel with the oil that trickles from its body. If one applies it to the soles of one's feet while **repeating the essence** mantra, **one will fly ten million leagues**, traveling in space **and returning**. If one forms into a drop or eats [a mixture of] the concretion of one born [a man] seven times[737] and the flesh of the desired living being,[738] one **can assume many thousands of forms**. Through the power of eating that flesh, one can **ascend palaces, trees,** and **houses**, and **one can travel ten million**

---

735 Tsong Khapa here follows Mardo's text, which understands "secret" (*guhya*, *gsang ba*) to be the object of the verb "I will explain" (*vakṣāmi*, *bshad kyis*). The Sanskrit, however, reads *guhya* in compound with *sādhaka*, i.e., "one who is adept in the secret," a reading supported by Bhavabhaṭṭa (Pandey 2002, 84).

736 Tsong Khapa's description of the *vetālasādhana* is based upon Vīravajra's commentary at PD 383b–384a.

737 Regarding this figure and his concretion (*rocanā*) see ch. 11 below.

738 That is, the flesh of the type of being whose form one wishes to assume.

leagues together with the yoginīs.[739] If one repeats the mantra ten thousand times over great fat and the oil of an old horse and rubs this on the soles of one's feet, one will **travel in space** and **return again**. **Aside from that, it will not occur** (**10.6.1**).[740]

Having performed the preliminaries of worship and sacrificial cake [offering], fill skulls of various beings with charnel ground earth during the waning fortnight. Grow white mustard [plants] in them, and for the sake of this, one should over time offer sacrificial cakes and repeat protective mantras such as *śumbha*, etc.[741] Later, wrap the white mustard seeds unerringly and repeat over each one hundred million mantras together with the name augment, forming them into a packet. Anyone to whom it is bound will be visible, be it oneself or another. If one wants to be **visible**, one will appear if one forms them into a drop or binds the packet [to oneself]. If one wants to be **invisible,** wipe off the drop or unbind the packet, and one will disappear. [Regarding the text] "**immature...as one wishes**," etc., [it is achieved] by undertaking the application of growing the white mustard in the respective skull, and so forth (**10.6.2**).[742]

Make an image with charnel ground dirt and dirt from the victim's footprint. Place a magical diagram with the injunction appropriate to the ritual action with the substances of fierce aggression[743] on the heart of

---

[739] Tsong Khapa appears to be following here the SM or SL translations, which reads "together with the yoginīs," *rnal 'byor ma rnams dang*. The Sanskrit reads the singular "together with a ḍākinī," *ḍākinyā saha*, while the PM translation reads the plural "together with the ḍākinīs," *mkha' 'gro ma rnams dang lhan cig*.

[740] This last line, *gzhan du mi 'gyur ro*, occurs in the translations but not in the extant Sanskrit text.

[741] Tsong Khapa here refers to the Trailokyavijaya mantra, which is coded in CT ch. 30.

[742] Tsong Khapa here is commenting on the line "One can take on immature, youthful, or elderly forms as one wishes." Evidently one can assume these forms by growing seeds in the appropriate type of skull.

[743] Literally, "cruel practice," *drag shul spyod pa*, which translates *abhicāra*, "black magic." Büton gives the following more detailed instructions concerning the *yantra*, injunction, and the accoutrements with which it should be drawn: "[Draw] the mandala of a moon that is like vermilion (*sindūra*) in the middle of the realm of space. In its midst is a sixteen-petaled lotus, and in the center of that is an eight-petaled lotus with stamens. Place on the sixteen petals [starting from] the east [the syllables of the mantra] *oṁ śrī he he ru ru kaṁ va jra ḍā ki nī j[ā] la saṁ va*. On the four [petals] in the cardinal directions of the eight-petaled lotus place [the syllables] *raṁ hūṁ hūṁ phaṭ*, counterclockwise

(cont'd)

that [figurine], wound with black thread. [Visualizing that] the victim is absorbed into that, repeat the mantra together with the injunction. If one stabs its mouth, etc., with an eight-inch spike of human bone, you will **steal** his **speech**, i.e., render him mute. One can **plunder** his **sight**, blinding him, [or] **steal** his **hearing**, making him deaf. One can **plunder** his nose,[744] making him insensate to smells, [or] **snatch the tongue**, making him insensate to tastes.

With regard to [the text] from "One can assume many thousands of forms" up to "snatch the tongue," there are explanations of many other rites in the commentaries of Kambala and Devagupta.[745] Fearing prolixity, I have set forth here those that occur in the oral instructions of the previous translators. I have already explained [how to] **draw out the blood of** whichever victim **one wishes**, and [how to] **immobilize him (10.6.3)**.[746]

3.3.3. 2.2.2. 2.2.2. 1.3. Showing the name of the chapter

In the *Concise* ***Śrī Herukābhidhāna Tantra***, [this] is **the tenth chapter** on **the achievement of the triple body and the procedure of the** host of **ritual actions of the essence [mantra]**. This is the explanation of the tenth chapter in the *Illumination of the Hidden Meaning, A Detailed Exegesis of the Concise Saṁvara Tantra Called "The Cakrasaṁvara."*

[from the east]. On the four ordinal [petals] draw skull receptacles on top of pots. In the center write *svāhā*, with the name augmented, inserted between [the syllables], as follows: *svā* "steal the speech of so-and-so" *hā*. Draw a universal vajra on the circle of mountains outside of the eight-petaled lotus, and draw the vajra wall and fiery mountains outside of the sixteen-petaled lotus. One should draw [these] with a mixture of the red fluid of a corpse (*ro'i sen rtsi'i khu ba*), red sandalwood, and blood, visualizing oneself as naked with bone ornaments" (NS 369–370).

744 Tsong Khapa follows the standard Tibetan translation, *sna* (PM, SL, SM), which is a translation of *ghrāṇa*, which can also designate the sense of smell.

745 See SN 27a–b and SS 96a–97a.

746 See ch. 9 above.

CHAPTER 11

Chapter 11 Outline

3.3.3. 2.2.2. 2.2.2. 2. Chapter eleven
3.3.3. 2.2.2. 2.2.2. 2.1. The promise to explain
3.3.3. 2.2.2. 2.2.2. 2.2. The method of examining the one born seven times
3.3.3. 2.2.2. 2.2.2. 2.3. Ritual success relying upon the concretion of the one born seven times
3.3.3. 2.2.2. 2.2.2. 2.4. Showing the name of the chapter

3.3.3. 2.2.2. 2.2.2. 2. Chapter eleven

The second part, chapter eleven, has four sections: (1) the promise to explain, (2) the method of examining the one born seven times, (3) ritual success in dependence upon the concretion of the one born seven times, and (4) showing the name of the chapter.

3.3.3. 2.2.2. 2.2.2. 2.1. The promise to explain

Now, after the tenth chapter, since there are also ritual actions of essence [mantra] to be achieved other than those previously explained, I will **speak of** the attainment of **power**, [and that thing] by which **there is rapid engagement in power** by the **adept**. What is that [thing]? It is the concretion (*rocanā*), etc., that exists, i.e., arises, in people who [are human] for seven lives without interruption. Power is attained **by means of** service[747] **only** by the adept (**11.1**).

3.3.3. 2.2.2. 2.2.2. 2.2. The method of examining the one born seven [times]

[The following] are the signs of one born seven times as a human without interruption. (1) There arise atoms of **pleasant fragrance** from the body of a person born as a human and (2) he **speaks the truth**. (3) With regard to **blinks after a long time**, there are three exegetical traditions. [These are], according to Bhavyakīrti, the positions that his semen is not quickly emitted, that his eyes open wide for a long time, and that he blinks

[747] The Tibetan translations here read "service," while the Sanskrit reads *prāśita*, "eating." This may be a genuine variant, perhaps from the Sanskrit *prasita*, although it may be an emendation to avoid the transgressive implications of this chapter.

rapidly.[748] If the text is like that in the Tibetan [translations], it seems that the middle [interpretation is best], as the former and latter approaches are meaningless. As for the meaning of that, it is said that [his eye] does not blink during the interval in which an ordinary person's eye blinks seven times. (4) His mind has **no anger** and (5) he has **fragrant breath in his mouth (11.2.1)**. Since this sort of pleasant fragrance is an effect of the concretion, this can identify him. [The text] "He must be one with a sevenfold shadow, who has a goose's gait and a compassionate disposition" is absent in Lochen and Mal's translations, but it occurs in the dual and solo Mardo translations.[749]

3.3.3. 2.2.2. 2.2.2. 2.3. Ritual success relying upon the concretion of the one born seven times

With regard to "serving him," Bhavabhaṭṭa explains that the existence of the concretion is identified by smelling that pleasant fragrance.[750] The equivalent term to that is *bsnams pa*. When the one born seven times dies, one **takes this concretion** that **is in his heart**. If one repeats **Śrī Heruka's essence mantra** over it **one hundred** and eight times and **makes** it into a **drop**, **one will fly up** into the sky **and travel tens of millions of leagues** from the ground **(11.2.2)**. **Just through** relying on

---

[748] Bhavyakīrti mentions several interpretations of this line, as follows: "Regarding **blinks after a long time**, some say that [it means that] his fluid is not quickly emitted. Others say that his eyes open wide for a long time. Someone else says that he blinks rapidly" (BC 19a: *yun ring por mig mi 'dzums pa dang / zhes bya ba ni rdzas myur du 'byung bar mi 'gyur ro zhes la la zer ro/ /gzhan dag ni mig yun ring bar bgrad pa yin no zhes zer ro/ /yang kha cig ni myur du 'dzum bar byed do zhes zer ro/*). Note that Tsong Khapa replaces Bhavyakīrti's ambiguous use of the term "substance"/"fluid" (*dravya*, *rdzas*) with the less ambiguous *khu ba*, "semen."

[749] As Tsong Khapa notes, this quote does occur in the PM and SM translations, but is not found in the extant Sanskrit or the SL translation. This text was probably added in consultation with the AU, in which it occurs as follows in ch. 65: *saptachāyo haṁsagatiko karuṇāśayato bhavet* (H 185b.4, I 618b.3–4, J 304.1–2).

[750] Section 2.2 of ch. 11 opens with the text, in Sanskrit, *taṁ bhakṣayitvā*, "Eating him." The Mardo translations follow the pattern established in v. 1, reading, "Serving him" (PM: *de bsten na*; SM: *de bsten nas*). Bhavabhaṭṭa likewise has a third reading, "smelling him" (*taṁ ghrāṇayitvā*). He commented, "Having smelled him, he can be recognized" (Pandey 2002, 86: *taṁ grāṇayitvā jñātavyam iti jñeyam*). This reading also occurs in the SL translation, *de bsnams na*.

that, i.e., smelling that, **one will become one who has** the supramundane **knowledge of the triple world. One will travel five hundred million** leagues **in a day**, and return. One will also attain **a divine body** that is long-lived and does not age.

Durjayacandra explains that the concretion has the color of saffron.[751] The previous lamas have said that is just [like] the eye of a bull, with the shape of a pouch of lymph. The followers of the Lama Mal have stated that, according to Pamting-pa's spiritual sons and the exegetical system that adheres to their [view], "since [the concretion bearer] is a bodhisattva, if the adept venerates and supplicates him, he will bestow his body [to the adept]. It is said [by some] that one needs the method of liberating him, following the Newari guru Kanakaśrī."[752] However, Bhavyakīrti explains that one takes the concretion from one born seven times who is deceased, which is excellent.[753]

Durjayacandra explains that even the entire collection of ritual actions of chapter ten can be performed relying upon the one born seven times.[754] It is evident that one can perform all of those up to "assuming the form that one desires."[755] The adept **who knows** the performance of the ritual actions relying upon the one born seven times with **Śrī Heruka's essence will be given whatever** powers **he desires (11.2.3)**.

3.3.3. 2.2.2. 2.2.2. 2.4. Showing the name of the chapter

In the ***Concise Śrī Herukābhidhāna Tantra***, [this] is **the eleventh chapter on the procedure** for achieving power relying upon the **characteristics** and body of **the one born seven times**. This is the explanation of the eleventh chapter in the *Illumination of the Hidden Meaning, A Detailed Exegesis of the Concise Saṁvara Tantra Called "The Cakrasaṁvara."*

---

751 See RG 279a.

752 Tsong Khapa here directly quotes Sachen's text at PG 216.2.

753 See BC 19a.

754 See RG 279a.

755 See ch. 10 above. This includes all of the rites in ch. 10 except for the rite of depriving a person of his or her senses.

CHAPTER 12

Chapter 12 Outline

3.3.3. 2.2.2. 2.2.3. Accomplishing ritual actions with the quintessence [mantra]

The third part, accomplishing ritual actions with the quintessence [mantra], has three sections: (1) the promise to explain, (2) the actual ritual applications, and (3) showing the name of the chapter.

3.3.3. 2.2.2. 2.2.3. 1. The promise to explain

Next, after the eleventh chapter, **I will explain** the **accomplishment in an instant**, i.e., quickly, those powers that **might exist in the triple world**, by means of ritual actions depending upon the **quintessence that perfects all powers (12.1)**.

3.3.3. 2.2.2. 2.2.3. 2. The actual ritual applications

The second part has six sections: (1) showing the four ritual applications of earthquakes, etc., (2) the ritual applications depending on the eye, (3) the ritual application of the pill that achieves flight, (4) the six rites of drawing blood, etc., together with their remedies, (5) the seven rites of invisibility, etc., together with their remedies, and (6) the five rites of reversing the flow of a river, etc., together with their remedies.

3.3.3. 2.2.2. 2.2.3. 2.1. Showing the four ritual applications of earthquakes, etc.

In order to obstruct those who would enter into the Tantra as they please, the arrangement [of the mantra] is reversed, from **ṭaph** up until **oṁ**. *Oṁ hrīḥ ha ha hūṁ hūṁ phaṭ*: **this is the quintessence of** Śrī Heruka's **essence** mantra.

As **one can cause the triple world** of the heavens, the earth's surface, and the underworld **to tremble with one hundred thousand repetitions of this** essence **mantra**, what else need one say with the word "**even**?"[756] It is said that this ritual action was accomplished by Nāropā.[757]

Draw on the middle of a piece of birch bark a six-petaled lotus with stamens at its center using ink that is a mixture of the red fluid of a corpse, concretion, and one's own semen. Its middle should be adorned with a lunar mandala, and it should be encircled by a row of vajras. Outside of that draw a white wheel with six spokes. Place the seven syllables counterclockwise[758] on the six petals of the lotus. Draw the essence of the six

[756] That is, the term is superfluous, but it is clearly added for emphasis, which is one of the uses of the term *api*.

[757] Sachen makes this claim at PG 321.1. He also provides a fuller description of the rite based on Kambala's commentary and an oral instruction attributed to Nāropā, as follows: "One who has completed the 400,000 service in the essence should draw the following magical diagram at the time of the ritual application: draw a six-petaled lotus with stamens that is ornamented by a moon disk inside of it. Draw encircling vajra rows both inside and outside it. This is the system of master Kambala. The guru Nāropā states that it is encircled by the vowels, outside of which are the consonants on the encircling mountain range. Outside of that draw the wheel with six spokes endowed with moonbeams. Draw an encircling vajra row outside of that. Place the syllables *oṁ*, etc., counterclockwise on the six petals, and place a *hūṁ* at the center. Outside of that place the armor mantras of the six yoginīs counterclockwise on the wheel's six spokes. Having thus placed the syllables and consecrated [the diagram], etc., one can also perform [rites of] protection or averting [negative forces]. At this point, if one especially desires to cause the triple world to tremble, one should attach that wheel to one's body and repeat this mantra 100,000 times. Or, one can draw it in this fashion on the palm of one's left hand, consecrate it, and then plant one's hand on the ground and repeat this mantra 100,000 times. [In either case,] the entire triple world will tremble. It is said that the guru Nāropā accomplished this" (PG 321.1; see also Kambala's commentary at SN 28b).

[758] A minority of the KS editions that I consulted (BQ) read "counterclockwise," *g.yon skor du*, while the majority read "clockwise," *g.yas skor du*. I have adopted the former reading because it is the reading found in all other sources that describe this ritual, including Sachen (quoted above), Kambala (SN 28b), Devagupta (SS 97b), and Büton (NS 374).

yoginīs, which is their armor [mantras], on the spokes of the wheel. The [text] "in the middle is the seventh, Heruka"[759] means that one places the seventh syllable on the lotus, that is, places the [syllable] *hūṁ* at the center of the lotus. The previous lamas say that one should write the victim's name together with an injunction.[760] Then utter the quintessence and gaze in the direction in which the victim is located with a passionate mental state, and raise and shake both hands. If one clearly visualizes oneself facing the victim, and one invokes him with the passion of being equipoised with the seal, **one can summon** whomever one desires, [such as] **gods, titans, *yakṣa*s, demons, serpent deities,**[761] **celestial musicians, and *kinnaras*.**[762] This being the case, there is no need to mention terrestrial beings.

Likewise, make an image with the earth of the victim's footprint, red sandalwood, salt, and mustard seeds, and draw the magical diagram on birch bark as previously explained. If one inserts it into [the image's] heart and repeats [the mantra] together with the name augment, one will subjugate the king together with his wealth and retinue.

Regarding **one can dry up rivers, oceans, ponds**, springs, **and so forth,** or **immobilize them**, one who has attained the power of mantra will accomplish [these powers] by changing the augment in the previous magical diagram and repeating the mantra with the augment.

In that place where one has **repeated** the quintessence [mantra] seven hundred thousand [times], draw a wheel engraved on copper, etc., and a magical diagram for subjugation with red sandalwood and the blood of one's left ring finger. If one consecrates it, repeats the mantra over it, and carries it upon one's body, **all ḍākinīs will be the adept's servants (12.2.1)**, i.e., they will listen to his commands, and will be unable to hinder him.

---

759 This occurs in Kambala's commentary at SN 28b.

760 This instruction does not occur in any of the Indian sources I have consulted, nor is it in Sachen's or Büton's commentaries. This, however, is standard procedure in rites of this sort.

761 The term *nāgas* does not occur in the Sanskrit, but does occur in all of the Tibetan translations.

762 *Kinnara* are legendary creatures with a horse head and a human body.

3.3.3. 2.2.2. 2.2.3. 2.2. The ritual applications depending on the eye

Draw the previously [described] wheel with white sandalwood on a lunar disk on one's left hand. Place the emanating light rays in accordance with the ritual action.[763] **Enchant water with this** quintessence, and wash the wheel with it. **If one rinses one's eyes with** [this] water, **one will recognize the one born seven times**, and you will come to know the past and future as well. Likewise, if one touches one's eyes with the hand that has the wheel and repeats the mantra, **those whose life is exhausted will appear as if dead**. That is, even one who has this sign will avert previous evil omens, and one will have the signs of **appearing long-lived** and **full of life.**[764] As in the dual translation, "Those whose life is exhausted will appear as if dead; the long-lived will appear to be full of life,"[765] one will know the signs of long and short lifespan.

Enchanting the eyes with the quintessence **mantra** together with the augment with [the hand] that has the wheel, **he whom one sees will be** injured and **immobilized (12.2.2)**.

3.3.3. 2.2.2. 2.2.3. 2.3. The ritual application of the pill that achieves flight

Take the skin of the sole of the foot of a hero who died in battle and **pulverize it with the blood** of the very person who died on the hero's sword. With regard to "malachite medicine" (*lig bu mig sman*), it occurs as "ear salve" (*rna ba'i mig sman*) in the dual translation.[766] While there

---

[763] That is, accord with the color correspondence, such as white for peaceful (*śānta*) operations.

[764] I do not believe that this was the earliest import of this passage. The text "Those whose life is exhausted will appear as if dead; the long-lived will appear to be full of life" does not refer to a rite of averting omens of death, but rather is connected to the issue of identifying the one born seven times. As ch. 11 above indicates, as do other texts such as Śubhakarasiṁha's account of the *Ḍākinī mantra* in his *Mahāvairocana-abhisambodhi Sūtra Commentary*, identifying the time of death of those who bear the *rocanā* was an essential aspect of the lore concerning them. Regarding this see Gray 2005, as well as T.1796.39.687.b17–c11.

[765] This is the PM translation.

[766] These are erroneous translations of *srotoñjana*, which is the kohl or black antimony (technically *stibnite*, Sb_2S_3) used as eye shadow in India. The translation "malachite medicine" (*lig bu mig sman*) occurs in the SM translation. This may reflect the use of malachite as a pigment in cosmetics. The translation *rna ba'i mig sman* (PM 223a) is

(cont'd)

are other explanations of the meaning of this, *lig bu* means "ear," and Devagupta explains that by mere contact of it to the ear, the eyes become clear.[767] It is said to be a type of stone that is found at the end of the continent.[768] It is also said that it is found on another continent.[769]

Saturate it with realgar, bovine concretion, saffron, and the heart **blood** of a hero. Place the pill that has been repeatedly soaked in these [substances] in a skull and **dry it in the shade**. As Bhavabhaṭṭa explains, "*Veda*s, three, four *māṣa* of gold, moon, and sun, the pill is gradually bound with an excess of sage, three, five *raktikā*."[770] That is, it should be **encased in the three metals**, gold, silver, and copper. This pill should **also be made habitable**. Since [the verb here] "**made habitable**" (*lhag gnas*, *adhivāsya*) is explained to mean "consecrate," it should be consecrated.[771]

---

based on the misreading of *srotoñjana* as *śrotrāñjana*, *śrotra* meaning "ear" and *añjana* "eye salve." The SL translation transliterated the term as *sru sta a dza na*. Antimony is clearly the intended meaning, as *śrotrāñjana/rna ba'i mig sman* is nonsensical. Nonetheless, some Sanskrit texts may have read *śrotrāñjana*, as Devagupta's commentary, translated below, attests.

767 Devagupta comments here as follows: "As for *li gu mig*, *li gu* is *srotra*, the ear. Through mere contact with the ear, the eye, i.e., both eyes, is cleared. It is found on another continent" (SS 98a; cf. SN 29a).

768 This is Kambala's explanation (SN 29a).

769 This is Devagupta's explanation (SS 98a). It is expanded upon as follows by Sachen: "Malachite is a type of stone that occurs on other islands (*gling*, *dvīpa*) such as Śrī Laṅka (*zangs gling*, *tāmradvīpa*)" (PG 321.3).

770 Bhavabhaṭṭa's verse reads as follows: *kanakaśaśidinakarāṇāṁ vedatricatuḥ pramāṇakā māṣāḥ / gulikābandhakramaśo munitriśararaktikābhyadhikāḥ* / (Pandey 2002, 88). It gives the measurements for the metals in code. The term *kanaka* means gold, while "moon and sun" evidently refer to silver and copper, which, Jayabhadra informs us, are the other two metals employed for the pill casing (Sugiki 2001, 122: *triloha iti suvarṇarajatatāmrāṇi*). The term *Veda* codes the number 4, *muni* "sage" the number 7, and *śara* "arrow" the number 5. A *māṣa* is a measure equal to 17 grains Troy, and a *raktikā* is one sixth of a *māṣa*. The weights should be understood as corresponding to the respective metals, gold, silver, and copper.

771 This is the explanation of Kambala and Devagupta. See SN 29a and SS 98a.

The **Puṣya lunar mansion** is connected to "making it habitable" in the dual and solo Mardo translations.[772] In the translations of Lochen it is connected to what follows, [reading] "When [the moon] is in Puṣya, put it in Śrī Heruka's mouth," which is better.[773] When [the moon] is in Puṣya or some other auspicious lunar mansion, draw a mandala with paints of the five types of color in an isolated spot such as a charnel ground. After it is prepared and worshipped, place in its center a victim, i.e., a clean corpse. Insert the pill into its mouth. This is the meaning of "**putting it in Śrī Heruka's mouth**."

Next, fumigate the corpse with bdellium and **cover its mouth with one's left hand**. Once one **repeats** the quintessence **one hundred and eight times**, the corpse will expel the pill from its mouth. If the adept puts it into his mouth, **from that moment one is rendered invisible**, and one's body will be **without any shadow**. If **one cannot even be seen by gods,** what need is there to mention being seen **by humans?** Mardo explains:

> Imagine that a *hūṁ* that emanates from the *hūṁ* of one's heart is installed in the corpse's heart. It completely transforms [the corpse] into Saṁvara with one face and two hands, ornamented with the six insignia (*ṣaṇmudrā*), etc. Visualize that light rays emanate from the *hūṁ* of his heart, worshipping the deities of the primordially established seven syllables [of the quintessence.] These turn into light and recollect in the *hūṁ* in the Hero's heart, merging with the seven syllables that are the reality of the deities. Next one should insert the pill in the Hero's mouth and utter the repetitions.[774]

---

[772] The text in the PM translation, *skar ma rgyal la bya ba yang*, corresponds to the first part of the Sanskrit text, *punaḥ puṣyasādhita puṣyeṇa ca kārayet*. The latter part, *puṣyeṇa ca kārayet*, may be an explanatory gloss. This obviously connects not only with the act of consecration but also with the entire process of pill production.

[773] This translation is preserved in both the SL and SM translations. However, the Sanskrit corresponds to the PM reading, and clearly connects Puṣya to the act of pill preparation.

[774] I presume that Tsong Khapa is quoting Mardo's CT commentary, the *Mar do lo tsa ba chos kyi dbang phyug gi bde mchog rtsa rgyud kyi bsdus don dang tikka rgyas pa*, a presumably lost work, discussed in the notes to the introduction section 3.2.3.3 above.

Likewise, **taking** the pill **out of the mouth, one will be visible. This pill of the power of flight was taught in this** *Laghusaṁvara* **Tantra by the Hero** Heruka **himself (12.2.3)**.

3.3.3. 2.2.2. 2.2.3. 2.4. The six rites of drawing blood, etc., together with their remedies

With this mantra of seven syllables, **the quintessence of** the twenty-two-syllable **essence** of **Śrī Heruka's** root mantra, prepare a human **skull** that is free of scars, **devoid of flesh**, and undefiled. One who has done the prior ritual service and who has the yoga of Adamantine Fury Heruka should visualize that Khaṇḍarohā bearing a sword, who arises from the utterance of *hūṁ*, is expelled from one's right nostril and bores into the five channels of the anus, vajra, heart, throat, and forehead of that victim whose name is held by her. Visualize that the streams of his blood completely fill the skull bowl. If one **rubs** the skull **with the tip of one's** right **forefinger** and repeats **the mantra** many times, **his blood will be drawn out**, and his body's flesh will be consumed. Should one wish to revive him, **rubbing it** again and again **with the** tip of the **left** forefinger with a peaceful mind, visualize that Khaṇḍarohā, emerging[775] from one's left nostril, fills the victim's body with the blood in the bowl [she holds] in her hand. [Thus] he is revived.

If one repeats the quintessence together with the augment and **strikes the skull with one's fist**, visualizing that it is the skull of the victim's head, the brain **of him whose name one utters** will sicken.[776] Should one who **calls the mantra to mind** with a peaceful intention actually **fill the skull with milk** while visualizing that [the victim's head] is insubstantially filled [by it], then **he will be relieved (12.2.4)**.

Repeat the quintessence over **cow concretion and form it into a drop** on one's forehead. **He whom one sees will be bound**, i.e., transfixed. Draw the previously explained wheel with corpse char, poison, and blood with a human bone pen on charnel ground cloth or a leaf of the

[775] Büton's commentary has the correct reading here, *phyung ba* (NS 377). Tsong Khapa here reverses the meaning with the incorrect verb *zhugs pa*.

[776] Tsong Khapa here gives the translation attested in the SL and SM translations, *de'i klad pa na bar 'gyur ro*. The PM translation reads "his brain will burst," *de'i klad pa 'gas par 'gyur*. The Sanskrit reads "his head will ache," *tasya śiro vedanā bhavati*.

sacrifice tree,[777] with a fervent mind at noon. Insert that wheel into the heart of an image of the victim made from corpse char. Rub it with black mustard seeds and heat it thoroughly in a fire of thorn briars. Draw or visualize the wheel on one's left hand as well, and **enchant one's fore-finger** with the mantra. The victim **at whom one brandishes it will instantly** be stricken with plague and will **fall down**, i.e., tumble to the ground.

Place that image in a hole within a burnt corpse and strike it with a human bone spike. Fill it with thorns without respite, and pour hot water on its heart. **If one strikes the earth with one's foot, repeating the mantra** with an augment, **he whose name one utters will instantly perish.** If one repeats the mantra over **water**, **sprinkles** it **on the earth**, and bathes the image in milk, he or she will be revived.

Draw a magical diagram on charnel ground cloth with turmeric or realgar, and with it wrap scorched, powdered iron and a mixture of red sandal powder, salt, black mustard seeds, and the earth of the victim's footprint. Dig one's eight fingers into the ground at a crossroad and hide it there, having repeated seven times the mantra augmented with the name of one's enemy. **If one brandishes one's** quintessence **mantra-enchanted forefinger at as many as one thousand** people, **they all will** be suppressed, i.e., **become immobilized**. It does not mean that one brandishes it one thousand times, as [someone] explained.[778] Lochen and Mal translate [*sarve* as] "they all," which is felicitous.[779] Take out the magical diagram and wash it with milk, and **they will be released with a word** of the reviving mantra (**12.2.5**).

Make an image of the victim with the **ash of a caṇḍāla**'s—i.e., outcaste's—burnt corpse. Draw a magical diagram augmented with the victim's name, and insert it into its heart. **Enchanting** that ash seven or **one hundred times**, if one **strikes** that previous image **thinking** of that sentient **being** whose form he will assume, then he will take on the form

---

777 The *yajñavṛkṣa*, *mchod sbyin gyi shing*, namely the Banyan-tree, *Ficus indica*.

778 This comment was made by Büton at NS 378. Tsong Khapa is clearly correct here, for in the Sanskrit, *mantrajaptena tarjatyāgrena sahasram api tarjayati*, the "thousand" (*sahasram*) are the object of the verb *tarjayati*.

779 The translation of *sarve* as *de thams cad* occurs in the SL translation, as Tsong Khapa reports. It is also translated thus in the PM translation. The SM translation reads simply *thams cad*.

that one desires he assume. Lochen and Mal's translations read "Struck, [he will assume] the form of that being of which one thinks," which is excellent.[780]

3.3.3. 2.2.2. 2.2.3. 2.5. The seven rites of invisibility, etc., together with their remedies

Make an image of the victim as previously explained **with the ash of a sacrificial fire** made with medicines such as sandalwood. Insert the wheel into its heart. Make **one hundred** repetitions of the quintessence [mantra] augmented with the victim's name over the ash.

He whom it strikes will not be seen even by the gods of the Trayastriṁśa [heaven]**. Should one**, with a restorative intention, **strike him with water enchanted seven times** with the augmented quintessence [mantra], **he will be seen again (12.2.6)**.

Draw a wheel augmented with the victim's name. Prepare the seeds, roots, stalk, leaves, and branches of the datura plant,[781] and put it in the closed mouth of a rabid dog's **skull. Bind** its fissures with mud [made of] charnel ground ash, and **repeat** the augmented quintessence [mantra] seven times **without breathing**. If you put it in a charnel ground, **he whose name** one [utters] **will become mad. As many as one thousand people will be maddened.** If one bathes [the skull] with milk reciting with a peaceful mind, they will be **released (12.2.7)**.

Having gone to an empty house, call out the **name** of any ḍākinī and repeat [the quintessence] **ten times** over **one's hair crest**, and **bind it up.** Then one may consort with **all** of the wicked **ḍākinīs.** And if one repeats it with the augment "Come!", they **will come**. **Go to an empty house**, and repeating the quintessence **one hundred times, tie up one's hair crest** on one's crown. **Opening one's eyes, one will be invisible as long as one repeats [the mantra].** If one **releases** one's hair crest, **one will be visible again (12.2.8)**.

---

780 The translation Tsong Khapa quotes, *sems can gang rjes su dran te bsnun pa de'i gzugs*, does occur in the SL translation. A close variant, *sems can gang rjes su dran pa de la bsnun pa de'i gzugs*, occurs in the PM and SM translations.

781 Tsong Khapa gives the Tibetan translation, *smyo byed*, and also attempts to transliterate its Sanskrit name, *dhattūra*, which he represents as *dadura*. This refers to the plant Datura alba, which is both a powerful hallucinogen and poison.

Enchant a clay saucer or **skull bowl** on which a magical diagram has been drawn with the quintessence together with an injunction. Reduce the clay saucer, etc., to powder. If one **casts it above, below, and in the** four **directions and** four **quarters**, **all of the gods, titans,** ***yakṣas***, **demons**, **celestial musicians,** ***kinnaras***, **and even the sea monsters will be bound.** One who enchants gravel and scatters it in the directions and quarters **can steal all the** harmful **yogas of the ḍākinīs**.

Hide the tail of a dog or jackal under the victim's bed. **Seeing a woman or man** on a seat or bed, **if one repeats the mantra one hundred** and eight **times**, **one can cause him or her to be stuck [there].** If one repeats the quintessence [with the injunction] "Tail begone!" with a mind desiring release, **[he or she] is released.**

3.3.3. 2.2.2. 2.2.3. 2.6. The five rites of reversing the flow of a river, etc., together with their remedies

Enchant with the augmented quintessence a magical diagram together **with a skull bowl**.[782] If one **casts it into** the water of a **river**, it is **forced to flow upstream**. **With** this very **skull bowl** ritual application **one can immobilize the waves**. And if one repeats [the quintessence] with the intention of reversal, **one can cause them to turn**. **Should one repeat** the augmented quintessence, repeating it **one thousand [times] gazing above**, **one can suppress a tremendous storm** (**12.2.9**).

Make one thousand repetitions over gravel **facing an enemy army**, and scatter it in the ten directions. If one **enters into battle**, **the pain of being struck by a hundred weapons will not arise**, **nor will one be cut by weapons**. **One will develop an adamantine body** that is unbreakable by weapons (**12.2.10**).

3.3.3. 2.2.2. 2.2.3. 3. Showing the name of the chapter

In the *Concise* ***Śrī Herukābhidhāna Tantra***, [this] is **the twelfth chapter on the procedure** of the host **of ritual actions of the quintessence**. This is the explanation of the twelfth chapter in the *Illumination of the Hidden Meaning, A Detailed Exegesis of the Concise Saṁvara Tantra Called "The Cakrasaṁvara."*

---

[782] Vīravajra explains the text "with a skull bowl" as follows: "Regarding **with a skull bowl**, should one write the magical diagram within a skull bowl, and place it into a river; it will be **forced to flow upstream**" (PD 387b).

CHAPTER 13

Chapter 13 Outline

3.3.3. 2.2.2. 2.2.4. Ritual success with the armor mantras
3.3.3. 2.2.2. 2.2.4. 1. The promise to explain
3.3.3. 2.2.2. 2.2.4. 2. The actual collection of rites
3.3.3. 2.2.2. 2.2.4. 2.1. The eight rites of dispelling fear, etc., together with subsequent release
3.3.3. 2.2.2. 2.2.4. 2.2. The collection of rites of subjugating and relying on cotton clothing
3.3.3. 2.2.2. 2.2.4. 2.3. The ordinary methods of accomplishing ritual actions
3.3.3. 2.2.2. 2.2.4. 2.4. The two rites of turning into a tree, etc., together with the subsequent release
3.3.3. 2.2.2. 2.2.4. 3. The name of the chapter

3.3.3. 2.2.2. 2.2.4. Ritual success with the armor mantras

The fourth part, ritual success with the armor mantras, has three sections: (1) the promise to explain, (2) the actual collection of rites, and (3) the name of the chapter.

3.3.3. 2.2.2. 2.2.4. 1. The promise to explain

Next, after the twelfth chapter, **I will explain** the achievement of **ritual actions** by means of mantras of the Hero's **armor in accordance with their regular order**. Moreover, one will attain **all those things one's mind fancies, whatever might exist in the triple world** (**13.1**).

3.3.3. 2.2.2. 2.2.4. 2. The actual collection of rites

The second part has four sections: (1) the eight rites of dispelling fear, etc., together with subsequent release, (2) the collection of rites of subjugating and relying on cotton clothing, (3) the ordinary methods of accomplishing ritual actions, and (4) the two rites of turning into a tree, etc., together with the subsequent release.

3.3.3. 2.2.2. 2.2.4. 2.1. The eight rites of dispelling fear, etc., together with subsequent release

With regard to the performance of ritual actions with the armor mantra, there is the ritual application of repeating the armor mantra such that **should one proceed on the road repeating the armor [mantra],**

there will be no fear of brigands or tigers. The adept should draw a three-pronged, opened vajra in the center of a lunar mandala with saffron, corpse lac, one's own blood, and concretion on birch bark on Sunday during the Puṣya conjunction. At the edge of the center draw two encircling rims, and at the center draw a six-syllable lotus together with its central [disk]. In its center write "*hūṁ* protect so-and-so from robbers and thieves *hūṁ*," and write on the six petals starting from the east, *oṁ*, *namaḥ*,[783] *svāhā*, *vauṣat*, *hūm hūṁ*, and *phaṭ*. Arrange on the circumference of the vajra's navel [the syllables] *ha*, *hi*, *hu*, *he*, *ho*, and *haṁ*, excluding *hā*, *hī*, *hū*, *hai*, *hau*, and *haḥ*.[784]

The method of drawing is not clear in Kambala's commentary, with the exception of a quote from the text of the *Vajraḍāka*.[785] Devagupta explains that the six shorter [syllables], *ha*, etc., are placed on the circumference of the vajra's navel, and there does not seem to be a placement of the [other] six such as long *hā*, etc.[786] But this does not accord with the explanation in the *Vajraḍāka* commentary that there are two six-petaled lotuses, and the six syllables, *hā*, etc., are placed [on one of them.][787]

One should consecrate it, and repeat [the mantra] and worship it during the three watches [of the night]. Repeating [the mantra] seven times, knot the ends of one's clothes. If one proceeds upon the road repeating the mantra, there will be no fear of brigands, and so forth. The [word] **just** (*api*, *yang*) does not occur in the translations of Lochen and Mal, but does

---

783 Tsong Khapa gives *nama* here, but the mantric syllables occur as *namaḥ* in CT ch. 6.

784 See ch. 6 above for a discussion of the omission of the syllables from the list of vowels to yield the six *h* syllables.

785 Tsong Khapa refers to Kambala's commentary at SN fol. 32a, which is similar but not identical to a passage at VD 43a.

786 See SS 101a.

787 Bhavabhaṭṭa, in his commentary on this text, does not seem to call for two lotuses, but rather a single lotus, with the six armor mantras written on the six petals, namely *oṁ ha*, *namaḥ hi*, *svāhā hu*, *vauṣaṭ he*, *hūṁ hūṁ ho*, and *phaṭ haṁ*. He then calls for the six long syllables to be placed along the circumference of the vajra's navel. See VV fol. 106b. This appears to be a different system than that described by the CT commentators such as Devagupta, in which the long syllables are excluded, as both CT ch. 6 as well as VD ch. 16 (at fol. 43a) recommend.

occur in the dual and solo Mardo translations.[788] Kambala's commentary reads [here], "if one proceeds on the road of fright."[789]

With regard to the ritual application of invisibility, if one proceeds on the road repeating the armor [mantra] while visualizing that the rim of the center of that wheel is encircled with drop shapes forming the augment "Delude the victim together with his retinue!", **one will not be seen** by others. **Nor will one be seen entering into the harem of a royal palace if one is repeating the armor [mantra]. One** can go and **take** from that place **that which one likes**, and one **will not even be seen by the gods (13.2.1)**.

Draw the previous[ly described] wheel notably encircled by drops with an aśoka[790] wood pen and realgar and turmeric juice [ink] on a shroud. Repeat the armor mantra one hundred times, and then repeat it with the augment of the names of the victim together with his army and steed. Form an image of the victim with the earth of his footprint, the dust of an elephant's footprint, and charnel ground ash. Insert that wheel into its heart. Scatter yellow flowers [over it] and press it with one's left foot. Repeat the mantra one hundred and eight times, and place it in a hole in the ground. Place it above the cover, having made a semblance of a house up to its heart. The army that **one touched with** one's right **hand will be immobilized** as if **impaled by a** spear that has been implanted deeply. **Even the thirty-three** gods **will not be able to move** them. If one **strikes** them **with one's foot** over which **the mantra** has been **repeated**, and takes the wheel out from under the earth and washes it with milk, they **will be released (13.2.2)**.

Repeat the armor mantra over **one's own blood** three times. Put it in one's mouth, and then spit it out and form it into a drop. **All those with whom one speaks, who see** oneself, and **whom one sees will have their blood drawn out**.

Should one visualize the Fierce King in one's enemy's **house**, and **repeat** the augmented armor mantra **one thousand times filled with**

---

[788] As Tsong Khapa reports, the term occurs in the PM and SM translations, but is absent in the SL translation. It also occurs in the Sanskrit, where it serves to emphasize that the action of repeating the armor mantra is sufficient to protect one against these dangers.

[789] That is, *ya nga ba'i lam du zhugs na* (SN 31b).

[790] That is, the wood of the aśoka tree, *Jonesia asoka*.

ferocity, everyone will come down with fever. If one sprinkles water enchanted five times with a peaceful intention, **they will recover**.

If one is to debate with another person, make an image of the victim with a mixture of the three soils, namely, that of the victim's footprint, that of a charnel ground, and that of an anthill. Draw a wheel with the augment "steal the speech of so-and-so," and insert it into the heart [of the image]. Press it with one's right foot, and mentally visualize the wheel within one's own heart. Visualize that light rays, which have the nature of the mantra, radiate from one's right nostril and pierce the victim's tongue, stacked one on top of another as high as Mt. Sumeru. By **gazing** at the victim's **face** and **repeating** the augmented mantra, **one will steal** his **speech (13.2.3)**.

Standing at **a river**bank **or pond**, and visualizing the Fierce King, imagine that all of the water molecules are in the shape of a hair lock or crown that arises in the form of the mandala deities. **If one repeats** the mantra **one thousand** [times], **one can** stay **on the water**.[791] **One will walk on the water as if it were firm ground.** If one **enters the water**, **one can stay in the river or even in the ocean** without moving (**13.2.4**).

3.3.3. 2.2.2. 2.2.4. 2.2. The collection of rites of subjugating and relying on cotton clothing

Visualize that one's right hand gives rise to the six heroes, and one's left hand to the six heroines, and that the deity couples are equipoised in union. If one, **rubbing both hands**, i.e., rubbing them back and forth, **repeats** the armor mantra **one thousand** [times], **the yoginīs will be subdued. The yoginīs have various forms; they are famed as** being born into the clans of those who have the nature of **Ḍākinī, Lāmā, Khaṇḍarohā, and Rūpiṇī. They will all**, i.e., every one of these yoginīs such as Pracaṇḍā, etc., **be under the power** of that adept (**13.3**).

Obtain the king of snakes[792] and divide [its body] at the junctures of white and black [coloration]. Separate the white and black [portions].

---

[791] Tsong Khapa here follows Mardo's translation (PM, SM: *chu'i steng du gnas*), which is incorrect. Sumatikīrti gives the correct translation, "one can walk on the water" (SL 109a: *chu'i steng du 'gro*), which corresponds exactly to the Sanskrit, *udakopari vrajet*.

[792] I presume this title refers to the king cobra (*Ophiophagus hannah*), which frequently exhibits alternating bands of lighter and darker coloration, or perhaps some related cobra species.

On the day of the **lunar conjunction of Puṣyā** during the waxing fortnight, get some cotton seeds and rub them with the flesh and clotted blood of the white portion, and then plant them in the ground. On a day of Puṣyā during the waning fortnight, rub seeds with the flesh and clotted blood of the black portion, and plant them. Saturate the earth as well with the clotted blood and flesh of these [snake sections].

When it is fully grown, the cotton that was rubbed by the white portion should be spun on a day of Puṣyā of the waxing fortnight by light yellow yoginīs, and it should be woven by light yellow weavers by the day's end. Pick the cotton grown with the black portion on a day of Puṣyā during the waning fortnight, and it should be spun by dark yoginīs, and woven by dark weavers on that day. In this way, the white and black cloth is produced during the lunar conjunction of Puṣyā. Repeat the armor mantra thirty-nine thousand [times] over the cloth. Fumigate the cloth produced with the black [portion] with [incense made from] black aloe wood[793] and the flesh and bones of the black portion, and fumigate the cloth produced with the white [portion] with conch blossom[794] and the flesh and bones of the white portion.

Then worship the guru, the heroes, and yoginīs, perceiving them in terms of deity yoga. By the command of the yoginīs, one wears the white cloth during the waxing fortnight, and the black cloth during the waning fortnight. **One's body covered with it, should** the yogin who is equipoised in meditative concentration **repeat it ten thousand times**, he **will thenceforth** attain invisibility. One's body covered with it, **one will be invisible** even to the gods, **in the sky for** as many as **a thousand leagues**, such that even one's shadow will not be seen. **One will go wherever one desires. With it one will travel** to lands at the edge of the outer **ocean. One will arrive via the upward flow (13.4),** that is, at the region between the Akaniṣṭha and Anabhraka [heavens].[795]

---

[793] That is, *kṛṣṇāgaru*, the black variety of the aloe wood or agar wood, *Amyris agallocha*.

[794] That is, the medicinal plant *śaṅkhapuṣpī*, *Canscora decussata*.

[795] That is, the highest region of the form realm corresponding to the fourth *dhyāna*, consisting of eight heavens, with Akaniṣṭha at the top and Anabhraka at the bottom; see Sadakata 1997, 58, 66–67.

3.3.3. 2.2.2. 2.2.4. 2.3. The ordinary methods of accomplishing ritual actions

One should experience whatever, i.e., form, etc., **comes within the path of the sense powers**, the eye, etc., namely the sense objects, which accord with the **nature** of those sense objects. That is, if one experiences the savor of sense objects, one is **poised** in the spirit of awakening of the inseparability of emptiness and compassion, in the **equality** of which conceives in terms of the **ultimate**, i.e., highest, truth. **Through the yoga** or union that apprehends the self in those terms, one should be engaged in the reality of all **buddhas (13.5)**. It should be thus.

As is stated in the *Caturyoginī Saṁpuṭa Tantra*, "One who enjoys all that he desires by means of the nature of what is on the path of the sense powers achieves the nature of all buddhas."[796] This means that those who aspire to the actuality of the inseparability of emptiness and bliss will achieve the host of ritual actions by means of the enjoyment of all desired objects. This is just like the demonstration of the need to know the reality of mantra [discussed] in chapter nine.[797]

3.3.3. 2.3.2. 2.2.4. 2.4. The two rites of turning into a tree, together with the subsequent release

Take **the sap gathered** from the **tree** that, by means of a rite previously undertaken, grown from the mouth of a corpse.[798] **Enchant it one thousand times**. **He whom one** visualizes as a tree while **forming it into a drop will turn into a tree**. **He is restored if one sprinkles him with water enchanted seven times.**

Take white mustard seeds grown in the skull of a brahmin by means of the previously explained rite,[799] and plant these again in an elephant's skull. **Taking** the powder of the ripened seeds of these [mustard plants] and **the dust formed on an elephant's foot, enchant it one thousand times**. **Whoever is struck by it will become an elephant (13.6)**. If one rides it, one will be victorious over [an army of] as many as one thousand elephants.

---

796 See the *Caturyoginīsaṁpuṭatantra*, D fol. 45a.

797 See ch. 9, section 3.3.3.2.2.2.2.2.1.3.

798 The Sanskrit text simply calls for the sap of the coral tree, *pārijāta* (*Erythrina indica*).

799 See section 3.3.3.2.2.2.2.2.2.1.2.2 in ch. 10 above.

3.3.3. 2.2.2. 2.2.4. 3. The name of the chapter

In the *Concise* ***Śrī Herukābhidhāna Tantra***, [this] is **the thirteenth chapter on the procedure** of the host ritual actions **of the armor mantra**. This is the explanation of the thirteenth chapter in the *Illumination of the Hidden Meaning, A Detailed Exegesis of the Concise Saṁvara Tantra Called "The Cakrasaṁvara."*

CHAPTER 14

Chapter 14 Outline

3.3.3. 2.2.2. 2.2.5. Showing other rites accomplished with the essence
3.3.3. 2.2.2. 2.2.5. 1. The promise to explain
3.3.3. 2.2.2. 2.2.5. 2. The actual ritual applications
3.3.3. 2.2.2. 2.2.5. 2.1. The literal explanation
3.3.3. 2.2.2. 2.2.5. 2.2. The symbolic explanation
3.3.3. 2.2.2. 2.2.5. 3. The benefits of attainment
3.3.3. 2.2.2. 2.2.5. 4. The method of attainment
3.3.3. 2.2.2. 2.2.5. 5. Praise for that
3.3.3. 2.2.2. 2.2.5. 6. The name of the chapter

3.3.3. 2.2.2. 2.2.5. Showing other rites accomplished with the essence

The fifth part, showing other rites accomplished with the essence, has six sections: (1) the promise to explain, (2) the actual ritual applications, (3) the benefits of attainment, (4) the method of attainment, (5) praise for that, and (6) the name of the chapter.

3.3.3. 2.2.2. 2.2.5. 1. The promise to explain

Next, [after] showing the armor's ritual actions, there is the text "**I will explain the spiritual discipline** (*sādhana*) **whereby the adepts** rapidly **attain** power, **the yoga of the donkey**-faced **form**." What need is there to meditate on this? Durjayacandra explains as follows:

> In answer to [the question] "If Heruka is attractive, why did he assume an unattractive visage?" It is taught that one meditates on the donkey form that causes **the cessation of the movement of the mind**, for [otherwise] one would not be able to achieve the previously explained ritual actions, on account of the difficulty of restraining the mind, which moves everywhere.[800]

[800] I have translated this passage as it occurs in Tsong Khapa's text. It diverges considerably from what Durjayacandra actually wrote. The passage occurs as follows in his commentary: "If Heruka is attractive, why did he assume an unattractive visage? [The text] states that [he did] **for the sake of the cessation of the movement of the mind**, etc. The movement of mind is swift, and this shows the need for restraining it. The ritual actions explained by the learned will not be achieved, as it is said: 'the adept will not

(cont'd)

This is in agreement with the systems of both translators, [one of whom] explained that "This yoga is taught for the sake of rapidly attaining the previously explained ritual actions."[801] Bhavabhaṭṭa also explains in terms of the cessation of the movement of mind.[802] The three commentaries explain **for the sake of the cessation of the movement of the mind (14.1)** as causing the cessation of the movement of mind.[803] This is like what [Tathāgatarakṣita] explains in his *Ubhayanibandha*, namely that "There is cessation by means of the donkey form yoga."[804] Regarding that from which one turns back and how it is done, Kambala stated that:

> [**For the sake of the cessation of the movement of the mind** means that one who has the proper procedure] turns back [the **movement of mind**, i.e.,] all wrong views and obscurations, and quickly transforms into a

---

succeed by means of ineptitude, for that yogī will not succeed on account of the difficulty of restraining the mind, which moves everywhere.' It is therefore taught for the sake of perfecting oneself; hence one should meditate on the donkey form that causes the cessation of the movement of mind" (RG 280a: *dpal he ru ka shin tu mdzes pa yin na/ ci'i phyir mi sdug pa'i gdong du bsgyur zhes na/ yid kyi shugs las bzlog bya'i phyir/ /zhes bya ba la sogs pa smos te/ yid kyi shugs ni mgyogs pa'o/ /de bzlog pa'i phyir zhes dgos pa bstan to/ /gang gi phyir yid ni thams cad du song zhing bzlog dka' ba des rnal 'byor pa de grub par mi 'gyur ba de'i phyir ma grub pas bsgrub pa de ni ma grub pa zhes pa'i rig pa las bshad pa'i sngar bshad pa'i las rnams 'grub par mi 'gyur ro/ /de bas na bdag nyid sgrub pa'i phyir dang yid kyi shugs zlog par byed pa'i bong bu'i rnam pa bsgom par bya'i phyir nye bar bstan to/*). The Sanskrit of this line reads *manoveganivṛttaye*, in which occurs the term *vega*, which usually means "movement." It is translated into Tibetan, however, as *shugs*, meaning "power, force, impulse." I follow the Sanskrit when citing the root text, but later in Tsong Khapa's commentary I translate it as "force," which seems to be the sense in which he understood and used the term.

[801] Sachen argues this at PG 324.4.

[802] See Pandey 2002, 94, and CV 188a.

[803] Tsong Khapa appears to be referring to Bhavabhaṭṭa's commentary, which explains this text as follows: "What is the meaning of [the text] **mind**, etc.? One achieves the **cessation of the movement of mind,** i.e., mental mastery" (Pandey 2002, 94: *kim artham ity āha—mana ityādi / manovego manorājyaṁ tasya nivṛttiḥ siddhatvāt /*). These comments do not occur in the commentaries that often agree with Bhavabhaṭṭa (i.e., Jayabhadra, Bhavyakīrti, and Vīravajra), so I am not sure to which other two commentaries Tsong Khapa is referring here.

[804] See UN 226a.

dreamlike, purified body, and is thereby free of movement and indestructible.[805]

Devagupta's commentary on "wrong views," etc., is excellent, as follows: "Through this procedure all erroneous obscurations are transformed. Through this there is the 'purified body,' which is, like a dream body, unobstructed and indestructible."[806] Erroneous obscurations impede the purified body's transformation into the magic body, hence their abandonment is transformative. [The following] is an example of the transformation of the purified body though abandoning this impediment: Arising in the manner of a dream body of mere wind-mind that appears to be separated from the coarse body, one will achieve the magic body of mere wind-mind that is separated from the coarse body. Regarding "transforms," the ripened coarse body that does not exist apart from the form of having limbs is transformed into the magic body. This body is not obstructed anywhere like a magically emanated body, and as it cannot be destroyed by anything, it is the adamantine body. While it is not exclusively necessary to meditate upon the donkey-faced one [to achieve] this, it is a general necessity of creation stage meditation on Heruka.

Furthermore, [in] the first stage it just develops as the cause that gives rise to the continuum that characterizes the magic body. With regard to the extraordinary cause in the context of the perfection stage, Kambala [wrote] at the end of his explanation of the mandala that "All mandala [deities] arise from the selflessness of things that is embraced by great compassion."[807] This shows that they arise from the compassion of the

---

805 Tsong Khapa omits the first portion of his commentary, which I have included here in square brackets. It occurs as follows: */yid kyi shugs kyis bzlog bya'i phyir/ /zhes ba ba yid kyi shugs ni yid kyi shugs te de'i chog dang ldan pas lta ba ngan pa dang sgrib pa thams cad las bzlog nas dag par 'gyur ba'i lus rmi lam ltar myur du yongs su brje bas g.yo ba dang bral te mi shigs pa'o/* (SN 33b–34a).

806 Tsong Khapa here emends slightly Devagupta's commentary, which occurs as follows *in toto*: "With regard to the **movement of mind**, through this procedure all erroneous obscurations are transformed. What is the 'purified body' that arises through that like? It quickly revolves like a dream body, and is unobstructed and indestructible" (SS 103a,b: *de la yid kyi shugs te cho ga 'dis phyin ci log gi sgrib pa thams cad rnam par bsgyur ba'o/ /des de dag pa'i lus su ji lta ba bzhin du 'gyur ba ni myur bar yongs su 'gyur ba rmi lam gyi lus bzhin du thogs pa med cing mi shigs pa'o/*).

807 This is a shortened version of the following text: */dkyil 'khor thams cad kyang spyan gsum pa la spyan dmar zhing snying rje chen pos yongs su gzung ba chos bdag med pa*

(cont'd)

selflessness of things, i.e., the gnosis of clear light that is embraced by great bliss. That is, the magic body arises from the mere wind-mind of clear light. Although there are some correspondences to this [process] in the creation stage, it primarily takes place in the context of the perfection stage.

Devagupta's commentary reads "the reality of the selflessness of things."[808] This is a translation error due to a failure to distinguish the terms "nature" (*rang bzhin*, *svabhāva*) and "to arise, become, exist" (*'byung ba*, *bhavanti/saṁbhavanti*).[809] The explanation by Kambala and Devagupta that the magic body, which transforms itself like a dream body, arises from clear light is also extremely important in the *Saṁvara* [tradition].

3.3.3. 2.2.2. 2.2.5. 2. The actual ritual applications

The second part has two sections: (1) the literal explanation and (2) the symbolic explanation.

3.3.3. 2.2.2. 2.2.5. 2.1. The literal explanation

Since the text states "donkey form [yoga for] becoming Śrī Heruka"[810] in the context of the chapter's name, and "essential yoga of the donkey" [in the first verse], it is the [chapter's] primary point. In accordance with the donkey-faced primary deity, the four [yoginīs]—**Ḍākinī,**

---

las byung ba'o/ (SN 34a). Note that Tsong Khapa reads *dkyil 'khor pa thams cad*, "all mandala deities," while Kambala's commentary reads *dkyil 'khor thams cad*, "all mandalas," although the text that follows, concerning eyes, implies that Tsong Khapa's reading is correct.

808 Devagupta's commentary here reads, referring to the mandala deities, "They all also have the nature of the selflessness of things" (SS 103b: *kun kyang chos bdag med pa'i ngo bo nyid do*). In place of the text *ngo bo*, Kambala's commentary reads *byung ba'o*.

809 I presume that Tsong Khapa is comparing here the text *ngo bo* and *byung ba'o* that occur at the end of the passage in question in the two commentaries. However, he uses the synonym *rang bzhin* here, rather than *ngo bo*; he may be relying on a different translation of Devagupta's commentary.

810 The Sanskrit chapter title reads "the procedure of the donkey-form yoga for becoming Śrī Heruka" *gardabhākarayogaśrīherukīkaraṇavidhi*. The PM and SM translations, which Tsong Khapa follows here, do not translate *yoga*, making the title somewhat ambiguous. The SL translation, however, does translate it.

Lāmā, Khaṇḍarohā, and Rūpiṇī—have **donkey-shaped faces** from which **blood** trickles. As Durjayacandra explains, "**donkey** appertains to their **faces** only."[811] Hence, their heads are not round.

The translations of Lochen and Mal read, "As for the yoginīs, there is Lāmā's Rūpiṇī...."[812] It is explained that **yoginīs** are the yoginīs who reside in the triple wheel [mandala], and their **desired forms** are donkey-faced.[813] Someone explains that they can assume other forms through the power of desire.[814]

In this way, previous scholars have held that there are two systems that assume that there are six and thirty deities on the basis of the root Tantra.[815] As for the remainder, the explanatory Tantra fills the deficiency, taking it to be sixty-two.[816] With regard to this, the heroes of the mind, speech, and body wheels are, respectively, garuḍa-faced, peacock-faced, and lion-faced. The four gatekeepers have the faces [indicated by their

---

811 Tsong Khapa quotes Durjayacandra as follows: *gdong tsam gyi bong bu yin te*. The text occurs differently in his commentary, as follows: "Their donkey faces are donkey-shaped" (RG 210a: *bong bu'i gdong ni bong bu'i rnam pa'o*).

812 The SL translation skips three lines, from 14.1d–2c, perhaps due to scribal error, and thus omits this text. Sachen confirms that Mal's translation contained this text (PG 325.1). This is only the beginning of a list, followed by Ḍākinī and Khaṇḍarohā. The Sanskrit here reads *yoginīlāmārūpiṇīḍākinī tathā khaṇḍarohā yoginyaḥ*. It is not clear if this is a list of five yoginīs beginning with Yoginī, or four beginning with Lāmā, although the commentaries point to the later interpretation. The PM and SM translations give only four, omitting the first *yoginī*, and moving *ḍākinī* to the foremost position, while the SL omits this list entirely.

813 Kambala explains this in terms of the three-wheeled mandala, and assigns different theriomorphic figures to them. He states that the heroes of the mind wheel are garuḍa-faced deities, those of the speech wheel are peacock-faced, and the body wheel's are lion-faced. He explains that the four gatekeepers, Kākāsya, etc., have the faces indicated by their names, and that the four quarter guardians have the following forms: buffalo-faced, antelope-faced, tiger-faced, and leopard-faced. See SN 34a, as well as the commentaries on this by Devagupta (SS 103b) and Büton (NS 390–391).

814 Sachen comments that they "can assume whatever form they desire, of which having a donkey head is one" (PG 226.2).

815 These are Ghaṇṭapā's system of five or six deities, consisting of the central couple surrounded by the four essence yoginīs, and Kāṇha's system of three thirty-deity mandalas (for each wheel), consisting of the central couple, the four essence yoginīs, sixteen heroes and heroines, and the eight gate and quarter goddesses.

816 I presume that here Tsong Khapa refers to Lūipa's full mandala of sixty-two deities.

names, which are] Crow Face (*kākāsyā*), etc. In regard to four quarter guardians, it says in the *Abhidhānottara* and many [other sources] that they have buffalo and antelope faces.[817] It is explained thus also by Durjayacandra and [Tathāgatarakṣita in his] *Ubhayanibandha*.[818] Kambala states that they have the faces of the buffalo, antelope, tiger, and leopard. Now, what are the faces of the yoginīs of the three wheels like? Bhavabhaṭṭa explains that they are donkey-faced.[819] It is explained in the *Vajraḍāka* commentary that there is also a tradition of not altering their faces.[820]

[The term] *mkha' 'gro* [in the root text] means **ḍākinī** (*mkha' 'gro ma*). [The ḍākinīs'] "three-pointed" is the **trident (14.2.1)**, which is encircled by a serpent.[821] Regarding "in the hand," it is held in the first of the right hands, in accordance with the explanation in which the trident is held and the curved knife left out.[822] The *Vajraḍāka* commentary explains that the [first] left hand holds a trident and the second a skull, and the first right hand holds a skull staff and the second a curved knife.[823] This

---

817 The AU's *gardabhākārasvecchāsiddhinimittasādhana* chapter is clearly the source for the commentaries of Kambala, Devagupta, and others here. This chapter does state this, as follows: "In the corners are Yamadāhī, [etc.], all of whom have buffalo or antelope faces" (H 178b.2, I 615a.2: *koṇeṣu yamadāhyā tu sarveṣāṁ mahiṣamukha-mṛgānānām*; J omits; see also AU 358b).

818 Durjayacandra and Tathāgatarakṣita generally follow the system described by Kambala, but both state that the four quarter guardians have buffalo faces (RG 280b, UN 226b).

819 Bhavabhaṭṭa explains that "With the exception of the four [gatekeepers], Kākāsyā, etc., they all are characterized by their donkey forms" (Pandey 2002, 94: *kākāsyādi-catuṣṭayaṁ vihāya sarvā eva garbhākāraviśiṣṭāḥ*).

820 Bhavabhaṭṭa, in his VV commentary, noted that: "Some say that the five yoginīs of the great bliss wheel assume donkey shapes, and the remaining [goddesses] assume [their] ordinary [forms]" (VV 164b: *kha cig ni bde chen po'i 'khor lo'i rnal 'byor ma rnam pa lnga ni bong bu'i cha byad du byas la/ lhag ma tha mal par bya'o zhes zer ro*).

821 Tsong Khapa here plays upon the term *triśūla*, "trident," which was translated literally into Tibetan as *rtse gsum*, "three pointed."

822 Tsong Khapa here is commenting upon the Tibetan translation "held in the hand" (*lag na thogs*), the Tibetan translation of *veṣṭitā*, "invested with." There were different exegetical systems regarding exactly what the goddesses hold in the hands. Several of the commentaries noted above present this information.

823 Bhavabhaṭṭa does indeed state this. See VV 164a,b. *Śāśvatavajra also attributes these implements to the goddesses. See MV 289b.

is evidently also in agreement with Kambala.[824] With the exception of these special explanations, the remaining [details of the deities' appearances] should be visualized in accordance with Lūipa's *Abhisamaya*.

Bhavabhaṭṭa, as he also held with regard to achievement with repetition of the father's essence mantra, explains that one should perform the ritual actions having repeated the essence mantra seven hundred thousand [times].[825] It is, however, explained in the *Abhidhānottara* that the quintessence mantra is repeated.[826]

3.3.3. 2.2.2. 2.2.5. 2.2. The symbolic explanation

There is also a perfection stage explanation regarding this production of a pure magic body through the mental force of meditating upon the donkey-faced one. Kambala explains that:

> The two breaths, right and left, [that rise] from the navel channel are said to be the sun and moon. Rising from the navel channel like the flower of a banana tree, one should recognize that the donkey's form is a lotus [shaped] like a bull's hoof. It is said that the downward-facing full lotus is adorned with moonlike light. In the ever-empty space in its center is the syllable *hūṁ*, which has the nature of wind. Like a burning wick, it is completely filled with the lower wind, which moves up to the heart, going on to the cranial cavity.[827]

Regarding this, the breaths that move in the nostrils are explained to be the right solar and left lunar winds, which move from the navel channel in the right *rasanā* and left *lalanā* channels, respectively. This also indicates

---

824 Kambala mentions the trident, skull, and skull staff, but he does not mention the curved knife. See SN 34a.

825 Bhavabhaṭṭa wrote that "This *sādhana* should be performed once one has counted 700,000 repetitions of the essence mantra" (Pandey 2002, 94: *hṛdayamantrajaptasaptalakṣasaṁkhye sādhanam etat karaṇīyam iti bhavaḥ*).

826 This occurs in the AU's *gardabhākārasvecchāsiddhinimittasādhana* chapter, where the reader is informed that "the yogī should repeat the quintessence" (J 291.7–292.1: *upahṛdayaṁ japet yogī*; AU 359a: *rnal 'byor nye snying bzlas na ni*).

827 See SN 34a,b.

that both the *rasanā* and *lalanā* channels rise up from the navel channel. "Like the flower of a banana tree" refers to the central channel at the center of the heart channel wheel. The explanatory Tantra states that: "Within the heart there is an eight-petaled lotus with a corolla, within which there is a channel that has the nature of a lamp wick. It faces downward, hanging like a banana flower."[828] The last line shows what a banana flower is like.[829]

Since that channel is shown as being that which rises from the navel channel, it is taught that it is the central channel. "Like a bull's hoof" means that it is like a cloven hoof on which there are extensions to the left and right as well as an empty center. When the *rasanā* and *lalanā* are extended with wind, the center is devoid of moving wind. Its lotus is the channel wheel. Although there are many [channel wheels] along it, here it is the channel wheel that is the navel's lotus. Since it is said that its outer shape is triangular, and as it exists in the form of the donkey face, it is taught that one should know that it is donkey-shaped. Thus, as in Lūipa's perfection stage, the penetrating of the vital points relying on that navel wheel, and the perfection stage meditation that arises relying on that, are the force of mind of the meditation on the donkey-faced one.

The bull hoof-like lotus is the lotus of the reality wheel (*dharma-cakra*) that faces downward from the heart. With regard to the syllable *hūṁ* in the middle of that lotus that is ornamented as if with moonbeams, it says in the explanatory Tantra that the syllable *hūṁ* appears upside down, and that it drips snow-like nectar.[830] The term "ever" [in Kambala's text "in the ever-empty space"] means "continually." It is "empty" of the wind inserted into the *dhūtī* by the force of yoga when one is not meditating. That which has "the nature of wind" is the life force that comes to have

[828] This passage occurs in kalpa 6, section 2 of the *Saṁpuṭa Tantra*, as follows: *hṛd-madhyagatapadmam aṣṭapatraṁ sakarṇikaṁ / tasya madhyagatanāḍī tailavarti-svarūpikā // kadalīpuṣpasaṁkāśā lambamānā tv adhomukhā /* (L 391a.9–b.1; see also ST 112a).

[829] This comment, naturally, would be important for Tsong Khapa's Tibetan readers, few of whom would have seen a banana flower. A simile such as this would have been clear to Indian readers.

[830] Tsong Khapa refers to text that is also in ST kalpa 6, section 2, shortly after the preceding quote. It reads "The syllable *hūṁ*, the unbeaten seed, is like falling dew" (L 391b.1–2: *hūṁkāro 'nāhatābījaṁ ava[śyā]pātasannibhaṁ*). The term *avaśyā* "dew" or "frost," is translated in Tibetan as "snow" (ST 112a: *kha ba*).

the nature of wind, since it is inserted into the *dhūtī* by the force of yoga. Then the fury fire blazes in the central channel from the navel "like a burning wick." The cause of the ignition of the navel's fury fire is the action of wind of the secret place below the navel "completely filling," i.e., moving to and fro. The fury fire goes up to the cavities of the four wheels, first to the navel, and then to the heart, and up to the throat and cranium. Once the fire reaches the cranium, the awakening spirit is drawn forth and trickles to the tip of the secret place. One should be able to understand by virtue of what came previously.[831]

Then, at the end [of the process of the awakening spirit] descending from above and being supported from below, subjective, natural great bliss apprehends the reality of objective selflessness. That is, the selflessness of objects is apprehended by the previously explained great compassion. It should be said that the magic body of the thirty-seven deities[832] will be attained just like the dream body that is like it, and that is produced from mere wind-mind. Kambala explains that if one abandons all distractions, observes silence, and practices the two previously explained processes for six months, one will attain the *ḍāka* of the donkey. And if one achieves that, one will attain the explanations of the powers of knowing the length of one's life, etc.[833] But he does not even begin to explain the creation stage's collection of ritual actions.

It says in four other commentaries that one should place an image of a donkey made of rice flour in the center of a mandala in which the deities' mantras are written, drawn with colored powders in the manner of the consecration mandala. Should the one who has the donkey-faced yoga repeat the mantra continually and gaze at the image in the center, whatever knowledge he desires will appear to him. It is said that this is the oral instruction.[834]

---

[831] I presume that Tsong Khapa is referring to his previous discussions of *caṇḍālī* meditation in chapter 1 above.

[832] These are the 37 goddesses of the CT mandala.

[833] Tsong Khapa here loosely paraphrases Kambala's commentary, which occurs as follows: "For the sake of that, should one abandon all distraction and assume the state of silence for six months, one will succeed. One who has this attainment will obtain all yogas" (SN 34b).

[834] Tsong Khapa here briefly summarizes Jayabhadra's description of this *sādhana*. For a translation of the full text of his commentary, see Gray 2007, 217–218, n. 3. See also

(cont'd)

3.3.3. 2.2.2. 2.2.5. 3. The benefits of attainment

If one is successful through the practice of the donkey yoga in this way, **one will foresee the end of one's life, and also the length of one's life**. That is, one will know the length of one's own and others' lives. **In this,** if **the yogī** himself has previously been a donkey, he will **see a donkey**, and **he will see**[835] the form of the **elephant**, and so forth, whatever **he was before (14.2.2)**, i.e., in a previous life. [These forms] are seen by the donkey **yogī** in order to appear in those forms that existed **in a previous life (14.3)**, the lives of himself or another.[836] In particular, you will know those who were human for their past seven lives. **Should there be** the flesh of **a power-bestowing person who was a man for seven lives, a sacrificial cake burnt oblation should be made with him**, i.e., eaten, secretly and without discursive thought at night.[837] Then **the adept will attain (14.4)** the power of transforming into a divine body, etc. Likewise, relying on that flesh, **one will ascend hundreds of thousands of leagues in an instant**.

This donkey **yoga** [of the] **supreme mantra is the best** or is excellent, i.e., very powerful. How is this so? It is very powerful because **it achieves union with the ḍākinīs (14.5)**, i.e., with the vajrayoginīs in the seats (*pīṭha*), subsidiary seats (*upapīṭha*), etc.

Sugiki 2001, 123, and CP 54b–55a. Versions of this *sādhana* also occur in the commentaries of Bhavabhaṭṭa (Pandey 2002, 94–95, CV 188b–189a), Bhavyakīrti (SM 20a), and Vīravajra (ST 186a,b).

[835] Tsong Khapa, following the PM and SM translations, uses passive constructions such as "seen in the form of," *gzugs can du mthong*. The Sanskrit, however, makes it clear that the *yogī* is the grammatical and logical subject here, e.g., "the yogī should see," *yogī paśyet*.

[836] Tsong Khapa here follows the reading given in Mardo's translations, which differs somewhat from the SL translation, as well as the extant Sanskrit. See Gray 2007, 218–219, nn. 6, 7. This translation is rather ambiguous and problematic. The commentaries make it clear that the practice being described here involves the contemplation of a consecrated image of the donkey-shaped Heruka, for the purpose of gaining visions of one's previous lives, and gaining the power to assume those forms.

[837] Tsong Khapa somewhat cryptically condenses one of Kambala's instructions. Kambala wrote here, "Free of discursive thought oneself, stay in a secret [place at] night" (SN 35a: *rnam par mi rtog bdag nyid kyis // mtshan mo gsang ba la gnas te /*).

3.3.3. 2.2.2. 2.2.5. 4. The method of attainment

If the donkey yogī **repeats** the mantra with the **sign**, i.e., conch shell rosary, he **will succeed within a month**.[838] This sort of attainment is due to the **supreme essence of** the father's **mantra** of this **secret supreme** bliss Tantra (**14.6**).

3.3.3. 2.2.2. 2.2.5. 5. Praise for that

This yogī who knows the supreme **reality**[839] of the two stages of donkey yoga is, **no doubt**, a yogī who unites in particular art and wisdom **in this** supreme bliss. And while all of the above explanations are stated in this *Ḍākinījālasaṁvara*) Tantra, they are held to be precious because they do not occur elsewhere other than in this literature.[840]

3.3.3. 2.2.2. 2.2.5. 6. The name of the chapter

In the *Concise* ***Śrī Herukābhidhāna Tantra***, [this] is **the fourteenth chapter on the procedure of the donkey-form yoga for becoming Śrī Heruka**. This is the explanation of the fourteenth chapter in the *Illumination of the Hidden Meaning, A Detailed Exegesis of the Concise Saṁvara Tantra Called "The Cakrasaṁvara."*

---

838 Here the Sanskrit reads, "Whoever repeats the sign of yoga will succeed within a month," *yoganimittaṁ japed yas tu māsenaikena sidhyati*. Here *yoganimittaṁ* is the object of the verb *japet*; it may be an oblique reference to the mantra. The Tibetan, however, reads it as instrumental, as "whoever repeats with a sign of yoga" (PM, SM: *rnal 'byor mtshan mas gang zlos pa*; SL: *rnal 'byor mtshan mas gang bzlos pa*). Tsong Khapa here follows Devagupta's commentary, namely that "'whoever repeats with a sign of yoga' means repeating with a conch rosary" (SS 104b).

839 Mardo's translations reads "this yogī who knows the supreme reality" (PM: *de nyid mchog shes gang de 'dir/ /rnal 'byor pa*; SM: */de nyid mchog shes pa de 'dir/ /rnal 'byor pa*), while the Sanskrit reads "this yogī who knows by means of reality" (*yo jānāti tattvena sa yogī*). Sumatikīrti's translation is closer to the Sanskrit, omitting *mchog* (SL 110a: *gang zhig de nyid shes pa ni*).

840 Tsong Khapa comments on the PM and SM translation of this text, which is "All these are stated in the *Ḍākinījālasamvara*" (*/mkha' 'dro dra ba'i sdom par ni/ /de dag thams cad brjod pa yin/*). The Sanskrit, however, reads, "The Hero Heruka obtains the Binding of the Ḍākinīs' Net," *eṣate heruko vīro ḍākinījālasamvaraṁ*. See my comments concerning this at Gray 2007, 220–221, n. 16.

CHAPTER 15

Chapter 15 Outline

3.3.3. 2.2.2. 3. The detailed exegesis of worship of the clanswoman

The third part, the detailed exegesis of worship of the clanswoman, has five sections: (1) the syllabic speech signs for generally recognizing the ḍākinīs, (2) the method of recognizing the particular ḍākinī clans, (3) physical signs for generally recognizing the ḍākinī clans, (4) things to know for ascertaining [the messenger's] devotion to oneself, and (5) verbal signs that are combinations of multiple syllables for generally recognizing the ḍākinīs.

3.3.3. 2.2.2. 3.1. The syllabic speech signs for generally recognizing the ḍākinīs

The first part has four sections: (1) the syllabic speech signs for generally recognizing the ḍākinīs, (2) the method of recognizing the particular ḍākinī clans, (3) physical signs for generally recognizing the ḍākinī clans, and (4) things to know for ascertaining [the messenger's] devotion to oneself.

3.3.3. 2.2.2. 3.1.1. The promise to explain

Now, after the fourteenth [chapter], I will explain that the adept, **he who knows the secret signs** of the yoginīs, **will succeed** in his desired aim **by means of** the **reality** of knowing the secret signs. **All** *saṁvaras* (**15.1**) refer to the yogī [adept] in the Tantras of the *Cakrasaṁvara* literature as is explained in the previously discussed explanatory Tantras.[841]

[841] This text, *sarvasamvareṣu*, is understood by Bhavabhaṭṭa as referring to the places where the yogins and yoginīs gather (Pandey 2002, 97). For this reason, I translate this as "in all sanctuaries." Büton, however, understands it in terms of the texts of the Cakrasaṁvara

(cont'd)

Someone said that this is "for the sake of protecting [all of the] saṁvara [vow]s that should be hidden from the [monastic] disciples, and so forth."[842]

3.3.3. 2.2.2. 3.1.2. The actual display of the signs

Ḍā is explained by the buddhas as [referring to] a "**person**," i.e., a man. ***Ḍī*** is the sign for "**woman**." These signs are not well known in the world as being applicable to these respective meanings, and they are also absent in other treatises such as works of grammar, and so forth. Yet it is established that these meanings were taught by the Tathāgata himself.

However, how does one recognize the ḍākinīs by means of these signs? It is not the case that one recognizes them by one saying "*ḍā*" and the other party replying "*ḍī*." Well, how then is it done? It is as Durjaya-candra explains, namely that "the utterances ['*ḍā*' and] '*ḍī*' are signs for the purpose of signifying whether one is a man or a woman, [respectively]. Realizing the signification thus makes it a sign. All of them should be regarded in this manner."[843] If one person utters "*ḍā*," the other person knows that it is a sign indicating that he is a man. Furthermore, as Kambala stated, "they are delighted due to [both parties] having the same intention."[844] If one understands thus [the signs], since both parties' minds accord, the ḍākinīs are delighted. One should also understand via this method the way of recognizing them by means of the following signs.

---

literature, which he lists as the "*Abhidhānottara* (AU), *Saṁpuṭa* (ST), *Vajraḍāka* (VD), *Sarvabuddhasamāyoga* (JS), *Ḍākārṇava* (DA), *Yoginīsaṁcāra* (YS), etc." (NS 394). Tsong Khapa appears to accept this interpretation.

842 This "someone" is Büton. See NS 394. The text in brackets translates the *thams cad* from the root text that Büton includes in his comment but which Tsong Khapa omits in his restatement of it. Büton's commentary, in turn, is based upon Bhavabhaṭṭa's. See Pandey 2002, 97.

843 Tsong Khapa omits a portion of the RG commentary for the sake of brevity, but this omission makes the text more difficult to understand. I have included the omitted text in brackets. The unabridged text occurs as follows: *ḍā zhes bya ba smos te skyes pa'am bud med du bshad par bya ba la ḍī zhes brjod pa ni brda ste/ de ltar bshad pa rtogs pa ni brda'o/ /de bzhin du yang thams cad du blta bar bya'o/* (RG 280b–281a).

844 See SN 35a. Kambala's text reads the singular pronoun *de* rather than the plural *de rnams*.

Pu[845] is the sign for "**restraint**," i.e., immobilization. ***Su*** means "**eating**" (15.2). ***Mā* is known to mean "mother,"** ***yā*** **"wife,"**[846] ***bhi*** **"sister**."[847] Likewise, ***vī*** means "**girlfriend**" (15.3), ***lu*** "**daughter**," **and *stri* should be known as "blood."**[848] Likewise,[849] ***so, pe, he,***[850] ***bha, bhu,***[851] ***pī, bhu,***[852] ***ḍhi,***[853] ***ga, stri,***[854] ***ku,***[855] ***ha,***[856] ***ja, ka, bha, svā,***[857] [as

---

845 Tsong Khapa reads here *phu*, following the SM translation. However, the Sanskrit manuscripts read *pu*. The PM translation reads *pū*, and the SL translation reads *pi*.

846 Tsong Khapa here follows the PM and SM reading. The SL reads *ya*, and the Sanskrit manuscripts *yo*. Bhavabhaṭṭa reads *ye* (Pandey 2002, 97), but all of the commentaries in Tibetan translation support the reading *yo* (CV 189b, TV 290b, IC 62b).

847 Tsong Khapa, following the Tibetan translations, reads *bhi* here. The Sanskrit reads *bhī*.

848 Tsong Khapa gives the reading *stri*, following the SM translation, which is close to the Sanskrit reading, *strī*. This is superior to the PM (*śrī*) and SL (*tri*) readings.

849 From this point onward Tsong Khapa lists all of the signs, followed by all of their meanings in a separate list. Unfortunately, this makes it very difficult to correlate the two. See my translation of the root Tantra to more easily make this link (Gray 2007, 222–225).

850 Tsong Khapa here follows the Tibetan translations. The CT manuscripts read *pi*, but Bhavabhaṭṭa reads *hī*, a reading supported by *Śāśvatavajra (TV 290b), as well as by Vīravajra, who reads *hi* (PD 393b).

851 Tsong Khapa follows the Tibetan translations in reading *bhu*. The Sanskrit manuscripts all read *bhū* here.

852 Tsong Khapa follows the SL and SM translations, which read *bhu*. However, the CT manuscripts read here *dū*, while Bhavabhaṭṭa's commentary reads *hū* (Pandey 2002, 98). Yet the Tibetan translation of the AU reads *du* (fol. 327a), as does Vīravajra's commentary (PD 393b). The parallel passage in the AU, however, reads *prī* (I 591b.7, J 210.4). The PM translation reads *dhu*, and, a reading also found in the commentaries of *Śāśvatavajra (TV 290b) and Indrabhūti (IC 63a).

853 Tsong Khapa's reading is very close to what I consider the best reading, *ḍī*, which is preserved in the AU manuscripts (I 591b.7, J 210.4), and supported by Śāśvatavajra (TV 290b) and Indrabhūti (IC 63a). The CT manuscripts read *hī* here, as do the manuscripts of Bhavabhaṭṭa's commentary (cf. Gray 2012, 107), which Pandey strangely misreads as *dhī* (2002, 98), apparently out of a desire to accord with Mardo's text and the Tibetan translation of this commentary, both of which read *dhī* (PM 225a, CV 190a). The SL and SM translations read *dhi*, and Vīravajra *di* (PD 393b).

854 The CT manuscripts and Bhavabhaṭṭa read *trī* here. The AU manuscripts, however, read *strī* (I 591b.7, J 210.4). The CT translations all read *stri*. Indrabhūti reads *tri* (IC 63a), and *Śāśvatavajra *stri* (TV 290b). *Trī* seems to be the best reading, as *strī* would be repetitive.

855 Tsong Khapa follows the Tibetan translations in reading *ku*, although the Sanskrit texts read *kū*.

well as the signs:][858] ***mi***,[859] ***ba***,[860] ***pe***, ***gha***,[861] ***ka***, ***sa***, ***ra***, ***du***, ***su***, ***na***, ***sa***, ***a***, ***ā***, ***na***,[862] and ***so***. The significations are, respectively, "**drinking soma**," "**beverage**" or a liquid substance (**15.4**), "**meat**," "**eating**," "**mixture**," i.e., assembly,[863] "**charnel ground**" (**15.5**), "**corpse**," "**yoginī**," the **Lāma** clan, "**Rūpiṇī**" (**15.6**), the **Ḍākinī** clan, "**Khaṇḍarohā**," "**both shanks**," "**the pair of forearms**" (**15.7**), **a salutation**, "**welcome**" (**15.8ab**), "**fish**," "**eating**," "Drinking the drinkable"[864] (**15.A1**), "Is [he

---

856 Tsong Khapa follows the Tibetan translations in reading *ha*, although the Sanskrit texts read *hā*.

857 Tsong Khapa here follows the SM translation. The PM translation reads *sva*, and the SL translation *su*, the reading that also occurs in the Sanskrit texts.

858 In Tsong Khapa's text the list occurs unbroken, as it does in the Tibetan translation he follows. However, the CT manuscripts and Bhavabhaṭṭa's commentary end with *su* (*svā* as read by Tsong Khapa). The remainder of the list occurs in the text of the AU, which is probably the source of the text that follows here.

859 Tsong Khapa, with the Tibetan translations, gives *mi*, but the AU manuscripts read *mī* (I 591b.8, J 210.5).

860 Tsong Khapa follows Mardo here (PM, SM). The AU manuscripts give the better reading *bha* (I 591b.8, J 210.5). This line is omitted in the SL translation. He also follows Mardo in omitting the next line, "*bhyo* is fasting," *bhyo abhakṣaḥ* (I 591b.8, J 210.5). This line is attested but mistranslated (or, perhaps, conflated with the previous line) in the SL translation (SL 110b: *bhyo zhes bya ba bza' ba yin*). It is accurately translated in *Śāśvatavajra's commentary (TV 290b: *bhyo zhes pa mi za ba'o*). Vīravajra comments that it indicates "consecrating and eating the five ambrosias" (PD 393b).

861 Tsong Khapa follows Mardo in reading *gha* (PM, SM). The SL translation and the Sanskrit read *ga*.

862 Tsong Khapa, with the Tibetan translation, gives *na*, but the AU manuscripts read *ṇa* (I 591b.9, J 210.7).

863 Tsong Khapa here gives Mardo's infelicitous translation for *melāpaka* ("meeting place"), namely *'dres pa* (PM, SM). Sumatikīrti gives "meeting," *phrad pa* (SL 110b). Neither translation expresses particularly well the meaning of the term, which is, generally, a place where the yoginīs gather, and, particularly, one of the ten classes of pilgrimage place.

864 Tsong Khapa is unable to properly interpret the text here, as *peyāpeyaṁ* (I 591b.8–9, J 210.5–6) is mistranslated in both versions of the Tibetan, which fail to acknowledge the interrogative expressed by the gerundive and its negation, meaning "Is it drinkable?" He gives "drinking the drinkable," *btung bya btung ba*, which correctly translates only a portion of this text.

or she] approachable?",[865] "desirable,"[866] "a **woman** who does not go to another man," "widow"[867] (**15.A2**), "**wicked woman**," "**beautiful woman**," "**ugly woman**," "**committed person**" (**15.A3**), "**uncommitted person**," "**has come**," "**has not come**," and "attachment"[868] (**15.A4**).

3.3.3. 2.2.2. 3.1.3. The synopsis and showing the method of imparting [the signs]

Every single one of these previously stated **syllabic signs** is that which **heroes**, i.e., brothers, **and sisters should know** (**15cd**). This means that these signs bring very close together one's own and the ḍākinīs' minds. Another translation lacks "to cognize" [here], which is excellent.[869] Since these signs, as Bhavyakīrti explains, are the signs of the accomplished yoginīs,[870] they are the signs of the messenger (*dūtī*) who procures the powers.

Regarding [Mardo's translation] "devoted and," etc., [the text that] occurs in Lochen's translation, "These should not be communicated to those who lack faith," is better.[871] It is the explanations of the signs and

---

[865] Here the Tibetan translations again fail to properly translate the gerundives, but Tsong Khapa does give the correct translation of *gamyāgamyam* (I 591b.9, J 210.6), namely *bgrod bya dang bgrod bya min*. He may have relied here on *Śāśvatavajra's commentary, which does translate it correctly (TV 290b).

[866] Here again the Tibetan translation fails to correctly translate the gerundive *kāmya*, reading *'dod pa* rather than *'dod bya*.

[867] Tsong Khapa follows Mardo here in reading "widow," *khyo med mo* (PM, SM). "Widow" is one of the meanings of the Sanskrit term *raṇḍā* (I 591b.9, J 210.6). This term is mistranslated as *khro med ma* in the SL translation.

[868] The Sanskrit reads "virtuous master," *sajjanaḥ ācāryaḥ*, here (I 592a.1, J 210.7). The Tibetan translations read "attachment," *chags pa*, but this is clearly due to a misinterpretation of *sajjana*. The translation of *Śāśvatavajra's commentary gives the correct and very literal translation "excellent person," *skye bu dam pa* (TV 290b).

[869] Tsong Khapa here refers to Mardo's apparently incorrect translation of *jñeyā* as *'du shes par byed pa* (PM, SM). Sumatikīrti's text, however, gives the correct reading, *shes par bya* (SL 110b).

[870] See BC 20a,b.

[871] This translation is preserved in Sumatikīrti's ed. (SL 110b: *dad pa dang mi ldan pa rnams la sbyin par mi bya'o*). Mardo's version is less consistent, reading: "[They] should be communicated to the devoted and undevoted" (PM: *gus pa dang mi gus pa la sbyin par bya*; SM: *gus pa dang mi gus pa la sbyin par bya ba ni*). This text does not occur in the extant CT manuscripts.

their meanings that are not communicated. These signs **should be communicated to those who** have the **pleasing, supreme commitment** and **are devoted to** benefiting, i.e., serving, the guru (**15.A5**).

3.3.3. 2.2.2. 3.1.4. Showing the name of the chapter

In the *Concise* ***Śrī Herukābhidhāna Tantra***, [this] is **the fifteenth chapter on the procedure of the syllabic signs**. This is the explanation of the fifteenth chapter in the *Illumination of the Hidden Meaning, A Detailed Exegesis of the Concise Saṁvara Tantra Called "The Cakrasaṁvara."*

CHAPTER 16

Chapter 16 Outline

3.3.3. 2.2.2. 3.2. The way to recognize the particular ḍākinī clans

The second part, the way to recognize the particular ḍākinī clans, has four sections: (1) showing each of the clans of the six ḍākinīs, (2) enumeration of the names of the seven ḍākinīs, (3) the classification of the ḍākinī clans, and (4) the classification of the lāmā clans.

3.3.3. 2.2.2. 3.2.1. Showing each of the clans of the six ḍākinīs

The first part has three sections: (1) the promise to explain, (2) the actual disclosure of that to be explained, and (3) showing the name of the chapter.

3.3.3. 2.2.2. 3.2.1. 1. The promise to explain

Next, after the fifteenth [chapter], **I will explain** concisely about the fortunate ones who have the characteristics to be explained below, as well as the unfortunate ones who lack these characteristics.[872] Although

---

[872] Here the Sanskrit reads, "Next I will impart here [for] the adept the secret of what should and should not be enjoyed" (*atha guhya bhakṣyam abhakṣyaṁ vai pravakṣyāmīha sādhakaḥ*). This reading is attested in commentaries such as Vīravajra's (PD 394a), Durjayacandra's (RG 281a), and Tathāgatarakṣita's (UN 227b). Tsong Khapa here follows Mardo's translation, which reads, "Next I will explain concisely about the fortunate and unfortunate ones" (PM: */de nas skal ldan skal ldan min/ /mdor bsdus nas ni rab bshad bya/*; SM: */de nas skal ldan skal ldan min/ /mdor bsdus nas ni bshad par bya/*). This seems to be based upon a (mis)reading of *bhavyam abhavyaṁ*. One the other hand, there is an additional reading preserved in the SL translation, namely "Next I will impart for the adept the secret of great power" (SL: */de nas dngos grub chen po gsang / /bsgrub pa po la bshad bya ba/*). This variant is also attested by Bhavabhaṭṭa (Pandey 2002, 100) and Kambala (SN 35a).

the unfortunate ones are not actually shown below, it means that one can understand the unfortunate ones by inferring from what is taught about the characteristics of the fortunate ones. The fortunate one[873] **resides within the supreme commitments** of the messenger, is **pleasing** to the adept, and is an **assistant** for him (**16.1**). Their characteristic is that which should be given only to one who is devoted to the guru. With regard to the first two lines, there also occurs [the following]: "Next I will impart concisely the secret, that is, what should and should not be enjoyed."[874] While two of the commentaries also explain [the text in this way], it seems that there were many differences in the Indian texts.

Then, having communicated to the devotee, if one adheres to the **distinctions** of one's **class** when the heroes and yoginīs are assembled, then the nondual, i.e., both, heroes and yoginīs will exist in six clans that are explained as being seven. **The adept** rapidly **attains** both **power**s **merely through recognizing that** (**16.2**). [This should be] connected to [the text] "I will impart." There are many different translations of the text "and then the class [distinctions]," etc.[875]

3.3.3. 2.2.2. 3.2.1. 2. The actual disclosure of that to be explained

The second part has two sections: (1) the division into seven clans and (2) the abridgement into six clans.

---

873 Here again, Tsong Khapa follows Mardo in reading *skal ldan* here. Pandey emends the Sanskrit on this basis to *bhavyāḥ* (2002:100). However, the CT manuscripts read *bhaktyā* (mss. A, B), a reading supported by the SL translation (SL: *dad pa rab dang ldan pa*). The reading *bhakṣyāḥ*, "those who are to be enjoyed," occurs in CT ms. C and the AU manuscripts (J 211.1; I 592a.2: *bhakṣā*). This reading is attested in the commentaries of Durjayacandra (RG 281a), Tathāgatarakṣita (UN 227b), and Indrabhūti (IC 64a).

874 Tsong Khapa here quotes Büton's commentary, at NS 398. This quote is quite close to the readings found in the Sanskrit and several of the Indian commentaries, as noted above.

875 Tsong Khapa here cites a line of the text as *de nas rigs kyi zhes sogs*. This version of the text occurs in Mardo's translations, as follows: "Then, if one apprehends the class distinctions" (PM, SM: *de nas rigs kyi dbye bzung na*). The Sanskrit here reads *varṇa-bhedaṁ tu yaṁ guhyaṁ*, so it appears that Mardo read *guhyaṁ* as *gṛhya*. Pandey emends this to accord with Mardo's reading (Pandey 2002, 100: *varṇabhedaṁ tu pragṛhya*), but this is unwarranted, as both commentaries that comment on this line support the former reading (RG 281a: *kha dog dbyes bas gsang ba gang*; IC 64a: *rigs kyi bye brag gsang ba dang*). The SL translation gives a very different reading, namely "color, scent, and so forth" (SL: *kha dog dri la sogs pa dang*).

3.3.3. 2.2.2. 3.2.1. 2.1. The division into seven clans

Even though one might know just the Ḍākinī clan as previously explained, if one does not know the particular clans, then one will not recognize a gathering of the ḍākinīs of one's own clan. On account of this, the particular clans are taught.

[1] **A woman**, i.e., ḍākinī, **who**se color **is pale like the lotus root**, the shape of whose **eyes** are **long like lotus petals**, **who always prefers white clothing**, **who** has the **fragrance of fresh sandalwood** on her head, *śirṣa*,[876] **and who delights**, i.e., has faith, **in** Vajrasattva, who **assembles** into one all of the **sugatas**. **She should be known as one born into the clan** of Vajrasattva who assembles the sugatas (**16.3**).

[2] **A woman who**se [complexion] **is like** the color of **refined gold**, **who prefers red and yellow garments**, **who has the scent of** the **jasmine** flower of the *Jāti* plant,[877] **and** the scent of **campaka** [flowers],[878] should be **a companion**, i.e., attached, **to the Heroes**, that is, in the clan of Ratnasambhava (**16.4**).

[3] A woman **who is dark blue** in color **like the Indīvara lotus**,[879] **who prefers wearing indigo clothing**, **and who has the scent of the utpala lotus,**[880] which is **indigo** in appearance, **is indeed a companion of the Hero** Heruka-**Rudra**,[881] i.e., is of his clan (**16.5**).

[4] **A woman** of beautiful appearance[882] **whose skin is the color of white lotus petals**, **and who always has the** delicious **scent of lotus**

---

876 Tsong Khapa is evidently attempting to give the Sanskrit equivalent for *mgor*, which would be *śirasi*. This does not occur at this line, but later, where it appears to be a corruption of *śirīṣa*, a type of flower.

877 *Jasminum grandiflorum*.

878 The yellow, fragrant flowers of the tree *Michelia campaka*.

879 *Nymphaea stellate*.

880 *Nymphaea caerulea*.

881 The CT and AU manuscripts read here *vīrarudrānugā hi sā*. Bhavabhaṭṭa, howver, reads *śrīherukānugā* (Pandey 2002, 101). Jayabhadra equated Rudra with Heruka, writing: "**A companion of the Hero Rudra** means one born in Śrī Heruka's clan" (Sugiki 2001, 124: *vīrarudrānugā iti śrīherukakulasambhūtety arthaḥ*). Tsong Khapa follows this interpretation, giving both names here.

882 Tsong Khapa here glosses as *gzugs mdzed ma* the term *mdzed ma*, "beautiful," that occurs in Mardo's translations (PM, SM) but not in the CT or AU manuscripts. The SL translation also glosses *nārī* here, but differently. In his text, she is "very pure" (*shin tu rnam dag*).

root[883] **is one who has a hero's resolve**, i.e., is of Amitābha's clan. As for **thus** (*tathā*), this means that [this identification] is just like the previous instruction [placing her] in Śrī Heruka's clan (**16.6**).

[5] **A woman who is red and** white,[884] since she has a red and white complexion, who prefers **red garments** on her **shapely figure**,[885] **and who smells like jasmine**[886] **and utpala lotus**, **is one born into the Vajra clan**, the clan of Akṣobhya. In another translation there occurs [the text] "[who has] a shapely figure and red face"[887] (**16.7**).

[6] **A woman who is yellow and dark blue** colored, **who prefers wearing white clothing**, and who has the scent of flowers on her head[888] **is known to be a companion of the Tathāgata** Amoghasiddhi, that is, she is of his clan (**16.8**).

[7] **A woman who is of reddish hue**, **who wears clothes of that color**, i.e., red, **and who always smells of camphor is a companion of Vairocana's clan,** that is, she is of his clan (**16.9**).

Thus **seven are the yoginīs' clans spoken by me**, Heruka. Vajrasattva is the causal Vajradhara, and Heruka is the resultant Vajradhara. If you distinguish these two, there are seven clans, but if you assimilate them, there are six. This I explain in the manner of the exegetical tradition of Nāropā's oral instructions.[889] Another commentary explains that the five

---

883 While the lotus root is certainly delicious, its scent is rather subdued and earthy, in my experience. However, as it is off-white or light tan in color, it fits the pattern of the text.

884 The Sanskrit reads here *raktagaurā*, translated in Mardo's texts as "red and white" (PM, SM: *dmar zhing dkar ba*). The SL translation, however, reads "red and light yellow" (*dmar shing ser skya*). Note that *gaura* can also mean "yellow" or "pale red."

885 Here Tsong Khapa follows the reading of the SL and SM translations, *gzugs bzang gos ni dmar ba dang*, which correctly translates *raktavastrasurūpiṇī*. The PM translation contains the erroneous *gzugs bzang kha ni dmar ba dang*.

886 That is *mallikā*, *Jasminum zambac*.

887 This is the PM translation's *gzugs bzang kha ni dmar ba dang*, discussed above.

888 Tsong Khapa here follows the PM and SM translation, *mgo la me tog dri dang ldan*, which appears to be an accurate translation of a faulty Sanskrit text. The extant CT manuscripts are defective here, reading *śirasipuspagandhā*. This AU preserves a better reading, "[who] has the scent of śirīṣa blossoms," *śirīṣapuspagandhā* (J 211.7; H missing folia; I defective), on which the SL's somewhat garbled translation appears to be based (SL 111a: *śrī shi dri yi me tog ldan*). The flowers of the śirīṣa tree, *Acacia sirissa* or *Mimosa lebbeck*, are white, which accords well with this passage.

889 Sachen is the source of this commentary; see PG 326.4.

clans with [Vajra]vārāhī make six, and with Vajradhara's clan, there are seven clans.[890] Kambala explains that the seven clans are [as follows] :

> Vairocana is said to [correlate to] the brahmin [class]; Ratna[sambhava] should be known to be the caṇḍāla. Amitābha is the lord of the dancers, and Amogha[siddhi], who has the vajra, with the dyers. The ḍombis are [associated] with Akṣobhya, and one should recognize the sixth, Vajrasattva's, as the kshatriya class. The seventh is the shudra [class], which gives rise to the universal clan of Heruka. (SN 35a)

This accords with the previous gurus.

Although here [the text] principally refers to the seven classes of seals who are ḍākinīs, the messengers who are human are also explained in terms of seven clans. Thus, the yogī should know his own clan according to the deity onto whom his flower was cast [during the consecration ceremony], and he should worship the yoginīs who are of the same clan as he is.

The seven [clans] are explained as **always take pleasure in** [the left-handed] **heteropraxy**,[891] such as eating with the left hand, moving the left foot first, etc. These seven are **each** marked by the **gesture** of her **own** clan, **and each has her own color (16.10)**.[892]

3.3.3. 2.2.2. 3.2.1. 2.2. The abridgement into six clans

With respect to those who **here** become followers of in each one of the six clans by speaking the **magic syllables of** their respective **clans**, *oṁ*, etc., and *oṁ jina jik*, etc., they **occur as six** "colors," i.e., **classes**.

---

[890] Tsong Khapa here is depending on Büton's characterization of Durjayacandra's commentary (NS 400). Durjayacandra's actual comments occur as follows: "With Vajravārāhī there are seven. The six are Vajrasattva together with Vairocana, etc." (RG 281a).

[891] That is, "the conduct of the left," *vāmācāra, g.yon pa'i kun spyod*. While this behavior might seem innocuous in other social contexts, it would seem less so in the Indian social world, in which the left side is considered inauspicious and associated with impurity.

[892] Tsong Khapa's text reads here "class of color," *mdog gi rigs*, which seems to reflect indecision concerning the proper translation of *varṇa*, since the term can be translated either as *mdog* or *rigs*.

This is the concise explanation. The equivalent term for "color" (*kha dog*), *varṇa*, can designate "class," "color," "syllable," or "utterance," and it would be better to translate it here as "class."[893] Since one **forms**, i.e., solicits,[894] one's **own gesture**, i.e., hand implement, of Vajrasattva, and since one **speaks the** mantric **speech that arises in** one's **own lineage** of Vajrasattva (**16.11**), it is the clan of Vajrasattva.[895]

A woman who goes to the left is always to the left of the yogī, i.e., circumambulates [him] to the left.[896] **She speaks** with an impressive voice,[897] **and looks gazing to the left (16.12)**, and **speaks** much when **women** are seen.[898] It is explained that she is a **committed** messenger of Ratnasambhava's clan.[899]

---

893 Tsong Khapa, following Büton (NS 401), corrects here the translation error found in the Tibetan translations.

894 I am not sure why Tsong Khapa glosses the verb *'ching* from *rang gi phyag rgya 'ching*, *badhnāti hi svakāṁ mudrāṁ*, with *'dri ba*, "solicit." The verb *badhnāti* clearly refers to forming the *mudrā* with one's hand.

895 Tsong Khapa adds the gloss Vajrasattva here because he interprets this and the following lines with respective clans. The root text here, however, seems to be speaking generally without reference to the specific clans.

896 Tsong Khapa here follows the SL and SM translations (SL: *rnal 'byor pa'i g.yon la brtag*; SM: *rnal 'byor pa yang g.yon la rtag*), which follows the AU reading (I 592a.8, J 212.3: *yogināṁ vāmatas sadā*). The CT manuscripts read, however, *yoginyo vāmatas sadā*, and this reading is followed by the PM translation (*rnal 'byor ma la'ang g.yon la brtag*) and the commentators, namely Bhavabhaṭṭa (Pandey 2002, 102), Durjayacandra (RG 282a), and Vīravajra (PD 395b).

897 Tsong Khapa follows the PM and SM translations here, *skad ni chen por rab smra ba*, which is attested in the AU manuscripts (I 592a.8; J 212.3: *vācāmahatprabhāṣī*) and also Bhavabhaṭṭa's commentary (Pandey 2002, 102). However, the CT manuscripts read here *vāmahastaprabhāṣī*, "She speaks by means of her left hand," which is meaningful given the text's focus on sign language. It is attested in the parallel passage of the SU (Tsuda 1974, 103), and also the somewhat defective SL translation (*lag pa gyon gyis mtshan pa dang*).

898 Tsong Khapa here follows PM and SM translations *bud med rnams mthong rab smra ba*, which seems to be defective, mistaking the *hṛṣṭa* of the Sanskrit for *dṛṣṭa*. The CT manuscripts read "He who speaks eagerly with women" *strīṇāṁ hṛṣṭaprabhāṣī ca*. Bhavabhaṭṭa reads *hṛṣṭaprahāṣī*, "eagerly laughs," but this reading is unattested elsewhere. Note that here and in subsequent lines the Sanskrit shows the masculine case, and may here be describing behavior proper for the male adept. The Tibetan does not indicate this, and thus Tsong Khapa reads the text as continuing to refer to the behavior of different classes of yoginīs.

899 Here again the Sanskrit text, *samayī so vidhīyate*, points to the male adept.

She who **solicits women**, who **speaks** her own **clan**'s **seed syllables (16.13)**, such as *hri*, etc., who **does not disregard the actions** and conduct **of** the lotus **clan**, and who preserves **that which is enjoined in the treatises** that teach the actions **of** her **own** clan, and who **repeats the** quintessence **spell of** her **clan**, is said to be a **committed** woman of Amitābha's clan **(16.14)**.[900]

[Those] who, **when saluting** holding their fingers to their foreheads, **always bow** with **the left**, with the **left** [side] of **one's body**, and who are **truthful**, i.e., true for their own sake, when **speaking with** goddesses, i.e., **women**,[901] are [members of] Akṣobhya's clan **(16.15)**.

[Those who] **draw** pictures **on the ground with** their **left big toe**, **scratch** their **heads**, **look askance**, and instruct **with** their **left hand**s [belong to] Amoghasiddhi's clan **(16.16)**.

When seeing her, the adept should particularly **recollect** that woman who is of **one's own** clan. One who **points with a finger to one's cheek, chin, or nostril (16.17)**, who **glances obliquely**, **repeats once** the King of Spells **mantra**, and **examines** the adept of **the** spell **consort**, i.e., of her own clan,[902] is a **yoginī** who **goes to the real thing**, i.e., speaks no falsehood. She is a messenger who **has the commitments** of Vairocana's clan **(16.18)**. This explanation of the six clans explains in the manner stated in Nāropā's oral instructions.[903]

3.3.3. 2.2.2. 3.2.1. 3. Showing the name of the chapter

In the *Concise* ***Śrī Herukābhidhāna Tantra***, [this] is **the sixteenth chapter on the procedure of examining the characteristics of the seven yoginīs** and six clans. This is the explanation of the sixteenth chapter in the *Illumination of the Hidden Meaning, A Detailed Exegesis of the Concise Saṁvara Tantra Called "The Cakrasaṁvara."*

---

900 Here again the Sanskrit, *samayī so vidhīyate*, uses a masculine pronoun and declension.

901 The Tibetan translations read *lha mo rnams* here, translating the Sanskrit *strīṇāṁ*.

902 The Sanskrit reads *vidyāṁ nirīkṣayet*, which seems to presume the male adept as subject and the female *vidyā* as object. Here Tsong Khapa resorts to commentatorial gymnastics to consistently read this text as referring to the behavior of the *yoginī*s.

903 Once again Tsong Khapa follows Sachen's text. See PG 327.3–328.2.

CHAPTER 17

Chapter 17 Outline

3.3.3. 2.2.2. 3.2.2. Enumeration of the names of the seven ḍākinīs

The second part, enumeration of the names of the seven ḍākinīs, has four sections: (1) the promise to explain, (2) showing the characteristics of the seven ḍākinīs, (3) showing their symbolic insignia, and (4) showing the name of the chapter.

3.3.3. 2.2.2. 3.2.2. 1. The promise to explain

Thence, after the sixteenth [chapter], I will explain concisely[904] in this chapter the characteristics of each one of the seven ḍākinīs, namely **Yāminī**,[905] **Trāsanī**,[906] Kānanī,[907] **Bhīmarūpā**,[908] **Saṁcārā**,[909] "She who

---

[904] The Sanskrit and Tibetan versions of this chapter all omit the usual "I will explain," which Tsong Khapa adds to conform to his usual commentatorial pattern.

[905] "She who is the night."

[906] "She who is terrifying."

[907] Here Tsong Khapa follows Mardo's translation *nags tshal ma* (PM, SM), "She who is of the forest," which is attested in the AU manuscripts as *kānanī* (I 592b.3; J 213.1), and he also lists the variant *shing ldan ma*. The CT manuscripts, however, read *kāminī*, "She who is impassioned," a reading that is also attested in Bhavabhaṭṭa's commentary (Pandey 2002, 104) as well as the SL translation (*'dod ldan ma*).

[908] Tsong Khapa follows Mal in conflating *'jigs* and *gzugs ma*, reading **bhīmarūpā*, "She of formidable form" (PG 328.3: *'jigs gzugs ma*; SL: *'jigs gzugs can*). They are read as two different names, "Formidable" and "Shapely," by Bhavabhaṭṭa (Pandey 2002, 104: *bhimā-rūpā*) and Mardo (PM, SM: *'jigs/ gzugs*). *Rūpā* does not occur in the CT manuscripts, and *bhimā* does not occur in the AU manuscripts (I 592b.3; J 213.1).

[909] Tsong Khapa here reads *gzugs kun spyod ma*, which is based upon Mardo's text (PM, SM), which is ambiguous in not clearly distinguishing the two names. All other sources clearly read *saṁcārā/kun tu spyod ma*, "She who transits."

is beautiful" or "She who devours life,"[910] and **Bhāsurā**. Regarding **assembled**,[911] Bhavabhaṭṭa explains that they are "concisely taken to be seven."[912] In Lochen's translation there also occurs: "The ḍākinīs have seven types. Their characteristics will be stated concisely here."[913] Durjayacandra also comments that "While no others aside from these seven are stated in this Tantra, there is also no mention of 'She who assembles' or 'She who dances.' Therefore, there are seven yoginī clans."[914] In the text [of this Tantra] they are twice stated to be seven, and, as there are no explanations that they are eight elsewhere in the extensive commentaries either, they should be taken as seven (**17.2**).[915]

Regarding "She who assembles," it occurs in Mal's translation as "...and Bhasurā, the seven clans. She who assembles will be stated here,"[916] it was explained that "She who assembles" is the eighth, in

---

910 Since Tsong Khapa follows Mal/Sumatikīrti and Sachen in conflating *bhimā* and *rūpa*, it was necessary to add an additional name to complete the list. Following them again he reads *mdzed ma* (SL, PG 233.1), which is not attested elsewhere. He also attests the alternate *tshe za ma*, the source of which appears to be Büton's commentary (NS 407).

911 The text that Tsong Khapa cites, *bsdus ma*, occurs only in Mardo's translation, and it appears to be a translation of *saṁhṛtāḥ*. Its feminine nominalization seems to indicate that Mardo mistook it as a proper name.

912 Tsong Khapa here comments on Bhavabhaṭṭa's explanation of the root text's *ḍākinyaḥ saptasaṁhṛtāḥ*, which occurs as follows: "As for the **seven assembled ḍākinīs**, it is the assembled ones, Yāminī, etc., that are are concisely declared to be the seven" (Pandey 2002, 104: *ḍākinyaḥ saptasaṁhṛtā iti etā yāminyādayaḥ saṁhṛtāḥ saṁkṣepeṇa sapta vyāhṛtā iti bhāvaḥ*).

913 The text attributed by Tsong Khapa to Lochen, */mkha' 'gro ma ni rnam pa bdun/ /mdor bsdus mtshan nyid 'dir bshad bya/*, is an expanded version of the text contained in the extant translations.

914 This translates the text as Tsong Khapa relates it. It occurs somewhat differently in the Tengyur, as follows: "While no others aside from these seven are stated in this Tantra, there is also mention of 'she who assembles.' Therefore, there are seven yoginī clans" (RG 283a).

915 Tsong Khapa is clearly correct here; the mistaken notion that there are eight clans seems to have derived from faulty translations in which *saṁhṛtāḥ* was taken as a proper name.

916 Tsong Khapa attributes to Mal the following text: */bha su ra dang rnam pa bdun/ /sdus pa mo ni 'dir bshad bya/*. This is close, but not identical, to the text preserved in the Phug-brag ms. Kangyur: */bha su ra dang rnam pa bdun/ /rang gi mtshan 'dir nyid bshad bya/*. Notice that there is no mention of "She who assembles" in this translation. However, Sachen does comment on the name *sdud pa mo* (PG 328.3), so other versions of this translation must have contained it.

addition to the seven assembled ḍākinīs. Furthermore, this does not mean that she is Vajravārāhī, because in the three translations of the *Abhidhānottara*, Vajravārāhī is counted as one of the seven,[917] and because of the root Tantra's statement that the clans are seven.[918] Thus, since the statement in the *Herukābhyudaya*, "Aihikī and Narteśvarī are said to be the eighth,"[919] differs from the root Tantra, were one to serve as the eighth here, Narteśvarī would fill the gap.[920]

Moreover, what are these ḍākinīs like? As the **yoginīs** have the nature of great passion, they are very **difficult to obtain** by those who advocate vehicles that are devoid of passion, etc. Likewise, the clans of **ḍākinīs** are also very difficult to obtain—this refers to their samaya mandalas. The **five ambrosias** should be read as "the ambrosia of the five." The elements of the body are five. The **real thing** refers to the things compounded with those five (**17.1**). The ambrosia of the five is explained as the indivisibility of bliss and emptiness that is the essence of these. Bhavyakīrti, and so forth, state, "since meetings with the yoginīs arise for one skilled in the service of the five ambrosias, they are not difficult to obtain."[921]

3.3.3. 2.2.2. 3.2.2. 2. Showing the characteristics of the seven ḍākinīs

Rūpikā,[922] **Cumbikā**—that is, "kisser"—**Lāmā**, **Parāvṛttā**,[923] **Sabālikā**,[924] **Anivartikā**,[925] and **Aihikīdevī**—"She who is of this

---

[917] The translation of Lochen and Atiśa does indeed include *phag mo*, presumably for *vārāhī*, among the list, although this is not supported by the extant Sanskrit manuscripts. See AU 328a.

[918] Tsong Khapa here criticizes Sachen's identification of "She who assembles" (*sdus pa mo*) with Vajravārāhī. See PG 328.3.

[919] See HA 11a.

[920] Tsong Khapa here paraphrases Büton's argument. See NS 407.

[921] Bhavyakīrti's comment here is more succinct, reading: "[They] are easy to obtain for one who is skilled with the five ambrosias." (BC 21a) Vīravajra also repeats this comment (ST 187b).

[922] "Beautiful."

[923] "She who returns."

[924] "She who is with child."

[925] "She who does not turn back."

[world]"[926]—are stated in the Tantras as the **seven ḍākinīs** (**17.3**). This is the concise presentation. This is an enumeration of [alternate] names for the seven, Yāminī, and so forth. The previous gurus have said that the former seven are transcendent, and that the latter seven are the names by which they are known to the worldly.[927]

Rūpikā should be known as **she** who **gazes** with attachment, i.e., **passionately**, **and furrows her** arched **brows**. She **first** displays her appealing **form**, **assembling** [people], then she later displays her ugly form, terrifying them (**17.4**).[928] She should also taken to be Yāminī. **She** should be **served** nondually, i.e., through union of the two, **by the** yogī who is a supreme bliss **Hero**.

She [who] **embraces and kisses a child**, be it "near," i.e., a close relative, or "not near," i.e., not [even] a distant relative (**17.5**),[929] **should be known to be Cumbikā**. She is also called Trāsanī. In a certain translation "whether agreeable or disagreeable" also occurs.[930] If one serves this **ḍākinī**, one's **sins**, i.e., obscurations, are destroyed. Thus she should be served.

She looks askance and **has**, i.e., has amassed, **frowns** on her **face**. Her brows are changed, i.e., moved, and she **threatens** (**17.6**). At some other times she expels **breath** and again **terrifies**. Moreover, she sometimes terrifies without exhaling. She is **called Lāmā**, and she is also called

---

926 The name *Aihikī* appears to derive from *aihika*, an abstract term derived from *iha* meaning "of this world, terrestial." See Monier-Williams 2002, 235.1. Tsong Khapa represents her name here as *e hi ki lha mo*, which is closer to the Sanskrit than the transliteration found in the Tibetan translations. *e hi ka lha mo*. He also correctly provides a literal Tibetan translation, *'di pa ma*.

927 This claim is made by Sachen at PG 233.1–2.

928 Tsong Khapa here follows the defective SM translation in reading "terrifies," *'jigs par byed pa*. The PM translation reads "destroys," *'jig par byed pa yin*, which likely reflects the extant Sanskrit in the CT manuscripts, *nāsaṁ karoti*. However, the SL translation contains what I believe is the best reading, "abandons, sets down," *'jog par byed pa*, which accurately translates the Sanskrit preserved in the AU manuscripts, *nyāsaṁ karoti*.

929 Tsong Khapa here follows Mardo's reading, *drung pa'am yang na mi drung pa* (PM, SM). The Sanskrit here reads *iṣṭaṁ vā yadi vāniṣṭaṁ*, "whether it is desired or not," which is far more meaningful here. The SL translation reads *sdug pa'am yang na mi sdug pa*. Note that *sdug pa* and *mi sdug pa* are possible translations for *iṣṭaṁ* and *aniṣṭaṁ*, respectively.

930 This is the SL text *sdug pa'am yang na mi sdug pa* discussed above.

Kānanī. Since [the Tantra] states clearly that Anivartā is not to be served, Lāmā also should be served.[931]

Pigs, bears,[932] **cats**, **jackals**, antelope,[933] and horses[934] (**17.7**), and **all** species like these **will be frightened on account of her**, i.e., when they see that woman. **She is known to be Parāvṛttā**. She is also called Bhīmarūpā.

She who laughs with extreme **delight**, **and having gone** for some purpose **does not return** again (**17.8**), i.e., does not come back quickly, **and who is open** in her **passion** for the adept, i.e., who desires to see him, **is known to be Khaṇḍarohā**. One Indian text states here "is known to be Sabālikā," which is excellent.[935] She is also called Saṁcārā.

Since **she is distraught**, i.e., unhappy, **whomever she touches, with her hand, a clod of earth,**[936] **her foot (17.9), the hem of her garment, or** even **with sticks,**[937] **will not live**. **She should be recognized as Anivartā**. It states that she is **not to be invoked (17.10)**, i.e., should not be served. She is also called "Beautiful" (*mdzed ma*). The

---

[931] In other words, the Tantra does not state that Lāmā should be served, but as it does not warn against this as it does with Anivartā below, Tsong Khapa argues that Lāmā too should be served.

[932] Tsong Khapa here follows Mardo in reading *dred* (PM, SM), the red bear (*Ursus isabellinus*). The Sanskrit reads *śarabha*, a term that originally designated a species of deer, but the term is also applied to the young elephant and also to a mythical mountain-dwelling beast; the Tibetan translations seem to incline toward the latter meaning but vary in its interpretation; the SL translation reads *seng ge*, the lion.

[933] Tsong Khapa follows the SM translation in reading *ce spyang ri dvags*, "jackals and antelopes." The PM and SL translations however, read here *ce sbyang ra*, "jackals and goats," which more accurately translates the Sanskrit *śṛgālājā*.

[934] The Tibetan reading here, *rta dag*, translates a particularly troublesome Sanskrit text, *śivāhayā*. Regarding this see Gray 2007, 234, n. 23.

[935] Tsong Khapa here repeats Büton's observation at NS 410.

[936] Tsong Khapa here inexplicably reads *lag pa'i bong pa'am*, "the clod of her hand," whereas the Sanskrit, *kāreṇātha loṣṭena*, and Mardo's Tibetan, *lag pa'am / bong pa'am* (226b) read them as two items in the list.

[937] Tsong Khapa here follows the reading of the Tibetan translations, *shing dag gis*. Both CT ms. A and the AU manuscripts are more specific, reading, *vārukāṣṭeṇa*, "or with a stick of the Āru tree" (*Lagerstroemia regina*). Pandey reads *vā kāṣṭeṇa* here (2002:105), perhaps due to influence from the Tibetan.

[alternate text] "beginners cannot invoke [her]" is not in the translations of Lochen, Mal, or the dual translation.[938] Were that the case, then it should be explained as meaning that she is not to be invoked by beginners.

She laughs, mutters, weeps, etc., **or flies into a rage** without a cause. Since it is said that she stays for a while in this region, she **is known to be Aihikā**. **The goddess** Aihikā **speaks sincerely**[939] (**17.11**), **and always speaks with Buddhists**, i.e., yoginīs who are Buddhist. **She is born in the Vajra clan**. She is also called Bhāsurā.

The seal **consort** (*mudrāṁ*, *phyag rgya mo*)[940] of the **ḍākinīs' clan** should be "marked," i.e., **recognized**, so that she might be **served by the hero**, i.e., adept (**17.12**). Regarding their affiliations with clans of the seven or six buddhas, it is as [was discussed] in [chapter] sixteen [above]. Regarding the particular identification of the clans of Yāminī, Rūpikā, etc., it should be known in accordance with the explanation in this chapter. If one wishes to know their placement in the mandala, their body colors, hand implements, and so forth, and their applicability to human girls, this should be known from Kambala's commentary.[941] How the yoginīs are assembled by them should be known from other commentaries.[942]

3.3.3. 2.2.2. 3.2.2. 3. Showing their symbolic insignia

It is explained that the **eight** hand implements of the first right hand of Rūpikā, etc., are, respectively, **a skull, an axe, a** boar's **tusk**, a **wheel, a** crocodile **banner, a sword, a terrible** knife or vajra,[943] and the

---

[938] This line, */las dang po la sgrub mi nus/*, occurs only in the SM translation.

[939] "Speaks sincerely" is a translation of the Tibetan *gsong por smra ba*. The Sanskrit here reads *prahasitavadanā*, "cheerful countenance."

[940] It is not clear whether the term *mudrāṁ* in the Sanskrit text refers to the consort or to the emblems that she might bear, depending on her affiliation. Tsong Khapa clearly takes this first instance as referring to the consort. The next instance, however, clearly refers to the emblems.

[941] See SN 35b–37a.

[942] Tsong Khapa here refers to the categorization of the mandala's twenty-four yoginīs into six clans. This is described, for example, by Durjayacandra at RG 282b–283a.

[943] The CT manuscripts read "terrible," *saṁtrāsanī*, here, which is glossed by Bhavabhaṭṭa as a knife, *kartrī* (Pandey 2002, 107) and by Jayabhadra as *vajra* (Sugiki 2001, 124).

conch[944] (**17.13**). In their left hands are a skull staff and offerings of semen and blood in a skull bowl.[945] The conch here is the hand implement of Narteśvarī who fills the gap, [for a total of eight goddesses.]

3.3.3. 2.2.2. 3.2.2. 4. Showing the name of the chapter

It is intended that these previously explained seven [goddesses] thoroughly transform into the **forms** of all of the yoginīs of the Triple Wheel [mandala]. That is, they assume their forms. Their **signs and emblems** are the skull, and so forth.

In the *Concise* ***Śrī Herukābhidhāna Tantra***, [this] is **the seventeenth chapter on the procedure of** showing this. This is the explanation of the seventeenth chapter in the *Illumination of the Hidden Meaning, A Detailed Exegesis of the Concise Saṁvara Tantra Called "The Cakrasaṁvara."*

---

944 "Conch," *dung*, only occurs in the Tibetan translation; the CT manuscripts read *kavaca*, "armor," instead. The CT manuscripts and Bhavabhaṭṭa, however, do read *saṁkhyāś cāṣṭamī smṛtāḥ*, which I translate as "counting them they are known to be eight." The only problem, of course, is that there are seven items in the list. The Tibetan translators seem to have been reading *śaṁkhā* here instead.

945 Tsong Khapa here expands upon Kambala's commentary at SN 37b.

CHAPTER 18

Chapter 18 Outline

3.3.3. 2.2.2. 3.2.3. The classification of the ḍākinī clans

The third part, the classification of the ḍākinī clans, has four sections: (1) the promise to explain, (2) the characteristics of each of the yoginī [clans], (3) summarizing the meaning of these, and (4) showing the name of the chapter.

3.3.3. 2.2.2. 3.2.3. 1. The promise to explain

Now, after the seventeenth [chapter], **I will explain**, **moreover**, the characteristics aside from the previous ones. Why is this necessary? It is because the **ḍākinīs abide by the commitments** to attend the yogī with that adept who **correctly discerns** the basis or cause of the **supreme state of the ḍākinīs (18.1**).

3.3.3. 2.2.2. 3.2.3. 2. The characteristics of each of the yoginī [clans]

The second part has six sections: (1) Padmanarteśvara's clan, (2) Heruka's clan, (3) Vajravārāhī's clan, (4) Khaṇḍarohā's clan, (5) Heruka's clan, and (6) Vināyaka's clan.

3.3.3. 2.2.2. 3.2.3. 2.1. Padmanarteśvara's clan

A woman who is reddish golden, i.e., light red, **is redolent with**, i.e., emits, **the scent of lotus**. **Her look is naturally placid**, and **it is accompanied**, i.e., followed by, the **appearance** of being **impassioned** toward, i.e., attached to, the adept (**18.2**). **The woman whose fingernails**

and eyes are reddened, **who loves all men**,[946] **and who** worships the **lotuses drawn in her house is** a ḍākinī **who is born into the clan of Padmanarteśvara**, i.e., Amitābha (**18.3**).

3.3.3. 2.2.2. 3.2.3. 2.2. Heruka's clan

A woman who has the mark of **a trident between her eyebrows, has a body that is dark blue and** slightly **pale**,[947] **is always intent upon** the yoga of **the Vajra clan** (**18.4**), and **always honors the vajra drawn in her house** is a **ḍākinī born into Śrī Heruka's clan** (**18.5**). **The woman who appears with a** trident[948] **on her forehead**, and with **a spear** as well, has **eyes** that **are red as well as reddish yellow**, **and her feet and hands are likewise red** (**18.6**). **She constantly exhibits affection for a goat or a chicken, and she always worships the vajra sign** drawn **in her house** (**18.7**). **There is no doubt that** this woman is a **ḍākinī born into Śrī Heruka's clan** (**18.8ab**).

3.3.3. 2.2.2. 3.2.3. 2.3. Vajravārāhī's clan

A woman on whose **forehead** or **hand a wheel is visible** (**18.8cd**) has a complexion **swarthy as a cloud**, and **always wears a silk headband**. **She is a woman of perfected good fortune** with respect to wealth, **and of exemplary happiness**[949] (**18.9**). She who has **drawn** a **wheel in her house**, and who **constantly worships** it, is **a ḍākinī born into Vajravārāhī's clan**, **and is proud of**, i.e., has pride regarding, **her power** (**18.10**). This **contrarian** woman's body color is **dark as black**

---

946 Tsong Khapa here follows Mardo, whose translations read *de bzhin skye bo kun la brtse* (PM, SM). The Sanskrit reads "her eyes are likewise reddened" (*saṁraktanayane tathā*), as does the SL translation (*mig ni kun tu dmar ba dang*).

947 Tsong Khapa here cites the text *lus ni sngo bsangs cung zad skya*, which is not the text that occurs in any of the extant Tibetan translations, none of which contains the qualifier *cung zad*.

948 Tsong Khapa follows the Tibetan translations in reading "trident" (*rtse gsum*). The extant Sanskrit reads *śūla*, "lance," rather than *triśūla*, "trident."

949 Tsong Khapa here follows Mardo's translation, which reads *mchog tu bde ba* (PM, SM). However, the extant Sanskrit reads "exemplary virtue," *sādhvī paratarā* (I 593a.5, J 215.1), which is the reading found in the SL translation (*mchog tu bden pa*).

kohl, and her teeth are white and prominent, i.e., long.[950] **She is constantly cruel and** highly **courageous**[951] **(18.11). She always takes pleasure in bathing**. A **vajra** sign is **drawn in her house**, and she **constantly worships** the drawing with a pure and virtuous intention (**18.12**).[952] **She is** a ḍākinī **born in Vajravārāhī's clan**, and has a retinue of ten thousand. Another [text] reads **fifteen thousand**[953] (**18.13ab**).

3.3.3. 2.2.2. 3.2.3. 2.4. Khaṇḍarohā's clan

A woman who **is yellow like** the color of **gold, with unmoving eyes**, i.e., who does not blink, has yellow facial **hair (18.13cd). On her forehead or hand a vajra** mark **is visible. She always maintains a state of** wealth like **royalty, is haughty** with pride, and is **truthful (18.14)**. Her body **is scented with jasmine perfume**. She **continuously** and greatly **worships the vajra** drawn **in her house (18.15). She is a supreme lady of great yogīs**,[954] **born into Khaṇḍarohā's clan** (**18.16ab**). Thus there are four [clans], [consisting of] Heruka's two clans, the second Vajravārāhī clan, and Khaṇḍarohā's clan, that are alike in worshipping drawings of vajras, but differ in terms of body color. In particular, there are also other [differences].[955]

---

950 The Tibetan translations all agree that her teeth are "white" and "prominent," *mtho ba*. The Sanskrit here is *daśanonnatā*, which I translated as "bucktoothed" in Gray 2007.

951 The Sanskrit adds here that she is "contrarian," *vāmā*. For some reason Tsong Khapa moves this term up to the front of this section as a gloss for "woman."

952 The Sanskrit here reads *vajraṁ gṛhe pūjyate satataṁ likhitaṁ śubham*, and I read *śubham* as declined with *vajraṁ* and *likhitaṁ*. Mardo, however, takes it as adverbial, and thus translates it as *dge bas* (PM, SM).

953 The extant Sanskrit reads "fifteen thousand," *sahasrāṇi daśapañcakam*; Bhavabhaṭṭa explains that "**fifteen thousand** refers to the fifteen thousand yoginīs" (Pandey 2002, 110: *sahasrāṇi daśapañcakam iti pañcadaśasahasrāṇi yoginya ity arthaḥ*). This reading occurs in the SL translation, which reads *stong phrag bcu lnga*. Mardo alone reads "ten thousand," *stong phrag bcu* (PM, SM).

954 The Sanskrit here reads *mahāyogīśvarī parā*, literally "supreme lady of great yogins." The Tibetan translations, however, read *rnal 'byor ma yi dbang phyug mchog*, "supreme lady of great yoginīs" (PM 227a; SL 113b).

955 Tsong Khapa refers to the five "clans" discussed so far. The descriptions of Heruka's clan and Vajravārāhī's clan each seem to include descriptions of two different types of women. As Tsong Khapa notes, both of those associated with Heruka worship vajras, but only the second associated with Vajravārāhī does; the first one worships a wheel.

3.3.3. 2.2.2. 3.2.3. 2.5. Heruka's clan

There is a woman who **is ever fond of meat**, whose body **is lean, and who has the color of black kohl (18.16cd). She has the form of a lance on her forehead**, and she is a woman who **takes delight in cruel deeds. She always goes to the charnel ground, and she is fearless** and **free of** filth, i.e., free of purity[956] **(18.17)**. She has the drop-like figure **on her forehead**,[957] and she **worships the skull drawn in her house. She is a ḍākinī born into the clan of the deity Śrī Heruka (18.18)**.

3.3.3. 2.2.2. 3.2.3. 2.6. Vināyaka's clan

There is a **woman who is** like the **color** of a blue **cloud and has teeth** that are **uneven** in length. **She always delights in cruel**, i.e., fierce, **deeds, and bares her left incisors (18.19). The axe drawn in her house is always worshipped. Have no doubt that she is a ḍākinī born in the clan of** Cakra-**Vināyaka**, i.e., the principal deity Saṁvara[958] (**18.20**). Someone explains that Vināyaka is Vighnāntaka.[959]

Thus, among the eight clans,[960] the first is clear. The second is Heruka's clan. The third is the Ratna clan.[961] The fourth is Vairocana's

---

[956] Tsong Khapa first gives Mardo's reading, *rtsog med* (PM, SM), then gives the SL reading, *gtsang sbra med*. Both appear to be attempts to translate the Sanskrit *nirghṛṇā*, meaning here "free of disgust."

[957] All of the Tibetan translations agree that she has a "drop," *thig le*, on her forehead, but the parallel passage in the AU indicates that she has a lance there (H 133b.3, I 593b.1, J 215.6–7: *yasyā lalāṭe śūlaṁ*). Given that the text already indicated that she has a lance on her forehead, it is hard to know which reading is superior; the former is contradictory and the latter repetitive.

[958] Literally meaning "remover," *vināyaka* is a name of Gaṇeśa. Bhavabhaṭṭa comments that Vināyaka refers to Vignāri, "foe of obstacles" (Pandey 2002, 110), which is another name of Gaṇeśa. Tsong Khapa follows Büton in identifying him with the Buddhist deity Saṁvara (NS 417).

[959] As noted above, Bhavabhaṭṭa as well as Büton (NS 417) identify him with Vighnāri (*bgegs dgra*), but neither identifies him with the Buddhist deity Vighnāntaka (*bgegs mthar byed*).

[960] The clans are eight in number if the first set of "Heruka's clan" and "Vajravārāhī's clan" are each divided into two, which is natural, given that each contains descriptions of two different types of women.

[961] This is the second type labeled as belonging to Śrī Heruka's clan.

clan, and the fifth Akṣobhya's clan.[962] The sixth is Vajrasattva's clan.[963] The seventh is Heruka's clan, which is taught twice.[964] The eighth is the clan of Amoghasiddhi.[965] The scholar Mardo stated that there are also the clans of the inner ḍākinīs of the four essence yoginīs.[966] There is also the method of recognizing their particular clans. But since the method for doing so is not different from the previous method, I will not repeat it.

3.3.3. 2.2.2. 3.2.3. 3. Summarizing the meanings of these

There is a distinctively different explanation that **these** previously explained **troops of ḍākinīs** were also born **into Śrī Heruka's clan**. Their **characteristics**, which are extremely secret vis-à-vis those who are not suitable vessels, are emanated, i.e., **stated, for the sake of benefiting** Saṁvara **adepts**[967] (**18.21**). Elsewhere it is also said that they do not emanate.

3.3.3. 2.2.2. 3.2.3. 4. Showing the name of the chapter

In the *Concise* ***Śrī Herukābhidhāna Tantra***, [this] is **the eighteenth chapter on the procedure of** ascertaining each of the clans relying on the **characteristic colors** and the **signs** drawn and worshipped by all eight yoginī clans. This is the explanation of the eighteenth chapter in the *Illumination of the Hidden Meaning, A Detailed Exegesis of the Concise Saṁvara Tantra Called "The Cakrasaṁvara."*

---

962 These two are labeled as Vajravārāhī's clan by the root text.

963 This is labeled Khaṇḍarohā's clan in the root text.

964 Indeed, it is taught three times, but different types of women are correlated to it in each case.

965 Or the clan of Vināyaka, according to the root text.

966 I presume that he made these comments in his apparently lost commentary.

967 These comments were made by Sachen at PG 331.4. Büton expands upon his comments, adding the idea of "emanation," which is absent in Sachen's commentary. See NS 417.

CHAPTER 19

Chapter 19 Outline

3.3.3. 2.2.2. 3.2.4. The classification of the lāmā clans

The fourth part, the classification of the lāmā clans, has three sections: (1) the promise to explain, (2) stating the characteristics of each of the lāma clans, and (3) showing the name of the chapter.

3.3.3. 2.2.2. 3.2.4. 1. The promise to explain

Furthermore, after the eighteenth chapter, **I will explain** truly, i.e., clearly,[968] **the** particular **defining marks of the lāmās, through which the adept can recognize their actual physical characteristics**, such as face, eyes, etc. (**19.1**).

3.3.3. 2.2.2. 3.2.4. 2. Stating the characteristics of each of the lāma clans

The second part has five sections: (1) Amitābha's clan, (2) Ratnasambhava's clan, (3) Akṣobhya's clan, (4) Vairocana's clan, and (5) Amoghasiddhi's clan.

[968] Tsong Khapa here glosses the *yang dag* of *yang dag bshad*, which is attested by Bhavabhaṭṭa as *saṁyakpravakṣāmi* (Pandey 2002, 112). The term *saṁyak* seems to be a later addition. It is not attested by Jayabhadra (Sugiki 2001, 124) or the AU mss. (H 134a.1, I 593b.3, J 216.3).

3.3.3. 2.2.2. 3.2.4. 2.1. Amitābha's clan

(**122**) A woman whose **face appears** broad[969] and **round**, who **always has a beard**, and has **long** body hairs and **eyebrows**[970] (**19.2**). **She** likes being **well dressed**, is very **clean**, is of **gentle** conduct, is **imperturbable**, i.e., has a stable mind, speaks **truthful** speech, **and always delights in the true Dharma**. The Buddha said that she is **a sister of the heroes**, i.e., adepts (**19.3**). When one sees her, **the gesture** of two hands encircling a **lotus should be presented**, i.e., displayed. Furthermore, one should display the **turtle gesture** in which one joins the palms of both hands.

It is held that her countergestures are [the following.] The **hide** gesture is acting as if one is holding the hide of a spotted **antelope** (*kṛṣṇasāra*). The **water vessel**, i.e., skull bowl, [gesture] is acting as if one is holding that (**19.4**). She is a woman who **draws a lotus in her house** on the **tenth lunar day**. These are **characteristics of women who are** of the **lāmā** clan of Amitābha's clan (**19.5**).

3.3.3. 2.2.2. 3.2.4. 2.2. Ratnasambhava's Clan

Her two **lips** hang,[971] and her two **eyes** are of long length and **reddish-yellow**. **She is** endowed with the good qualities of enjoying **wealth**, **fortune**, and **auspiciousness**, and she appears **yellow like the campaka flower** (**19.6**). Her stature is **not** very **tall nor short**, but just right. **She prefers variegated clothing**. She has **three lines on her forehead** that **reach up**, i.e., exist, **toward the part of her hair** (**19.7**). **She laughs and is pleased, seizes and stays** upon **the road. She always takes delight in tales of death in battle**, due to the clashes of opposing armies (**19.8**).

---

[969] The adjective "broad," *yongs rgyas par*, occurs in Mardo's translations only.

[970] The Tibetan translation read *spu dang smin ma ring ba*, apparently reading a substantive *lomāḥ* along with *bruvoḥ*. However, the Sanskrit, as attested by Bhavabhaṭṭa, reads the adjectival *lomaśāḥ*, "hairy," which seems to modify *bruvoḥ*.

[971] Tsong Khapa quotes the SM translation, *mchu gnyis rlo*. This, along with the SL translation *mchu ni 'phyang*, correctly translates the Sanskrit *lamboṣṭhī*. The majority of editions of the Kangyur give the corrupt reading *mchu gnyis glo* for the PM translation. The erroneous *glo* was corrected to *rlo* in the Lhasa edition, however. See Gray 2012, 314.

Seeing such a wanton, i.e., haughty, **one**, **display the** three-pronged **lance gesture**, in which one presses the thumb on the middle joint of the little finger and raises the remaining three [fingers]. One should also **exhibit the dance** posture **in which the** right leg is extended and the **left foot is drawn up** (**19.9**). In the case of this and the former gesture, it is not certain that this is the only way of doing them.[972]

Regarding the way in which she faces, she **turns**, i.e., circles, from the **left**. It is said that this is the yoginī's **countergesture**. **The eighth and fourteenth days** of the waning fortnight are said to be the times when the yoginīs meet with their male adepts (**19.10**). They are also the times for drawing images. Whoever **draws** a three-pronged **lance** in her house and **continually worships** it is one who is **characterized** as a **lāmā** of the clan of **Lokeśvara** or the Lord Ratnasambhava, as previously explained (**19.11**).

3.3.3. 2.2.2. 3.2.4. 2.3. Akṣobhya's Clan

There is a woman on whose **cheeks** appear, i.e., are, cavities. Her body color is **red** with a **yellowish** tint, and her **eyes** are greenish **yellow** (**19.12**). **Her hair** is swirled, i.e., **curled**,[973] **and her head** and forehead are **turbaned**. She has a **single line** on **her brow** (**19.13**). **Moreover, her neck** is **long**, **and she always prefers red clothing**. **She laughs** and **sings**, **and becomes instantly fierce** (**19.14**). **Her mind wavers, and she is particularly attracted to quarrels. Seeing such a wanton one** who is a seal consort (*phyag rgya ma*) of Akṣobhya's clan, **display the spear gesture** (**19.15**), in which the index finger in brandished with the thumb pressing all of the other fingers. Regarding **the second gesture**, **present** the gesture in which one acts as if **eagerly** ringing a **bell**; it is not certain that this is the only way of doing this.[974] As for **turning**, i.e.,

---

[972] Indeed, many of the commentators give diverging explanations of these gestures. For translations of some of these see the notes to my translation of the root text (Gray 2007, 239–242).

[973] Tsong Khapa here glosses the translation *skra ni de bzhin 'khyil ba dang* (PM, SM), from *kuñcitāś ca tathā keśā*, with the more colloquial *skra li ba*.

[974] For example, Vīravajra explained that "cupping the hand over the left knee is displaying the **bell gesture**" (PD 398a).

circling, her body **to the left** direction, it is said that this is **her counter-gesture (19.16)**.

3.3.3. 2.2.2. 3.2.4. 2.4. Vairocana's Clan

There is a woman who is of **short** stature, **with thick calves**. She **always prefers yellow garments, and drapes cloth over her shoulders (19.17). Seeing such a wanton one, display the wheel gesture** in which you join the thumb and index finger and open, i.e., extend, the other fingers. Then one **should eagerly present the second gesture**, **the conch gesture** in which the index finger is extended and the other fingers a contracted just a bit, with the [palm of the hand] facing up (**19.18**). **It is held that turning** her body **to the left is her countergesture**. **The fourteenth** of the waning fortnight is the time that they gather. She who **draws a vajra** mark **in her house (19.19) is characterized** as a **lāmā** of the clan of **Śrī Heruka**, i.e., Akṣobhya (**19.20ab**).

3.3.3. 2.2.2. 3.2.4. 2.5. Amoghasiddhi's Clan

There is a woman who has a lot of **hair all** over her body. **Her eyes are dark yellow (19.20cd)**. Her body is thick,[975] **deformed**, and unbearable, i.e., **terrible**.[976] Her face is expansive and her **mouth large**.[977] Her belly hangs,[978] **she is black colored, and she has** bulbous

---

[975] Tsong Khapa here follows the Tibetan translations, which read "thick" (PM, SL, SM: *sbom*), which does not agree with the Sanskrit *karālā*, "dreadful." Tsong Khapa interprets this and the following two adjectives as referring to her body in general. Sachen, however, interprets "thick" as referring to her body, and "deformed" to her face (PG 332.4). The SL translation also adds another somewhat strange line here, unattested elsewhere, which might be translated as "She who displays the great she-skeleton" (SL: *keng rus chen mo ngom pa mo*).

[976] Tsong Khapa here provides an accurate gloss on Mardo's inaccurate translation (PM, SM: *mi bzad pa*, for *ghorā*).

[977] Tsong Khapa here reproduces Mardo's translation, which accurately represents the text of the CS mss., namely *sthūlāsyā sthūlavaktrā*, which is redundant since both *āsya* and *vaktra* mean "mouth" or "face." This redundancy is eliminated in the AU version of the text, which is "she has a large mouth and large teeth," *sthūlāsyā sthūlavaktrakajā* (J 218.2; I 594a.4: *-vaktrajāḥ*; H 135a.2: *-vaktragāḥ*).

[978] Tsong Khapa again follows Mardo's translation, which reads *gsus pa rlo* (PM, SM) here. The Sanskrit, however, again indicated that she has a "large lower lip," *lamboṣṭhī*, which is accurately translated in the SL translation (*mchu 'phyang*).

eyes[979] **and a broken nose (19.21)**. She is always skilled in song.[980] She has the **color** of a rain **cloud**. **Seeing such a wanton one** who is **charming**, i.e., fascinating, **display the serpent deity gesture (19.22)**, in which the left arm is bent, and the right elbow is placed on top of it. The thumb and index finger [of the left hand] are extended, and the other three fingers contracted and held by the right [hand]. One **should present eagerly the second gesture**, i.e., the **spear** gesture. **It is held that turning** her body from **the left is her countergesture (19.23)**. **The eleventh is her** gathering **day**, and an image of **a tusk is drawn in her house**. These **characterize** a **lāmā** born in **Vajravārāhī**'s clan (**19.24**).

Although the method of assigning the five lāmā [classes] to the five clans is not clear in the root Tantra, the *Abhidhānottara*, or the *Saṁpuṭa*, they are arranged as is stated in the Guhyasamāja explanatory Tantra, the *Vajramālā*. Although they are also recognized as particular ḍākinī clans, the way of recognizing the particular [ḍākinī] clans is not like [the method of] the previous commentaries.

3.3.3. 2.2.2. 3.2.4. 3. Showing the name of the chapter

In the *Concise* ***Śrī Herukābhidhāna Tantra***, [this] is **the nineteenth chapter on pointing out the gestures of** all five **yoginīs** of the lāmā clans, and pointing out the countergestures. This is the explanation of the nineteenth chapter in the *Illumination of the Hidden Meaning, A Detailed Exegesis of the Concise Saṁvara Tantra Called "The Cakrasaṁvara."*

979 The Tibetan translations read *mig zlum*, "bulbous eyes," but the Sanskrit reads *kotarākṣī*, "sunken eyes."

980 Tsong Khapa here follows Mardo's nonliteral translation, *rtag tu glu la mkhas pa dang* (PM, SM). The Sanskrit here reads "[she is] always conversant with the celestial musicians," *gandharvakuśalā*.

Chapter 20

Chapter 20 Outline

3.3.3. 2.2.2. 3.3. The physical signs for generally recognizing the ḍākinī clans

The third part, the physical signs for generally recognizing the ḍākinī clans, has three sections: (1) the hand seal signs, (2) the signs characterized by the limbs, and (3) the characteristics of the distinctive gestures.

3.3.3. 2.2.2. 3.3.1. The hand seal signs

The first part has four sections: (1) the promise to explain, (2) the actual display of the signs, (3) what should be done once the signs are displayed, and (4) the name of the chapter.

3.3.3. 2.2.2. 3.3.1. 1. The promise to explain

Now, having explained the characteristics of the lāmās in the nineteenth [chapter], **I will explain above all** the **signs** that are displayed with **the left hand**. Why are these displayed? [They are displayed] in order that one who correctly **discerns** the displayed signs may control the dearly beloved ones such the **brothers and sisters** (**20.1**), so that they do everything that they are bidden. As it says in the *Abhidhānottara*, "The yoginī should proceed with the signs with the left hand."[981] Bhavabhaṭṭa

---

[981] Tsong Khapa here quotes two lines from the AU as follows: */rnal 'byor ma yis lag g.yon gyis/ /brda rnams la ni 'jug par bya/*. The Tibetan trans. of the AU, however, reads: "One should proceed with the signs with the left hand of a yogī" (AU 252a: */rnal 'byor pa yi lag g.yon gyis/ /brda rnams la ni 'jug par bya/*). This is actually a disjointed quotation of a verse that occurs as follows in the Sanskrit: "The hero should display the sign with the left hand of a yogī, proceeding with the signs that point out the heroes' abode" (H 9b.6, I 535b.3–4, J 15.6: *chommakāṁ darśayed vīra[ḥ] vāmāhastena yoginaḥ vīrānām ālayoddeśachommakānāṁ pravartanaṁ*).

likewise explains that the yogī should make signs in response to the yoginī's symbolic display.[982]

3.3.3. 2.2.2. 3.3.1. 2. The actual display of the signs

A ḍākinī who **shows her left hand is saying, "I salute [you]."** As it says in the *Vajraḍāka*, "Displaying the left hand is making a salutation."[983] The yogī showing the **ring finger** of the left hand is **the salutatory response (20.2)**. Moreover, as is stated in the *Vajraḍāka*, "Displaying the ring finger is the salutatory response."[984]

A yoginī **slapping her belly** is indicating, "I am **hungry**." Thus, one should give her food. A woman who **shows her brow** is saying, "**I come from space**" (**20.3**). A woman who **places her finger in her mouth** is saying, "**I am eating** food." Women who **loll** their **tongues** are saying, "**I have eaten** food" (**20.4**). The [feminine pronoun] "who" (*yā*, *gang zhig*) should be understood as referring to the yoginī.

If, having traveled a bit, **should she touch her knee** and calf, this indicates, "**I am exhausted**." **Touching** the **tips** of her other **fingers** with her left thumb **is to say, "I have rested"** (**20.5**). **Gnashing her teeth**, i.e., with her teeth, indicates, "**I am eating flesh**."[985] **Showing a frown** indicates that **"I am bound"** (**20.6**). **Displaying** the arms like the wings of an **eagle** indicates, **"I am free."** These are the meanings of the sign displays of the nine [beginning with] "belly slapping," etc. The adept, understanding them, responds in kind.

---

982 Bhavabhaṭṭa comments as follows in the context of this first verse. "**Now**, i.e., immediately after relating the gestures and counter gestures, **I will explain above all** the hand seals immediately after the syllabic signs." (Pandey 2002, 116: *atheti mudrāprati-mudrākathanānantaram / anyatamam iti / akṣarachommakānantaraṁ hastachommakaṁ vakṣya iti sambandhaḥ*) Bhavabhaṭṭa clearly is referring to the text's sequence of explaining the secret signs. However, the Tibetan translation of this commentary differs significantly from the Sanskrit here, lending support to Tsong Khapa's reading. See Pandey 2002, 442.

983 Portions of CT ch. 20 also occur in VD ch. 8. See Sugiki 2003, 74 and VD 20a.

984 See Sugiki 2003, 74 and VD 20a.

985 The Sanskrit here, *māṁsaṁ bhakṣayāmi*, is accurately translated in the SL (*sha za ba*) and SM (*sha za'o*) translations. The PM translation, with its reading *bza' yi*, lacks an equivalent to *māṁsaṁ*.

If she shows the fist of her left hand, **display the trident** (*pa ti sa, paṭṭiśa*) **to her** (**20.7**); that is, touch the three fingers[986] to one's forehead in the manner of a skull. **Show your khatvanga staff**, held by your left hand, to her who **gazes** in a **strange** manner, and **indicates** by holding **her hair** with her left hand[987] (**20.8**). **To her who shakes her limbs, display** the gesture of **two fangs**, in which one, with two vajra fists,[988] straighten the two little fingers and place them at both sides of one's mouth. **Indicating** the right **hand with** the left **hand is to say, "The sacrificial cake should be eaten"** (**20.9**). **Showing her right hand is to say, "Do thus!" Touching**, i.e., indicating, **her ear**, shows, "**Stay** together with me" (**20.10**). **Touching** the **fingernails** of her other fingers with the **fingernail** of her left thumb is to say, "Carry **the corpse**!"[989] Drawing an image on **the earth is to say, "Today I will enter the mandala**" (**20.11**). **Touching her** breast[990] **is to say, "Protect my son."**

---

[986] That is, the index, middle, and ring fingers.

[987] Tsong Khapa here follows Mardo's translation (PM, SM), which gives an anomalous two-part sign followed by a response. It reads: */rnam par 'gyur ba bltas nas ni/ /gang zhig skra ni ston pa la/ /kha ṭvāṁ ga ni de la bstan/*. These three lines correspond to a Sanskrit verse, one of the lines of which is omitted. The Sanskrit reads "If she indicates her hair, gaze with a strange [expression]. If she displays her fingernail, show her your khatvanga staff." (*keśān darśayed yā tu vikṛtaṁ ca nirīkṣayet / nakhaṁ darśayed yā tu khaṭvāṅgaṁ tasyā darśayet //*). Mardo also reverses the order of the first verse half. The SL translation, in two lines, also translates three of the Sanskrit *pāda*s, as follows: */skra ston pa ni rnam par khro/ /de ston kha ṭvāṁ ga ni bstan/*. Here *rnam par khro* may be a translation of *vikṛtaṁ*, but it lacks an equivalent to *nirīkṣayet* or *nakhaṁ*.

[988] The "vajra fist" is a fist made by bending both the thumb and forefinger, touching the tip of the forefinger to the thumb's knuckle, and grasping the top joint of the thumb with the other three fingers.

[989] There are several variant translations for this injunction. The Sanskrit in the CT manuscripts has the passive reading "The corpse is being conducted," *mṛto nīyate*. Tsong Khapa reads it as "Carry the dead corpse" (*shi ba'i ro khyer zhig*). This seems to be a clarification of the SM translation, *shi ba khyer*. This reading is supported by Śāśvatavajra, who glosses it as "Carry the corpse to the charnel ground." (TV 295b: *shi ba dur khrod du khyer zhig*). The PM translation has the defective reading *shi yis khyer*. However, there is an alternate reading in the AU, namely "Death is certain." (H 135b.7: *mṛtyo niyatam*). This reading is supported by Mal's translation, as reported by Sachen (PG 333.3: *shi bar nges*). The SL translation, however, reads here "S/he is dead" (*'di ni 'chi ba*).

[990] Tsong Khapa here follows Mardo's reading (PM, SM: *nu ma*). The Sanskrit, however, reads "chin," *cibukaṁ*, a reading also attested in Mal and Sumatikīrti's translation (PG 333.3: *kos ko*; SL 115b: *ko sko*).

Drawing an image on **the earth with the thumb of her left** hand is to say, **"The elder protects me" (20.12)**. **Opening her eyes** is **saying, "Do thus!"** Touching[991] the **knuckles** of her fingers with her left hand is to say, "**Lying in bliss** together" (**20.13**). Any of these whatsoever may be displayed for the messengers. The meaning [of the signs] from "indicating a hand with a hand" on down[992] are also like the previous [signs].[993] Although there are also numerous nonhand signs in this chapter, since it primarily shows hand signs, as the majority [of signs shown], it is said that this is called "the chapter on hand signs."

3.3.3. 2.2.2. 3.3.1. 3. What should be done once the signs are displayed

It will be shown that one should practice together with all of those previously explained messengers.

3.3.3. 2.2.2. 3.3.1. 4. The name of the chapter

In the *Concise* ***Śrī Herukābhidhāna Tantra***, [this] is **the twentieth chapter on the procedure of** the **symbolic gestures**, which are primarily **hand** signs, **of** all **yoginīs**. This is the explanation of the twentieth chapter in the *Illumination of the Hidden Meaning, A Detailed Exegesis of the Concise Saṁvara Tantra Called "The Cakrasaṁvara."*

---

991 The verb *reg pa* is attested in both Mardo's and Mal's translations (PM, SM, PG 333.3), which is likely an interpretive translation of the Sanskrit *lekhayed*, attested in the AU mss. (I 594b.5; H omits; J 220.2: leṣayed). The CS mss., however, read "should lick," *lehayed*, here.

992 That is, from verse 9 onward.

993 That is, the yogī is expected to recognize them and respond accordingly.

Chapter 21

Chapter 21 Outline

3.3.3. 2.2.2. 3.3.2. The signs characterized by the limbs

The second part, the signs characterized by the limbs, has three sections: (1) the promise to explain, (2) the actual display of the signs, and (3) showing the name of the chapter.

3.3.3. 2.2.2. 3.3.2. 1. The promise to explain

Next, after the twentieth [chapter], **I**, Vajradhara, **will explain,** through the power of great compassion, **the characteristic of the great secret** that is not the experiential scope of [monastic] disciples, and so forth,[994] and that is the easy method through which the adept attains success. Regarding the text that appears as "the vision of the great secret,"[995] the **great secret** refers to the ḍākinīs, and the **vision** refers to the signs that are to be viewed with the eye, the corporeal signs (**21.1ab**).

3.3.3. 2.2.2. 3.3.2. 2. The actual display of the signs

A yogī **should show his head to a woman who touches her crown** (**21.1cd**). [The pronoun] "who" (*yā*, *gang zhig*) refers to the ḍākinīs, and the responses are displayed by the yogī. Since Kambala

---

[994] Tsong Khapa here seems to be referring to the *Saṁpuṭa Tantra*'s gloss of the "secret," which is: "It is secret because it is not the experiential scope of Viṣṇu, Śiva, Brahmā, the disciples, or the solitary buddhas" (Skorupski 1996, 217: *hariharahiraṇyagarbha-śrāvaka-pratyekabuddhānām agocaratvād rahasyaṁ*).

[995] Tsong Khapa follows Mardo here, who reads */de nas gsang ba chen po yi/ /lta ba nga yis bshad par bya/* (PM, SM). The Sanskrit, however, reads, "Next I will explain the characteristic[s] that are the great secret of vision," *atha darśanamahāguhyaṁ lakṣaṇaṁ pravadāmy ahaṁ*. This reading is more accurately reflected by the SL translation, */de nas mthong ba chen po'i gsang / /mtshan nyid rab tu bshad par bya/*.

explains these signs literally, it is acceptable that there is no additional explanation [of them].[996]

Show your cheek to her who **shows her forehead**. Likewise, **show your tongue** to her who **shows her tooth (21.2)**, [your] **chin** to her who **displays her lips**, [your] **belly to her who touches her neck (21.3)**, [your] **forearm**[997] **to her who shows her hands**, [your] back[998] **to her who displays her buttocks**[999] **(21.4)**, [your] **chin to her who displays her breasts**, [your] **navel to her who shows her belly (21.5)**, [your] **penis to her who displays her secret** place, [your] **anus to her who shows her thigh (21.6)**, [your] **shank to her who displays her knee**, **the sole of** [your] **foot to her who displays her feet (21.7)**, [your] **finger**[nail][1000] **to her who shows her finger** [joint],[1001] **the sky to her who points to the earth (21.8)**, **the sun to her who points out the sky**. **To her who indicates**, i.e., makes, curvy **river**-like lines in space with her hands, display the **ocean** gesture, in which, spreading your fingers on both hands, you move them in the manner of waves **(21.9)**.

Regarding these that were just explained, **have no doubt** that [they] are **the gestures** of the **ḍākinīs' body** parts. Regarding displaying

---

996 Kambala, after quoting this first line, simply comments that this and the others "are easy to understand as they [should be understood] literally" (SN 38b).

997 The Sanskrit here reads "forearm," *bāhu*, but this is translated into Tibetan as *dpung*, which usually designates the shoulder or upper arm.

998 The Sanskrit texts here all read *pṛthvīṁ*, which Bhavabhaṭṭa explains refers to the "earth-touching gesture," *bhūsparśamudrā* (Pandey 2002, 119), in which, in seated position, one rests one's upper right arm on one's right knee and touches the ground with the tips of one's fingers. The Tibetan texts indicate that it is the back (*rgyab*, *pṛṣṭhaṁ*) that is indicated here, which very well may represent a genuine textual variant.

999 The Sanskrit here, *trikaṭikā*, is obscure; *kaṭi* or *kaṭikā* refer to the hips or buttocks, but the prefix *tri*, "three, triple," makes the referent obscure. According to Bhavabhaṭṭa, "*trikaṭikām* is a [textual] difficulty connected to the two buttocks" (Pandey 2002, 119: *trikaṭikām iti sphigdvayasambandhigranthiḥ*). The Tibetans translated this literally as "triple waist" (PM: *sum rked*; SM: *sum rked*) and "waist" (SL: *bsked pa*). Tsong Khapa follows Bhavabhaṭṭa in identifying it with the buttocks.

1000 Tsong Khapa follows the Tibetan translations in reading *sor mo*, "finger." The Sanskrit, however, reads "fingernail," *nakhaṁ*, here.

1001 The Tibetan translations here read *sor tshigs*, "finger joint," while the Sanskrit reads *aṅguliṁ*, "finger."

the previously explained [gestures], they should always be kept secret[1002] from those who are not suitable vessels. **One should display** the signs and symbolic responses truly, i.e., unerringly, to those who are suitable vessels (**21.10**).

3.3.3. 2.2.2. 3.3.2. 3. Showing the name of the chapter

In the *Concise* ***Śrī Herukābhidhāna Tantra***, [this] is **the twenty-first chapter on the procedure of** the **characteristics of the body**. This is the explanation of the twenty-first chapter in the *Illumination of the Hidden Meaning, A Detailed Exegesis of the Concise Saṁvara Tantra Called "The Cakrasaṁvara."*

[1002] Tsong Khapa follows Mardo's translation here of *gsang ba*, "secret" (PM, SM), which appears to be a mistranslation of *guhyakāḥ*, "secret ones," i.e., the yoginīs, as Jayabhadra explains in the context of chapter 22 below (Sugiki 2001, 124: *gukhyakā iti yoginyaḥ*).

CHAPTER 22

Chapter 22 Outline

3.3.3. 2.2.2. 3.3.3. The characteristics of the distinctive gestures

The third part, the characteristics of the distinctive gestures, has four sections: (1) the promise to explain, (2) the actual display of the signs, (3) their summary, and (4) showing the name of the chapter.

3.3.3. 2.2.2. 3.3.3. 1. The promise to explain

Then,[1003] after the twenty-first [chapter], the [text] reads **I will explain with respect to the distinct limb gestures**, which are the "other," i.e., supreme, [means] whereby the yoginīs are pleased.[1004] Since Kambala explains that "'distinct' means distinct from the hands in general, i.e., the fingers,"[1005] it should be read as "the gestures distinct to the hand." As for the method, they are explained according to the procedure stated in the Tantra.[1006] Why is this necessary? It is because through knowledge of the display of gestures, the yoginī **recognizes** the adept as a **brother**, and the adept, the yoginī as a **sister**, **without doubt (22.1)**. Knowing thus, they become trusting like siblings, and they will do as they are bidden. The signs and responses are necessary [for this].

[1003] Tsong Khapa breaks up the Tibetan *de nas gzhan yang*, which is a translation of *ataḥ paraṁ*, "furthermore," and treats them as separate words.

[1004] Tsong Khapa here follows Kambala's commentary, which glosses *gzhan/paraṁ* as *dam pa* (SN 38b), which Tsong Khapa paraphrases as *mchog*.

[1005] See SN 38b.

[1006] Tsong Khapa is conflating here two distinct textual variants. The CT manuscripts here, attested by Bhavabhaṭṭa (Pandey 2002, 121), read *ataḥ paraṁ pravakṣyāmi aṅga-mudrāviśeṣataḥ*. The AU manuscripts (I 595a.2, J 221.2), however, read *yathāvidhiḥ* in place of *viśeṣataḥ*, and this reading is also attested by Bhavabhaṭṭa as a variant text, as well as by Mardo (PM, SM: *cho ga bzhin*). The SL translation attests an additional variant, *ji bzhin...mchog*.

3.3.3. 2.2.2. 3.3.3. 2. The actual display of the signs

Any yogin or yoginī who **shows one finger is saying, "Welcome."** The other party, **showing two fingers**, the index and middle finger, **replies, "Welcome" (22.2)**. This thus explains the **gestures** distinct to **the limbs of all yoginīs. One should know the eye gesture (22.3), in which the forefinger is slightly contracted**, as the response to one who displays the extended middle finger of the left hand.[1007] The yoginī **to whom the mantrin shows this** gesture **will instantly come under his control for as long as he lives, have no doubt (22.4)**.

Likewise, **show one's forefinger to her who shows her middle finger**, and **one's tongue to her who displays her ring finger (22.5)**, the three-pronged **lance** [gesture] **to her who shows the** previously explained **trident** (*pa ti sa, paṭṭiśa*) [gesture],[1008] **the part of one's hair to her who displays her head (22.6)**, **one's mouth**[1009] **to her who points to the ground**, **the part of one's hair to her who frowns (22.7)**, **one's lips to her who shows her teeth**, **one's mouth to her who shows her neck**,[1010] and **one's eye to her who shows her forehead (22.8)**. When one indicates with the fingers of one's hands to those who display their foreheads, and so forth, it is explained that these are gestures of the fingers that are parts of the hands.

[1007] Tsong Khapa here follows Mardo's translation, which differs from the reading given in all other sources. Moreover, he appears to misconstrue Mardo's text, which is clearly a description of the *netramudrā*: "The left middle finger is extended, and the forefinger contracted slightly" (PM: */g.yon gyi gung mo brkyang pa la/ /cung zad mdzub mo bskum pa ni/*; SM: */g.yon gyi gung mo brkyang ba la/ /cung zad mdzub mo bskums pa ni/*). Sachen, who follows Mal's translation, correctly reads this as a description of the *mudrā* (PG 344.1). Tsong Khapa attempts to read into this both a sign and response, presumably to fit the pattern set by the rest of the chapter.

[1008] This gesture was described by Tsong Khapa in chapter 20, section 3.3.3.2.2.2.3.3.1.2, above.

[1009] Tsong Khapa here gives the correct reading, *kha*, attested in the SL translation as well as the AU (I 595a.5: *vaktraṁ*). Mardo gives the reading "sky" (PM, SM: *mkha'*), which is unattested elsewhere.

[1010] This sentence is present in all of the Tibetan translations, but is not attested in the surviving Sanskrit texts.

3.3.3. 2.2.2. 3.3.3. 3. Their summary

These gestures that were thus respectively explained **are the gestures** distinct to **the limbs of all yoginīs**. As for the **display** of these gestures, the **secret ones**, i.e., ḍākinīs, always **proceed** to display, i.e., realize, **the true**, i.e., unerring, **vision** (**22.9**).

3.3.3. 2.2.2. 3.3.3. 4. Showing the name of the chapter

In the *Concise* ***Śrī Herukābhidhāna Tantra***, [this] is **the twenty-second chapter on the procedure of the characteristics of the** yoginīs' **distinctive gestures**. This is the explanation of the twenty-second chapter in the *Illumination of the Hidden Meaning, A Detailed Exegesis of the Concise Saṁvara Tantra Called "The Cakrasaṁvara."*

CHAPTER 23

Chapter 23 Outline

3.3.3. 2.2.2. 3.4. Things to know for ascertaining [the messenger's] devotion to oneself
3.3.3. 2.2.2. 3.4.1. The promise to explain
3.3.3. 2.2.2. 3.4.2. Worshipping for the sake of devotion
3.3.3. 2.2.2. 3.4.3. Displaying the signs of devotion
3.3.3. 2.2.2. 3.4.4. The drawn signs that should be known
3.3.3. 2.2.2. 3.4.5. Showing the name of the chapter

3.3.3. 2.2.2. 3.4. Things to know for ascertaining [the messenger's] devotion to oneself

The fourth part has five sections: (1) the promise to explain, (2) worshipping for the sake of devotion, (3) displaying the signs of devotion, (4) the drawn signs that should be known, and (5) showing the name of the chapter.

3.3.3. 2.2.2. 3.4.1. The promise to explain

Next, after the twenty-second [chapter], the [text] states, "**I will explain** the method **whereby** the adept **recognizes the characteristics** of the **ḍākinīs'** display. Why is this necessary? This is because once one has recognized the distinctive characteristics of the ḍākinīs, then, even **from afar**, one will consider [her] to be a **sister of the heroes and heroines**[1011] (**23.1**).

3.3.3. 2.2.2. 3.4.2. Worshipping for the sake of devotion

The devoted woman who is pleased with the adept is **the hero's**, i.e, adept's, **enjoyment**, like **the earth**, since she is the ground that gives rise to the good qualities. The translations "**devoted woman who is pleased with him**" and "**like the earth**" are easy to understand. "Earth"

[1011] Tsong Khapa follows the PM translation (PM: *dpa' bo dpa' mo'i sring mo*), which is unattested elsewhere. The Sanskrit reads *vīrāṇāṁ vīrabhaginī*, which is more closely approximated by the other translations (SM: *dpa' bo dpa' bo'i sring mo*; SL: *dpa' bo yis/ /dpa' bos bsring mor*).

indicates the yoginī who is like the earth.[1012] **Taking her as one's support** means taking her as one's seal, who, having been relied upon, is the site for the accomplishment of awakening. Regarding the Saṁvara yogī's **worship** of the yoginī, it means rising from one's seat and embracing [her] tightly, and kissing [her]. **Binding** (*saṁvara*, *bde mchog*), i.e., supreme bliss, is the worship of her. Furthermore, the body of supreme bliss is produced through the **union** (yoga) of the great seal[1013] (**23.2**).

3.3.3. 2.2.2. 3.4.3. Displaying the signs of devotion

These [things], explained below, are the **signs of the yoginī's** attachment. This line is not in Lochen's or Mal's translations.[1014] What are they? **Gazing backward** is the opposite of gazing with the right eye, i.e., gazing with the left. Or, abandoning gazing in front, one gazes behind. [There is] **the alteration of her face**, i.e., her **brows raise** with slight embarrassment, and quiver. Her inner and outer **bliss always** shines[1015] (**23.3**). One **should recognize** the **rapid** displays of **various** actions such as the different gazes, etc. Likewise, one should also recognize the other indications that **thus arise from the ḍākinīs**. Regarding the display of **three circular lines** between the eyebrows;[1016] **through their turning and transformations** (**23.4**), they cause one to **go** to, i.e., realize, **the ḍākinīs**.[1017] **One should recognize** all of **their sign**s.

[1012] This could be a commentary on either *vasuṁdharā*, which I translate as "[like] the earth," or *medinī*, "ground," both of which are translated by Mardo as *sa gzhi*, which he distinguishes from *ādhāraṁ* with the translation *gzhi* (PM, SM). The SL translation is even worse, translating all three terms as *gzhi*.

[1013] Tsong Khapa here glosses the compound *yogasamvara*, incorrectly translated into Tibetan as *rnal 'byor pa yi sdom pa*, which he seems to understands as *yoginīsamvara*. This is understood by commentators such as Bhavabhaṭṭa to refer to sexual yoga. See Pandey 2002, 123–124, and my translation of that at Gray 2007, 251 n. 5.

[1014] Tsong Khapa refers here to Mardo's line *'di dag rnal 'byor ma rnams kyi* (PM, SM), which does not occur in the other translations or the commentaries.

[1015] Tsong Khapa follows the Tibetan translations here (PM, SM: *bde ba rtag pa*; SL: *rtag tu bde bas*). However, the majority of Sanskrit texts read "unchanging countenance," *śāśvataṁ mukham*. Regarding this see Gray 2007, 252 n. 7.

[1016] Tsong Khapa's text literally reads "at or on the *ūrṇā* (*mdzod spu na*)," the swirl of hair between the eyebrows.

[1017] Tsong Khapa takes the ḍākinīs in the line *mkha' 'gro ma rnams nges 'gro ba'i* (PM, SL, SM) as the object of the action of going. In the Sanskrit, however, they are clearly the

(cont'd)

Regarding the inner explanation of the two lines beginning with **transformations**, Kambala stated that:

> In order to achieve the bliss of the perfected [spirit of awakening], one ignites the fury fire that draws forth great bliss **through** the **transformation** of the yogic posture (*yantra*, *'khrul 'khor*) for the sake of **turning**, i.e., binding the life force and vital energy [so that it does not] go outside. The mantrin who inserts these into the central channel that is devoid of the life force mixes the **three circular lines**, i.e., three worlds, in experiential unity. In that moment, the conceptions and sensations of self and other, and likewise earth, water, wind, fire, and space, are all not conceived. [They] **return in an instant,** i.e., one experiences bliss.[1018]

Suddenly, although there is no need, she **goes** a little **and returns** again, **and her previous face is destroyed,**[1019] i.e., her previous countenance is composed (**23.5**). The text **her previously uttered speech is impaired**[1020] means that, having acknowledged that her previously uttered

---

agents of the actions of movement, since the present participle *gacchantyaḥ* and the verb *vinivartante* both agree with *ḍākinyaḥ*.

1018 Tsong Khapa quotes Kambala's commentary with a number of omissions and additions. The text occurs as follows in the Kangyur: *phul du byung ba'i bde ba bsgrub pa'i don bskor ba ni byang chub kyi sems la yongs su bskor ba ste/ srog dang rtsol ba sdom pa'i 'khrul 'khor gyis yang dag par phul du 'byung ba'i bde chen po'i lte ba'i dkyil 'khor du 'bar bas stong pa dbus su chad pa'i sngags pas 'jig rten gsum po dang lhan cig tu 'dre ba ste/ sa dang chu dang rlung nyid dang / /me dang nam mkha' nyid dang ni/ /bdag dang gzhan du rtog tshor dang / /skad cig de la kun mi dmigs/ /de yi mod la ldog 'gyur te/ /bdag gis bde ba nyams su myong /* (SN 39a). For a translation of the Kangyur version of this text see Gray 2007, 253 n. 11.

1019 Tsong Khapa here glosses CT 23.5cd as it occurs in the SM translation, */glo bur rnam par ldog 'gyur te/ /sngar gyi gdong ni 'jig gyur pa/*. There are numerous variant readings here. The PM translation reads */glo bur rnam par bzlog 'gyur te/ /sngar bzhin gdong ni 'jig gyur pa/*. The SL translation reads */sngar tshig gi ni nyams pa nyid/ /de yi gdong ni 'dzigs 'gyur ba/*. For a detailed discussion of these variants see Gray 2007, 254 n. 12.

1020 Tsong Khapa give a variant reading of Mal's translation, *sngar brjod tshig ni nyams par byed*. Very similar versions of this are attested elsewhere (SL: *sngar tshig gi ni nyams pa yin*; PG 245.2: *ngar bshad tshig nyams pa*).

speech has a contradiction, the former is destroyed. The line "Her shape like that" is not in the other translations or commentaries.[1021] If [this text] is like a [translation of] the *Abhidhānottara* that reads, "Her face is beautiful, bright like a vajra," it would seem [to read] "the beautiful face of that" ḍākinī is a "bright" drawing that is like **a vajra**.[1022] The **voice of that** ḍākinī is **always** clear like the call **of a cuckoo (23.6)**. The text "always clear" occurs in the *Abhidhānottara* [translations].[1023]

3.3.3. 2.2.2. 3.4.4. The drawn signs that should be known

The **sign** of this ḍākinī is that she draws **the form of a vajra, together with a mirror, in her house**; this is the first. The drawing of **the form of a sword, together with a mirror,** is likewise the second drawn sign (**23.7**). It **should be known** that forms of a **flag** and a **spear** are **always** drawn, as is a concave **mirror**.[1024] The drawing of **forms** in the house that are taken to be **signs**, in short, the vajra, etc., **should be known (23.8)**. She who is **endowed with these** previously explained **distinguishing marks should be recognized as being the supreme ḍākinī (23.9)**.

In Kambala's commentary there is [an explanation of] the symbolic implements, such that "one should know clearly the symbolic implements"

[1021] Tsong Khapa is correct in noting that this defective line, *rnam pa de lta de yi de*, occurs only in Mardo's translations (PM, SM).

[1022] The AU text that Tsong Khapa cites, */de'i gdong ni mdzas gyur pa/ /rdo rje lta bur gsal ba yin/*, is not the same as the text in the translation preserved in the Kangyur, which reads, "Her mouth is cleft, split in the shape of a vajra," */de'i dngos ni 'jig gyur pa/ /rdo rje lta bur gsal ba yin/* (AU 331b), in trans. of *vadanaṁ ca khaṇḍitaṁ tasyā vajrākṛtir iva sphuṭam*. Note that *sphuṭam*, here as in the CT translation, was inaccurately translated as *gsal ba*, which was a source of difficulty for commentators such as Tsong Khapa.

[1023] A close variant of the line Tsong Khapa quotes, *gsal ba de ni rtag tu 'gyur*, occurs in the canonical AU translation (AU 331b: *gsal ba de ni rtag tu gyur*).

[1024] Tsong Khapa here comments on the Tibetan translation *me long kha sbyar ba*, which would appear to be a translation of *saṁpuṭadarpaṇa*. However, Bhavabhaṭṭa explains that these terms are not in compound or agreement. He commented as follows: "**intercourse**...**by means of a mirror** means that [she is] gazing incessantly at the state of intercourse with a mirror." (Pandey 2002, 125: *saṁpuṭaṁ darpaṇeneti saṁpuṭatvaṁ darpaṇena satataṁ nirīkṣaṇam ity arthaḥ*). Regarding the meaning of *saṁpuṭa* here, see Kambala's comments below.

from the summary in two lines "the form taken to be a sign," etc. They are the vajra, wheel, jewel, lotus, sword, universal vajra, flag, and spear. As for their meaning, which should be clearly known, through the divisions of the clans, the vajra, flag, sword, and spear are a mere measure of barley, and the wheel, jewel, lotus, and universal vajra are a mere measure of peas, i.e., *caṇaka*. That is, in accordance with the stages of Akṣobhya, etc., it is said that through subtle yoga meditation, in which the wheels of the mandala are inserted with a firm mind within each of the five symbols and colors of one's clan, one will attain the success of the great seal.[1025] Thus, **in her house** indicates the house of the vajra, i.e., the vulva, which also indicates the tip of the vajra's aperture. With respect to these two [the penis and vulva], the mandala meditation of one's clan within the subtle implements is shown.

[The statement] "mere measure of barley" refers to the four implements shown in the root Tantra, and "mere measure of peas" refers to the four wheels, and so forth. How should they be taken? Here there is a portion applicable to the creation process, and two portions connected with the creation of natural bliss once one has inserted the life force into the central channel, by means of visualizing the implements within the yogin and yoginī's lower apertures of the central channel. As I have explained such matters extensively elsewhere, I will not go into this here.

One should know that these [lines] in the root Tantra indicate the Ghaṇṭapā tradition's process of the universal vajra together with the seed. Additionally, an explanation of the four implements, vajra, etc., was stated by Kambala, as follows:

> As for the meditation on utter emptiness of the **vajra** inserted within the vulva: everything is sky-like. Misknowledge, and so forth, are suddenly [seen to be] faults of thought arising from conceptualization. The mind, naturally pure clear light, is regarded as **mirror**-like, and all things as if reflections. They are clear and pure like the sky. The **sword** cuts away the afflictions; it is sharp in achieving the aims of sentient beings. Hoisting [them] by means of merit like a **flag**, the **spear** pierces the

[1025] Tsong Khapa here summarizes Kambala's commentary at SN 39a,b.

afflictions. The mind is one-pointed, and with its pinnacle of flame the yogī [undertakes] **intercourse** (*saṁpuṭa*), achieving bliss."[1026]

With regard to drawing the **vajra** that is inserted **in the house** there, one meditates on the emptiness of all entities equal to the sky that arises depending upon the visualization of the insertion of the vajra at the vajra tip, illustrated by that within the vulva of the seal. The sky-like clarity and purity of all things, like reflected images, is the **sword** that cuts all afflictions, and is sharp in fulfilling the aims of sentient beings. The **flag** is hoisted high with merit. The **spear** is piercing the afflictions with the one-pointed mind. The mind of natural clear light that is suddenly uncovered with respect to the faults of conceptualization such as misknowledge, etc., which arise from mistaken thoughts, is like a polished **mirror**. That very mind, since it attains bliss by means of the yoga of the sharp tongue of the fury fire, illuminates reality, which is the two extremely clear mirrors conjoined.

3.3.3. 2.2.2. 3.4.5. Showing the name of the chapter

In the *Concise* ***Śrī Herukābhidhāna Tantra***, [this] is **the twenty-third chapter on the procedure of** the characteristics of the distinctive **ḍākinīs'** devotion and **signs and insignia** such as the vajra, etc. This is the explanation of the twenty-third chapter in the *Illumination of the Hidden Meaning, A Detailed Exegesis of the Concise Saṁvara Tantra Called "The Cakrasaṁvara."*

1026 This text occurs as follows in Kambala's commentary: *bha ga'i dbus tshud rdo rje ni/ /shin tu stong par bsgoms pa ni/ /thams cad nam mkha' mnyam pa'o/ /ma rig la sogs glo bur ba/ /rtog pa'i nyes pa rtog las byung / /rang bzhin 'od gsal rnam dag pa/ /sems ni me long bzhin du blta/ /chos rnams gzugs brnyan lta bu ste/ /gsal zhing dag pa nam mkha' mtshungs/ /ral gri nyon mongs gcod byed pa/ /sems can don byed rno ba'o/ /bsod nams kyis 'degs rgyal mtshan bzhin/ /mdung thung nyon mongs 'bigs byed pas/ /sems ni rtse gcig pa nyid do/ /de nyid me lce rno sbyor pas/ /kha sbyar bde ba thob pa'o/* (SN 39a). I follow Tsong Khapa here in connecting "meditation on utter emptiness" and "the vajra inserted within the vulva" with the genitive particle *yi*, but I follow Kambala's commentary in reading *rnal 'byor pas* instead of Tsong Khapa's *rno sbyor bas*.

CHAPTER 24

Chapter 24 Outline

3.3.3. 2.2.2. 3.5. Verbal signs that are combinations of multiple syllables for generally recognizing the ḍākinīs

The fifth part has five sections: (1) the promise to explain, (2) the actual verbal signs that are combinations of multiple syllables, (3) summarizing their meaning, (4) showing the extraordinary distinguishing features of this Tantra, and (5) showing the name of the chapter.

3.3.3. 2.2.2. 3.5.1. The promise to explain

Now, after the twenty-third [chapter], **I will explain**, for the sake of benefiting **the adept**, **the secret signs** of an **alternate language** of the Tathāgata other than those known in the world and in other treatises. Regarding the need for this, **know without a doubt** that **through** the use of the secret signs, the yogī is a **brother** to the yoginī, and the yoginī a **sister** to the yogī, since they are intimate like siblings (**24.1**).

3.3.3. 2.2.2. 3.5.2. The actual verbal signs that are combinations of multiple syllables

Displaying [the gesture of] holding the fringe of one's garment with one's hand and **respectfully** saying "***potaṅgī***"[1027] is a **salutation**.

[1027] In this chapter, Tsong Khapa provides transliterations for most of the signs and translations for others. He mainly relies on the SM translation. Although the SM reading is often identical to the PM, when they diverge, Tsong Khapa follows the SM reading here. He also takes the SL readings into consideration. For the transliterated words, I put Sanskrit "reconstructions" in bold. For Tsong Khapa's actual transliterations, see the edition for this section. Note that the Sanskrit "reconstructions" often differ from the actual Sanskrit readings. See Gray 2012, 141–148, for the actual Sanskrit text here.

The **reply** is to **respectfully** say "***pratipotaṅgī***" while indicating the shaking of the fringe of one's garment. Likewise, [the signs are:][1028] ***gamu***, ***lumpa***, ***dehaṁ***, or *dehi*,[1029] ***caṭhūka***,[1030] ***pīraṇa***, ***kaurava***,[1031] ***karṇika***, ***āli***,[1032] ***vārāha***,[1033] ***śravaṇa***, ***amṛtasthāna***, ***samagamā***, ***tālikā***, ***narakaṁ***, ***amukaṁ***, ***kakhila***, ***śvasanaṁ***, ***paridhi***, ***virati***, *kru ta*,[1034] *an tya stha*,[1035] ***paśulika***, ***bhaginī***, ***medaka***, ***gṛhāṇi***, **touching the teeth with the tongue**, ***gandhavāsinī***, ***kuta***, ***kiraṇa***, ***tulampa***, ***daro***, ***nirodha***, ***tripti***, ***dhuryu***, ***dhūpapriyā***,[1036] ***sānu***, ***sarita***, ***aṅguli***, ***vadana***, ***rājikā***, ***ādanā***,[1037]

[1028] Tsong Khapa's method here of listing all of the signs followed by all of the responses is not particularly conducive to understanding. For the presentation of the two lists together along with detailed commentary and discussions of variant readings of the signs, see my translation of the root text in Gray 2007, 256–262.

[1029] Tsong Khapa gives the reading of the PM and SM translations, *de haṁ*, followed by the SL reading, *de hi*.

[1030] Tsong Khapa reads *tsa ṭhū ka* here, following the SM translation. The PM translation reads here *catuka*, and the Sanskrit texts all read *caṭuka* here, and take it as the signified of *gṛhānaṁ*.

[1031] Tsong Khapa, following the SM translation, gives what is certainly the right reading, i.e., *kauravā* as a code for "death" (*māraṇaṁ*). This reading is preserved by Bhavabhaṭṭa (Pandey 2002, 127). They are reversed in the AU manuscripts, and the Tibetan translations follow suit, taking *māraṇaṁ* as code for *kauravā*. *Kauravā* is not particularly meaningful; they translate it as "evil word/utterance," (PM: *smra ngan*; SL, AU 332a: *sgra ngan*), as if translating *krūraravā*.

[1032] The Sanskrit here reads *śiro 'liḥ*, although Tsong Khapa, following the SM translation, reads *āli* instead of *ali*. The PM translation omits this line, but the SL and AU translation agree with the Sanskrit in taking *śiras* as a code for *ali*, which is nonsensical. Tsong Khapa follows Büton (NS 440) in reversing these terms, which makes more sense.

[1033] Tsong Khapa, following the SM translation, transliterates this term as *ba rā ha*. The Tibetan translations and Bhavabhaṭṭa's commentary appear to be defective here. The most likely reading appears to be that preserved in the AU manuscripts, *karaṇam udara[m] vārāhaṁ keśaḥ* (H 138a.1, I 595b.3, J 223.3), taking the terms *karaṇam* and *vārāhaṁ* as codes for body parts.

[1034] Tsong Khapa here follows the SM translation's defective reading *kru ta*. The Sanskrit here reads "cruel" (*krūra*), which is more accurately transliterated in the PM and SL translations as *kru ra*.

[1035] Tsong Khapa again follows the SM translation's defective transliteration, *an tya stha*. The Sanskrit *antastha* is better reflected by the PM's reading, *an ta stha*. The SL's reading, *yan ta*, is even worse.

[1036] Tsong Khapa gives the SM reading, *dhu pa spri ya*, which represents an attempt to transliterate *dhūpapriyā*, the sign preserved in Bhavabhaṭṭa's commentary (Pandey 2002, 126).

paṅkti*, *chando*, *cala*,**[1038] *pra bha ha*,[1039] ***paśu*, *yānti*, *sasaṁ*, *phalguṣaṁ*, *mahākṣaraṁ*, *ga*, *nā*, *go*, *ma*, *bhā*, *hā, *a sba ka*,[1040] **touching the breast, touching the mouth, touching the teeth**, and *dhri*.[1041]

[These mean,] respectively, **"I go," "I come," town**, "Take!,"[1042] **heart, death, bell, head, hair, ears, churning stick, man, ḍākinī, mandala, charnel ground, gate**, the **brahmin** class, the **kshatriya** class, the **vaishya** class, the **shudra** class, the **caṇḍāla** [class], **house, ḍākinī, water**, the **seals, "I am hungry," thirst, "coming from such and such a place," flower, laughter, teeth, rain**, an **entreaty, outside, cloud, mountain, rivers, limbs, face, tongue, teeth, flag, rosary, wind, wild animal** (*mṛga, ri dvags*), **mandala, crossroad, living being, great beast**,[1043] **goat, human, bull, buffalo, eating, royal officials, dwelling in the forest**, "[I have] **eaten**," "[I am] **satisfied**," and **shame**.

***Hā* is its synonym** (*paryāyāḥ*) means that it is a synonym for the term "eating."[1044] ***Ho* is sometimes its synonym** means that it is a synonym for the term "[I am] satisfied."[1045] That is the case in some contexts. Although [the syllable] *dhri* occurs in Mardo's solo translation,

---

1037 Tsong Khapa, following Mardo (PM, SM), reads *ādanā*, while the Sanskrit reads *adanā*.

1038 Tsong Khapa, following Mardo (PM, SM), reads *cala*, while the Sanskrit reads *cāla*.

1039 Mardo's translations add an additional line, "carrying along (*pravaha*) means a boat" (PM: *pra ba ha ni gru'o*; SM: *pra bha ha ni gru'o*), which is not attested elsewhere. Tsong Khapa follows the SM's defective reading *pra bha ha*.

1040 Tsong Khapa follows the defective reading *a sba ka*, which is one of two defective readings found in extant copies of the SM translation (see Gray 2012, 524). The best reading, attested in multiple Sanskrit and Tibetan sources, appears to be *adhyakā*. See Gray 2007, 261 n. 32.

1041 Tsong Khapa follows the SM translation in reading *dhri* here. The Sanskrit reads *hrī*.

1042 Tsong Khapa here follows Mardo's translation (PM: *zung zhig*; SM: *zung cig*), which is evidently a translation of the imperative *gṛhāṇa*, a reading close to the *gṛhānaṁ* preserved in most manuscripts.

1043 The Tibetan translations all read *phyugs chen po'o*, "great beast" or "great sacrificial victim." The Sanskrit here reads *mahāsavaṁ*, "great corpse."

1044 Tsong Khapa comments on this line out of its proper order. It follows the code pair *bhā iti bhakṣaṇaṁ* above.

1045 Tsong Khapa here comments on a line immediately following *dantasparśanaṁ tṛptam iti*.

the [reading] *hri* occurs in the dual translation,[1046] and it accords with the other translations of the root Tantra and with the *Abhidhānottara*.[1047] The *Vajraḍāka* and *Ḍākārṇava* read "*hrika* means 'shame.'"[1048]

Mardo's solo translation contains [the following text]: "**Touching the void** means 'nothing.' As for **'Let's engage in sexual union**,' there is **touching the thigh**. **'[Do it] thus above!' It is not [done] from below**."[1049] The first verse of the dual translation is similar [to that], and then it reads: "In touching the thigh, 'Let's engage in sexual union' [is meant]. '[Do it] thus above!' '*Eva*' means 'it is not [done] from below.'"[1050] Although the *Abhidhānottara* is unlike this,[1051] in the *Vajraḍāka* it says: "In touching the void, 'Let's engage in sexual union' [is meant]. Touching the thigh means 'Let's [do it] now.'"[1052] The *Ḍākārṇava* also reads: "Touching the void [indicates] sexual union; touching the thigh [means] '[Do it] thus now!'"[1053] The *Herukābhyudaya* states, "In touching the secret, sex [is indicated]."[1054]

Thus, in touching the void in the midst of the genitals, "Let's engage in sexual union!" [is indicated]; these two, touching the void and sexual union, are linked. Regarding "touching the thigh [means] '[Do it] thus now!,'" "thus" and "touching the thigh" are linked. "Above" and "below" should be taken as stated in the *Herukābhyudaya*: "If one looks below, there is nothing below. If one looks above, there is something."[1055] This

---

1046 As Tsong Khapa reports, the correct reading *hrī* does occur in the PM translation, while the SM translation preserves the defective reading *dhri*.

1047 See AU 332a.

1048 See VD 20b, DA 208a.

1049 Tsong Khapa accurately quotes the SM translation here.

1050 Tsong Khapa likewise accurately quotes the PM translation here.

1051 The AU version of this text differs somewhat from the CT reading. See AU 332a. The extant Sanskrit of the AU also differs from its Tibetan translation. See my edition of the Sanskrit for a full account of the latter.

1052 See VD 20b.

1053 See DA 208a.

1054 See HA 19a.

1055 See HA 19a. Unfortunately, this passage clarifies this text only slightly. Büton gives a better explanation, as follows: "As for **touching the thigh**, [it means] 'I should be

(cont'd)

chapter's signs and responses are also like those explained in chapter fifteen.

3.3.3. 2.2.2. 3.5.3. Summarizing their meaning

The **gestures**, i.e., signs, and **countergestures**, i.e., symbolic responses, are the very **signs** that are **secret** to those who are not proper vessels. They are the means of knowing the **characteristics of the four classes**, i.e., clans, **spoken by the Hero** Heruka.[1056] Bhavabhaṭṭa maintains that they are the symbolic speech of all of them, namely the four clans of the four essence yoginīs, and that all of the signs of the four yoginī clans are shown by this chapter.[1057]

3.3.3. 2.2.2. 3.5.4. Showing the extraordinary distinguishing features of this Tantra

Here the Yoginī Tantras teach primarily the inseparability of bliss and emptiness from the perspective of wisdom. The view of the reality of emptiness is taught in brief in the Tantras, since the Lord Nāgārjuna intended that there would be nothing left to explain aside from what he established extensively.

---

below; you should do it from above.' **Thus**, in this way it should be done. Do it as the uppermost, that is, in the unobjectifying *samādhi* of all things. **It is not [done] from below**, meaning doing other than this is not one of the gestures, countergestures, or signs. These explanations of the definitive meaning are the esoteric instructions of Padmavajra" (NS 444). Büton here follows and expands upon the briefer comments contained in Padmavajra's commentary on the *Ḍākārṇava* (To. 1419, D fol. 219b–220a). Mardo's interpolation in his line "'*Eva*' means 'it is not [done] from below'" seems to point toward this interpretation, since the Sanskrit letter *e*, shaped like a downward-pointing triangle, is typically understood as a sign for the vulva, while the letter *va*, shaped like an upward-pointing triangle in some older scripts, is often understood to refer to the penis; the term *eva* or *evaṁ* thus represents their union, typically with the woman on top.

1056 Tsong Khapa here follows Mardo's translation, which is also attested in the Tibetan AU translation (PM, SM: *dpa' bos gsungs pa*; AU 332a: *dpa' bo'i gsung gi*). However, there is an alternate reading, "Hero's wife," attested in the SL (*dpa' bo'i btsun mo*) and the AU Sanskrit manuscripts (I 595b.9, J 224.4: *vīrabhāryā*).

1057 Bhavabhaṭṭa wrote that "[These] are all the symbolic speech signs of these four clans, namely [of] Ḍākinī, Lāmā, Khaṇḍarohā, and Rūpiṇī" (Pandey 2002, 129: *ḍākinī ca tathā lāmā khaṇḍarohā ca rūpiṇī catvāro vargās teṣāṁ sarvasaṁketabhāṣā chommakā*).

With regard to the need for explaining with an emphasis on great bliss, [there are] two [topics]: (1) meditation in which one concentrates upon vital points in the adamantine body that are part of the art of drawing forth great bliss, and (2) the drawing forth of great bliss in reliance upon one who manifests in the form of wisdom (*prajñā*). The former is taught in many different ways in the distinguished class of Unexcelled Tantra. The latter has three [types, namely] drawing forth [great bliss] relying upon (1) the actual seal, (2) the gnostic seal that is visualized, and (3) the great seal, whose form is empty. The first two occur in many Tantras. The third is clearly taught in the "bodhisattva commentary" literature. The *Commentary Praising Saṁvara* explains the import of this Tantra in the same way.[1058]

One rapidly encounters the consummation with the actual seal, the distinctive messenger of the twenty-four places, and so forth, and depending upon her one makes rapid and great progress on the path. Regarding this, there is the method of visualizing the heroes and heroines of the seats, etc., in the outer and inner mandalas, and so forth, and also the methods of relying on the conduct of the left. Since [these methods] do not occur elsewhere in the manner that they occur in the literature of this Tantra, one should know that the distinctive Saṁvara teachings are great.

Thus, the topic of uniting with the distinctive messenger is taught in many chapters, and [this text] teaches again and again, from beginning to end, the system of making progress on the path through the kindness of the messenger. Although, taking into account the text of this Tantra, the words [that mention] bliss are not as numerous as they are in the *Hevajra Tantra*, since the previous explanations derive from the perspective of great bliss itself, it is not the case that [this text] does not teach the mastery of great bliss. Therefore, one should ascertain these principal distinctive teachings that are unlike those in other Tantras.

Furthermore, the import of this Tantra is conceptualized as the great seal of emptiness as reality (*dharmatā*). Thus, the ultimate definitive meaning of drawing forth the natural great bliss was stated by

---

[1058] Tsong Khapa here refers to Vajrapāṇi's *Laghutantraṭīkā*, which does discuss the attainment of bliss via the *karma-* and *jñāna-mudrās* (Cicuzza 2001, 136). He then discusses the *mahāmudrā* in the following section on *ṣaḍaṅgayoga* (2001, 137–143). Regarding this see Gray 2009.

Ghaṇṭapā in his *Pañcakrama*. You should understand it according to how I explained it in my commentary on that.[1059]

3.3.3. 2.2.2. 3.4.5. Showing the name of the chapter

In the *Concise* ***Śrī Herukābhidhāna Tantra***, [this] is **the twenty-fourth chapter on the procedure of** designating as signs **the symbolic speech** that illustrates the characteristics of all **four** of the **classes**, i.e., clans. This is the explanation of the twenty-fourth chapter in the *Illumination of the Hidden Meaning, A Detailed Exegesis of the Concise Saṁvara Tantra Called "The Cakrasaṁvara."*

[1059] See Tsong Khapa's *bde mchog rim lnga'i bshad pa sbas don lta ba'i mig rnam par 'byed pa*.

APPENDIXES, GLOSSARIES, BIBLIOGRAPHIES, AND INDEXES

Appendix I

Tsong Khapa's General Outline (sa bcad) of the Entire Illumination of the Hidden Meaning (Chs. 1–51)

[VOLUME ONE]	
[Introduction]	
1.	The general arrangement of all the teachings
2.	The particular arrangement of the great bliss Tantras
2.1.	Identifying the root Tantra, explanatory Tantras, and intertextual Tantras
2.1.1.	Identifying the noncontroversial Tantras
2.1.2.	Discussing the controversial explanatory Tantras
2.2.	Showing the time and place of the original proclamation of the *Cakrasaṁvara Tantra*
2.3.	The way in which the explanatory Tantras explain the root Tantra
2.3.1.	Identifying the main points by which the explanatory Tantras explain the root Tantra

2.3.2.	How the uncommon explanatory Tantras explain
2.3.2. 1.	How the *Abhidhānottara* and *Vajraḍāka* explain
2.3.2. 1.1.	How the *Abhidhānottara* explains
2.3.2. 1.1.1.	How the creation stage is explained
2.3.2. 1.1.1. 1.	How the creation stage is not clear in the root Tantra
2.3.2. 1.1.1. 2.	How this explanatory Tantra explains clearly
2.3.2. 1.1.2.	How the perfection stage is explained
2.3.2. 1.2.	How the *Vajraḍāka* explains
2.3.2. 2.	How the *Saṁvarodaya* and the *[Yoginī]saṁcāra* explain
2.3.2. 2.1.	How the *Saṁvarodaya* explains
2.3.2. 2.2.	How the *[Yoginī]saṁcāra* explains
2.3.3.	How the common explanatory Tantras explain
3.	Introduction to the way in which the concise root Tantra is explained
3.1.	The explanation based on the instructions of the mahāsiddhas
3.2.	Showing the method of explanation based upon them [the instructions of the mahāsiddhas]
3.2.1.	Significance of the count of fifty-one chapters

3.2.2.	Applying the threefold explanation to the fifty-one chapters
3.2.3.	Showing the relevance of the summary of each chapter
3.2.3. 1.	Showing the summary of each [chapter]
3.2.3. 1.1.	Summary of bestowing consecration and showing reality therein
3.2.3. 1.2.	The summary of the selection of mantras and achieving the powers
3.2.3. 1.3.	The summary of attaining both powers through the kindness of the messengers
3.2.3. 1.4.	The summary of impact-heightening conduct and the vow as a friend on the path
3.2.3. 1.5.	The summary of the four mudrās such as mahāmudrā
3.2.3. 1.6.	The summary on understanding the signs of the rapid attainment of the powers
3.2.3. 2.	The arrangement in one of the stages of the path
3.2.3. 3.	The method of the lineage from Nāropā
[Chapter 1]	
3.3.	The actual method of explaining the root Tantra
3.3.1.	The meaning of the name
3.3.1. 1.	The translation of the name

3.3.1. 2.	The explanation of the name
3.3.2.	The salutation of the translators
3.3.3.	The meaning of the text
3.3.3. 1.	The reason "Thus have I heard" is not stated in the beginning
3.3.3. 2.	The actual explanation of the text's meaning
3.3.3. 2.1.	The first chapter's introduction to the significance of the entire Tantra
3.3.3. 2.1.1.	The actual text
3.3.3. 2.1.1. 1.	The promise to explain the secret
3.3.3. 2.1.1. 2.	The exhortation to listen to the secret
3.3.3. 2.1.1. 2.1.	The secret that should be heard
3.3.3. 2.1.1. 2.1.1.	Showing in brief the presentation of the secret
3.3.3. 2.1.1. 2.1.1. 1.	Explaining the interpretable meaning
3.3.3. 2.1.1. 2.1.1. 2.	Explaining the definitive meaning
3.3.3. 2.1.1. 2.1.2.	Explaining the presentation somewhat more extensively
3.3.3. 2.1.1. 2.1.2. 1.	The actual meaning

3.3.3. 2.1.1. 2.1.2. 1.1.	Explaining the two lines [that begin with] "the secret…supreme" [1.2cd]
3.3.3. 2.1.1. 2.1.2. 1.1.1.	Explaining in terms of the interpretable meaning
3.3.3. 2.1.1. 2.1.2. 1.1.1. 1.	Explaining as applicable to the narrative preface "Thus have I heard…"
3.3.3. 2.1.1. 2.1.2. 1.1.1. 1.1.	Stating the exact words of the narrative preface
3.3.3. 2.1.1. 2.1.2. 1.1.1. 1.2.	Explaining their meaning
3.3.3. 2.1.1. 2.1.2. 1.1.1. 2.	The explanation applicable to the creation stage
3.3.3. 2.1.1. 2.1.2. 1.1.2.	Explaining in terms of the definitive meaning
3.3.3. 2.1.1. 2.1.2. 1.1.2. 1.	The definitive meaning as applied to the narrative preface
3.3.3. 2.1.1. 2.1.2. 1.1.2. 2.	The definitive meaning as applied to the creation stage
3.3.3. 2.1.1. 2.1.2. 1.1.2. 3.	Explaining the sixteen syllables in reference to alchemy
3.3.3. 2.1.1. 2.1.2. 1.2.	Explaining the four lines [that begin with] "made of all ḍākinīs" [1.3]

3.3.3. 2.1.1. 2.1.2. 1.2.1.	The explanation applied to the goal
3.3.3. 2.1.1. 2.1.2. 1.2.2.	The explanation applied to the perfection stage of the path
3.3.3. 2.1.1. 2.1.2. 1.3.	Explaining the two lines that begin with *arising* [1.4a–b]
3.3.3. 2.1.1. 2.1.2. 1.3.1.	Explaining the interpretable meaning
3.3.3. 2.1.1. 2.1.2. 1.3.2.	Explaining the definitive meaning
3.3.3. 2.1.1. 2.1.2. 2.	The difficult to obtain
3.3.3. 2.1.1. 2.1.2. 3.	Showing an example of the union of bliss and emptiness
3.3.3. 2.1.1. 2.2.	The actual exhortation to listen
3.3.3. 2.1.1. 3.	The method for making progress in the secret of the path
3.3.3. 2.1.1. 3.1.	Worship of the clanswoman
3.3.3. 2.1.1. 3.1.1.	General worship of the clanswoman
3.3.3. 2.1.1. 3.1.2.	The attainment of power depending upon the clanswoman, together with worship
3.3.3. 2.1.1. 3.1.3.	The benefits of worshipping the clanswoman
3.3.3. 2.1.1. 3.2.	Protecting the commitments

3.3.3. 2.1.1. 3.2.1.	Maintaining the commitments to be protected
3.3.3. 2.1.1. 3.2.2.	Protecting the food commitments
3.3.3. 2.1.1. 3.3.	Meditation on the four seals
3.3.3. 2.1.1. 4.	Showing the place for practicing the secret
3.3.3. 2.1.2.	Showing the name of the chapter
[Chapter 2]	
3.3.3. 2.2.	The detailed exegesis of the meaning by the remaining forty-nine [chapters]
3.3.3. 2.2.1.	Becoming a suitable vessel for meditating on the two stages, and so forth
3.3.3. 2.2.1. 1.	Drawing the mandala, and its worship upon completion
3.3.3. 2.2.1. 1.1.	The characteristics of the master
3.3.3. 2.2.1. 1.2.	How he performs the rite
3.3.3. 2.2.1. 1.2.1.	The rites of the ground
3.3.3. 2.2.1. 1.2.1. 1.	Purifying the ground
3.3.3. 2.2.1. 1.2.1. 2.	Occupying the ground
3.3.3. 2.2.1. 1.2.2.	The rite of drawing and completing the mandala

3.3.3. 2.2.1. 1.2.2. 1.	Drawing the mandala
3.3.3. 2.2.1. 1.2.2. 1.1.	Drawing with marking string
3.3.3. 2.2.1. 1.2.2. 1.2.	Drawing with color
3.3.3. 2.2.1. 1.2.2. 2.	Completing the mandala
3.3.3. 2.2.1. 1.2.3.	Making and placing the vases
3.3.3. 2.2.1. 1.2.4.	The rite of mandala worship
3.3.3. 2.2.1. 1.2.4. 1.	Ornamenting the mandala
3.3.3. 2.2.1. 1.2.4. 2.	Worshipping the mandala
3.3.3. 2.2.1. 1.3.	Showing the name of the chapter
[Chapter 3]	
3.3.3. 2.2.1. 2.	Bestowing consecration in the completed mandala
3.3.3. 2.2.1. 2.1.	Pleasing the guru and the deities in the beginning
3.3.3. 2.2.1. 2.2.	Entering the mandala and bestowing consecration
3.3.3. 2.2.1. 2.2.1.	Entering the mandala
3.3.3. 2.2.1. 2.2.2.	Bestowing consecration upon the entrant
3.3.3. 2.2.1. 2.2.2. 1.	The actual consecration bestowal
3.3.3. 2.2.1. 2.2.2. 1.1.	Bestowing the vase consecration

3.3.3. 2.2.1. 2.2.2. 1.2.	Bestowing the higher consecrations
3.3.3. 2.2.1. 2.2.2. 2.	The salutation at the end of that
3.3.3. 2.2.1. 2.3.	Offering the fee and its benefit
3.3.3. 2.2.1. 2.3.1.	Offering the fee
3.3.3. 2.2.1. 2.3.2.	The benefit of offering
3.3.3. 2.2.1. 2.4.	Showing the definite need for consecration
3.3.3. 2.2.1. 2.5.	Showing the significance of consecration
3.3.3. 2.2.1. 2.5.1	Showing the supremacy of this consecration
3.3.3. 2.2.1. 2.5.2.	Addendum on the difficulty of getting this consecration
3.3.3. 2.2.1. 2.6.	Showing the name of the chapter
[Chapter 4]	
3.3.3. 2.2.2.	The detailed exegesis of the secret for suitable vessels
3.3.3. 2.2.2. 1.	The detailed exegesis of the secret of the path
3.3.3. 2.2.2. 1.1.	The four realities of the creation stage
3.3.3. 2.2.2. 1.2.	The four realities of the perfection stage
3.3.3. 2.2.2. 1.3.	Showing the name of the chapter

[Chapter 5]	
3.3.3. 2.2.2. 2.	The detailed exegesis of attainment by means of mantra and meditation
3.3.3. 2.2.2. 2.1.	Selecting the mantra to be repeated
3.3.3. 2.2.2. 2.1.1.	Selecting the root mantra's consonants
3.3.3. 2.2.2. 2.1.1. 1.	The actual text
3.3.3. 2.2.2. 2.1.1. 1.1.	Preparing the basis for mantra selection
3.3.3. 2.2.2. 2.1.1. 1.1.1.	The interpretable explanation
3.3.3. 2.2.2. 2.1.1. 1.1.2.	The definitive explanation
3.3.3. 2.2.2. 2.1.1. 1.2.	Selecting the mantra from that [basis]
3.3.3. 2.2.2. 2.1.1. 1.2.1.	Selecting the eight-line root mantra
3.3.3. 2.2.2. 2.1.1. 1.2.1. 1.	Selecting the first four lines
3.3.3. 2.2.2. 2.1.1. 1.2.1. 2.	Selecting the latter four [lines]
3.3.3. 2.2.2. 2.1.1. 1.2.2.	Selecting the *kara kara* root mantra
3.3.3. 2.2.2. 2.1.1. 1.2.2. 1.	Selecting the mantra's first set of eight [lines]
3.3.3. 2.2.2. 2.1.1. 1.2.2. 2.	Selecting the mantra's middle set of eight

3.3.3. 2.2.2. 2.1.1. 1.2.2. 3.	Selecting the mantra's final set of eight [lines]
3.3.3. 2.2.2. 2.1.1. 1.3.	Showing the greatness of the selected mantra
3.3.3. 2.2.2. 2.1.1. 2.	Showing the name of the chapter
[Chapter 6]	
3.3.3. 2.2.2. 2.1.2.	Selecting the hero's armor mantra
3.3.3. 2.2.2. 2.1.2. 1.	The actual text
3.3.3. 2.2.2. 2.1.2. 1.1.	The enumeration of the two mantras' syllables together with the selection of the armor mantra
3.3.3. 2.2.2. 2.1.2. 1.2.	Showing the places on which the armor [mantras] are set down
3.3.3. 2.2.2. 2.1.2. 2.	The name of the chapter
[Chapter 7]	
3.3.3. 2.2.2. 2.1.3.	Selecting the root mantra's vowels
3.3.3. 2.2.2. 2.1.3. 1.	The actual selection of the auxiliary vowels
3.3.3. 2.2.2. 2.1.3. 1.1.	Selecting the vowels of the eight-line [mantra]

3.3.3. 2.2.2. 2.1.3. 1.1.1.	Selecting the vowels of the first four lines
3.3.3. 2.2.2. 2.1.3. 1.1.2.	Selecting the vowels of the last four [lines]
3.3.3. 2.2.2. 2.1.3. 1.2.	Selecting the vowels of the *kara*, etc., [mantra]
3.3.3. 2.2.2. 2.1.3. 1.2.1.	Selecting the vowels of the first set of eight [lines]
3.3.3. 2.2.2. 2.1.3. 1.2.2.	Selecting the vowels of the middle set of eight [lines]
3.3.3. 2.2.2. 2.1.3. 1.2.3.	Selecting the vowels of the final set of eight [lines]
3.3.3. 2.2.2. 2.1.3. 2.	The greatness of the selected mantra
3.3.3. 2.2.2. 2.1.3. 3.	Selecting the root mantra's first and last syllables
3.3.3. 2.2.2. 2.1.3. 4.	Showing the name of the chapter
[Chapter 8]	
3.3.3. 2.2.2. 2.1.4.	Selecting the reversed order essence mantra and the heroine's armor mantra
3.3.3. 2.2.2. 2.1.4. 1.	The essence mantra
3.3.3. 2.2.2. 2.1.4. 2.	The armor mantras together with the four treasures

3.3.3. 2.2.2. 2.1.4. 3.	The method of performing the mantra authorization
3.3.3. 2.2.2. 2.1.4. 4.	The name of the chapter
[Chapter 9]	
3.3.3. 2.2.2. 2.2.	The way of achieving the powers through mantra repetition
3.3.3. 2.2.2. 2.2.1.	Ritual success with the root mantra
3.3.3. 2.2.2. 2.2.1. 1	The promise to explain, and its greatness
3.3.3. 2.2.2. 2.2.1. 2	Detailed exegesis of the actual host of ritual actions
3.3.3. 2.2.2. 2.2.1. 2.1.	The general principles of the methods for performing the ritual actions
3.3.3. 2.2.2. 2.2.1. 2.2.	Showing each of the methods for performing ritual actions
3.3.3. 2.2.2. 2.2.1. 2.2.1.	The rites that largely destroy and incidentally benefit
3.3.3. 2.2.2. 2.2.1. 2.2.2.	The host of destructive rites
3.3.3. 2.2.2. 2.2.1. 2.2.3.	Showing the way to perform rites that incidentally benefit

3.3.3. 2.2.2. 2.2.1. 2.2.4.	The destructive rites of killing and restoring life
3.3.3. 2.2.2. 2.2.1. 2.2.5.	Showing other beneficial rites
3.3.3. 2.2.2. 2.2.1. 3.	Showing the necessity of understanding the reality of mantra for those [rites]
3.3.3. 2.2.2. 2.2.1. 4.	Showing the name of the chapter
[Chapter 10]	
3.3.3. 2.2.2. 2.2.2.	Ritual success with the essence [mantra]
3.3.3. 2.2.2. 2.2.2. 1.	Chapter ten
3.3.3. 2.2.2. 2.2.2. 1.1.	Accomplishing the triple body
3.3.3. 2.2.2. 2.2.2. 1.1.1.	The promise to explain
3.3.3. 2.2.2. 2.2.2. 1.1.2.	Showing the adept's accomplishment of the triple body
3.3.3. 2.2.2. 2.2.2. 1.1.2. 1.	The general meaning
3.3.3. 2.2.2. 2.2.2. 1.1.2. 2.	The auxiliary meaning
3.3.3. 2.2.2. 2.2.2. 1.2.	The collection of rites of the essence [mantra]
3.3.3. 2.2.2. 2.2.2. 1.2.1.	The promise to explain

3.3.3. 2.2.2. 2.2.2. 1.2.2.	The actual collection of rites
3.3.3. 2.2.2. 2.2.2. 1.3.	Showing the name of the chapter
[Chapter 11]	
3.3.3. 2.2.2. 2.2.2. 2.	Chapter eleven
3.3.3. 2.2.2. 2.2.2. 2.1.	The promise to explain
3.3.3. 2.2.2. 2.2.2. 2.2.	The method of examining the one born seven times
3.3.3. 2.2.2. 2.2.2. 2.3.	Ritual success relying upon the concretion of the one born seven times
3.3.3. 2.2.2. 2.2.2. 2.4.	Showing the name of the chapter
[Chapter 12]	
3.3.3. 2.2.2. 2.2.3.	Ritual success with the quintessence [mantra]
3.3.3. 2.2.2. 2.2.3. 1.	The promise to explain
3.3.3. 2.2.2. 2.2.3. 2.	The actual ritual applications
3.3.3. 2.2.2. 2.2.3. 2.1.	Showing the four ritual applications of earthquakes, etc.
3.3.3. 2.2.2. 2.2.3. 2.2.	The ritual applications depending on the eye

3.3.3. 2.2.2. 2.2.3. 2.3.	The ritual application of the pill that achieves flight
3.3.3. 2.2.2. 2.2.3. 2.4.	The six rites of drawing blood, etc., together with their remedies
3.3.3. 2.2.2. 2.2.3. 2.5.	The seven rites of invisibility, etc., together with their remedies
3.3.3. 2.2.2. 2.2.3. 2.6.	The five rites of reversing the flow of a river, etc., together with their remedies
3.3.3. 2.2.2. 2.2.3. 3.	Showing the name of the chapter
[Chapter 13]	
3.3.3. 2.2.2. 2.2.4.	Ritual success with the armor mantras
3.3.3. 2.2.2. 2.2.4. 1.	The promise to explain
3.3.3. 2.2.2. 2.2.4. 2.	The actual collection of rites
3.3.3. 2.2.2. 2.2.4. 2.1.	The eight rites of dispelling fear, etc., together with subsequent release
3.3.3. 2.2.2. 2.2.4. 2.2.	The collection of rites of subjugating and relying on cotton clothing
3.3.3. 2.2.2. 2.2.4. 2.3.	The ordinary methods of accomplishing ritual actions

3.3.3. 2.2.2. 2.2.4. 2.4.	The two rites of turning into a tree, etc., together with the subsequent release
3.3.3. 2.2.2. 2.2.4. 3.	The name of the chapter
[Chapter 14]	
3.3.3. 2.2.2. 2.2.5.	Showing other rites accomplished with the essence
3.3.3. 2.2.2. 2.2.5. 1.	The promise to explain
3.3.3. 2.2.2. 2.2.5. 2.	The actual ritual applications
3.3.3. 2.2.2. 2.2.5. 2.1.	The literal explanation
3.3.3. 2.2.2. 2.2.5. 2.2.	The symbolic explanation
3.3.3. 2.2.2. 2.2.5. 3.	The benefits of attainment
3.3.3. 2.2.2. 2.2.5. 4.	The method of attainment
3.3.3. 2.2.2. 2.2.5. 5.	Praise for that
3.3.3. 2.2.2. 2.2.5. 6.	The name of the chapter
[Chapter 15]	
3.3.3. 2.2.2. 3.	The detailed exegesis of worship of the clanswoman
3.3.3. 2.2.2. 3.1.	The syllabic speech signs for generally recognizing the ḍākinīs

3.3.3. 2.2.2. 3.1.1.	The promise to explain
3.3.3. 2.2.2. 3.1.2.	The actual display of the signs
3.3.3. 2.2.2. 3.1.3.	The synopsis and showing the method of imparting [the signs]
3.3.3. 2.2.2. 3.1.4.	Showing the name of the chapter
[Chapter 16]	
3.3.3. 2.2.2. 3.2.	The way to recognize the particular ḍākinī clans
3.3.3. 2.2.2. 3.2.1.	Showing each of the clans of the six ḍākinīs
3.3.3. 2.2.2. 3.2.1. 1.	The promise to explain
3.3.3. 2.2.2. 3.2.1. 2.	The actual disclosure of that to be explained
3.3.3. 2.2.2. 3.2.1. 2.1.	The division into seven clans
3.3.3. 2.2.2. 3.2.1. 2.2.	The abridgement into six clans
3.3.3. 2.2.2. 3.2.1. 3.	Showing the name of the chapter
[Chapter 17]	
3.3.3. 2.2.2. 3.2.2.	Enumeration of the names of the seven ḍākinīs
3.3.3. 2.2.2. 3.2.2. 1.	The promise to explain
3.3.3. 2.2.2. 3.2.2. 2.	Showing the characteristics of the seven ḍākinīs

3.3.3. 2.2.2. 3.2.2. 3.	Showing their symbolic insignia
3.3.3. 2.2.2. 3.2.2. 4.	Showing the name of the chapter
[Chapter 18]	
3.3.3. 2.2.2. 3.2.3.	The classification of the ḍākinī clans
3.3.3. 2.2.2. 3.2.3. 1.	The promise to explain
3.3.3. 2.2.2. 3.2.3. 2.	The characteristics of each of the yoginī [clans]
3.3.3. 2.2.2. 3.2.3. 2.1.	Padmanarteśvara's clan
3.3.3. 2.2.2. 3.2.3. 2.2.	Heruka's clan
3.3.3. 2.2.2. 3.2.3. 2.3.	Vajravārāhī's clan
3.3.3. 2.2.2. 3.2.3. 2.4.	Khaṇḍarohā's clan
3.3.3. 2.2.2. 3.2.3. 2.5.	Heruka's clan
3.3.3. 2.2.2. 3.2.3. 2.6.	Vināyaka's clan
3.3.3. 2.2.2. 3.2.3. 3.	Summarizing the meaning of these
3.3.3. 2.2.2. 3.2.3. 4.	Showing the name of the chapter
[Chapter 19]	
3.3.3. 2.2.2. 3.2.4.	The classification of the lāmā clans
3.3.3. 2.2.2. 3.2.4. 1.	The promise to explain

3.3.3. 2.2.2. 3.2.4. 2.	Stating the characteristics of each of the lāma clans
3.3.3. 2.2.2. 3.2.4. 2.1.	Amitābha's clan
3.3.3. 2.2.2. 3.2.4. 2.2.	Ratnasambhava's clan
3.3.3. 2.2.2. 3.2.4. 2.3.	Akṣobhya's clan
3.3.3. 2.2.2. 3.2.4. 2.4.	Vairocana's clan
3.3.3. 2.2.2. 3.2.4. 2.5.	Amoghasiddhi's clan
3.3.3. 2.2.2. 3.2.4. 3.	Showing the name of the chapter
[Chapter 20]	
3.3.3. 2.2.2. 3.3.	The physical signs for generally recognizing the ḍākinī clans
3.3.3. 2.2.2. 3.3.1.	The hand seal signs
3.3.3. 2.2.2. 3.3.1. 1.	The promise to explain
3.3.3. 2.2.2. 3.3.1. 2.	The actual display of the signs
3.3.3. 2.2.2. 3.3.1. 3.	What should be done once the signs are displayed
3.3.3. 2.2.2. 3.3.1. 4.	The name of the chapter

[Chapter 21]	
3.3.3. 2.2.2. 3.3.2.	The signs characterized by the limbs
3.3.3. 2.2.2. 3.3.2. 1.	The promise to explain
3.3.3. 2.2.2. 3.3.2. 2.	The actual display of the signs
3.3.3. 2.2.2. 3.3.2. 3.	Showing the name of the chapter
[Chapter 22]	
3.3.3. 2.2.2. 3.3.3.	The characteristics of the distinctive gestures
3.3.3. 2.2.2. 3.3.3. 1.	The promise to explain
3.3.3. 2.2.2. 3.3.3. 2.	The actual display of the signs
3.3.3. 2.2.2. 3.3.3. 3.	Their summary
3.3.3. 2.2.2. 3.3.3. 4.	Showing the name of the chapter
[Chapter 23]	
3.3.3. 2.2.2. 3.4.	Things to know for ascertaining [the messenger's] devotion to oneself
3.3.3. 2.2.2. 3.4.1.	The promise to explain
3.3.3. 2.2.2. 3.4.2.	Worshipping for the sake of devotion
3.3.3. 2.2.2. 3.4.3.	Displaying the signs of devotion

3.3.3. 2.2.2. 3.4.4.	The drawn signs that should be known
3.3.3. 2.2.2. 3.4.5.	Showing the name of the chapter
[Chapter 24]	
3.3.3. 2.2.2. 3.5.	Verbal signs that are combinations of multiple syllables for generally recognizing the ḍākinīs
3.3.3. 2.2.2. 3.5.1.	The promise to explain
3.3.3. 2.2.2. 3.5.2.	The actual verbal signs that are combinations of multiple syllables
3.3.3. 2.2.2. 3.5.3.	Summarizing their meaning
3.3.3. 2.2.2. 3.5.4.	Showing the extraordinary distinguishing features of this Tantra
3.3.3. 2.2.2. 3.5.5.	Showing the name of the chapter
[VOLUME TWO]	
[Chapter 25]	
3.3.3. 2.2.2. 4.	Showing the root mantra, and the detailed explanation of the commitments to be protected
3.3.3. 2.2.2. 4.1.	The clear exposition of the root mantra
3.3.3. 2.2.2. 4.1.1.	The way in which the root mantra is made unclear

3.3.3. 2.2.2. 4.1.2.	The way in which the root mantra is clarified in this chapter
3.3.3. 2.2.2. 4.1.2. 1.	Explaining in terms of the interpretable meaning
3.3.3. 2.2.2. 4.1.2. 2.	Explaining in terms of the definitive meaning
3.3.3. 2.2.2. 4.1.2. 2.1.	The definitive meaning of the first set of eight
3.3.3. 2.2.2. 4.1.2. 2.2.	The definitive meaning of the latter set of eight
3.3.3. 2.2.2. 4.1.3.	Showing the name of the chapter
[Chapter 26]	
3.3.3. 2.2.2. 4.2.	Showing the eight commitments
3.3.3. 2.2.2. 4.2.1.	Demonstrating the greatness of the root mantra
3.3.3. 2.2.2. 4.2.2.	The bestowal of all powers through the worship of the messenger
3.3.3. 2.2.2. 4.2.3.	The procedures of the commitments and vows
3.3.3. 2.2.2. 4.2.3. 1.	The promise to explain
3.3.3. 2.2.2. 4.2.3. 2.	Heteropraxy together with worship
3.3.3. 2.2.2. 4.2.3. 3.	Showing each of the commitments

3.3.3. 2.2.2. 4.2.3. 4.	Their concise meaning
3.3.3. 2.2.2. 4.2.4.	The cause of delighting the messenger
3.3.3. 2.2.2. 4.2.5.	The procedure of examining the disciple
3.3.3. 2.2.2. 4.2.6.	Showing the name of the chapter
[Chapter 27]	
3.3.3. 2.2.2. 5.	The detailed exegesis of the conceptually elaborate practices
3.3.3. 2.2.2. 5.1.	The general arrangement of practices
3.3.3. 2.2.2. 5.2.	The conceptually elaborate practices shown by three chapters
3.3.3. 2.2.2. 5.2.1.	The practice of the observances together with the offerings and sacrificial cakes
3.3.3. 2.2.2. 5.2.1. 1.	The promise to explain
3.3.3. 2.2.2. 5.2.1. 2.	The actual explanation
3.3.3. 2.2.2. 5.2.1. 2.1.	The way of practicing the conduct and observances
3.3.3. 2.2.2. 5.2.1. 2.1.1.	Having sought the messenger, the way in which one conducts oneself toward her

3.3.3. 2.2.2. 5.2.1. 2.1.2.	How the rites and observances should be practiced
3.3.3. 2.2.2. 5.2.1. 2.1.2. 1.	How the rites should be practiced
3.3.3. 2.2.2. 5.2.1. 2.1.2. 2.	How the observances should be practiced
3.3.3. 2.2.2. 5.2.1. 2.1.3.	The worship of the purities, and its benefit
3.3.3. 2.2.2. 5.2.1. 2.1.3. 1	The worship of the purities
3.3.3. 2.2.2. 5.2.1 .2.1.3. 2	The benefit of doing thus
3.3.3. 2.2.2. 5.2.1. 2.2.	The sacrificial procedure
3.3.3. 2.2.2. 5.2.1. 3.	Showing the name of the chapter
[Chapter 28]	
3.3.3. 2.2.2. 5.2.2.	The procedure of the inner fire sacrifice together with one clan
3.3.3. 2.2.2. 5.2.2. 1.	The inner fire sacrifice, along with a section on what should and should not be done
3.3.3. 2.2.2. 5.2.2. 1.1.	The procedure of inner fire sacrifice
3.3.3. 2.2.2. 5.2.2. 1.2.	Showing the difference between appropriate and inappropriate actions
3.3.3. 2.2.2. 5.2.2. 2.	Heteropraxy and the one clan procedure

3.3.3. 2.2.2. 5.2.2. 2.1.	Heteropraxy
3.3.3. 2.2.2. 5.2.2. 2.2.	The one clan procedure
3.3.3. 2.2.2. 5.2.2. 3.	Showing other procedures of fire sacrifice
3.3.3. 2.2.2. 5.2.2. 4.	The one clan procedure together with its benefit
3.3.3. 2.2.2. 5.2.2. 5.	Showing the name of the chapter
[Chapter 29]	
3.3.3. 2.2.2. 5.2.3.	The characteristics of the messenger and procedures for the state of heat or power
3.3.3. 2.2.2. 5.2.3. 1.	The promise to explain
3.3.3. 2.2.2. 5.2.3. 2.	The actual explanation
3.3.3. 2.2.2. 5.2.3. 2.1.	The characteristics of the messenger
3.3.3. 2.2.2. 5.2.3. 2.2.	The procedure of power
3.3.3. 2.2.2. 5.2.3. 2.3.	Praise for Mahāyoga
3.3.3. 2.2.2. 5.2.3. 2.3.1.	The consequences of hating and rejecting Mahāyoga
3.3.3. 2.2.2. 5.2.3. 2.3.2.	The benefits of establishing oneself in Mahāyoga
3.3.3. 2.2.2. 5.2.3. 3.	Showing the name of the chapter

[Chapter 30]	
3.3.3. 2.2.2. 6.	Selecting the protective mantra that removes obstacles
3.3.3. 2.2.2. 6.1.	The promise to explain
3.3.3. 2.2.2. 6.2.	Explaining the promised import
3.3.3. 2.2.2. 6.2.1.	Performing ground cleansing, etc., and selecting the mantra
3.3.3. 2.2.2. 6.2.1. 1.	Assembling the basis on which the mantra is selected
3.3.3. 2.2.2. 6.2.1. 2.	Showing the yoga by which one selects
3.3.3. 2.2.2. 6.2.1. 3.	Placing the basis from which one selects
3.3.3. 2.2.2. 6.2.1. 4.	The actual method of mantra selection
3.3.3. 2.2.2. 6.2.1. 4.1.	Summary of mantra selection
3.3.3. 2.2.2. 6.2.1. 4.2.	The definitive meaning of the basis of selection and the summary
3.3.3. 2.2.2. 6.2.1. 4.3.	Detailed exegesis of mantra selection
3.3.3. 2.2.2. 6.2.1. 4.3.1.	Selecting the mantra's first line
3.3.3. 2.2.2. 6.2.1. 4.3.2.	Selecting the mantra's second line
3.3.3. 2.2.2. 6.2.1. 4.3.3.	Selecting the mantra's third line

3.3.3. 2.2.2. 6.2.1. 4.3.4.	Selecting the mantra's fourth line along with the first and final syllables
3.3.3. 2.2.2. 6.2.2.	The greatness of the selected [mantra] and its procedure
3.3.3. 2.2.2. 6.2.2. 1.	The mantra's greatness
3.3.3. 2.2.2. 6.2.2. 2.	The mantra's procedure
3.3.3. 2.2.2. 6.2.3.	Arranging the four mantras in a series and showing them
3.3.3. 2.2.2. 6.3.	Showing the name of the chapter
[Chapter 31]	
3.3.3. 2.2.2. 7.	The detailed exegesis of the food commitments
3.3.3. 2.2.2. 7.1.	The chapter on the procedure of the hand signs
3.3.3. 2.2.2. 7.1.1.	Explanation of the scope of engagement of heteropraxy
3.3.3. 2.2.2. 7.1.2.	Detailed exegesis of heteropraxy
3.3.3. 2.2.2. 7.1.2. 1.	Heteropraxy in general
3.3.3. 2.2.2. 7.1.2. 2.	Worship with the left hand in particular
3.3.3. 2.2.2. 7.1.3.	Acting to hide and disclose this method

3.3.3. 2.2.2. 7.1.4.	Showing the name of the chapter
[Chapter 32]	
3.3.3. 2.2.2. 7.2.	The chapter on the procedures of the achievement of the sacrificial victim and zombie, and the creation stage
3.3.3. 2.2.2. 7.2.1.	The promise to explain
3.3.3. 2.2.2. 7.2.2.	Explaining the promised import
3.3.3. 2.2.2. 7.2.2. 1.	The achievement of the sacrificial victim for the sake of fire sacrifice
3.3.3. 2.2.2. 7.2.2. 2.	The achievement of the zombie for the sake of great power
3.3.3. 2.2.2. 7.2.2. 3.	Showing the yoga of the creation stage that is essential for all of them
3.3.3. 2.2.2. 7.2.2. 3.1.	Creation of the habitat
3.3.3. 2.2.2. 7.2.2. 3.2.	Creation of the inhabitant deities
3.3.3. 2.2.2. 7.2.3.	Showing the name of the chapter
[Chapter 33]	
3.3.3. 2.2.2. 7.3.	The chapter on the secret and reverential worship

3.3.3. 2.2.2. 7.3.1.	The promise to explain
3.3.3. 2.2.2. 7.3.2.	Explaining the promised import
3.3.3. 2.2.2. 7.3.2. 1.	The reverential worship
3.3.3. 2.2.2. 7.3.2. 2.	The secret worship
3.3.3. 2.2.2. 7.3.2. 3.	The benefit of worship
3.3.3. 2.2.2. 7.3.3.	Showing the name of the chapter
[Chapter 34]	
3.3.3. 2.2.2. 8.	The detailed exegesis of the secret of the four [types of] worship
3.3.3. 2.2.2. 8.1.	The chapter that shows the great seal
3.3.3. 2.2.2. 8.1.1.	The promise to explain
3.3.3. 2.2.2. 8.1.2.	Explaining the promised import
3.3.3. 2.2.2. 8.1.2. 1.	Detailed exegesis of the import to be explained
3.3.3. 2.2.2. 8.1.2. 1.1.	Explaining in terms of the interpretable meaning
3.3.3. 2.2.2. 8.1.2. 1.2.	Explaining in terms of the definitive meaning

3.3.3. 2.2.2. 8.1.2. 1.2.1.	The explanation that occurs in the oral instructions of previous gurus
3.3.3. 2.2.2. 8.1.2. 1.2.2.	Kambala the Blanketed's explanation
3.3.3. 2.2.2. 8.1.2. 1.2.2. 1.	The explanation in terms of the yoga of the drop
3.3.3. 2.2.2. 8.1.2. 1.2.2. 2.	The explanation in terms of subtle yoga
3.3.3. 2.2.2. 8.1.2. 2.	Summary of the explained import
3.3.3. 2.2.2. 8.1.3.	Showing the name of the chapter
[Chapter 35]	
3.3.3. 2.2.2. 8.2.	The chapter that shows the reality seal
3.3.3. 2.2.2. 8.2.1.	The promise to explain
3.3.3. 2.2.2. 8.2.2.	Explaining the promised import
3.3.3. 2.2.2. 8.2.2. 1.	Explaining in terms of the interpretable meaning
3.3.3. 2.2.2. 8.2.2. 1.1.	The method of repeating [the mantra]
3.3.3. 2.2.2. 8.2.2. 1.2.	The method of achieving ritual actions with Khaṇḍarohā
3.3.3. 2.2.2. 8.2.2. 2.	Explaining in terms of the definitive meaning
3.3.3. 2.2.2. 8.2.3.	Showing the name of the chapter

[Chapter 36]	
3.3.3. 2.2.2. 8.3.	The chapter that shows both the symbolic and actual seals through a single approach
3.3.3. 2.2.2. 8.3.1.	The promise to explain
3.3.3. 2.2.2. 8.3.2.	Explaining the promised import
3.3.3. 2.2.2. 8.3.2. 1.	The worship of reality
3.3.3. 2.2.2. 8.3.2. 1.1.	Worship depending on the two [types of] seals
3.3.3. 2.2.2. 8.3.2. 1.2.	Explaining somewhat the classification of the four seals
3.3.3. 2.2.2. 8.3.2. 2.	The procedure for ritual success depending on that
3.3.3. 2.2.2. 8.3.3.	Showing the name of the chapter
[Chapter 37]	
3.3.3. 2.2.2. 8.4.	The chapter on subjugating the actual seal (consort)
3.3.3. 2.2.2. 8.4.1.	The promise to explain
3.3.3. 2.2.2. 8.4.2.	Explaining the promised import
3.3.3. 2.2.2. 8.4.2. 1.	Subjugating the victim relying upon food

3.3.3. 2.2.2. 8.4.2. 2.	Subjugating the victim relying upon fire sacrifice
3.3.3. 2.2.2. 8.4.2. 3.	Showing praise for the subjugation procedure
3.3.3. 2.2.2. 8.4.3.	Showing the name of the chapter
[Chapter 38]	
3.3.3. 2.2.2. 9.	The detailed exegesis the two remaining [modes of] conduct
3.3.3. 2.2.2. 9.1.	The promise to explain
3.3.3. 2.2.2. 9.2.	The promised import explained
3.3.3. 2.2.2. 9.2.1.	Showing the commitment to protect the performance of conduct, etc.
3.3.3. 2.2.2. 9.2.1. 1.	Showing the commitments that pertain to what the yogī should not do
3.3.3. 2.2.2. 9.2.1. 2.	Showing the commitments that pertain to what should be done
3.3.3. 2.2.2. 9.2.2.	Showing conduct performance together with the locations
3.3.3. 2.2.2. 9.3.	Showing the name of the chapter
[Chapter 39]	
3.3.3. 2.2.2. 10.	Examining the signs of the attainment of success

3.3.3. 2.2.2. 10.1.	The chapter on vision and "ha ha" laughter
3.3.3. 2.2.2. 10.1.1.	The promise to explain
3.3.3. 2.2.2. 10.1.2.	Explaining the promised import
3.3.3. 2.2.2. 10.1.2. 1.	The method of giving rise to vision through laughter
3.3.3. 2.2.2. 10.1.2. 2.	Showing the consequence of fear when [they] are seen
3.3.3. 2.2.2. 10.1.2. 3.	Showing the benefit of not being afraid when [they] are seen
3.3.3. 2.2.2. 10.1.3.	Showing the name of the chapter
[Chapter 40]	
3.3.3. 2.2.2. 10.2.	The chapter on subjugating the five classes, and serving the great seal
3.3.3. 2.2.2. 10.2.1.	The promise to explain
3.3.3. 2.2.2. 10.2.2.	Explaining the promised import
3.3.3. 2.2.2. 10.2.2. 1.	Outer and inner fire sacrifice
3.3.3. 2.2.2. 10.2.2. 2.	The number relative to each [type of] victim
3.3.3. 2.2.2. 10.2.2. 3.	The benefit of doing so

3.3.3. 2.2.2. 10.2.3.	Showing the name of the chapter
[Chapter 41]	
3.3.3. 2.2.2. 10.3.	The chapter on the placement of the mandala of twenty-four syllables
3.3.3. 2.2.2. 10.3.1.	The promise to explain
3.3.3. 2.2.2. 10.3.2.	Explaining the promised import
3.3.3. 2.2.2. 10.3.2. 1.	Classifying the ritual actions to be achieved
3.3.3. 2.2.2. 10.3.2. 2.	Showing the cause of their achievement
3.3.3. 2.2.2. 10.3.2. 2.1.	The concise exposition
3.3.3. 2.2.2. 10.3.2. 2.2.	The detailed exposition
3.3.3. 2.2.2. 10.3.2. 2.2.1.	Showing in detail the places with the ḍākinīs
3.3.3. 2.2.2. 10.3.2. 2.2.2.	Recognizing the chief among the places
3.3.3. 2.2.2. 10.3.2. 2.2.2. 1.	Showing the twenty-four places
3.3.3. 2.2.2. 10.3.2. 2.2.2. 2.	The way to engage with the blessings of the yoginīs there
3.3.3. 2.2.2. 10.3.2. 2.2.2. 3.	Those who are included with the yoginīs
3.3.3. 2.2.2. 10.3.2. 2.2.3.	Showing protection by means of meditation and worship

3.3.3. 2.2.2. 10.3.3.	Showing the name of the chapter
[Chapter 42]	
3.3.3. 2.2.2. 10.4.	The chapter on the laughter mantra and the cause of the ḍākinīs' forms
3.3.3. 2.2.2. 10.4.1.	The promise to explain
3.3.3. 2.2.2. 10.4.2.	The actual explanation
3.3.3. 2.2.2. 10.4.2. 1.	The first exegetical method
3.3.3. 2.2.2. 10.4.2. 1.1.	The method of laughter
3.3.3. 2.2.2. 10.4.2. 1.2.	The signs of laughter together with the remainder
3.3.3. 2.2.2. 10.4.2. 2.	The second exegetical method
3.3.3. 2.2.2. 10.4.3.	Showing the name of the chapter
[Chapter 43]	
3.3.3. 2.2.2. 11.	Showing other methods for the attainment of mundane powers
3.3.3. 2.2.2. 11.1.	Ritual success with the father's quintessence and armor [mantras]
3.3.3. 2.2.2. 11.1.1.	Success relying upon the father's quintessence

3.3.3. 2.2.2. 11.1.1. 1.	The promise to explain
3.3.3. 2.2.2. 11.1.1. 2.	The promised explanation of the meaning
3.3.3. 2.2.2. 11.1.1. 2.1.	Places in which they glance
3.3.3. 2.2.2. 11.1.1. 2.2.	Naked worship
3.3.3. 2.2.2. 11.1.1. 2.3.	The mantra that protects against obstacles
3.3.3. 2.2.2. 11.1.1. 2.4.	Ritual success relying on the attainment of mantric power
3.3.3. 2.2.2. 11.1.1. 2.4.1.	Methods for gaining particular mantric powers
3.3.3. 2.2.2. 11.1.1. 2.4.2.	Methods for success in rites relying upon them
3.3.3. 2.2.2. 11.1.1. 2.4.2. 1.	Ritual success in invisibility and tree summoning
3.3.3. 2.2.2. 11.1.1. 2.4.2. 2.	Ritual success in dream interpretation and the descent of the divinatory image
3.3.3. 2.2.2. 11.1.1. 2.4.2. 3.	Ritual success in the pacification of illness, etc.
3.3.3. 2.2.2. 11.1.1. 2.4.2. 3.1.	Pacifying illness relying upon mantra and a wheel

3.3.3. 2.2.2. 11.1.1. 2.4.2. 3.2.	Fire sacrifice for subjugation, along with the options
3.3.3. 2.2.2. 11.1.1. 2.4.2. 3.3.	Showing the different colors for the different ritual actions
3.3.3. 2.2.2. 11.1.1. 2.4.2. 3.4.	Methods for destroying poison, plague, etc.
3.3.3. 2.2.2. 11.1.1. 2.4.2. 3.5.	Victory in gambling and fighting, and additional matters
3.3.3. 2.2.2. 11.1.1. 2.5.	Techniques for achieving ritual power
3.3.3. 2.2.2. 11.1.1. 3.	Showing the name of the chapter
[Chapter 44]	
3.3.3. 2.2.2. 11.1.2.	Success relying upon his and the mother's armor
3.3.3. 2.2.2. 11.1.2. 1.	The promise to explain
3.3.3. 2.2.2. 11.1.2. 2.	The promised explanation of the meaning
3.3.3. 2.2.2. 11.1.2. 2.1.	The rite of summoning from the perspective of dominion
3.3.3. 2.2.2. 11.1.2. 2.1.1.	Summoning relying on a wheel
3.3.3. 2.2.2. 11.1.2. 2.1.2.	Summoning relying on fire sacrifice

3.3.3. 2.2.2. 11.1.2. 2.2.	The rite of suppression and subsequent release
3.3.3. 2.2.2. 11.1.2. 2.3.	The rite of maddening and subsequent release
3.3.3. 2.2.2. 11.1.2. 3.	Showing the name of the chapter
[Chapter 45]	
3.3.3. 2.2.2. 11.2.	Ritual success relying on the heroine's armor and five *ha* [syllables]
3.3.3. 2.2.2. 11.2.1.	Procedures for achieving the heroine's armor and the power of speech
3.3.3. 2.2.2. 11.2.1. 1.	The promise to explain
3.3.3. 2.2.2. 11.2.1. 2.	Explaining the promised import
3.3.3. 2.2.2. 11.2.1. 2.1.	The method for achieving the power of speech
3.3.3. 2.2.2. 11.2.1. 2.2.	Success in multiple rites of summoning relying on that
3.3.3. 2.2.2. 11.2.1. 2.2.1.	Summoning in reliance on binding the vulval seal
3.3.3. 2.2.2. 11.2.1. 2.2.2.	Summoning in reliance on fire sacrifice

3.3.3. 2.2.2. 11.2.1. 2.2.3.	Ritual success relying on the Oleander flower
3.3.3. 2.2.2. 11.2.1. 2.3.	Achieving the power of speech relying on other methods
3.3.3. 2.2.2. 11.2.1. 2.4.	Having obtained that, achieving many different rites with speech
3.3.3. 2.2.2. 11.2.1. 2.4.1.	Rites of summoning and destroying
3.3.3. 2.2.2. 11.2.1. 2.4.2.	Explaining the rite of summoning in particular
3.3.3. 2.2.2. 11.2.1. 3.	Showing the name of the chapter
[Chapter 46]	
3.3.3. 2.2.2. 11.2.2.	Ritual success relying on the five ha [syllables]
3.3.3. 2.2.2. 11.2.2. 1.	The promise to explain
3.3.3. 2.2.2. 11.2.2. 2.	Explaining the promised import
3.3.3. 2.2.2. 11.2.2. 2.1.	The rite of killing
3.3.3. 2.2.2. 11.2.2. 2.2.	The rite of shape changing
3.3.3. 2.2.2. 11.2.2. 2.3.	The rite of womb transference
3.3.3. 2.2.2. 11.2.2. 3.	Showing the name of the chapter

[Chapter 47]	
3.3.3. 2.2.2. 11.3.	Success with the *Buddhaḍākinī* mantra and continual performance of deity visualization
3.3.3. 2.2.2. 11.3.1.	Ritual success with the *Buddhaḍākinī* mantra
3.3.3. 2.2.2. 11.3.1. 1.	The promise to explain
3.3.3. 2.2.2. 11.3.1. 2.	Explaining the promised import
3.3.3. 2.2.2. 11.3.1. 2.1.	Success with rites of controlling and destroying
3.3.3. 2.2.2. 11.3.1. 2.2.	Success with the rite of transforming into another [state]
3.3.3. 2.2.2. 11.3.1. 2.2.1.	Transforming into another gender
3.3.3. 2.2.2. 11.3.1. 2.2.2.	Transforming into another life form
3.3.3. 2.2.2. 11.3.1. 2.2.3.	Transforming into another substance
3.3.3. 2.2.2. 11.3.1. 2.2.4.	Transforming into another mental state
3.3.3. 2.2.2. 11.3.1. 2.2.5.	Transforming into another form
3.3.3. 2.2.2. 11.3.1. 2.2.6.	Turning another man's wealth [into one's own]
3.3.3. 2.2.2. 11.3.1. 3.	Showing the name of the chapter

[Chapter 48]	
3.3.3. 2.2.2. 11.3.2.	Continual visualization of the heroes and yoginīs
3.3.3. 2.2.2. 11.3.2. 1.	The promise to explain
3.3.3. 2.2.2. 11.3.2. 2.	Explaining the promised import
3.3.3. 2.2.2. 11.3.2. 2.1.	The mantra that achieves rites, with its benefit
3.3.3. 2.2.2. 11.3.2. 2.2.	Visualizing the secret mandala
3.3.3. 2.2.2. 11.3.2. 2.2.1.	Visualizing the habitat
3.3.3. 2.2.2. 11.3.2. 2.2.2.	Visualizing the inhabitant deities
3.3.3. 2.2.2. 11.3.2. 2.3.	Summarizing the meaning
3.3.3. 2.2.2. 11.3.2. 3.	Showing the name of the chapter
[Chapter 49]	
3.3.3. 2.2.2. 11.4.	Detailed exposition of the examination of the one born seven times
3.3.3. 2.2.2. 11.4.1.	The promise to explain
3.3.3. 2.2.2. 11.4.2.	Explaining the promised import
3.3.3. 2.2.2. 11.4.2. 1.	Making an image of the sacrificial victim from rice powder

3.3.3. 2.2.2. 11.4.2. 2.	The rite of relying on one who has the characteristics of the supreme sacrificial victim
3.3.3. 2.2.2. 11.4.2. 2.1.	The promise to explain the two meanings
3.3.3. 2.2.2. 11.4.2. 2.2.	Showing the characteristics of the supreme sacrificial victim
3.3.3. 2.2.2. 11.4.2. 2.3.	Showing the ritual application relying on him
3.3.3. 2.2.2. 11.4.2. 2.3.1.	Success through the rite relying on the supreme sacrificial victim
3.3.3. 2.2.2. 11.4.2. 2.3.2.	Success through the rite relying on another sacrificial victim
3.3.3. 2.2.2. 11.4.2. 3.	Showing the supremacy of that ritual application
3.3.3. 2.2.2. 11.4.3.	Showing the name of the chapter
[Chapter 50]	
3.3.3. 2.2.2. 11.5.	Ritual success with the mother's essence mantra
3.3.3. 2.2.2. 11.5.1.	Explaining the fire sacrifice
3.3.3. 2.2.2. 11.5.1. 1.	The promise to explain
3.3.3. 2.2.2. 11.5.1. 2.	Explaining the promised import

3.3.3. 2.2.2. 11.5.1. 2.1.	The fire sacrifice for controlling
3.3.3. 2.2.2. 11.5.1. 2.2.	The violent fire sacrifices
3.3.3. 2.2.2. 11.5.1. 2.2.1.	The fire sacrifice for dividing
3.3.3. 2.2.2. 11.5.1. 2.2.2.	The fire sacrifices for killing and expelling
3.3.3. 2.2.2. 11.5.1. 2.3.	The method for continually pacifying obstacles
3.3.3. 2.2.2. 11.5.1. 2.4.	The fire sacrifice for enriching
3.3.3. 2.2.2. 11.5.1. 2.4.1.	Expanding wealth
3.3.3. 2.2.2. 11.5.1. 2.4.2.	Expanding power
3.3.3. 2.2.2. 11.5.1. 2.4.3.	Expanding dominion
3.3.3. 2.2.2. 11.5.1. 2.4.4.	Extending life
3.3.3. 2.2.2. 11.5.1. 2.5.	The fire sacrifice for paralyzing
3.3.3. 2.2.2. 11.5.1. 3.	Summarizing the meaning and showing the mantra that achieves the rites
3.3.3. 2.2.2. 11.5.2.	Explaining the ten seats, etc.
3.3.3. 2.2.2. 11.5.2. 1.	The promise to explain
3.3.3. 2.2.2. 11.5.2. 2.	Explaining the promised import

3.3.3. 2.2.2. 11.5.2. 2.1.	Showing the ten seats, etc.
3.3.3. 2.2.2. 11.5.2. 2.1.1.	The general meaning
3.3.3. 2.2.2. 11.5.2. 2.1.1. 1.	The way that the names of the grounds such as the Joyous are each stated
3.3.3. 2.2.2. 11.5.2. 2.1.1. 2.	Avoiding contradiction of stating [the grounds] out of harmony with the seats, etc.
3.3.3. 2.2.2. 11.5.2. 2.1.1. 3.	The types of disciples for whom they are stated
3.3.3. 2.2.2. 11.5.2. 2.1.2.	The auxiliary meanings
3.3.3. 2.2.2. 11.5.2. 2.2.	Showing that the ten seats, etc., are all pervading
3.3.3. 2.2.2. 11.5.3.	Summarizing the meaning
3.3.3. 2.2.2. 11.5.4.	Showing the name of the chapter
[Chapter 51]	
3.3.3. 2.3.	The chapter's summary of the previous [chapters]
3.3.3. 2.3.1.	The promise to explain
3.3.3. 2.3.2.	Explaining the promised import

3.3.3. 2.3.2. 1.	Showing the esoteric instruction for this Tantra that is very difficult to obtain
3.3.3. 2.3.2. 2.	Showing the fourteen realities that are the method for easily obtaining it
3.3.3. 2.3.2. 2.1.	Explaining the literal meaning of the fourteen realities
3.3.3. 2.3.2. 2.2.	The explanation applicable to the two stages
3.3.3. 2.3.2. 3.	The benefits of practice in the fourteen, and the fault of lacking faith
3.3.3. 2.3.2. 3.1.	The benefits of practice in the fourteen realities
3.3.3. 2.3.2. 3.1.1.	Showing in general the outer benefits of this
3.3.3. 2.3.2. 3.1.2.	Showing in particular the benefit that arises at the time of death
3.3.3. 2.3.2. 3.2.	The fault of lacking faith in this path
3.3.3. 2.3.2. 4.	The method of comprehensive meditation in the fourteen realities
3.3.3. 2.3.2. 5.	Showing the method for not forsaking any of the Buddha's scriptures
3.3.3. 2.3.3.	Showing the chapter count

[Colophon]	
3.3.4.	The meaning of the conclusion
3.3.4. 1.	How the text concluded
3.3.4. 2.	How [the text] was translated in Tibet

APPENDIX II

Sumatikīrti's Laghusaṁvaratantrapaṭalābhisandhi

Introduction

Here I have provided a complete translation of Sumatikīrti's *Laghusaṁvaratantrapaṭalābhisandhi*. As the title suggests, it presents a chapter outline of the root Tantra. It was composed in the eleventh century by Sumatikīrti, a disciple of Nāropā who played a pivotal role in the transmission of the *Cakrasaṁvara Tantra* to Tibet, and who was directly involved in the production of two of the three extant translations of this text.[1060] This text was translated by him and the Tibetan translator Drakchok Sherab.

Tsong Khapa was clearly very fond of this text. It is a concise outline of the CT, so quoting it in its entirety served a useful purpose. Tsong Khapa was likely also attracted to the prestige of Nāropā's lineage, as is indicated by his frequent invocation of Nāropā's exegetical system. As a direct disciple of Nāropā, Sumatikīrti was no mere scholar, but also occupied a premier spot in an extremely popular practice lineage. Moreover, Tsong Khapa's proper name, blo-bzang grags pa, is also the Tibetan translation of the Sanskrit name Sumatikīrti, so he may have felt a personal connection to this scholar as well.

This translation not only is complete and uninterrupted, it also differs somewhat from the translations of the passages quoted in Tsong Khapa's commentary. While Tsong Khapa's version of the text is generally quite close to that preserved in the Tengyur, there are some significant differences. In the translation embedded in Tsong Khapa's commentary above, I followed Tsong Khapa's text unless otherwise noted. Here I attempt to provide the overall best reading; however, when all other things are equal, I have privileged here the "best reading" that I have selected for my edition. All significant variants are discussed in the notes to the translation below.

[1060] Regarding Sumatikīrti and his involvement with the translation of the CT into Tibetan, see Gray 2012.

Translation

In Sanskrit: *Laghusaṁvaratantrapaṭalābhisandhi*
The Intended Import of the Chapters of the Concise Saṁvara Tantra

Homage to Śrī Vajraḍāka.

I will state the intended import of the *Laghusaṁvara Tantra*. First, all of the concise meanings with respect to the creation and perfection stages are summarized by the first chapter, stated in detail by the chapters from the second up to the fiftieth, and are brought together by the last chapter. This explanation, which is applied to the three parts of the *Laghu[saṁvara] Tantra*[1061] that was abridged by the Blessed Lord, is the intention of Nāropā.[1062] "Having conferred consecration, show reality to him."[1063] This means that in the esoteric Mahāyāna,[1064] first there is consecration bestowal. The mandala is the preliminary stage for this, thus the second chapter shows the mandala, while the third shows consecration bestowal. The fourth [chapter shows] the reality that is the aim of consecration conferral. Thus the three chapters explain [the meaning summarized by the lines in chapter one] from **And now... the secret** (**1.1a**) up until **Listen** (**1.5d**). This [indicates] the detailed exegesis of the

---

1061 Tsong Khapa here is referring to Sumatikīrti's division of the Root Tantra into three parts, i.e., chapter 1, chapters 2–50, and chapter 51.

1062 There are two alternate readings here. The Tengyur reads */bcom ldan 'das kyis bsdus pa'i rgyud chung ngu 'di'i kha sbyor gsum pa'i bshad pa 'di ni nā ro ta pa'i dgongs pa'o/*, while Tsong Khapa reads *bcom ldan 'das kyis gsungs pa'o/ /zhes rgyud chung ngu 'di gsum du sbyar ba'i bshad pa 'di ni nā ro pa'i dgongs pa'o/*. I generally follow the former, but I follow Tsong Khapa's reading *gsum du sbyar ba'i bshad pa*, as *kha sbyor gsum pa'i bshad pa* does not seem to make sense.

1063 Sumatikīrti appears here to be quoting CT ch. 1 here; however, there is no passage in this chapter in the extant versions of the text corresponding to his quote, *de la dbang bskur nas ni 'di nyid bstan*. Note, however, that Sachen quotes a close variant of this line, *de yang dbang bskur nas ni de nyid bstan* (PG 308.2) at the opening of his commentary on CT ch. 4. However, this line is not found in any extant version of the CT.

1064 This translates the Tengyur reading, *theg pa chen po gsang sngags*. Tsong Khapa reads "Mantrayāna," *theg pa gsang sngags*.

mandala that is visualized by means of the preliminary [visualizations] such as **the dried** [dung] **in a cattle pen (32.10cd)**, and so forth, which are thus stated [in the root text]. Since [this topic] is completed with this, it is not stated elsewhere than this [text]. Then, in commenting upon [the text] **is successful with mantra repetition and meditative states (1.10.ab)**, one must show the selection of the mantras that are to be repeated, which are set forth in a scrambled order in the four chapters from the fifth through the eighth and in the twenty-fifth and thirtieth [chapters]. You should understand that this is for the sake of preventing the repetition of the mantra [by someone who] lacks a master in the lineage. In this way, one should understand that the mundane powers are shown in the characteristics of the supreme and ordinary powers of repetition [that are described] from the ninth chapter until the end of the fourteenth, and from the forty-third until the fiftieth. By applying the three bodies to the above [descriptions],[1065] the supreme, supramundane success is revealed. In that way, the [chapters] from the fifteenth to the twenty-fourth explain **the messengers are natural and accomplished (1.7a)**, etc., in order to show here that the mundane and supramundane successes are based on the kindness of the yoginīs. So that one might understand the differentiation of the yoginīs,[1066] one should know the syllabic signs, the differentiation of the six classes, the enumeration of names, the characteristics of the ḍākinī clans and the lāma clans, the hand signs, the gazes, the body gestures, the signs and insignia, and the verbal signs. These ten particularities show the characteristics of the messengers in the ten chapters, respectively. After that, in order to fulfill the meaning of [statements] such as **...should always protect the commitments (1.10c)**, chapter twenty-six shows the commitments that are guarded so as to please the messenger whom one has recognized. Chapter twenty-seven shows the conduct (*spyod pa*, *caryā*) performed at the command of

[1065] I follow here Tsong Khapa's reading, *gong du sku gsum sbyar bas*. The Tengyur text reads "through consecration in which," *gang du dbang bskur nas*, but this makes somewhat less sense.

[1066] Tsong Khapa's text here reads "three [types] of yoginīs," *rnal 'byor ma gsum gyi*, but the Tengyur text reads simply *rnal 'byor ma'i*. The former reading makes sense in the context of CT 1.7a only, since the chapters in question differentiate more than three types of yoginī.

the pleased seal that one has achieved. [It also demonstrates] the contrived conducts that fulfill the import of characteristic [statements] such as **the state of being a yogī (1.9c)**. Chapters twenty-eight and twenty-nine show the performance of the contrived conduct. Then, as an explanation of [the text] **there are honey and vermilion,...with camphor (1.11c)**, etc., the three chapters from the thirty-first show the commitments of eating necessary for all [modes of] conduct. Furthermore, one should also know hand worship, the names of the distinctive substances, and the differentiation of the three types of food procedures. After that, the four chapters from the thirty-fourth onward are commentaries on **there are the four [types of] worship; thus the great hero (1.14ab)**, etc. One should investigate them in the order of the great seal (*mahāmudrā*), the reality seal (*dharmamudrā*), the actual seal (*karmamudrā*), and the subjugation of the actual seal.[1067] The symbolic seal (*samayamudrā*) is shown elsewhere[1068] as the characteristics of visualizing the wheel of the mandala. Therefore, here it is not very extensively discussed separately from them. Then the thirty-eighth extensively illustrates the uncontrived and extremely uncontrived conduct in order to fulfill the import of [statements] such as **the state of being a yogī**, etc. With respect to that, the signs of the powers common to the three yoginīs[1069] are taught from chapter thirty-nine to chapter forty-two. On the basis of what was shown in summary and in detail, the fifty-first chapter brings [these points] together.[1070] [This] is the guru's oral instruction.

1067 The text Tengyur texts read "the actual seal and the subjugation of the actual seal," *las kyi phyag rgya dang las kyi phyag rgya dbang du bya ba*, while Tsong Khapa reads simply "the subjugation of the actual seal," *las kyi phyag rgya dbang du bya ba*. The former reading makes more sense, since, as Tsong Khapa explains, the actual seal and her subjugation are explained in two different chapters, the thirty-sixth and thirty-seventh.

1068 Here I follow the Tengyur texts' *gzhan du* rather than Tsong Khapa's *bzhin du*.

1069 This translates the Tengyur texts' *rnal 'byor ma gsum*. Tsong Khapa reads *rnal 'byor gsum*.

1070 This translates the Tengyur texts' *de ltar mdo dang rgyas par bstan pa'i sgo nas le'u lnga bcu rtsa gcig tu bsdus nas bstan to*. Tsong Khapa reads *de ltar mdo dang rgyas par bstan pa'i don rnams kyi mtshan nyid le'u lnga bcu rtsa gcig pas gcig tu bsdus nas / bcom ldan 'das kyis bstan to*.

This completes the *Intended Import of the Concise Saṁvara Tantra*, composed in the presence of Śrī Nāropā's successor, the scholar Sumati-kīrti. It was translated by the Indian preceptor himself, and the translator-monk Drakchok Sherab.

Appendix III

Tibetan Names (Phonetic-Transliterated Equivalents)

Phonetic Rendition	**Wylie Transliteration**
Aday Chenpo	A-des-pa Chen-po
Akuching Sherab Gyatso	A-khu-ching Shes-rab-rgya-mtsho
Büton	Bu-ston
Chö Pelzangpo	Chos-dpal-bzang-po
Chogro Chökyi Gyaltsen	Cog-ro Chos-kyi-rgyal-mtshan
Chökyi Pelwa	Chos-kyi-dpal-ba
Cholay Namgyal	Phyogs-las-rnam-rgyal
Dechenpa (Chö Pelzangpo)	bDe-chen-pa (Chos-dpal-bzang-po)
Demchok Dorje	bDe-mchog-rdo-rje
Drakchok Sherab	Grags-mchog Shes-rab
Dro Lotsawa Sherab Drak (*See* Prajñākīrti)	'Bro Lo-tsā-ba Shes-rab-grags
Drogmi (Lotsawa)	'Brog-mi (Lo-tsā-wa)
Gampopa	sGam-po-pa
Gö Hlaytsay	'Gos Lhas-btsas
Hla Lama Yeshe Ö	Lha bLa-ma Ye-shes-'od
Hlodrak Namka Gyaltsen	Lho-brag Nam-mkha' rGyal-mtshan
Jigmay Lingpa	'Jigs-med gLing-pa
Kashipa Rinchen Pel	bKa'-bzhi-pa Rin-chen-dpal
Khön Könchok Gyalpo	'Khon dKon-mchog rGyal-po
Kunga Nyingpo (*See* Sachen [Kunga Nyingpo])	Kun-dga' sNying-po
Kyungpo (Lotsawa)	Khyung-po (Lo-tsā-wa)
Lochen (Rinchen Zangpo)	Lo-chen (Rin-chen bZang-po)

Phonetic Rendition	**Wylie Transliteration**
Lodrö Drakpa (*See* Malgyo [Lotsawa])	bLo-gros-grags-pa
Malgyo (Lotsawa)	Mal-gyo (Lo-tsā-ba)
Mardo (Lotsawa)	Mar-do (Lo-tsā-ba)
Marpa Chökyi Wangchuk (*See* Mar-do [Lotsawa])	Mar-pa Chos-kyi-dbang-phyug
Marpa Dopa (*See* Mardo [Lotsawa])	Mar-pa Do-pa
Marpa Hlodrakpa (Lotsawa)	Marpa Lho-brag-pa (Lo-tsā-wa)
Namka Wangchuk	Nam-mkha'-dbang-phyug
Ngok Lochung Legpay Sherab	rNgog-lo-chung legs-pa'i-shes-rab
Padma Karpo	Padma dKar-po
Pamting-pa	Pham-thing-pa
Phakpa Ö	'Phags-pa-'od
Pitong Hamdu	Phi-tong-haṁ-du
Rinchen Namgyal	Rin-chen-rnam-rgyal
Rinchen Zangpo (*See* Lochen)	Rin-chen bZang-po. *See* Lo-chen
Sachen (Kunga Nyingpo)	Sa-chen (Kun-dga' sNying-po)
Shönu Pel	gZhon-nu-dpal
Shönu Sönam	gZhon-nu-bsod-nams
Sönam Gyaltsen	bSod-nams-rgyal-mtshan
Tang Chungpa	Thang-chung-pa
Yeshe Zangpo	Ye-shes bZang-po
Yönten Gyatso (*See* Phakpa Ö)	Yon-tan rGya-mtsho
Zewa (blo-ldan)	gZe-ba (blo-ldan)

Glossaries

English-Sanskrit-Tibetan Glossary

English	**Sanskrit**	**Tibetan**
accomplished, achieved	siddha	grub pa
accomplishment, achievement	siddhi	dngos grub
action	kriyā	bya ba
adept	sādhaka	sgrub pa po
aerial state	khecarīpada	mkha' spyod gnas
		mkha' la 'gro ba'i gnas
affliction	kleśa	nyon mongs
ambrosia	amṛta	bdud rtsi
appendix	uttaratantra	rgyud phyi ma
armor	kavaca	go cha
art	upāya	thabs
asceticism	tapas	dka' thub
astral spirit	graha	gdon
auspicious	śubha	dge ba
awakening spirit	bodhicitta	byang chub sems
narrative preface	nidāna	gleng gzhi
barbarian	mleccha	kla klo
beast	paśu	phyugs
being	sattva	sems dpa'
beneficiary	sādhya	bsgrub bya
benefit, benefiting	anugraha	phen 'dogs
binding	saṁvara	sdom pa
birth place	yoni	skye gnas
Blessed Lady	bhagavatī	bcom ldan 'das ma
Blessed Lord	bhagavān	bcom ldan 'das
bliss	sukha	bde ba

English	Sanskrit	Tibetan
blood	rakta, rudhira	khrag
body	aṅga	lus
	kāya	sku, lus
	gātra, deha, mūrti, vigraha, śarīra	lus
body wheel	kāyacakra	sku kyi 'khor lo
cake	saṁkulikā	snum 'khur
celestial musician	gandharva	dri za
centaur	kinnara	mi'am ci
central channel	avadhūti	rtsa dbu ma
characteristic	lakṣaṇa	mtshan nyid
charnel ground	śmaśāna	dur khrod
chastity	brahmacārya	tshangs spyod
clan	kula	rigs
clanswoman	kulikā	rigs ldan
commitment	samaya	dam tshig
communal enjoyment body	sambhogakāya	longs spyod rdzogs pa'i sku
concentration	samādhi	ting nge 'dzin
conception, conceptualization	vikalpa	rnam par rtog pa
concretion	rocanā	gi wang
conduct	caryā	spyod pa
consecration	abhiṣeka	dbang bskur ba
countergesture	pratimudrā	phyag rgya'i lan
creation stage	utpattikrama	bskyed rim
cyclic existence	saṁsāra	'khor ba
dead person	preta	yi dags
death	mṛtyu	'chi ba
death	māra	bdud
demon	rākṣasa	srin po
demoness	rākṣasī	srin mo
destroying	nigraha	tshar gcod

English	Sanskrit	Tibetan
devil	māra	bdud
divinatory image	prasena	pra se na
divine consort		yum
divine couple		yab yum
disciple	śrāvaka	nyan thos
disposition	śīla	mos pa
dissatisfaction	duḥkha	sdug bsngal
distinguishing mark	lakṣaṇa	mtshan nyid
dryad	yakṣiṇī	gnod sbyin mo
emanation	nirmāṇa	sprul pa
enveloping	saṁpuṭa	kha sbyar ba
esoteric instruction	āmnāya	man ngag
essence	hṛdaya	snying po
experiential scope	gocara	spyod yul
experiential unity	ekarasa	ro gcig
explanatory Tantra	vyākhyātantra	bshad rgyud
Father Tantra		pha rgyud
fee	dakṣiṇā	yon
field	kṣetra	zhing
fierce one	khrodha	khro bo
fire sacrifice	homa	sbyin sreg
vase	kalaśa	bum pa
flight	khecaratvaṁ	nam mkhar rgyu
floating	khecara	mkha' spyod, mkha' la rgyu ba
flying	khecara	mkha' spyod, mkha' la rgyu ba
	khecarī	mkha' la spyod
fury fire	caṇḍālī	gtum mo
gesture	mudrā	phyag rgya
ghost	preta	yi dags

English	Sanskrit	Tibetan
goblin	pīśāca	sha za
gnosis	jñāna	ye shes
gnosis hero	jñānasattva	ye shes sems dpa’
great seal	mahāmudrā	phyag rgya chen po
great serpent	mahoraga	lto ’phye chen po
habitual propensity	vāsanā	bag chags
happiness	sukha	bde ba
heretic	tīrthika	mu stegs
hero	vīra	dpa’ bo
	sattva	sems dpa’
Heruka	heruka	he ru ka, khrag ’thung ba
heteropraxy	vāmācāra	g.yon pa’i kun spyod
inauspicious	aśubha	mi dge ba
insight	vipaśyanā	lhag mthong
insignia	mudrā	phyag rgya
intercourse	saṁpuṭa	kha sbyar ba
joy	ānanda	dga’ ba
joy of cessation	viramānanda	dga’ bral
khatvanga staff	khaṭvāṅga	kha ṭvāṁ ga
knowledge	jñāna	she pa
lady	yoṣit	btsun mo
left channel	lalanā	rtsa rkyang ma
life force	prāṇa	srog
limb	aṅga	yan lag
magical diagram	yantra	’khrul ’khor
manifestation body	nirmāṇakāya	sprul pa’i sku
means of achievement	sādhana	sgrub byed
means of achieving	sādhaka	sgrub byed
meditation, meditative state	dhyāna	bsam gtan
meeting place	melāpaka	’dus pa

English	**Sanskrit**	**Tibetan**
menstruating	puṣpavatī	me tog dang ldan pa
messenger	dūtī	pho nya mo
mind wheel	cittacakra	thugs kyi 'khor lo
Mother Tantra		ma rgyud
natural	sahaja	lhan cig skyes pa
natural joy	sahajānanda	lhan cig skyes pa'i dga' ba
nature	ātman	bdag nyid
	prakṛti	rang bzhin
net, network	jāla	dra ba
nonconceptual	nirvikalpa	rnam par mi rtog pa
nonconceptuality	nirvikalpatvam	mi rtog pa nyid
nondual	advaya	gnyis med
observance	vrata	brtul zhugs
obstacle demon	vināyaka	log 'dren
		rnam par log 'dren
omen	utpāta	ltas ngan
oral instruction	upadeśa	man ngag
origin of things	dharmodaya	chos 'byung ba
penis	liṅga	ling ga
perfected one	siddha	grub pa
perfection stage	niṣpannakrama	rdzogs rim
power	siddhi	dngos grub
	śaktika	nus pa
practice	caryā	spyod pa
procedure	vidhi	cho ga
quiescence	śamathā	zhi gnas
quintessence	upahṛdaya	nye snying
race	yoni	skye gnas
reality	tattva	de nyid
	dharmatā	chos nyid
red	rakta	dmar po

English	**Sanskrit**	**Tibetan**
reality body	dharmakāya	chos kyi sku
right channel	rasanā	rtsa ro ma
rite	vidhi	cho ga
ritual action	karma	las
	kriyā	bya ba
root Tantra	mūlatantra	rtsa rgyud
sacred knowledge	vidyā	rig pa
sacrificial cake	bali	gtor ma
sacrificial victim	paśu	phyugs
sea monster	makara	chu srin
seal	mudrā	phyag rgya
seal consort	mudrā	phyag rgya ma, phyag rgya mo
seat	pīṭha	gnas
secret	guhya, rahasya	gsang ba
seed syllable	bīja	sa bon
semen	śukra	khu ba
seminal fluid	retas	rdzas
sentient being	sattva	sems dpa'
serpent deity	nāga	klu
serpent	uraga	lto 'phye
	sarpa	sbrul
solitary buddhas	pratyekabuddha	rang rgyal ba
speech wheel	vākcakra	gsung gi 'khor lo
spell	vidyā	rig pa
spell consort	vidyā	rig ma
sphere of reality	dharmadhātu	chos kyi dbyings
spiritual discipline	sādhana	sgrub byed
strategy	upāya	thabs
subsidiary charnel ground	upaśmaśāna	nye ba'i dur khrod
subsidiary field	upakṣetra	nye ba'i zhing

English	Sanskrit	Tibetan
subsidiary meeting place	upamelāpaka	nye bar 'dus pa
subsidiary seat	upapīṭha	nye gnas
suffering	duḥkha	sdug bsngal
supreme bliss	saṁvara	bde mchog
supreme joy	paramānanda	mchog dga'
tantric feast	gaṇacakra	tshogs kyi 'khor lo
titan	asura, dānava	lha min
tree spirit	yakṣa	gnod sbyin
triple wheel	tricakra	'khor lo gsum
triple world	triloka, trailokya	'jig rten gsum
Unexcelled Yoga	*anuttarayoga	rnal 'byor bla med
unification	samāyoga	mnyam 'byor
union	yoga	rnal 'byor
	saṁyoga	yang dag 'byor
	saṁvara	sdom pa
universal monarch	cakravartin	'khor los sgyur ba
untimely death	apamṛtyu	dus min 'chi
uterine blood	rakta, rajas	khrag
vassal lord	sāmanta	rgyal phran
vermilion	rakta	dmar
victim	sādhya	bsgrub bya
victor	jina	rgyal ba
vow	saṁvara	sdom pa
vulva	yoni	skye gnas
	dharmodaya	chos 'byung ba
	bhaga	bha ga
war machine	yantra	'khrul 'khor
wisdom	prajñā	shes rab
wisdom consort	prajñā	shes rab ma
yogic posture	yantra	'khrul 'khor
zombie	vetāla	ro langs

Sanskrit-Tibetan-English Glossary

Sanskrit	Tibetan	English
aṅga	lus	body
	yan lag	limb
advaya	gnyis med	nondual
anugraha	phen 'dogs	benefit, benefiting
apamṛtyu	dus min 'chi	untimely death
abhiṣeka	dbang bskur ba	consecration
amṛta	bdud rtsi	ambrosia
avadhūti	rtsa dbu ma	central channel
aśubha	mi dge ba	inauspicious
asura	lha min	titan
ātman	bdag nyid	self, nature, oneself
ānanda	dga' ba	joy
āmnāya	man ngag	esoteric instruction
uttaratantra	rgyud phyi ma	appendix
utpattikrama	bskyed rim	creation stage
utpāta	ltas ngan	omen
upakṣetra	nye ba'i zhing	subsidiary field
upadeśa	man ngag	oral instruction
upapīṭha	nye gnas	subsidiary seat
upamelāpaka	nye bar 'dus pa	subsidiary meeting place
upaśmaśāna	nye ba'i dur khrod	subsidiary charnel ground
upahṛdaya	nye snying	quintessence
upāya	thabs	art, strategy
uraga	lto 'phye	serpent
ekarasa	ro gcig	experiential unity
karma	las	ritual action
kalaśa	bum pa	vase
kavaca	go cha	armor

Sanskrit	Tibetan	English
kaya	sku, lus	body
kāyacakra	sku kyi 'khor lo	body wheel
kinnara	mi'am ci	cfentaur
kula	rigs	clan
kulikā	rigs ldan	clanswoman
kriyā	bya ba	action, ritual action
kleśa	nyon mongs	affliction
kṣetra	zhing	field
khaṭvāṅga	kha ṭvāṁ ga	khatvanga staff
khecara	mkha' spyod, mkha' la rgyu ba	flying, floating
khecaratvaṁ	nam mkhar rgyu	flight
khecarī	mkha' la spyod	flying
khecarīpada	mkha' spyod gnas, mkha' la 'gro ba'i gnas	aerial state
khrodha	khro bo	fierce one
gaṇacakra	tshogs kyi 'khor lo	tantric feast
gandharva	dri za	celestial musician
gātra	lus	body
guhya	gsang ba	secret
gocara	spyod yul	experiential scope
graha	gdon	astral spirit
cakravartin	'khor los sgyur ba	universal monarch
cakrasaṁvara	'khor lo sdom pa	
caṇḍālī	gtum mo	fury fire
caryā	spyod pa	conduct, practice
cittacakra	thugs kyi 'khor lo	mind wheel
jāla	dra ba	net, network
jina	rgyal ba	victor
jñāna	ye shes	gnosis
	shes pa	knowledge

Sanskrit	Tibetan	English
jñānasattva	ye shes sems dpa'	gnosis hero
tattva	de nyid	reality
tapas	dka' thub	asceticism
tricakra	'khor lo gsum	triple wheel
triloka, trailokya	'jig rten gsum	triple world
ḍākinī	mkha' 'gro ma, phra men ma	
dakṣiṇā	yon	fee
dānava	lha min	titan
duḥkha	sdug bsngal	dissatisfaction, suffering
dūtī	pho nya mo	messenger
deha	lus	body
dharmakāya	chos kyi sku	reality body
dharmatā	chos nyid	reality
dharmadhātu	chos kyi dbyings	sphere of reality
dharmodaya	chos 'byung ba	origin of things, vulva
dhyāna	bsam gtan	meditation, meditative state
nāga	klu	serpent deity
nigraha	tshar gcod	destroying
nidāna	gleng gzhi	narrative preface
nirmāṇa	sprul pa	emanation
nirmāṇakāya	sprul pa'i sku	manifestation body
nirvikalpa	rnam par mi rtog pa	nonconceptual
nirvikalpatvam	mi rtog pa nyid	nonconceptuality
niṣpannakrama	rdzogs rim	perfection stage
paramānanda	mchog dga'	supreme joy
paśu	phyugs	beast, sacrificial victim
pīṭha	gnas	seat
pīśāca	sha za	goblin
puṣpavatī	me tog dang ldan pa	menstruating
prakṛti	rang bzhin	nature

Sanskrit	**Tibetan**	**English**
prajñā	shes rab, shes rab ma	wisdom, wisdom consort
pratimudrā	phyag rgya'i lan	countergesture
prasena	pra se na	divinatory image
prāṇa	srog	life force
preta	yi dags	ghost, dead person
bali	gtor ma	sacrificial cake
bīja	sa bon	seed syllable
bodhicitta	byang chub sems	awakening spirit
brahmacārya	tshangs spyod	chastity
bhaga	bha ga	vulva
bhagavatī	bcom ldan 'das ma	Blessed Lady
bhagavān	bcom ldan 'das	Blessed Lord
makara	chu srin	sea monster
mahāmudrā	phyag rgya chen po	great seal
mahoraga	lto 'phye chen po	great serpent
māra	bdud	devil, death
mudrā	phyag rgya, phyag rgya ma, phyag rgya mo	seal, seal consort, gesture, insignia
mūrti	lus	body
mūlatantra	rtsa rgyud	root Tantra
mṛtyu	'chi ba	death
melāpaka	'dus pa	meeting place
mleccha	kla klo	barbarian
yakṣa	gnod sbyin	tree spirit
yakṣiṇī	gnod sbyin mo	dryad
yantra	'khrul 'khor	magical diagram, yogic posture, war machine
yoga	rnal 'byor	union
yogin	rnal 'byor pa	
yoginī	rnal 'byor ma	

Sanskrit	**Tibetan**	**English**
yoni	skye gnas	vulva, birth place, race
yoṣit	btsun mo	lady
rakta	dmar, dmar po, khrag	red, vermilion, blood, uterine blood
rajas	khrag	uterine blood
rasanā	rtsa ro ma	right channel
rahasya	gsang ba	secret
rākṣasa	srin po	demon
rākṣasī	srin mo	demoness
rudhira	khrag	blood
retas	seminal fluid	rdzas
rocanā	gi wang	concretion
lakṣaṇa	mtshan nyid	characteristic, distinguishing mark
lalanā	rtsa rkyang ma	left channel
liṅga	ling ga	penis
vākcakra	gsung gi 'khor lo	speech wheel
vāmācāra	g.yon pa'i kun spyod	heteropraxy
vāsanā	bag chags	habitual propensity
vikalpa	rnam par rtog pa	conception, conceptualization
vigraha	lus	body
vidyā	rig pa, rig ma	spell, sacred knowledge, consort
vidhi	cho ga	procedure, rite
vināyaka	log 'dren, rnam par log 'dren	obstacle demon
vipaśyanā	lhag mthong	insight
viramānanda	dga' bral	joy of cessation
vīra	dpa' bo	hero
vetāla	ro langs	zombie
vyākhyātantra	bshad rgyud	explanatory Tantra

Sanskrit	**Tibetan**	**English**
vrata	brtul zhugs	observance
śaktika	nus pa	power
śamathā	zhi gnas	quiescence
śarīra	lus	body
śīla	mos pa	disposition
śukra	khu ba	semen
śubha	dge ba	auspicious
śmaśāna	dur khrod	charnel ground
śrāvaka	nyan thos	disciple
sattva	sems dpa'	(sentient) being, hero
samaya	dam tshig	commitment
samādhi	ting nge 'dzin	concentration
samāyoga	mnyam 'byor	unification
saṁkalpa	rnam par rtog pa	conception, conceptualization
saṁkulikā	snum 'khur	cake
saṁpuṭa	kha sbyar ba	enveloping, intercourse
saṁyoga	yang dag 'byor	union
saṁvara	sdom pa	binding, sanctuary, vow, union
	bde mchog	supreme bliss
saṁsāra	'khor ba	cyclic existence
sarpa	sbrul	serpent
sahaja	lhan cig skyes pa	natural
sahajānanda	lhan cig skyes pa'i dga' ba	natural joy
sādhaka	sgrub pa po	adept
	sgrub byed	means of achieving
sādhana	sgrub byed	means of achievement, spiritual discipline
sādhya	bsgrub bya	victim, beneficiary
sāmanta	rgyal phran	vassal lord

Sanskrit	**Tibetan**	**English**
siddha	grub pa	accomplished, achieved, perfected one
siddhi	dngos grub	power, accomplishment, achievement
sukha	bde ba	bliss, happiness
hṛdaya	snying po	essence
heruka	he ru ka, khrag 'thung ba	Heruka
homa	sbyin sreg	fire sacrifice

Tibetan-Sanskrit-English Glossary

Tibetan	Sanskrit	English
kla klo	mleccha	barbarian
klu	nāga	serpent deity
dka' thub	tapas	asceticism
sku	kaya	body
skye gnas	yoni	vulva, birth place, race
bskyed rim	utpattikrama	creation stage
kha ṭvāṁ ga	khaṭvāṅga	khatvanga staff
kha sbyar ba	saṁpuṭa	enveloping, intercourse
khu ba	śukra	semen
khrag	rakta	blood, uterine blood
	rajas	uterine blood
	rudhira	blood
khro bo	khrodha	fierce one
mkha' 'gro ma	ḍākinī	
mkha' spyod	khecara	flying, floating
mkha' spyod gnas, mkha' la 'gro ba'i gnas	khecarīpada	aerial state
mkha' la rgyu ba	khecara	flying, floating
'khor ba	saṁsāra	cyclic existence
'khor lo sdom pa	cakrasaṁvara	"binding of the wheels"
'khor lo gsum	tricakra	triple wheel
'khor los sgyur ba	cakravartin	universal monarch
'khrul 'khor	yantra	magical diagram, yogic posture, war machine
gi wang	rocanā	concretion
go cha	kavaca	armor
grub pa	siddha	accomplished, achieved, perfected one
gleng gzhi	nidāna	narrative preface

Tibetan	Sanskrit	English
dga' ba	ānanda	joy
dga' bral	viramānanda	joy of cessation
dge ba	śubha	auspicious
rgyal phran	sāmanta	vassal lord
rgyal ba	jina	victor
rgyud phyi ma	uttaratantra	appendix
sgrub pa po	sādhaka	adept
sgrub byed	sādhaka	means of achieving
	sādhana	means of achievement
bsgrub bya	sādhya	victim, beneficiary
dngos grub	siddhi	accomplishment, achievement, power
bcom ldan 'das	bhagavān	Blessed Lord
bcom ldan 'das ma	bhagavatī	Blessed Lady
chu srin	makara	sea monster
cho ga	vidhi	procedure, rite
chos kyi dbyings	dharmadhātu	sphere of reality
chos kyi sku	dharmakāya	reality body
chos nyid	dharmatā	reality
chos 'byung ba	dharmodaya	origin of things, vulva
mchog dga'	paramānanda	supreme joy
'chi ba	mṛtyu	death
'jig rten gsum	triloka, trailokya	triple world
nyan thos	śrāvaka	disciple
nye snying	upahṛdaya	quintessence
nye gnas	upapīṭha	subsidiary seat
nye ba'i dur khrod	upaśmaśāna	subsidiary charnel ground
nye ba'i zhing	upakṣetra	subsidiary field
nye bar 'dus pa	upamelāpaka	subsidiary meeting place
nyon mongs	kleśa	affliction
gnyis med	advaya	nondual

Tibetan	**Sanskrit**	**English**
mnyam 'byor	samāyoga	unification
snying po	hṛdaya	essence
ting nge 'dzin	samādhi	concentration
gtum mo	caṇḍālī	fury fire
gtor ma	bali	sacrificial cake
ltas ngan	utpāta	omen
lto 'phye	uraga	serpent
lto 'phye chen po	mahoraga	great serpent
brtul zhugs	vrata	observance
thabs	upāya	art, strategy
thugs kyi 'khor lo	cittacakra	mind wheel
dam tshig	samaya	commitment
dur khrod	śmaśāna	charnel ground
dus min 'chi	apamṛtyu	untimely death
de nyid	tattva	reality
dra ba	jāla	net, network
dri za	gandharva	celestial musician
gdon	graha	astral spirit
bdag nyid	ātman	self, nature, oneself
bdud	māra	devil, death
bdud rtsi	amṛta	ambrosia
bde mchog	saṁvara	supreme bliss
bde ba	sukha	bliss, happiness
'dus pa	melāpaka	meeting place
sdug bsngal	duḥkha	dissatisfaction, suffering
sdom pa	saṁvara	binding, sanctuary, vow, union
nam mkhar rgyu	khecaratvaṁ	flight
nus pa	śaktika	power
gnas	pīṭha	seat
gnod sbyin	yakṣa	tree spirit
gnod sbyin mo	yakṣiṇī	dryad

Tibetan	**Sanskrit**	**English**
rnam par rtog pa	vikalpa, saṁkalpa	conception, conceptualization
rnam par mi rtog pa	nirvikalpa	nonconceptual
rnam par log 'dren	vināyaka	obstacle demon
rnal 'byor	yoga	union
rnal 'byor pa	yogin	
rnal 'byor bla med	*anuttarayoga	Unexcelled Yoga
rnal 'byor ma	yoginī	
snum 'khur	saṁkulikā	cake
pra se na	prasena	divinatory image
dpa' bo	vīra	hero
spyod pa	caryā	conduct
spyod yul	gocara	experiential scope
sprul pa	nirmāṇa	emanation
sprul pa'i sku	nirmāṇakāya	manifestation body
pha rgyud		Father Tantra
phen 'dogs	anugraha	benefit, benefiting
pho nya mo	dūtī	messenger
phyag rgya	mudrā	seal, insignia, gesture
phyag rgya ma	mudrā	seal consort
phyag rgya mo	mudrā	seal consort
phyag rgya chen po	mahāmudrā	great seal
phyag rgya'i lan	pratimudrā	countergesture
phyugs	paśu	beast, sacrificial victim
phra men ma	ḍākinī	
bag chags	vāsanā	habitual propensity
bum pa	kalaśa	vase
byang chub sems	bodhicitta	awakening spirit
dbang bskur ba	abhiṣeka	consecration
sbyin sreg	homa	fire sacrifice
sbrul	sarpa	serpent
bha ga	bhaga	vulva

Tibetan	Sanskrit	English
ma rgyud		Mother Tantra
man ngag	upadeśa	oral instruction
	āmnāya	esoteric instruction
mi dge ba	aśubha	inauspicious
mi rtog pa nyid	nirvikalpatvam	nonconceptuality
mi'am ci	kinnara	centaur
mu stegs	tīrthika	heretic
me tog dang ldan pa	puṣpavatī	menstruating
mos pa	śīla	disposition
dmar	rakta	vermilion
dmar po	rakta	red
btsun mo	yoṣit	lady
rtsa rkyang ma	lalanā	left channel
rtsa rgyud	mūlatantra	root Tantra
rtsa dbu ma	avadhūti	central channel
rtsa ro ma	rasanā	right channel
tshangs spyod	brahmacārya	chastity
tshar gcod	nigraha	destroying
tshogs kyi 'khor lo	gaṇacakra	tantric feast
mtshan nyid	lakṣaṇa	characteristic, distinguishing mark
rdzas	retas	seminal fluid
rdzogs rim	niṣpannakrama	perfection stage
zhi gnas	śamathā	quiescence
zhing	kṣetra	field
yan lag	aṅga	limb
yang dag 'byor	saṁyoga	union
yab yum		divine couple
yi dags	preta	ghost, dead person
yum		divine consort
ye shes	jñāna	gnosis
ye shes sems dpa'	jñānasattva	gnosis hero

Tibetan	**Sanskrit**	**English**
yon	dakṣiṇā	fee
rang bzhin	prakṛti	nature
rig pa	vidyā	spell, sacred knowledge
rig ma	vidyā	spell consort
rigs	kula	clan
rigs ldan	kulikā	clanswoman
ro gcig	ekarasa	experiential unity
ro langs	vetāla	zombie
las	karma	ritual action
ling ga	liṅga	penis
lus	aṅga, kāya, gātra, deha, mūrti, vigraha, śarīra	body
log 'dren	vināyaka	obstacle demon
sha za	pīśāca	goblin
shes pa	jñāna	knowledge
shes rab	prajñā	wisdom
shes rab ma	prajñā	wisdom consort
bshad rgyud	vyākhyātantra	explanatory Tantra
sa bon	bīja	seed syllable
sems dpa'	sattva	(sentient) being, hero
srin po	rākṣasa	demon
srin mo	rākṣasī	demoness
srog	prāṇa	life force
gsang ba	guhya, rahasya	secret
gsung gi 'khor lo	vākcakra	speech wheel
bsam gtan	dhyāna	meditation, meditative state
lha min	asura, dānava	titan
lhag mthong	vipaśyanā	insight
lhan cig skyes pa	sahaja	natural
lhan cig skyes pa'i dga' ba	sahajānanda	natural joy

Selected Bibliographies

Indian and Tibetan Texts

Abhayākaragupta. *Āmnāyamañjarī*. *Śrīsaṁpuṭatantrarājaṭīkāmnāya-mañjarī-nāma* (AM). To. 1198, D rgyud 'grel vol. cha, 1b–316a.

Advayavajra. *Pañcatathāgatamudrāvivaraṇa*. (To. 2242.) Sanskrit edited in Shastri 1927, 23–27.

Abhidhānottara Tantra

(AU) To. 369, D rgyud 'bum vol. ka, 247a–370a.

(H) Institute for Advanced Studies of World Religions (Carmel, NY) microfiche no. MBB-I-100. Incomplete; consisted of a total 194 folia, 6 of which are missing. Written on palm leaves in Bhujimol script by the scribe Paramānanda. Dated N. S. 258, 1138 CE.

(I) Institute for Advanced Studies of World Religions (Carmel, NY) microfiche no. MBB-I-26. Consists of 92 folia on Nepali paper in Nevārī script. Dated N. S. 863, 1743 CE.

(J) A late ms. of 160 folia in Devanāgarī on Nepali paper, reproduced in Lokesh Chandra, ed. *Abhidhānottara-Tantra: A Sanskrit Manuscript from Nepal*. Śata-piṭaka series vol. 263. New Delhi: Sharada Rani, 1981.

Alaṁkakalaśa. *Śrīvajramālāmahāyogatantraṭīkā-gambhīrārthadīpikā-nāma*. To. 1795, D rgyud 'grel vol. gi, 1b–220a.

Āryadeva. *Śrīcatuṣpīṭhatantrarāja-maṇḍalavidhisārasamuccaya*. To. 1613, D rgyud 'grel vol. ya, 113a–138a.

Atiśa Dīpaṅkaraśrījñāna. *Abhisamayavibhaṅga* (AV). To. 1490, D rgyud 'grel vol zha 186a–202b.

Bhavabhaṭṭa. *Cakrasaṁvaravivṛtti* (CV). To. 1403, D rgyud 'grel vol. ba, 141a–246b. Sanskrit and Tibetan edited in Pandey 2002.

———. *Śrīvajradāki-nāma-mahātantrarājasya vivṛtti* (VV). To. 1415, D rgyud 'grel vol. tsha, 1–208b.

Bhavyakīrti. *Śrīcakrasaṁvarapañjikā Śūramanojñā-nāma* (BC). To. 1405, D rgyud 'grel vol. ma, 1–41a.

Buddhaśrījñānapāda. *Dvikramatattvabhāvana-nāma-mukhāgama*. To. 1853, D rgyud 'bum vol. di, 1b–17b.

Bu-ston Rin-chen-grub. *rgyud sde spyi'i rnam par gzhag pa rgyud sde rin po che'i mdzes rgyan zhes bya ba* (RP). In *The Collected Works of Bu-ston*, ed. Lokesh Chandra. New Delhi: International Academy of Indian Culture, 1966, vol. ba, pp. 1–610.

———. *bde mchog rtsa rgyud kyi rnam bshad gsang ba'i de kho na nyid gsal bar byed pa* (NS). In *The Collected Works of Bu-ston*, ed. Lokesh Chandra. New Delhi: International Academy of Indian Culture, 1966. vol. cha, pp.141–718.

Cakrasaṁvara Tantra (CT). Sanskrit and Tibetan edited in Gray 2012.

Caturyoginīsaṁpuṭatantra. To. 376, D rgyud 'bum vol. ga, 44b–52b.

*Candrakumara. (zla-ba gzhon-nu). *Śrīherukābhyudaya-mahāyoginitantrarāja-katipayākṣarapañjikā*. To. 1421, D rgyud 'grel vol. wa, 101b–120a.

Ḍākārṇava-mahāyoginītantrarāja (DA). To. 372, D rgyud-'bum, vol. kha, 137a–264b.

Ḍākinīvajrapañjara. *Āryaḍākinīvajrapañjara-mahātantrarājakalpa* (DV). To. 419, D rgyud 'bum vol. nga, 30a–65b.

Dārika. *Śrīcakrasaṁvarasādhanatattvasaṁgraha*. To. 1429, D rgyud 'grel vol. wa, 197b–203b.

Devagupta. *Śrīcakrasaṁvara-sarvasādhana-sanna-nāma-ṭīkā* (SS). To. 1407, D vol. ma, 69a–156b.

Durjayacandra. *Ratnagaṇa-nāma-pañjikā* (RG). To. 1404, D rgyud 'grel vol. ba, 246b–315a.

Ghaṇṭapā. See Vajraghaṇṭa.

Guhyasamāja Tantra. *Sarvatathāgatakāyavākcittarahasya-guhyasamāja-nāma-mahākalparāja*. To. 442, 443. D rgyud 'bum vol. ca, 90a–157b. Sanskrit edited in Matsunaga 1978.

Herukābhyudaya (HA). To. 374, D rgyud 'bum vol. ga, 1b–33b.

Hevajra-tantrarājā. To. 417, D rgyud 'bum vol. nga, 1b–30a. Sanskrit and Tibetan edited in Snellgrove 1959.

Indrabhūti. *Śrīcakrasaṁvaratantrarāja-saṁvarasamuccaya-nāma-vṛtti* (IC). To. 1413, D rgyud 'grel vol. tsa, 1a–119b.

———. *Śrīsaṁpuṭatilaka-nāma-yoginī-tantrarājā-ṭīkā-saṁdarśanāloka-nāma*. To. 1197, D rgyud 'grel vol. ca, 94b–313a.

Jayabhadra. *Cakrasaṁvarapañjikā* (CP). To. 1406, D rgyud 'grel vol. ma, 41a–69a. Sanskrit edited in Sugiki 2001.

Kambala. *Śrīcakrasaṁvaramaṇḍalopāyikā-ratnapradīpodyota*. To. 1444, D rgyud 'grel vol. wa, 251a–272b.

———. *Sādhananidhi-śrīcakrasaṁvara-nāma-pañjikā*

(K) National Archives of Nepal, ms. no. 4-122, *bauddhatantra* 87. Mf. B31/20, Moriguchi #610. This work consists of 73 palm leaf folia, in Newārī script. No date. Note that it is catalogued under the title *Herukāvidhāna*.

(SN) To. 1401, D rgyud 'grel vol. ba, 1b–78a; PTT. 2118, vol. 48, pp. 173.5–207.5.

Kambalāmbara. *Śrīcakrasaṁvarābhisamayaṭīkā*. PTT. 4661, vol. 82, pp. 90.1–98.1.

Kāṇha. *Ālicatuṣṭaya* (AC). To. 1451, D rgyud 'grel vol. wa, 355b–358b.

———. *Ālicatuṣṭaya-vibhaṅga*. To. 1452, D rgyud 'grel vol. wa, 358b–367b; PTT. 2168, vol. 51, pp. 228.3–229.5.

———. *Guhyatattvaprakāśa*. To. 1450, D rgyud 'grel vol. wa, 349a–355b; PTT. 2167, vol. 51, 224.4–228.1.

———. *Vasantatilakā-nāma*. To. 1448, D rgyud 'grel vol. wa, 298b–306b; PTT. 2166, vol. 51, starting p. 220.5; Sanskrit and Tibetan edited in Samdhong and Dwivedi 1990.

———. *Śrīcakrasaṁvarasādhana*. To. 1445, D rgyud 'grel vol. wa, 272b–276b.

Khyāvajravārāhī-abhidhāna-tantrottara-vārāhyabhibodhi (KV). To. 377, D rgyud 'bum vol. ga, 52b–60a.

Lūipa. *Śrībhagavad-abhisamaya*. To. 1427, D rgyud 'grel vol. wa, 186b–193a.

Mahāmudrātilaka. *Śrīmahāmudrātilakaṁ-nāma-mahāyoginī-tantrarāja-adhipati*. To. 420, D rgyud-'bum, vol. nga, 66a–90b.

Mahātantrarāja-śrīsaṁpuṭatilaka-nāma. To. 382, D rgyud 'bum vol. ga, 158b–184a; PTT. 27, vol. 2, 280.2–290.1.

Nāgabodhi. *Śrīguhyasamājamaṇḍalaviṁśatividhi*. To. 1810, D rgyud 'grel vol. ngi, 131a–145b.

———. *Samājasādhanavyavasthāna*. PTT. 2674, Q vol. 62, pp. 7.3–12.1.

Padmavajra. *Śrīḍākārṇavamahāyoginī-tantrarāja-vāhikaṭīkā*. To. 1419, D rgyud 'grel vol. dza, 1b–318a.

Puṇḍarīka. *Vimalaprabhā-nāma-mūlatantrānusāriṇīdvādaśasāhasrikā-laghukālacakra-tantrarāja-ṭīkā*. To. 1347, D rgyud 'grel vol. tha, 107b–277a.

Prajñārakṣita. *Śrī-abhisamaya-nāma-pañjikā*. To. 1465, D rgyud 'grel vol. zha, 34a–45b.

Sa-chen Kun-dga' sNying-po. *dpal 'khor lo bde mchog gi rtsa ba'i rgyud kyi ṭīka mu tig phreng ba* (PG). In *The Complete Works of the Great Masters of the Sa Skya Sect of the Tibetan Buddhism. Vol. 1. The Complete Works of Kun dga' snying po*. bSod nams rgya mtsho, compiler. Tokyo: The Toyo Bunko, 1968, 288.3–380.3.

Saṁpuṭa Tantra

(ST) To. 381, D rgyud ’bum vol. ga, 73b–158b; PTT. 26, vol. 2, pp. 245.5–280.1.

(L) Microfiche scan of Sanskrit manuscript; Institute for Advanced Studies of World Religions (Carmel, NY) microfiche no. MBB-I-17.

Sanskrit partially edited in Skorupski 1996 and Sugiki 2003.

Saṁvarodaya Tantra (SU). To. 373, D rgyud ’bum vol. kha, 265a–311a. Sanskrit and Tibetan partially edited in Tsuda 1974.

Sarvabuddha-samāyoga-ḍākinījālasamvara-nāma-uttaratantra (JS). To. 366, D rgyud ’bum vol. ka, 151a–193a.

*Śāśvatavajra (rtag-pa’i rdo-rje). *Śrītattvaviśada-nāma-śrīsaṁvaravṛtti* (TV). To. 1410, D rgyud ’grel vol. ma, 253a–352a.

Subāhuparipṛcchā-tantra. To. 805. D rgyud ’bum vol. wa, 118a–140b; 蘇婆呼童子請問經, translated by Śubhakarasiṁha. T.895.18.719a–746b.

Śubhakarasiṁha and Yi-xing (一行). 大毘盧遮那成佛經疏。(*Mahāvairocana-abhisambodhi Sūtra Commentary*) T.1796. 39.579a– 789c.

Sumatikīrti. *Laghusaṁvaratantrapaṭalābhisandhi*. To. 1411, D vol. ma, 352a–353a; PTT. 2127, Q vol. 49, pp. 161.4–162.2.

Śūraṅgavajra. *Mūlatantrahṛdaya-saṁgrahābhidhānottaratantramūlamūlavṛtti* (MV). To. 1414, D rgyud ’grel vol. tsa, 120a–232a.

Tathāgatarakṣita. *Ubhayanibandha* (UN). To. 1409. D rgyud ’grel vol. ma, 207a–253a.

———. *Yoginīsaṁcāranibandha*. To. 1422, D rgyud ’grel vol. wa, 120a–139a. Sanskrit edited in Pandey 1998.

Tathāgatavajra. *Lūipābhisamayavṛttiṭīkā-viśeṣadyota-nāma*. To. 1510. D rgyud ’grel vol. zha, 285a–308b.

Tsong Khapa. *rje tsong kha pa'i gsung 'bum*. sku 'bum par ma. 19 vols. TBRC work number 22272.

———. *rgyud kyi rgyal pod pal gsang ba 'dus pa'i rgya cher bshad pa sgron ma gsal ba'i dka' ba'i gnas kyi mtha' dpyod rin po che'i myu gu,* vol. ca.

———. *sngags rim chen mo. rgyal ba khyab bdag rdo rje 'chang chen po'i lam gyi rim pa gsang ba kun gyi gnad rnam par phye ba*, vol. ga.

———. *bcom ldan 'das dpal 'khor lo bde mchog gi mngon par rtogs pa'i rgya cher bshad pa 'dod pa 'jo ba*, vol. ta.

———. *bde mchog bsdus pa'i rgyud kyi rgya cher bshad pa sbas pa'i don kun gsal ba*.

(B) TBRC scan of the *bla brang bkra shis 'khyil* print of the KS; vol. nya, *sbas don* 1a–248a; pp. 485–979. TBRC work number W22273.

(D) TBRC scan of the *de dge dgon chen* print of the KS; vol. nya, *sbas don* 1a–254a; pp. 407–909. TBRC work number W22274.

(Q) The Otani reprint of the KS in the Tibetan Tripitaka, Beijing edition. *Btsoṅ-kha-pa Bkaḥ-ḥbum* vol. da, 1a–229b. Photoreproduced in *The Tibetan Tripitaka: Peking Edition,* ed. Daisetz T. Suzuki, 168 vols. Tokyo-Kyoto: Tibetan Tripitaka Research Institute, 1955–1961. PTT 6157, vol. 157, pp. 2.1–94.1.

(T) *bkra shis lhun po par rnying* edition of the KS. Photographic reprint. Delhi: Ngawang Gelek Demo, 1980, vol. nya, *sbas don* 1a–251b.

———. *bde mchog rim lnga'i bshad pa sbas don lta ba'i mig rnam par 'byed pa*, vol. tha.

Vajraḍāka Tantra. *Śrīvajraḍāka-nāma-mahātantrarāja* (VD). To. 370, D rgyud-'bum vol. kha, 1b–125a. Sanskrit partially edited in Sugiki 2002 and 2003.

Vajraghaṇṭa. *Śrīcakrasaṁvarapañcakrama* (PK). To. 1433, D rgyud 'grel vol. wa, 224b–227a.

———. *Śrīcakrasaṁvarasādhana*. To. 1432, D rgyud 'grel vol. wa, 222b–224b.

———. *Śrīcakrasaṁvaraṣekaprakriya-upadeśa*. To. 1431, D rgyud 'grel vol. wa, 219b–222b.

Vajragarbha. *Hevajrapiṇḍārthaṭīkā*. To. 1180, D rgyud 'grel vol. ka 1b1-46a7.

Vajrapāṇi. *Laghutantraṭīkā*. *Lakṣābhidhānāduddhṛta Laghutantra-piṇḍārthavivaraṇa* (LT). To. 1402, D rgyud 'grel vol. ba, 78b–141a; PTT. 2117, vol. 48, pp. 143.1–173.5. Sanskrit edited in Cicuzza 2001.

Vidyādharīvajrayoginīsadhāna. To. 380, D rgyud 'bum vol. ga, 72b–73a.

Vīravajra. *Padārthaprakāśikā-nāma-śrīsaṁvaramūlatantraṭīkā* (PD). To. 1412, D rgyud 'grel vol. ma, 353b–450a.

———. *Yoginīsaṁcāraṭīkā*. To. 1423, D rgyud 'grel vol. wa, 139a–153a.

———. *Samantaguṇaśālina-nāma-ṭīkā* (SG). To. 1408, D rgyud 'grel vol. ma, 156b–207a.

———. *Sarvatantranidānamahāguhyaśrīsaṁpuṭa-nāma-tantrarājaṭīkā-ratnamālā-nāma*. To. 1199, D rgyud 'grel vol. ja, 1b–111a.

Yoginīsaṁcāra Tantra (YS). To. 375, D rgyud 'bum vol. ga, 34a–44b. Sanskrit and Tibetan edited in Pandey 1998.

Editions and Secondary Sources

Bentor, Yael. 1997. "Interiorized Fire Offerings of Breathing, Inner Heat and the Subtle Body." In *Tibetan Studies: Proceedings of the 7th Seminar of the International Association for Tibetan Studies, Graz 1995*, edited by Ernst Steinkellner, 51–58. Wein: Verlag der Österreichischen Akademie der Wissenschaften.

Broido, Michael M. 1983a. "*bShad Thabs*: Some Tibetan Methods of Explaining the Tantras." In *Contributions on Tibetan and Buddhist Religion and Philosophy. Proceedings of the Csoma de Körös Symposium Held at Velm-Vienna, Austria, 13–19 September 1981 vol. 2*, edited by Ernst Steinkellner and Helmut Tauscher, 15–45. Wiener Studien Zur Tibetologie und Buddhismuskunde. Heft 11. Wein: Arbeitskreis für Tibetische und Buddhistische Studien, Universität Wien.

———. 1983b. "A Note on dGos-'Brel." *Journal of the Tibet Society* 3: 5–19.

Chandra, Lokesh. 1963. *Materials for a History of Tibetan Literature*. New Delhi: International Academy of Indian Culture.

Chimpa, Lama and Alaka Chattopadhyaya. 1970. *Tāranātha's History of Buddhism in India*. Simla: Institute of Advanced Studies. Reprint, Delhi: Motilal Banarsidass, 1990.

Cicuzza, Claudio. 2001. *The Laghutantraṭīkā by Vajrapāṇi: A Critical Edition of the Sanskrit Text*. Serie Orientale Roma 86. Roma: Istituto Italiano per l'Africa e l'Oriente.

Cozort, Daniel. 1986. *Highest Yoga Tantra: An Introduction to the Esoteric Buddhism of Tibet*. Ithaca, NY: Snow Lion.

Davidson, Ronald M. 2002. *Indian Esoteric Buddhism: A Social History of the Tantric Movement*. New York: Columbia University Press.

———. 2005. *The Tibetan Renaissance: Tantric Buddhism in the Rebirth of Tibetan Culture*. New York: Columbia University Press.

Doniger, Wendy. 1996. "Sexual Masquerades in Hindu Myths." In *The Transmission of Knowledge in South Asia: Essays on Education, Religion, History, and Politics*, edited by Nigel Crook, 28–48. Delhi: Oxford University Press.

George, Christopher S. 1974. *The Caṇḍamahāroṣaṇa Tantra: Chapters I-VIII: A Critical Edition and English Translation*. American Oriental Series vol. 56. New Haven: American Oriental Society.

Gray, David B. 2001. "On Supreme Bliss: A Study of the History and Interpretation of the Cakrasamvara Tantra." PhD diss., Columbia University.

———. 2005a. "Eating the Heart of the Brahmin: Representations of Alterity and the Formation of Identity in Tantric Buddhist Discourse." *History of Religions* 45.1: 45–69.

———. 2005b. "Disclosing the Empty Secret: Textuality and Embodiment in the Cakrasamvara Tantra." *Numen* 52.4: 417–444.

———. 2007. *The Cakrasamvara Tantra: A Study and Annotated Translation*. New York: American Institute of Buddhist Studies / Columbia University Press.

———. 2009. "The Influence of the *Kālacakra*: Vajrapāṇi on Consort Meditation." In *As Long as Space Endures: Essays on the Kālacakra Tantra in Honor of His Holiness the Dalai Lama*, edited by Edward A. Arnold. Ithaca, NY: Snow Lion.

———. 2012. *The Cakrasamvara Tantra: Editions of the Sanskrit and Tibetan Texts*. New York: American Institute of Buddhist Studies / Columbia University Press.

Gutschow, Kim. 2004. *Being a Buddhist Nun: The Struggle for Enlightenment in the Himalayas*. Cambridge: Harvard University Press.

Huber, Toni. 1999. *The Cult of Pure Crystal Mountain: Popular Pilgrimage and Visionary Landscape in Southeast Tibet*. Oxford: Oxford University Press.

Jamgön Kongtrul Lodrö Tayé. 1995. *Myriad Worlds: Buddhist Cosmology in Abhidharma, Kālacakra and Dzog-chen*. Ithaca, NY: Snow Lion.

Kalff, Martin M. 1979. "Selected Chapters from the Abhidhānottara-Tantra: The Union of Female and Male Deities." Ph.D. diss., Columbia University.

Kaschewsky, Rudolf. 1974. *Das Leben des Lamaistischen Heiligen Tsongkhapa Blo-bzaṅ-grags-pa (1357–1419), Dargestellt und erläutert anhand seiner Vita, Quellort allen Glückes*, 1 Teil, Asiatische Forschungen band 32. Wiesbaden: Otto Harrassowitz.

Lo Bue, Emberto F. 1997. "The Role of Newar Scholars in Transmitting the Indian Buddhist Heritage to Tibet (c. 750–c.1200)." In *Les habitants du toit du monde: Études recueillies en hommage à Alexander W. Macdonald*, edited by Samten G. Karmay and Philippe Sargant, 629–658. Nanterre: Societé d'Ethnologie.

Matsunaga, Yukei. 1978. *The Guhyasamāja Tantra*. Osaka: Toho Shuppan.

Monier-Williams, Sir Monier. 2002. *A Sanskrit-English Dictionary*. Corrected edition, Delhi: Motilal Banarsidass.

Pandey, Janardan Shastri. 1998. *Yoginīsaṁcāratantram with Nibandha of* Tathāgatarakṣita *and Upadeśānusāriṇīvyākhyā of Alakakaśala*. Rare Buddhist Texts Series no. 21. Sarnath: Central Institute of Higher Tibetan Studies.

———. 2002. *Śrīherukābhidhānam Cakrasaṁvaratantram with the Vivṛti Commentary of* Bhavabhaṭṭa. Rare Buddhist Texts Series no. 26. Sarnath: Central Institute of Higher Tibetan Studies, 2 vols.

Roerich, Goerge N. 1959. *Biography of Dharmasvāmin (Chag lo tsa-ba Chos-rje-dpal), A Tibetan Monk Pilgrim*. Patna: K. P. Jayaswal Research Institute.

———. 1976. *The Blue Annals*. 2nd ed., Delhi: Motilal Banarsidass.

Ruegg, David Seyfort. 1966. *The Life of Bu ston Rin po che with the Tibetan Text of the Bu ston rNam thar. Serie Orientale Roma* vol. 34. Roma: Istituto Italiano per il Medio ed Estremo Oriente.

Sadakata, Akira. 1997. *Buddhist Cosmology: Philosophy and Origins*. Trans. Gaynor Sekimori. Tokyo: Kosei Publishing Co.

Samdhong Rinpoche and Vrajvallabh Dwivedi. 1990. *Vasantatilakā of Caryāvratī Śrīkṛṣṇācārya with Commentary: Rahasyadīpikā by Vanaratna*. Rare Buddhist Text Series 7. Sarnath, Varanasi: Central Institute of Higher Tibetan Studies.

———. 1992. *Mahāmāyātantraṁ Ratnākaraśāntiviracitaguṇavatīṭīkāsayutam*. Rare Buddhist Text Series 10. Sarnath, Varanasi: Central Institute of Higher Tibetan Studies.

Samuel, Geoffrey. 1993. *Civilized Shamans: Buddhism in Tibetan Societies*. Washington, D.C.: Smithsonian Institute Press.

Schoening, Jeffrey D. 1996. "*Sūtra* Commentaries in Tibetan Translation." In *Tibetan Literature: Studies in Genre*, edited by José Ignacio Cabezón and Roger R. Jackson, 111–124. Ithaca, NY: Snow Lion.

Shastri, Hariprasad. *Advayavajrasaṁgraha*. Baroda: Oriental Institute, 1927.

Skorupski, Tadeusz. 1996. "The *Saṁpuṭa-Tantra*: Sanskrit and Tibetan Versions of Chapter One." In *The Buddhist Forum volume IV Seminar Papers 1994–1996*, ed. Tadeusz Skorupski, 191–244. London: School of Oriental and African Studies, University of London.

Smith, Jonathan Z. 1987. "The Domestication of Sacrifice." In *Violent Origins*, edited by Robert G. Hamerton-Kelly, 191–205. Stanford: Stanford University Press.

Snellgrove, David L. 1959. *The Hevajra Tantra: A Critical Study*. London: Oxford University Press, 2 vols.

Sobisch, Jan-Ulrich. 2002. *Three-Vow Theories in Tibetan Buddhism: A Comparative Study of Major Traditions from the Twelfth through Nineteenth Centuries*. Wiesbaden: Dr. Ludwig Reichart Verlag.

Sugiki Tsunehiko. 2001. "On the Making of the *Śrīcakrasaṁvaratantra*, with a Critical Sanskrit Text of Jayabhadra's *Śrīcakrasaṁvarapañjikā*." *Chisan Gakuho* (智山学報) 50: 91–141.

———. 2002. "A Critical Study of the Vajraḍākamahātantrarāja (I): Chapter 1 and 42." *Chisan Gakuho* (智山学報) 51: 81–115.

———. 2003. "A Critical Study of the Vajraḍākamahātantrarāja (II): Sacred Districts and Practices Concerned." *Chisan Gakuho* (智山学報) 52: 53–106.

SUZUKI Daisetz T., ed. *The Tibetan Tripitaka: Peking Edition*. 168 vols. Tokyo-Kyoto: Tibetan Tripitaka Research Institute, 1955–1961.

Thurman, Robert A.F. 1976. *The Holy Teaching of Vimalakīrti, A Mahāyāna Scripture*. University Park: Pennsylvania State University Press.

———. 1982. *Life & Teachings of Tsongkhapa*. Dharamsala: Library of Tibetan Works and Archives.

———. 1984. *The Central Philosophy of Tibet*. Princeton, NJ: Princeton University Press.

———. 2011. *Brilliant Illumination of the Lamp*. New York: American Institute of Buddhist Studies/Columbia University Press.

TSUDA Shiníchi. 1974. *The Saṁvarodaya-Tantra: Selected Chapters*. Tokyo: The Hokuseido Press.

UI Hakuju, et al. 1934. *A Complete Catalogue of Tibetan Buddhist Canons (Bkaḥ-ḥgyur and Bstan-ḥgyur)*. Sendai: Tōhoku Imperial University.

Vaidya, P. L. *Aṣṭasāhsrikā Prajñāpāramitā with Haribhadra's Commentary Called Āloka*. The Darbhanga: Mithila Institute of Post-Graduate Studies and Research in Sanskrit Learning, 1960.

Vogel, Claus. 1965. *Vāgbhaṭa's Aṣṭāṅgahṛdayasaṁhitā: The First Five Chapters of its Tibetan Version*. Wiesbaden: F. Steiner.

Vose, Kevin A. 2009. *Resurrecting Candrakīrti: Disputes in the Tibetan Creation of Prāsaṅgika*. Boston: Wisdom Publications.

Wedemeyer, Christian K. 2006. "Tantalizing Traces of the Labours of the Lotsāwas: Alternative Translations of Sanskrit Sources in the Writings of Rje Tsong kha pa." In *Tibetan Buddhist Literature and Praxis: Studies in its Formative Period, 900–1400*, edited by Ronald M. Davidson and Christian K. Wedemeyer, 149–182. Leiden: Brill.

White, David Gordon. 1996. *The Alchemical Body: Siddha Traditions in Medieval India*. Chicago: University of Chicago Press.

Yarnall, Thomas Freeman. 2013. *Great Treatise on the Stages of Mantra (sngags rim chen mo), Chapters XI-XII, The Creation Stage, by* Tsong Khapa *Losang Drakpa*. New York: American Institute of Buddhist Studies/Columbia University Press.

———. *The Emptiness that is Form*, forthcoming.

Zysk, Kenneth G. 2002. *Conjugal Love in India: Ratiśāstra and Ratiramaṇa*. Leiden: Brill.

INDEXES

Index of Canonical Texts Cited

Index of Canonical Authors Cited

Tibetans

General Index

A

accomplishment
of the triple body, 253, 254, 258, 259, 261
accomplishment of…. *See also* achievement of…
accomplishment(s) (*siddhis*), 19, 20, 29–31, 57, 61–64, 71, 73, 77, 122, 123, 125, 145, 152, 155, 156, 163, 171, 174, 175, 179, 180, 184, 192, 193, 213–216, 221, 224, 225, 232, 239, 245, 247, 250, 251, 259, 264, 267, 291, 297, 299
supreme, 17, 65, 71, 72, 94, 125, 128, 132, 156, 214, 223, 233, 250
two, 66, 67, 72, 94, 125, 127, 132, 300
worldly/ordinary, 17, 65, 66, 72, 94, 125, 132, 163, 170, 175, 214, 223, 233, 250, 259, 265, 268, 271, 290
achievement
of pleasure/joy, 67, 115, 125, 126, 338
of ritual actions, 65, 121, 204, 216, 233, 236, 247, 265, 266, 275, 280, 282
achievement of…. *See also* accomplishment of…
achievement(s) (*siddhis*). *See* accomplishment(s) (*siddhis*)
Akṣobhya Buddha, 122, 165, 302, 303, 305, 317, 318, 320, 321, 337
alchemy, 76, 101, 110, 111, 123, 130, 132, 163, 170, 240
Amitābha Buddha, 165, 302, 303, 305, 314, 318, 319
Amoghasiddhi Buddha, 165, 302, 303, 305, 317, 318, 321
appendix Tantra (*uttaratantra*) (genre), 32, 35, 36, 38, 54, 81, 82, 85, 95, 233
auxiliary Tantra (*yan lag gi rgyud*) (genre), 35, 37, 38

B

bodhisattva(s), 12, 86, 124, 126, 127, 185, 192, 264
commentaries, 8, 23, **40**, 57, 121, 344
body mandala, 45, 47, 52, 53, 54, 58, 106, 126, 136, 144, 161, 168, 176, 178, 180, 256
Brahmā, 327
Buddha bodies
communal enjoyment body (*sambhogakāya*), 254–259
manifestation body (*nirmāṇakāya*), 254, 256
reality body (*dharmakāya*), 254–259
triple body, 253, 254, 257–259, 261

C

caṇḍāla(s), 247, 248, 272, 303, 341
caru oblation(s), 251
channel(s), 43, 48, 49, 51, 54, 56, 86, 88–90, 101–104, 106–109, 113, 114, 116, 124, 131, 132, 168, 180, 181, 189–191, 237, 243, 244, 256, 271, 288–290, 335, 337

D

Ḍ

E

[explanatory Tantra (*vyākhyātantra*) (genre) (*cont'd*)]
146, 148, 152–154, 166, 183, 190, 192, 197, 200, 208, 286, 289, 293, 322

F

fire sacrifice, 56, 58, 121, 139, 205, 233, 235, 247
fury fire, 20, 48, 51, 56, 89, 101, 103, 108, 113, 116, 191, 245, 290, 335, 338

G

gaṇacakra, 251
Geluk (order, tradition, lama, etc.), 3, 7, 24, 25
gnosis, 12, 21, 47, 55, 80, 85, 90, 112, 115, 120, 163, 164, 179, 181, 250, 257, 258
  body, 180, 259
  from the descent of the awakening spirit, 90, 114
  line (in mandala), 146
  natural, 54, 86, 91, 104, 119, 189
  nondual, 78
  of clear light, 93, 181, 182, 285, *See also* clear light
  of exact objective reality, 99
  of great bliss, 107, 256
  of natural joy, 181
  of the indivisibility of bliss and emptiness, 48, 90
  wheel, 143, 154
  wisdom-gnosis consecration, 115, 160, 168
gnosis hero. *See* hero(es)/heroine(s), gnosis

H

habitat. *See* mandala, habitat
Hayagrīva, 123, 208
hero(es)/heroine(s), 30, 33, 40, 41, 45, 67, 70, 71, 81, 97, 99, 104, 112–114, 117, 118, 134, 141, 148–150, 157, 177–179, 187–189, 207, 209, 213, 268–271, 278, 279, 286, 292, 297, 300–302, 309, 311, 319, 323, 333, 343, 344, 398
  commitment, 46, 143, 145, 149, 153, 154
  gnosis, 46, 47, 143, 145, 154
  mandala, 31, 46, 126, 183
  mantra(s) of, 65, 184, 188, 206, 209, 210, 225, 275
  solitary, 47, 154, 177
  twenty-four, 45, 52, 66, 88, 152, 179, 225
Heruka, 30, 40, 51, 52, 86, 91, 105, 113, 123, 131, 142, 150, 162, 163, 204, 207, 240, 270, 271, 282, 292, 343
  as natural joy, 116
  causal, 45
  clan of, 301–303, 313–317, 321
  color of, 45
  creation of, 105–107, 109
  donkey-faced, 65, 282, 284, 285, 288, 291, 292
  empty aspect, 93, 109, 257
  four-faced, 45, 156
  mantra of, 142, 204, 223, 224, 229, 263, 264, 266, 267, 271

N

O

P

R

S

Ś

T

U

V

W

Y

Z